just
JAVA™ 1.2

FOURTH EDITION

THE SUN MICROSYSTEMS PRESS
JAVA SERIES

▼ ***Core Java 1.2, Volume 1 - Fundamentals***
Cay S. Horstmann & Gary Cornell

▼ ***Core Java 1.2, Volume 2 - Advanced Features***
Cay S. Horstmann & Gary Cornell

▼ ***Graphic Java 1.2, Volume I: AWT***
David M. Geary

▼ ***Graphic Java 1.2, Volume II: Swing***
David M. Geary

▼ ***Graphic Java 1.2, Volume III: Advanced Swing***
David M. Geary

▼ ***Graphic Java 1.2, Volume IV: 2D API***
David M. Geary

▼ ***Inside Java Workshop 2.0***
Lynn Weaver

▼ ***Instant Java, Third Edition***
John A. Pew & Stephen G. Pew

▼ ***Java by Example 1.2***
Jerry R. Jackson & Alan L. McClellan

▼ ***Java Studio by Example***
Lynn Weaver & Leslie Robertson

▼ ***Jumping JavaScript***
Janice Winsor & Brian Freeman

▼ ***Just Java 1.2***
Peter van der Linden

▼ ***More Jumping JavaScript***
Janice Winsor, Brian Freeman, & Bill Anderson

▼ ***Not Just Java, Second Edition***
Peter van der Linden

just JAVA™ 1.2

FOURTH EDITION

PETER van der LINDEN

Sun Microsystems Press
A Prentice Hall Title

The publisher offers discounts on this book when ordered in bulk quantities.
For more information, contact: Corporate Sales Department, Phone: 800-382-3419;
Fax: 201-236-7141; E-mail: corpsales@prenhall.com; or write: Prentice Hall PTR,
Corp. Sales Dept., One Lake Street, Upper Saddle River, NJ 07458.

Editorial/production supervision: *Joanne Anzalone*
Cover designer: *Anthony Gemmellaro*
Cover design director: *Jerry Votta*
Manufacturing manufacturer: *Alexis R. Heydt*
Marketing manager: *Kaylie Smith*
Acquisitions editor: *Gregory G. Doench*
Editorial Assistant: *Mary Treacy*
Sun Microsystems Press publisher: *Rachel Borden*

10 9 8 7 6 5 4 3 2 1

ISBN 0-13-010534-1

Sun Microsystems Press
A Prentice Hall Title

Contents

Chapter 6

More OOP —Extending Classes, 141

Chapter 7

Java Statements, 171

Chapter 8

Interfaces, 201

Using the Just Java CD-ROM

About the CD-ROM

Welcome to the *Just Java* CD-ROM—a disk packed with all the Java tools and source code discussed in the book and lots more.

This CD is for any system that can read an ISO 9660 CD with the Rockridge/Joliet extensions (i.e., a system that can handle CDs with deep directories, symbolic links, and more than just 8.3 filenames, on Unix, Windows, and the Macintosh).

There is a huge amount of useful, entertaining, or educational material on this CD. Some of the content (and there is a *lot* more) is:

•	**Useful**	Java Development Kits for Windows, Macintosh, and Solaris. Java Programmer's FAQ and Glossary. Decompilers and obfuscators.
•	**Educational**	Translators for Perl, TCL, Eiffel, C, C++, Python, etc. CIA World Fact Book—your tax dollars at work. The Linux operating system for x86 (Debian 2.0 release).
•	**Entertaining**	Java program to solve crossword puzzles. Java Digital Simulator. The Sherlock Holmes books. Java Bible Code software. Look for hidden messages.

You can explore the CD-ROM quite effectively using a browser. Mount the CD on your computer, and point your browser at the index.html file in the root.

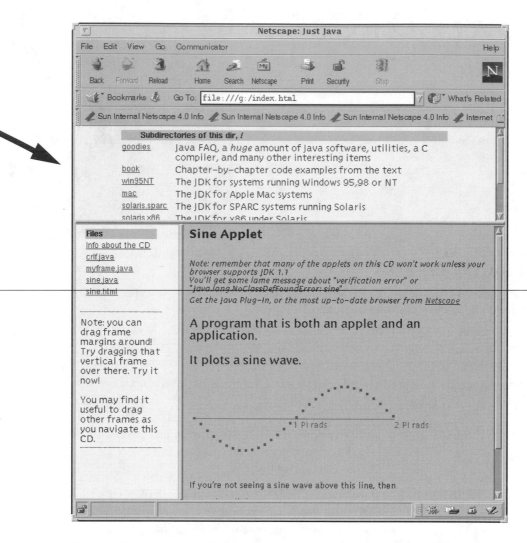

You'll see a display like that shown above. Notice the three frames.

- The top frame is a list of directories in this directory, plus a short description of each. You can click on a directory name to move the browser into that directory. That's what the arrow above shows.

- The left-hand frame is a list of useful files in this directory. You can click on a filename to display that file in the right-hand frame.

- The right-hand frame is an area for displaying files. Sometimes an applet runs in that frame, as shown in the figure above.

You can drag the frame boundaries around if it helps you to read the contents. If you click on, for example, the "goodies" directory name indicated by the arrow in the previous diagram, the browser will take you to that directory, and the display will now look like this:

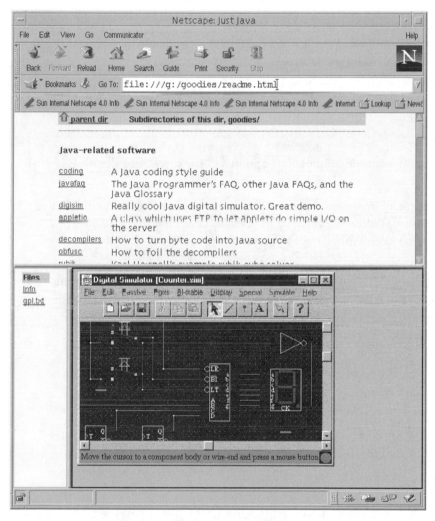

You can carry on exploring this way. You can also use the "back" and "forward" buttons in the browser if you want. There are hundreds of megabytes of data of interest to a professional programmer on this CD, including many freeware or shareware compilers for other programming languages.

Before you tackle the other languages, you'll want to install and try Java as explained in the following pages. Choose the latest (highest version number) JDK for your system, and check for a more recent one on the web.

Using the CD-ROM on Windows 95, 98, and NT

Installing the JDK on Windows 95, 98, or NT:

1. Put the CD in the CD drive, and in a shelltool go to the directory win95NT.

    ```
    d:\win95NT
    ```

    Your CD drive letter may be d: or e: or something else. You need around 65MB of disk space for the release.

2. Choose the highest version number release. If there is a more recent one at http://java.sun.com, download and use that instead. Execute the self-extracting archive.

    ```
    jdk12-win32
    ```

    This will ask you a couple of questions and install the Java compiler and tools. A good place to install the compiler is in c:\jdk1.2.

3. Once the JDK files have been unpacked onto your hard drive, you will need to add (or modify) the PATH variable in your autoexec.bat file. Use a text editor to add the jdk1.2\bin directory to your path:

    ```
    SET PATH=c:\jdk1.2\bin; (...the rest of your path)
    ```

4. Save the change to your autoexec.bat and restart your computer so the new variable takes effect. Earlier versions of the JDK required you to set an additional variable, CLASSPATH. From JDK 1.2 this is needed only if there are user classes outside your current directory. For now, ignore this shell variable.

5. There is a file called "docs/install.html" in the JDK directory. It contains a longer explanation of installation, along with a troubleshooting guide. Please refer to it as necessary.

This CD-ROM does not have a Java compiler for Windows 3.1. A Windows 3.1 version of Java can be downloaded from http://www.alphaworks.ibm.com/formula, but I don't recommend it. Win3.1 and typical Win3.1 hardware lack too many features to be truly satisfactory.

Note: Many of the files on this CD use long file names, which is one of the features of Windows 95. If you are unable to see the long file names on the CD, your Windows 95/NT system may not be configured correctly. Check by double-clicking on the "System" icon in the Control Panel and then clicking on the "Performance" tab. If the "Performance" section does not indicate that "Your system is configured for optimal performance," then there is a configuration issue. See Windows Help or contact Microsoft Technical Support for further assistance.

Using the CD-ROM on Macintosh

Installing the JDK on a Macintosh:

Apple's Java, bundled with Mac OS 8.1 and later, only has the runtime library, not the compiler. So you'll need to install it from this CD. Apple (one of the companies with the most to gain from portable software) is regrettably not current with the latest Java. So the JDK 1.2 libraries described in this text won't yet run on your Macintosh. If you'd like to see an up-to-date version of Java on Apple's computers, be sure to let Apple know about it by letter, phone call, or e-mail.

Table 1: Apple Java Releases

Java Release	Apple Name	Works on Mac OS
JDK 1.0.2	MRJ 1.0	Mac OS 7.5.3 rev 2 or later
JDK 1.1.3	MRJ 2.0	Mac OS 8.0 or later; Mac OS 7.6.1 or later with custom install
JDK 1.2	Not avail, Nov. 1998	N/A

1. Put the CD in the CD drive, and review the directory called "mac." Look at the highest version number JDK there, e.g., JDK 1-0-2. As this book went to press, I was still waiting for Apple's permission to bundle the compiler.

2. Then use a browser to look at the following:

    ```
    http://www.apple.com/macos/java/
    ```

    Choose the highest version number release from the CD and the Apple site. Download the self-mounting image to your hard drive and double-click to open. You need around 30MB of disk space for the release.

3. The Apple Java compiler currently consists of two files, MRJSDK2.0.1.bin and MRJ_2.0.smi.bin, both of which need to be installed. Do the usual clicking to expand them. You can compile and run Java programs by dragging and dropping the appropriate files onto the Java tools javac and JBindery.

Note: You should note that Macintosh, Windows, and Unix text files have different conventions for end-of-line. Macintosh expects a carriage return, Windows expects a carriage return and a linefeed, and UNIX expects a newline character (linefeed). Even though some text files may not appear to be properly formatted, the Java compiler handles source files created under any of these conventions.

You should also note that file names longer than twenty-six characters will be truncated on a Mac. Therefore, some of the sample Java programs on this CD will have to be renamed and recompiled to execute properly on a Macintosh.

Using the CD-ROM on Solaris

Installing the JDK (Solaris 2.5.1 or Later):

This CD uses the Rockridge extensions, so Solaris users may get a warning message saying the CD doesn't conform to the ISO 9660 specification. Ignore it.

The solaris.sparc directory contains the JDK for Sparc. The solaris.x86 directory contains the Intel version. Installation instructions are the same for Solaris for SPARC and Solaris for x86. On Intel systems, use "x86" instead of "sparc" in the filenames below. Insert the Just Java CD into your CD-ROM drive.

1.   If Volume Manager is running on your machine, the CD is automatically mounted to the /cdrom/just_java directory when you insert it. If the Volume Manager is not running on your machine, mount the CD manually by becoming root and typing:

```
# mkdir -p /cdrom/just_java
# mount -rF hsfs /dev/dsk/c0t6d0s0 /cdrom/just_java
```

2.   Choose the highest version number release. If there is a more recent one at http://www.sun.com, download and use that instead. Copy the file to your hard disk. Assume you're putting it in /home/linden, it would go here:

```
cd /cdrom/just_java/solaris.sparc
cp jdk1.2-solaris2-sparc.bin /home/linden
```

This is about a 20MB file, so it will take a few seconds to copy.

3.   Execute the self-extracting archive, e.g.:

```
cd /home/linden
./jdk1.2-solaris2-sparc.bin
```

This will ask a couple of questions and install the Java compiler/tools.

4.   Add the java "bin" directory to your path. The exact filename and syntax depends on the shell you are using. If you are a C shell user, the file is .cshrc and the syntax is as shown:

```
setenv JAVAHOME  /home/linden/jdk1.2
set path=( $JAVAHOME/bin  ... rest of path ... )
```

Log out then log in so the new variables take effect.

Earlier versions of the JDK required you to set an additional variable, CLASSPATH. From JDK 1.2 this is needed only if you are trying to run user classes outside your current directory. For now, ignore this shell variable.

5.   There is a file called "docs/install.html" in the JDK directory. It contains a longer explanation of installation along with a troubleshooting guide. Please refer to it as necessary.

Pathnames Used Throughout This Book

The source code for the Java runtime library is part of the JDK that you have on this CD. From time to time, I will refer you to particular files.

The first part of the pathname will depend on where you installed JDK, and I'll represent this by "$JAVAHOME."

The separators in a pathname are different on Unix than on Windows. For example, I may recommend you look at a file located here:

$JAVAHOME/src/java/awt/Windows.java

If you installed Java on your PC at C:\jdk1.2fcs, then the file to review is here:

C:\jdk1.2fcs\src\java\awt\Window.java.

CHAPTER

1

- Compiling and Executing a Sample Program

- The Biggest Java Benefit: Portability

- The "Java Platform"

- The Java Language

- Java Libraries

- Releases of the JDK to Date

- Java Virtual Machine

- The World Wide Web and Java

What Is Java?

J ava is a new programming language from Sun Microsystems, but Java is much more than just a programming language. Java works well with web browsers and has great features like Object-Oriented Programming, GUI programming, database access, network support, and built-in security.

Java software's biggest asset is its capacity to run on all computers. Java achieves this by layering libraries on top of any operating system. Java is really a full computing platform, just as the Macintosh, Windows 98, and OS/390 are platforms.

The computer industry has adopted Java for pragmatic reasons. Java provides a robust way for organizations to streamline and integrate incompatible computer systems. Java provides a framework for systems that people are *very* interested in building, such as reusable component software, thin client/server software, network programming (TCP/IP sockets), secure browser-based software (a basic requirement for e-commerce), and threaded, multimedia code.

And yet, Java is not complicated. Programmers seem to enjoy working in Java because they can accomplish more, more quickly. You hear many stories about C++ programmers who try Java and never switch back. You can be more productive in Java than in other similar languages for two reasons:

- Java has a large (almost overwhelming) set of rich libraries. These libraries are "building blocks" for your systems. The libraries are identical on all Java implementations on all computers. There are libraries for database access, for networking, for running in a browser, for GUI programming, and many more.

- The language was designed so that some common bugs either can't happen, or are caught as soon as they occur. For example, array indexes are always checked to be within bounds; the language is strongly-typed; type conversions are checked for validity at runtime; and memory address arithmetic, a common bug in C, is not allowed.

Java was released to the public in the summer of 1995, and its popularity has grown faster than anyone thought possible. In a 1996 meeting of the Mountain View, California, Java Users Group, I asked the designer of Java, James Gosling, how long it would be before we could throw away our C++ books in favor of Java. He started laughing because the question seemed so audacious at that time. No one is laughing now.

This free release of Java on the web in mid-1995 coincided with the enormous, continuing surge of interest in the Internet. Within six months, Java was in use by more than 100,000 programmers. Two years later, Java had around 400,000 programmers, the same number of developers as the Windows platform. The number of Java developers increases by tens of thousands each month. By summer 1998, over half a million programmers had registered with Sun's Java Developer group, and more than twice as many had downloaded the compiler. Since Java runs anywhere, the total potential market for all these developers is the 317+ million computer systems in the world. Java is well positioned to replace Windows as the high-volume platform of the computer industry. With only one exception, Java has united all the players in the software industry behind it.

No programming language in the past has ever gathered so many adherents in such a short space of time. Because of the speed of acceptance, you sometimes hear people complain about "Java hype." It is easy to overlook that sometimes a new development gets attention because it really is better than its predecessors. Due to the attention it has received, programmers (especially students) frequently ask, "Should I learn Java or Perl, C++, C, or Fortran?" The answer is, "Yes." You should learn several programming language and be familiar with several more. (That's why I put compilers for several other languages besides Java on the CD that comes with this book). Luckily, the Java language is easy to learn, and is covered in the first few chapters of this book. The remainder of the book covers the Java libraries, which are extensive.

Compiling and Executing a Sample Program

For those who want to get off to a quick start, this section walks through the compilation and execution of a Java program. Just follow these numbered steps:

1. Install the Java system from the CD as described in the previous section, "Installing the CD-ROM."

2. When you write and compile your own programs, follow these rules *very carefully:*

    *   Use an editor to create a file with your source code. My advice is not to use a development environment at first—it just adds another thing to learn. Use an editor that saves in an ASCII text format, not a word processor format, and one that doesn't change the file name. On a PC, EDIT works. Notepad works if you put quotes around the filename when you save it, as in "myframe.java".

    *   The name of your Java class or module must match the name of the file that it is in. This means *exactly* match, including letter case and spelling! If you call your Java class `TrYmE`, then it *must* be in a source file called `TrYmE.java`. Letter case matters throughout Java such that, for example, the word "System" is different from the word "system," and you cannot use one in place of the other.

3. Type the program on the next page into a file called `myframe.java`, or you can simply copy the file off the CD.

    Note: I am tempting fate by printing these lines in a book and asking readers to exactly copy them exactly. Such examples are notoriously prone to proofreading and printing errors. Just copy this file off the top directory of the CD if you have trouble. This program is explained in detail in Chapter 3, "Explanation of a Sample Program."

    Ensure that you follow the rules about the file name matching the class name, even to the letter case! The file name has the suffix of `.java`, too. If you are using a system that doesn't permit 4-character file extensions (probably Windows 3.1), read the documentation accompanying its Java compiler on the correct way to format names.

```
// 40 line Java demo, Peter van der Linden
// rolls colored text across the screen
import java.awt.*;
class myframe extends Frame {
    static int x=0,y=120; // x,y position to display message
    static int i=0;
    static int LtoR=1;      // 1->we are moving msg L-to-R

    Font fb = new Font("TimesRoman", Font.BOLD, 36);
    String msg[]={"Java", "Portable", "Secure", "Easy"};
    Color color[]={Color.blue, Color.yellow, Color.green, Color.red};

    public void paint(Graphics g) { // gets called by runtime library
        g.setFont( fb );
        g.setColor( color[i] );
        g.drawString(msg[i],x,y);
    }

    static public void main(String s[]) throws Exception {
        myframe mf = new myframe();
        mf.setSize(200,200);
        int pixelsPerLine=200, totalLines=4;
        mf.setVisible(true);
        for (int j=0;j<pixelsPerLine*totalLines; j++) {
            Thread.sleep(25);
            mf.repaint();
            if (LtoR==1) {
                if ( (x+=3) < 200) continue;
                i = ++i % 4;          // move index to next msg/color
                x=50; y=0; LtoR=0;  // move msg top to bott next time
            } else {
                if ( (y+=3) < 200) continue;
                i = ++i % 4;          // move index to next msg/color
                x=0; y=120; LtoR=1; // move msg L-to-R next time
            }
        }
        System.exit(0);
    }
}
```

Figure 1-1: Sample Java program to compile and run.

4.   Open a command-line window by getting a DOS prompt onWindows or a command shell on Unix. Compile the program by typing:

```
javac myframe.java
```

There should be no error messages from this compilation. If there are, you probably typed something wrong in the file or the command.

Correct it and try again.

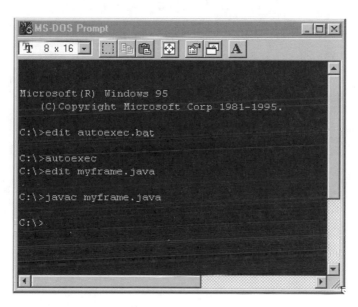

Figure 1-2: The process of compilation

5. A successful compilation will create file `myframe.class`. Execute the Java class file like this:

```
java myframe
```

If you have entered everything correctly, your results will look like Figure 1-3, which shows a screen capture of the program running on Windows 95.

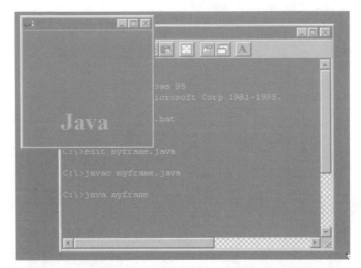

Figure 1-3: Running the program on Windows 95.

It's exciting that such a program can be written in less than a page of code. Copy the `myframe.class` file onto a floppy disk, and walk it over to a different system. Run it on the Java system you install there, and marvel at the possibilities of universally portable software.

Book Web Site/ Author E-Mail

If you find an error in this text, please let me know by e-mail to pvdl@afu.com. I used to offer a $1 bounty for the first report of each error. I've dropped that due to the financial burden of paying taxes on all that extra income. So, no bounty, but you do get the benefit of knowing you are helping other programmers. There is an errata sheet at http://www.afu.com, where you can also find the freshest copy of the Java Programmers FAQ.

The Biggest Java Benefit: Portability

Java executables run on all computer systems. You compile a Java program once on any system and can run it anywhere—on a Macintosh, on Windows 95, on any of the varieties of Unix, on DEC's VMS, on IBM's mainframe operating systems, and even on cell phones, Personal Digital Assistants (PDAs), embedded processors, and smart cards (credit cards with a microprocessor and memory).

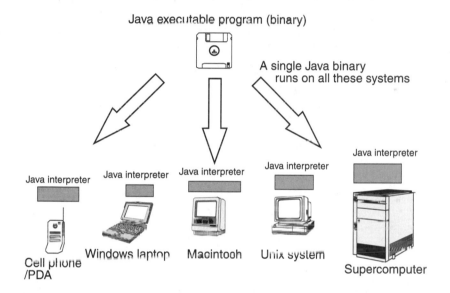

Figure 1-4: Total platform independence: Your Java application runs on every system that supports Java. No more "123 for DOS, 123 for Windows 3.1, 123 for Windows 95;" just "123 for Java," and you're done.

Why Software Portability Matters

You may be thinking that portability does not affect you: Your software runs on your PC and that's all you ever use. You are correct, right up until the time you want to buy a new system. Then you are faced with the "choice" of totally discarding your investment in software or choosing only from systems that offer some compatibility with your previous system. You've been locked in.

For businesses the problem is worse and far more expensive. Even if your whole organization has standardized on, say, Microsoft Windows, there have been multiple releases over the past five or six years: MS-DOS, Win3.1, Win3.11, Win95A, Win95B, Win98, NT 3.1, NT3.5, NT3.51, NT4, and WinCE. These platforms have incompatibilities between them, too. Even applications running on a single platform have limited interoperability. Office 95, for example, cannot read files produced by default from Office 97, even when the files don't use any of the new Office 97 features.

In the rapidly-growing world of distributed processing over the Internet, portability becomes critical. You may have one kind of platform internally, but you have no control over other departments on the intranet or over your customers, suppliers, and partners on the extranet. If you have arbitrary restrictions on the operating systems that run your applications, you will lose customers and alienate partners.

Rather than throwing out everything and chasing the moving target of operating system compatibility, Java lets you "Write Once, Run Anywhere." Portability is the reason IBM is such a strong supporter of Java. IBM has six incompatible product lines: mainframes, minicomputers, workstations, two kinds of PC, and a network computer. There is limited interoperability between them, but Java changes all that. Portability also makes it easier for Java programmers to transfer their skills to new jobs, and thus gives employers a wider pool of candidates from which to choose.

Portable software gives everyone more choices. Many software vendors develop for the platform with the greatest market share first, the Macintosh as an afterthought, and other systems not at all. Java's portability makes it the highest-volume platform of all and thus the first platform for which to develop. Costs will decrease for everyone if software vendors can spread their development expenses over a potential market of over 317 million computers, instead of the 91 million Windows 3.1 systems, the 20 million Macintosh systems, or the 12 million Unix systems.

Software portability is about "future proofing" your software. Rewrite it in Java, and that's the last port you'll ever need to do. Portability is the Holy Grail of the software industry. It has long been sought, but never before attained. Java brings the industry closer to true software portability than any previous system has.

Software Portability Case Studies

Java portability was originally a work-in-progress, and platform differences showed through in some libraries. Today the issue has been overcome. The most troublesome area was GUI code portability. Even that has now been solved by a new library written in Java. The following are Java portability experiences of two developers.

Gene McKenna works for a software company in San Francisco producing e-commerce applications. He recently took a complex distributed database Java application with a web front end, and ported it from NT to Solaris with no recompilation at all. This is a real enterprise system from the database to the web interface to everything in between; the port involved simply reinstalling the software and fixing up a batch script. Occasionally bugs are fixed on the deployed system, and the code is transferred back. The portability of source and binaries works both ways.

This system was developed and tested on an NT box, but deployed on Solaris and Linux. "Anyone new to programming may think nothing of this," Gene commented, "but before Java, it was time-consuming and expensive to port a system. With Java, our applications now run on all platforms."

Jason Shattu works for Saudi International Bank in London and took part in the bank's first Java project. The system was initially developed on an NT-based server that used multi-threading, database access, and the CORBA middleware technology.

Code portability was not made a priority on the project, but when finished, Jason was asked to port the system to Solaris. To everyone's surprise and delight, there were no source changes needed to get the code to run on Unix. The code didn't even need recompiling; Jason moved the binary files across to the Unix system and it all just ran the first time. Java has since become the bank's main development language replacing VB and FoxPro.

Java portability poses a real threat to Microsoft. Software that can run on any operating system has a larger market than software that is Windows-only. Over time ISVs should move their products away from Windows-only to Java—unless Java can somehow be spoiled or broken. It is unfortunate for you, me, and all computer users that Microsoft's Java strategy is to try to undermine Java portability. The 1998 federal anti-monopoly case against Microsoft revealed a Microsoft internal memo stating that Microsoft's strategic goal was to "kill cross-platform Java." You might want to bear that in mind when choosing your Java supplier.

The "Java Platform"

The Java platform has several pieces:

- Java programming language

- Java Virtual Machine (interpreter)

- Software libraries accompanying the system

- The World Wide Web and Java

While mentioning the pieces that make up Java, I should also note some software that includes the Java name but is only marginally related to Java. I am talking about JavaScript, the scripting language developed by Netscape Communications Corporation. JavaScript is used in the Netscape browser to prompt the user for input and then to read it, open and close additional windows, and so on. JavaScript supports an elementary browser programming capability, but is not a general-purpose applications language as Java is. You don't need to learn JavaScript to be a Java programmer. If you already know JavaScript, it neither helps nor hurts.

As you read through the following sections describing the features of Java, you may recognize various good ideas that were pioneered by earlier systems. Java does not introduce many things that are wholly new; the innovation is in the blending of so many established good ideas from several sources.

The Java Language

Java is an object-oriented programming language in the same family as C++, Pascal, or Algol 60. It adopts ideas from non-mainstream languages like Smalltalk and Lisp, too. Java is a strongly-typed language, has data declarations, and has statements that operate on the data. The statements are grouped into what other languages call functions, procedures, or subroutines. Since Java is an object-oriented language, we call the functions *methods*. Methods can call other methods and can be recursive (call themselves). Program execution begins in a method with the special name main().

If you are already familiar with Object-Oriented Programming, great! If not, Chapter 2, "The Story of O: Object-Oriented Programming," explains the terminology, the ideas behind it, and how the ideas are expressed in Java.

Java is immediately recognizable to many programmers. The statements and expressions are similar to those in other languages and, in most cases, identical to those of C or C++.

Although Java adds some new things, it is equally notable for what is left out. The designer of C++ actually wrote, "Within C++, there is a much smaller and cleaner language struggling to get out." (Stroustrup, Bjarne, *The Design and Evolution of C++*, Addison-Wesley, 1994: 207). Of the people who agree with that prophetic statement, many think that the name of that smaller and cleaner language is Java.

How Java Is Simpler Than C or C++

Compared with C, Java does *not* have

- Memory address (pointer) arithmetic
- Preprocessor
- Automatic type conversion
- Global functions and variables
- Type definition aliases (typedefs)

Compared with C++, Java does *not* have

- Templates (although people are talking about adding them)
- Operator overloading
- Multiple inheritance
- Multiple ABIs

If you are not a C++ programmer and you don't know what some of these things are, don't worry. Even if you are a C++ programmer, you might not be fully conversant with all these features. With Java, you don't need to know.

The size of the basic datatypes, such as integers, characters, and floating-point numbers, is laid down in the language and is the same on all platforms. If a computer system doesn't support, say, 64-bit long integers, it must simulate them in software for Java. In this way, you get the same numeric results no matter what computer runs your program. The Java specification was adjusted recently to provide a better fit for the Intel x86 platform that does some floating-point calculations in 80 bits, even though it only has 64-bit registers to store the results.

We'll be covering these other Java language features, too, in later chapters:

- **Garbage collection.**   With garbage collection, the runtime library, not the programmer, reclaims dynamic storage no longer in use in a program.

- **Threads.** Threads let a program do more than one thing at once, just as timesharing lets a computer system do more than one thing at once.

- **Exceptions.** Exceptions let a programmer deal with error conditions when most convenient, instead of cluttering up the main flow of control with lots of error-checking and code-handling.

For those who like to study language reference manuals, the Java specification is online at http://java.sun.com/docs/books/jls/html/index.html.

It is also published in book form as *The Java Language Specification,* but I don't recommend buying it until it is updated with the Java 1.1 language additions, such as inner classes and blank final variables.

Note that there are no royalties due for the use of Sun's Java compilers, runtimes, or the software you build with them. Sun has written a perpetual, irrevocable, free, and royalty-free license for the Java specification. Sun realizes that Java has the best chance of succeeding if everyone in the computer industry can share in the benefits. In other words, use of Java does not exchange one monopoly for another. Instead, Java enables open competition on a level playing field, with participation by all.

Java Libraries

Much of the real value of Java is in the set of cross-platform APIs (described in the following box) that come with the system. Java has possibly the easiest-to-use networking and windowing (GUI) of any language, and that has helped its widespread adoption. For example, there is a library function to read a JPEG file and display it on the screen. There is another library function to make a method call to a Java program running on another computer, making distributed systems easy to build. A GUI application written in Java has the same portability as other Java programs. It, too, runs on all computer systems. A network program written in Java is much the same as any other kind of I/O. You create an object of the appropriate type and read or write it. The runtime system does all the painful low-level work for you, such as making the socket connections and sending the bytes over TCP/IP.

Application Programmer Interface (API)

This is the set of libraries the programmer sees and uses when writing source code. An API consists of the names of the routines in a library and the number and types of arguments they take. For example, the POSIX 1003.1 standard says that every system complying with the standard will have a function with the following prototype that returns nonzero if c is in the range of the 7-bit ASCII codes:

```
int isascii(int c);
```

A program that uses only the routines specified in an API can be ported to any OS that implements the API simply by recompiling it. APIs are for software vendors. Java supports a common API on all computers.

The Java libraries can be divided into two categories:

- **Core libraries bundled with the Java Development Kit (JDK):** These are the class libraries that every JDK must support.

- **Optional standard additions to the JDK:** These are the class libraries that are optional. If the feature is supported, however, it must be supported with this API.

Note that subset implementations are not allowed. If an API is in the core set, all Java execution environments must have it. If an API is in the Standard Extension (optional) set, an implementation can choose whether to include all of it or omit all of it.

There are so many additional libraries and packages announced for Java at this point, that alone they would make a topic for a pretty thick book. The following tables provide an overview of the Java libraries; in the second half of the book, we'll cover the use of the mainstream class libraries.

I'm showing you these now to give you some idea of the richness of the Java platform. I suggest you glance over them at this time. Later, when you have mastered the basics of the language and are looking to try different application areas, you can return and take a longer look.

The following API families were public when JDK 1.2 was released. Sun occasionally adds a library or uses a different grouping. You can always find the most up-to-date information on Sun's Java web page http://java.sun.com.

Table 1-1: Core APIs and Their Purposes

Core API	Purpose
Java runtimes	Standard runtime libraries for I/O, networking, applets, basic windowing, data structures, internationalization, math operations, and more.
Java Foundation Classes	"Swing" GUI library, Java 2D graphics, and accessibility (GUI support for people with visual and other impairments).
Security	Support for digital signatures, X.509 certificates, and message digests, explained later in the book. Exportable worldwide.
Java IDL	(Java Interface Definition Language) Used to talk to CORBA middleware
JDBC	(Java Database Connectivity) Library for database access.
JavaBeans	Software component library.
Java RMI	(Java Remote Method Invocation) For communicating with other Java processes, possibly on other systems.

The next table shows some of the Standard Extension APIs—optional additional libraries.

Table 1-2: Extension APIs and Their Purposes

Extension API	Purpose
Java Communications	Support for reading and writing the RS232 serial and IEEE 1284 parallel ports on a computer. Enables faxing, voice mail, and smart cards.
Infobus	A library contributed to Java by Lotus. Used to send data between communicating components and applets.
JavaHelp	Platform-independent framework for online help. Can be embedded in a program or used stand-alone in a browser for online documentation. Content can be client-side (fast) or server-side (shared).
JavaMail	Protocol-independent framework for building Java-based mail and messaging applications. Supports IMAP (client/server mail) and SMTP (Internet mail transfer).
Java Media	Large API set containing individual packages for 3D imaging, MIDI sound, remote collaboration, ech processing, telephony, and video and audio streaming,.
JNDI	(Java Naming and Directory Interface) A standard to get information from LDAP, NIS, or other enterprise directory service.

The Java Media libraries are Standard Extensions because they make heavy demands on the hardware (like video streaming) or require special peripherals (like the telephony library). If your low-end laptop can't do this, there is no value in burdening it with the libraries.

There are also three levels of application environments defined for very low-end systems. These are specifications aimed at hardware, rather than software functionality. These APIs are shown in Table 1-3.

Table 1-3: Device APIs and Their Purposes

Device APIs	Purpose
PersonalJava	An application environment for consumer devices that may be mobile and may be connected to a network, such as PDAs now and portable network computers in the future. PersonalJava has core and (optional) standard extension APIs, and it is fully upward compatible with Java, which means your PDA programs can be debugged and will run on a PC.
EmbeddedJava	A subset of PersonalJava with upward compatibility. It's intended for dedicated embedded devices that are severely resource-constrained, such as process controllers, laser printers, network routers, cell phones, and pagers. It allows you to write the software in Java and is designed to sit on top of any real-time operating system.
JavaCard	A specification of an environment for Java software that runs on smart cards.
	Note: Smart cards are not common in the U.S. but are very popular in the rest of the world. Imagine a credit card where the retailer doesn't have to dial up for authorization because the card can securely hold a record of value and transactions. On my desk as I write I have a signet ring that contains a Java interpreter chip and enough memory to hold a small program. It cost less than $15. The technology is here today: Who will be first to invent a Java wristwatch with a wireless video feed?

While the low-end APIs are a world of their own, this book is about Java applications programming for general purpose desktop systems. There are plenty of other Java APIs and products from Sun. Take a look at the web site for the most up-to-date information.

Each API family generally contains several related APIs, and each API (termed a *package* in Java) may be composed of several classes. This hierarchy is shown in Figure 1-5.

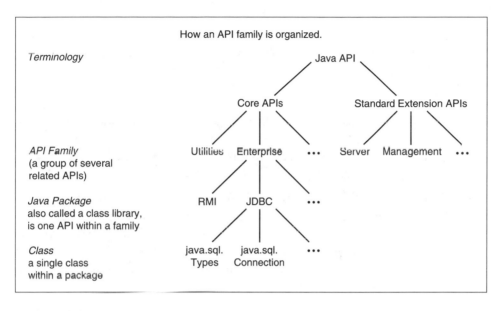

Figure 1-5: The hierarchy of an API family.

Releases of the JDK to Date

The major releases of the Java Development Kit (JDK) are listed below. The goal is to make all releases upward compatible (older code runs on newer systems) and downward compatible (newer code that only uses older features runs on older systems).

- **JDK 1.0.2** was the original May 1996 FCS (First Customer Ship) release of Java. There were two quick maintenance updates ("dot-dot" releases) bumping the version number from 1.0 to 1.0.2. The release supported basic GUI code, applets, and networking.

- **JDK 1.1** came out in February 1997. There has been a maintenance release about every quarter, taking the current version number to JDK 1.1.7. Release 1.1 of Java introduced a new event model for the window system to enable JavaBeans (component software). I/O was changed to better support internationalization and a feature called inner, or *nested*, classes was added to the language.

- **JDK 1.2** shipped in November 1998. It greatly improved GUI portability by adding the Swing library written in Java. It had better support for security, and many more libraries including 2D processing, CORBA interoperability, and the Java media framework. Some minor changes to the language were made to bring x86 numerics within the fold.

You should install and run the most up-to-date version of the JDK available to you, but don't use a beta release for a production system. Check Sun's Java web site for the latest releases. If you use Solaris, be aware that Sun offers a "Reference release" and a "Production release." The Reference release might be a little newer, but the Production release has been more extensively tested and tuned for Solaris and is the version you should use for development work.

Java Virtual Machine

Java source code is compiled to produce object code, known as *bytecode*. So far, this is just like any other language. The critical difference is that bytecode is not the binary code of any existing computer. It is an architecture-neutral machine code that can quickly be interpreted to run on any specific computer. You execute a Java program by running another program called the Java Virtual Machine, or JVM. The JVM is typically invoked by running the program called `java`. The JVM reads the bytecode program and interprets or translates it into the native instruction set.

This feature is highly significant! Running bytecode on a JVM is the reason that Java software is "Write Once, Run Everywhere." A Java executable is a binary file that runs on every processor. A Java program is compiled on any computer, and run on any computer.

Application Binary Interface (ABI)

This is the environment that a program sees at runtime. It is the format of an executable file; the OS specifics such as process address space, and hardware details such as the number, sizes, and reserved uses of registers.

Only a compiler-writer has to know the details of an ABI, but an ABI allows a hardware clone market to exist. A program that conforms to a system's ABI will run on any processor that complies with the ABI, regardless of who built the system—original manufacturer, clone maker, or OEM.

Binary standards, such as the SPARC Compliance Definition, specify an ABI. Every processor architecture, such as Intel x86, Apple/Motorola Power PC, and Sun SPARC, has its own native ABI. Java supports the same ABI on all computers.

The Java Virtual Machine—a fancy name for the interpreter—needs to be implemented once for each computer system; then all bytecode will run on that system. There are several alternative JVMs available for the PC and the Macintosh, and they differ in speed, cost, and quality.

Program portability through use of an interpreter for common bytecodes is not a new idea. The UCSD Pascal system ran the same way. Smalltalk, popularized a while back at Xerox PARC and more recently by IBM, uses the same approach.

Bytecode is not just for Java. If you modify a compiler for some other language, such as Ada, COBOL, or Visual Basic, so that it outputs bytecode, you can run it equally well on the JVM on any computer. A number of companies are retargeting their compilers to do exactly that. Not all languages are a good fit to the JVM; for example, the pointer arithmetic in C and C++ makes them a poor fit. However, being able to run your code on the JVM that is now standard with every new computer system on the planet is a powerful inducement to change. Companies designing new kinds of computer systems will be able to count on having a large volume of Java application software available from day one. Java greatly helps innovation, while retaining the investment in hardware, software, and training.

Java takes several other steps to ensure portability.

- It offers the same Application Programmer Interface (API) on all platforms.

- Java has the same Application Binary Interface (ABI) on all platforms. The Java Virtual Machine implements that common ABI.

- The Java Language specification mandates several things that are normally left to the discretion of the compiler writer. By requiring that operands are evaluated in a strict left-to-right order and stipulating the sizes of all the primitive types (ints are 32 bits, doubles are 64 bits, etc.), Java offers not just program portability but identical program behavior on different systems. In other words, not only does the program run everywhere, but it will get the same arithmetic results everywhere, despite different hardware models of arithmetic and overflow.

- Java uses the Unicode character set, which is a 16-bit superset of ASCII. Unicode can represent the symbols in most of the alphabets in the world, including Russian Cyrillic characters and Asian ideograms.

Performance

Portability initially comes at the cost of some performance. It's a reasonable bargain. Imagine if all the systems that had been built over the years had not tried to shave off the costs of two extra bytes of storage and had stored 4-byte years instead of 2-byte years. We would not now have a year-2000 problem.

If a binary is not compiled down to a specific machine code, extra work is needed at runtime to finish the job. The first Java programs were about 10 to 20 times slower than equivalent C++ code. People are very interested in making Java as fast as possible, and the performance difference is now much smaller. On some codes it is negligible.

Some JVMs can compile the bytecode as they run it, a technique known as "Just In Time" compilation, or JIT. The first time through, the code is run at interpreted speed. It is also compiled in a separate thread and subsequent passes through a loop are executed at native binary speed. Since a JIT compiler knows the exact details of the execution environment, such as cache sizes, whether floating-point is emulated, and amount of main memory, it can conceivably generate higher performance code than a C compiler, targeting a more general environment.

There are also compilers that translate directly to native code (.exe format on a PC, for example) instead of or as well as bytecode. The bytecode specification allows native code to be stored in the binary, as well as the portable bytecode.

If you have questions about whether performance is an issue for you, a pilot project should get you the answers. Performance also depends on the application environment. If you are doing any kind of database access, the performance bottleneck there will dwarf any other delay in the system. The Sun JDK 1.2 comes with a JIT compiler switched on by default. Performance is typically no longer an issue.

The World Wide Web and Java

There are three kinds of Java programs:

- Stand-alone programs, known as *applications*.

- Programs that run in web browsers, known as *applets*. An applet is simply an application program that runs inside a browser.

- Programs that run in a web server, known as *servlets*. A servlet is simply an application program that is run on demand by a web server.

Applets

There are very few differences between programming an applet versus programming an application. In fact, a single binary can even be both. Everything you learn about Java application programming carries over to applet programming, and vice versa.

You can put a web page on a server, and browser clients can download the page on demand to see the formatted text. Applets work in the same way. You write and compile a Java applet program, then place a URL or HTML reference to it in the web page. When a client browses that page, the Java applet binary is downloaded to the client along with the text and graphics files. The browser contains a JVM, and it executes the applet on the client computer.

This sounds simple and perhaps not very interesting. In fact, it is galvanizing the computer industry. Before Java, the World Wide Web (WWW) was a read-only interface. You browsed URLs, it served you pages. Now that web pages can cause programs to run, the browser is on the way to becoming the universal computer interface. Originally, an applet was considered a little application, but in fact there is no size restriction on applets. Because the model is useful, applets of all sizes exist. Java applets fit very neatly into the client/server model of computing. A later chapter is devoted to applets.

Applets in general are more popular for in-house enterprise systems than for high-profile ISV software. Don't make the mistake of ignoring applets because they haven't revolutionized office suite software. It's a question of using the right tools for the job. There are some excellent applets on the CD accompanying this book.

Server-Side Java

Java is becoming hugely popular on the server, where it is being used to replace CGI scripts. This kind of program is called a *servlet*. Sun Microsystems has a Java Web Server product that provides a convenient framework for invoking servlets.

A servlet is a Java program whose input comes from a server and whose output goes to a server. Other than that, it is virtually no different from a regular Java program. Think of a servlet as an application that, like an applet, requires a web server software environment in which to run. When the web server starts up a servlet when its URL is referenced, the applets can use this to talk to the server via sockets to write files, open connections to other servers, or whatever.

On the CD, there is a web server that supports servlets, including source code, so you can easily experiment with it if you wish. One of the benefits of servlets is that you can now use one language consistently on the client, on the server, in your middleware, and for accessing the corporate database. It replaces a muddle of different languages and scripts, and the "Write Once, Run Anywhere" feature is a bonus that makes Java servlets irresistible.

CHAPTER
2

- Abstraction

- Encapsulation

- The One-Minute Object Manager

- Classes

- Per-Instance and Per-Class Members

- The "final" Modifier

- Access Modifiers

- Some Light Relief

The Story of O: Object-Oriented Programming

It's a surprising but accurate observation that software development trends seem to be running in the opposite direction from the universe in general. The universe has entropy—it is gradually "winding down," or proceeding to a less and less coherent state. By way of contrast software development methodologies over the past 30 years have become more disciplined and more organized. The prime example of this is Object-Oriented Programming (OOP), an old idea enjoying a powerful revival at present.

Java is an object-oriented language, and to understand Java you have to understand OOP concepts. Fortunately, the big, well-kept secret of Object-Oriented Programming works in our favor here: Object-Oriented Programming is based on simple ideas. If you already know OOP, you can breeze through this chapter to pick up the Java way of doing things. If you haven't done any OOP before, this chapter will explain it from first principles.

Object-Oriented Programming is based on a small number of common-sense fundamentals.Unfortunately OOP has some special terminology, and it suffers from the "surfeit of Zen" problem: to fully understand any one part, you need to understand most of the other parts. Most programmers can understand OOP instinctively when it is explained clearly.

The Big Well-Kept Secret of Object-Oriented Programming

Although there are zillions of language-specific details, Object-Oriented Programming is based on a few simple ideas.

It is not usually explained clearly, however. Look at the turbo-babble you can find in the introduction to any book on C++, for example:

> Object-Oriented Programming is characterized by inheritance and dynamic binding. C++ supports inheritance through class derivation. Dynamic binding is provided by virtual class functions. Virtual functions provide a method of encapsulating the implementation details of an inheritance hierarchy.

Completely accurate, but also completely incomprehensible to someone encountering the topic for the first time. Here we describe OOP in simple English, and relate it to familiar programming language features.

Teach Yourself OOP the Hard Way

Alan Kay, an OO expert who is now an Apple distinguished Fellow, began studying the topic in the early 1970s. He was leafing through eighty pages of Simula-67 listing. Simula was the first OO language, but Alan hadn't seen it before and didn't know that. He thought it was Algol or an Algol-variant.

He literally taught himself the principles of OOP from reading eighty pages of code in the first object-oriented language. Not everyone will want to duplicate that achievement, so this chapter provides the missing background.

Object-Oriented Programming is not a new idea; Simula-67 pioneered it around thirty years ago. Most experts agree that OOP is based on four key principles: abstraction, encapsulation, inheritance, and polymorphism.

We'll deal with the two in this chapter, and another two in a later chapter. We'll describe these concepts in terms of real-world examples, and then through programming abstractions. At the end of this chapter, you'll have enough knowledge to read and write basic object-oriented programs. You'll need to read the second OOP chapter to properly understand OOP, though.

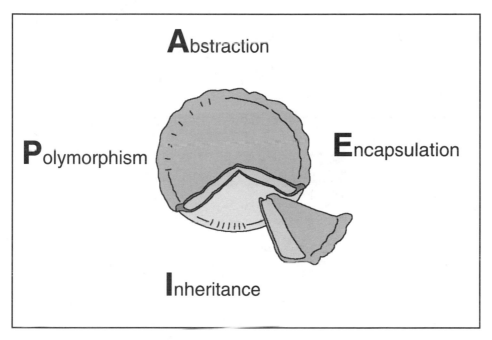

Figure 2-1: OOP has four key concepts which you can remember by thinking of A PIE: Abstraction, Polymorphism, Inheritance, and Encapsulation.

Abstraction

To process something from the real world on a computer, we have to extract the essential characteristics. The data representing these characteristics are how we will process that thing in a system.

The characteristics that we choose will depend on what we are trying to do. Take a car, for example. A registration authority will record the Vehicle Identification Number (the unique code assigned by the manufacturer), the license plate, the current owner, the tax due, and so on. When the car checks into a garage for a service, however, the garage will represent it in their computer system by license plate, work description, billing information, and owner. In the owner's home budgeting system, the abstraction may be the car description, service history, gas mileage records, and so on.

These are all examples of data abstractions. Data abstraction is the process of refining away the unimportant details of an object, so that only the appropriate characteristics that describe it remain. These, together with the operations on the data, form an abstract data type. We just mentioned three different data abstractions for a car. Abstraction is where program design starts. All mainstream programming languages provide a way to store pieces of related data together. It is usually called something like a structure or record.

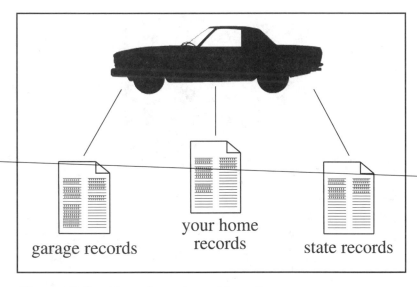

garage records   your home records   state records

Figure 2-2:   Three abstractions of "a car."

The One-Minute Object Manager

You have already covered two of the four cornerstones of Object-Oriented Programming. Now is a good time to show what this means with programming examples. We'll use C to start out because it's an enormously popular language, and because if you know any algorithmic language, it's pretty easy to map that to C. Let's begin with an explanation that will take no more than one minute to follow.

We'll build our example around a C struct (a record or structure in other languages) that we'll call "fruit." Since it is our user-defined data type that stores information abstracted from the qualities of fruit, we'll declare variables like plum, apple, and banana that are instances of fruit type. Fruit isn't usually something that is data processed, but this example keeps everything focused on the new abstraction, rather than the bits and bytes.

Assume we are primarily concerned with the nutritional value of fruit. As a result the characteristics that we abstract out and store might go into a structure like this:

```
typedef struct {                         C CODE
        int grams;
        int cals_per_gram;
} Fruit;
```

We also have a function that can calculate the total calories, given a pointer to a fruit structure:

```
int total_calories (Fruit *this)
{
        return (this->grams) * (this->cals_per_gram);

}
```

Encapsulation

One step beyond abstraction is the recognition that, equally as important as data, are the operations that are performed on it. Encapsulation simply says that there should be a way to associate the two closely together and treat them as a single unit of organization. In language terms, data and related functions should be bundled together somehow, so you can say, "This is how we represent a blurf object, and these are the only operations that can be done on blurfs."

This is a subtle principle because non-OOP languages support encapsulation well for built-in types and not at all for user-defined types. For example, take floating-point numbers. In most languages, the only valid thing you can do with them is arithmetic operations and I/O. Even in C, if you try to shift left the bits of a floating-point number the compiler will print out an error message, as shown below:

```
float         f = 2.0;              C EXAMPLE
int           i,j = 1;

i = f << j;
        ^^ operand must have integral type
```

The valid operations for a float are encapsulated, or bundled together, as part of the type information, and shifting isn't one of them. You cannot directly get your hands on the bits that represent the internal fields of the type, such as the significand, the sign bit, or the exponent. The compiler enforces the rule that "the operation must be compatible with the type."

Although C provides header files that group together variables, types (typedefs), and function declarations, this is not true encapsulation. C header files do not enforce the integrity of a type (i.e., preventing invalid operations, like assigning a float to an int that represents month_number), nor do they provide any information hiding. Any program that includes the header file has full details of what is in the type, can access individual fields as desired, and can create new functions that operate on the internals of the structs.

Support for encapsulation—bundling together types and the functions that operate on those types and restricting access to the internal representation—is extended in OOP-languages to cover user-defined types. They enforce the integrity of a type by preventing programmers from accessing individual fields in inappropriate ways. Only a predetermined group of functions can access the data fields. The collective term for datatype and operations bundled together with access restrictions is a *class*. An individual variable or constant data item in a class is a *field*. A variable of some class type is called an *instance* or an *object*. It's pretty much the same as a variable of an ordinary type, except the valid functions that can be invoked for it are tied to it. In a way, OOP is a misnomer; we should really say "Class-Based Programming."

Explanation for Non-Native Speakers of C

The definition of the Fruit struct should be self-explanatory. It has two fields that are integers. One records the weight; the other, the unit calories.

The function "total_calories" has one parameter that is the address of a Fruit variable. The parameter is called "this", and the asterisk before it says it is an address variable. The body of the function says to get the "grams" field of the structure pointed to by the argument called "this" and multiply it (here the asterisk has the conventional meaning) by the "cals_per_gram" field. Return the result as the value of the function.

In the example below, the declaration "Fruit pear ..." creates and initializes a variable of the Fruit type. Finally, the last line creates an integer variable called "total_cals". The variable is initialized with the value returned by calling the function on the pear argument. The function expects the address of a Fruit, rather than the Fruit itself, so we pass it "&pear" — the address of pear.

Note: "Pointer to" and "address of" mean exactly the same thing in C, except on really strange computers of a type that nobody builds anymore.

Here's a C example of calling it:

```
Fruit pear = {5, 45};                          C CODE
int total_cals = total_calories( &pear );
```

So far, so good. But the function and the Fruit type that it operates on, are not closely coupled together. It's too easy to get inside the struct and adjust fields independently. It's possible for anyone to add their own extra functions that operate on the fields of the Fruit type.

We seek the quality of *encapsulation*, so let's bundle together the type definition with all the functions that operate on it. In C, we bundle things together by enclosing them in curly braces. Our example would then look like:

```
struct Fruit {
        int grams;                             PSEUDO C
        int cals_per_gram;

           // we have moved the function inside the struct
        int total_calories (Fruit *this)
        {
                return (this->grams) * (this->cals_per_gram);
        }
};
```

Note that "//" makes the rest of the line a comment in Java (and C++). We'll often annotate code examples using that. You cannot actually declare a function inside a struct in C, but let's imagine you could. To simplify things we now impose a rule or convention about function arguments: all the functions that we declare inside the Fruit datatype will always take a pointer-to-a-fruit as the first parameter. This first parameter will point to the fruit that we are going to do the operation on.

So let's save some writing and have the compiler make that first parameter implicit. We won't mention the fruit pointer either in the parameter list or before the fields it points to. We'll just assume that it exists implicitly, and its name is always "this". Think of it as saying, "This here pointer points to the specific piece of fruit you are working on." We'll provide the fruit variable explicitly in the call, but it is implicit in the method declaration.

At this point, we have created a class. Replace the word "struct" with the word "class". Our three modifications are to do the following:

1. Bundle together the functions with the datatypes in a struct template.

2. Give all the functions an implicit first parameter called "this" that points to an actual struct instance with the data.

3. Replace the word "struct" with "class".

```
class Fruit {
        int grams;
        int cals_per_gram;                          C++ CODE

        int total_calories ( )
        {
                return grams * cals_per_gram;
        }
};
```

There. Those are the elements of C++. The rest are just details (although there are rather a lot of them). That should have taken about one minute to read, although it may take a little longer to re-read and sink in. We get some other benefits from organizing the namespaces: the data fields are implicitly recognized inside the functions without having to say from which struct they came. They come from the same kind of struct that contains the function. In other words, the compiler assumes the missing pieces. Here's how the same code looks in Java. Try compiling it.

```
class Fruit {
    int grams;
    int cals_per_gram;                    Java CODE

    int total_calories ( ) {
        return grams * cals_per_gram;
    }
}
```

There are plenty of keywords—public, private, and protected—to control whether other classes can access the fields and methods, or the *members*. We'll cover those later. Let's make explicit the important distinction between a class and an object.

Table 2-1: Differences Between a Class and an Object

Name	Description	Example Java Code

Class	A *template* or type, describing the field and methods that we group together to represent something.
	A class is comparable to a datatype. A class is also known as a *non-primitive type*.
		```class Fruit {```
		 ``` int grams;```
		 ``` int cals_per_gram;```
		
		 ``` int total_calories ( )```
		 ``` {```
		 ``` return grams *```
		 ``` cals_per_gram;```
		 ``` }```
		 ```}```

Object	A variable constructed according to a class template, able to hold values in its fields, and able to have its methods called.
	An object is comparable to a variable like "x". There are typically many objects for any given class. We say an object is an *instance* of a class or *belongs to* a class.
		```Fruit apple;```
		
		 ```Fruit orange, lemon, plum;```

Primitive Type	A primitive type is one of the eight basic data types in Java, such as int, char, boolean, and more.
	A primitive type is not composed of any other types, and it contrasts with the non-primitive, or class types.
		```int grams;```
		 ```int cals_per_gram;```
		
		 ```char c = 'X';```
		
		 ```double pi = 3.142;```

There are no structs, typedefs, or records in Java. The most important way to group related things together is to put them in a class. You can also put classes together into a package.

Here's a neat thing: a class can be related to another class in a parent/child relationship. This means that you can say "this class is exactly like that class over there, but with these additional members or changes." All classes that you write have a parent class, either one that you specify or the root system class known as *Object*. A class is a type, and a child class is just a subtype. We'll talk a lot more about this in the second OOP chapter.

Here is how you declare object variables:

```
Fruit   plum, apple, pear;
```
                                                            Java CODE

You need to create objects before you can invoke methods on them, and that information is coming up. For now, here is how to call the methods, after you have created the objects:

```
// call total_calories() on the plum object
 int c = plum.total_calories();

// call total_calories() of several different objects
 int i = plum.total_calories() +
          apple.total_calories() +
          pear.total_calories();
```

The programming language takes care of the housekeeping of sending a pointer to the variable as the implicit first parameter and of using that pointer to find the object variables. If it helps, you can think of the compiler as translating this:

```
plum.total_calories()                        /* Java */
```

into this:

```
total_calories(&plum)                        /* C */
```

It's actually doing quite a bit more than that; making sure the method is only called for objects of the correct type, enforcing encapsulation, supporting inheritance, and so on. The new notation is useful to convey all these overtones. We refer to the functions that are in the class as "methods" because they are the method for processing some data of that type. There aren't any global functions or data. Everything is in some class in Java.

Classes

The preceding section described the philosophy of OOP. Now we'll dive into the details of Java, and look at objects, how to create them, and how to call methods on them.

You Always Get to an Object with a "Reference Variable"

All objects in Java are always accessed through memory references all the time. This is termed *indirect addressing*. You never deal with an object directly; you always deal with the address of an object.

> ### References, Pointers, Addresses—The Same Thing
>
> Some people say that Java doesn't have pointers, it has references. They mean that references are a refinement of pointers with restricted semantics.
>
> The same people say that C doesn't have memory addresses, it has pointers. That is splitting hairs: a reference is another name for a pointer, which is another name for a memory address. If Java doesn't have pointers, why is a common error condition called a "Null**Pointer**Exception"?
>
> Java doesn't have arbitrary arithmetic on pointers (the source of so many bugs in C++) and Java automatically dereferences pointers as needed, making it easy to use.

When you declare a variable, what you get depends on the type. If you declare a primitive type (simple built-in types like int, char, boolean, and float), you actually get the variable and you can immediately read, write, and process it. An example follows:

```
int i;
i =0;  i++; i=myNumber; // all fine.
```

If, however, you declare a variable of any class type, since you do *not* immediately get an object of that class, you cannot immediately read, write, or call its methods! What you get is a *reference variable*—a location that can hold a reference to the desired object *when you fill it in*. A reference to something is just its address in memory.

```
Fruit i;    // "i" is a Fruit reference, we must still create it
i.grams =0; // Not fine. The "i" Fruit does not exist yet
            // executing the statement will cause a runtime error
```

Note that this is a big difference from C++, where declaring an object reserves space for the object then and there. The Java way allows useful implementation simplifications—object sizes never have to be known on compilation, because they are *all* simply dealt with as a reference to the actual object. The point you should take away is that objects of non-primitive types—objects and arrays—need to be created before use, and are always and exclusively referenced indirectly. *Dereferencing*, or going first to the reference variable to get the memory address and then going to that address to get the fields, is done automatically for you. When the compiler needs an address, it uses the address; when the compiler needs an object, it dereferences the address.

If you have had to grapple with C or C++ pointers this is an incredible boon, and is one reason that people are so productive in Java. The concept that variables are really references to objects is so strong in Java, that "reference type" is used synonymously for "class" in the language specification.

This declaration gets a variable myName that can reference an object of String:

```
String myName;
```

This is after you have filled in the reference so it points to such an object. Create a String object for myName, or you can make it point to an existing String object.

So when you compare two reference variables, you are actually comparing whether the address in yourName matches the address in myName; meaning, do these two variables point to the same object?

```
String yourName = "Anne";
if (yourName == myName) ... // compares String addresses
```

Frequently you are more interested in comparing two different objects for equal data fields. That kind of comparison is done using a method call. The standard Java String class defines a method equals(), and you might use it like this:

```
if ( yourName.equals(myName) ) // compares String contents
```

If you have two variables, the assignment shown does not *copy* the apple object:

```
Fruit apple = ... some value... ;
Fruit myfruit;
... myfruit = apple;
```

It takes the memory address that is in apple and copies it into myfruit. The variables myfruit and apple now reference the same object. Changes made through myfruit will be seen by apple!

```
myfruit.grams = 37;
```

The field `apple.grams` (that is, the field `grams` in the object that `apple` references) is now 37, too.

The "null" Reference

References can be assigned a special value that says, "I don't refer to anything." In Java, this is called the *null* value. When you declare a reference type, it is initialized with the value "null," usually represented as zero in the underlying system. You can explicitly assign null or check for it using the literal value "null" like this:

```
Window MyWindow;  // MyWindow has the value null
MyWindow = new Window(); // MyWindow points to a Window object

if (MyWindow==null) . . .
```

There is a similar keyword for the return type of methods to say "this method doesn't return any value". The keyword is `void`.

Summary: Object Variables Hold References to Objects, Not Objects

This summarizes the implications of Java's philosophy that non-primitive variables hold references to objects, meaning that they hold the address of an object.

- Declaring an object variable does not create a corresponding object.

- Comparing two object variables with the "`==`" operator really compares the pointers held in the variables, not the objects pointed to. You usually want to define an `equals()` method for comparisons.

- An object is passed as a parameter by pushing a copy of the reference to it on the stack. The fields in the original object may therefore be changed or updated by the method, and you cannot make the original version of the reference point to a different object.

- It's easy to declare a class that has an instance of itself as a field. For example, a linked list contains a linked list, and a binary tree contains two binary trees. If you declare the field "Foo", it will be a" reference to Foo".

- Since a reference variable is dereferenced automatically to get the contents of fields in the object, it's easy for you to overlook that assignments and comparisons are of pointers, not objects.

Creating New Objects: Constructors

Whenever you declare an object variable, before you can actually do anything with it, you must make it point to an object instance. You can assign an existing object reference into it, or you can create a new object using a constructor—a process known as *instantiation*, like so:

```
myVariable = new MyClass();
```

You may also combine the declaration and instantiation into one like this:

```
MyClass myVariable = new MyClass();
```

A constructor is like a special kind of method that can be used only to create and initialize a new object. Rather than "constructor," "Create_and_Initialize" would be a better, though long, name, but the OOP world has already settled on constructor. One reason a constructor (or at least an ordinary method) is needed is because no one outside the class is able to access data whose scope is limited to the class (we call this private data—there is a keyword to label data in this way). Therefore you need a privileged function inside the class to fill in the initial data values of a newly-minted object. This is a bit of a leap from C, where you just initialize a variable with an assignment in its definition, or even leave it uninitialized.

Constructor functions always have the same name as the class, and have this general form

```
optionalAccessModifier ClassName ( parameterlist ) optionalThrows {

        statements

}
```

We can ignore the optional parts for now. Note that there is no explicit return type, nor the keyword "void". In some sense, the constructor name (the same as the classname) *is* the return type.

Here is the Fruit class with some constructors added:

```
class Fruit {                           Java CODE
    int grams;
    int cals_per_gram;

    Fruit() {                    // constructor
        grams=55;                // no-arg constructor - has no arguments
        cals_per_gram=0;
    }

    Fruit(int g, int c) {    //another constructor
        grams=g;
        cals_per_gram=c;
    }
}
```

Here are some examples of objects being constructed:

```
    . . .
    // invoking constructor in a declaration
    Fruit melon=new Fruit(4,5);

    Fruit banana - new Fruit();

    Fruit lime, kumquat=new Fruit(), raspberry;

    // invoking constructor in a statement
    melon=new Fruit(60,3);
    // melon now points to a different newly created object
```

In the first line, a Fruit object referenced by melon is created with grams = 4 and cals_per_gram = 5.

Similarly a Fruit object, referenced by banana, is created with grams = 55 and cals_per_gram = 0. We get that because those are the defaults that the no-arg (no arguments) constructor uses.

A Fruit object, referenced by kumquat, is created using the no-arg constructor. Reference variables lime and raspberry are created, each with the value null.

Most classes have at least one explicit constructor. You can define several different constructors, and tell them apart by their parameter types. Sometimes you may want one constructor to call another. You may have a series of constructors that accept several different types of arguments and call a single constructor with the arguments in a standardized form to do all the rest of the processing in one place, which is quite common. You may use `this(...)` to call a different constructor in the same class. Normally `this` in a method means "the object I was invoked on." Here it is re-used to mean "one of my other constructors; pick the one with the matching signature."

When one constructor explicitly invokes another, that invocation must be the very first statement in the constructor. This is true for a couple of reasons. First, something is fully created after a constructor has been completed, and second, something must be fully created before you can start playing around with its fields.

Here is an example of one constructor invoking another with `this()`:

```
class Fruit {
        // data fields
    int grams;
    int cals_per_gram;

    Fruit() {            // constructor
        this(55, 0);
    }

    Fruit(int g, int c) {    //another constructor
        grams=g;
        cals_per_gram=c;
    }

        // ... other methods ....

}
```

Calls the sibling constructor whose arguments match.

A constructor cannot be invoked explicitly by the programmer other than in object creation, although this might otherwise be quite a useful operation to, say, reset an object to a known initial state. This is because a constructor is deemed to magically create an object, as well as to set values in its fields. The language specification says that constructors are not counted as members of a class. Other than that they are like methods and have ordinary statements.

Declaring a class does not create any objects. For example:

```
class Employee {
    . . . // does not create any object
}
```

Declaring a variable of that class type does not create any objects, either.

```
Employee you; // does not create an object
```

Declaring a variable of a class type gives you a variable that can point to an object when you fill it in.

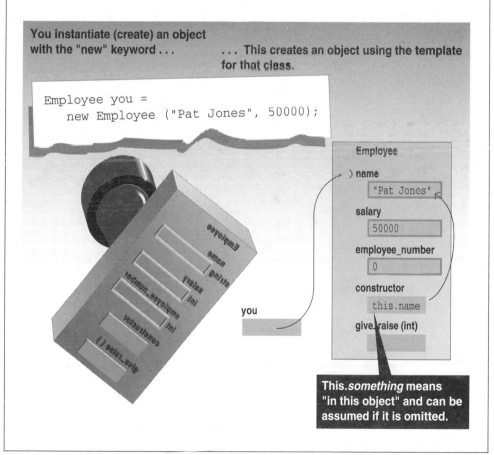

Figure 2-3: An object is created with a "new" keyword.

Since almost everything in Java is an object, almost everything is created by a call to a constructor. Constructors have the same name as the class, so it is very common to see something declared and initialized with calls like this:

```
Bicycle schwinn = new Bicycle();
Cheese cheddar = new Cheese(matured);
Beer ESB = new Beer(London, bitter, 1068);
Fruit lime = new Citrus(); // Fruit is the superclass of Citrus
```

The repeated classname looks quite odd to some programmers at first.

One way to visualize classes and objects is to think of a class as like a rubber stamp. The rubber stamp (class) can create many imprints (objects).

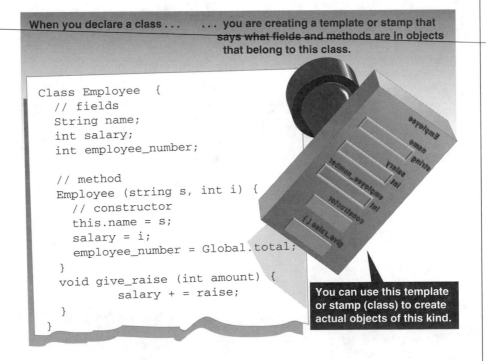

When you declare a class . . .   . . . you are creating a template or stamp that says what fields and methods are in objects that belong to this class.

```
Class Employee  {
   // fields
   String name;
   int salary;
   int employee_number;

   // method
   Employee (string s, int i) {
     // constructor
     this.name = s;
     salary = i;
     employee_number = Global.total;
   }
   void give_raise (int amount) {
          salary + = raise;

   }
}
```

You can use this template or stamp (class) to create actual objects of this kind.

The class defines the "shape" or fields that each object has. On paper, the fields are just areas of paper bordered by ink. You can write different values in those areas. In a programming language, the fields are variables and methods. The methods can calculate and assign new values to the variables.

Figure 2-4:   A class is like a rubber stamp. It is a template or mold for creating objects.

How Constructors Are Invoked

When you do not provide any explicit constructors for your class (you are allowed to do this), then the default no-arg constructor is assumed for you. The *default no-arg* (meaning "no arguments") constructor for a class takes no arguments and does nothing, but it does ensure that every class always has at least one constructor. Some classes shouldn't have a no-arg constructor, so when you provide any constructor at all, you do not get the default no-arg constructor. In this case if you also want a no-arg constructor, you provide one explicitly.

When an object is instantiated, this is the order in which things happen:

1. The memory for the object is allocated.

2. The memory is cleared before being allocated to an object, causing data fields to be filled in with the default values zero, 0.0, null, and so on. Thus all objects start with a known state.

3. The constructor is called and might explicitly call another constructor in the same class. For example, a no-arg constructor might call one of the other constructors with some preset values for arguments, like this:

    ```
    Fruit() {              // constructor
        this(55, 0); // explicitly calls
    }                      // the Fruit(int, int) constructor
    ```

4. A constructor in the object's parent class is *always* called, either explicitly with super(*someArguments*), or implicitly. This is recursive, meaning that it calls a constructor in its parent and so on back to the Object class.

    ```
    Fruit(int g, int c) {    //another constructor
        // super();    parent constructor implicitly called here
        grams=g;
        cals_per_gram=c;
    }
    ```

5. Any data fields with explicit initializers have those initial assignments executed. Any *Instance Initializers* are executed, which are a hack introduced with JDK1.1 so that anonymous classes (which cannot have constructors) can be initialized. We'll say what anonymous classes are later. The executions take place in the order in which they appear in the source code.

6. The rest of the statements in the object's constructor are executed.

No Destructors

Java has automatic storage management, including automatic reclamation of objects no longer in use. The runtime system does not therefore need to be told when an object has reached the end of its lifetime. Accordingly, there are no destructor methods to reclaim an object. Just delete, overwrite, or null out the last reference to an object and it becomes available for destruction so the memory can be reused. We'll cover more about this when we discuss garbage collection further on.

Methods

Methods are the OOP name for functions. A method is always declared inside a class; methods can't exist outside a class. A method has this general form:

This part is known as the "method signature"

```
optAccess returnType ( methodName ( optArgumentList ) ) optionalThrowsClause {
      ... statements...
}
```

The parts marked "opt" in the example above are optional. So an example method may look like this:

```
void someMethod() {
      i = this.total_calories();
}
```

Or it could look like this,which is how the main routine looks where execution starts.

The "method signature"

```
public static void ( main ( String[] args ) ) {
      ... statements...
}
```

You invoke a method by its name. You can have several methods with the same name in a class. The same-named methods are said to *overload* the name.

```
void someMethod(int i) {
    ... // some statements
}
void someMethod(double d, char c) {
    ... // some statements
}
```

The two methods above are overloaded. As long as they have different arguments, the compiler will be able to tell which one you intend to call. The ten-dol-
lar way of saying this is, "The method signature is used to disambiguate
overloaded method calls."

Methods with the same name should do the same thing. Don't have a method
called `validate()` that validates a customer record, and another one in the same
class called `validate(int i)` that calculates the square root of its argument.

Primitive variables declared inside a method have an undefined initial value. For
those familiar with compiler internals, as with most other programming languages, it's too big a performance hit to keep clearing stackframes, so it's not
done. Primitive local variables get an initial value of whatever old junk was left
on the stack.

You can call other methods in the same class without explicitly saying what object
you are invoking the method on. It assumes the "this" object.

```
class Fruit {
    int total_calories() { ... }

    void someMethod() {
        int i = total_calories();
        ... // more statements
    }
// ... rest of class omitted
```

You can write the "this" reference explicitly, with the exact same meaning, but
most people don't.

```
class Fruit {
    int total_calories() { ... }

    void someMethod() {
        int i = this.total_calories();
        ... // more statements
    }
}
```

You can also prefix "this." onto a data member name. One reason for writing it
that way is if you gave a parameter the same name as a data member. The param-

eter name hides the simple data member name, so you qualify it by saying it is the so-and-so field of this object:

```
class Fruit {
    int i;                // the field "i"
    void someMethod(int i) {
        this.i = i; // "i" is the parameter, "this.i" is the field
    }
```

The following boxes summarize how to call a method in the same class versus another class.

Calling a Method in the Same Class	Calling a Method in Another Class
| ```
class Fruit {
    int total_calories() { ... }

    void someMethod() {
        int i = total_calories();
        // it knows you mean this.
    }
``` | ```
class Cooking{

    Fruit lime = ...

    void otherMethod() {
        int i = lime.total_calories();
        // tell it which object

    }
``` |

An Alternative Rationale for OOP

Another way of looking at this class thing is that it's just a way of giving user-defined types the same privileges as types that are built in to the language.

Just as the compiler knows what may and may not be done with a float, classes provide a way to specify the same information and constraints for new types.

Since data can only be changed in disciplined ways, the result is software that is more reliable and quicker to debug. A piece of the program that "owns" (declares) an object cannot break it open and fool around with the individual fields.

OOP stresses the importance of objects rather than procedural statements. Consider it analogous to the C statement "i++", indicating "take the object called 'i' and do the '++' operation on it." Here we have "take the object called 'plum' and do the 'total_calories()' method on it."

In the Java code above, Fruit is a class.The variables apple, plum, and pear are instances of the class, or objects. The variables grams and cals_per_gram are instance variables. The function total_calories() is a method. The declarations of grams, cals_per_gram, and total_calories() are fields. The class as a whole forms a user-defined type.

A class can be used to "stamp out" or create any number of objects.

Each object keeps its own values in its data fields.

The template or class can turn out any number of objects of that kind.

Employee

name

Eugene Desmond

Employee

name

Pat

salary

65

employee

0

con

giv

Employee

name

"Bill Mudflap"

salary

75000

employee_number

0

constructor

give_raise (int)

name = ...

Each object has the same set of fields. Here the fields are "name", "salary", "employee_number", "Employee" (a constructor) and "give_raise" (a method). Whenever one of these names is used, it refers to the field in this particular object.

A constructor is always called to initialize the object. There can be several constructors, and they are distinguished by their arguments. If you didn't provide any constructors, a default one with no arguments is provided for you.

. . means the "name" field of this object, not any of the other objects.

Conceptually, each object has its own copy of the methods in the class. In practice, methods don't change (unlike the values in data fields), so we don't need to keep multiple copies of them. We do need to make sure that when a method references a field, it refers to that field in that object. The compiler takes care of it for you.

Figure 2-5:   A class can stamp out any number of objects belonging to that class.

Reference Variables and Passing Parameters to Methods

The difference between variables of primitive types and objects (reference types) has implications for parameter passing to methods, too. Variables of primitive types are passed by value; objects are passed by reference.

"Passing by value" means that the argument's value is copied, and is passed to the method. Inside the method this copy can be modified at will, and doesn't affect the original argument.

"Passing by reference" means that a reference to (i.e. the address of) the argument is passed to the method. Using the reference, the method is actually directly accessing the argument, not a copy of it. Any changes the method makes to the parameter are made to the actual object used as the argument. After you return from the method, that object will retain any new values set in the method.

What's really going on here is that a *copy* of the value that references an object argument is passed to the method. This is why some Java books say "everything is passed by value"—the *object reference* is passed by *value* which effectively passes the *object itself* by *reference*.

Dynamic Data Structures

The first question that most programmers ask when they hear that Java does not feature pointers is, "How do you create dynamic data structures?" How, for instance, do you create a binary tree class in which objects of the class can point to each other?

The answer is that reference variables can do this. Here are the data members for a Tree class in Java:

```
class Tree {
    private Object data;
    private Tree left;
    private Tree right;
        . . .
```

Java scores in allowing memory references, but disallowing the unsafe behavior frequently associated with them. By allowing arithmetic on pointers, unchecked deallocation, dangling pointers, pointers into the stack, and other evils, C/C++ gives the programmer too much rope. Sooner or later, most of us end up tying ourselves in knots with it.

Per-Instance and Per-Class Members

We have seen how a class defines the fields and methods that are in an object, and how each object stores its own version of these members. That is usually what you want. Sometimes, however, you have some fields of which you want only one copy, no matter how many instances of the class exist. A classic example of this is a field that represents a total. The objects contain the individual amounts, and it would be handy to have a single field that represents the total over all the objects for the class. This is the purpose of the keyword "static" — it makes something exist per-class, not per-instance. There are four varieties of static thing (once-only) in Java:

- **Data.** This is one set of data that belongs to the class, not individual objects.

- **Methods.** These are methods that belong to the class.

- **Blocks.** These are blocks that are executed only once.

- **Classes.** These are classes that are nested in another class. Static classes were introduced with JDK 1.1.

Static Is a Crummy Name

Of all the many poorly-chosen names in Java, "static" is the very worst. It comes from the confusing and confused static keyword in C. Static never made much sense as a keyword in C either. The term originated with data that was allocated statically in the data segment at compile time, but the term was re-used with other meanings, too. Whenever you see "static" in Java, think "once-only" or "per-class".

Static Data

Static data belongs to the class, not an individual object of the class. There is exactly one instance of static data, regardless of how many instances of the class there are. To make a field "per-class" apply the keyword "static", as shown below.

```
class Employee {
    String name;                // per-object field
    long     salary;            // per-object field
    short    employee_id;       // per-object field

    static int total_employees; // per-class field (one only)

        . . .
}
```

The purpose of the Employee class is to store and process data on an individual employee. However, we also use the class to hold the total number of employees that we have on the payroll. The variable `total_employees` is a quantity associated with employees in general, so this class might be a good home for it. It's wasteful, however, and error-prone to duplicate this value in every employee object. While `total_employees` is a value associated with the class as a whole, it is not associated with each object of it. Applying the storage modifier "static" to a data field makes that happen.

The "static" keyword means that there is just one of these fields, and it is shared by all objects in the class.

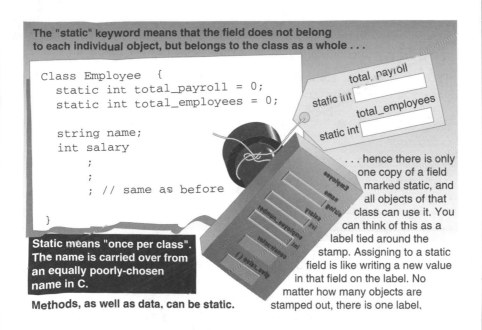

The "static" keyword means that the field does not belong to each individual object, but belongs to the class as a whole . . .

```
Class Employee   {
   static int total_payroll = 0;
   static int total_employees = 0;

   string name;
   int salary
       ;
       ;
       ; // same as before

}
```

total payroll

static int [____]

total_employees

static int [____]

. . . hence there is only one copy of a field marked static, and all objects of that class can use it. You can think of this as a label tied around the stamp. Assigning to a static field is like writing a new value in that field on the label. No matter how many objects are stamped out, there is one label.

Static means "once per class". The name is carried over from an equally poorly-chosen name in C.

Methods, as well as data, can be static.

Static (think "one per class") data is useful for any data that belongs to the class as a whole rather than any instance of it. A version id, and a running total are two examples of this kind of data.

Figure 2-6: "Static" means "only one for the whole class."

Inside the class, static data is accessed by giving its name. Outside the class, static data can be accessed by prefixing it with the name of an object or the name of the class. Either works as the following example shows:

```
Employee newhire = new Employee();
newhire.total_employees++; // reference through an instance

Employee.total_employees = 0; // reference through the class
```

The second form, referencing static variables through the class name, is preferred because it provides a cue that this is not instance data. Static variables are also called class variables.

Static Methods

Just as there can be static data that belongs to the class as a whole, there can also be static methods, also called *class methods*, that do some class-wide operations and do not apply to an individual object. Again, these are highlighted by using the "static" modifier before the method name. Again, you can call a static method by prefixing it with the name of an object or the name of the class.

It is always better to call a static method using the name of the class so that people don't confuse it with per-instance methods. Here is an example:

```
class Employee {
    String name;
    long      salary;
    short     employee_number;

    static int total_employees;

    static void clear() {
        total_employees = 0;
    }
}
    . . .

    newhire.clear();   // reference through an instance

    Employee.clear();  // better: reference through the class
```

Methods, as well as data, can be labeled as "static", meaning "there is only one of these for the class", not "one per object". The "main( )" method, where execution begins in an application is a static method.

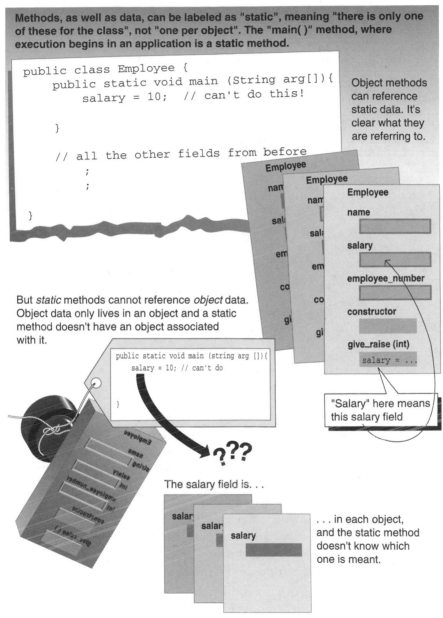

```
public class Employee {
    public static void main (String arg[]){
        salary = 10;   // can't do this!

    }

    // all the other fields from before
        ;
        ;

}
```

Object methods can reference static data. It's clear what they are referring to.

But *static* methods cannot reference *object* data. Object data only lives in an object and a static method doesn't have an object associated with it.

```
public static void main (string arg []){
    salary = 10; // can't do

}
```

"Salary" here means this salary field

???

The salary field is. . .

. . . in each object, and the static method doesn't know which one is meant.

Figure 2-7:   Static methods cannot directly reference per-object data.

A common pitfall is to reference *per-object* data from a *static* method. This "does not compute," since a static method is associated with a class, not an object. A static method doesn't have the implicit "this" object. The compiler won't know which object you want and will emit an error message if you try to access an instance variable from a static method, such as:

```
Can't make static reference to non-static variable
```

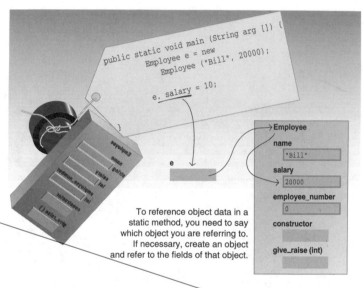

One way to reference instance (per-object) data and methods from a static method is to declare and instantiate an object in the static method. You can then access the data and methods of that instance. We've already let the cat out of the bag about not really keeping "per instance" copies of instance methods. So what is a static method used for? You declare a method static when it does something relating to the class as a whole, rather than specific to one instance. The class `java.lang.String` has several `valueOf()` methods that take a primitive type (boolean, int, etc.) argument and return its value as a String. These methods are static, so you can invoke them without needing a string instance, as in:

```
String s=String.valueOf(123.45); // OK
```

The `java.lang.Math` package is all static methods: abs(), sin(), cos(), exp(), and so on.

Finally, the main() method where execution starts is static. If it weren't, some bogus magic would be needed to create an instance before calling it.

Figure 2-8: Static methods must specify the object containing the per-object data that they want to reference.

Methods, as well as data, can be labeled as "static", meaning "there is only one of these for the class", not "one per object". The "main( )" method, where execution begins in an application is a static method.

```
public class Employee {
    public static void main (String arg[]){
        salary = 10;  // can't do this!

    }

    // all the other fields from before
        ;
        ;


}
```

Object methods can reference static data. It's clear what they are referring to.

But *static* methods cannot reference *object* data. Object data only lives in an object and a static method doesn't have an object associated with it.

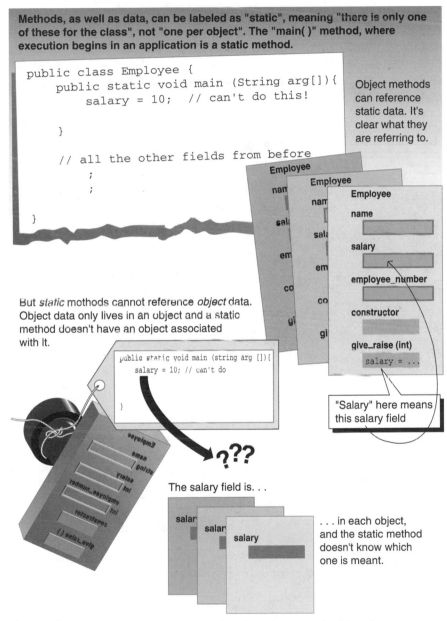

```
public static void main (string arg []){
    salary = 10; // can't do
}
```

???

"Salary" here means this salary field

The salary field is. . .

. . . in each object, and the static method doesn't know which one is meant.

Figure 2-7: Static methods cannot directly reference per-object data.

A common pitfall is to reference *per-object* data from a *static* method. This "does not compute," since a static method is associated with a class, not an object. A static method doesn't have the implicit "this" object. The compiler won't know which object you want and will emit an error message if you try to access an instance variable from a static method, such as:

```
Can't make static reference to non-static variable
```

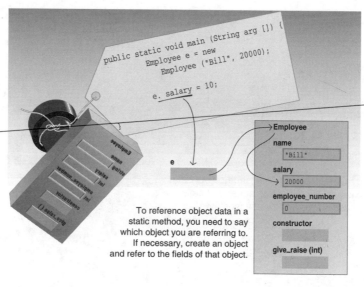

To reference object data in a static method, you need to say which object you are referring to. If necessary, create an object and refer to the fields of that object.

One way to reference instance (per-object) data and methods from a static method is to declare and instantiate an object in the static method. You can then access the data and methods of that instance. We've already let the cat out of the bag about not really keeping "per instance" copies of instance methods. So what is a static method used for? You declare a method static when it does something relating to the class as a whole, rather than specific to one instance. The class `java.lang.String` has several `valueOf()` methods that take a primitive type (boolean, int, etc.) argument and return its value as a String. These methods are static, so you can invoke them without needing a string instance, as in:

```
String s=String.valueOf(123.45); // OK
```

The `java.lang.Math` package is all static methods: abs(), sin(), cos(), exp(), and so on.

Finally, the main() method where execution starts is static. If it weren't, some bogus magic would be needed to create an instance before calling it.

Figure 2-8: Static methods must specify the object containing the per-object data that they want to reference.

The "static" keyword means that there is just one of these fields, and it is shared by all objects in the class.

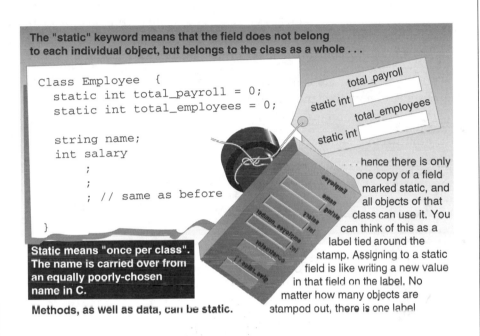

The "static" keyword means that the field does not belong to each individual object, but belongs to the class as a whole . . .

```
Class Employee {
    static int total_payroll = 0;
    static int total_employees = 0;

    string name;
    int salary
        ;
        ;
        ; // same as before

}
```

static int [total_payroll]

static int [total_employees]

. . . hence there is only one copy of a field marked static, and all objects of that class can use it. You can think of this as a label tied around the stamp. Assigning to a static field is like writing a new value in that field on the label. No matter how many objects are stamped out, there is one label

Static means "once per class". The name is carried over from an equally poorly-chosen name in C.

Methods, as well as data, can be static.

Static (think "one per class") data is useful for any data that belongs to the class as a whole rather than any instance of it. A version id, and a running total are two examples of this kind of data.

Figure 2-6: "Static" means "only one for the whole class."

Inside the class, static data is accessed by giving its name. Outside the class, static data can be accessed by prefixing it with the name of an object or the name of the class. Either works, as the following example shows:

```
Employee newhire = new Employee();
newhire.total_employees++; // reference through an instance

Employee.total_employees = 0; // reference through the class
```

The second form, referencing static variables through the class name, is preferred because it provides a cue that this is not instance data. Static variables are also called class variables.

Static Methods

Just as there can be static data that belongs to the class as a whole, there can also be static methods, also called *class methods,* that do some class-wide operations and do not apply to an individual object. Again, these are highlighted by using the "static" modifier before the method name. Again, you can call a static method by prefixing it with the name of an object or the name of the class.

It is always better to call a static method using the name of the class so that people don't confuse it with per-instance methods. Here is an example:

```
class Employee {
      String name;
      long      salary;
      short     employee_number;

      static int total_employees;

      static void clear() {
          total_employees = 0;
      }
}
    ...

    newhire.clear();   // reference through an instance

    Employee.clear();  // better: reference through the class
```

Static Blocks

The third kind of static thing is a static block. A block of code is a series of state-ments contained in a pair of curly braces. It can occur anywhere in a class that a member declaration can occur. A static block is a block prefixed by the keyword static. A static block must be inside a class, and outside all methods. A static block belongs to the class, and is most commonly used for initialization. It is exe-cuted when the class is first loaded into the JVM. *Loading a class* means reading in and converting a stream of bits from a file or URL into a known class inside the JVM. A class is loaded on demand, when another class references it.

The keyword "static" precedes the curly braces that delimit the static block, as shown here:

```
public class Employee {
    String name;
    long     salary;
    short    employee_number;

    static int total_payroll;

    static {
        System.out.println("Calculating payroll total ");
        if ( weAreIncludingTempsAndContractors ) // some condit'n
            total_payroll = ... // some value
        else total_payroll = ... // some other value
    }
}
```

> **Reloading Classes and Re-Executing Static Blocks**
>
> There was a subtle bug in pre-JDK 1.2 compilers. If a class dropped out of use, meaning that there were no instances of it left, it could be completely removed from the VM to save memory. If you later created an instance of the class, it would be loaded again, and the static initializers would execute again.
>
> This was potentially disastrous if you were relying on the "once only" semantics. The bug was fixed in JDK1.2, and the language specification was clarified: Classes are guaranteed not to be unloaded unless the class that loaded them is also unloaded. Essentially, classes stay in memory unless you are starting over from scratch.

Once again, static blocks can only access static data. There can be multiple static blocks in a class, and they are executed in the order in which they occur in the source. They are most useful for initializing data or guaranteed one-time only initialization. You can do more in a block of code than you can in an initializer expression that is attached to a variable declaration.

Static Classes

The final kind of static thing is a static class, also known as a *nested top-level class*. A static class is just the declaration of an entire class—constructors, methods, fields, and all—as a static member of another class.

A nested top-level class is typically used as a handy way to group some related classes tightly together—even more tightly than simply putting them in the same source file. An example of a nested top-level class might look like this:

```
class Hashtable {
        // data fields
        private Entry[] myTable;
        private int count=0;

        Object get() { return myTable[--count]; }

        void put(Object key, Object value) {
            Entry e = new Entry(key, value);
            myTable[count++] = e;
        }

        // a nested top-level class
        static class Entry {
            int hash;
            Object key;
            Object data;
            Entry(Object k, Object v) { ... }
            int hashCode() { ... }
            // various Entry management methods
        } // end of nested class "Entry"

    // ... other Hashtable methods ....
    } // end of class Hashtable

    // in yet another class entirely
        ... Hashtable.Entry he = new Hashtable.Entry(myk, myv);
            int i = he.hashCode();
```

Nested top-
level class.

The usual static limitation applies: The static class cannot access any of the instance data of an object belonging to the class in which it is nested. The static class, like the static method, does not have a "this" reference to an instance.

In the example above, the top-level class called `Entry` is nested inside the class called `Hashtable`. Here the nested class is used for organization. Everything to do with a hashtable entry is put into the nested class, and everything to do with the hashtable as a whole is in the containing class. Notice how you can make a forward reference to the nested class before you have defined it in the file. The name is `Entry` inside the containing class, and is `Hashtable.Entry` outside. By the way, this example comes from the Java runtime library.

The "final" Modifier

The last part of this chapter deals with some keywords that can be used to modify declarations. While the next section looks at several other keywords which make a class or the members of a class more visible or less visible to other classes, this section looks at final, which makes something constant. Why was the word "const" or "constant" not chosen? Because "final" can also be applied to code, as well as data, and the term "final" makes sense for both.

A class or a class member (that is, a data field or a method) can be declared final, meaning that this is the immediate value to use, and it won't change. We will look at what it means for a class or a method not to change in the advanced OOP chapter. A couple of final declarations are:

```
final static int myTotal = 100000;
final Fruit banana = new Fruit(200, 35);
```

When a reference variable is declared final, it means that you cannot make that variable point at some other object. You can, however, access the variable and change its fields through that final reference variable. The reference is final, not the referenced object. JDK 1.1 introduced the ability to mark method arguments and variables local to a method as final, such as:

```
void someMethod(final MyClass c, final int a[]) {
    c.field = 7; // allowed
    a[0] = 7; // allowed
    c = new MyClass(); // final means this is NOT allowed
    a = new int[13]; // final means this is NOT allowed
}
```

Marking a declaration as final is a clue to the compiler that certain optimizations can be made. In the case of final primitive data, the compiler can substitute the value in each place the name is used.

The "blank final variable"

JDK 1.1 also introduced something called a *blank final variable* which is simply a final variable (of any kind) that doesn't have an initializer. A blank final variable must be assigned an initial value, and that can be assigned only once. If you give a value to a blank final in a constructor, every constructor must give it a value. This is because you don't know which constructor will be called, and it must end up with an initialization. You could also initialize it in an instance initializer, as follows:

```
class Fruit {
    ... // stuff
    final String consumer;// blank final variable - has no initializer

    Fruit (String s) {  // constructor
        consumer = s;  // the blank final is initialized
    }

    ... // more stuff
}
```

Use a blank final when you have a value that is too complicated to calculate in a declaration, or that might cause an exception condition (more on that later), or where the final value depends on an argument to a constructor.

Access Modifiers

There are several keywords that control the visibility of a class and the members of a class. The table below explains these modifiers (private, no keyword, protected, and public). There are plenty of other keywords (static, final, abstract, native, and so on) that affect other things about a member or class. We have already seen static. Some of the other keywords can occur together, such as "static final".

You can have only one access modifier though, and if you leave it off, you get the default which is "the field can be accessed by anything in the same package." We'll talk more about packages later, but a package is just a group of related classes that you want to bundle together. Think "package = directory."

Table 2-2 is just a summary to look over. We'll be seeing it in action when we start some programming. Do notice how the modifiers form a logical increasing progression from no access to maximum access. Each is a true superset of the previous modifier. That will help you remember them.

In general you should give fields the most restricted visibility that still makes it possible for them to work. Don't make any fields public without good reason. Doing so destroys encapsulation.

Here is an OOP code idiom allowing read-only access to a field:

```java
public class Employee {
    private long salary;// is NOT visible to other classes

    public long getSalary() { // is visible to other classes
        return salary;
    }
}

class somOtherClassEntirely {

    public void main() {
        Employee e = ...

        long pay = e.getSalary();// gets the salary field of e
```

In the example above the salary field is private and cannot be accessed outside the Employee class. However, the Employee class can define an accessor function which is not private and that reads the value and returns it. Accessor functions frequently occur in pairs, with the name getSomething() to read it, and setSomething(x newValue) to set it.

Table 2-2: Keywords and Their Effects

Keyword	Effect	Example of Use

private	Members are not accessible outside this class.
	Making a constructor private prevents the class being instantiated.
	Making a method private means that it can only be called from within the class.
		```class Fruit {```
		``` private static int tot_grams;```
		``` private int grams;```
		``` private int cals_per_gram;```
		
		``` private Fruit() { // constructor```
		``` grams=55;```
		``` cals_per_gram=0;```
		``` }```
		```}```

(none)
often called
"package
access"
	Members are accessible in classes in the same package (loosely, directory) only.
	A class can be given package access or public access.
		```class Employee { // package access```
		``` String name;```
		``` long salary;```
		``` static int total_employees;```
		
		``` static void clear() {```
		``` total_employees = 0;```
		``` }```
		```...```

protected	Members are accessible in the package and in subclasses of this class.
	Note that protected is *less* protected than the default of package access.
		```class Employee {```
		``` protected String name;```
		``` protected long salary;```
		
		``` protected void```
		``` give_raise(int amount) {```
		``` salary = salary+amount;```
		``` }```
		```...```

public	Members are accessible anywhere the class is accessible.
	A class can be given package access or public access.
		```public class Employee {//public access```
		
		``` public static void main() {```
		``` }```
		```...```
		```}```

Some Light Relief

The Binary Burger: One Byte Is All You Need

That brings us to the end of the first part of OOP. We digress a little now and end this chapter with a software anecdote. Sometimes I'll end a chapter this way as a reward for reaching the end of the chapter.

Not too long ago, the fast food chain Burger King was proudly advertising the many choices they offer a customer. Burger King ads boasted of the 1024 ways a customer could order their WHOPPER burger; not "hundreds of ways" or "over 1000 ways," but "1024 ways." The number 1024 immediately jumps out to experienced programmers because it is 2^{10}, also known as a K, as in "They're offering a \$5K sign-on bonus at Flibbertigibbet Software, so I need you to at least match that, 'K?"

Naturally, a few programmers with too much imagination and free time on their hands tried to decode what the ten binary variables were in the Burger King world of choices. Here's what we came up with:

- single or double
- mayo
- lettuce
- cheese
- pickles
- onion
- tomato
- mustard
- ketchup

That's only nine. The tenth variable? It's something only a hacker would expect—it's the beef! Yep, one of the parameters that Burger King was apparently counting among its 1024 choices for the WHOPPER burger was "no burger." You heard it: Go to Burger King and order a veggie burger and see what you get. Even better, order a "double patty, with no patty." This kind of boolean confusion is precisely why Hamburger University just does not get the same kind of respect as, say, MIT or Caltech. Actually, a reader in Australia e-mailed to say that some of the burger joints there feature veggie burgers, so you just never know.

CHAPTER

3

Explanation of a
Sample Program

E ver since *The C Programming Language* (Kernighan, Brian and Dennis Ritchie, Prentice-Hall) was published in 1978, writers of programming text books have been using the "Hello World" program as an introductory example. Programmers deserve a bit of innovation. Java is the first popular language to support graphics, networking, multimedia, multi-threaded code, and software portability. Surely we can do a bit better than a first example that spits up a bit of text on the screen?

Chapter 1, "What is Java?," introduced an example program that did some GUI work to display a window and to roll some text across it in several directions and colors. What we'll do in this chapter is look at that code in more detail, and explain how it works. Then we'll round off the chapter with a discussion of the stack and the heap and what they do.

If you haven't yet installed the JDK and tried running the `myframe` example from chapter 1, now would be an excellent time to do that. As the great Arnold Schwarzenegger once said, "You can't get muscles by watching me lift weights."

The source listing appears on the following page with the annotations appearing on the page after that.

```
// 40 line Java demo, Peter van der Linden
// rolls colored text across the screen
```
1
```
import java.awt.*;
```
2
3 `class myframe extends Frame {`
```
    static int x=0,y=120; // x,y position to display message
```
4 `static int i=0;`
```
    static int LtoR=1;      // 1->we are moving msg L-to-R
```

5
```
    Font fb = new Font("TimesRoman", Font.BOLD, 36);
    String msg[]={"Java", "Portable", "Secure", "Easy"};
    Color color[]={Color.blue, Color.yellow, Color.green, Color.red};
```

6
```
    public void paint(Graphics g) { // gets called by runtime library
        g.setFont( fb );
        g.setColor( color[i] );
        g.drawString(msg[i],x,y);
    }
```

7
```
    static public void main(String s[]) throws Exception {
```
8
```
        myframe mf = new myframe();
        mf.setSize(200,200);
        int pixelsPerLine=200, totalLines=4;
        mf.setVisible(true);
        for (int j=0;j<pixelsPerLine*totalLines; j++) {
```
9
```
            Thread.sleep(25);
            mf.repaint();
            if (LtoR==1) {
                if ( (x+=3) < 200) continue;
                i = ++i % 4;              // move index to next msg/color
                x=50; y=0; LtoR=0;   // move msg top to bott next time
            } else {
```
10
```
                if ( (y+=3) < 200) continue;
                i = ++i % 4;              // move index to next msg/color
                x=0; y=120; LtoR=1; // move msg L-to-R next time
            }
        }
        System.exit(0);
    }
}
```

Explanation of the Example Program

1. The `import` keyword saves the programmer from having to write out the full package names of all the library classes that will be used in this source file. Here we are importing `java.awt.*` which means all the classes in the java.awt package, just as * means all the files in a directory. It means we can write `Frame` or `Font` instead of `java.awt.Frame` or `java.awt.Font`. The `java.awt` package contains basic windowing support.

2. This box encloses the class we have written. The class is called `myframe`, and it has some field members (boxes 4 and 5) and two method members (boxes 6 and 7).

3. To say that we want this class to be a subclass of the Frame class, use `extends Frame`. Frame is a class in the AWT package that displays a basic window on the screen. By saying we extend Frame, we get all the things that Frame can do, plus we can add our own specializations or variations.

4. These four fields (`x, y, i, ItoR`) are declared static so that we can reference them without an instance of the class existing.

5. These three fields represent the text that we are going to move across the screen, and its color and font. `Font` and `Color` are two classes from the java.awt package. We declare a Font variable called `fb` and create an instance of it using a constructor from the Font class. The variables `msg` and `color` are both four-element arrays which we initialize here.

6. The `paint()` method is a standard part of many classes in the awt package. The convention is that the Java runtime will call it when the window system needs to update what is on the screen. Since we *extended* the Frame class, our version of `paint()` here *replaces* the basic one in Frame. (This is a piece of OOP that we haven't covered yet).

    When you call `setVisible(true)` on a `Frame`, the window system knows it has to display it. It does that by calling our `paint` method at the right times to put it up on the screen. It will call `paint` when execution starts and any time after that when we request it. The statements inside `paint` set the default font and color, and then write some text from `msg[i]` onto the graphics context argument at location `x,y`. The window system translates that into pixels on the screen.

7. The `main()` method has a special *signature*, or method name and arguments that is recognized as the place where a program starts executing when you run the class that it is in. More about this in the next section.

8. The first variable we declare inside the main routine is a `myframe`. That gives us an instance variable on which we can invoke the ordinary (non-static) methods of `myframe` and its parent `Frame`. The first statement is a method call, `mf.setSize(200,200)`, to set `mf`'s size to 200 pixels wide and 200 pixels high. Again, this is a method we inherit by virtue of extending `java.awt.Frame`.

9. This is in the body of a loop that is executed a few hundred times. Our first action is to go to sleep and delay the program for 25 milliseconds. Since the method `sleep()` is a static method of the standard Java runtime class `Thread`, we can just invoke it with the classname. Animation looks better if you pace it out.

   After the loop delay, we ask for the `mf` instance of `myframe` to be scheduled for repainting on the screen. What we are going to do here is change the location where we display the text a little bit each time through the loop. The overall effect will be to make the text appear to glide across the screen.

10. This is the "else" part of an "if...then...else" statement that is in the body of the big loop. Just for fun, the program alternates between rolling the text across the screen horizontally and vertically. This "if" statement is where the choice is made. If the LtoR variable has the value 1, we execute the "then" part. Otherwise, we execute the "else" part that drops the text vertically.

    First, we increase y by three and check that the result is less than 200, that being the height of the screen. The variable y, of course, is used in paint as one of the coordinates for locating the text message. By changing its value, we change where the text is drawn. If y is less than 200, then `continue`. That means branch immediately to the head of the loop. If y is greater than 200, then we are at the end of scrolling the text down, and we want to select another message and color, and scroll the other way. We increment `i`, ensuring it stays in the range 0–3, we reset x,y and we change LtoR so that the "then" part of the "if" statement before 10 will be chosen. That clause is similar to the "else" clause, but increments the x variable, instead of y, to move text horizontally.

Applications Versus Applets Versus Servlets

A Java program can be written to run in these three different ways:

- As a stand-alone program that can be invoked from the command-line, termed an *application*. The sample program we were reviewing is an application.

- As a program embedded in a web page, to be downloaded to the client and run in the browser when the page is browsed, termed an *applet*. Just as a booklet is a little book, an applet is a little application.

- As a program invoked from a web server, to be run on the server when a particular URL is browsed, termed a *servlet*.

The execution vehicles differ in the default execution privileges they have and the way in which they indicate where to start execution. Almost all the code and examples are the same whether you are writing an application, an applet, or a servlet. Only a few trivial startup details differ. We will deal with applications here, and applets in a later chapter. How and why to set up a servlet is a bit too far off-topic for the scope of this text.

Where an Application Starts

Looking at the signature[1] of main(), which is the method in which every application starts execution, we see the following:

```
public static void main(String args[]) {
```

The keywords say that the function is:

- **`public`**, namely visible everywhere.

- **`static`**, namely a class method that can be called using the classname without needing an object of the class. Static methods are often used where you would use a global function in C or C++. That is, you are not doing something to some specific object, you are just doing something that generally needs doing.

- **`void`**, namely the method does not return a value.

That last point is a difference between Java and C/C++. In C, main() is defined to return an int. In Java, main() is defined to return a void, that is "no value." Java has a better way to indicate program failure, namely throwing an exception.

A Common Pitfall

A very common and frustrating pitfall is trying to access an object member from the static method called main(), as we mentioned in chapter 2, "The Story of O: Object-Oriented Programming." There are two ways to get past this. The simplest way is to make a referenced field static, too. If the field has to be non-static because each object needs its own copy, then instantiate an object whose purpose is to be an instance variable allowing you to reference the member or invoke a call on it.

```
class myframe { ...
    public static void main(String args[]) {
        // we want to invoke the instance method setSize()
        myframe mf = new myframe(); // so declare an instance
        mf.setSize(200,200); // then use it for the call
```

It looks weirdly recursive the first time you see it. Think of it this way: The class definition is a datatype. All you are doing is instantiating an object of that type at a point when you need one, which happens to be inside the original datatype definition.

---

1. Strictly speaking, the signature doesn't include the access modifiers or return type.

The `main()` routine where execution starts is a static method. That means it can be invoked before any individual instance objects have been created.

Passing over the modifiers, the actual function is as follows:

```
void main(String args[]) {
```

It declares a function called "main" that has no return value, and takes just one argument here called "args" (the parameter name doesn't matter, just its data type) which is an array of Strings. The empty array bracket pair are a reminder that the function is not restricted to any one size of array. The Strings are the command-line arguments with which the program was invoked. "String" is a class in Java, with more to it than just the nul-terminated character array it is in C.

You don't need a separate count of the number of arguments, because all arrays have a length field holding the size of the array. Simply use `args.length`, which gets the number of Strings in the `args` array.

The zeroth argument in the args array is the first command-line argument, *not* the program name as in C and C++. The program name is already known inside the program: It is the name of the class that contains the "main()" function. The name of this class will match the name of the file it is in. This framework is all that is needed to indicate the entry point program where execution will start.

We're working from the middle out here. Having seen our first reasonable Java program, in the next chapter we'll look at the small building blocks of individual tokens that the compiler sees.

For the rest of this chapter we'll mention the stack and the heap—which are a couple of popular runtime data structures, common to many programming languages, and we'll finish up with some light relief.

Runtime Internals: Stack and Heap

The *stack* is a runtime data structure for keeping track of memory to support functions and recursive function invocation. All modern block-structured languages use a stack. Many processors have some hardware support for them.

When you call a method, some housekeeping data, known as an *activation record* or *stack frame*, is pushed onto the stack. The activation record contains the return address, the arguments passed to the function, the space for local variables, and so on. When you return from a function, the record is popped from the stack. The next function call will push another record into the same space.

If you have any pointers back into the old activation record on the stack, memory can be corrupted, a common problem in C/C++. In other words, the lifetime of stack-based storage is tied to the scope in which it was allocated, and although some languages let you get this wrong, Java doesn't!

The *heap* is another compiler runtime data structure. It is a large storage area that is managed dynamically. Many programming languages support heap-based memory allocation. Different pieces of storage can be allocated from and returned to the heap in no particular order. Whenever something is allocated on the heap, its lifetime is independent of the scope in which is was allocated.

```
Fruit saveIt;
void foo() {
    Fruit f = new Fruit();
    saveIt = f;
}

... foo();
saveIt.grams = 23; // is it valid? f was allocated in foo
// and foo is no longer live
```

In the code above, a Fruit object is allocated in a method and a reference to that Fruit is stashed away for later use. Later, after the method has returned, the reference is used to access the Fruit. This is valid for heap-based storage. It is not valid in stack-based storage and is the source of a large number of high-profile bugs and failings in C/C++ code. The Internet Worm of 1988 used this flaw to subvert a system. Ten years later, the Hotmail bug of 1998 fell vulnerable to the same flaw! Since Java uses only heap-based storage for variables accessed through references, objects can happily live on after the scope in which they were created.

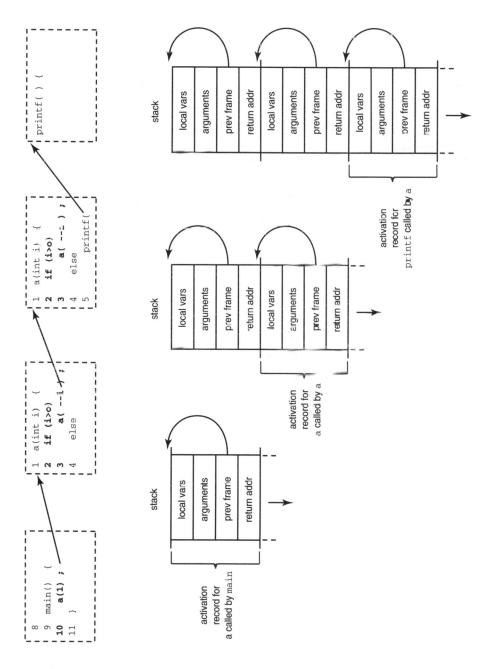

Figure 3-1: Stacks in Java.

Since the heap and the stack both grow dynamically on demand, they are usually put at opposite ends of the address space and grow into the hole between them.

Looking for an Argument?

Here is a little bit of compiler terminology, common to most languages.

A *parameter* is a variable declared in a method declaration. It provides a name for referring to the different arguments with which the method will later be called. In the following code, the variables param1 and param2 are parameters:

```
void foo(int param1, char param2) {
    param 1 = ... ;
    ... = param2;
}
```

Some people call a parameter a *formal parameter.*

Notice how the String array parameter to the `main` routine is usually called "arg" even though it is a parameter, not an argument. This is a carryover from the same mistaken convention in C.

An *argument* is a value used in a particular call to a method. In the following code the values 23 and c are arguments:

```
plum.foo( 23, c );
```

Some people call an argument, an *actual parameter.*

The Class "Object"

Most of the following chapters will end with a brief listing of one of the standard built-in classes. You should just scan the list, look at the typical methods, and then go on. Later when you want to refer to the class in detail, you can look back at the end of the chapters.

We've mentioned a couple of times that there is a class called "Object" that is the ultimate superclass (parent class) of all other classes in the system. The members that exist in Object are thus inherited by every class in the system. Whatever class you have, an instance of it can call any of these methods. Here is what Object has:

```
public class Object {
    public java.lang.Object();
    public java.lang.String toString();

    protected native java.lang.Object clone() throws
                             CloneNotSupportedException;

    public boolean equals(java.lang.Object);
    public native int hashCode();

    protected void finalize() throws Throwable;
    public final native java.lang.Class getClass();

    // methods relating to thread synchronization
    public final native void notify();
    public final native void notifyAll();
    public final void wait() throws InterruptedException;
    public final native void wait(long) throws
                                     InterruptedException;
    public final void wait(long, int) throws
                                     InterruptedException;
}
```

The "throws SomeException" clause is an announcement of the kind of unexpected error return that the method might give you.

There are several variations on the standard OS synchronization primitives `wait()` and `notify()`. These are described in the chapter on Threads. The remaining methods in Object, and thus in every class, are further highlighted below.

In each case, the method offers some useful, though somewhat elementary, functionality. Programmers are supposed to provide their own version of any of these methods to replace the basic one, if necessary. When an object (any object) calls a method, its own version of that method is preferred, over an identically-named method in a parent class, as we'll see in the second chapter on OOP.

```
public java.lang.String toString();
```

This is a very handy method! You can call it explicitly and it will return a string that "textually represents" this object. Use it while doing low-level debugging to see if your objects really are what you thought they were. Here's what I get for Fruit:

```
public class Fruit {
    int grams;
    int cals_per_gram;

    public static void main (String args[]) {
        Fruit f = new Fruit();
        System.out.println( " f = " + f.toString() );
    }
}
```

When you run the program, the output is as follows:

```
f = Fruit@a04c8d82
```

It is also invoked implicitly when any object and a String object are joined in a "+" operation. That operation is defined as *String concatenation.* To turn the other object into a String, its toString() method is called. It constitutes a piece of "magic" extra operator support for type String.

```
protected native Object clone() throws CloneNotSupportedException
```

The "native" keyword says that the body of this method is not written in Java, but will be provided in a native library linked in with the program.

Java supports the notion of cloning, meaning to get a complete bit-for-bit copy of an object. Java does a shallow clone, meaning that when an object has data fields that are other objects, it simply copies the reference. The alternative is to recursively clone all referenced classes, too, known as a *deep clone.*

As a programmer, you can choose the exact cloning behavior you want. If a class wants to support deep cloning on its objects, it can provide its own version of clone(). When you provide your own version of clone, you can also change the access modifier to public (so other classes can call it and hence clone this object) rather than the default protected (outside this package, only subclasses can clone).

Note that `clone()` returns an Object. The object returned by `clone()` is usually immediately cast (type converted) to the correct type, as in this example:

```
Vector v = new Vector();
Vector v2;

v2 = (Vector) v.clone(); // cast it back to Vector type
```

Not every class should support the ability to clone. If I have a class that represents unique objects, such as employees in a company, the operation of cloning doesn't make sense. Since methods in Object are inherited by all classes, the system places a further requirement on classes that want to be cloneable—they need to implement the cloneable interface to indicate that cloning is valid for them. Implementing an interface is described later.

```
public boolean equals(Object obj)
```

The method does a comparison of reference types, such as:

```
        if (obj1.equals(obj2) ) ...
```

This is equivalent to the following:

```
        if (obj1 == obj2 ) ...
```

The point is that you can provide your own version of `equals()` to give it whatever semantics make sense for your class. This has been done for String, because two Strings are usually considered equal if they contain the exact same sequence of characters, even if they are different objects. When you override `equals()`, you'll want to override `hashCode()` to make certain equal Objects get the same hashcode.

```
public native int hashCode ()
```

A hashcode is a value that uniquely identifies an individual object. For example, you could use the memory address of an object as its hashcode if you wanted. It's used as a key in the standard `java.util.Hashtable` class. We'll say more about hashtables later.

```
protected void finalize() throws Throwable
```

The method `finalize()` is a hook you can override to help with memory management. For more information, see the chapter on garbage collection. That "throws Throwable" is an indication of what error conditions (exceptions) this method can potentially raise. For more on this topic, see the chapter on exceptions.

```
public final native Class getClass()
```

Java maintains a runtime representation for all classes, known as *Run Time Type Identification* or RTTI. This method gets that information, which is of type Class. The class whose name is Class has several methods to tell you more about the class to which an arbitrary object belongs. You invoke the getClass method in the usual way:

```
Class whatAmI = myobject.getClass();
```

Having seen our first reasonable Java program, in the next chapter we'll look at the small building blocks of individual tokens that the compiler sees.

Some Light Relief

Animation Software

This is a story I got from the friend of a friend who works for a Hollywood special-effects company. In other words, it's a FOAF-tale (Friend Of A Friend) and may have as much credibility as Burt Reynolds's toupee. Remember the cheesy 1970s TV series *Battlestar Galactica?* It did well enough to spawn a movie with the same name.

When filming of the *Battlestar Galactica* movie began, the specification of the spaceship bridge set called for lots of CRTs with animated wire-frame displays. Since the displays should show pictures of various space craft and look futuristic, the images had to rotate wildly.

When the staff at the special-effects company started to generate these displays, they discovered that programming real-time animated computer graphics is quite a bit more difficult than stop-motion photography of clay animation models. Shocking as it sounds, these people were not really programmers at all; what they did was create motion-control sequences to "fly" model spaceships through combat maneuvers for the camera. Writing real software to display wire-frame images on the monitors was a venture into the unknown.

Their attempts to write code proved fruitless. Finally, they reverted to doing what they knew best: They got the model shop to build them some wire-frame models out of actual wire, sprayed them with fluorescent paint, and hooked them up to servomotors inside dummy CRTs illuminated with ultra-violet lamps. Then they wrote a little code to run the servomotors. The wire models rotated, tilted up and down, glowed brightly, and apparently looked very realistic on film, even to people who knew what wire-frame graphics should look like.

All this cost only a small fraction more than it would have cost to learn the graphics programming or to hire someone who already knew how to do it. The great thing is that Hollywood's reputation was upheld for having, underneath all that fake tinsel and glitter, real tinsel and glitter. *Battlestar Galactica* was still a cheesy movie, but in this case at least it the cheese was real.

CHAPTER

4

Identifiers,
Keywords, and
Types

The great majority of operating systems in use today employ the ASCII code set to represent characters. ASCII, the American Standard Code for Information Interchange, started out as a 7-bit code that represented uppercase and lowercase letters, the digits 0–9, and a dozen or so control characters like NUL and EOT. As computing technology became pervasive in Western Europe, users demanded the ability to represent all characters in their national alphabets. ASCII was extended to 8 bits, with the additional 128 characters being used to represent various accented and diacritical characters not present in English. The extended 8-bit code is known as the ISO 8859-1 Latin-1 code set. It is reproduced for reference as an appendix at the end of this book.

Java and Unicode

A more general solution was needed for Java that included support for Asian languages with their many thousands of ideograms. The solution that was chosen is Unicode. It is an ISO[1] standard 16-bit character set supporting 65,536 different

---

1. ISO is the International Organization for Standardization, a federation of national standards bodies.

characters. About 21,000 of these are devoted to Han, the ideograms seen in Chinese, Japanese, and Korean. The ISO Latin-1 code set forms most of the first 256 values, effectively making ASCII a subset of Unicode.

Java uses Unicode to represent characters internally. The external representation of characters, which is what you get when you print something and what you offer up to be read, is totally dependent on the services of the host operating system. On Unix, Windows 95, and the Macintosh, the character sets are all 8-bit based. When Java gets a character on these systems, the operating system gives it 8 bits, but Java immediately squirrels it away in a 16-bit datatype and always processes it as 16 bits. This does away with the horrid multibyte char complications in C and the special wide versions of the string-handling routines. If at some future point the host system adopts Unicode, then user code doesn't need to change and only a few routines in its Java I/O library will need to be modified to accommodate it.

You can read more about the Unicode standard at http://www.unicode.org. Be warned: For something that is conceptually so simple, the Unicode standard sets some kind of world record in obscurity and all-around lack of clarity. An example can be seen at http://www.unicode.org/unicode/standard/utf16.html, reproduced in the box below.

Extended UCS-2 Encoding Form (UTF-16)

The basic Unicode character repertoire and UCS-2 encoding form is based on the Basic Multilingual Plane (BMP) of ISO/IEC 10646. This plane comprises the first 65,536 code positions of ISO/IEC 10646's canonical code space (UCS-4, a 32-bit code space). Because of a decision by the Unicode Consortium to maintain synchronization between Unicode and ISO/IEC 10646, the Unicode Character Set may some day require access to other planes of 10646 outside the BMP. In order to accommodate this eventuality, the Unicode Consortium proposed an extension technique for encoding non-BMP characters in a UCS-2 Unicode string. This proposal was entitled UCS-2E, for extended UCS-2. This technique is now referred to as UTF-16 (for UCS Transformation Format 16 Bit Form).

Another way of saying all that is "Unicode characters are 16 bits, and UCS-4 characters are 32 bits. Right now, Unicode forms the least significant 16 bits of the 32-bit code, but that might get jumbled up in future in a new coding system called UTF-16." It's ironic—some programmers would say "predictable"—that a standard whose purpose is to foster communication is so poorly written that it actually hinders the ready transmission of meaning.

Scanning

When a Java compiler reads in program source, the very first thing that it does, before even forming tokens out of the characters, is to look for any six character sequences of the form \uxxxx where xxxx is exactly four hexadecimal digits, as in \u3b9F. These six-character sequences are translated into the corresponding one Unicode character whose value is xxxx, which is pushed back into the input stream for rescanning. Because this early scanning takes place before tokens are assembled, the six character sequence \uxxxx will be replaced even if it appears in a quoted string or character literal. It is done so that Java programs with arbitrary Unicode characters in them can be translated to and from ASCII and processed by ASCII tools with no loss of information. Relax though: You never see this in practice.

Identifiers

Identifiers, which are names provided by the programmer, can be any length in Java. They must start with a letter, underscore, or dollar sign, and in subsequent positions, can also contain digits.

A letter that can be used for a Java identifier doesn't just mean uppercase and lowercase A–Z. It means any of the tens of thousands of Unicode letters from any of the major languages in the world including Bengali letters, Cyrillic letters, or Bopomofo symbols. Every Unicode character above hex 00C0 is legal in an identifier. The table below shows some example valid Java identifiers:

Table 4-1: Legal Java Identifiers

calories	Häagen_Dazs	déconnage
_99	Puñetas	fottío
i	$__	p

Comments

Java has comment conventions that are similar to C++. Comments starting with "//" go to the end of the line, as follows:

```
i = 0;   // the "to end-of-line" comment
```

Comments starting with "/*" end at the next "*/", as follows:

```
/* the "regular multiline" comment
 */
```

There's a third variety of comment starting with "/**". This indicates text that will be picked up by javadoc, an automatic documentation generator. This is an implementation of the *literate programming* system invented by Donald Knuth. The Javadoc tool (part of the JDK) parses source code with these special comments and extracts them into a set of HTML pages describing the API.

```
/** the API comment for HTML documentation
    @version 1.12
    @author A.P.L. Byteswap
    @see SomeOtherClassName
    HTML tags can also be put in here.
 */
```

The javadoc comments must be outside a method. Take a look at the source of the java runtime library (distributed with the JDK) to see examples. There is a whole set of comments preceding each class, and each individual method in the class. Try javadoc. Javadoc works on .java files, not .class files, because the .java files contain the comments. Add some of the javadoc tags to the myframe example and run javadoc like this:

```
javadoc myframe.java
```

This will create several files and it will list their names as it generates them. They can be viewed in your web browser. It shows the chain of class inheritance and all the public fields in the class.

Commenting Out Code

Since comments do not nest in Java, to comment out a big section of code, you must either put "//" at the start of every line, or use "/*" at the front and immediately after every embedded closing comment, finishing up with your own closing comment at the end.

You can also use the following around the section you want to temporarily delete:

```
if ( false ) {
    ...
}
```

Each of these approaches has drawbacks. My preference is to use a smart editor that knows how to add or delete "//" from the beginning of each line. That way it is absolutely clear what is commented out.

Whether you agree with the idea of using web pages to store program documentation or not, it offers some compelling advantages. Documentation automatically generated from the program source is much more likely to be available, accurate, (what could be more accurate than the documentation and the source being two views of the same thing?) and, complete (the documentation is written at the same time as the code and by the same person).

Keywords

Keywords are reserved words, and they cannot be used as identifiers. ANSI C has only 32 keywords. Java has almost 50 keywords, including some reserved for future use in case the language designers add to the language. The "gang of seven" in Sun's Java group is kicking around some alternative proposals for templates (generic classes) at present. The keywords can be divided into several categories according to their main use:

Used for built-in types:

```
boolean
char
byte       short       int         long
float      double      widefp²     strictfp
void
```

Used in expressions:

```
new        this        super
```

Used in statements:

selection statements	if else
	switch case break default
iteration statements	for continue
	do while
transfer of control statements	return
	throw
exception statements	try catch finally
thread statements	synchronized

Used to modify declarations (visibility, sharing etc.):

```
static
abstract   final
private    protected  public
```

Used for other method or class-related purposes:

```
class      instanceof    throws     native
transient  volatile
```

2.   widefp and strictfp are provisionally introduced in JDK 1.2, pending industry discussion.

Used for larger-than-class building blocks:

```
extends
interface    implements
package      import
```

Reserved for possible future use:

```
const    goto
```

The Primitive Types

Java has eight built-in, non-object types, also known as primitive types. They are:

- boolean (for truth values)

- int, long, byte, short (for arithmetic on integers)

- double, float (for arithmetic on the real numbers)

- char (for character data, ultimately to be input or printed)

All class types are ultimately represented in terms of primitive types. Primitive types are simpler than class types, and are directly supported in hardware on most computers. That is, most of the operations on primitive types are a single machine instruction, like ADD, whereas the operations on class types are specified as statements in a method.

Most other high-level languages don't specify the sizes of primitive data types. This allows compiler writers the freedom to select the best sizes on each architecture for performance. The freedom turns out to be a false economy since it greatly impedes program portability, and programmer time is a lot more expensive than processor time. Java does away with all the uncertainty by rigorously specifying the sizes of the basic types and making clear that these sizes are identical on all platforms. Let us examine the properties of each of these in turn.

boolean

This is the data type used for true/false conditions. To optimize memory access time, more than one bit is used to store a boolean value. In the Sun JVM all integer types smaller than 32 bits are promoted to 32 bits when pushed on the stack during execution. An array of booleans is treated as an array of bytes.

range of values: false, true

literals: A "literal" is an integer value provided at compile-time. Just write down the number that you mean, and that's the literal. Literals have types just like variables have types. For boolean, the literals are false, true. In the code below, the assignment will always occur.

```
if (true) x = 33;
```

You cannot cast (convert) a boolean value to any other type. However you can always get the same effect by using an expression:

```
if (bool) i=1; else i=0; // set int according to bool value.
bool = (i==0? false:true); // set bool according to int value.
```

In Java, the boolean type is not based on integers. In particular, the programmer cannot increment, decrement, or add boolean values. Inside a JVM, there are no instructions dedicated to booleans, and integer operations are used.

int

The type int is a 32-bit, signed, two's-complement number, as used in virtually every modern cpu. It will be the type that you chose by default whenever you are going to carry out integer arithmetic.

range of values: −2,147,483,648 to 2,147,483,647

literals: Int literals come in any of three varieties:

- A decimal literal, e.g., 10 or −256

- With a leading zero, meaning an octal literal, e.g., 077777

- With a leading 0x, meaning a hexadecimal literal, e.g., 0xA5 or 0Xa5

Uppercase or lowercase has no significance with any of the letters that can appear in integer literals. If you use octal or hexadecimal and you provide a literal that sets the leftmost bit in the receiving number, then it represents a negative number. (Brush up on two's-complement format if you don't know why.)

An integer literal is a 32-bit quantity. But provided its actual value is within range for a smaller type, an int literal can be assigned directly to something with fewer bits, such as byte, short, or char. If you try to assign an int literal that is too large into a smaller type, the compiler will insist that you write an explicit conversion, termed a "cast".

Integer literals can be assigned to floating-point variables without casting. When you cast from a bigger type of integer to a smaller type, the high-order bits are just dropped.

A Word About Casts (Type Conversion)

All variables have a type in Java, and the type is checked so that you can't assign two things that are incompatible. You cannot directly assign a floating point variable to an integer variable.

It is reasonable, however, to convert between closely-related types. That is what a cast does. Although casting can be used between two objects of related classes, and between two primitives, you cannot cast an object to a primitive value or vice versa.

You cast an expression into another type by writing the desired new type name in parentheses before the expression:

```
float f = 3.142;

int i = (int) f; // a cast
```

Some numeric conversions don't need a cast. You are allowed to directly assign from a smaller-range numeric type into a larger range—as in, byte to int, or int to long, or long to float—without a cast.

---

long

The type long is a 64-bit, signed, two's-complement quantity. It should be used when calculations on whole numbers may exceed the range of int. Using longs, the range of values is -2^{63} to $(2^{63}-1)$. Numbers up in this range will be increasingly prevalent in computing, and 2^{64} in particular is a number that really needs a name of its own. In 1993, I coined the term "Bubbabyte" to describe 2^{64} bytes. Just as 2^{10} bytes is a Kilobyte, and 2^{20} is a Megabyte, so 2^{64} bytes is a Bubbabyte. Using a long, you can count up to half a Bubbabyte less one.

range of values: −9,223,372,036,854,775,808 to 9,223,372,036,854,775,807

literals: The general form of long literals is the same as int literals, but with an "L" or "l" on the end to indicate "long." However, never use the lower case letter "l" to indicate a "long" literal as it is too similar to the digit "1." Always use the upper case letter "L" instead. The three kinds of long literals are:

- A decimal literal, e.g., 2047L or −10L

- An octal literal, e.g., 0777777L

- An hexadecimal literal, e.g., 0xA5L or OxABADCAFEDEADBE30L

All long literals are 64-bit quantities. A long literal must be cast to assign it to something with fewer bits, such as byte, short, int, or char.

byte

The byte type is an 8-bit, signed, two's-complement quantity. The reasons for using byte are to hold a generic 8-bit value, to match a value in existing data files, or to economize on storage space where you have a large number of such values. Despite popular belief, there is no speed advantage to bytes, shorts, or chars— modern CPUs take the same amount of time to load or multiply 8 bits as they take for 32 bits.

range of values: −128 to 127

literals: There are no byte literals. You can use, without a cast, int literals provided their values fit in 8 bits. You can use char, long, and floating-point literals if you cast them.

You always have to cast a (non-literal) value of a larger type if you want to put it into a variable of a smaller type. Since arithmetic is always performed at least at 32-bit precision, this means that assignments to a byte variable must always be cast into the result if they involve any arithmetic, like this:

```
byte b1=1, b2=2;
byte b3 = b2 + b1; // NO! NO! NO! compilation error
byte b3 = (byte) (b2 + b1); // correct, uses a cast
```

People often find this unexpected. If I have an expression involving only bytes, why should I need to cast it into a byte result? The right way to think about it is that most modern computers do all integral arithmetic at 32-bit or 64-bit precision (there is no "8-bit add" on modern CPUs). Java follows this model of the underlying hardware. An arithmetic operation on two bytes potentially yields a bigger result than can be stored in a byte. The philosophy for numeric casts is that they are required whenever you assign from a more capacious type to a less capacious type.

short

This type is a 16-bit signed, two's-complement integer. The main reasons for using short are to match external values already present in a file, or to economize on storage space where you have a large number of such values and they will be able to fit in the limited range of values.

range of values: −32,768 to 32,767

literals: there are no short literals. You can use, without a cast, int literals provided their values will fit in 16 bits. You can use char, long, and floating-point literals if you cast them.

As with byte, assignments to short must always be cast into the result if the right hand side of the assignment involves any arithmetic.

The next two types, double and float, are the floating-point arithmetic types:

double

The type double refers to floating-point numbers stored in 64 bits, as described in the IEEE[3] standard reference 754. The type double will be the default type you use when you want to do some calculations that might involve decimal places (i.e. not integral values).

range of values: These provide numbers that can range between about −1.7E308 to +1.7E308 with about 14 to 15 significant figures of accuracy. The exact accuracy depends on the number being represented. Double precision floating-point numbers have the range shown in Figure 4-1.

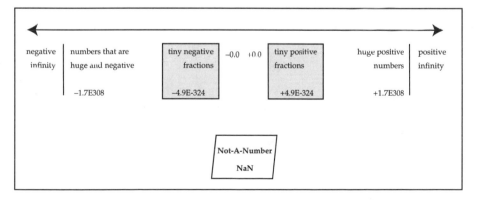

Figure 4-1: Type double should be used when calculations involve decimal places.

IEEE 754 arithmetic has come into virtually universal acceptance over the last decade, and it would certainly raise a few eyebrows if a computer manufacturer proposed an incompatible system of floating-point numbers now. IEEE 754 is the standard for floating point arithmetic, but there are several places where chip designers can choose from different alternatives within the standard, such as rounding modes and extended precision. Java originally insisted on consistency on all hardware by specifying the alternatives that must be used. That is now being loosened somewhat (strictfp/widefp is an example) but the details were still under discussion when JDK 1.2 shipped.

IEEE 754 has an ingenious way of dealing with the problem of representing on limited hardware the unlimited amount of infinite precision real-world numbers. The problem is resolved by reserving a special value that says, "Help! I've fallen off the end of what's representable and I can't get up." You're probably familiar with infinity, but the "Not-a-Number" might be new if you haven't done much numerical programming. Not-a-Number, or NaN, is a value that a floating point can take to indicate that the result of some operation is not mathematically well-defined, like dividing zero by zero.

If you get a NaN as an expression being evaluated, it will contaminate the whole expression, producing an overall result of NaN—*which is exactly what you want!* The worst way to handle a numeric error is to ignore it and pretend it didn't happen.

You may never see a NaN if your algorithms are numerically stable, and you never push the limits of your datasets. Still, it's nice to know that NaN is there, ready to tell you your results are garbage, if they head that way.

literals : It is easiest to show by example the valid formats for double literals:

```
1e1  2.   .3   3.14 6.02e+23d
```

The format is very easy-going; just give the compiler a decimal point, or an exponent, and it will recognize that a floating-point literal is intended. A suffix of "D", "d", or no suffix, means a double literal. In practice, most people omit the suffix.

It is also permissible to assign any of the integer literals or character literals to floats or doubles. The assignment doesn't need a cast, as you are going from a less capacious type to a more capacious type. So a line like this, while perverse, is valid:

```
double cherry = '\n';
```

Make Mine a Double: How Large Is 1.7E308?

The largest double precision number is a little bit bigger than a 17 followed by 307 zeroes.

How large is that? Well, the volume of the observable universe is about $(4pi/3)(15$ billion light-years$)^3 = 10^{85}$ cm^3. The density of protons is about 10^{-7} cm^{-3}. This value seems so sparse because it is an average for all space— on a planet the value is much, much denser of course. The number of protons in the observable Universe is about 10^{78}, or "only" 1 followed by 78 zeros, give or take two-fifty.

The largest double precision number is even bigger than a googol. A googol is the number description suggested by 9 yr. old Milton Sirotta in 1938 at the request of his uncle, mathematician Edward Krasner. A googol is 10^{100}, meaning that it is only a 1 followed by 100 zeroes. Is the largest double precision number bigger than Madonna's capacity for self-promotion? No, we have to admit, it probably isn't that big.

It's possible to come up with problems where you want accuracy to 14 significant figures, such as figuring the national debt, but it is most unusual to need to tabulate numbers that are in orders of magnitude greater than the number of protons in the universe.

It takes the integer value of the literal (0x0a in this case), floats it to get 10.0d, and assigns that to "cherry." Don't ever do this

float

The type float refers to floating-point numbers stored in 32 bits, as described in the IEEE standard reference 754.

The justification for using single precision variables used to be that arithmetic operations were twice as fast as on double precision variables. With modern extensively-pipelined processors and wide data buses between the cache and CPUs, the speed differences are inconsequential. The reasons for using floats are to minimize storage requirements when you have a very large quantity of them or to retain compatibility with external data files.

range of values: The type float provides numbers that can range between about −3.4E38 to 3.4E38 (i.e. 340,000,000,000,000,000,000,000,000,000,000,000,000) with about 6–7 significant figures of accuracy. The exact accuracy depends on the number being represented.

literals: The simplest way to understand what is allowed is to look at examples of valid float literals, as follows:

```
1e1f 2.f  .3f  3.14f 6.02e+23f
```

A suffix of "F" or "f" is always required on a float literal. A common mistake is to leave the suffix off the float literal, as follows:

```
float cabbage = 6.5;
 Error: explicit cast needed to convert double to float.
```

The code must be changed to the following:

```
float cabbage = 6.5f;
```

Also, a double literal cannot be assigned to a float variable without a cast even if it is within the range of the float type. This is because some precision in decimal places may potentially be lost. The next section explains more about this interesting, and sometimes subtle, topic.

char

This type is a 16-bit unsigned quantity that is used to represent printable characters. Since it is an integer-based type, all the arithmetic operators are available on it. Unlike all the other arithmetic types, char is unsigned—it never takes a negative value. You should only use char to hold character data or bit values. If you want a 16-bit quantity for general calculations, don't use char, use short. This will avoid the possible surprise of converting between signed and unsigned types. Otherwise a cast of a negative value into char will magically become positive without the bits changing.

Java provides the framework that is capable of handling characters from just about any locale in the world. The cost is that we store and move 16 bits for each character instead of just 8 bits.

range of values: a value in the Unicode code set 0 to 65,535

You have to cast a 32- or 64-bit result if you want to put it into a smaller result. This means that assignments to char must always be cast into the result if they involve any arithmetic. An example would be:

```
char c = (char) (i + 42); // cast
```

literals: Character literals appear between single quotes or in Strings. They can be expressed in four ways, and can be used for all of the types char, byte, short, int, and long.

- A single character, `'A'`

- A character escape sequence. The allowable values are:

  `'\n'` (linefeed)   `'\r'` (carriage return)   `'\f'` formfeed

  `'\b'` (backspace)   `'\t'` (tab)   `'\\'` (backslash)

  `'\"'` (double quote)   `'\''` (single quote)

- An octal escape sequence. This has the form `'\nnn'` where nnn is one-to-three octal digits in the range 0 to 377. Note the odd fact that you can only set the least significant 8 bits of a 16-bit char when using an octal escape sequence. Some examples are `'\0'` or `'\12'` or `'\277'` or `'\377'`.

- A Unicode escape sequence. This has the form `'\uxxxx'` where xxxx is exactly four hexadecimal digits. An example is:

  ```
  '\u0041' is the character A
  ```

Choosing Unicode for the char type was a bold and forward-looking design choice. Although a few people complain about the cost and waste of using 16 bits per character, these are the same pikers who a few years ago didn't want to shift from two-digit years to four-digit years, and who still hold onto their abacuses while they evaluate the "cutting edge" slide rules.

> **Switching to Unicode**
>
> OS vendors missed a big opportunity to move from ASCII to Unicode as the native character set of various operating systems. It could all have been done as part of the transition to 64-bit software. Since that didn't happen, we'll all have two big "flag-days" in our future: one to make our applications 64-bit compatible, and one to make our applications globally compatible. The extra storage requirements of Unicode are a no-brainer. Rotating magnetic media just keeps getting cheaper and cheaper. Even if my 1GB of data doubled in size—which it won't because I have a lot of non-text files—that is only about another $25 worth of disk.
>
> When the operating system vendors do catch up, Java is already there.

Designers of forward-looking systems like Java have a responsibility to include proper support for more than just Western alphabets. Apart from anything else, customers are more likely to buy your software if it supports their native language. Until all systems have adopted Unicode, however, handling it on an ASCII system is clumsy, so avoid sprinkling Unicode literals through your code.

String

To round out this chapter, here is the standard Java class String. As a class type, it contrasts with the primitive types described up to this point in the chapter.

As the name suggests, String objects hold a series of adjacent characters like an array. It takes a method call, however, (not an array reference) to pull an individual character out. You will use String instances a lot—whenever you want to store zero or more characters in a sequence or do character I/O. Arrays of char do some of these things, too, but String is a lot more convenient for comparing several characters, and using literal values.

literals: A string literal is zero or more characters enclosed in double quotes, like this:

```
"" // empty string
"That'll cost you two-fifty \n"
```

Because Strings are used so frequently, Java has some special built-in support. Everywhere else in Java, you use a constructor to create an object of a class, such as:

```
String filmStar = new String( "Arnold Alois Schwarzenegger" );
```

String literals count as a short cut for the constructor. So this is equivalent:

```
String filmStar = "Arnold Alois Schwarzenegger";
```

Each string literal behaves as if it is a reference to an instance of class String, meaning that you can invoke methods on it, copy a reference to it, and so on. For the sake of performance, the compiler can implement it another way, but it must be indistinguishable to the programmer.

Like all literals, string literals cannot be modified after they have been created. Variables of class String have the same quality—once you have created a String, you cannot change a character in the middle to something else. Some people refer to this by saying, "Strings are immutable." You can always discard any String and make the same reference variable refer to a different one in its place. You can even construct a new String out of pieces from another, so being unable to change a given String after it has been created isn't a handicap in practice.

String Concatenation

The other String feature with special built-in support is concatenation. Whenever a String is one operand of the "+" operator, the system does not do addition. Instead the other operand (whatever it is, object or primitive thing) will be converted to a String by calling its toString() method, and the result is the two Strings joined together. You will use this feature in many places. Here's a couple of them:

- To print out a variable, and some text saying what it is:

```
System.out.println( "x has value " + x
            + " and y has value " + y );
```

- to break a long String literal down into smaller strings, and continue it across several lines:

```
"Thomas the Tank Engine and the naughty "
+ "Engine-driver who tied down Thomas's Boiler Safety Valve"
+ "and How They Found Pieces of Thomas in Three Counties."
```

- To convert the value to a String, (concatenating an empty String with a value of a primitive type is a Java idiom):

```
int i = 256;
    ...
... "" + i // yields a String containing the value of i.
```

That's much shorter than the alternative of using the conversion method of the String class `String.valueOf( i )`.

String Comparison

Just a reminder about String comparisons. Compare two Strings like this:

```
if ( s1.equals(s2)) ....
```

Not this:

```
if (s1 == s2) ....
```

The first compares string contents, the second string addresses. Failing to use "equals()" to compare two strings is probably the most common single mistake made by Java novices.

String uses another built-in class called StringBuffer to help it operate. String-Buffer differs from String in that you can change characters in the middle of a StringBuffer after it has been instantiated. StringBuffer doesn't have any support for searching for individual characters or substrings though. StringBuffer is widely used by the compiler to implement support for concatenating two Strings into a longer String. You'll use the class String a lot more than StringBuffer.

The following code shows the important methods of the String class. You can look at the entire source in file $JAVAHOME/java/src/lang/String.java.

```
public final class String {
        // constructors with various arguments
    public String();
    public String(java.lang.String);
    public String(java.lang.StringBuffer);
    public String(byte[]);
    public String(byte[],int);
    public String(byte[],int,int);
    public String(byte[],int,int,int);
    public String(byte[],int,int,java.lang.String)
                              throws UnsupportedEncodingException;
    public String(byte[],java.lang.String) throws UnsupportedEncodingException;
    public String(char[]);
    public String(char[],int,int);
        // comparisons
    public char charAt(int);
    public int compareTo(java.lang.Object);
    public int compareTo(java.lang.String);
    public int compareToIgnoreCase(java.lang.String);
    public boolean endsWith(java.lang.String);
    public boolean equals(java.lang.Object);
    public boolean equalsIgnoreCase(java.lang.String);
    public boolean regionMatches(int, java.lang.String, int, int);
    public boolean regionMatches(boolean, int, java.lang.String, int, int);
    public boolean startsWith(java.lang.String);
    public boolean startsWith(java.lang.String, int);
        // search, extract and other routines
    public String concat(java.lang.String);
    public static String copyValueOf(char[]);
    public static String copyValueOf(char[], int, int);
    public byte [] getBytes();
    public void getBytes(int, int, byte[], int);
    public byte [] getBytes(java.lang.String)throws UnsupportedEncodingException;
    public void getChars(int, int, char[], int);
    public int hashCode();
    public int indexOf(int);
    public int indexOf(int, int);
    public int indexOf(java.lang.String);
    public int indexOf(java.lang.String, int);
    public native java.lang.String intern();
    public int lastIndexOf(int);
    public int lastIndexOf(int, int);
    public int lastIndexOf(java.lang.String);
    public int lastIndexOf(java.lang.String, int);
    public int length(); // gets the length of the string
    public String replace(char, char);
    public String substring(int);
    public String substring(int, int);
    public char toCharArray()[]; public java.lang.String toLowerCase();
    public String toLowerCase(java.util.Locale);
    public String toString();
    public String toUpperCase();
    public String toUpperCase(java.util.Locale);
    public String trim(); // chops off leading & trailing spaces
        // conversion to String
    public static String valueOf(char);
    public static String valueOf(double);
    public static String valueOf(float);
    public static String valueOf(int);
    public static String valueOf(long);
    public static String valueOf(java.lang.Object);
    public static String valueOf(boolean);
    public static String valueOf(char[]);
    public static String valueOf(char[], int, int);
}
```

Some Light Relief

Hatless Atlas

Here's a cheery song that has been circulating around the Internet for more than a few years. It's sung to the tune of *Twinkle, Twinkle, Little Star*, but to sing it you have to know how some programmers pronounce the shifted and control characters on a keyboard. The "^" character above the "6" is often pronounced "hat" because it looks like a little hat. Some people give the name "huh" to "?", and "wow" to "!". Both of those are a lot shorter than more conventional names.

The song is called *Hatless Atlas* and it goes like this:

^ < @ < . @ *	Hat less at less point at star,
} " _ # ⊦	backbrace double base pound space bar.
- @ $ & / _ %	Dash at cash and slash base rate,
!(@ | = >	wow open tab at bar is great.
; ' + $? ^?	Semi backquote plus cash huh DEL,
, # " ~ |) ^G	comma pound double tilde bar close BEL.

This song can be enjoyed on more than one level. While the theme is not wholly recognizable, key elements come through. The bare-headed strong man relishes nature ("point at star"), and then enjoys the full hospitality of a tavern ("Wow, open tab at bar is great"). Soon he finds that the question of payment does arise, after all; hence, the veiled reference to Alan Greenspan ("slash base rate") and the finality overshadowing that closing lament "bar close BEL"!

I like to think that in the years to come, wherever programmers gather in the evening, after the pizza is all eaten and a sufficient quantity of beer has been drunk, a piano may start to play softly in the corner. Quietly, one member of the group will sing, and then more and more of the programming staff will join in. Any systems analysts who haven't yet quaffed themselves unconscious might sway unsteadily with the beat. Soon several choruses of *Hatless Atlas* will roll lustily around the corners of the room. Old timers will talk of the great bugs they have overcome and the days of punching clocks, cards, and DOS.

Or maybe we'll all stay home and watch re-runs of *Star Trek: Kirk Violates the Prime Directive with Xena, Warrior Princess* instead, who knows?

CHAPTER
5

Names, Arrays, Operators, and Accuracy

T his chapter covers more of the language basics: names, arrays, how operators work, and the accuracy you can expect in arithmetic. The chapter finishes up by presenting the standard class java.lang.Math.

Names

What is the difference between an *identifier* and a *name?* As we saw in Chapter 4, "Identifiers, Keywords, and Types," an identifier is just a sequence of letters and digits that don't match a keyword or the literals "true," "false," or "null." A name, on the other hand, can be prefixed with any number of further identifiers to pinpoint the namespace from which it comes. An identifier is thus the simplest form of name. The general case of name looks like the following:

```
package1.Package2.PackageN.Class1.Class2.ClassM.memberN
```

Since packages can be nested in packages, and classes nested in classes, there can be an arbitrary number of identifiers separated by periods, as in:

```
java.lang.System.out.println( "goober" );
```

That name refers to the `java.lang` package. There are several packages in the `java` hierarchy, and `java.lang` is the one that contains basic language support. One of the classes in the `java.lang` package is `System`. The class `System` contains a field that is an object of the `PrintStream` class, called `out`. `PrintStream` supports several methods, including one called `println()` that takes a `String` as an argument. It's the way to get text output to the standard output of a program.

By looking at a lengthy name in isolation, you can't tell where the package identifiers stop and the class and member identifiers start. You have to do the same kind of evaluation that the compiler does. Since the namespaces are hierarchical, if you have two identifiers that are the same, you can say which you mean by providing another level of name. This is called *qualifying the name.* For example, if you define your own class called `BitSet`, and you also want to reference the class of the same name that is in the `java.util` package, you can distinguish between them like this:

```
        BitSet mybs = new BitSet();
java.util.BitSet yourbs = new java.util.BitSet();
```

A *namespace* isn't a term that occurs in the Java Language Specification. Instead, it's a compiler term meaning "place where a group of names are organized as a whole." By this definition, all the members in a class form a namespace. All the variables in a method form a namespace. A package forms a namespace. Even a local block inside a method forms a namespace. A compiler will look for an identifier in the namespace that most closely encloses it. If not found, it will look in successively wider namespaces until if finds the first occurrence of the correct identifier. Java also uses the context to resolve names. You won't confuse Java if you give the same name to a method, to a data field, and to a label. It puts them in different namespaces. When the compiler is looking for a method name, it doesn't bother looking in the field namespace.

When Can an Identifier Be Forward-Referenced?

A forward reference is the use of a name before that name has been defined, as in the following:

```
class Fruit {
    void foo() { grams = 22; } // grams not yet declared
    int grams;
}
```

A primitive field needs to appear before it is used only when the use is in the initialization of a field. In the example above, the use is in a method, so this is a valid forward reference to the field `grams`. The declaration of a class never needs to appear before the use of that class, as long as the compiler finds it at some point during that compilation.

Expressions

There's a lengthy chapter in the Java Language Specification on expressions, covering many cases that would be interesting only to language lawyers. What it boils down to is that an expression is any of the alternatives shown in Table 5-1.

Table 5-1: Expressions in Java

Expression	Example of Expression
a literal	`245`
this object reference	`this`
a field access	`plum.grams`
a method call	`plum.total_calories()`
an object creation	`new Fruit( 3.5 )`
an array creation	`new int[27]`
an array access	`myArray[i][j]`
any expression connected by operators	`plum.grams * 1000`
any expression in parens	`( plum.grams * 1000 )`

You *evaluate* an expression to get a result that will be a variable (as in, evaluating `this` gives you an object you can store into), a value, or nothing (a void expression). You get the last by calling a method with a return value of void.

An expression can appear on either side of an assignment. If it is on the left-hand side of an assignment, the result designates where the evaluated right-hand side should be stored.

The type of an expression is known either at compile time or checked to be compatible with whatever you are doing with the expression at runtime. There is no escape from strong typing in Java.

Arrays

In this section we introduce arrays and describe how to use them. Some people claim that the support and syntax for arrays is much the same in Java as it is in C. That is a little misleading as the similarities are superficial ones based on syntax alone. Java has neither the complexities nor the "size fixed at compile time" of C arrays. The Java array model is more like Ada with arrays of arbitrary bounds as parameters, and dynamically-allocatable arrays, each with information about their own length.

Array Subscripts Start at Zero

Array subscripts always start at zero. People coming to Java from another language often have trouble with that concept. After all, when you're counting anything, you always start "one, two, three"—so why would array elements be any different?

This is one of the things carried over from C. C was designed by and for systems programmers, and in a compiler, a subscript is translated to "offset from array base address." You can save a step in subscript-to-address translation if you disallow subscripts with an arbitrary starting point. Instead, directly use offset-from-base-address, and the first offset is zero.

Watch out! It means that when you declare the following, valid subscripts for "day" are in the range 0 to 364:

```
int day[] = new int[365];
```

A reference to "day(365)" is invalid. If this causes distress in terms of program readability (perhaps you want days numbered from 1 to 365 to match the calendar), simply declare the array one larger than it needs to be, and don't use element zero.

Array indexes are all checked at runtime. If a subscript attempts to access an element outside the bounds of its array, it causes an exception and the program ceases execution rather than corrupt memory. Exceptions are described in a later chapter.

Array types are reference types in Java; that is, your array variable is really a reference to an array. Arrays are objects.

Here are some ways in which arrays *are* like objects:

- They are because the language says they are (section 4.3.1).

- Array types are reference types, just like object types.

- Arrays are allocated with the "new" operator, similar to constructors.

- Arrays are always allocated on the heap, never on the stack.

- The parent class of all arrays is `Object`, and you can call any of the methods of `Object`, such as `toString()`, on an array.

On the other hand, here are some ways arrays *are not* like objects:

- You can't give a different parent class to an array.

- Arrays have a different syntax from other object classes.

- You can't define your own methods for arrays.

Regard arrays as funny kinds of objects that share some key characteristics with regular objects. Operations that are common to all objects can be done on arrays. Operations that require an object as an operand can be passed an array. The length of an array (the number of elements in it) is a data field in the array class. For example, you can get the size of an array by referencing the following:

```
a.length        // yes
```

People always want to treat that as a method call, and write the following:

```
a.length()      // NO! NO! NO!
```

Think of it this way: For an array, length is just a final data field, set when the array object is created. There is no need to have the overhead of a method call.

The Length of an Entire Array Versus a String in an Array

Think back to the String argument array and the main() routine. You may be wondering how to get the length of the array (the total number of Strings) versus the length of a given String in the array. Here is some code that demonstrates the two scenarios.

```
public static void main(String args[]) {
    int i=0;
    System.out.println( "number of String args:" + args.length );
    System.out.println( "length of i'th String:" +args[i].length()
);
}
```

Contrast how "length" is a data field for arrays and is a method for the class String. This is a frequent point of confusion for beginners.

Creating an Array

When you declare an array, as in the following example, that declaration says the "carrot can hold a reference to any size array of int."

```
int carrot [];
```

You have to make the reference point to an array before you can use it, just as with class types. You might make it point to an existing array, or you might create the array with a new expression, just as with objects.

Array Size

You can never specify the size of an array in a C-style declaration like this:

```
int sprout [256];                          // NO! NO! NO!
```

The array's size is set when you assign something to it, either in an initializer or a regular assignment statement.

```
carrot [] = new int[256];
```

Once an array object has been created with a given size, it cannot change for that array, although you can replace it by assigning a differently-sized array object to it.

When you create an object, although the primitive types in it are created, the non-primitive types are just references that must be filled in before they refer to an object. It is the same with arrays. If the elements are a primitive type, they are created.

```
carrot = new int [256]; // creates 256 ints
carrot[7] = 32;         // ok
```

If the elements are a reference type, you have 256 *references* to objects *after* you fill them in.

```
Fruit carrot [] = new Fruit[256]; // creates 256 references
carrot[7].grams = 32; // NO! NO! NO!
```

You still need to make each individual reference element point to an object before you can access the object. You need to do something like this:

```
Fruit carrot [] = new Fruit[256];
    for (int i=0; i<carrot.length; i++) {
        carrot[i] = new Fruit();
    }
```

Failing to create the objects in an array of reference types is the most common novice mistake with arrays, and it causes a NullPointerException error.

Initializing an Array

You can create and initialize an array in one declaration, like this:

```
byte b[] = new byte[] { 0, 1, 1, 2, 3 };
String wkdays[] = new String [] {
                        "Mon", "Tue", "Wed", "Thu", "Fri", };
Fruit orchard[] = new Fruit [] {new Fruit(),
                                new Fruit(4,3),
                                null };
```

A superfluous trailing comma is allowed in an initialization list—an unnecessary carryover from C. The permissible extra trailing comma is claimed to be of use when a list of initial values is being generated automatically.

That `new type[] {values... }` is called an *array creation expression* and it is new with JDK 1.1. In all versions of Java, you can also initialize an array in its declaration with an array initializer like this:

```
byte b [] = { 0, 1, 1, 2, 3 }; // {...} is array initializer
```

You can't use an array initializer anywhere else, like in an assignment statement. There wasn't a good reason for that restriction, so array creation expressions were brought to the rescue. You *can* use an array creation expression anywhere, such as:

```
b = new byte[] { 5, 5, 5 }; // assignment statement
```

There is a method called `arraycopy()` in class `java.lang.System` that will copy part or all of an array, like this:

```
String midweek[] = new String[3];
System.arraycopy ( wkdays /*src*/, 1 /*offset*/,
                   midweek /*dest*/, 0 /*offset*/, 3 /*len*/ );
```

You can clone an array, like this:

```
int p[] = new int[10];
int p2[] = (int[]) p.clone(); // makes a copy of p
```

Whereas cloning creates the new array, arraycopy just copies elements into an existing array. As with the clone of anything, you get back an Object which must be cast to the correct type. That's what (`int[]`) is doing.

Arrays of Arrays of ...

The language specification says there are no *multidimensional* arrays in Java, meaning the language doesn't use the convention of Pascal or Ada of putting several indexes into one set of subscript brackets. Ada allows multidimensional arrays like this:

```
year : array(1..12, 1..31) of real;        Ada code for
                                            multi-dimensional array.
year(i,j) = 924.4;
```

Ada also allows arrays of arrays, like this:

```
type month is array(1..31) of real;        Ada code for array of
                                            arrays.
year : array(1..12) of month;
year(i)(j) = 924.4;
```

What "Multidimensional" Means in Different Languages

The Ada standard explicitly says arrays of arrays and multidimensional arrays are different. The language has both.

The Pascal standard says arrays of arrays and multidimensional arrays are the same thing.

The ANSI C standard says C has what other languages call arrays of arrays, but it also calls these multidimensional.

The Java language only has arrays of arrays, and it only calls these arrays of arrays.

Java arrays of arrays are declared like this:

```
Fruit plums [] [] ;
```

Array "plums" is composed of an array that is composed of an array whose elements are Fruit objects. You can allocate and assign to any arrays individually.

```
plums = new Fruit [23] [9]; // an array[23] of array[9]
plums [i] = new Fruit [17]; // an array[17]
plums [i][j] = new Fruit(); // an individual Fruit
```

Because object declarations do not create objects (I know I am stressing this repeatedly—it's an important point), you will need to fill out or *instantiate* the elements in an array before using it. If you have an array of arrays, like the one below, you will need to instantiate both the top-level array and at least one bottom level array before you can start storing ints:

```
int cabbage[][];
```

The bottom level arrays do not have to all be a single uniform size. Here are several alternative and equivalent ways you could create and fill a triangular array of arrays:

• Use several array creation expressions, like this:

```
int myTable[][] = new int[][] {
                        new int[] {0},
                        new int[] {0,1},
                        new int[] {0,1,2},
                        new int[] {0,1,2,3},
            };
```

• Lump all the initializers together in a big array initializer, like this:

```
int myTable[][] = new int[][] {
                {0},
                {0,1},
                {0,1,2},
                {0,1,2,3}, };
```

• Initialize individual arrays with array creation expressions, like this:

```
int myTable[][] = new int[4][];
... // later in statements
myTable[0] = new int[] {0};
myTable[1] = new int[] {0, 1};
myTable[2] = new int[] {0, 1, 2};
myTable[3] = new int[] {0, 1, 2, 3};
```

• Use a loop, like this:

```
int myTable[][] = new int[4][];
... // later in statements
for( int i=0; i<myTable.length; i++) {
    myTable[i] = new int [i+1];
    for (int j=0; j<=i; j++)
        myTable[i][j]=j;
}
```

This could be done in a static block (if myTable is static) or in a constructor.

If you don't instantiate all the dimensions at one time, you must instantiate the most significant dimensions first. For example:

```
int cabbage[][] = new int[5][];    // ok
int cabbage[][] = new int[5][3];   // ok
```

but:

```
int cabbage[][] = new int[][3];    // NO! NO! NO!
```

Arrays with the same element type, and the same number of dimensions (in the C sense, Java doesn't have multidimensional arrays) can be assigned to each other. The arrays do not need to have the same number of elements because what actually happens is that one reference variable is copied into the other. For example:

```
int eggs[] = {1,2,3,4};
int ham[] = new int[2] {77, 96};
ham = eggs;
ham[3] = 0;      // OK, because ham now has 4 elements.
```

This doesn't make a new copy of eggs; it makes ham and eggs reference the same array object.

Watch the size of those arrays of arrays. The following declaration allocates an array of 4 * 250 * 1000 * 1000 = 1GB.

```
int bubba[][][] = new int[250][1000][1000];
```

Do you have that much virtual memory on your system?

Practical Example of Array Reference Types

Changes made to the array through references by one variable will be seen by references through the other variable.

```
// show example of what is a copy, and what is a ref.
    Integer beer[] = new Integer[10];
    Integer lager[];

    beer[3] = new Integer(3);
```

In diagram form, this code is depicted in Figure 5-1.

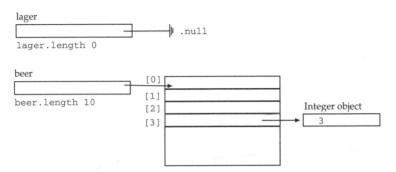

Figure 5-1: Pre-"lager=beer" assignment.

If we now execute the assignment shown below, we will get the result shown in Figure 5-2.

```
lager = beer;
```

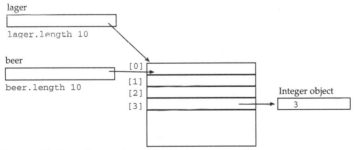

Figure 5-2: "lager=beer" has been assigned.

It simply copies the beer reference variable into the lager reference variable.

After the assignment shown below, we have the results shown in Figure 5-3.

```
beer[3] = new Integer(256);
```

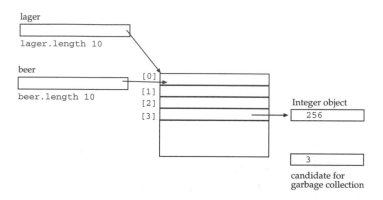

Figure 5-3: Post-assignment of "beer[3] = new Integer (256)".

By executing the following statements, the println message will be printed out.

```
if (lager[3].intValue() == 256)
        System.out.println("It just copied the reference" +
                           " -- they point at same Object" );
```

When one element of the array at which beer points is changed, naturally the change is seen by both array reference variables.

Have Array Brackets, Will Travel

There is a quirk of syntax in that the array declaration bracket pairs can *float*, to be next to the element type, to be next to the data name, or to be in a mixture of the two. The following are all valid array declarations:

```
int a [] ;
int [] b = { a.length, 2, 3 } ;

char c [][] = new char[12][31];
char[] d [] - { [1,1,1,1}, {2,2,2,2} }; // creates d[2][4]
char[][] e;

byte f [][][] = new byte [3][3][7];
byte [][] g[] = new byte [3][3][7];

short [] h, i[], j, k[][];
```

If array brackets appear next to the type, they are part of the type, and apply to *every* variable in that declaration. In the code above, "j" is an array of short, and "i" is an array of arrays of short.

This is mostly so declarations of functions returning arrays can be read more normally. Here is an example of how returning an array value from a function would look following C rules (you can't return an array in C, but this is how C syntax would express it if you could):

```
int funarray()[] { ... }                Pseudo-C CODE
```

Here are the alternatives for expressing it in Java, (and it is permissible in Java), first following the C paradigm:

```
int ginger ()[]  { return new int[20]; }        Java CODE
```

A better way is to express it like this:

return type

```
int []    ginger () { return new int[20]; }        Java CODE
```
method

The latter allows the programmer to see all the tokens that comprise the return type grouped together.

Arrays are never allocated on the stack in Java, so you cannot get into trouble returning an array stack variable. If you declare an array as a local variable (perhaps in a method), that actually creates a reference to the array. You need a little more code to create the array itself and that will allocate the array safely on the heap. In C, it is too easy to return a pointer to an array on the stack that will be overwritten by something else pushed on the stack after returning from the method.

Indexing Arrays

Arrays may be indexed by "int" values. Arrays may not be indexed by "long" values. That means arrays are implicitly limited to no more than the highest 32-bit int value, namely 2,147,483,647. That's OK for the next couple of years—but the lack of 64-bit addressing will eventually make itself felt in Java.

Values of types "byte," "short," and "char" are promoted to "ints" when they are used as an index, just as they are in other expression contexts.

Operators

Most of the operators in Java will be readily familiar to any programmer. One novel aspect is that the order of operand evaluation in Java is well-defined. For many older languages, including C and C++, the order of evaluation has been deliberately left unspecified. In other words, in C the following operands can be evaluated and added together in any order:

```
i + myArray[i] + functionCall();
```

The function may be called before, during (on adventurous multiprocessing hardware), or after the array reference is evaluated, and the additions may be executed in any order. If the functionCall() adjusts the value of i, the overall result depends on the order of evaluation. The trade-off is that some programs give different results depending on the order of evaluation. A professional programmer would consider such programs to be badly written, but they exist nonetheless.

The order of evaluation was left unspecified in earlier languages so that compiler-writers could re-order operations to optimize register use. Java makes the trade-off in a different place. It recognizes that getting consistent results on all computer systems is much more important than getting varying results a trifle faster on one system. In practice, the opportunities for speeding up expression evaluation through reordering operands seem to be quite limited in many programs. As processor speed and cost improve, it is appropriate that modern languages optimize for programmer sanity instead of performance.

Java specifies not just left-to-right operand evaluation, but the order of everything else, too, such as:

- The left operand is evaluated before the right operand of a binary operator. This is true even for the assignment operator, which must evaluate the left operand (where the result will be stored), fully before starting on the right operand (what the result is).

- In an array reference, the expression before the square brackets "[]" is fully evaluated before any part of the index is evaluated.

- A method call for an object has this general form:

  objectInstance.methodName(arguments);

- The objectInstance is fully evaluated before the methodName and arguments. This can make a difference if the objectInstance is given to you by a method that has side effects. In that case, any arguments are evaluated one by one from left to right.

- In an allocation expression for an array of several dimensions, the dimension expressions are evaluated one by one from left to right.

The Java Language Specification (Gosling, James, Bill Joy, and Guy L. Steele, Addison-Wesley, 1996) uses the phrase, "Java guarantees that the operands to operators *appear to be* evaluated from left-to-right." This is an escape clause that allows clever compiler-writers to do brilliant optimizations, as long as the appearance of left-to-right evaluation is maintained.

For example, compiler-writers can rely on the associativity of integer addition and multiplication. This means that a+b+c will produce the same result as (a+b)+c or a+(b+c). This is true in Java even in the presence of overflow, because what happens on overflow is well-defined. We have a section on overflow later in this chapter.

If one of the subexpressions occurs again in the same basic block, a clever compiler-writer might be able to arrange for its re-use. In general because of complications involving infinity and not-a-number (NaN) results, floating-point operands cannot be trivially reordered.

Note that the usual operator precedence still applies. In an expression like the one below, the multiplication is always done before the addition.

```
b + c * d
```

It has to be done first, because the result is one operand of the addition.

What the Java order of evaluation says is that for all binary (two argument) operators the left operand is always fully evaluated before the right operand. Therefore, the operand "b" above must be evaluated before the multiplication is done (because the multiplied result is the right operand to the addition).

Left-to-right evaluation means in practice that all operands in an expression (if they are evaluated at all) are evaluated in the left-to-right order in which they are written down on a page. Sometimes an evaluated result must be stored while a higher precedence operation is performed. Although the Java Language Specification only talks about the apparent order of evaluation of operands to individual operators this is a necessary consequence of the rules.

Java Operators

The Java operators and their precedence are shown in Table 5-2. The arithmetic operators are undoubtedly familiar to the reader. We'll outline some of the other operators in the next section.

Table 5-2: Java Operators and Their Precedence

Symbol	Note	Precedence (highest number= highest precedence)	COFFEEPOT Property (see next section)
++ --	pre-increment, decrement	16	right
++ --	post-increment, decrement	15	left
~	flip the bits of an integer	14	right
!	logical not (reverse a boolean)	14	right
- +	arithmetic negation, plus	14	right
(typename)	type conversion (cast)	13	right
* / %	multiplicative operators	12	left
- +	additive operators	11	left
<< >> >>>	left and right bitwise shift	10	left
instanceof < <= > >=	relational operators	9	left
== !=	equality operators	8	left
&	bitwise and	7	left
^	bitwise exclusive or	6	left
|	bitwise inclusive or	5	left
&&	conditional and	4	left
||	conditional or	3	left
? :	conditional operator	2	right
= *= /= %= += -= <<= >>= >>>= &= ^= |=	assignment operators	1	right

The ++ and -- Operators

The pre- and post-increment and decrement operators are shorthand for the common operation of adding or subtracting one from an arithmetic type. You write the operator next to the operand, and the variable is adjusted by one.

```
++i; // pre-increment
j++; // post-increment
```

It makes a difference if you bury the operator in the middle of a larger expression, like this:

```
int result = myArray[++i]; // pre-increment
```

This will increment i *before* using it as the index. The post-increment version will use the current value of i, and after it has been used, add one to it. It makes a very compact notation. Pre- and post-decrement operators work in a similar way.

The % and / Operators

The division operator "/" is regular division on integer types and floating point types. Integer division truncates towards zero, so -9/2 is -4.5 which is truncated to -4.

The remainder operator "%" is what is left over after dividing the right operand into the left operand a whole number of times. Thus, -7%2 is -1. This is because 2 * -3 = -6 and the difference between -6 and -7 is -1.

This equality is true for division and remainder on integer types:

```
(x / y) * y + x%y == x
```

If you need to work out what sign some remainder will have, just plug the values into that formula.

The << >> and >>> Operators

In Java the ">>" operator does an arithmetic or signed shift right, meaning that the sign bit is propagated. In C, it has always been implementation-defined whether this was a logical shift (fill with 0 bits) or an arithmetic shift (fill with copies of the sign bit). This occasionally caused grief as programmers discovered the implementation dependency when debugging or porting a system. Here's how you use the operator in Java:

```
int eighth = x >> 3; // shift right 3 times same as div by 8
```

One new Java operator is ">>>" which means "shift right and zero fill" or "unsigned shift" (do not propagate the sign bit). The ">>>" operator is not very useful in practice. It works as expected on numbers of canonical size, ints and longs. It is broken, however, for short and byte, because negative operands of these types are promoted to int (with sign propagation) before the shift takes place. The zero fill starts at bit 31, not bit 7 or 15 as you might think.

If you want to do unsigned shift on a short or a byte, mask the bits you want and use >>.

```
byte b = -1;
b = (byte)((b & 0xff) >> 4);
```

That way programs won't mysteriously stop working when someone changes a type from `int` to `short`.

The *instanceof* Operator

The other new operator is instanceof. We've said a couple of times that a class can be set up as a subclass of another class. The `instanceof` operator is used with superclasses to tell if you have a particular subclass object. For example, we may see the following:

```
class vehicle { ...
class car extends vehicle { ...
class convertible extends car { ...

vehicle v; ...
if (v instanceof convertible) ...
```

The `instanceof` operator is often followed by a statement that casts the object from the base type to the subclass, if it turns out that the one is an instance of the other. Before attempting the cast, instanceof lets us check that it is valid. There is more about this in the next chapter.

The & | and ^ Operators

The "&" operator takes two boolean operands, or two integer operands. It always evaluates both operands. For booleans, it ANDs the operands producing a boolean result. For integer types, it bitwise ANDs the operands, producing a result that is the promoted type of the operands (as in, long or int).

```
int flags = ... ;
int bitResult = (flags & 0x0F );
```

"|" is the corresponding bitwise OR operation. "^" is the corresponding bitwise XOR operation.

The && and || Operators

The "&&" is a conditional AND that takes only boolean operands. It avoids evaluating its second operand if possible. If a is evaluated to false, the AND result must be false and the b operand is not evaluated. This is sometimes called *short-circuited evaluation.* "||" is the corresponding short-circuited OR operation. There is no short-circuited XOR operation.

You often use a short-circuited operation to check if a variable refers to something before calling a method on it.

```
if ((anObject != null) && (anObject instanceof String)) { ...
```

In the example above, if the variable anObject is null, then the second half of the expression is skipped. Possible mnemonic: The longer operators "&&" or "||" try to shorten themselves by not evaluating the second operator if they can.

The ? ... : Operator

The "? ... :" operator is unusual in that it is a ternary or three-operand operator. It is best understood by comparing it to an equivalent if statement:

```
if (someCondition) truePart else falsePart
    someCondition ? trueExpression : falseExpression
```

The conditional operator can appear in the middle of an expression, whereas an if statement cannot. The value of the expression is either the true expression or the false expression. Only one of the two expressions is evaluated. If you do use this operator, don't nest one inside another, as it quickly becomes hard to follow. This example of ? is from the Java runtime library:

```
int maxValue = (a >= b) ? a : b;
```

The parentheses are not required, but they make the code more legible.

The Assignment Operators

Assignment operators are another notational shortcut. They are a combination of an assignment and an operation where the same variable is the left operand and the place to store the result. For example, these two lines are equivalent:

```
i += 4;        // i gets increased by 4.
i = i + 4;     // same thing.
```

There are assignment operator versions of all the arithmetic, shifting, and bit-twiddling operators where the same variable is the left operand and the place to store the result. Here's another example.

```
ypoints[i] += deltaY;
```

Assignment operators are carried over from C into Java, where they were originally intended to help the compiler-writer generate efficient code by leaving off a repetition of one operand. That way it was trivial to identify and reuse quantities that were already in a register.

The Comma Operator Is Gone

Finally, note that Java cut back on the use of the obscure comma operator. Even if you're quite an experienced C programmer, you might never have seen the comma operator, as it was rarely used. The only place it occurs in Java is in "for" loops. The comma allows you to put several expressions (separated by commas) into each clause of a "for" loop.

```
for (i=0, j=0; i<10; i++, j++)
```

It's not actually counted as an operator in Java, so it doesn't appear in Table 5-2. It's treated as an aspect of the for statement.

Associativity

Associativity is one of those subjects that is poorly explained in many programming texts, especially the ones that come from authors who are technical writers not programmers. In fact a good way to judge a programming text is to look for its explanation of associativity. Silence is not golden.

There are three factors that influence the ultimate value of an expression in any algorithmic language, and they work in this order: precedence, associativity, and order of evaluation.

Precedence says that some operations bind more tightly than others. Precedence tells us that the multiplication in a + b * c will be done before the addition, i.e. we have a + (b * c) rather than (a + b) * c. Precedence tells us how to bind operands in an expression that contains different operators.

Associativity is the tie breaker for deciding the binding when we have several operators of equal precedence strung together. If we have 3 * 5 % 3 should we evaluate it as (3 * 5) % 3, that is 15 % 3, which is 0? Or should we evaluate it as 3 * (5 % 3), that is 3 * 2, which is 6? Multiplication and the "%" remainder operation have the same precedence, so precedence does not give the answer. But they are left-associative, meaning when you have a bunch of them strung together you start associating operators with operands from the left. Push the result back as a new operand, and continue until the expression is evaluated. In this case, (3 * 5) % 3 is the correct grouping.

Associativity is a terrible name for the process of deciding which operands belong with which operators of equal precedence. A more meaningful description would be, *"Code Order For Finding/Evaluating Equal Precedence Operator Textstrings."* This is the "COFFEEPOT property" mentioned in Table 5-2.

Note that associativity deals solely with deciding which operands go with which of a sequence of adjacent operators of equal precedence. It doesn't say anything about the order in which those operands are evaluated.

Order of evaluation, if it is specified in a language, tells us the sequence for each operator in which the operands are evaluated. In a strict left-to-right language like Java, the order of evaluation tells us that in (i=2) * i++, the left operand to the multiplication will be evaluated before the right operand, then the multiplication will be done, yielding a result of 4, with i set to 3. Why isn't the auto-increment done before the multiplication? It has a higher precedence after all. The reason is because it is a *post* increment, and so by definition the operation is not done until the operand has been used. In C and C++ this expression is undefined because it modifies the same i-value more than once. It is legal in Java because the order of evaluation is well defined.

How Accurate Are Calculations?

The accuracy when evaluating a result is referred to as the *precision* of an expression. The precision may be expressed either as number of bits (64 bits), or as the data type of the result (double precision, meaning 64-bit floating-point format). In Java, the precision of evaluating each operator depends on the types of the operands. Java looks at the types of the operands around an operator, and picks the biggest of what it sees: double, float, and long, in that order of preference. Both operands are then promoted to this type, and that is the type of the result. If there are no doubles, floats, or longs in the expression, both operands are promoted to int, and that is the type of the result. This continues from left to right through the entire expression.

A Java compiler follows this algorithm to compile each operation:

- If either operand is a double, do the operation in double precision.

- Otherwise, if either operand is a float, do the operation in single precision.

- Otherwise, if either operand is a long, do the operation at long precision.

- Otherwise, do the operation at 32-bit int precision.

In summary, Java expressions end up with the type of the biggest, floatiest type (double, float, long) in the expression. They are otherwise 32-bit integers.

Most programmers already understand that floating-point numbers are approximations to real numbers. They may inherently contain tiny inaccuracies that can mount up as you iterate through an expression. (Actually, most programmers learn this the hard way.) Do not expect ten iterations of adding 0.1 to a float variable to cause it to exactly equal 1.0F! If this comes as a surprise to you, try this test program immediately, and thank your good fortune at having the chance to learn about it before you stumble over it as a difficult debugging problem.

```
public class inexact1 {
    public static void main(String s[]) {
        float pear = 0.0F;
        for (int i=0; i<10; i++) pear = pear + 0.1F;

        if (pear==1.0F) System.out.println("pear is 1.0F");
        if (pear!=1.0F) System.out.println("pear is NOT 1.0F");
    }
}
```

You will see this results in the following:

```
pear is NOT 1.0F
```

Since 0.1 is not a fraction that can be represented exactly with powers of two, summing ten of them does not exactly sum to one. This is why you should never use a floating-point variable as a loop counter. A longer explanation of this thorny topic is in "What Every Computer Scientist Should Know about Floating Point" by David Goldberg, in the March 1991 issue of *Computing Surveys* (volume 23, number 1). Note that this is a characteristic of floating-point numbers in all programming languages, and not a quality unique to Java.

Accuracy is not just the range of values of a type, but also (for real types) the number of decimal places that can be stored. Since the type float can store about six to seven digits accurately, when a long (which can hold at least 18 places of integer values) is implicitly or explicitly converted to a float, some precision may be lost.

```
public class inexact2 {
    public static void main(String s[]) {
        long  lasagna = 9000000000000000000L;
        float fructose = lasagna; // assign the long into a float

        lasagna = (long) fructose; //cast the float back into a long
        System.out.println(
            "lasagna (started as 9e18, assigned to float) is: \n"
            +lasagna);
    }
}
```

The output is as follows:

```
lasagna (started as 9e18, assigned to float) is: 9000000202358128640
```

As you can see, after being assigned to and retrieved back from the float variable, the long has lost all accuracy after six or seven significant figures. The truth is that if a float has the value shown, it could stand for any real value in the interval between the nearest representable floating-point number on each side. The library is entitled, within the bounds of good taste and consistency, to print it out as any value within that interval. If all this makes you fidget uncomfortably in your seat, maybe you better take a look at that Goldberg article. There is a hyperlink to it in the Java Programmers FAQ that is on the CD.

Floating-Point Extension Proposal

Two new keywords were added to JDK 1.2 in the beta 4 release: `strictfp` and `widefp`. The `widefp` keyword lets you specify that a method or class should use IEEE 754 extended precision (80-bit) when calculating intermediate results. This matches what the hardware does by default in an Intel x86 processor or an IBM PowerPC. The other keyword, `strictfp`, just says to use standard precision. The two alternatives can produce slightly different results.

Since things didn't quite sync up between the release of JDK 1.2, and the agreement of this proposal by all interested parties, Sun added the keyword in anticipation of industry agreement. If that is not forthcoming, or someone comes up with a better way, these keywords will be taken out. Right now, the keywords do nothing in the JVM, but you can write them in your code.

Here's the proposal for telling a method to use the wide format:

```
widefp void doCalc (float x, float y) {
      // some calculations to be done in extended precision...
}
```

What Happens on Overflow?

When a result is too big for the type intended to hold it, because of a cast, an implicit type conversion, or the evaluation of an expression, something has to give! What happens depends on whether the result type is integer or floating-point.

Integer Overflow

When an integer valued expression is too big for its type, only the low end (least significant) bits get stored. Because of the way two's-complement numbers are stored, adding one to the highest positive integer value gives a result of the highest negative integer value. Watch out for this (it's true for all language that use standard arithmetic, not just Java).

There is one case in which integer calculation ceases and overflow is reported to the programmer: division by zero (using / or %) will throw an exception. To "throw an exception" is covered in a later chapter.

There is a class called Integer that is part of the standard Java libraries. It contains some useful constants relating to the primitive type int.

```
public static final int    MIN_VALUE = 0x80000000; // class Integer
public static final int    MAX_VALUE = 0x7fffffff; // class Integer
```

There are similar values in the related class Long. Notice how these constants (final) are also static. If something is constant you surely don't need a copy of it in every object. You can use just one copy for the whole class, so make it static.

One possible use for these constants would be to evaluate an expression at long precision, and then compare the result to these int endpoints. If it is between them, then you know the result can be cast into an int without losing bits, unless it overflowed long, of course.

Floating Point Overflow

When a floating-point expression (double or float) overflows, the result becomes infinity. When it underflows (reaches a value that is too small to represent) the result goes to zero. When you do something undefined like divide zero by zero, you get a NaN. Under no circumstances is an exception ever raised from a floating-point expression.

The class `Float`, which is part of the standard Java libraries, contains some useful constants relating to the primitive type `float`.

```
public static final float POSITIVE_INFINITY;
public static final float NEGATIVE_INFINITY;
public static final float NaN;
public static final float MAX_VALUE = 3.40282346638528860e+38f;
public static final float MIN_VALUE = 1.40129846432481707e-45f;
```

One pitfall is that it doesn't help to compare a value to NaN, for NaN compares false to everything (including itself)! Instead, test the NaNiness of a value like this:

```
if (Float.isNaN( myfloat ) ) ... // It's a NaN
```

There are similar values in the class Double.

Overflow Summary

- Integer arithmetic
    Division by zero (using / or %) will throw an exception.

    Out of range values drop the high order bits from the result.

- Floating point arithmetic
    Never throws an exception.

    Out of range values are indicated by a NaN result.

Arithmetic That Cannot Overflow

There is a class called `java.math.BigInteger` that supports arithmetic on unbounded integers and a class called `java.math.BigDecimal` that does the same thing for real numbers. We'll give some examples of these classes later. They simulate arbitrary precision arithmetic in software. They are not as fast as arithmetic on the primitive types, but they offer arbitrary precision operands and results.

The Math Package

Let's introduce another of the standard classes. This one is called `java.lang.Math` and it has a couple of dozen useful mathematical functions and constants, including trig routines (watch out—these expect an argument in radians, not degrees), pseudorandom numbers, square root, rounding, and the constants pi and e.

There are two new methods in Math, introduced in JDK 1.2, to convert between degrees and radians.

```
public static double toDegrees(double); // new in JDK 1.2
public static double toRadians(double); // new in JDK 1.2
```

You'll need these when you call the trig functions if your measurements are in degrees.

You can review the source of the Math package at $JAVAHOME/src/java/lang/Math.java.

How to Invoke a Math.method

All the routines in the Math package are static, so you typically invoke them using the name of the class, like this:

```
double cabbage = java.lang.Math.random(); // value 0.0..1.0
```

There is a way to shorten the method call to name just the class and method, using the `import` statement, explained later.

```
double cabbage = Math.random();
```

The Math.log() function returns a natural (base e) logarithm. Convert natural logarithms to base 10 logarithms with code like this:

```
double nat_log = ...

double base10log = nat_log / Math.log(10.0);
```

The list of members in the java.lang.Math class is:

```java
public final class Math {
    public static final double E = 2.7182818284590452354;
    public static final double PI = 3.14159265358979323846;
    public static native double IEEEremainder(double, double);
    public static double abs(double);
    public static float abs(float);
    public static int abs(int);
    public static long abs(long);

// trig functions
    public static double toDegrees(double); // new in JDK 1.2
    public static double toRadians(double); // new in JDK 1.2
    public static native double sin(double);
    public static native double cos(double);
    public static native double tan(double);
    public static native double asin(double);
    public static native double acos(double);
    public static native double atan(double);
    public static native double atan2(double, double);
    public static native double exp(double);
    public static native double pow(double, double);
    public static native double log(double);
    public static native double sqrt(double);

// rounding and comparing
    public static native double ceil(double);
    public static native double floor(double);
    public static double max(double, double);
    public static float max(float, float);
    public static int max(int, int);
    public static long max(long, long);
    public static double min(double, double);
    public static float min(float, float);
    public static int min(int, int);
    public static long min(long, long);
    public static long round(double);
    public static int round(float);

// returns a random number between 0.0 and 1.0
    public static synchronized double random();

// rounds the argument to an integer, stored as a double
    public static native double rint(double);
}
```

Some Light Relief

Too Much Bread

Dough. Spondulicks. Moolah. Cabbage. Oof. Bread.

It's what we get for writing programs that other people want, instead of spending all our time writing programs that interest us. Since we program for money, we might as well try to maximize the flow that comes our way. There are various ways to do that, all involving trade-offs. One way, not unusual in Silicon Valley where I work, is to put the perfection of the programming craft above all other life-style considerations. That can get a bit dire in the long run, though. This story concerns a programmer who tried to maximize his income with unexpected results. We'll call him "Archie" here, because that's his name.

Archie made a vast pile of loot by contract programming. Archie wasn't all that good at programming and often had to skip to a new contract every few months. He was very good at selling himself, though, and giving the appearance of competence, which is how he survived as a contract programmer for so long. He fiddled his taxes by fixing things so that he appeared to be an employee of a shell company in an offshore tax haven. Actually, he was a *partner* in that shell company, paid himself a pittance in the taxable country, and stashed a tax-free fortune offshore. He did this for a number of years.

So, Archie lived a jet-set life and never missed a chance to rub it in the faces of us wage slaves. Archie had everything: badly-written code, oodles of cash, regular ski trips, and many girlfriends (whom he gleefully two-timed). In short, he was a bit of a reptile who thought he'd figured out a way to beat the system.

Eventually Archie had so much stashed away in his offshore bank account that he decided to put the money to use. Since he couldn't easily spend the money domestically, he bought a sandwich shop franchise in Barcelona. The sandwich shop was doing fine under its current owner and was almost certain to continue to prosper. Archie hired a local manager to replace the old owner, and everything ran well for about a month.

Then Archie received an urgent call from the bank in Spain saying that the venture wasn't generating enough cash to meet its payroll. Archie transferred the funds and put it down to start-up costs. The same thing happened the next month. At great cost, Archie hired a local auditor who eventually determined the local manager was skimming from the profits! Archie flew to Barcelona, fired the manager, and stayed in a hotel for three weeks until he was able to hire a new manager. This investment was already proving expensive.

The new manager wasn't any more honest than the last one, and Archie had to fly out and hire another one. That manager only lasted a couple of weeks, and Archie realized that he had a serious problem on his hands. So far all the flights, hotels, payroll, auditing, and advertising had cost him about as much again as his original investment. He needed to put more cash in every month to keep the venture solvent. He didn't have a new manager, and worst of all, since it now had a track record of six months of losses, he could no longer sell the business as a going concern.

Archie quickly figured out that he'd have to take charge personally to solve these problems. This is why you could find Archie—jet-setter and lavishly-paid contract programmer—waiting tables in a sandwich shop in Barcelona throughout 1998. While he's serving sandwiches and trying to build up a record of profitability for the business so he can unload it, Archie has no time to work as a contract programmer. Thus his losses also include what he'd make in a year of contract programming. It couldn't happen to a nicer guy.

The last time I passed through Barcelona on business, I felt like having a snack, so I called in at the sandwich store. Archie was neatly dressed in a green apron and a hair net, and he was standing behind a counter slicing a towering pile of loaves. "Hi Archie. How's things?" I called out. Archie glanced up and gestured at the loaves all around him. "Too much bread," he muttered. I could only nod my silent agreement with his pronouncement. Yes, way too much bread.

Further Reading

"What Every Computer Scientist Should Know About Floating-Point Arithmetic"

by David Goldberg, *Computing Surveys*, March 1991, published by the Association for Computing Machinery.

It explains why all floating-point arithmetic is approximate and how errors can creep in. There is a hyperlink to an online copy of this paper in the Java Programmers FAQ which is on the CD.

ANSI/IEEE Standard 754-1985 for Binary Floating-Point Arithmetic

Institute of Electrical and Electronic Engineers, New York, published 1985. Reprinted in SIGPLAN 22(2) pages 9–25.

CHAPTER

6

More OOP — Extending Classes

We now come to the second part of Object-Oriented Programming where we cover another two parts of "A PIE": inheritance and polymorphism. You need a solid understanding of these to successfully use the Java library routines. Despite the unusual names, they describe some clean concepts.

Inheritance means building on a class that is already defined to extend it in some way. Inheritance is what you acquire from past generations. Just as inheritance in real life is "what you get from a parent," inheritance in OOP is "what you get from a parent class." Every class has one immediate parent class. This is either a parent that you name explicitly or the parent that you get implicitly. For example:

```
class A { ... }
```

actually means:

```
class A extends java.lang.Object { ... }
```

The class `java.lang.Object` is the root of all classes. The keyword `extends` followed by the name of some other class is how you indicate that the other class is the parent class of this class, also known as *superclass*. All the non-private members of the superclass are available in a subclass just as though they were declared directly in the subclass. Some terminology:

class	A data type
extend	To make a new class that inherits the contents of an existing class.
superclass	A parent or "base" class. Superclass wrongly suggests that the parent class has more than the subclass.
subclass	A child class that inherits, or extends, a superclass. It is called a subclass because it only represents a sub-part of the universe of things that make up the superclass. It usually has more fields to represent its specialization, however.

Inheritance

To see what inheritance means in practice, consider a real world example of the Linnaean taxonomy of the animal kingdom and a similar example using C types.

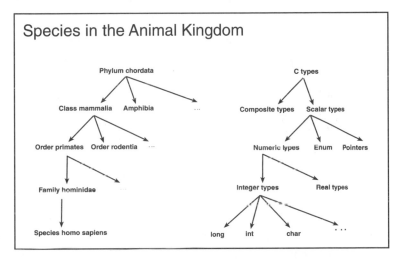

Figure 6-1:   Two real-world examples of an inheritance hierarchy.

In biology, animals are classified by whether they have a spinal cord or not. All mammals have a spinal cord. They inherit it as a characteristic because they are a subclass of the chordata phylum (fancy words for "the group with spines"). Mammals, like humans, also have specialized characteristics: they feed their young milk, they have hair, they have two generations of teeth, and so on. Primates inherit all the characteristics of mammals including the quality of having a spinal cord which mammals inherited from their parent type. The primate subclass is specialized with forward facing eyes, a large braincase, and so on to increasingly specialized subtypes.

We can also show how inheritance applies in theory to the C types, but that model is of no practical use. C doesn't have built-in inheritance, so a C programmer cannot use the type hierarchy in real programs. An important part of OOP is figuring out and advantageously using the hierarchies of the abstract data types in your application.

To summarize, inheritance occurs when a class adopts or adapts the data structures and methods of a base or *parent class*. That creates a hierarchy, similar to a scientific taxonomy. Each level is a specialization of the one above. Inheritance is one of the concepts people mean when they say Object-Oriented Programming requires a special way of thinking. Get ready to spring forward with that "conceptual leap."

A Java Example of Inheritance

There is a GUI library class in Java called Window that implements the simplest kind of window. The class Window doesn't even have borders or a menubar, so you can't move it or close it. The source for the Java runtime library is part of the JDK, and you can look at Window.java at $JAVAHOME/src/java/awt/Window.java. If you look at that file, you'll see the following code.

```
import several-packages;
public class Window ... {
... // about 900 lines of code of methods and fields

    public Window(Frame owner) { // a constructor
       ...

}
```

Read the code carefully on this and the following pages, as we're going to stick with this example for much of the chapter.

A Window object can be moved or written on by your code and can hold other GUI objects. Here's a program to instantiate a Window object and display it on the screen:

```
import java.awt.*.*;
public class example {
    public static void main(String args[]) {
        Frame f = new Frame();// Window must belong to a Frame
        Window w = new Window(f);
        w.setSize(200,100);
        w.setVisible(true);
        w.setLocation(50,50);
    }
}
```

The constructor for Window requires a more fully-featured GUI object, a Frame, so we create one here just to give it to the constructor. We don't do anything else with the Frame. If you compile and run the code, you will get the shown in the following screen capture.

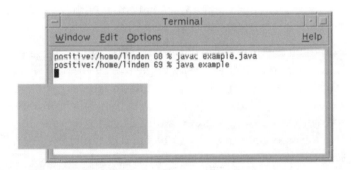

For the sake of this example, let's assume that your program needs a slightly different kind of window: a WarningWindow. The only change from Window is that you want WarningWindows to be colored red to highlight their importance. Everything else should work exactly like Window and should have all the same methods and fields.

There are at least three possible ways to implement WarningWindow:

1.   Change the Window class and add a constructor for a special Window that is colored red. This is a bad approach, because you never, ever want to change the standard runtime library, even if you get the source for it

2.   Copy all the code in Window.java into file WarningWindow.java, making the change you need. This is a bad approach because it is impossible to keep duplicated code in synchronization. Whenever the code for class Window changes in future releases, class WarningWindow will be out of sync and may well stop working.

3.   Make WarningWindow a *subclass* of Window, so it *inherits* all the functionality from Window. *Add* a small amount of code for the different behavior you want.

The preferred OOP approach is the third one: make WarningWindow *extend* the class Window, so WarningWindow inherits all the data and methods of Window.

```
class WarningWindow extends java.awt.Window {
    ... // put any additional members in here
}
```

This is exactly how the OOP process is supposed to work: find a class that does most of what you want, and then subclass it to provide the exact functionality.

There's nothing special about the libraries that come with Java. You are supposed to subclass system classes and your own classes as needed.

There are two points to watch here. First, (unlike real life) the child class chooses its parent class. The parent has some say in the matter in that it can control its visibility with access modifiers, and it can make itself final to say "no class is permitted to extend me." Second, you have to know what a class does and how it is implemented in order to extend it successfully. Despite the goals of encapsulation, you cannot treat a superclass like a black box and completely ignore its inner workings. This is because a subclass is essentially a statement that "I belong to the same black box as the superclass."

I happen to know that the Window class, like many graphical classes, has a method called setBackground() that can be used to change the color of its background[1]. All we have to do is make sure that every WarningWindow calls that method when it is being instantiated. A good way to ensure that is to put the call in a constructor. The code should go in a file called WarningWindow.java.

```
class WarningWindow extends java.awt.Window {

    WarningWindow(java.awt.Frame anyFrame) { //a constructor
        super(anyFrame);
        setBackground(java.awt.Color.red);
    }
}
```

We have to add a constructor anyway, because Windows take a Frame argument in their constructor, so we can't rely on the default no-arg constructor. We write a WarningWindow constructor with the Frame argument, have it call the constructor of its superclass (that's the "super(anyFrame)" statement), and then call setBackground() to set the window color to red.

Here's an example program that instantiates a regular window and a WarningWindow. As you can see, all the non-private members of the superclass are available in the subclass just as if they were declared directly in the subclass.

---

1. Actually, setBackground() and many of the other "Window" routines truly come from a superclass of Window; in this case, the class called Component.

```
import java.awt.*;
public class example { // example use of 2 kinds of Window

    public static void main(String args[]) {
        Frame f = new Frame();

        Window w = new Window(f); // standard Window
        w.setSize(200,100);
        w.setVisible(true);
        w.setLocation(300,300);

// The new red-hued WarningWindow we created
        WarningWindow ww = new WarningWindow(f);
        ww.setSize(200,100); // setSize is in a superclass
        ww.setVisible(true);
        ww.setLocation(370,370);
    }
}
```

We can call the three setSomething() methods, even though we didn't declare them in WarningWindow. We inherited them from Window.

Try running the program and you will see the result shown in the following screen capture. Since the red window won't show up red in a printed book, you're going to have to try it to prove I'm not kidding you

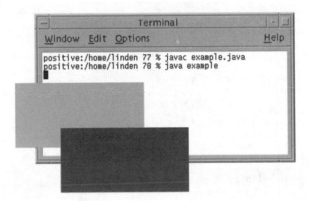

That's your first example of inheritance. We have reused the functionality of nine hundred lines of code, in a new six-line class that is in a separate file, and only contains the differences and specializations from its superclass. How is this any different from a library? What we have here is a powerful way to take an existing library and *modify* some of its behavior without modifying the library itself.

You might ask how this is any different from instantiating an ordinary Window and always remembering to color it red. The answer is that inheritance lets the compiler and runtime do the hard work of keeping track of what an object is, and whether it has the library behavior or the modified behavior. Inheritance lets you *superimpose* some new behavior on a class to create essentially a new library, but without copying everything. I use this all the time when debugging or prototyping some code. "What if I did it this way?" I ask myself, and I write a subclass that inherits the main class and contains my experimental changes. If the idea is bad, I just throw away the new class, and I haven't changed one line of source code in the underlying class.

Take another look at the constructor in the WarningWindow class. That line of code that reads `super(anyFrame)` is a common idiom when one class extends another. The code `super( )` is the way you express "call the constructor of my superclass." That's exactly what we want here: a regular Window is constructed, and its color is changed to red.

"Is a" Versus "Has a"

Don't confuse inheritance with having a data field that is another class.

It's very common to have a class that only implements a data structure such as a table. That arrangement is known as a container class, because it "contains" the data structure. You attach that data structure to some other class by declaring an instance of it inside the class as a field.

Declaring a class inside another just sets up a reference variable to the class with no special privileges or relationship. In contrast, inheritance says the subclass is a variation of the superclass that extends its semantics in some way.

The way to distinguish between these two cases is to ask yourself the "is a" versus "has a" question. Let's assume you have a "car" class and an "engine" class, and you want to decide whether to use inheritance or nesting to associate the two. Would you say "a car has an engine" or "a car is an engine?" If the answer is "has a," use nesting. If the answer is "is a," use inheritance. Similarly, if we have a "mammal" class and a "dog" class, we know that a "dog is a mammal." We would use inheritance to add the canine specializations to the mammal class resulting in the dog class.

The rule of thumb is that inheritance is for specialization of a type or changing its behavior. Container classes are for data structure re-use.

As we saw in chapter 2, a superclass constructor is *always* invoked when you create a subclass object. If you don't explicitly call a superclass constructor, then the no-arg constructor of the superclass is called for you. If the superclass doesn't have a no-arg constructor (either an implicit one because you didn't provide any constructors or an explicit no-arg constructor that you did provide), then you will get a compilation error along the lines of "no constructor found in superclass."

The most common use of `super` is the call `super()` which invokes a constructor in the superclass. The keyword is also used to access fields of any superclass (not just the immediate superclass) that are hidden by an identically-named feature in the subclass.

Java Does Not Use Multiple Inheritance

You may have heard about "multiple inheritance." That means having more than one immediate parent class. The resulting subclass thus has characteristics from all its immediate parent types.

Multiple inheritance is much less common than single inheritance. Where it has appeared in languages (like C++), it has been the subject of considerable debate on whether it should be in the language at all. Multiple inheritance poses additional problems in both implementation and use. Say there is a class A with some data members, and classes B and C inherit from A. Now have a class D that multiply-inherits from B and C. Does D have one copy of A's data members, or two identical copies? When you access something else in A, do you get B's or C's version of it? All this can be worked out, if you don't mind having a language reference manual the size of the Gutenberg Bible.

Some people say that no convincing examples have been produced where there was no alternative design avoiding multiple inheritance. Java bypasses any difficulties by not permitting multiple inheritance. The interface feature described in a later chapter fills in the gap left by multiple inheritance.

There is no way to "chain" several supers together, however, and reach back higher into the parent class hierarchy. Do not think that because `super.x` means "the x of a superclass" therefore "`super.super.x`" means "the x of grandparent." This is a very common mistake. There is no `super.super.x`.

Inheritance usually provides increasing specialization as you go from a general superclass class (e.g., vehicle) to a more specific subclass (e.g., passenger car, fire truck, or delivery van). It can equally well restrict or extend the available operations, though.

Be sure to note that a cast of something to its superclass makes it see the super-class variables where there is name hiding. The reason Java allows name duplication is to permit new fields to be added later to superclasses without breaking existing subclasses that might already use that name. The subclasses will continue to use their own copies of those fields, except when you tell them to behave like superclass objects.

A variable may have the same name as a method in its own class or superclass without either hiding the other.

```
class Example {
    public int total = 22;// overloading field and method is dumb,
    public int total () {   // but it works OK
        . . .
```

Name duplication should be rare, because the Java Language Specification says that method names should be based on verbs, while field names should be based on nouns (JLS, sect. 6.8).

In the case of a method with the same name in both a superclass and the subclass, the runtime system figures out exactly what class this object really is, and calls the method that is a member of that particular class. This dealt with in the section on overriding later in this chapter.

It turns out that all objects carry around a little bit of extra information about their type and the characteristics of that type. The runtime system needs to keep track of the type of an object reference to check casts to invoke the right version of over-loaded methods. The information is known as Run Time Type Information (RTTI), and it is kept in an object of its own. You get to the RTTI object through the get-Class() method that is in class Object and thus inherited by every class. The type of an RTTI object is a reference type whose name is Class. That class called Class is featured at the end of this chapter.

Compatibility of Superclass and Subclass

One of the nice things about inheritance is that it lets you treat a specialized object as a more general one. In other words, my WarningWindow, by virtue of being a subclass of Window, counts as a Window and can be used anywhere in code where a Window is used. If you have a method that expects a Window as an argument, you can pass it a WarningWindow, and it will work fine.

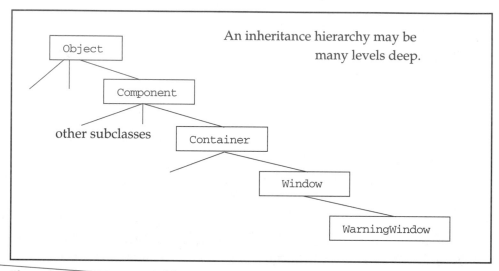

If you have a `Window` variable, you can assign a `WarningWindow` into it, like this:

```
WarningWindow ww = new WarningWindow( new Frame() );
Window w = ww; // the Window obj now refers to a WarningWindow
```

Here's the really magical thing: that `Window` object will continue to behave as a `WarningWindow`! It will display with a red background whenever someone invokes a `Window` operation on it that causes it to be updated on the screen.

This is a *key point* of OOP. When you have a variable of SomeClass, it might actually be referring to a much more specialized subclass. If a method takes some particular superclass type as a parameter, you can actually call it with any of its subclasses, and it will do the right thing. Add some lines of code to the example class a few pages back to try this. You can even assign a `WarningWindow` object to an `Object`, then later cast it back to a `WarningWindow`, and it won't have lost its type information.

Casting

Let's look a little more closely into compatibility between subclass and superclass. We'll use the following code for examples:

```
public class Mammal { ... }
public class Dog extends mammal { ... }
public class Cat extends mammal { ... }
Mammal m;
Dog fido = new Dog();
Cat kitty = new Cat();
      ... m = fido;
```

Notice the assignment of `fido` (a `Dog` object) into `m` (a `Mammal` variable). You can always make a more general object hold a more specialized one, but the reverse is not true without an explicit type conversion. All dogs are mammals, but not all mammals are dogs. Cats, horses, pigs, and people are also mammals. You can assign m=fido, but not (directly) fido=m because m could be referring to a `Cat` object. Just as you can cast (convert) an integer into a double, you can cast a superclass into one of its more specialized subclasses. You can't directly assign the following:

```
fido = m;      // causes compilation error
```

You can, however, cast it. To cast any type, write the typename in parentheses immediately before the object being cast. In this case:

```
fido = (Dog) m;     // The cast allows the compilation to work
                    // and the conversion is checked at runtime
```

Type hierarchies are often drawn as tree diagrams with `Object` (the ultimate superclass) at the top, and all subclasses beneath their superclass as Figure 6-1 exemplifies. In a drawing of this kind, you can only cast "downward" from a superclass to some subclass (or subclass of a subclass, and so on). You can never cast "sideways" to force an object to become something it is not.

The general rules for casting classes are:

- You can always assign parent = child; a cast is not needed, because a specific child class also belongs to its general parent class. You can assign several levels up the hierarchy; that is the parent may be a more remote ancestor. `Chordata c = new Dog()` is valid.

- You can cast child = (child) parent, and it will be checked at runtime. If the parent is referring to the correct child type, the assignment will occur. If the parent refers to some unrelated subclass, an exception `ClassCastException` will be raised. Exceptions are a recoverable interruption to the normal flow of control. They are described later.

- You cannot assign or cast at all between arbitrary unrelated classes, as in `fido=kitty;`.

Because every class is a subclass of the built-in system class `Object`, every object can be assigned to something of type `Object`, and later cast back to the type that it really is. In this way, the type `Object` can be used as a general reference to anything.

Some Java utility classes store and manipulate `Object`. You can use them for any object, later casting to get back the same type that you put in. You can be certain that, if a cast succeeds, you really have an object of the type you cast to. This is another illustration of the point that there is no evading strong typing in Java.

You can probably guess how the `instanceof` operator is used. We met `instanceof` in the last chapter. It allows you to compare a reference variable with a type, and it returns a value at runtime based on what type of object the variable is truly pointing to at that moment.

```
Mammal m;
if (Math.random() < 0.5) m = new Dog(); else m = new Mammal();
if (m instanceof Dog) // Check the type before attempting cast
    fido = (Dog) m; // the cast will always succeed.
```

Summary: Superclass/Subclass Compatibility

They must really love this topic on the Java Certification exam, because they ask it in several different questions. Make sure you have it down before taking that test. Here are possible assignments and a note about their compatibility:

superclass = subclass // *always valid*

subclass = (subclass) superclass // *valid at compile time, checked at runtime*

subclass = superclass // *not valid as written, requires a cast to compile*

someClass = someUnrelatedClass // *won't even compile*

someClass = (someClass) someUnrelatedClass // *won't even compile*

Polymorphism

Polymorphism is a complicated name for a straightfoward concept. It is Greek for "many shapes," and it merely means using the same one name to refer to different methods. "Name reuse" would be a better term. There are two types of polymorphism in Java: the really easy kind (overloading) and the interesting kind (overriding).

Overloading

The really easy kind of polymorphism is called *overloading* in Java and other languages, and it means that in any class you can use the same name for several different (but hopefully related) methods. The methods must have different signatures, however, so that the compiler can tell which of the synonyms is intended. Here are two overloaded methods:

```
public static int parseInt(String s, int radix)
                              throws NumberFormatException;
public static int parseInt(String s) throws NumberFormatException
```

These methods come from the class java.lang.Integer, which is a class wrapper[2] for the primitive type int and has some helper functions like these. The first method tries to interpret the String as an int. The second method does the same thing, but uses an arbitrary base. You could parse a hexadecimal String by supplying 16 as the radix argument.

The return type and the exceptions that a method can throw are not looked at when resolving same-named functions in Java.

The I/O facilities of a language are one typical place where overloading is used. You don't want to have an I/O class that requires a different method name depending on whether you are trying to print a short, an int, a long, and so on. You just want to be able to say "print(thing)." Note that C fails to meet this requirement. Although it's the same routine, "printf," it also needs a format specifier (which is a statement in a particularly ugly programming language in its own right) to tell printf what argument types to expect and to output. If you change the type of the C value you are outputting, you usually need to change the format specifier, too.

---

2.   A *class wrapper* is a class wrapped around a primitive type so you can treat that primitive type as an object, and send it to data structures and methods that process only objects.

Overriding

The second, more complicated kind of polymorphism, true polymorphism, is resolved dynamically at runtime. It occurs when a subclass class has a method with the same signature (number, type and order of parameters) as a method in the superclass. When this happens, the method in the derived class overrides the method in the superclass. Methods cannot be overridden to be more private; only to be more public.

An example should make this clear. Let's go back to our base class Window, and our subclass WarningWindow. I happen to know that one of the operations you can do with a Window is setSize() on it. That's even in our example program. We will give WarningWindow its own version of setSize(), to reflect the fact that Warning-Windows are more important, and should be bigger than regular Windows. We add a setSize() method to our subclass:

```
class WarningWindow extends java.awt.Window {

    WarningWindow(java.awt.Frame apple) { // constructor
        super(apple);
        setBackground(java.awt.Color.red);
    }

    public void setSize(int x, int y) { // overriding method
        int bigx = (int) (x*1.5);
        int bigy = (int) (y*1.5);
        super.setSize(bigx, bigy);
    }
}
```

The method setSize() in WarningWindow replaces or overrides the superclass's version of setSize() when the method is invoked on a WarningWindow object. C++ programmers will note that you do not need to specifically point out to the compiler (with the C++ "virtual" keyword) that overriding will take place. Here's some example code:

```
public static void main(String args[]) {
        Frame f = new Frame();
      { Window w = new Window(f);
        w.setSize(200,100);
        w.setVisible(true);
        w.setLocation(300,300);
      }
      { Window w = new WarningWindow(f); // the only change
        w.setSize(200,100);
        w.setVisible(true);
        w.setLocation(370,370);
      }
}
```

I have simply duplicated some code and put it in separate blocks (separate scopes) so that the duplication of the variable w doesn't cause a compiler error. In the first block, I assign a regular window to w; in the second, I assign a Warning-Window. Even though w remains a Window object, different methods are called on it.

When you try running this, you will note that when we apply the setSize() method to a Window, we get the base class version, meaning it comes out the regular size. When we apply the setSize method to a WarningWindow, we get the WarningWindow specialized version which it displays 50% bigger in each direction. Wow!

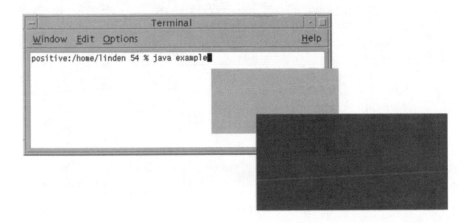

When we invoke the method on something that started out as a general Window, but may have been assigned a WarningWindow at runtime, the correct method is chosen at runtime based on what the object actually is. And *that* is polymorphism. It is a powerful tool for letting a class implement an operation in a way that is unique to itself.

It would clearly be bad design to override a method in a way that fundamentally changes what it does. You probably wouldn't *really* want to make setSize() use different values from its arguments. It makes a great demonstration for teaching purposes, though, because the difference is so visible.

The Difference Between Overloading and Overriding

Overloading, the shallow kind of polymorphism, is resolved by the compiler at compile time. Overloading allows several methods to have the same one name, and the compiler will choose the one you mean by matching on argument types.

Overriding, the deep kind of polymorphism is resolved at runtime. It occurs when one class extends another, and the subclass has a method with the same signature (exact match of number and argument types) as a method in the superclass.

Question: Which of them gets invoked?

Answer: If it's an object of the subclass, the subclass one; if it's an object of the superclass, the superclass one. The reason this is "fancy" is that sometimes you cannot tell until runtime, so the compiler must plant code to work out which method is appropriate for whatever this object turns out to be, then call that at runtime.

The technical term for "choosing the correct method for whatever object this is at runtime" is *late binding* or *delayed binding*. Polymorphism is the language feature that allows two methods to have the same name, such that late binding may be applied.

Constructor declarations are not members. They are never inherited and therefore are not subject to hiding or overriding.

Inheriting from Object

So the meaning of inheritance is that a class has access to the members of a parent class. If a class has its own version of a method in a parent class, its own version will be called.

This has implications for program maintenance. When you see a class accessing some member, if you cannot find the declaration in the class itself, look in the parent class, and then in the parent of the parent class, all the way back to the ultimate base class Object, if necessary.

Inheritance is the reason why you can call toString() on any object. If you look back at the listing of Object at the end of chapter 3, you'll see it has a number of methods that are inherited by every class. The method toString() is one of these.

When to override Object. toString()

The method toString() has some magic language support. The language rule is that when the compiler sees a String and any other object whatsoever as the two operands to a "+" operator, the system will call a method with the name toString to create a String representation of that object and then concatenate the two Strings. You thus have two choices for the toString method for any class:

- You can let the inheritance hierarchy pick up the toString method from superclass Object. This will return a String containing the classname and something that looks like the address of the instance.

- You can provide in your class your own version of a method with this signature:

```
public String  toString()
```

You will write the method to print out the value of key fields, nicely formatted. It will override the Object version of toString.

It's better to take the second alternative and provide more meaningful output. The method toString() will be invoked on any object that is concatenated with a String.

Fruit lemon = new Fruit();

String s = "Your object is " + lemon;

// the + invokes method lemon.toString()

Defining toString for your classes and printing an object this way is a useful debugging technique.

Forcing Overriding off: Final

There are two further adjustments to fine-tune inheritance: abstract and final. You will be able to use this to great advantage when you become more expert. Lets go back to the class java.lang.Math that we met at the end of chapter 5. One feature of the class is that all trig operations are done in radians, not degrees. Would it be possible to *extend* java.lang.Math and *override* just the trig functions so that they worked with degrees instead? You could leave all the other rounding and comparing Math functions alone, and you would have specialized the subclass for your needs.

Your code might look like this:

```
public class DegreeMath extends java.lang.Math { // won't work
    public double sin(double d) {
        double degToRad = super.toRadians(d);
        double result = super.sin(degToRad);
        return super.toDegrees(result);
    }
// an experienced programmer might smoosh everything together as:
//        return super.toDegrees( super.sin( super.toRadians(d) ));
    ...
    }
```

That is a great idea in theory, but it cannot be done this way for the Math class in practice for two reasons. One, all the Math methods are static. Two, the Math class is labelled as final.

```
public final class Math { ...
    public static native double sin(double a);
```

All the methods in Math are static (class-based) methods. Static methods do not participate in overriding. Overriding is used when an object might be one type or might be a more specialized sub-type. Class methods don't belong to an object and never have this possible ambiguity. Acting as a reminder that a method will not be overridden is another reason why you should always invoke class methods using the name of the class, not an instance of it.

When the keyword final appears at the start of a class declaration, it means "no one can extend this class." Similarly, an individual method can be made final preventing it being overridden when its class is inherited. It is final in the sense that it is a leaf of an inheritance tree. Typically, you might wish to prevent further inheritance to avoid further specialization: you don't want to permit this type to be further adjusted. A "final" method is also a clue to the compiler to inline the code. Inlining the code means optimizing out the overhead of a method call by taking the statements in the body of the method and duplicating them inline instead of making the call. This is a classic space versus time trade-off.

The class `java.lang.Math` is labelled as `final` for reasons of performance. Overriding can be "turned off" on a method or class by using the keyword `final` on a method or class. A method call can be made much more quickly if the compiler can compile it in, rather than having the runtime system figure out which is the right overriding method at execution time. (This performance cost is the reason overriding is off by default in C++).

The class `java.lang.String` is labelled as `final` for reasons of security and performance. As well as being a final class, String objects are read-only. If you could override String, you could write a subclass that was not read-only, but could be used in all the places that String is used. Specifically, you could change the String pathname to a file after it had been checked for access permission, but before the open operation had been done.

Forcing Overriding: Abstract

Just as `final` tells the compiler "this thing is complete and must not be changed or extended or overridden," there is a keyword to force overriding to take place. The keyword `abstract` tells the compiler "this thing is incomplete and must be extended to be used." You can think of `final` and `abstract` as opposites of each other, as they cannot occur together for a method or class. The keyword `final` or `abstract` can be applied to an individual method or an entire class. We have already seen `final` applied to data.

When the keyword `abstract` appears at the start of a class declaration, it means that zero or more of its methods are abstract. An abstract method has no body; its purpose is to *force* some subclass to override it and provide a concrete implementation of it. Labelling a method `abstract` requires you to label the class `abstract`.

You make a class `abstract` when three conditions are fulfilled:

- There will be several subclasses.
- You want to handle all the different subclasses as an instance of the superclass.
- The superclass alone does not make sense as an object.

That set of conditions for deciding when to use an abstract class probably made no sense at all yet, so I'll try to show what it means in terms of an example. Think back to the GUI class Window. We showed a few pages back how Window is a subclass of Component (not directly, but two levels down). It turns out that Component is the window toolkit superclass for many Java library objects that you can display on the screen. In particular, many screen widgets (Unix terminology) or controls (Microsoft terminology) are Components. Scrollbars, panels, dialogs, tabbed panes, cursors, labels, textfields, and so on are all subclasses of Component. Thus it meets the first condition of abstract classes: there is more than one subclass.

There are many operations that we can do on a control without precisely knowing or caring which control it is. One common operation is to add it to a container for display. A container is a GUI backdrop or pinboard whose purpose is to arrange and display the group of components it is given. We don't want to have umpteen individual methods, one for adding each individual type of control to a panel. We just want to be able to say the following:

```
myContainer.add(Component c);
```

We have the second condition: for convenience, you want to handle all the different subclasses as an instance of the superclass. The most frequently seen case is where the superclass is a parameter to a method, as it is here.

Finally, all the subclasses of Component are real, concrete objects. You can actually display them on the screen. Component itself is not a concrete object. You cannot sensibly display the Component superclass on the screen (what would be drawn?). Only the subclasses have the actual semantics of shape, behavior, and look. An instance of Component itself doesn't really make sense. You need an instance of a concrete subclass of Component. In this way, the third condition has been met, an instance of the superclass does not make sense as an object.

Although making a class `abstract` forces a programmer to extend it and fill in some more details in the subclass before it can be instantiated, it allows the class to stand in for any of the concrete subclasses. Saying a class is abstract imposes the requirements "you must implement the abstract method(s) in a subclass" and "you cannot instantiate an object of the abstract class, it is incomplete in some way." Abstract has no connection with data abstraction we saw in chapter 2.

Here's the general form that Component has in source code:

```
public abstract class Component {
    public void setBackground(java.awt.Color){...}
    public void setVisible(boolean) { ...}
    public void setLocation(int, int){ ...}
    ... // 3800 lines of code omitted
    public abstract void DrawMeOnScreen();
}


// some concrete subclasses of Component
public class Button extends Component {
    public void DrawMeOnScreen(){ ...}
}

public class Scrollbar extends Component { ...
    public void DrawMeOnScreen(){...}
}


// Some other class entirely that wants to operate
// on any of the above subclasses
public class Container {
    public void remove(Component comp) { ...}
    public Component add(Component comp){ comp.DrawMeOnScreen(); }
    void setFocusOwner(Component c) { .. }
}
```

I have fudged a bit on the name and use of DrawMeOnScreen() to make the example simpler. That's what the method does, but it is called something less intuitive— paint(), if you must know. We'll meet it in a later chapter.

The use of extends is at least twenty times more common than the use of abstract to fine-tune class hierarchies in the Java runtime library.

The Class Whose Name Is `Class`

Here's where the terminology admittedly can get a little confusing. We saw a few pages back that every object has some Run Time Type Information associated with it. The RTTI for any object is stored in an object whose class is called "Class." Class could certainly use a better, less self-referential name.

A big use of `Class` is to help with loading new classes during program execution. A lot of other languages load an entire program before they start execution. Java encourages dynamic loading. Classes only need to be loaded on demand when they are first referenced.

When you compile the class `Fruit`, it creates the bytecode file Fruit.class. Fruit.class contains the bytecode for `Fruit` and also a `Class` object describing `Fruit`. To load class `Fruit`, the runtime system first looks for its `Class` object. `Class` also provides the information for checking casts at runtime. Finally, it lets a program look at all the members of a class—the data fields and the methods. These are all systems programming activities, unlikely to occur in your programs, but providing `Class` makes it easy to program them without stepping outside the Java system. You can safely skim over the rest of this section, returning when you have a specific need to look at RTTI.

To access the runtime type information for a class, you need an object of type Class. You can get one in three ways. Here's some code showing the alternatives:

```
Fruit lemon = new Fruit();

Class which = lemon.getClass(); // getClass is a method in Object
```
   or
```
Class which = Class.forName("Fruit"); // forName is a static method
```
   or
```
Class which = Fruit.class; // class literal
```

The last alternative is called a *class literal*. You can jam the characters `.class` onto the end of any type at all, even a primitive type like `int`, and it gets you the Class RTTI associated with the type. You'll choose which of the alternatives to use depending on whether you have an object, the classname in a String, or the class.

Once you have the class object you can invoke its methods. The strict left-to-right evaluation of Java allows method calls to be chained together in one statement. You can do this with any methods where the result of one method is the reference used in the next:

```
String name = myobject.getClass().getName();
```

```
public final class java.lang.Class  {
     public java.io.InputStream getResourceAsStream(java.lang.String);
     public java.net.URL getResource(java.lang.String);

     public native String getName();
     public static native java.lang.Class forName(java.lang.String);
     public native java.lang.Object newInstance();

     static native Class getPrimitiveClass(java.lang.String);

     public native boolean isInstance(java.lang.Object);
     public native boolean isAssignableFrom(java.lang.Class);
     public native boolean isInterface();
     public native boolean isArray();
     public native boolean isPrimitive();

// security related
     public native ClassLoader getClassLoader();
     public native Object getSigners()[];
     native void setSigners(java.lang.Object[]);

// introspection on the class, its ancestors, members and constructors
     public native Class getSuperclass();
     public native Class getInterfaces()[];
     public native Class getComponentType();
     public native int getModifiers();
     public Class getDeclaringClass();
     public Class getDeclaredClasses()[];
     public Class getClasses()[];
     public reflect.Constructor getConstructors()[];
     public reflect.Constructor getConstructor(java.lang.Class[]);
     public reflect.Constructor getDeclaredConstructors()[];
     public reflect.Constructor
getDeclaredConstructor(java.lang.Class[]);

     public reflect.Field getFields()[];
     public reflect.Field getField(java.lang.String);
     public reflect.Field getDeclaredFields()[];
     public reflect.Field getDeclaredField(java.lang.String);

     public reflect.Method getMethods()[];
     public reflect.Method getMethod(java.lang.String,
java.lang.Class[]);
     public reflect.Method getDeclaredMethods()[];
     public reflect.Method getDeclaredMethod(
                          java.lang.String, java.lang.Class[]);

     public java.lang.String toString();
}
```

It can be useful to print out the names of classes while debugging code that deals with arbitrary objects. This and other popular methods of class follow. The first returns the name of the Class.

```
public native String getName();
```

The next method takes a String that should be the name of a class and retrieves the Class (RTTI) object for that class. It's an alternative to getClass(), used when you have the name of the class in a String, rather than having any objects of it.

```
public static native Class forName(String className)
throws ClassNotFoundException
```

This next example is a surprising method—it allows you to create an object of the class for which this is the RTTI. Coupled with the forName() method, this lets you create a object of any class whose name you have in a String. Highly dynamic! The no-arg constructor of the appropriate class is called, so it better have one.

```
public native Object newInstance()
throws InstantiationException, IllegalAccessException
```

In the following example, if you have an instance of a class, and you cast it to the class that you know it is, you can call its methods!

```
        String s = "Fruit";
           ...
        Object f = Class.forName(s).newInstance();
```

Use the classloader that loaded this next class to get a resource (e.g., a file) from the same place. That place might be a zip or Jar file, a local filesystem, or a network connection.

```
public InputStream getResourceAsStream(String name)
```

Similar to the previous method, this one returns a URL that can access the resource, rather than a Stream with its contents.

```
public java.net.URL getResource(String name) {
        name = resolveName(name);
```

This checks if the Class it is invoked on is the same as, or a superclass of, the obj. This is the dynamic equivalent of the instanceof operator. If true, it means you could assign the obj, possibly with a cast, into the object for whom this is the RTTI.

```
public native boolean isInstance(Object obj);
```

Some Light Relief

Hank the Angry, Drunken, Beautiful Person

The email to me was brief. It just read:

```
From billg@Central Mon May  4 11:57:41 PDT 1998
Subject: Hank the Angry Dwarf
To: jokes@Sun.COM

Hey everyone.  If you've got five seconds to spare, go to the
following url:
     http://www.pathfinder.com/people/50most/1998/vote/index.html

and vote for:
     Hank the Angry, Drunken Dwarf

This is a huge joke.  We want to try to get Hank way up there on
the People Magazine 50 most beautiful people of the year list.  As
of 2:00AM, he's already up to number 5!
```

Well, I can recognize a high priority when I see one. I put down the critical bug fix I was working on, went right to the web site, and checked what this was all about.

Every year the celebrity gossip magazine *People* prints a list of "the 50 most beautiful people in the world," and this year they were soliciting votes on their web site. *People* had started the ball rolling with nominations for actors like Kate Winslet and Leonardo DiCaprio, who were in the public eye because of their roles in the Titanic movie. (What a drag that movie was. I guessed the ending after an hour or so. Not to spoil it for anyone, but the boat hits an iceberg and sinks.)

People magazine gave web surfers the opportunity to write in names of people for whom they wanted to vote. A fan of the Howard Stern radio show nominated "Hank the angry, drunken dwarf" for *People*'s list. When Stern heard about Hank's nomination as one of the most beautiful people in the world, he started plugging the candidacy on the radio. A similar phenomenon took place on the Internet, and many people received e-mail like I did. Another write-in stealth candidate widely favored by netizens was flamboyant, blond-haired, veteran pro-wrestler, Ric Flair.

Hank the angry, drunken dwarf is an occasional guest on Stern's syndicated radio program. Hank is a 36-year old dwarf who lives in Boston with his mother and has made a name for himself as a belligerent, if diminutive, devotee of beer, tequila, and Pamela Anderson.

The *People* web site soon crashed under the strain of incoming votes for Hank, and there were dark allegations of automated voting programs, or votebots. I was shocked.[3] When the *People* poll closed on May 8, 1998, the results were as follows:

230,169 votes	Hank the dwarf	Angry, drunken dwarf and Stern radio guest
17,145 votes	Ric Flair	25-year pro-wrestling performer
14,471 votes	Leonardo DiCaprio	High school drop out, actor
7,057 votes	Gillian Anderson	College graduate, actress
5,941 votes	Kate Winslet	High school drop out, actress

Hank Nassif the angry, drunken dwarf was officially the most beautiful person in the world, by a margin of more than 10-to-1 over the runner-up! Unhappily, *People* magazine showed their true colors at this point, ignored the clear mandate from the web site and went ahead with a cover story naming the guy who came in third as the official "most beautiful person in the world" for 1998. What a rip-off.

In Fall 1998, Time Magazine was running a poll for "Person of the Century" at http://cgi.pathfinder.com/time/time100/poc/century.html. It's really a pity that Time Magazine lent its prestigious name to something so meaningless as an Internet poll. If someone ever tries to justify something to you using data from an Internet poll, just clue them in about Hank. The last time I checked the Time poll, Ric Flair was number 3, right behind Adolf Hitler and Jesus (numbers 2 and 1, respectively). You know what to do.

Time

---

3.   I am not shocked enough to mention that there is enough information in the Java Programmers FAQ on the CD that comes with this book and in the network chapter of this book to enable you to write your own Java votebot. Please send me a copy to put on the CD.

Exercises

1. What are the four attributes that distinguish Object-Oriented Programming? What are some advantages and disadvantages of OOP?

2. Give three examples of primitive types and three examples of pre-defined Java classes (i.e., object types).

3. What is the default constructor, and when is it called? What is a no-arg constructor?

4. Describe overriding, and write some code to show an example.

5. Consider the following three related classes:

```
class Mammal {}
class Dog extends Mammal { }
class Cat extends Mammal { }
```

There are these variables of each class:

```
Mammal m;
Dog d = new Dog( );
Cat c = new Cat( );
```

6. Which of these statements will cause an error at compile time and why? Which of these statements may cause an error at runtime and why?

```
m = d; // 1.
d = m; // 2.
d = (Dog) m; // 3.
d = c; // 4.
d = (Dog) c; // 5.
```

CHAPTER
7

Java Statements

Statements are the way we get things done in a program. Statements live in methods and in blocks. Any statement may be prefixed by a label, as shown here:

```
months: for(int m = 1; m <= 12; m++) { ...
```

The general syntax is this:

```
identifier: statement
```

Java doesn't have a `goto` statement. If a label appears, it is either just empty documentation (rare—use a comment instead), or it is used to break out of certain enclosing statements in a clean way.

Statements in Java can be conveniently divided into several groups:

- "Organizing" statements
- Expression statements
- Selection, Iteration, and Transfer statements
- Guarding statements

First we will describe all but the guarding statements. We will then introduce the topic of exceptions, which provides the context in which to talk about guarding statements.

Most of Java's statements are pretty much identical to their counterparts in other languages and will be readily recognizable to any programmer. Accordingly we can limit our discussion to showing the general form of each statement and noting any special rules or "gotchas" that apply.

"Organizing" Statements

There are two statements whose use is primarily to organize your code. It is convenient to group them in with the other statements, because the Java Language Specification says they are regular statements. The two *organizing* statements (my term) are the block statement and the empty statement.

A block statement is a pair of curly braces, "{ ... }", that contains zero or more statements and local variable declarations in any order. Wherever you can legally put one statement, you can put a block statement. We've seen block statements many times. Use them to put a whole group of statements in an "if" branch or to declare a variable that will be used just within the block. A block statement looks like this:

```
{
    Window w = new WarningWindow(f);
    w.setSize(200,100);
    w.setVisible(true);
}
```

An empty statement is simply a semicolon by itself. The empty statement does nothing. Wherever you can legally put a statement, you can put an empty statement. In the example below, we are saying "if the condition is true, do nothing; otherwise invoke the method."

```
boolean noRecordsLeft = ...
if (noRecordsLeft)
      ; // empty statement
else {
        alertTheMedia(); ...
```

The code is written this way for a reason: rewriting it so the "else" part becomes the "then" part causes the condition to become a double negative ("not no records left"). It's usual to comment the empty statement and put it on a line by itself.

Expression Statements

Certain kinds of expression are counted as statements. You write the expression, put a semicolon after it, and voila, it's an expression statement. In particular, an assignment, method invocation, the instantiation of a class, and pre-increment, post-increment, and decrement are all expressions that can be statements.

```
new WarningWindow(f); // instance creation
w.setSize(200,100);// method invocation
i++;                    // post increment
a = b;                  // assignment
```

An expression statement is executed by evaluating the expression. Any ultimate result after an assignment has taken place is discarded. Usually you save a reference to something that you create an instance of. For example, you have:

```
foo = new WarningWindow(f); // instance creation
```

not:

```
new WarningWindow(f); // instance, but no ref saved
```

However, there are certain classes that you can instantiate for which you don't necessarily need to save a reference, like Threads and inner classes. So, you might see this either way.

Selection Statements

The general form of the "if" statement looks like this.

if

```
if ( Expression ) Statement  [ else  Statement ]
```

Statement Notes

✔ The `Expression` must have boolean type. This has the delightful side-effect of banishing the old "if (a=b)" problem, where the programmer does an assignment instead of a comparison, (a==b). If that typo is written, the compiler will give an error message that a boolean is needed in that context—unless a and b are booleans. At least you're protected for all the other types.

✔ The Statement can be any statement, in particular a block statement, { ... }, is normal.

The general form of the "switch" statement is impossible to show in any meaningful form in a syntax diagram with less than about two dozen production rules. That tells you something about the statement right there. If you look at Kernighan and Ritchie's C book, you'll note that even they were not up to the task of showing the syntax in any better way than this:

switch

```
switch (Expression) Statement
```

Neither has had a C book since. Ignoring syntax diagrams, the switch statement is a poor man's "case" statement. It causes control to be transferred to one of several statements depending on the value of the Expression, which must be of type `char`, `byte`, `short`, or `int`. It generally looks like this:

```
switch (Expression) {
      case constant_1 : Statement; break;
      case constant_5 :
      case constant_3 : Statement; break;
            ...
      case constant_n : Statement; break;
            default : Statement; break;
}
```

Statement Notes

✔ If you omit a "break" at the end of a branch, after that branch is executed control falls through to execute all the remaining branches! This is almost *never* what you want.

✔ There can be only one "default" branch, and it doesn't have to be last. The "default" branch can be omitted. If it is present, it is executed when none of the "case" values match the Expression.

✔ A Statement can be labelled with several cases. (This is actually a trivial case of fall-through).

✔ If none of the cases match, and there is no default case, the statement does nothing.

✔ Implicit fall-through (in the absence of "break") is a bug-prone misfeature.

Switch Is Badly Designed

Looking through about 100,000 lines of the Java Development system source, there are about 320 switch statements. Based on a random sample of files, implicit fall-through is used in less than 1% . A statement in which you must take explicit action 99% of the time to avoid something is a disaster. Death to the switch statement!

Iteration Statements

The "for" statement looks like this:

for (*Initial; Test; Increment*) *Statement*

Statement Notes

✔ Initial, Test, and Increment are all Expressions that control the loop. Any or all of them is optional. A typical loop will look like this:

```
for( i=0; i<100; i++ ) { ...
```

A typical infinite loop will look like:

```
for (;;)
```

✔ As in C++, it is possible to declare the loop variable in the "for" statement, like this:

```
for( int i=0; i<100; i++ ) { ...
```

This is a nice feature created for the convenience of the programmer. Unlike most C++ compilers, the lifetime of the Java loop variable concludes at the end of the "for" statement. The continued existence of loop variables in C++ was an artifact of the original implementations that simply translated the language to C. It was convenient to collect all declarations and move them to the beginning of the block without trying to impose a finer granularity of scope. This sloppy approach is now being tightened up for ANSI C++.

✔ The comma separator "," is allowed in the Initial and Increment sections of loops. This is so you can string together several initializations or increments, like this:

```
for(i=0,j=0; i<100; i++, j+=2 ) { ...
```

The "while" statement looks like this:

> while (*Expression*) *Statement*

Statement Notes

✔ While the boolean-typed expression remains true, the Statement is executed.

✔ This form of loop is for iterations that take place zero or more times. If the Expression is false on the first evaluation, the Statement will not execute.

The "do while" statement looks like this:

> do *Statement* while (*Expression*) ;

Statement Notes

✔ The Statement is executed, and then the boolean-typed expression is evaluated. If it is false, execution drops through to the next statement. If it is true, you loop through the Statement again.

✔ This form of loop is for iterations that take place at least one time. If the Expression is false on the first evaluation, the Statement will already have executed once.

There may be "continue" statements in a loop. These look like:

> continue;

> continue *Identifier* ;

Continue statements occur only in loops. When a continue statement is executed, it causes the flow of control to pass to the next iteration of the loop. It's as though you say, "Well, that's it for iteration N; increment the loop variable (if this is a "for" loop), do the test, and continue with iteration N+1."

The "continue *Identifier*" form is used when you have nested loops, and you want to break out of an inner one altogether and start with the next iteration of the outer loop.

The loop with which you want to continue is labelled at its "for" statement with the matching identifier, and it does the same trick. Namely, that's it for iteration N of the labelled loop, increment the loop variable (if this is a "for" loop), do the test, and continue with iteration N+1. You continue with the *next iteration*, even though the label is (confusingly) at the beginning, rather than labelling, say, the end of the loop. Here is an example "continue" statement:

```
months: for (int m=1; m<=12; m++) {
                // do something
                // nested loop
                for (int d=1; d<=31; d++) {
                        // some daily thing
                        if (m==2 && d==28) continue months;
                        // otherwise something else
                }
                // more guff
        }
```

There may be "break" statements in a loop or switch. These look like this:

break

```
break;
```

Or they look like this:

```
break identifier;
```

Break is like a more dramatic version of continue. Break with no identifier causes control to pass to just after the end of the enclosing "for, do, while," or "switch" statement. The loop or switch statement is "broken out of." Break with no identifier can appear only in a statement by virtue of the whole thing being nested in an iteration or switch statement. You will break to the end of the iteration or switch, *not* the statement it's immediately nested in.

```
for (int i=1; i<=12; i++){
    if (LeapYear()) {
        if (i==2) break;
    }
    getTotalforMonth(i);
}
// break to here. Is that what you want?
```

If an identifier is included, it must be an identifier matching the label on some enclosing statement. The enclosing statement can be *any* kind of statement, not just an iterative or switch statement. In other words, it's OK to break out of any kind of enclosing block as long as you explicitly indicate it with a label. In practice, it's almost always a loop or switch that you break out of, not an if or block.

Again, there is the slightly confusing feature that statements are labelled at their *beginning*, but "break" causes you to jump to their *end*. Here is an example:

```java
months: for (int m=1; m<=12; m++) {

            // do something
            // nested loop
            for (int d=1; d<=31; d++) {
                // some daily thing
                if (cost > budget)  break months;
            }
    }
    cost=0;
```

Transfer of Control Statements

A "return" statement looks like this:

```
        return;

    return   Expression;
```

Statement Notes

✔ "Return" gets you back to where you were called from.

✔ A "return *Expression*" can be used only with something that actually does return a value, meaning never with a "void" method. There is another statement that causes transfer of control: the "throw" statement that raises an exception. We will cover this in the chapter that deals with exceptions.

There is a reserved word "goto" in Java, but there is no goto statement. The designers grabbed the keyword to ensure that no one uses it as a variable name in case it later turns out to be convenient to support (perhaps for automatically generated code).

How to Look at Bytecode Instructions for a Statement

You can look at the Java code output by the compiler by using the javap command, like this:

        javap -c *class*

The javap command is an abbreviation for "java print." It can be instructive and fun to look at the bytecode output for various Java statements. You can find answers to questions about the code something is compiled into. You can find out more about bytecode by looking at the JVM specification at http://docs.sun.com:80/ab2/coll.127.1/@Ab2CollToc?subject=java.

Javap will also tell you the sourcefile from which the class came, which is sometimes a useful check that you are executing the code you want. Here's the result of running javap on the WarningWindow class we compiled in the last chapter:

```
javap -c WarningWindow
Compiled from example.java // first it lists the class API
class WarningWindow extends java.awt.Window {
    WarningWindow(java.awt.Frame);
    public void setSize(int, int);
}

Method WarningWindow(java.awt.Frame) // really a constructor
   0 aload_0
   1 aload_1
   2 invokespecial #6 <Method java.awt.Window(java.awt.Frame)>
   5 aload_0
   6 getstatic #7 <Field java.awt.Color red>
   9 invokevirtual #8 <Method void setBackground(java.awt.Color)>
  12 return

Method void setSize(int, int)
   0 iload_1
   1 i2d
   2 ldc2_w #10 <Double 1.5>
   5 dmul
   6 d2i
   7 istore_3
   8 iload_2
   9 i2d
  10 ldc2_w #10 <Double 1.5>
  11 ... etc
```

Exceptions

At several points in the preceding text I mentioned exceptions, only to defer discussion. This is where I deliver on the promise of describing the purpose and use of exceptions following this order:

1. The purpose of exceptions.

2. How to cause an exception (implicitly and explicitly).

3. How to handle ("catch") an exception within the method where it was thrown.

4. Handling groups of related exceptions.

5. How the exception propagates if not handled in the method where it was thrown.

6. How and why methods declare the exceptions that can propagate out of them.

7. Fancy exception stuff.

The Purpose of Exceptions

Exceptions are for changing the flow of control when some important or unexpected event, usually an error, has occurred. They divert processing to a part of the program that can try to cope with the error, or at least die gracefully. The error can be any condition at all, ranging from "unable to open a file" to "array subscript out of range" to "no memory left to allocate" to "division by zero." Java exceptions are adapted from C++ which itself borrowed them from the research language ML. Like C and C++, ML (Meta Language) was developed at Bell Labs. Java exception terminology is presented in Table 7-1.

Table 7-1: Exception Terminology of Java

Note	Java	Some Other Languages
An error condition that happens at runtime	Exception	Exception
Causing an exception to occur	Throwing	Raising
Capturing an exception that has just occurred and executing statements to resolve it in some way	Catching	Handling
The block that does this	Catch clause	Handler
The sequence of method calls that brought control to the point where the exception happened	Stack trace	Call chain

An exception can be set in motion explicitly with the "throw" statement, or implicitly by carrying out some illegal or invalid action. The exception then diverts the normal flow of control (like a goto statement).

If the programmer has made provision, control will transfer to a section of the program that can recover from the error. That section can be in the same method, in the method that called the one where the exception occurred, or in the one that called that method. If no handler clause if found there, the thrown object continues up the stack of calls that were made at runtime. You might want to refresh your memory on how the stack is used to keep track of method invocations by looking at the diagram that was presented back in chapter 3.

If the thrown object gets to the top where your program execution started, and no handler for the exception has yet been found, then program execution will cease with an explanatory message.

Therefore, the places that you can jump to are strictly limited. You even must explicitly stipulate, "In this block, I will listen for and deal with this type of exception."

How to Cause an Exception (Implicitly and Explicitly)

Exceptions are caused in one of two ways: the program does something illegal (common case), or the program explicitly generates an exception by executing the throw statement (less common case). The throw statement has this general form:

```
throw  ExceptionObject;
```

The *ExceptionObject* is an object of a class that extends the class java.lang.Exception.

How to Handle ("Catch") an Exception Within the Method Where It Was Thrown

Of the types of statements we defined at this chapter's opening, here is where *guarding statements* fit in.

Here is the general form of how to catch an exception.

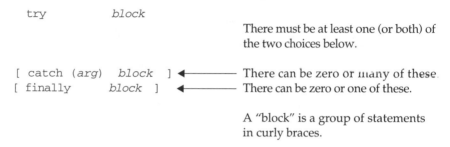

```
try          block
```
There must be at least one (or both) of the two choices below.

```
[ catch (arg)  block  ]
[ finally      block  ]
```
There can be zero or many of these.
There can be zero or one of these.

A "block" is a group of statements in curly braces.

The "try" statement says, "Try these statements, and see if you get an exception." The "try" statement must be followed by at least one "catch" clause or the "finally" clause.

Each catch says, "I will handle any exception that matches my argument." Matching an argument means that the thrown exception could legally be assigned to the argument exception. There can be several successive catches, each looking for a different exception. Don't try to catch *all* exceptions with one clause, like this:

```
catch (Exception e) { ...
```

That is way too general to be of use and you might catch more than you expected. You are better off letting the exception propagate to the top and give you a reasonable error message.

The "finally" block, if present, is a "last chance to clean up" block. It is *always* executed—even if something in one of the other blocks did a "return!" The "finally" block is executed whether an exception occurred or not and whether it was caught or not. It is executed after the catch block, if present, and regardless of the path taken through the try block and the catch block.

The "finally" block can be useful in the complete absence of any exceptions. It is a piece of code that is executed irrespective of what happens in the "try" block. There may be numerous paths through a large and complicated "try" block. The

© 1996 Matthew Burtch

User-Defined Exceptions

Here is an example of how to create your own exception class by extending
System.exception:

```
class OutofGas extends Exception {}

class banana {
        :

    if (fuel < 0.1) throw   new OutofGas();
}
```

Any method that throws a user-defined exception must also either catch it, or
declare it as part of the method interface. What, you may ask, is the point of
throwing an exception if you are going to catch it in the same method? The
answer is that exceptions don't *reduce* the amount of work you have to do to handle errors. Their advantage is they let you collect it all in well-localized places in
your program, so you don't obscure the main flow of control with zillions of
checks of return values.

Some Predefined Exceptions and How They Extend More Basic Classes

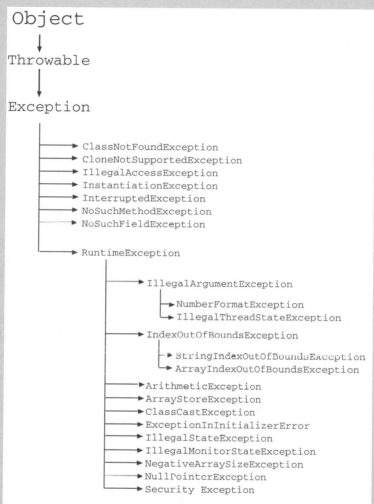

```
Object
  │
  ▼
Throwable
  │
  ▼
Exception
  │
  ├──► ClassNotFoundException
  ├──► CloneNotSupportedException
  ├──► IllegalAccessException
  ├──► InstantiationException
  ├──► InterruptedException
  ├──► NoSuchMethodException
  ├──► NoSuchFieldException
  │
  └──► RuntimeException
         │
         ├──► IllegalArgumentException
         │      ├──► NumberFormatException
         │      └──► IllegalThreadStateException
         │
         ├──► IndexOutOfBoundsException
         │      ├──► StringIndexOutOfBoundsException
         │      └──► ArrayIndexOutOfBoundsException
         │
         ├──► ArithmeticException
         ├──► ArrayStoreException
         ├──► ClassCastException
         ├──► ExceptionInInitializerError
         ├──► IllegalStateException
         ├──► IllegalMonitorStateException
         ├──► NegativeArraySizeException
         ├──► NullPointerException
         └──► Security Exception
```

The names are intended to suggest the condition each represents. The source files for these can be found in $JAVAHOME/src/java/lang.

Why is there a class "Throwable?" Why doesn't Exception extend Object directly? The reason is that there is a second class called "Error," which also extends Throwable. In other words, both Exceptions and Errors can be thrown, but Errors are not meant to be caught. They usually indicate some catastrophic failure. Typical Errors are: LinkageError, OutOfMemoryError, VerifyError, and IllegalAccessError. Throwable is the common superclass for all.

Triggering an Exception

Here is a simple program that causes a "division by zero" exception:

```
class melon {
    public static void main(String[] a) {
        int i=1, j=0, k;

        k = i/j;     // Causes division-by-zero exception
    }
}
```

Compiling and running this program gives this result:

```
> javac melon.java
> java melon
      java.lang.ArithmeticException: / by zero
            at melon.main(melon.java:5)
```

There are a certain number of predefined exceptions, like ArithmeticException, known as the runtime exceptions. Actually, since *all* exceptions are runtime events, a better name would be the "irrecoverable" exceptions. They mean "runtime" in the sense of "thrown by the runtime library code, not your code."

Runtime exceptions contrast with the user-defined exceptions which are generally held to be less severe, and in some instances can be recovered from. If a filename cannot be opened, prompt the user to enter a new name. If a data structure is found to be full, overwrite some element that is no longer needed. You don't have to make provision for catching runtime exceptions. You do have to make provisions for catching other exception types.

"finally" block can contain the housekeeping tasks that must always be done (counts updated, locks released, and so on) when finishing this piece of code.

Here is an example of an exception guarding statement in full adapted from the window toolkit code:

```java
public void printComponents(Graphics g) {
    // ... some code omitted ...
    Graphics cg = g.create();
    try {
        cg.clipRect(i.left, i.top, vs.width, vs.height);
        cg.translate(p.x, p.y);
        c.printAll(cg);
    } finally {
        cg.dispose();
    }
}
```

The method prints components in a scrolling window. It puts a pixel representation of the components onto g, the Graphics context. Graphics contexts are an operating system concept, not a Java concept. The finally clause was designed for recycling (releasing) resources like this.

Cleaning Up with finally

Most resources in a program are simply memory, but there are a few resources known to the operating system outside the program. Graphics contexts are one example. They are used to keep track of something on the screen and carry around a lot of information about font, resolution, size, color, and pixel data. There are usually a limited number of graphics contexts available at any one time.

Sockets, file descriptors, and window handles are other common examples. The dispose() method here hands the context back to the operating system. (It is probably implemented as a native code routine.) By putting the call to dispose in the finally clause, we can be certain that the scarce resource will always be given back to the operating system, regardless of any exceptions raised or avoided.

After the whole *try ... catch ... finally* series of blocks are executed, if nothing else was done to divert it, execution continues after the last catch or finally (whichever is present). The kinds of things that could make execution divert to elsewhere are the regular things: a continue, break, return, or the raising of a different exception. If a "finally" clause also has a transfer of control statement, then that is the one that is obeyed.

Handling Groups of Related Exceptions

We mentioned before that "matching an argument" means that the thrown exception can be assigned legally to the argument exception. This permits a subtle refinement. It allows a handler to catch any of several related exception objects with common parentage. Look at this example:

```
class Grumpy extends Exception {}
class TooHot    extends Grumpy {}
class TooTired extends Grumpy {}
class TooCross extends Grumpy {}
class TooCold   extends Grumpy {}

    .
    :

    try {
       if ( temp > 40 ) throw (new TooHot() );
       if ( sleep < 8 ) throw (new TooTired() );
    }
    catch (Grumpy g) {
          if (g instanceof TooHot)
             {System.out.println("caught too hot!"); return;}
          if (g instanceof TooTired)
             {System.out.println("caught too tired!"); return;}
    }
    finally {System.out.println("in the finally clause.");}
  }
```

The catch clauses are checked in the order in which they appear in the program. If there is a match, then the block is executed. The instanceof operator can be used to learn the exact identity of the exception.

How the Exception Propagates if Not Handled in the Method Where It Was Thrown

If none of the catch clauses match the exception that has been thrown, then the finally clause is executed (if there is one). At this point (no handler for this exception), what happens is the same as if the statement that threw the exception was not nested in a try statement at all. The flow of control abruptly leaves this method, and a premature return is done to the method that called this one. If that call was in the scope of a try statement, then we look for a matching exception again, and so on.

Figure 7-1 shows what happens when an exception is not dealt within the routine where it occurs. The runtime system looks for a "try . . . catch" block further up the call chain, enclosing the method call that brought us here. If the exception propagates all the way to the top of the call stack without finding a matching exception handler, then execution ceases with a message. You can think of this as Java setting up a default catch block for you, around the program entry point that just prints an error message and quits.

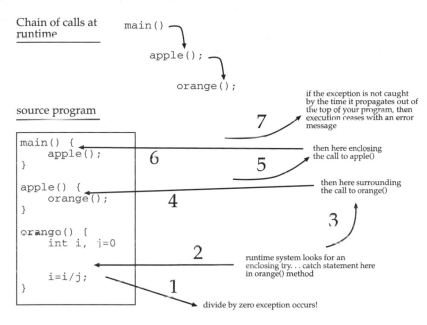

Figure 7-1: The result of an exception not dealt within the occurring routine.

There is no overhead to putting some statements in a "try" statement. The only overhead comes when an exception occurs.

How and Why Methods Declare the Exceptions That Can Propagate Out of Them

Earlier we mentioned that a method must either catch the exceptions that it throws or declare it along with its signature[1], meaning it must announce the exception to the outside world. This is so that anyone who writes a call to that method is alerted to the fact that an exception might come back instead of a normal return.

---

1. The exceptions a method throws are not part of the signature, though.

This allows the programmer calling that method to make the choice between handling the exception or allowing it to propagate further up the call stack. Here is the general form of how a method declares the exceptions that might be propagated out of it:

```
modifiers_and_returntype name (params)  throws e1, e2, e3  { }
```

The names e1 through e3 must be exception or error names (that is, any type that is assignable to the predefined type Throwable). Note that just as a method signature specifies the return *type*, it specifies the exception *type* that can be thrown, rather than an exception object.

An example, taken from the Java I/O system follows:

```
 byte readByte() throws IOException;
short readShort() throws IOException;
 char readChar() throws IOException;

void writeByte(int v) throws IOException;
void writeShort(int v) throws IOException;
void writeChar(int v) throws IOException;
```

The interesting thing to note here is that the routine to read a char can return a char—not the int that is required in C. C requires an int to be returned so that it can pass back any of the possible values for a char, plus an extra value (traditionally –1) to signify that the end of file was reached. Some of the Java routines just throw an exception when the EOF is hit. Out-of-band-signalling can be effective in keeping your code well organized. The EOF exception is a subclass of the IOException so the technique suggested above for handling groups of related exceptions can be applied.

The rules for how much and what must match when one method that throws an exception overrides another work in the obvious way. Namely, if you never do this, you will never be obviously bothered by it. Well, OK, another way to think about it is to consider the exception as an extra parameter that must be assignment-compatible with the exception in the class being overridden.

Fancy Exception Stuff

When you create a new exception by subclassing an existing exception class, you have the chance to associate a message string with it. The message string can be retrieved by a method. Usually the message string will be some kind of message that helps resolve the problem or suggests an alternative action.

```
class OutofGas extends Exception {
    OutofGas(String s) {super(s);}  // constructor
}


    ...
// in use, it may look like this
try {
        if (j<1) throw  new OutofGas("try the reserve tank");
    }
catch ( OutofGas o) {
        System.out.println( o.getMessage() );
    }
  ...


//At runtime, this message will appear:
  try the reserve tank
```

Another method that is inherited from the superclass Throwable is
"printStackTrace()." Invoking this method on an exception will cause the call
chain at the point where the exception was thrown (not where it is being handled)
to be printed out. For example:

```
// catching an exception in a calling method

class test {
    static int myArray[] = {0,1,2,3,4};

    public static void main(String[] a) {
        try {
            bob();
        } catch (Exception e) {
            System.out.println("caught exception in main()");
            e.printStackTrace();
        }
    }

    static void bob() {

        try {
          myArray[-1] = 4; //obvious out of bounds exception
        }
        catch (NullPointerException e) {
            System.out.println("caught a different exception");
        }

    }
}
```

At runtime it will look like this:

```
caught exception in main()
java.lang.ArrayIndexOutOfBoundsException: -1
    at test.bob(test5p.java:19)
    at test.main(test5p.java:9)
```

Summary of Exceptions

- Their purpose is to allow safer programming by providing a distinct path to deal with errors.

- Use them. They are a useful tool for organized error-handling.

- The main use of exceptions is getting a decent error message explaining what failed, where, and why. It's a bit much to expect recovery. Graceful degradation is often the most you can obtain.

We will now conclude this chapter with a look at our featured class, Integer.

The Class Integer

In the previous chapter we referred to the class `java.lang.Integer` as a class wrapper for the primitive type `int`. There is a similar class wrapper for all the primitive types boolean, char, int, long, etc., as shown in Table 7-2. The classes for Byte and Short were added in JDK 1.1.

Table 7-2: Primitive Types and Their Corresponding Classes

Primitive Type	Corresponding Class (in src/java/lang)
boolean	Boolean
char	Character
byte	Byte
short	Short
int	Integer
long	Long
float	Float
double	Double

There are three purposes for having a class version of each basic type:

- To provide an object wrapper for data values. A wrapper is useful because most of Java's utility classes require the use of Objects. Since variables of the primitive types are not objects in Java, it's convenient to provide a simple way to "promote" them when needed.

- To support some useful constants and methods associated with the type, like range boundaries, and conversion to and from String.

- To give primitive types the same kind of introspection as non-primitive types. "Introspection" is a Java term for looking at the characteristics of a Java object. It allows you to write component software, debuggers, class inspectors, and other systems programs, in Java.

Here is an example of moving an int to an Integer object and back again, using methods from the Integer class.

```
// changes int to Integer and back
Integer myIntObj;
int i=42;

myIntObj = new Integer(i);   // int to an Integer object
i = myIntObj.intValue();     // Integer object to an int
```

As with Strings, once one of these objects have been created with a given value, that value cannot be changed. You can throw away that object and create a new one, but the object itself doesn't change its identity once assigned. If you need a class that can hold an int that changes, it is trivial to declare. Here it is:

```
public class AnyInt { public int i; }
```

Here is the declaration of class java.lang.Integer:

```
public final class java.lang.Integer extends java.lang.Number
                            implements java.lang.Comparable {
    public static final int MIN_VALUE = 0x80000000; // -2147483648
    public static final int MAX_VALUE = 0x7fffffff; // +2147483647
    public static final java.lang.Class TYPE; // synonym for Integer.class
// constructors
    public java.lang.Integer(int);
    public java.lang.Integer(java.lang.String) throws
                            java.lang.NumberFormatException;
// integer/string conversion
    public static int parseInt(java.lang.String) throws
                                    NumberFormatException;
    public static int parseInt(java.lang.String, int) throws
                                    NumberFormatException;
    public static java.lang.String toBinaryString(int);
    public static java.lang.String toHexString(int);
    public static java.lang.String toOctalString(int);
    public java.lang.String toString();
    public static java.lang.String toString(int);
    public static java.lang.String toString(int, int);
    public static java.lang.Integer valueOf(java.lang.String)
                        throws java.lang.NumberFormatException;
    public static java.lang.Integer valueOf(java.lang.String, int)
                        throws java.lang.NumberFormatException;
    // converts between Integer values & system properties
    public static java.lang.Integer getInteger(java.lang.String);
    public static java.lang.Integer getInteger(java.lang.String, int);
    public static java.lang.Integer getInteger(java.lang.String, Integer);
    public static java.lang.Integer decode(java.lang.String) throws
                            java.lang.NumberFormatException;
    public int compareTo(java.lang.Integer);
    public int compareTo(java.lang.Object);
    public byte byteValue();
    public short shortValue();
    public int intValue();
    public long longValue();
    public float floatValue();
    public double doubleValue();

    public boolean equals(java.lang.Object);
    public int hashCode();
}
```

You might be wondering about that "implements Comparable" clause at the start of the class. That says, "This class has the methods demanded by the interface whose name is Comparable. It is the subject of the very next chapter.

Some Light Relief

MiniScribe: The Hard Luck Hard Disk

Most readers will know the term "hard disk" which contrasts with "floppy disk," but how many people know about MiniScribe's pioneering efforts in the fields of *very* hard disks, inventory control, and accounting techniques?

MiniScribe was a successful start-up company based in Longmont, Colorado, that manufactured disk drives. In the late 1980s, Miniscribe ran into problems when IBM unexpectedly cancelled some very big purchasing contracts. The venture capitalists behind MiniScribe, Hambrecht & Quist, brought in turnaround expert Q.T. Wiles to get the company back on track.

Wiles mercilessly hounded company executives to meet revenue targets, even as sales fell still further. In desperation, the beleaguered executives turned to out-right record falsification. It must have seemed so easy. Over the space of a couple of years they came up with an impressive range of fraudulent techniques for making a failing company have the appearance of prospering.

The Miniscribe executives started off with the easy paper-based deceit, like:

- Counting raw inventory as finished goods (with a higher value).
- Anticipating shipments before they were made to customers.
- Counting imaginary shipments on non-existent ships.

When they were not found out, they graduated to more brazen activities like parading inventory past the accountants twice, so it would be counted twice, and shipping obsolete product to a fake customer called "BW." "BW" stood for "Big Warehouse" and was a MiniScribe storage building. And so it went on, with smaller crimes leading to bigger crimes, just the way your kindergarten teacher warned it would.

Miniscribe employed more than 9,000 people worldwide at the height of its fortunes, so this was no fly-by-night, two-guys-in-a-garage undertaking. This was a fly-by-night, 9000-guys-in-a-Big-Warehouse undertaking. The companies that supplied Miniscribe were doing less and less business with them and were finding it hard to get paid. One analyst surveyed the entire computer industry and found only one large MiniScribe customer. At the same time MiniScribe was issuing press releases talking about "record sales."

The most breathtaking coup, though, was the brick scam. Desperate to show shipments on the books, executives brought in their assistants, spouses, and even children for a crazy weekend of filling disk shipping boxes with house bricks. They also created a special computer program called "Cook book" (these guys were well aware of what they were doing) that facilitated shipping the bricks to good old "BW" and recognizing the "revenue" from that customer. These bricks were surely the ultimate hard drive.

Of course, it all came unglued in the end. On January 1, 1990, MiniScribe announced massive layoffs and filed for bankruptcy. Chief Financial Officer Owen Taranto, the genius who devised the brick shipment plan, was granted immunity for his testimony. The stock went into a precipitous decline, but not before the aptly-named Wiles had unloaded a parcel of it at premium prices.

There was plenty of blame to go around. After a trial, Cooper & Lybrand, Hambrecht & Quist, and sixteen MiniScribe executives were ordered to pay $568 million in restitution to defrauded stockholders. Wiles was sentenced to three years in the Big House. The remains of MiniScribe were bought out by rival Maxtor. The later Maxtor model 8541s looked just like Miniscribe 8541s, so they were still being made, but any resemblance to a brick was long since gone.

CHAPTER

8

Interfaces

Interfaces are an important concept in Java. Interfaces are in the language to allow a class to say it behaves like some other class and can be used in place of the other class.

We already saw that with inheritance, but you can inherit only from one class. Interfaces allow a class to say, "I have the same kind of behavior as A, and B, and C, and you can use me wherever you are using an A, or B, or C." Interfaces provide much of the functionality of multiple inheritance, but without the difficulties.

In C++, a class can inherit from multiple superclasses, as shown in Figure 8-1.

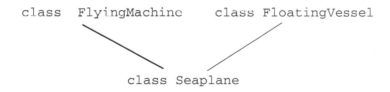

Figure 8-1: Multiple inheritance.

Problems arise when there are name clashes in the base classes. Class FlyingMachine may have a method called navigate() that does navigation in three dimensions. Class FloatingVessel may have a method with the same name that only navigates in two dimensions. Seaplane inherits both methods, which immediately results in a name clash error. You don't want to be forced to change the names in one base class because of the names in some other base class. There is no general way to say which of the two navigate() methods Seaplane should have and which it should forget. Worse, the common fields may have to be laid out in a different place in the parent class and one subclass, because the common fields of the other subclasses already grabbed those locations.

Interfaces avoid this kind of kind of multiple-inheritance problem. An interface is a skeleton of a class showing the methods the class will have when someone implements it. An interface may look like this:

```
public interface Comparable {
    public int compareTo(Object o); // method declarations...
}
/**
 * Compares this object with the specified object for order.
 * Returns a negative integer, zero, or a positive integer
 * if this object is less than, equal to, or greater than the
 * specified object.<p>
 */
```

An interface looks a bit like a class (actually, more like an abstract class), is counted as a reference type, and can generally be used in a lot of the same places as a class. It doesn't have any behavior, though: it's just a description of promised behavior. The declarations in an interface—the fields and methods—are always public, even if you don't label them. You can declare only constant data in an interface. Even if you don't label it "final," it is assumed that it is.

Although avoiding multiple-inheritance problems is useful, the fundamental reason for having interfaces is to decouple or *separate some behavior* that you know some classes have from the classes that *use that behavior*. Some uses of interfaces follow:

- Interfaces are a way of saying, "You need to plug some code in here for this thing to fully work." The interface specifies the exact signatures of the methods that must be provided.

- Use the interface type as a parameter for a method. *Inside the method you can invoke any of the methods promised by the interface parameter.* When you actually call the method, you will have to provide an object that has all the methods promised by the interface. It might help to think of this as a bit like passing in a subclass as an argument and having the correct over-riding methods called (or it might not be helpful—opinions vary).

```
void howBigIsIt(Comparable c) {
    ...
    Object somethingElse = ...
    if ( c.CompareTo(somethingElse) ) ...
}
    ...
```

With interfaces, you can write code that makes calls on classes that haven't even been written yet. A class can come along later and be used in the places where you have used the interface—if it has all the methods and matching signatures that are in the interface. If you think interfaces are used frequently in the Java runtime library, you are right. To help programmers, a class has to say when it fulfills an interface, which it does with the keyword "implements" like this:

```
public class Double implements Comparable { ...
```

If we see the line above, we know at once that Double has a method with the compareTo signature, because that's what the Comparable interface promises. Objects of class Double can be used anywhere you have used the Comparable interface. A class can extend only one superclass, but it can implement any number of interfaces. Two interfaces can make the same demand for a method of the same name in a class.

Here's some more code from the Double class. If you want to peek ahead, this is the standard java.lang.Double class featured at the end of this chapter. Double is an object wrapper for double precision floating-point numbers, meaning that it provides a thin object layer over the primitive type. Because of this, it can be used by all the classes that require an object as an argument. The class Double implements the Comparable interface by providing a body for the compareTo method.

```
public class Double implements Comparable { ...

    public int compareTo(Object o) {
        anotherDouble = (Double) o;
        double anotherVal = anotherDouble.value;
        double thisVal = value;

        if (thisVal < anotherVal)
            return -1; // Neither val is NaN, thisVal is smaller
        if (thisVal > anotherVal)
            return 1; // Neither val is NaN, thisVal is larger
        // trickiness because of NaN's omitted
        return 0;
    }
// other methods in the class omitted ...
}
```

Look at the source in $JAVAHOME/src/java/lang/Double.java if you are curious about the NaN trickiness. Several different classes can implement the same interface, each in their own special way.

The code above says that if I see anything that takes a Comparable as an argument, I can actually call it with a Double object. The reason is that Double has all the behavior promised by Comparable. Here's an example:

```
void howBigIsIt(Comparable c) {
    ...
}
 ...
Double myDouble = new Double(22.0);
howBigIsIt( myDouble ); // can call method using a Double
```

Getting more detailed, I can write a data structure that sorts an array. Instead of making it an array of, say, Integer, I can make it an array of Comparables, and anything that implements the interface can use my sort class. Here's how some of the code might look:

```
// first, a reminder of the interface
public interface Comparable {
    public int compareTo(Object o);
}

// next, my sortingClass to sort anything that can be compared
// this make use of the Comparable interface
public class sortingClass {
    // holds the data
    static java.lang.Comparable [] d;

    // a constructor, to fill up the d array
    sortingClass(java.lang.Comparable data[]) { d=data; }

    int findLargest() {
        java.lang.Comparable largestSoFar = d[0];
        int where = 0;
        for (int i=1; i<d.length; i++) {
            if ( largestSoFar.compareTo(d[i]) == -1) {
                largestSoFar = d[i]; // new element is bigger
                where = i;           // so record where it is
            }
        }
        return where;
    }

    ... // more methods, omitted
```

There actually is a `java.lang.Comparable` interface, and that's what I'm using here. In the body of the `findLargest()` method, we look at successive elements of the array called d, and compare them *using the compareTo method*. This is a neat trick. We have promised only that method so far and not actually supplied a body for it. It's enough to allow compilation to take place. We can't actually run the code until we supply a class that implements the interface.

To keep the example small, I haven't filled up the page with code showing the rest of a sort algorithm. You'll have to believe me when I say that by taking away the largest thing in a pile of objects, you can sort them. That is how the bubblesort algorithm works.

Here's how the code to fulfill the interface might hook up with the sortingClass:

```
public static void main(String[] args) {
    Double data [] = new Double[] { new Double(4.0),
        new Double(10), new Double(9), new Double(0.6),
        new Double(1), new Double(99), new Double(6.00) };

    sortingClass s = new sortingClass( data );
    int i = s.findLargest();
    String val = s.d[i].toString();
    System.out.println("Largest is "+ val + " at element "+i);
}
```

We pass our Double array into the sortingClass in the constructor. Sure enough, when we run that code, it will print out the following message:

```
% java Try
Largest is 99.0 at element 5
```

This demonstrates that the correct substitution of Double's version of compareTo() was made in the sortingClass. Better than that, the very same sortingClass works if we instantiate it with Integer objects.

```
    Integer data2 [] = new Integer[] { new Integer(4),
        new Integer(10), new Integer(9), new Integer(6),
        new Integer(1), new Integer(99), new Integer(600) };

    sortingClass s = new sortingClass( data2 );
    int i = s.findLargest();
    String val = s.d[i].toString();
    System.out.println("Largest is "+ val + " at element "+i);
```

This results in the following:

```
% java Try
Largest is 600 at element 6
```

Don't be misled into thinking that interfaces are a replacement for C++ templates (i.e., providing generic types). The point is that the interface allows the class that uses it to be freed from any one specific datatype. If you can compare it, you can sort it. The interface lets you use sortingClass with any type that implements the Comparable interface, even a type that hadn't been thought of when sortingClass was written. If the class implements Comparable, you can use the sortingClass on it.

Think of interfaces as being like a library of stub bodies against which you can compile, but you have to supply a real library at runtime before you actually make the calls.

Interfaces Versus Abstract Classes

While an interface is used to specify the form that something *must* have, it does not actually provide the implementation for it. In this sense, an interface is a little like an abstract class that must be extended in exactly the manner that its abstract methods specify.

An interface differs from an abstract class in the following ways:

- An abstract class is an incomplete class that requires further specialization. An interface is just a specification or prescription for behavior.

- An interface doesn't have any overtones of specialization that are present with inheritance. It merely says, "We need something that does 'foo' and here are the ways that users should be able to call it."

- A class can implement several interfaces at once, whereas a class can extend only one parent class.

- Interfaces can be used to support callbacks (inheritance doesn't help with this). This is a significant coding idiom. It essentially provides a pointer to a function, but in a type-safe way. The next section explains callbacks.

Here's the bottom line: You'll probably use interfaces more often than abstract classes. Use an abstract class when you want to initiate a hierarchy of more specialized classes. Use an interface when you just want to say, "I need to be able to call methods with these signatures in your class."

Note that an interface can only extend another interface. While a class can legally implement an interface, it can only implement some of the methods. It then becomes an abstract class that must be further extended (inherited) before it can be instantiated.

Granting Permission through an Interface—Cloneable

When we looked at the Object class in chapter 3, we saw that it has this method:

```
protected native Object clone() throws CloneNotSupportedException;
```

Java supports the notion of *cloning*, meaning to retrieve a complete bit-for-bit copy of an object.

Not every class should support the ability to clone. If I have a class that represents a set of unique objects, such as employees in a company, the operation of cloning doesn't make sense, as it doesn't represent anything in the real world. Methods in Object, however, are inherited by all classes, including clone. So, the system places a further requirement on classes that want to be cloneable: they must implement the cloneable interface to indicate that cloning is valid for them. The cloneable interface is this:

```
public interface Cloneable { } // completely empty
```

This is not the most common use of interfaces, but you do see it in the system libraries. To have a class that can be cloned, you must state that the class implements the Cloneable interface.

```
public class copyme implements Cloneable { ...
```

Why wasn't the method clone() of Object made part of the Cloneable interface? That seems like the obvious place to put it, instead of in Object. The reason is that we have two conflicting aims. We want to provide a default implementation of clone so that any cloneable class can automatically inherit it. We also want individual classes to take an extra step to permit cloning on their object.

The end result is that we require at minimum an extra step of having cloneable classes implement the Cloneable interface. We provide a default implementation by putting the method clone, with a body, into the root superclass Object.

> **Shallow Versus Deep Clone**
>
> There is some subtlety to a class that has data fields that are other classes. Do you simply copy the reference, and share the referenced object (a *shallow clone*), or do you recursively clone all referenced classes, too (a *deep clone*)?
>
> While Object.clone() does a shallow clone, supplying the method in class Object and making it overridable allows you to choose the behavior you want. You can disallow any kind of clone. You can override clone as public rather than the default protected (outside this package, only subclasses can clone). You can even implement a deep clone, if you wish.

Note that `clone()` returns an `Object`. The object returned by `clone()` is usually cast immediately to the correct type, as in this example:

```
Vector v = new Vector();
Vector v2;

v2 = (Vector) v.clone();
```

Since Arrays are considered to implement Cloneable, they can be copied by System.arrayCopy or by clone().

Interfaces in the Java Runtimes

Interfaces are used in several other places in the Java runtimes. The utility class java.util.Vector implements three interfaces, as shown below:

```
public class Vector extends AbstractList
    implements List, Cloneable, java.io.Serializable { ...
```

The Cloneable class is described above. By implementing a List, the class is announcing that it can be used wherever a List is used. It can also do all the things a List can do, meaning it can have elements added or removed, can be checked for being empty, can tell you its size, and so on.

By implementing Serializable, the class Vector is saying that it and all of its sub-types have the ability to be serialized. Being serialized is the conversion into a stream of bytes that can be written out to disk and later reconstituted into an object. This is the same permission-granting use of an interface that we saw with Cloneable.

Using Interfaces Dynamically

The examples of interfaces thus far have solved compile time issues. There is an additional way that an interface can be used to obtain more dynamic behavior, which forms the basis of GUI programming in Java.

Once we have defined an interface, we can use it as the type of some parameter to a method. Inside the method we can use that parameter to invoke the operations that the interface promises. Whenever we make a call to that method, we can pass it a class that implements the interface, and it will call the appropriate method of that class. The following four steps should make this a little clearer.

1. Define an interface that promises a method called *run* like this:

    ```
    interface Runnable {
        public void run();
    }
    ```

2. Now sprinkle calls to "run" throughout our code, even though we don't yet have anything that fulfills the interface.

    ```
    void vitalSystemThing(Runnable r) {
        r.run();
    }
    ```

    This code can be compiled, and may even be part of the Java runtime library.

3. At a later time and in another file, provide a class (or several classes) that implements the following interface:

    ```
    class myCode implements Runnable {
        public void run() {
            System.out.println("You called myCode.run()");
        }
        // other code ...
    }
    ```

4. Pass myCode object to the vitalSystemThing:

    ```
    myCode myobj = new myCode()
    vitalSystemThing( myobj );
    ```

Whenever the vitalSystemThing is invoked, it results in `myCode.run()` being called back. This is therefore known as a *callback*. It's a drawn-out way of doing what you do with a function pointer in C or C++, and this has led some people to call for the addition of function pointers to Java. That won't happen since Java callbacks are type-safe, but function pointers might not be.

The main reason for writing your code this way is that it decouples the calling routine from the called-back routine. You could have several different classes that implement the Runnable interface. Callbacks allow any of them to be sent to the vitalSystemThing and hence to be called back. The correct class is called back, based on the type at runtime.

There actually *is* a built-in Java interface, called *Runnable* that is used in this way for threads. It is described in chapter 10. The use of an interface allows the runtime system to schedule and control threads that you implement and compile later. Here is another example of an interface used as a callback:

```java
interface runnable {
    public void run();
}

public class VeryDynamic {
    public static void main(String args[]) {
        runnable r;
        try {
            Class unknown = Class.forName(args[0]);
            r = (runnable) unknown.newInstance();
            r.run();
        } catch (Exception e){ e.printStackTrace();}

    }
}

class Coffee implements runnable {
    public void run() { System.out.println("Coffee.run called"); }
}

class Tea implements runnable {
    public void run() { System.out.println("Tea.run called"); }
}
```

The try and catch statements are required to accommodate the exceptions that the enclosed statements might cause. If you compile this program, you can run it like this:

```
java VeryDynamic Tea
```

Try executing it with an argument of "Coffee" and an argument of "Bogus." The three lines in bold simply get the runtime type information for the class whose name you give as an argument. They then create an instance of that class that is cast to runnable, and call the run() method of that class.

The example demonstrates how a callback can work for an object of a class that isn't known until runtime. It's used extensively in the Java GUI library to tell your code about events happening on screen.

Using Interfaces for Named Constants

There's another unorthodox way to use an interface that forms a useful programming idiom. If you have a group of related constants, perhaps of the kind you would put in an enumerated type (if the language has enumerated types), you might gather them in a class like this:

```
public class FightingWeight {
    public static final int          flyweight = 100;
    public static final int        bantamweight = 113;
    public static final int       featherweight = 118;
    public static final int         lightweight = 127;
    public static final int        welterweight = 136;
    public static final int        middleweight = 148;
    public static final int lightheavyweight = 161;
    public static final int         heavyweight = 176;
}
```

Then, to use the constants in another class, you would have to do something like this:

```
static int title = FightingWeight.heavyweight;
```

Let's say you make FightingWeight an *interface*, like this:

```
public interface FightingWeight {
    public static final int          flyweight = 100;
    public static final int        bantamweight = 113;
    public static final int       featherweight = 118;
    public static final int         lightweight = 127;
    public static final int        welterweight = 136;
    public static final int        middleweight = 148;
    public static final int lightheavyweight = 161;
    public static final int         heavyweight = 176;
}
```

You can then reference the names directly. Wow!

```
class gooseberry implements FightingWeight {
    ...
static int title = heavyweight;
```

The system interface `javax.swing.WindowConstants` uses this technique. This works for classes, too, but it's poor style to extend a class just for better name visibility.

The Class Double

Here is the declaration of class java.lang.Double.

```
public final class java.lang.Double extends java.lang.Number
                                implements java.lang.Comparable {
    // constructors
    public java.lang.Double(double);
    public java.lang.Double(java.lang.String)
                    throws java.lang.NumberFormatException;
    public static final double POSITIVE_INFINITY = 1.0 / 0.0;
    public static final double NEGATIVE_INFINITY = -1.0 / 0.0;
    public static final double NaN = 0.0d / 0.0;
    public static final double MAX_VALUE = 1.79769313486231570e+308;
    public static final double MIN_VALUE = longBitsToDouble(1L);
    public static final java.lang.Class TYPE=
Class.getPrimitiveClass("double");

    public byte byteValue();
    public short shortValue();
    public int intValue();
    public long longValue();
    public float floatValue();
    public double doubleValue();

    public int compareTo(java.lang.Double);
    public int compareTo(java.lang.Object);
    public boolean isInfinite();
    public static boolean isInfinite(double);
    public boolean isNaN();
    public static boolean isNaN(double);
    public boolean equals(java.lang.Object);
    public int hashCode();
    public static native long doubleToLongBits(double);
    public static native double longBitsToDouble(long);

    public static double parseDouble(java.lang.String) throws
                            java.lang.NumberFormatException;
    public java.lang.String toString();
    public static java.lang.String toString(double);
    public static java.lang.Double valueOf(java.lang.String) throws
                            java.lang.NumberFormatException;
}
```

Some Light Relief

To close out the chapter, let's peek at another example of naming and the confusion that can arise. There's a pervasive industry legend that the antihero computer HAL in the film *2001: A Space Odyssey* was so-named to indicate that he was one step ahead of IBM. Alphabetically "H," "A," and "L" precede "I," "B," and "M" by one letter.

Similarly, people say that Windows NT (WNT) is one step away from VMS. Dave Cutler designed VMS when he was at Digital and then joined Microsoft to become the chief architect of Windows NT. I believe that the name was chosen with this in mind. It's a moot point now that the product has been renamed Windows 2000 to make it look like a continuation of the Windows line.

Arthur C. Clarke, the author of *2001: A Space Odyssey*, emphatically denies the HAL legend in his book *Lost Worlds of 2001*, claiming that HAL is an acronym for "Heuristically-programmed Algorithmic Computer." Clarke even wrote to the computer magazine *Byte* to place his denial on record. Methinks he doth protest too much.

Certainly the claims of an involved party are one piece of evidence, but there is no particular reason why they should be accepted uncritically as complete truth. Consider them rather in the context of all pieces of evidence, as happens in courts of law every day. For one thing, "Heuristically-programmed Algorithmic Computer" is a contrived name that does not properly form the desired acronym. For another, most of the working drafts of the 2001 story had HAL named "Athena," and it would have remained so had not Clarke deliberately rechristened it. The odds of him accidentally latching onto the one name that mimics one of the world's largest computer companies are a few thousand to one.

Why would Clarke deny it if it were true? IBM logos appear in several places in the movie, and the filmmakers clearly cut a deal with IBM for product placement. It may be that Clarke decided to assert some artistic independence by deciding on name change as a subtle dig at IBM: HAL is a homicidal maniac who goes berserk. Perhaps he was just suggesting that his creation was one step ahead of IBM. Later, when the story got out, Clarke realized he would look foolish, or at the very least ungracious, by lampooning them. So, he denied the connection.

An interesting concern is why the name was changed at all. If Clarke provided an explanation of *that* along with his denials, the denials would have more credibility.

Exercises

1. Describe, without excessive hand-waving, two common uses for interfaces.

2. Take any class that you have written, and make it cloneable by making it implement the Cloneable interface. The Cloneable source code is at $JAVAHOME/src/java/lang/Cloneable.java.

3. Override Object.clone() to do a shallow copy for your class, and also keep count of the number of objects of your class that have been created. Don't forget to count those created via a constructor, too.

4. Write some code to clone an object of your class. Change your version of clone() to do a deep copy for your class. Run the clone program again, and make it print out enough details that you can tell the difference between a shallow clone and an deep clone.

CHAPTER
9

Packages and Visibility

In this chapter, we'll look at the "how" and "why" of packages. Java uses the term *package* to mean a collection of related .class files in a directory. Thus, a package is both a directory and a library. How do you tell the compiler that a class belongs to some package? It's simplicity itself—just write the first non-comment line in the file like this:

```
package identifier.identifier.identifier... ;
```

You can have one or more identifiers. They denote a deeper and deeper depth in the package and filesystem hierarchy. A package clause might be this:

```
package java.lang;
```

That says that the classes in the file belong to the java.lang package. It also says that the class file will be in directory `java\lang\` (on Windows) or `java/lang/` (on Unix). Java uses the computer's filesystem to organize and locate packages.

We already know that the name of a public class must match the name of the file containing the source code. Java also requires a *package name* to match the last part of the *directory name* where it is kept. Since it's most convenient to keep source and bytecode together, the source will usually be in the same directory.

The requirement means that if you know the name of a class, you also know where to find it. Classes that are part of the same package will be in the same directory. It simplifies things for the compiler-writer, and gives the programmer less to remember.

What Are Packages for?

Packages (as the name suggests) are for parcelling up several class files, and having a convenient way to give that group a name of its own. When you're just writing a few programs for your personal use, you can put them in any old directory and use any old names. When you have a team of twenty programmers working on five different software products that interact, you need a better way to organize your files than "putting them in any old directory."

Packages solve the problem of name conflicts. Unlike many other language or compiler systems, Java doesn't link all your code into one big freestanding program. Instead, it leaves everything in separate classfiles. When you say "java myclass" to run a program, the JVM follows a set of rules to locate the file myclass.class, and then loads that class into the execution environment. As execution proceeds, the JVM loads the classes that myclass references as it needs them, and then it loads all the classes that *those* classes reference, and so on throughout program execution.

If a class was identified purely by its classname and nothing else, we'd have to demand that classnames be unique. Otherwise, if I wrote a class called ReadData that was part of my program installed on a customer's system, and you wrote a class called ReadData that was part of your program installed on the same customer's system, the JVM wouldn't know which of the two classes to load when it hit a reference to ReadData.

Packages give the programmer a way to qualify a class name. The system can then use more than just the identifier that comes after "public class ..." to locate and name a class.

```
package java.util.zip;
public class ZipFile ... {
```

In the code above, you are actually specifying that the full name of this class is the following:

```
java.util.zip.ZipFile
```

That is what the JVM will look for at runtime, and that is how you distinguish the class from any other `ZipFile` class that someone else may have written. There is an algorithm for choosing package names that ensures we all end up with different fully-qualified class names. Part of the algorithm is that names starting with "java" are reserved for the Java system itself, and you may not write any packages that start with that name.

An additional function of packages is to provide namespaces to the programmer, and we review how that works a little later in the chapter.

How to Choose a Package Name

Package names are hierarchical, just like mailing addresses. If you want to send a letter, you can't just write "Mr. James Brown" on the envelope. There are thousands of people with that name. It's not even good enough to just include the street name. There are likely scores of men named "Mr. James Brown" living at the same number on Main Street in different towns in different countries. We make the address unique by giving enough further qualifiers. Two different addresses for two different people might have some components that match, like this:

Mr. James Brown,
27, Main Street,
Cricklewood,
London,
England

Mr. James Brown,
27 Main Street,
Hollywood,
California

As long as there is some identifier that is different, they are different addresses. A mailing address can identify satisfactorily which recipient is meant, and these different addresses can be different lengths. Reading from the bottom up, the address goes from most general to most specific. Package names are formed the same way.

The Java Language Specification tells us that package names should be formed from Internet domain names. If an organization that is writing software for sale doesn't have an Internet domain name, they should go into some other, slower-paced line of work. Domain names are guaranteed to be unique and the JLS tells us to reverse them so they are sorted from most general to least general. That means that all java class libraries coming out of IBM should be in packages whose names start with `com.ibm`.

IBM will probably want to impose further levels of package names, so that its different divisions don't conflict with each other. How, and how far, they subdivide it further is totally up to them. They'll probably want to add, at minimum, "division" and "product within division." Another example package name, representing the online real-time arbitrage system that I am coding for the software conglomerate AFU, Inc., is `com.afu.applications.arby`.

That distinguishes my arby package from all the other Java code on which AFU is working, namely `com.afu.applications.gambling.horses`, `com.afu.applications.office99`, and `com.afu.OSkernel`.

In this way, the most significant part of your package name has already been chosen for you, and the least significant part you can subdivide as you wish. Those parts of a package name are called the *members*. Just as classes have members, packages have members. The members of a class or interface are the fields (data) and methods (code). The members of a package are the subpackages and classes or interfaces.

By following this protocol, you can also easily create package names that are unique across the entire Internet, since domain names have this quality. It allows different vendors to provide class libraries with no danger of namespace collisions.

How the JVM Finds Classes

A couple of pages back we saw that the full name of a class included the package name and might be something like `com.afu.applications.arby.ReadData`.

We also saw that the JVM will expect the class file to be in `com\afu\applications\arby\ReadData.class` (on Windows) or `com/afu/applications/arby/ReadData.class` (on Unix). Clearly, that's the final part of a complete pathname. Where does the JVM start looking for the first part?

> **Rooting about for Packages**
>
> Java has seen a bit of evolution in the area of where to look for the roots of your packages. The support in JDK 1.0 was downright horrid. In JDK 1.1, it was only mildly ugly. In JDK 1.2, things are OK. To avoid confusion, I'll describe only the vastly improved JDK 1.2 support here. If you want to get things working under one of the earlier releases, read and follow the directions in the readme file that comes with that version of the JDK.

You no longer have to tell the JVM where to find the runtime library. For your own classes, either you have to tell the JVM the directories where it might find the roots of your packages, or you have to put your packages in a place where it looks automatically.

The first point to note is that you can gather all your class files into a *jar file*, so you don't really need umpteen levels of directory on the customer's system. A jar file (Java Archive) works exactly like a zip file and can be used to store a whole directory tree in a single file. In the case of my world-beating arbitrage program, I jar'ed everything into a file called all.jar. We now have to put the jar file (or the complete directory tree) where Java can find it, or tell Java the possible places to look for it.

Putting the Jar File Where Java Will Find It

Java looks in the directory $JAVAHOME/jre/lib/ext for jar files. You can install your programs by placing the jar file containing them in this directory. They will be found automatically without further action on the user's part.

Java looks in the directory $JAVAHOME/jre/classes for a directory hierarchy containing class files that corresponds to your package hierarchy. You may have to create the classes subdirectory the first time. If your program doesn't use packages, you can just dump the .class files in this directory, although that gets messy for more than a few files.

Telling Java Where to Look for the Jar File or Package Roots

Java will look at the CLASSPATH environment variable, typically set in the autoexec.bat file (on Windows) or in a shell initialization file (on Unix). CLASSPATH tells the class loader all the possible places (roots) to begin looking for Java packages to import in a compilation or to load at runtime.

The CLASSPATH will be set to a list of one or more pathnames separated by ";" (Windows) or ":" (Unix). It may look like this, for instance, on Windows:

```
SET CLASSPATH = c:\all.jar;c:\project\test;.
```

It may look like this on a Unix system using C shell:

```
setenv CLASSPATH /all.jar:/project/test/:.
```

That tells Java to look, in order, for the arby code in the following:

```
/all.jar
/project/test/com/afu/applications/arby/*.class
./com/afu/applications/arby/*.class
```

One of these had better be a match or the compilation or run will fail with the error, "Class not found." The first match found is the class for which it is looking. Java tools that expect classes can cope with package names. Thus, the following works to run a program:

```
java com.afu.applications.arby.go
```

Zip Files and Jar Files

Zip files were introduced in December 1995 for classes. A zip file is a collection of .class files grouped together in one physical file, as can be done on Windows with the standard Windows zip software.

Jar files replaced zip files in the JDK 1.1 release. Jar files are in zip format and can contain an extra "manifest" file listing all the files in the jar. The standard Java runtime library is kept in a 10MB jar file called *jre/lib/rt.jar*.

Jar files are convenient for a browser opening a connection to a remote URL applet. The browser need open only one connection for a package, not one for each class. Since opening the TCP/IP connection often takes more time than transmitting the data, this is a win. Jar files are a performance enhancement aimed mostly at browsers.

How Packages Support Namespaces

We mentioned above that another role packages play is to provide namespaces to the programmer. That is, the package has implications for the visibility of classes and fields. This is simply the access modifers that we met at the end of chapter 2. In order of most accessible to least accessible, they are:

1. **public**, world access.

2. **protected**, accessible in *this* package (think "directory") and also in subclasses in *other* packages.

3. Default, package access (any class in the package).

4. **private**, accessible only in this class.

The interaction between classes and subclasses, along with things in the same package and things in other packages, can be downright confusing. Figures 9-1 through 9-4 illustrate the interaction of public, protected, default (package), and private.

What about C++ "Friend"?

The keyword "friend" in C++ is a hack to allow a piece of code to access the protected or private member declarations of another class

Java does not permit access to private members from outside the class. If another class needs to see those members, you would do this by labelling not the friend, but the private members. Instead of making them private, give them either protected, package (no keyword), or public access.

Java has no exact equivalent of the C++ protected modifier that says, "This field can only be accessed by this class and its subclasses." The Java protected modifier has a slightly different meaning that says, "This field can be accessed only by this class and its subclasses, *plus anything else in the same package.*"

They love asking questions about this on the Java Certification exam, to try to catch out all the C++ programmers.

When you start to build bigger systems you will use a package statement at the top of each source file to say to which package the class belongs. The package names must match the directory names. The package name is concatenated with the class name and stored as the full name of the class.

KEY:
bolded code
means
"is visible in here"

/ fruits   / apple.java

```
package fruits;
public class apple {
    public int i;
}
```

pippin.java

```
package fruits;
class pippin extends apple {
    i = ...
}
```

plum.java

```
package fruits;
class plum {
    my_apple.i = ...
}
```

/ sun

     / sauces   / chutney.java

```
package sauces;
import fruits.*;
class chutney {
    my_apple.i = ...
}
```

applesauce.java

```
package sauces;
import fruits.*;
class applesauce extends apple {
    i = ...
}
```

Figure 9-1: Public—visible everywhere.

/ fruits   / apple.java

```
package fruits;
public class apple {
    protected int i;
}
```

pippin.java

```
package fruits;
class pippin extends apple {
    i = ...
}
```

plum.java

```
package fruits;
class plum {
    my_apple.i = ...
}
```

/ sun

/ sauces   / chutney.java

```
package sauces;
import fruits.*;
class chutney {

}
```

applesauce.java

```
package sauces;
import fruits.*;
class applesauce extends apple {
    i = ...
}
```

Figure 9-2: Protected—visible in same package and subclasses anywhere.

/ fruits   / apple.java

```
package fruits;
public class apple {
            int i;
}
```

pippin.java

```
package fruits;
class pippin extends apple {
            i = ...
}
```

plum.java

```
package fruits;
class plum {
        my_apple.i = ...
}
```

/ sun

/ sauces   / chutney.java

```
package sauces;
import fruits.*;
class chutney {

}
```

applesauce.java

```
package sauces;
import fruits.*;
class applesauce extends apple {

}
```

Figure 9-3: Default (package)—visible in this package.

/ fruits   / apple.java

```
package fruits;
public class apple {
    private int i;
}
```

pippin.java

```
package fruits;
class pippin extends apple {

}
```

plum.java

```
package fruits;
class plum {

}
```

/ sun

    / sauces   / chutney.java

```
package sauces;
import fruits.*;
class chutney {

}
```

applesauce.java

```
package sauces;
import fruits.*;
class applesauce extends apple {

}
```

Figure 9-4: Private—not accessible outside this class

The requirement that package name match the source file directory name also means that any given directory can contain files of at most one named package. If you don't put your classes into a package, they are compiled by default into an anonymous package in the current directory. When you are building a big system across several directories, you will want to make sure everything goes into a named package.

Using the host filesystem to structure a Java program, and particularly to help organize the program namespace, is a very good idea. It avoids unnecessary generality, and it provides a clear model for understanding.

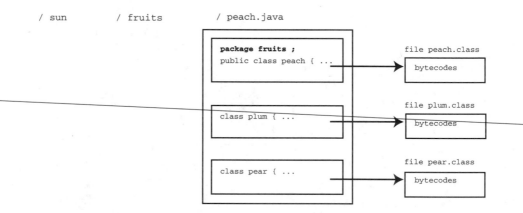

Figure 9-5: How package names relate to directory names.

Compilation Units

Since a source file is what you present to a Java compiler, the contents of a complete source file are known as a "Compilation Unit." Think of it as the unit of compilation, just as the gram is a unit of mass.

Java tries hard not to let you build a system using some components that are out-of-date. When you invoke the compiler on a source file, the compiler does not just translate that in isolation. It looks to see what classes it references, and tries to determine if they are up-to-date. If the compiler decides another class needs compiling, it adds it in, and recursively applies the same procedure to it.

In other words, Java has a "make"-like utility built into it. Say the class you are compiling makes reference to a class in another file. That utility is capable of noticing when the second .class file does not exist, but the corresponding .java does, and of noticing when the .java file has been modified without a recompilation taking place. In both these cases, it will add the second .java file to the set of files it is recompiling.

Here is an example. This is the contents of file plum.java:

```
public class plum {
    grape g;
}
```

This is the contents of file grape.java:

```
public class grape { }
```

If we now compile plum.java, the compiler will look for grape.class, check that it is up-to-date with respect to its source file, and if not, it will recompile grape.java for you!

Here is the output from such a compilation:

```
javac -verbose plum.java
[parsed plum.java in 1312 ms]
[loaded /home/linden/jdk1.2fcs/jre/lib/rt.jar(java/lang/Object.class) in
71 ms]
[checking class plum]
[parsed ./grape.java in 2 ms]
[wrote plum.class]
[checking class grape]
[wrote ./grape.class]
[done in 2718 ms]
```

As you can see, grape.java got compiled as well, creating grape.class.

What we're explaining here is how the rules work when you use the default case of source and object files in the same directory. If you use the "-d" option to javac to make your class files be written in a different directory to the source, then the rules below are modified accordingly.

A compilation unit (source file) has several rules:

1. It can start with a package statement, identifying the package (a library) to which the class will belong.

   A package statement looks like this:

   ```
   package mydir;
   ```

   When starting out, it's simplest not to use packages. Your class files will belong to a default anonymous package and be visible to other classes in the same directory.

2. Next can come zero or more import statements, each identifying a package or a class from a package that will be available in this compilation unit.

   An import statement looks like this:

   ```
   import java.io.*;
   ```

3. The rest of the compilation unit consists of class declarations and interface declarations.

4. At most, one of the classes in the file can be public. This class must have a name that corresponds to the file it is in, as shown in Figure 9-6.

   ```
   public class plum      // must be in file plum.java.
   ```

The underlying host system should allow filenames with the same form as Java classnames: unbounded length, contain "$" or "_" as well as Unicode alphabetics, and case sensitive. The more restrictions there are on filenames on your host system, the more restrictions there are on the classnames you can use. This will form a practical impediment to the total portability of the software. Avoid using characters in classnames that are problematic for any host file systems.

Each of the classes in a .java file will create an individual .class file to hold the generated bytecodes. If you have three classes in a source file, the compiler will create three . class files.

file peach.java

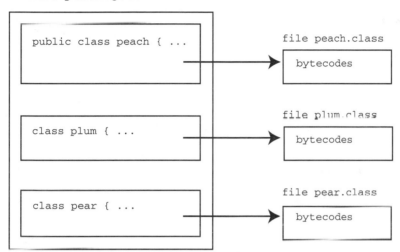

Figure 9-6: Classes and corresponding file names.

Simplicity is a major advantage of Java. Programmers can devote all their brain power to solving the problem, rather than trying to learn and remember the ten thousand complicated rules and the five thousand special cases of language or system. One of Silicon Valley's top programmers (and I mean really *top* programmers) confided to me, "Thank heavens for Java. It means I won't have to learn C++." A lot of programmers share that sense of relief at being able to leapfrog over C++ and go directly to a simpler language.

Import

Packages put classes into a group. Imports let you use a more convenient form for referring to a package or its members in your code. You never have to use the import clause. When you do use it, its effect is to allow you to use a class name directly, instead of fully qualifying it with the package name.

An import statement always has at least two components. The final component is either a class name, or a "*" (meaning all classes in that package), like this:

```
import package.classname;    or    import package.*;
```

You cannot import a subpackage, and expect to supply the rest of the name in your code. So you can do this:

```
import java.util.Date;              // no import used
class Pie {               or      class Pie {
    Date whenMade;                    java.util.Date whenMade;
```

but not

```
import java.*;
class Pie {
    util.Date whenMade // does not work!
```

Some people say, "Just use the 'import all classes' form." Others recommend that you import only the minimum number of packages and libraries you require, to provide a clear sign of what the actual dependencies are. Whatever you import, only the code that is needed is written to the .class file. Superfluous imports are discarded. You should be able to conclude this from what you already know about how Java loads a program dynamically. There is no compilation or runtime performance difference to the two forms.

All compilations import the standard Java package `java.lang.*` without specifically naming it. That package contains interactive I/O classes, objects representing some of the built-in types, predefined exceptions, and mathematical operations, among other useful items.

Now that we've looked at how you can group classes into packages and subpackages, we will look at how you can group classes within classes, namely *inner classes*.

Inner Classes

In JDK 1.0, Java had only *top-level classes* that had to be members of packages. In JDK 1.1, Java gained *inner classes*, which are classes that are members of other classes, or are nested inside a block, or in an expression. See the Table 9-1 for further explanation.

Table 9-1: Inner Classes in Java

Java Term	Description	Example Code

Nested Top-Level Class	A nested class that is declared "static." This is not an inner class, but a new kind of top-level class.	<pre>class Top {
		    int i,j;
		    static class MyNested {
		        int k, l;
		    }
		}</pre>

Member Class	A nested class that is not declared "static." This is an inner class.	<pre>class Top {
		    int i,j;
		    class MyInner {
		        int k, l;
		    }
		}</pre>

Local Class	This is an inner class, declared within a block, typically within a method.	<pre>void foo() {
		    int i,j;
		    class MyInner {
		        int k, l;
		    }
		}</pre>

Anonymous Class	A variation on a local class. The class is declared and instantiated within a single expression. This is an inner class.	<pre>void foo () {
		    JFrame jf = new JFrame();
		    jf.addKeyListener(
		        new KeyAdapter() {
		            public void
		            keyPressed(KeyEvent k){...}
		        }
		    );
		}</pre>

Table 9-1 summarizes the different kinds of class (and interface) that Java has in addition to top-level classes. We will look at the special features of each of these and how to use them in the pages ahead. Nested classes will make more sense when we have covered event-handlers (chapter 14), so you want to just glance over the table on the previous page. For now, you can note that there are ways you can nest classes inside each other like Russian dolls, and postpone an in-depth reading until you need it.

Nested Top-Level Classes

A nested top-level class is a static member of an enclosing top-level class (or interface). We saw nested top-level classes at the end of chapter 2, as one of the four "static" (once-only) things that a class can contain.

We mention nested top-level classes again here to contrast them with inner classes. A nested top-level class works exactly like any top-level class, the only distinction being that its name includes the name of the class in which it is nested. For example, you might see code like this:

```
class Top {
    int i,j;
    static class SomeClass {
        int k;
        void foo() { ... }
    }
    void bar () {
        SomeClass sc = new SomeClass();
    }
}

class someOther {
    Top.SomeClass mySc = new Top.SomeClass();
}
```

Since it is static and therefore does not have a "this" pointer to an instance of the enclosing class, a nested class has no access to the instance data of objects for its enclosing class.

You would typically use a nested top-level class when you have a significant data structure that strongly relates to the enclosing class, but contains enough substance to warrant a class of its own. You can see two examples of a nested top-level class used this way in the class `java.lang.Character` which is featured at the end of this chapter.

Member classes can be declared final, private, protected, or public, just like other members. Access protection protects against classes outside the enclosing class. It never affects the enclosing class or other classes inside it.

Member Classes

One of the criticisms that people sometimes (rightfully) make of OOP is that everything has to be a class. In particular, even if you just want a single function for some utilitarian purpose, you still have to create a class and instantiate an object of that class and invoke a method on that instance. The code for that class might have to be pages and pages away from the place in the source file where you use it. It's a bit heavyweight if your utility function is just a few lines of code. Inner classes are intended to improve the situation.

Java now supports one class being declared within another class, just as a method or data field is declared within a class. The three varieties of inner class are *member class*, *local class*, and *anonymous class*, each one being a refinement of the one before it.

A member class looks exactly like the nested top-level class—with the keyword `static` removed. That says, "The class appears in every instance." Just as any member in a class can see all the other members, the scope of the inner class is the entire parent in which it is directly nested. That is, the inner class can reference any members in its parent. The parent must declare an instance of an inner class, before it can invoke the inner class methods, assign to data fields (including private ones), and so on.

```
class top {
    int i=33;

    class myNested {    // member inner class
        int k=i;
        void foo() {}
    }

    void bar () {
        myNested mn1 = new myNested(); //instantiate member class
        myNested mn2 = new myNested(); // get another one too
        mn1.k = 564 * mn2.k;
    }

}
```

A colleague of mine pointed out that a good way to think of an inner class object is that it is associated with an instance of its enclosing class. It really has two "this" pointers it deals with: one to itself and one to its enclosing object.

Unlike nested top-level classes, inner classes are not directly part of a package and are not visible outside the class in which they are nested. Inner classes are intended for GUI event handlers, and we'll see plenty of real examples of them in chapter 14. They allow you to put the event handling class and method right next to the place where you declare the GUI objects.

Local Classes

A local class is an inner class. It is a class that is declared within a block of code, so it is not a member of the enclosing class. Typically, a local class is declared within a method.

Figure 9-7 shows a local inner class. The class is declared inside the method init(). This inner class is the event-handler for a button. You will find the code on the CD in the directory book\ch09\ and you can try compiling and running it. You could easily convert this local class to a member class by moving it outside the method. The distinction between member classes and local classes is a fine one. The most important limitation is that local classes can access only final variables or parameters. The reason for this apparently strange restriction is given later in the chapter. It has to do with the way it is implemented.

```
//<applet code=f.class height=100 width=200> </applet>
    import java.applet.*;
    import java.awt.*;
    import java.awt.event.*;

    public class f extends Applet {

        Button apple = new Button ("press me");
        public void init() {
```

> Inner Class

```
        class MyinnerBHClass implements java.awt.event.ActionListener {
                int i=1;
                public void actionPerformed (ActionEvent e) {
                // this gets called when button pressed . . .
                System.out.println ("button pressed" + i++ +" times");
                }
        }

            add (apple);
            apple.addActionListener (new MyinnerBHClass () );

    }

}
```

The inner class can be placed wherever any declaration can go, including inside the init ( ) method.

Figure 9-7: A local inner class.

Anonymous Classes

It's possible to go one step further from a local inner class to something called an *anonymous class*. An anonymous class is a refinement of inner classes, allowing you to combine the *definition* of the class with the *instance allocation*.

Instead of just nesting the class like any other declaration, you go to the "new SomeClass ()" statement where an object is instantiated and put the entire class there in brackets, as shown in Figure 9-8.

```
//<applet code=f.class height=100 width=200> </applet>
import java.applet.*;
import java.awt.*;
import java.awt.event.*;

public class f extends Applet {

        Button apple = new Button("press me");

        public void init() {
                add(apple);
                apple.addActionListener(
                        new ActionListener ()
        {
                public void actionPerformed(ActionEvent e) {
                    System.out.println ( e.paramString () +" pressed");
                }
        } // end anon class

        ); // end method call
    }
}
```

what kind of class or interface implementor it is

Anonymous Class

Figure 9-8: An anonymous class.

Try compiling and running this example. Your f.java file will generate class files called f.class and f$1.class. The second of these represents the anonymous ActionListener inner class.

Be sure you are clear on what is going on here, even if the code won't make sense until we reach chapter 14. This is saying that there is an Interface (or class—we can't tell from looking at the code here) called ActionListener. We are declaring an object of an anonymous class type that either implements the interface or extends the class. If it extends the class, then any methods we define may override the corresponding methods of the base class.

You should only use inner classes and anonymous classes where the event handler is just a few lines long. If the event-handler is more than a screenful of text, it should be in a named top-level class. We have to admit, however, that the notational convenience for smaller cases is considerable. Just don't get carried away with it.

How Inner Classes Are Compiled

You might be interested to learn that inner classes are completely defined in terms of a source transformation into corresponding freestanding classes, and that this is how the Sun compiler implements them. An inner class "pips" is defined to be transformed into JDK 1.0 compatible code.

```
public class orange {
     int i=0;
     void foo() {   }

     class pips {
          int seeds=2;
          void bar() { }
     }
}
```

First, separate out the inner class and prefix the containing class to its name.

```
public class orange {
     int i=0;
     void foo() {   }
}

class orange$pips {
     int seeds=2;
     void bar() { }
}
```

Then, give the inner class a private field that keeps a reference to the object in which it appears. Also, ensure all the constructors initialize this extra field.

```
class orange$pips { // the transformed inner class
    private orange this$0;    // the saved copy of orange.this

    orange$pips(orange o) {   // constructor
        this$0 = o; // initialize the ref to enclosing obj
    }
    int seeds=2;
    void bar() { }
}
```

The manufactured field this$0 allows the inner class to access any fields of its containing class, even private fields which could not otherwise be accessed. If you try compiling this example, you will note that the compiler produces class files with names like orange$pips.class.

That embedded dollar sign in the name of nested classes is part of the definition. Having a consistent explicit policy for naming inner classes allows everyone's tools (debugger, linker, and so on) to work the same way.

One restriction on inner classes is that they can't access variables of the method in which they are embedded. The reason is clear if you think it through. The source transformation shown above lets an inner class get back to its outer class, but the scoping rules don't give it any way to see the local variables of a method in that class. If you break this rule, as in the code below, the compiler will give an error message like the one shown:

```
public void init() {
    int i = 20; // local variable i
            ... // lines omitted
    s.addAdjustmentListener(
        new AdjustmentListener() {
            public void adjustmentValueChanged(AdjustmentEvent
ae) {
                something.setSize( i, ae.getValue()   );
^  Attempt to use a non-final variable i from a different method. From
enclosing blocks, only final local variables are available.
```

The simplest fix is to make the variable final if possible. A constant (final) variable can be used because the compiler will pass a copy of it to the inner class constructor as an extra argument. Since it is final, that value won't later change to something else.

Some people feel that inner classes take more away from the simplicity and purity of model than they provide. Don't make the problem worse by using them for large classes. We now finish the chapter by featuring the class Character.

The Class Character

Here is the declaration of class java.lang.Character. Notice the two examples of
a nested top-level class on the next page of the listing.

```
public final class java.lang.Character
        implements java.io.Serializable, java.lang.Comparable {
    public java.lang.Character(char); // constructor

    public static final int MIN_RADIX = 2;
    public static final int MAX_RADIX = 36;
    public static final char MIN_VALUE = '˜0000';
    public static final char MAX_VALUE = '˜ffff';
    public static final java.lang.Class TYPE =
Class.getPrimitiveClass("char");
    public static final byte UNASSIGNED;//about 20 other Unicode types
    public static final byte UPPERCASE_LETTER;
    public static int getType(char); // returns the Unicode type

    public char charValue();
    public int compareTo(java.lang.Character);
    public int compareTo(java.lang.Object);
    public static int digit(char, int);
    public boolean equals(java.lang.Object);
    public static char forDigit(int, int);
    public static int getNumericValue(char);
    public int hashCode();

    public static boolean isDefined(char);
    public static boolean isDigit(char);
    public static boolean isISOControl(char);
    public static boolean isIdentifierIgnorable(char);
    public static boolean isJavaIdentifierPart(char);
    public static boolean isJavaIdentifierStart(char);
    public static boolean isJavaLetter(char); // deprecated
    public static boolean isJavaLetterOrDigit(char); // deprecated
    public static boolean isLetter(char);
    public static boolean isLetterOrDigit(char);
    public static boolean isLowerCase(char);
    public static boolean isSpace(char);
    public static boolean isSpaceChar(char);
    public static boolean isTitleCase(char);
    public static boolean isUnicodeIdentifierPart(char);
    public static boolean isUnicodeIdentifierStart(char);
    public static boolean isUpperCase(char);
    public static boolean isWhitespace(char);
    public static char toLowerCase(char);
    public java.lang.String toString();
    public static char toTitleCase(char);
    public static char toUpperCase(char);

    // class Character is continued on the next page ...
```

```
       // class Character continued ...
       // Character contains two top-level nested classes

    public static class java.lang.Character.Subset {
// represents a particular subset of the Unicode characters
        protected java.lang.Character.Subset(java.lang.String);
        public final boolean equals(java.lang.Object);
        public final int hashCode();
        public final java.lang.String toString();
    } // end of Subset

    public static final class java.lang.Character.UnicodeBlock
                              extends java.lang.Character.Subset {
// Names for Unicode Blocks. Any given character is contained by
// at most one Unicode block.
        public static final UnicodeBlock BASIC_LATIN;
        public static final UnicodeBlock LATIN_1_SUPPLEMENT;
        public static final UnicodeBlock LATIN_EXTENDED_A;
        public static final UnicodeBlock LATIN_EXTENDED_B;
        public static final UnicodeBlock IPA_EXTENSIONS;
        public static final UnicodeBlock SPACING_MODIFIER_LETTERS;
        public static final UnicodeBlock COMBINING_DIACRITICAL_MARKS;
        public static final UnicodeBlock GREEK;
        public static final UnicodeBlock CYRILLIC;
        public static final UnicodeBlock ARMENIAN;
        public static final UnicodeBlock HEBREW;
        public static final UnicodeBlock ARABIC;
        public static final UnicodeBlock DEVANAGARI;
            ... there are about 65 of these in all ...
        public static final UnicodeBlock COMBINING_MARKS_FOR_SYMBOLS;
        public static final UnicodeBlock LETTERLIKE_SYMBOLS;
        public static final UnicodeBlock NUMBER_FORMS;
        public static UnicodeBlock of(char);
    } // end of UnicodeBlock class

} // end of Character class
```

Java Coding Style

This seems like a good point in the text to tell you about the recommended coding style for Java. These recommendations are actually in section 6.8, "Naming Conventions," in the Java Language Specification.

- Package names are guaranteed unique by using the Internet domain name in reverse order, as in com.afu.applications.arby. The com (or edu, gov, etc.) part used to be in uppercase, but now lowercase is the recommendation.

- Class and interface names should be descriptive nouns, with the first letter of each word capitalized, as in PolarCoords. Interfaces are often (not always) called *something*-able, e.g., Runnable, or Sortable. There is a caution here: java.util.Observable is not an interface, though java.util.Observer is. These two are not well designed.

- Object and field names are nouns or noun phrases with the first letter lowercase and the first letter of subsequent words capitalized, as in currentLimit.

- Method names are verbs or verb phrases with the first letter lowercase, and the first letter of subsequent words capitalized, as in calculateCurrentLimit.

- Constant (final) names are in caps, as in UPPER_LIMIT

If you keep to these simple conventions, you'll be giving useful stylistic hints to those who must maintain your code. Maybe they will do the same for you. There aren't any recommendations in the JLS on brace style, but all the Java runtime code I've ever seen uses this style:

```
compoundStatement {            void someMethod() {
    statement;                     statement;
    statement;                     statement;
}                              }
```

It's a slight variant of "K&R style" (it comes from Kernighan and Ritchie who developed C), known as "The Original One True Brace Style" (TOOTBS)[1]. With this style, the else part of an if-else statement and the while part of a do-while statement appear on the same line as the close brace. With most other styles, the braces are always alone on a line. When maintaining someone else's code, *always* use the style used in that code.

---

1. I'm not making another one of my acronym wisecracks here—this is all true.

The One True Brace style has methods formatted like this:

```
void someMethod()
{
        statement;
        statement;
}
```

The *Original* One True Brace Style, and Java, has them like this:

```
void someMethod() {
        statement;
        statement;
}
```

The Java way is more consistent, but makes it a little harder to find functions and review their signatures. You'll be enchanted to hear that there are many further styles and variations that different programmers champion. Stick with TOOTBS.

Some Light Relief

The Domestic Obfuscated Java Code Non-Competition

Readers of my book, *Expert C Programming*, will be aware of the International Obfuscated C Code Competition (IOCCC). It's an annual contest run over Usenet since 1984 to find the most horrible and unreadable C programs of the year. Not horrible in that it is badly written, but in the much subtler concept of being horrible to figure out what it does and how it works.

The IOCCC accepts entries in the winter, they are judged over spring, and the winners are announced at the summer Usenix conference. It is a great honor to be one of the dozen or so category winners at the IOCCC, as many very good programmers turn their talents to the dark side of the force for this event. If you know C pretty well, you might be interested in figuring out what this IOCCC past winner does:

```
main() {printf(&unix["\021%six\012\0"],(unix)["have"]+"fun"-0x60);}
```

Hint: It doesn't print "have fun."

Here, in the spirit of the IOCCC are two Java programs that I wrote for April Fool's Day. You should be pretty good at reading Java code at this point, so I won't spoil your fun. This program is on the CD in directory book/ch09/h.java. It looks like one big comment, so it should compile without problems. When you run it, it greets you! But how?

```
/*    Just Java
      Peter van der Linden
      April 1, 1996.

\u0050\u0076\u0064\u004c\u0020\u0031\u0020\u0041\u0070\u0072\u0039\u0036
 \u002a\u002f\u0020\u0063\u006c\u0061\u0073\u0073\u0020\u0068\u0020\u007b
  \u0020\u0020\u0070\u0075\u0062\u006c\u0069\u0063\u0020\u0020\u0020\u0020

\u0073\u0074\u0061\u0074\u0069\u0063\u0020\u0020\u0076\u006f\u0069\u0064

\u006d\u0061\u0069\u006e\u0028\u0020\u0053\u0074\u0072\u0069\u006e\u0067

\u005b\u005d\u0061\u0029\u0020\u007b\u0053\u0079\u0073\u0074\u0065\u006d

\u002e\u006f\u0075\u0074\u002e\u0070\u0072\u0069\u006e\u0074\u006c\u006e

\u0028\u0022\u0048\u0069\u0021\u0022\u0029\u003b\u007d\u007d\u002f\u002a

  */
```

The second program is my attempt to greatly improve program portability. This one source file can be compiled by an ANSI C compiler and executed. The same code can also be compiled by a Java compiler and executed, and by a C++ compiler! Am I having a great day, or what? True source portability! Every program should do as well. This program is on the CD.

```
/*  Peter van der Linden,    "Just Java"
    April 1, 1996
    Real portability: a Java program, C program and C++ program.

    Compile and run this Java program with:  javac b.java     java b
    Compile and run this C program with:     cc     b.c       a.out
    Compile and run this C++ program with:   CC     b.c       a.out
    \u002a\u002f\u002f*/

#define String char*
#define t struct
#include <stdio.h>
t{t{int(*print)(const char*,...);}out;}
System={{printf}};/*\u002a\u002f

public class b {
                            public static void
/* The main routine                        */     main (
/* The number of arguments \u002a\u002f\u002f*/        int     argc,
/* The array of argument strings           */        String argv[] )
                {
                        System.out.print("Hi!\n");
                }

/*\u002a\u002f}/**/
```

How does this trilingual program work?

Please don't suggest an International Obfuscated Java Code Competition! It works for C because there are so many opportunities to abuse the preprocessor, the expression semantics, the library calls, and so on. Computer consultant Mike Morton suggested to me that these *should* be an *O*bfuscated *J*ava competition, just so we could name it the "OJ trial."

Java doesn't offer half so many opportunities to unscrew the inscrutable, so let's keep things that way, OK?

CHAPTER
10

- What Are Threads?

- Two Ways to Obtain a New Thread

- The Lifecycle of a Thread

- Thread Groups

- Four Kinds of Threads Programming

- Some Light Relief

Doing Several
Things at Once:
Threads

Multithreading is not a new concept in software, but it is new to come into the limelight. People have been kicking around experimental implementations for a dozen years or more, but it is only recently that desktop hardware (especially desktop multiprocessors — if you don't have one tell your boss you need one today!) became powerful enough to make multithreading popular.

There is a POSIX[1] document P1003.4a (ratified June 1995) that describes a threads API standard. The threads described by the POSIX model and the threads available in Java do not exactly coincide. The Java designers didn't use POSIX threads because the POSIX model was still under development when they implemented Java. Java threads are simpler, take care of their own memory management, and do not have the full generality (or overhead) of POSIX threads.

---

1.   POSIX is an operating system standard, heavily weighted to a common subset of Unix.

What Are Threads?

Everyone is familiar with time-sharing: a computer system can give the impression of doing several things simultaneously by running each process for a few milliseconds, then saving its state and switching to the next process, and so on. Threads simply extend that concept from switching between several different programs to switching between several different functions executing simultaneously within a single program as shown in Figure 10-1. A thread isn't restricted just to one function. Any thread in a multi-threaded program can call any series of methods that could be called in a single-threaded program.

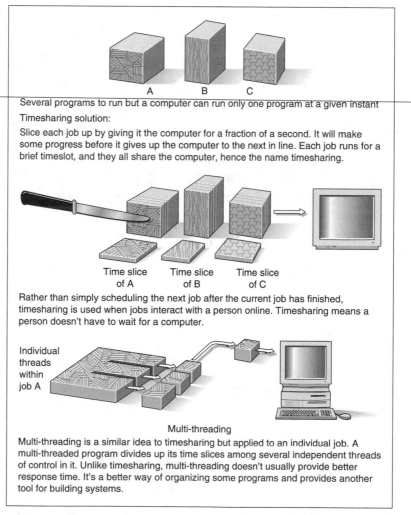

Several programs to run but a computer can run only one program at a given instant

Timesharing solution:

Slice each job up by giving it the computer for a fraction of a second. It will make some progress before it gives up the computer to the next in line. Each job runs for a brief timeslot, and they all share the computer, hence the name timesharing.

Time slice of A   Time slice of B   Time slice of C

Rather than simply scheduling the next job after the current job has finished, timesharing is used when jobs interact with a person online. Timesharing means a person doesn't have to wait for a computer.

Individual threads within job A

Multi-threading

Multi-threading is a similar idea to timesharing but applied to an individual job. A multi-threaded program divides up its time slices among several independent threads of control in it. Unlike timesharing, multi-threading doesn't usually provide better response time. It's a better way of organizing some programs and provides another tool for building systems.

Figure 10-1: An explanation of timesharing and multithreading.

When the operating system switches from running one process to running another for its time slice, there is a quite costly overhead of saving the program state (virtual memory map, file descriptors, interrupt settings, etc.). When the JVM switches from running one of your threads to running another of your threads, a low-overhead context switch (saving just a few registers, a stack pointer, the program counter, etc.) within the same address space is done. Threads can actually achieve the counterintuitive result of making a program run faster, even on uniprocessor hardware. This occurs when there are calculation steps that no longer have to wait for earlier output to complete, but can run while the I/O is taking place.

Threads (an abbreviation of "threads of control," meaning control flow) are the way we get several things to happen at once in a program. Why is this a good idea? In an unthreaded program (what you have been using to date in Java, and what you have always used in Fortran, Pascal, C, Basic, C++, COBOL, and so on), only one thing happens at a time. Threads allow a program to do more than one thing at a time. There are three reasons why you would do this:

- You will have interactive programs that never "go dead" on the user. You might have one thread controlling and responding to a GUI, while another thread carries out the tasks or computations requested, while a third thread does file I/O, all for the same program. This means that when one part of the program is blocked waiting on some resource, the other threads can still run and are not blocked.

- Some programs are easier to write if you split them into threads. The classic example is the server part of a client/server. When a request comes in from a client, it is very convenient if the server can spawn a new thread to process that one request. The alternative is to have one server program try to keep track algorithmically of the state of each client request.

- Some programs are amenable to parallel processing. Writing them as threads allows the code to express this. Examples include some sorting and merging algorithms, some matrix operations, and many recursive algorithms.

Two Ways to Obtain a New Thread

There are two ways to obtain a new thread of control in Java. Either extend the Thread class, or write a class to implement the runnable interface and use it in the Thread constructor. The first way can be used only if your class doesn't extend any other class (as Java disallows multiple inheritance).

1. Extend class "java.lang.Thread" and override "run()".

    ```
    class mango extends Thread {
        public void run() { ... }
    }
    ```

or

2. Implement the "Runnable" interface (the class "Thread" itself is an implementation of "Runnable"), and use that class in the Thread constructor.

    ```
    class pineapple implements Runnable {
        public void run() { ... }
    }

    Thread t1 = new Thread(new pineapple());
    ```

Your applets extend class Applet by definition, so threads in applets must always use the second way. If the thread doesn't have to run in the Applet object, it can use the first approach.

Figure 10-2 shows how a class Thread is created by extending Thread.

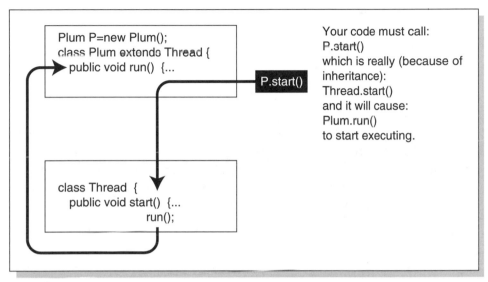

Plum P=new Plum();
class Plum extends Thread {
    public void run() {...

P.start()

Your code must call:
P.start()
which is really (because of inheritance):
Thread.start()
and it will cause:
Plum.run()
to start executing.

class Thread {
    public void start() {...
                    run();

Figure 10-2:   Class Thread created by an extending Thread.

Creating a thread by extending class Thread looks confusing, because you have to start the thread running by calling a method that you do not have, namely P.start() in Figure 10-2. You extended Thread with a subclass, so your class will inherit Thread.start() and all will be well.

Then, continuing to refer to Figure 10-2, declaring an object of class Plum gives you a new thread of control whose execution will start in the method "run()". That isn't an OOP mechanism, it's just a name convention you have to know. Declaring two Plums (or more likely one Plum and one object of some other thread subclass) will give you two independently executing threads of control, and declaring and filling an array of Plums will give you an entire array.length of threads of control.

New threads do not start executing on creation. For some applications, programmers (or maybe the runtime system—we'll talk about this in the chapter on applets) want to create threads in advance, then explicitly start them when needed, so this has been made the way it works. Create a thread like so:

```
Plum p = new Plum();
```

You start it running by calling the "start()" method, like so:

```
p.start();
```

Or you can create and start it in one step, like this:

```
new Plum().start();
```

Execution will then begin in the "run()" method, from whence you can call other methods in this and other classes as usual. Remember: "run()" is the place where it starts, and "start()" will get it running. Arrrgh! Perhaps another way to think of this is that "run()" is the equivalent of "main()" for a thread. You do not call it directly, but it is called on your behalf. There's a lot of this in Java!

A Few Words on Runnable

The Runnable interface just looks like this:

```
public interface Runnable {
    public abstract void run();
}
```

All it does is promise that an implementing class will have a method called run. The method is abstract to provide the absolute minimum of constraint on the classes that will implement Runnable. It allows them to be abstract classes and provide only an abstract method for run, deferring the details to a later subclass.

To get a Runnable object running, you pass it as an argument to a Thread constructor, like this:

```
class Pear implements Runnable {
    public void run() { ... }
}
...

Thread t1 = new Thread(new Pear());
```

You can then invoke all the Thread methods on t1, such as:

```
t1.start();
t1.stop();
```

You have to call start() to get the Runnable implementation executing (just as with a thread). It's common to instantiate and start in one statement like this:

```
new Thread (new Pear()).start();
```

However, you cannot have statements *within the Runnable interface implementation* of "run()" that invoke the Thread methods, like "sleep()" or "getName()" or "setPriority()." This is because there is no Thread "this" in Runnable, whereas there is in Thread. This perhaps makes an implementation of Runnable slightly less convenient than a subclass of Thread. There is a simple workaround shown after this code example.

```
// Show the two ways to obtain a new thread
//    1.   extend class java.lang.Thread and override run()
//    2.   implement the Runnable interface,

class example {
    public static void main(String[] a) {

        // alternative 1
        ExtnOfThread t1 = new ExtnOfThread();
        t1.start();

        // alternative 2
        Thread t2 = new Thread (now ImplOfRunnable());
        t2.start();
    }
}


class ExtnOfThread extends Thread {
    public void run() {
        System.out.println("Extension of Thread running");
        try {sleep(1000);}
        catch (InterruptedException ie) {return;}
    }
}


class ImplOfRunnable implements Runnable {
    public void run() {
        System.out.println("Implementation of Runnable running");

// next two lines will not compile
//          try {sleep(1000);}
//          catch (InterruptedException ie) {return;}
    }
}
```

The class Thread has many other methods, as well as run(). It has methods to stop(), sleep(), suspend(), resume(), setPriority(), and others. You can only call these Thread methods if you have a Thread object to invoke them on. You don't get that automatically in a class that implements Runnable.

To get a Thread object, you call the static method Thread.currentThread().Its return value is simply the currently running thread. Once you have that, you can easily apply any thread methods to it, as shown in the next example.

```
class ImplOfRunnable implements Runnable {
    public void run() {
        System.out.println("Implementation of Runnable running");
        Thread t = Thread.currentThread();
        try { t.sleep(1000); }
        catch  (InterruptedException ie) { return; }
    }
}
```

A call to currentThread() can appear in any Java code, including your main program or whatever. Once you have that thread object you can invoke the thread methods on it.

The official word from the Java team is that the Runnable interface should be used if the "run()" method is the only one you are planning to override. The thinking is that, to maintain the purity of the model, classes should not be subclassed unless the programmer intends to modify or enhance the fundamental behavior of the class.

As with exceptions, you can provide a string argument when you create a thread subclass. If you want to do this, you must provide a constructor to take that string and pass it back to the constructor of the base class. The string becomes the name of the object of the Thread subclass and can later be used to identify it.

```
class Grape extends Thread {
      Grape(String s){ super(s); } // constructor

      public void run() { ... }
}
    ...
   static public void main(String s[]) {
       new Grape("merlot").start();
       new Grape("pinot").start();
       new Grape("cabernet").start();
    ...
```

You cannot pass any parameters into the "run()" method because its signature would differ from the version it is overriding in Thread. A thread can, however, get the string with which it was started, by invoking the "getName()" method. This string could encode arguments or be an index into a static array of arguments as needed.

You have already seen enough to write an elementary Java program that uses threads. So do it. Write two classes that extend Thread. In one the run() method should print "I like tea" in a loop, while the other prints "I like coffee." Create a third class with a main() routine that instantiates and starts the other two threads. Compile and run your program.

The Lifecycle of a Thread

We have already covered how a thread is created, and how the "start()" method inherited from Thread causes execution to start in its run() method. An individual thread dies when execution falls off the end of "run()" or otherwise leaves the run method (through an exception or return statement). If an exception is thrown from the run method, the runtime system prints a message saying so, the thread terminates, but the exception does not propagate somehow back into the code that created or started the thread. What this means is that once you start up a separate thread, it doesn't come back to interfere with the code that spawned it.

Priorities

Threads have priorities that can be set and changed. A higher priority thread executes ahead of a lower priority thread if they are both ready to run.

Java threads are preemptible, meaning that a running thread will be pushed off the processor by a higher priority thread before it is ready to give it up of its own accord. Java threads might or might not also be time-sliced, meaning that a running thread might or might not share the processor with threads of equal priority.

A Slice of Time

Not guaranteeing time-slicing may seem a somewhat surprising design decision as it violates the "Principle of Least Astonishment"—it leads to program behavior that programmers find surprising (namely threads suffer from CPU starvation). There is some precedent in that time-slicing can also be missing in a POSIX-conforming thread implementation. POSIX specifies a number of different scheduling algorithms, one of which (round robin) does do time-slicing. Another scheduling possibility allows a local implementation. In the Solaris case of POSIX threads only the local implementation is used, and this does not do any time-slicing.

Many people think that the failure to require time-slicing is a mistake that will surely be fixed in a future release.

Since a programmer cannot assume that time-slicing will take place, the careful programmer assures portability by writing threaded code that does not depend on time-slicing. The code must cope with the fact that once a thread starts running, all other threads with the same priority might become blocked. One way to cope with this would be to adjust thread priorities on the fly. That is *not* recommended because the code will cost you a fortune in software maintenance.

A better way is to yield control to other threads frequently. CPU-intensive threads should call the "yield()" method at regular intervals to ensure they don't hog the processor. This won't be needed if time-slicing is made a standard part of Java. Yield allows the scheduler to choose another runnable thread for execution.

Up to and including the 1.2 version of Java, priorities run from 1 (lowest) to 10 (highest). Threads start off with the same priority as their parent thread (the thread that created them), and the priority can be adjusted like this:

```
t1.setPriority ( t1.getPriority() +1 );
```

On operating systems that have priorities, most users cannot adjust their processes to a higher priority (because they may gain an unfair advantage over other users of the system).[2] There is no such inhibition for threads, because they all operate within one process. The user is competing only with himself or herself for resources.

---

2.   Hence the infamous message from the system operator, "I've upped my priority, now up yours."

Thread Groups

A thread group is (big surprise!) a group of Threads. A Thread group can contain a set of Threads as well as a set of other Thread groups. It's a way of lumping several related threads together and doing certain housekeeping things to all of them, like starting them with a single method invocation.

There are methods to create a thread group and add a thread to it. Applets are not allowed to manipulate threads outside the applet's own thread group. You may want to save a reference to that group for later use:

```
public class myApplet extends Applet{
    private ThreadGroup mygroup;
    public void init(){
        mygroup=Thread.currentThread().getThreadGroup();
```

Thread groups exist because it turned out to be a useful concept in the runtime library. There was no reason not to just pass it through to application programmers, too.

How Many Threads?

Sometimes programmers ask, "How many threads should I have in my program?" Ron Winacott of Sun Canada has done a lot of thread programming, and he compares this question to asking, "How many people is it reasonable to fit in a vehicle?"

The problem is that so much is left unspecified. What kind of vehicle is it? Is it a minivan or a compact car? Are the people children or 250-pound wrestlers like Ric Flair? How many are needed to get to where you want to go in this car (e.g., driver, mechanic, navigator, fuel purchaser)? In other words, what kind of program is it, and what hardware are you running it on?

The bottom line is this. Each thread has a default stack size of 400K in the JDK current release. It will also use about 0.5K to hold its internal state, but the stack size is the limiting factor. A 32-bit Unix process (Unix is the most capable of all the systems that Java has been ported to) effectively has a 2GB user address space, so in theory you could have around 5000 threads. In practice you would be limited by CPU availability, swap space, and disk bandwidth before you got up there. In one experiment, I was able to create almost 2000 threads before my desktop system ground to a halt. That was just create them; I'm not making any claims about them doing any useful work.

Now, back to the real question. Overall there is no unique correct answer. How many is "reasonable?" There is only one person who can accurately answer this question, and that is the programmer writing the threaded application. The runtime library has a comment that mentions twenty-six threads as being the maximum concurrency that one might reasonably expect. That's just a rule of thumb.

The best estimate is "the number of threads needed to perform the task." If this number is too high for the address space or the CPU power, then you must redesign the tasks (and the number of threads) to use what is available. Use threads to achieve concurrency or to gain overlapping I/O. Do not try to create a new thread for every single method, class, or object in your program.

The CD contains a program that I wrote to solve crossword puzzles. The program reads in a big dictionary of words at the start of execution, and I put that file processing into a separate thread. The rest of the program can thus proceed with constructing the user interface, while the I/O is taking place in the background. Everything would otherwise just stall until the data had been read. It works well and is a good example of where to use threads effectively.

Inner Class Thread

One Java expert on the HotJava team pointed out that you can write the following to create and start a background thread close to the place where it's relevant:

```
(new Thread() {
    public void run() {
        // 2 or 3 lines to do in the background
    }
} ).start();
```

That's true, but for goodness sake, don't make your programs impossible to maintain by putting more than two or three lines in an inner class. In theory, you can nest an inner class in an inner class, but don't let me catch you doing it.

Four Kinds of Threads Programming

Coordination between different threads is known as *synchronization*. Programs that use threads can be divided into the following four levels of difficulty, depending on the kind of synchronization needed between the different threads.

1. Unrelated Threads

2. Related but Unsynchronized Threads

3. Mutually-Exclusive Threads

4. Communicating Mutually-Exclusive Threads

We will deal with the first two here and the last two in the next chapter. The following Figure 10-3 is the key for all illustrations dealing with this topic.

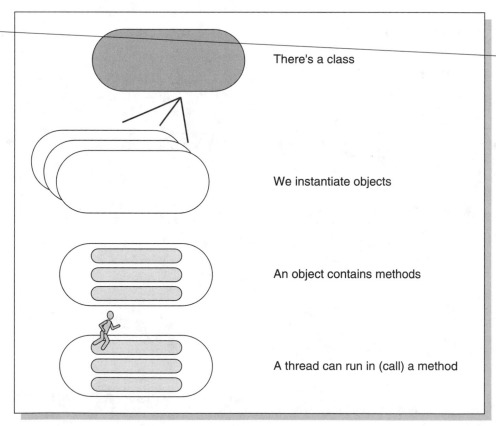

Figure 10-3: Key to threads diagrams.

1. Unrelated Threads

The simplest threads program involves threads of control that do different things and don't interact with each other.

A good example of unrelated threads is the answer to the programming challenge set a few pages back.

The code follows:

```
public class drinks {
   public static void main(String[] a) {
      Coffee t1 = new Coffee();
      t1.start();
      new Tea().start();  // an anonymous thread
   }
}

class Coffee extends Thread {
   public void run() {
        while(true) {
            System.out.println("I like coffee");
            yield();  // did you forget this?
        }
   }
}

class Tea extends Thread {
   public void run() {
        while(true) {
            System.out.println("I like tea");
            yield();
        }
   }
}
```

When you run this program, you will see the output:

```
I like coffee
I like tea
I like coffee
I like tea
I like coffee
I like tea
```

It is repeated over and over again until you press control-C or otherwise interrupt program execution. This type of threads programming is easy to get working, and it corresponds to Figure 10-4.

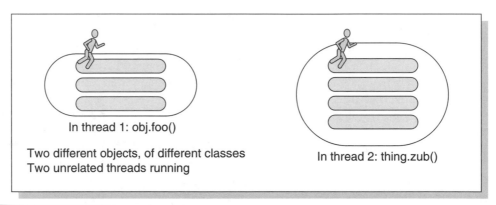

In thread 1: obj.foo()

Two different objects, of different classes
Two unrelated threads running

In thread 2: thing.zub()

Figure 10-4: Unrelated threads.

2. Related but Unsynchronized Threads

This level of complexity uses threaded code to partition a problem, solving it by having multiple threads work on different pieces of the same data structure. The threads don't interact with each other. Here, threads of control do work that is sent to them, but they don't work on shared data, so they don't need to access it in a synchronized way.

An example of this would be spawning a new thread for each socket connection that comes in. A Thread that just does "work to order" like that is a good example of a demon thread—its only purpose is to serve a higher master. See Figure 10-5 for a graphical representation of how this kind of thread interacts with objects.

Demon Threads

A thread can also be marked as a demon or daemon (the spelling varies) thread. If the program gets into a state where only demon threads are running, it terminates. Demon threads are those that exist only to carry out work on behalf of others. The following will mark a thread as a demon.

```
myThread.setDemon(true);
```

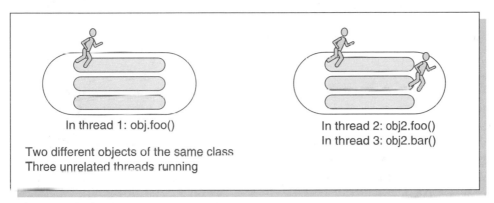

In thread 1: obj.foo()

In thread 2: obj2.foo()
In thread 3: obj2.bar()

Two different objects of the same class
Three unrelated threads running

Figure 10-5: Related but unsynchronized threads.

A less common but still interesting example of related but unsynchronized threads involves partitioning a data set, and instantiating multiple copies of the same thread to work on different pieces of the same problem. Be careful not to duplicate work, or even worse, to let two different threads operate on the same data at once.

Here is an example program that tests whether a given number is a prime number. That involves a lot of divisions so it's a good candidate for parcelling the work out among a number of threads. Tell each thread the range of numbers it is to test-divide into the possible prime. Then let them all loose in parallel.

The driver code is:

```
// demonstrates the use of threads to test a number for primality

public class testPrime {

    public static void main(String s[]) {
        long possPrime = Long.parseLong(s[0]);
        int centuries = (int)(possPrime/100) +1;

        for(int i=0;i<centuries;i++) {
            new testRange(i*100, possPrime).start();
        }

    }
}
```

This main program gets its argument, which is the value to test for primality, and then calculates how many 100s there are in the number. A new thread will be created to test for factors in every range of 100. So if the number is 2048, there are twenty 100s. Twenty one threads will be created. The first will check whether any of the numbers 2 to 99 divide into 2048. The second will check the range 100 to 199. The third will check 200 to 299, and so on, with the 21st thread checking the numbers 2000 to 2100.

The line "new testRange(i*100, possPrime).start();" instantiates an object of class testRange, using the constructor that takes two arguments. That object belongs to a subclass of Thread, so the ".start()" jammed on the end starts it running. This is the Java idiom of invoking a method on the object returned by a constructor or method invocation. The listing of class testRange follows:

```
class testRange extends Thread {

    static long possPrime;
    long from, to;

    // constructor
    //    record the number we are to test, and
    //    the range of factors we are to try.
    testRange(int argFrom,long argpossPrime) {
        possPrime=argpossPrime;
        if (argFrom==0) from=2; else from=argFrom;
        to=argFrom+99;
    }

    public void run() {
        for (long i=from; i<=to && i<possPrime; i++) {
            if (possPrime%i == 0) {   // i divides possPrime exactly
                    System.out.println(
                     "factor "+i+" found by thread "+getName());
                    this.stop();
            }
            yield();
        }
    }

}
```

The constructor just saves a copy of the number we are to test for primality, and it saves the start of the range of potential factors for this thread instance to test. The end of the range is the start plus 99.

All the run() method does is count through this range, trying each divisor. If one divides the number exactly, then print it out and stop this thread. We have the answer that the number is not prime. There are many possible improvements to the algorithm (for instance, we need only test for factors up to the square root of the possible prime). These improvements have been omitted so as not to clutter up the code example.

A sample run of this program might look like this:

```
% java testPrime 2048
  factor 2 found by thread Thread-4
  factor 512 found by thread Thread-9
  factor 1024 found by thread Thread-14
  factor 128 found by thread Thread-5
  factor 256 found by thread Thread-6
```

So, 2048 is not a prime number and five of the 21 threads found factors. The default name for the first thread you create is Thread-4 (not Thread-1) because there are already several threads running in your program, including the garbage collector and your main program.

The following code are the non-private members of the class `java.lang.Thread.`. You can look at the full source at $JAVAHOME\src\java\lang\Thread.java.

```
public class java.lang.Thread implements java.lang.Runnable {
    java.lang.InheritableThreadLocal$Entry values;
    public static final int MIN_PRIORITY;
    public static final int NORM_PRIORITY;
    public static final int MAX_PRIORITY;
// constructors
    public java.lang.Thread();
    public java.lang.Thread(java.lang.Runnable);
    public java.lang.Thread(java.lang.Runnable,java.lang.String);
    public java.lang.Thread(java.lang.String);
    public java.lang.Thread(ThreadGroup,java.lang.Runnable);
    public Thread(ThreadGroup, Runnable, String);
    public java.lang.Thread(ThreadGroup,String);

    public static int activeCount();
    public final void checkAccess();
    public static native java.lang.Thread currentThread();
    public void destroy();
    public static void dumpStack();
    public static int enumerate(java.lang.Thread[]);
    public java.lang.ClassLoader getContextClassLoader();
    public final java.lang.String getName();
    public final int getPriority();
    public final java.lang.ThreadGroup getThreadGroup();
    public void interrupt();
    public static boolean interrupted();
    public final native boolean isAlive();
    public final boolean isDaemon();
    public boolean isInterrupted();
    public final void join() throws java.lang.InterruptedException;
    public final synchronized void join(long) throws
                                        InterruptedException;
    public final synchronized void join(long, int) throws
                              InterruptedException;
    public void run();
    public void setContextClassLoader(java.lang.ClassLoader);
    public final void setDaemon(boolean);
    public final void setName(java.lang.String);
    public final void setPriority(int);
public static native void sleep(long) throws java.lang.InterruptedException;
public static void sleep(long, int) throws java.lang.InterruptedException;
    public java.lang.String toString();
    public static native void yield();
    public native synchronized void start();
// deprecated methods: do not use.
    public native int countStackFrames();               // deprecated
    public final void stop();                            // deprecated
    public final synchronized void stop(java.lang.Throwable); //deprecated
    public final void suspend();                         // deprecated
    public final void resume();                          // deprecated
}
```

Some Light Relief

The Motion Sensor Solution

A few weeks ago I moved into a new office building. This was good in that it gave me the motivation to discard all the flotsam and jetsam I had not yet unpacked from the previous such move. But it was bad in that there were a few things about the new office that didn't suit me.

Number one on the list was the motion sensor connected to the lights. All modern U.S. office buildings have power-saving features in the lighting, heating, and ventilation. These building services are usually installed above the top floor of a building, but that's another storey. Improving the energy efficiency of buildings is part of the federal government's Energy Star program. Energy Star is the reason that the photocopier is always off when you go to use it. There are Energy Star power management guidelines that apply to desktop computers, too. In fact, I'm responsible for Sun's desktop power management software, so I know how essential it is to allow users to retain control over power-saving features. Apparently, our building designers did not appreciate this.

The light in my new office was wired up to a motion sensor, and it would automatically switch itself off if you didn't move around enough. This was something of a nuisance as there are long periods in the day when the only thing moving in my office are my fingertips flying over the keyboard. Periodically my office would be plunged into darkness, a sharp transition which spoils my concentration. And concentration is very important to programmers.

After that unpleasant business clearing up the glitter trap[3] I installed in the VP's office, it would be futile to ask the facilities guys to replace the motion sensor with a regular switch. So I considered other alternatives. A gerbil on an exercise wheel? They're too high-maintenance, noisy, smelly, and they keep erratic hours. One of my colleagues suggested installing folks from the marketing department in my office and having them flap their arms intermittently, thus getting some productive use out of them. I did consider it, but they have some of the same disadvantages as the gerbil, and may not be so easy to train.

The final answer was one of those kitschy dippy bird things. I position it next to the sensor and dip the beak in the glass of water the morning. It continues to rock

---

3. Booby-trapped ceiling tile, hinged like a trapdoor and piled with confetti on top. The trap is triggered by a thread attached to the back of a desk drawer. It pulls out the safety latch when the drawer is opened. Treat your boss to one today.

backwards and forwards for a good long time, and everyone is happy. I plan to camouflage the dippy bird with a water lily in a dish, which motivates the housekeeping staff to keep the water level topped up. That makes it zero maintenance from my perspective and the closest we'll get to perpetual motion, but at least the lights no longer go out on me.

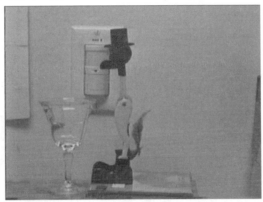

How Do Dippy Birds Work?

Dippy birds work on the same general principle as the steam engine, but with less splendor.

The bird is essentially two balanced globes connected by a small tube, with the lower globe full of a very volatile (easy to evaporate) liquid. You start it going by tipping the upper globe forward into a glass of water, and releasing it back upright.

Water evaporation from the outer surface of the upper globe soon cools it, causing the air inside the upper globe to contract, dropping its pressure, and sucking some of the fluid up the tube from the lower globe. That change in weight distribution causes the bird to tip over, dunk its beak in the water.

A bubble of air travels up the tube, thus releasing the column of fluid to the bottom of the bird. That weight change in turn makes the bird bob upright again.

As the water droplets left on its beak start to evaporate, the pressure in the higher globe drops again, and the cycle repeats until the water source is used up.

You can get a dippy bird of your own from Edmunds Scientific at http://www.edsci.com. Don't forget about the glitter trap, either.

CHAPTER 11

Advanced Thread Topics

In this chapter we will cover the advanced thread topics. Specifically we will explain how threads synchronize with each other when they have data that they must pass to each other. That is, they cannot solve the problem merely by staying out of each other's way, and ignoring each other.

In the last chapter, we saw the easy parts of thread programming as items 1 and 2. This chapter covers Items 3 and 4 from the same list and are the hard parts of thread programming. We are about to plunge into level 3: when threads need to exclude each other from running during certain times.

3. Mutually-Exclusive Threads

Here's where threads start to interact with each other, and that makes life a little more complicated. In particular we use threads which need to work on the same pieces of the same data structure.

These threads need to take steps to stay out of each others' way so they don't each simultaneously modify the same piece of data leaving an uncertain result. Staying out of each other's way is known as *mutual exclusion*. You may not believe mutual exclusion is necessary, or see why if I just say so, so we will motivate the discussion with some code, which you should type in and run.

This code simulates a steam boiler. It defines some values (the current reading of and the safe limit for a pressure gauge), and then instantiates ten copies of a thread called "pressure" storing them in an array. The main routine concludes by waiting for each thread to finish (this is the "join()" statement) and then prints the current value of the pressure gauge. Here is the main routine:

```java
public class p {
    static int pressureGauge=0;
    static final int safetyLimit = 20;

    public static void main(String[]args) {
        pressure []p1 = new pressure[10];
        for (int i=0; i<10; i++)   {
            p1[i] = new pressure();
            p1[i].start();
        }
        try{
            for (int i=0;i<10;i++)
                        p1[i].join();
        } catch(Exception e){ }

        System.out.println(
                "gauge reads "+pressureGauge+", safe limit is 20");
    }

}
```

Now let's look at the pressure thread. This code simply checks if the current pressure reading is within safety limits, and if it is, it waits briefly, then increases the pressure. Here is the thread:

```java
class pressure extends Thread {

    void RaisePressure() {
        if (p.pressureGauge < p.safetyLimit-15) {
            // wait briefly to simulate some calculations
            try{sleep(100);} catch (Exception e){}
            p.pressureGauge += 15;
        }  else ; // pressure too high -- don't add to it.
    }

    public void run() {
        RaisePressure();
    }
}
```

If you haven't seen this kind of thing before, it should look pretty safe. After all, before we increase the pressure reading we always check that our addition won't push it over the safety limit. Stop reading at this point, type in the two dozen lines of code, and run them. Here's what you may see:

```
% java p
   gauge reads 150, safe limit is 20
```

Although we always checked the gauge before increasing the pressure it is over the safety limit by a huge margin! Better evacuate the area! So what is happening here?

This is a classic example of what is called a *data race* or a *race condition*. A race condition occurs when two or more threads update the same value simultaneously. What you want to happen is:

- Thread 1 reads pressure gauge

- Thread 1 updates pressure gauge

- Thread 2 reads pressure gauge

- Thread 2 updates pressure gauge

But it may happen that thread 2 starts to read before thread 1 has updated, so the accesses take place in this order:

- Thread 1 reads pressure gauge

- Thread 2 reads pressure gauge

- Thread 1 updates pressure gauge

- Thread 2 updates pressure gauge

In this case, thread 2 will read an erroneous value for the gauge, effectively missing the fact that thread 1 is in the middle of updating the value based on what it read. For this example we helped the data race to happen by introducing a tenth-of-a-second delay between reading and updating. But whenever you have different threads updating the same data, a data race can occur even in statements that follow each other consecutively.

In this example we have highlighted what is happening and rigged the code to exaggerate the effect, but in general data races are among the hardest problems to debug. They typically do not reproduce consistently and they leave no visible clues as to how data got into an inconsistent state.

To avoid data races, follow this simple rule: Whenever two threads access the same data, they must use mutual exclusion. You can optimize slightly, by allowing multiple readers at one instant. A reader and a writer must never be running at the same time. Two writers must never be running at the same time. As the name suggests, mutual exclusion is a protocol for making sure that if one thread is touching some particular data, another is not. The threads mutually exclude each other in time.

In Java, thread mutual exclusion is built on data Objects. Every Object in the system has its own semaphore[1] (strictly speaking this will only be allocated if it is used), so any Object in the system can be used as the "turnstile" or "thread serializer" for threads. You use the `synchronized` keyword and explicitly or implicitly provide an Object, any Object, to synchronize on. The runtime system will take over and apply the code to ensure that, at most, one thread has locked that specific object at any given instant as shown in Figure 11-1.

The `synchronized` keyword can be applied to a class, to a method, or to a block of code. In each case, the mutex (mutual exclusion) lock of the named object is acquired, then the code is executed, then the lock is released. If the lock is already held by another thread, then the thread that wants to acquire the lock is suspended until the lock is released.

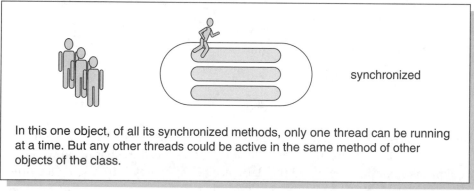

In this one object, of all its synchronized methods, only one thread can be running at a time. But any other threads could be active in the same method of other objects of the class.

Figure 11-1:   Mutually-exclusive threads.

---

1.   A semaphore is the basic operating system primitive that supports mutual exclusion. It's a hardware lock plus a couple of operations on it to maintain a queue of threads and let them through one at a time.

The Java programmer never deals with the low-level and error-prone details of creating, acquiring and releasing locks, but only specifies the region of code and the object that must be exclusively held in that region. You want to make your regions of synchronized code as small as possible, because mutual exclusion really chokes performance. Here are examples of each of these alternatives of synchronizing over a class, a method, or a block, with comments on how the exclusion works.

Mutual Exclusion Over an Entire Class

This is achieved by applying the keyword `synchronized` to a class method (a method with the keyword `static`). Making a class method synchronized tells the compiler, "Add this method to the set of class methods that must run with mutual exclusion," as shown in Figure 11-2. Only one `static synchronized` method for a particular class can be running at any given time, regardless of how many objects there are. The threads are implicitly synchronized using the class object.

In the preceding pressure example, we can make RaisePressure a static synchronized method, by changing its declaration to this:

```
static synchronized void RaisePressure() {
```

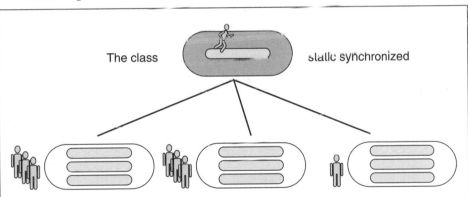

The class — static synchronized

Only one thread can be running in a synchronized static (class) method at a time, no matter how many objects of the class there are.

There is one lock for static synchronized methods, and a different lock for synchronized methods. So a thread could have exclusive access to a static synchronized method, while another thread has exclusive access to a synchronized method, for a given class and object. Yet other threads could be running in methods that are not marked as synchronized at all.

Figure 11-2: Mutual exclusion over a class.

Since there is only one of these methods for the entire class, no matter how many thread objects are created, we have effectively serialized the code that accesses and updates the pressure gauge. Recompiling with this change, and rerunning the code will give this result (and you should try it):

```
% java p
gauge reads 15, safe limit is 20
```

Mutual Exclusion Over a Block of Statements

This is achieved by attaching the keyword "synchronized" before a block of code. You also have to explicitly mention in parentheses the object whose lock must be acquired before the region can be entered. Reverting to our original pressure example, we could make the following change inside the method RaisePressure to achieve the necessary mutual exclusion:

```
void RaisePressure() {
    synchronized(O) {
        if (p.pressureGauge < p.safetyLimit-15) {
            try{sleep(100);} catch (Exception e){} // delay
            p.pressureGauge += 15;
        } else ; // pressure too high -- don't add to it.
    }
}
```

We will also need to provide the object O that we are using for synchronization. This declaration will do fine:

```
static Object O = new Object();
```

We could use an existing object, but we do not have a convenient one at hand in this example. The fields "pressureGauge" and "safetyLimit" are ints not Objects, otherwise either of those would be a suitable choice. It is always preferable to use the object that is being updated as the synchronization lock wherever possible. Recompiling with the change, and rerunning the code will give the desired exclusion:

```
% java p
gauge reads 15, safe limit is 20
```

Mutual Exclusion Over a Method

This is achieved by applying the keyword "synchronized" to an ordinary (non-static) method. Note that in this case the object whose lock will provide the mutual exclusion is implicit. It is the "this" object on which the method is invoked.

```
synchronized void foo { ...  }
```

This is equivalent to:

```
void foo {
   sychronized (this) {
      . . .
   }
}
```

Especially note that making the obvious change to our pressure example will not give the desired result!

```
// this example shows what will NOT work
synchronized void RaisePressure() {
      if (p.pressureGauge < p.safetyLimit 15) {
            try{sleep(100);} catch (Exception e){} // delay
            p.pressureGauge += 15;
      } else ; // pressure too high -- don't add to it.
}
```

The reason is clear: The "this" object is one of the ten different threads that are created. Each thread will successfully grab its own lock, and there will be no exclusion between the different threads at all. Synchronization excludes threads working on the *same* one object; it doesn't synchronize the same method on different objects.

Be sure you are clear on this critical point: Synchronized methods are useful when you have several threads that might invoke methods simultaneously *on the same one object*. It ensures that at most one of all the methods designated as synchronized will be invoked *on that one object* at any given instant.

In this case we have the reverse. We have one thread for each of several different objects calling the same method simultaneously. Some system redesign is called for here.

Note that synchronized methods all exclude each other, but they do not exclude a non-synchronized method, nor a (synchronized or non-synchronized) static (class) method from running.

4. Communicating Mutually-Exclusive Threads

> **Warning: Specialized Threads Topics Ahead**
>
> Here's where things become downright complicated, until you get familiar with the protocol. This is a complicated section, and you don't need to understand it unless you are tackling advanced concurrent programming. You can safely jump over this material to the section called "Swing Threads—A Caution!", returning to study it in depth when you see the words wait/notify in a program.

The hardest kind of programming with threads is when the threads need to pass data back and forth. Imagine that we are in the same situation as the previous section. We have threads that process the same data, so we need to run synchronized. In our new case, however, imagine that it's not enough just to say, "Don't run while I am running." We need the threads to be able to say, "OK, I have some data ready for you," and to suspend themselves if there isn't data ready. There is a convenient parallel programming idiom known as *wait/notify* that does exactly this. Figure 11-3 shows this in four stages.

Wait/notify is a tricky language-independent protocol that has been developed by ingenious minds. Wait/notify wasn't invented by Java, and it's not Java-specific. If you've ever taken a college-level course in operating system concurrency, you have probably seen it. Otherwise, you just need to appreciate it as the accepted solution to this problem. Wait/notify is used when synchronized methods in the same class need to communicate with each other. The most common occurrence of this is a producer/consumer situation—one thread is producing data irregularly and another thread is consuming (processing) it.

Methods in the threads are only ever called from within synchronized code, which means they are both only ever called when a mutex lock is held. However, simple synchronization is not enough. The consumer might grab the lock and then find that there is nothing in the buffer to consume. The producer might grab the lock and find that there isn't yet room in the buffer to put something. You could make either of these spin in a busy loop continually grabbing the lock, testing whether they can move some data, releasing the lock if not. But busy loops are never used in production code. They burn CPU cycles without any productive result.[2] The correct approach lies in the two method calls wait() and notify().

---

2.   Well, OK, one of my colleagues pointed out a research paper that showed a brief busy loop followed by a wait/notify was superior to either used alone. Let's leave research papers out of this for now.

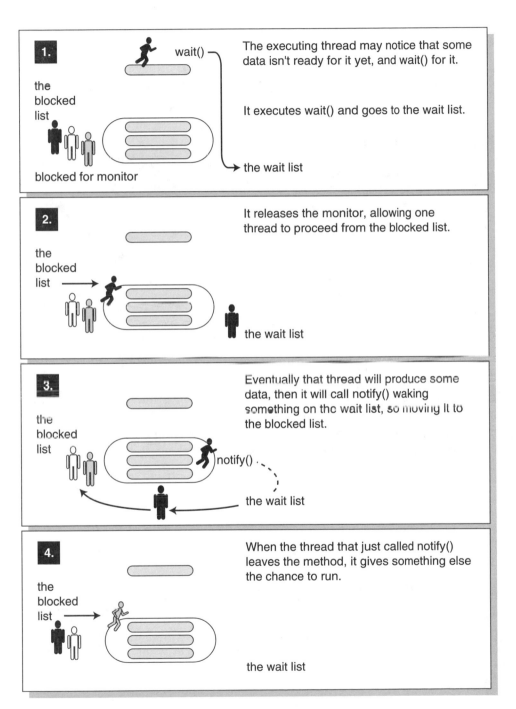

Figure 11-3: Communicating mutually-exclusive threads.

- Wait() says, "Oops, even though I have the lock I can't go any further until you have some data for me, so I will release the lock, and suspend myself here. One of you notifiers carry on!"

- Notify() says, "Hey, I just produced some data, so I will release the lock and suspend myself here. One of you waiters carry on!"

The pseudo-code for the way the producer works is:

```
// producer thread
enter synchronized code (i.e. grab mutex lock)
produce_data()
notify()
leave synchronized code (i.e. release lock)
```

The pseudo-code for the consumer is:

```
// consumer thread
enter synchronized code
while( no_data )
    wait()
consume_the_data()
leave synchronized code
```

The consumer waits in a loop because a different consumer may have grabbed the data, in which case it needs to wait again. As we have already seen, entering and leaving synchronized code is trivially achieved by applying the keyword "synchronized" to a method, so the templates become like this:

```
// producer thread
produce_data()
notify()
```

```
// consumer thread
while( no_data )
    wait()
consume_the_data()
```

Usually the producer is storing the produced data into some kind of bounded buffer, which means the producer may fill it up and will need to wait() until there is room. The consumer will need to notify() the producer when something is removed from the buffer.

The pseudo-code is:

```
// producer thread—produces one datum
while( buffer_full )
     wait()
produce_data()
notify()

// consumer thread—consumes one datum
while( no_data )
     wait()
consume_the_data()
notify
```

The reason we walked through this step-by-step is that it makes the following program a lot easier to understand. If you didn't follow the pseudo-code above, go back over the previous section again. This code directly implements the pseudo-code, and demonstrates the use of wait/notify in communicating mutually-exclusive threads.

There are three classes below. The first is a class that contains a main driver program. It simply instantiates a producer thread and a consumer thread and lets them go at it.

```
public class plum {
  public static void main(String args[]) {
     Producer p = new Producer();
     p.start();

     Consumer c = new Consumer(p);
     c.start();
  }
}
```

The second class is the Producer class. It implements the pseudo-code above and demonstrates the use of wait/notify. It has two key methods: one that produces data (actually just reads the number of millisecs the program has been running) and stores it into an array. The other method, called consume(), will try to return successive values from this array. The value of this set-up is that produce() and consume() can be called from separate threads: they won't overrun the array; they won't get something before it has been produced; they won't step on each other; and neither ever gets in a busy wait.

```
class Producer extends Thread {
    private String [] buffer = new String [8];
    private int pi = 0;   // produce index
    private int gi = 0;   // get index

    public void run() {
        // just keep producing
        for(;;) produce();
    }

    private final long start = System.currentTimeMillis();
    private final String banana() {
        return "" + (int) (System.currentTimeMillis() - start);
    }

    synchronized void produce() {
        // while there isn't room in the buffer
        while ( pi-gi+1 > buffer.length ) {
            try {wait();} catch(Exception e) {}
        }
        buffer[pi&0x7] = banana();
        System.out.println("produced["+(pi&7)+"] " + buffer[pi&7]);
        pi++;
        notifyAll();
    }

    synchronized String consume(){
        // while there's nothing left to take from the buffer
        while (pi==gi) {
            try {wait();} catch(Exception e) {}
        }
        notifyAll();
        return buffer[ gi++&0x7 ];
    }
}
```

Produce () puts a datum in the buffer, and consume () pulls something out to give
it to the consumer.

Those expressions like "pi&0x7" are a programming idiom to mask off the bits of the subscript we want. In this case it is cheap way to let the subscript be incremented without limit, but always get the value modulo 8. It requires the buffer size to be a power of two, which we can easily arrange. If this coding idiom makes you uneasy, change the program to use subscripts that are incremented modulo the buffer size. You'll see it is actually simpler this way.

Finally, the third class is another thread that will be the consumer in this example. It starts off with a common Java idiom: another class is passed into the constructor, and all the constructor does is save a copy of this object for later use. This is the way that the consumer can call the consume() method of the producer.

```
class Consumer extends Thread {
    Producer whoIamTalkingTo;
    // java idiom for a constructor
    Consumer(Producer who) { whoIamTalkingTo = who; }

    public void run() {
        java.util.Random r = new java.util.Random();
        for(;;) {
            String result = whoIamTalkingTo.consume();
            System.out.println("consumed: "+result);
            // next line is just to make it run a bit slower.
            int randomtime = r.nextInt() % 250;
            try{sleep(randomtime);} catch(Exception e){}
        }
    }
}
```

The idiom of passing an object into a constructor that saves the reference to it, for later communicating something back, is a common idiom. You should make especial note of it. Make sure you understand the example above, to see how this is written and used.

The run method of this consumer simply repeats over and over again a get, printing what it got, followed by a sleep for a random period. The sleep is just to give the producer some work to do in adapting to an asynchronous consumer.

When you compile these three classes together and try running them, you will see output like this:

```
% java plum      produced[0] 12
    produced[1]  18
    produced[2]  20
    produced[3]  22
    produced[4]  24
    produced[5]  26
    produced[6]  29
    produced[7]  31
    consumed: 12
    produced[0] 47
    consumed: 18
    produced[1] 213
    consumed: 20
    produced[2] 217
```

And so on. Notice that the producer filled up the buffer before the consumer ran at all. Then each time the slow consumer removed something from the buffer, the producer re-used that now empty slot. And always the consumer got exactly what was stored there with no data race corruption. If this explanation of wait/notify seems complicated, your impression is correct. Programming threaded code is hard in the general case and these methods supply a specialized feature that makes one aspect of it a little easier. The good news is that, for simple producer/consumer code, you don't have to bother with any of this. Two classes, PipedInputStream and PipedOutputStream, in the I/O library can be used in your code to support simple asynchronous communication between threads. We will look at this later.

Wait and notify are methods in the basic class Object, so they are shared by all objects in the system. There are several variants:

```
    public final native void notify();
    public final native void notifyAll();

    public final void wait() throws InterruptedException;
    public final void wait(long time, int nanos) throws
InterruptedException;
    public final native void wait(long timeout) throws
InterruptedException;
```

The difference between notify() and notifyAll() is that notifyAll() wakes up all threads that are in the wait list of this object. That might be appropriate if they are all readers or they are all waiting for the same answer, or can all carry on once the data has been written. In the example there is only one other thread, so notify() or notifyAll() will have the same effect. There are three forms of wait, including two that allow a wait to timeout after the specified period of milliseconds or milliseconds and nanoseconds(!) have elapsed. Why have a separate wait list or wait set for each object, instead of just blocking waiting for the lock? Because the whole point of wait/notifying is to take the objects out of contention for systems resources until they are truly able to run! A notify notifies an arbitrary thread in the wait list. You can't rely on FIFO order.

Interrupting a Thread

Now we have all that theory behind us, let's explain the minor point of why statements like this have an exception handler:

```
try {sleep(randomtime);} catch(Exception e){}
try {wait();} catch(Exception e) {}
```

It's quite easy. One thread can interrupt another sleeping thread by calling its interrupt() method. This will make the interrupted thread wake up and take the exception branch. The thread has to be able to tell the difference between waking up because it has been "notified" and waking up because it has been "interrupted." So the second case is detected by raising the exception InterruptedException in the thread. Statements like sleep(), join(), and wait() that are potentially prone to being interrupted in the middle need to catch this exception, or declare that their method can throw it.

The interrupt() method of Thread sets the interrupt state (a boolean flag) of a thread to "true". A thread can query and clear its own interrupt state using the Thread.interrupted() method. (You call it twice to clear it!) You can query the interrupted state of any thread using isInterrupted(). The method interrupt() will not wake a thread that is waiting to acquire a synchronization lock.

Two further points: In this text, I generally use the parent type Exception, instead of the correct subtype, InterruptedException. This is to minimize the size of the lines in the example. Always catch the narrowest type of exception you can or you may catch more than you bargained for. And do something sensible with it, like print an error message. Finally, note that the interrupt() method was not implemented in the first major release of the JDK.

Synchronized code isn't a perfect solution, because a system can still get into deadlock. Deadlock or *deadly embrace* is the situation where there is a circular dependency among several threads between resources held and resources required. In its simplest form, Thread "A" holds lock "X" and needs lock "Y," while Thread "B" holds lock "Y" and is waiting for lock "X" to become free. Result: that part of the system grinds to a halt. This can happen all too easily when one synchronized method calls another. The "volatile" keyword may also be applied to data. This informs the compiler that several threads may be accessing this simultaneously. The data therefore needs to be completely refreshed from memory (rather than a value that was read into a register three cycles ago) and completely stored back on each access.

Volatile is also intended for accessing objects like real time clocks that sit on the memory bus. It is convenient to glue them on there, because they can be read and written with the usual "load" and "store" memory access instructions, instead of requiring a dedicated I/O port. They can return the current time via a single cycle read, but the value will change unpredictably due to actions outside the program. Volatile isn't really intended for general use on arbitrary objects in applications. The keyword isn't used anywhere in the current version of the runtime library.

Generalized thread programming is a discipline in its own right and one that will become increasingly significant now that Java makes it so easy. The Solaris operating system kernel is a multi-threaded implementation, and multi-threaded is definitely the future trend. Consult the threads books listed at the end of this chapter for a thorough grounding in the topic of threads programming.

Swing Threads—A Caution!

A little later in the text we'll look at the Swing library that you can use to create GUI programs. But here we'll provide a word of warning relating to Threads. The GUI components are maintained on the screen by a thread of their own, separate to any threads that you have running in your code. This GUI thread is called the *event-dispatching thread*, and it handles rendering the GUI components and processing any GUI events that take place. An example of a GUI event would be a mouse click, or a selection from a menu, or a keystroke on a text field.

The problem of thread safety and synchronization occurs in the system libraries just as much as it does in your code. To work properly, **Swing requires that all codethatmightaffectGUIcomponentsbeexecutedfromtheevent-dispatching thread** . As you'll see in chapter 14, events are handled by a callback through an interface to a class you supply. That means that your event-handler code automagically executes in the event-dispatching thread, as it should. But if you then try to create new GUI components in *another* thread of yours, you are bringing hard-to-debug synchronization problems down on your own head.

There is one exception to the rule of doing only GUI work in the event dispatching thread, which fortunately allows us to write our programs in the most natural way. You are allowed to construct a GUI in the application's main method, or the Applet's init method, providing no GUI components are already on the screen from your program and providing you do not further adjust it from this thread after the GUI becomes visible. Most people obey these rules by accident, but you should know about them. For practical purposes, this means if you want to create a new GUI component in response to a GUI event, you should do the instantiation in the code that handles the GUI event. This will be clearer after reading the chapter on event-handling.

If you have to do some further GUI work from one of your own threads, you can put it into the correct thread by using the Runnable interface. There is a Swing utility that takes a Runnable as an argument, and runs it in the event dispatching thread. The code is as follows:

```
Runnable toDo= new Runnable() {
    public void run() {
        // things to do in the event-dispatching thread
        doTheWork();
    }
};
        ...
SwingUtilities.invokeLater( toDo );
```

The advice from the Swing team is, "If you can get away with it, avoid using threads" in GUI programs.

Green Threads Versus Native Threads

You may hear the terms *green threads* and *native threads*. This refers to the Unix implementations of Java. When Java 1.0 first came out on Solaris, it did not use the native Solaris library libthread.so to support threads. Instead it used runtime thread support that had been written in Java for an earlier project code-named "Green." That thread library came to be known as "green threads."

Thread support on WIndows used the native libraries from the start, but on Solaris, green threads were used. That meant that threaded programs running on Solaris didn't get the benefit of the native libraries. In particular, if your Java program was executing on a multiprocessor Solaris system, it was never the case that different threads could execute truly in parallel by being dispatched on different processors. There are other benefits, too, to do with more efficient mapping of I/O system calls.

Clearly people would really like that to happen, so a different team inside Sun cooperated with the main Java team to implement native threads. The native threads team customizes the green threads product within a month or two of FCS. The goal is to fold the work back into the Solaris port so no customization is needed.

Thread Local Storage

Thread local storage is a term for data which is accessible to anything that can access the thread, but which can hold a value that is unique in each thread. A common use for thread local storage is giving a different value to each of several newly-constructed threads that lets them identify themselves (as in, "if I am thread 5,...").

Thread local storage was introduced with JDK 1.2 and allows each thread to have its own *independently initialized* copy of a variable. It's easy enough to give threads their own variables. The bit that's tricky is in getting them initialized with a value that's different in each thread in a thread safe way. It's tough for the thread to do it because each copy of the same thread is (naturally) executing the same code. ThreadLocal objects are typically private static variables used to associate some state with a thread (e.g., a user id, session id, or transaction id).

You typically extend the ThreadLocal class and override variables as needed. Here's how you give your threads an int id. First, the subclass of ThreadLocal is:

```
class MyThreadLocal extends ThreadLocal {
    private static int id = 0;

    protected synchronized Object initialValue() {
        return new Integer(id++);
    }
}
```

If you look at the source code for java.lang.ThreadLocal, you'll see that this just overrides the initialValue() method to make it an Integer. The underlying int is incremented each time the method is called (so everyone gets a different initial value). You should override it to set up whatever value you want the thread local storage to be. Now have a program that creates a few threads:

```
public class t3 {
    private static MyThreadLocal tls = new MyThreadLocal();

public static void main(String args[]) {
    /* Start the threads */
    for(int i=0; i<5; i++) {
        Thread t = new Thread() {
        public void run() {
        System.out.println("I'm thread " + tls.get());
        System.out.println("That's thread " + tls.get());
        } };

        t.start();
    }
    }
}
```

The lines in italic are a thread anonymous inner class. The real point here is our tls thread local storage object. When you try running the program you'll see each different thread has its own value for the integer that MyThreadLocal maintains.

Here is some sample output:

```
java t3
    I'm thread 0
    That's thread 0
    I'm thread 1
    That's thread 1
    I'm thread 2
    That's thread 2
    I'm thread 3
    That's thread 3
    I'm thread 4
    That's thread 4
```

We make it print out the number twice to prove that the tls value is not simply being incremented in the get() routine. You can call the get() routine multiple times from the same thread and get the same value. How can that be?

What's happening behind the scenes is that the class ThreadLocal is maintaining a table of threads versus values. Any thread can get its local value from the table and any thread can set a new value for itself into the table. The access is through tls.get(0) and tls.set(). The ThreadLocal class translates that into table lookup, indexed by thread id. How does it know thread id? It's just the value returned by Thread.currentThread!

Wait—I hear you ask, "How does the initial value get set?" It doesn't! At least, it doesn't until you call ThreadLocal's get() for the first time. When you do, it calls initialValue() as its first action to put a value in the table for you to get.

You could have achieved the same effect without using ThreadLocal by extending Thread, but this doesn't scale. Suppose you have one package that wants to associate a numerical ID with a thread, and a second that wants to associate a userId. If both demand that you use a particular subclass of Thread, you're out of luck. You can't use both at the same time. This is exactly the problem that ThreadLocal solves.

Thread local storage is another thread idiom, and you won't use it in many (perhaps any) of your Java threaded programs. But when you want it, it is there. It's designed and implemented in a particularly clever way that makes it easy for the programmer to use, but also makes the maximum use of Java features to do all the work. The Thread API didn't change at all for the addition of thread local storage. It gets "two thumbs up" from this reviewer. We'll finish the chapter by reviewing memory management, a system feature that relies on threads.

Garbage Collection

Now that you've seen how a Java program can have more than one thing going on at once, we'll look at a practical place where that is used in the runtime library, namely automatic memory reclamation. Languages with dynamic data structures (structures that can grow and shrink in size at runtime) must have some way of telling the underlying operating system when they need more memory. C does this with the malloc() library call. Java does this with the "new" operator.

Conversely, you also need some way to indicate memory that is no longer in use (e.g., threads that have terminated, objects that are no longer referenced by anything, variables that have gone out of scope, etc.) and hand it back to the runtime system for reuse. C does this with the free() library call, C++ uses delete, but Java takes different approach to reclaiming memory.

C and C++ require explicit deallocation of memory. The programmer has to say what memory (objects) to give back to the runtime system, and when. In practice this has turned out to be an error-prone task. It's all too easy to create a "memory leak" by not freeing memory before overwriting the last pointer to it. It can then neither be referenced nor freed, and is lost to further use for as long as the program runs.

Compiler writers for algorithmic languages have the concept of a "heap" and a "stack." Pushing and popping on the stack takes care of dynamic memory requirements related to procedure call and return. The heap is responsible for all other dynamic memory. In Java, that's a lot because object allocation is always from the heap. The only variables allocated on the stack are the local variables of a method.[3]

To avoid the problems of explicit memory management, Java takes the burden off the shoulders of the programmer, and puts it on the runtime storage manager. One subsystem of the storage manager will be a "garbage collector." The automatic reclaiming of memory that is no longer in use is known as "garbage collection" in computer science. Java has a thread that runs in the background, whose task is to do garbage collection. It looks at memory, and when it finds objects that are no longer referenced, it reclaims them by telling the heap that memory is available to be reallocated.

---

3. Java actually has multiple stacks: it starts out with one for Java code and another stack for C native methods. Additional stacks are allocated for every thread created. This aspect of Java requires a virtual memory mapping system to operate efficiently.

Why Do We Need Garbage Collection?

Taking away the task of memory management from the programmer gives him or her one less thing to worry about, and makes the resulting software more reliable in use. It may take a little longer to run compared with a language like C++ with explicit memory management, because the garbage collector has to go out and look for reclaimable memory rather than simply being told where to find it. On the other hand, it's *much* quicker to debug and get the program running in the first place. Most people would agree that in the presence of ever-improving hardware performance, a small performance overhead is an acceptable price to pay for more reliable software.

What is the cost of making garbage collection an implicit operation of the runtime system rather than a responsibility of the programmer? It means that at unpredictable times, a potentially large amount of behind-the-scenes processing will suddenly startup when some low water mark is hit and more memory is called for. This has been a problem with past systems, but Java addresses it somewhat with threads. In a multi-threaded system, the garbage collector can run in parallel with user code and has a much less intrusive effect on the system.

We should mention at this point that there is almost no direct interaction between the programmer and garbage collection. It is one of the runtime services that you can take for granted, like keeping track of return addresses, or identifying the correct handler for an exception. The discussion here is to provide a little more insight into what takes place behind the scenes.

If you want to tell the system that you are done with a data structure, and it can be reclaimed, all you do is remove all your references to it, as in:

```
myBigDataStructure = null;
```

If there are other references to the data structure, it won't be garbage-collected. But as soon as nothing points to it, it is a candidate for sweeping away.

You might be wondering, "What about my threads?" What if you start a thread, and then overwrite the reference to it, as was shown in the thread local storage example a few pages back. Will that be reclaimed? The answer is no. You may not have a reference to the thread, but the runtime system still does, and the thread will not be reclaimed until it falls off the end of its run method. This is also the reason your GUI programs don't terminate when they come to the end of your main() method: there are still some window system threads running.

Garbage Collection Algorithms

A number of alternative garbage collection algorithms have been proposed and tried over the years. Three popular ones are "reference counting," "mark and sweep," and "stop and copy."

Reference counting keeps a counter for each chunk of memory allocated. The counter records how many pointers directly point at the chunk or something inside it. The counter needs to be kept up-to-date as assignments are made. If the reference count ever drops to zero, nothing can ever access the memory and so it can immediately be returned to the pool of free storage. The big advantage of reference counting is that it imposes a steady constant overhead, rather than needing a periodic bursts of the cpu. The big disadvantage of reference counting is that in its simplest incarnation it is fooled by circular references. If A points to B, and B points to A, but nothing else points to A and B they will not be freed even though they could be. It's also a little expensive in multi-threaded environments because reference counts must be locked for mutual exclusion before reference counts are updated.

Adjusting Garbage Collection

Up to JDK 1.1, you used to be able to turn off garbage collection by starting Java with this option:

```
java -noasyncgc  ...
```

One reason for doing this might be to experiment and see how much of a difference in performance it makes, if any. The commandline option is no longer supported in JDK 1.2. You should not turn off garbage collection in a program that may run for an extended period. If you do it is almost guaranteed to fail with memory exhaustion sooner or later.

You can call the following method to request to run the garbage collector at any point you choose.

```
system.gc();
```

The current Java implementation from Sun uses the "mark and sweep" garbage collection algorithm. The marker starts at the root pointers. These are things like the stack, and static (global) variables. You can imagine marking with a red pen every object that can be accessed from the roots. Then the marker recursively marks all the objects that are directly or indirectly referenced from the objects reachable from the roots. The process continues until no more red marks can be placed. The entire virtual process may need to be swapped in and looked at, which is expensive in disk traffic and time. A smart garbage collector knows it doesn't have to bring in objects that can't contain references like large graphics images and the like. Then the "sweep" phase starts, and everything without a red mark is swept back onto the free list for re-use. Memory compaction also takes place at this point. Memory compaction means jiggling down into one place all the memory that is in use, so that all the free store comes together and can be merged into one large pool. Compaction helps when you have a number of large objects to allocate.

Another garbage collection algorithm is "stop and copy." As the name suggests, it stops all other threads completely and goes into a garbage collection phase, which is simplicity itself. The heap is split into two parts: the currently active part and the new part. Each of these is known as a "semi-space." It copies all the non-garbage stuff over into the new semi-space and makes that the currently-active semi-space. The old currently-active semi-space is just discarded completely. Non-garbage is identified by tracing active pointers, just as in mark and sweep.

The advantage of "stop and copy" is that it avoids heap fragmentation, so periodic memory compaction is not needed. Stop and copy is a fast garbage collection algorithm, but it requires twice the memory area. It also can't be used in real time systems as it makes your computer appear to just freeze from time to time.

Finalizers

A "finalizer" is a Java term, related to but not the same as a C++ destructor. When there are no further references to an object, its storage can be reclaimed by the garbage collector.

A finalizer is a method from class Object that any class may override. If a class has a finalizer method, it will be called on dead instances of that class before the memory occupied by that object is re-used. You only need to use finalizers if you have some special reason for wanting to get hold of objects as they are garbage collected. You have no such reason 99.9% of the time, and you can ignore finalizers.

Interpose a finalizer by providing a body for the method finalize() in your class, to override the Object version. It will look like this:

```
class Fruit {

        protected void finalize() throws Throwable {
    // do finalization ...
};
```

It must have the signature shown (protected, void, and no arguments).

The Java Language Specification says:

> The purpose of finalizers is to provide a chance to free up resources (such as file descriptors or operating system graphics contexts) that are owned by objects but cannot be accessed directly and cannot be freed automatically by the automatic storage management. Simply reclaiming an object's memory by garbage collection would not guarantee that these resources would be reclaimed.

Finalization was carried over from the Oak language and justified on the grounds that it would help provide good resource management for long-running servers.

If present, a class's finalizer is called by the garbage collector at some point after the object is first recognized as garbage and before the memory is reclaimed, such that the object is garbage at the time of the call. A finalizer can also be called explicitly. In JDK 1.0 there is no guarantee that an object will be garbage collected, and hence there is no guarantee that an object's finalizer will be called. A program may terminate normally without garbage collection taking place. So you could not rely on a finalizer method being called, you cannot use it to carry out some essential final housekeeping (release a lock, write usage statistics, or whatever). If the method System.runFinalizersOnExit() is called (and accepted by the SecurityManager) before exit, Java 1.1 will guarantee that finalizers are run.

Finally (uh…), don't confuse "final" (a constant) or "finally" (a block that is always executed after a "try()") with "finalize"—the three concepts are unrelated.

Weak References

JDK 1.2 brought in the notion of *weak references*. Weak references allow a program to have a reference to an object, that does not prevent the object from being considered for reclamation by the garbage collector. This is an advanced technique that won't appear in your programs very often. I've been writing Java programs for a few years, and only needed something like this once or twice.

They also allow a program to be notified when the collector has determined that an object has become eligible for reclamation. Weak references are useful for building caches that are flushed only when memory is low, and for scheduling post-mortem cleanup actions in a more flexible way than is possible with the Java finalization mechanism.

If you studied the section on thread local storage a few pages back, you'll already have seen one place where weak references are used. The thread local storage used a table that connected threads with corresponding data items. Each thread has a regular reference to the thing that it uses for a key in the table, and to the entry. The table is a data structure that ties these together, allowing quick retrieval of an entry corresponding to a key. The thread has regular references, but the table just has weak references to all its keys/entries. A key and entry stay around as long as the strong references from the thread do. But when the thread ends, and is garbage collected, now there are only weak references to that key/entry in the table. Voila, key and entry are suddenly and automatically also candidates for garbage collection.

Design Patterns

There's an area of OOP technology that seems to be increasing in importance known as *design patterns*. A design pattern is a set of steps for doing something, like a recipe is a set of steps for cooking something.

There is a key book on the topic called *Design Patterns—Elements of Reusable Object-Oriented Software* by Erich Gamma, Richard Helm, Ralph Johnson, and John Vlissides (Addison Wesley, 1994: ISBN 0-201-63361-2). As the authors explain, design patterns describe simple, repeatable solutions to specific problems in object-oriented software design. They capture solutions that have been improved over time; hence, they aren't typically the first code that comes to mind unless you know about them. They are code idioms writ large. They are not unusual or amazing, or tied to any one language. Giving the common idioms names and describing them, helps reuse. Some common idioms/design patterns are shown in Table 11-1.

Table 11-1: Common Idioms and Design Patterns

Design Pattern	Purpose and Use
Factory Method	Supplies an interface to create any of several related objects, without specifying their concrete classes. The Factory figures out the precise class that is needed and constructs one of those for you.
Adapter	Converts the interface of a class into another interface that the client can use directly. Adapter lets classes work together that couldn't otherwise. Think "hose to sprinkler interface adapter."
Observer	Defines a many-to-one dependency between objects, so that when the observed object changes state, all the Observers are notified and can act accordingly. Think "monitoring the progress of something coming in over the network."
Strategy	Defines a family of algorithms and makes them interchangeable. Strategy lets the algorithm vary independently from the clients that use it. Think "let the client specify if speed or space is the preferred optimization."

The recommended book describes a couple of dozen design patterns, and it repays further study.

Some Light Relief

The Robot Ping-Pong[4] Player

Computer scientists are always looking for hard new problems to solve. They want the problems to be hard enough to be worth tackling, preferably capable of eventual solution, yet easy to describe (so that you don't have to spend too long educating grant-making organizations on what you'll do with their money).

Constructing a robot that could play ping-pong was proposed years ago as a particularly difficult computer science problem requiring solutions in vision, real-time control, and artificial intelligence.

Various other robots have been proposed and constructed over the years: robots that walk on jointed legs, robots that try to learn from their environment, robots that recognize facial expressions and so on. None has quite achieved the popularity of the ping-pong playing robots. A number of them have been built in the engineering labs of the finest universities around the globe. The researchers even published the official rules of robot ping-pong so they could have tournaments. Several of these were organized by Professor John Billingsley, of the E.& E.E. Department at Portsmouth University.

Extracts From The Official Rules of Robot Ping-Pong

Rule 11: Those parts of the robot visible to the opponent must be black including absorption of infrared in the region of 1 micron wavelength.

Rule 17: The judges may disqualify a robot on the grounds of safety, or penalize it for serious breaches of sportsmanship.

Naturally the students at M.I.T. built their share of robot ping-pong players. Some of the best work was done there, in the Artificial Intelligence labs where they used Lisp as the implementation language.

A story, probably apocryphal, is told of an early prototype at M.I.T. After several months of hard work, the students finally coaxed the robot into accurately serving a series of balls from its ball magazine. Eagerly the students reloaded it, and fetched their professor to witness the accomplishment. When the balding professor arrived, he stood expectantly at the far end of the table from the robot and gave the signal to proceed.

---

4.   "Ping-Pong" is a trademark of Parker Brothers.

Cheaters Never Prosper?

Table tennis is full of surprises. In one world championship after the Cultural Revolution, communist China seemed absolutely unbeatable at table tennis. They won every competition in sight, dominating their opponents with surprising spin shots.

Later the truth came out; they were cheating, or at least stretching the rules to breaking point. The communist regime had equipped its teams with special bats. Both sides of the bat looked identical, but they were made out of very different materials. One side of the bat would give a regular shot, the other would help impart a fierce spin. Opponents didn't even know about the trick bats, and had no way of knowing what kind of a shot was coming at them.

The tournament rules were changed. Trick bats were still allowed, but the faces had to be different colors. Communist Chinese domination of the sport came to an end.

As soon as the robot started, it launched a series of hard accurate lobs directly at the professor's cranium. No matter how the professor twisted and ducked, the machine kept him in its sights until at last it was out of balls. When all the tears and laughter had finally stopped, the students were cleared of any wrongdoing. It seems that the robot had been set up to target a large illuminated white patch on the wall representing the opponent, and when the luckless teacher stood within range, his bald brow showed up on the vision system as larger, whiter and shinier, so was preferred. This incident allegedly led to the aforementioned rule 11. No word on whether the robot was nailed under rule 17.

The name of Professor Marvin Minsky of MIT is often attached to this story. Professor Minsky is adamant that he was never bombarded with ping pong balls, but he concedes that an early ball catcher robot did once make a grab for his head. That seems to be the origin of this story.

There is an equally apocryphal coda to this story. It seems that the students went on to enter the robot in one of the tournaments where it played quite well for the first fifteen minutes. Suddenly, unaccountably, the robot froze completely and let several successive balls from the opponent bounce off its chest without even attempting a return serve. Then equally suddenly it started playing again. A furious debugging session was started, only to pinpoint the cause of the problem almost immediately. The robot was driven by Lisp software. It ran perfectly for a quarter hour until it had exhausted its free memory. At that point the garbage collector kicked in. Nothing else could run until the garbage collector had done its thing, not even the code to return a ball. That's why single threaded systems aren't very good at real-time processing. The workaround was simple: reboot the processor immediately prior to each tournament match.

Exercises

1. Give three examples of when threads might be used to advantage in a program. Describe a circumstance when it would not be advantageous to use threads.

2. What are the two ways of creating a new thread in Java?

3. Take your favorite sorting algorithm, and make it multi-threaded. *Hint*: A recursive partitioning algorithm like quicksort is the best candidate for this. Quicksort simply divides the array to be sorted into two pieces, then moves numbers about until all the numbers in one piece are smaller (or at least no larger) than all the numbers in the other piece. Repeat the algorithm on each of the pieces. When the pieces consist of just one element, the array is sorted.

Further Reading

Threads Primer: A Guide to Multithreaded Programming

by Daniel J. Berg and Bil Lewis (SunSoft Press/Prentice Hall, 1995)

ISBN: 0-13-443698-9

The definitive introduction to threads programming.

There is a survey of garbage collection techniques at ftp://ftp.cs.utexas.edu/pub/garbage/bigsurv.ps

A Robot Ping-Pong Player: an experiment in real-time intelligent control

by Russell L. Andersson (Cambridge, MA: M.I.T. Press, 1988)

ISBN: 0-262-01101-8

A rather stuffy book that completely shies away from the essential levity of the subject matter, in favor of dragging in a lot of guff about polynomials and trajectories. Doesn't mention either of the two stories above, but the system was written in C and the book includes several interesting C listings.

Programming with Threads

by Steve Kleiman, Devang Shah, and Bart Smaalders (SunSoft Press/Prentice Hall, 1996)

ISBN: 0-13-172389-8

Written by senior threads development engineers at Sun Microsystems, this is a comprehensive reference work on threads. This book was introduced in February 1996.

CHAPTER 12

Practical Examples Explained

The chapter contains a nontrivial Java program annotated with a running commentary. The program source appears on the CD accompanying this book, so you can look at it without the annotation, and you can try compiling and running it without typing it in.

The program generates anagrams (letter rearrangements). You give it a word or phrase, and it comes back with all the substring combinations that it can find in the dictionary. It uses a wordlist as a dictionary (there's one of those on the CD, too), and you can also specify the minimum length of words in the anagrams that it generates.

For any phrases more than a few letters long, there are a lot more anagrams than you would ever think possible.

Case Study Java Program: Fritter Engine Shunt

Here is an example of running the program on the infamous "surfing the Internet" phrase, specifying words of length four or longer. It finds dozens and dozens of them, starting like this:

```
java anagram "surfing the internet" 4
reading word list...
main dictionary has 25144 entries.
least common letter is 'f'

fritter engine shunt
fritter hung intense
surfeit Ghent intern
surfeit ninth regent
furnish greet intent
furnish egret intent
furnish tent integer
further stint engine
further singe intent
further tinge tennis
further gin sentient
freight nurse intent
freight runt intense
freight turn intense
freight run sentient
freight nun interest
freight sen nutrient
freeing Hurst intent
    ...
```

If you specify a length argument, it will try to use words with at least that many characters, but the final word it finds to complete the anagram may be shorter. This program is written as an application, so there is no issue about accessing files.

Here is the annotated program source:

```
/*
 * Usage: anagram string-to-anagram [[min-len] wordfile]
 * Java Anagram program, Peter van der Linden .
 */

import java.io.*;
```

Note, the "using an interface to hold useful constants" idiom was explained in chapter 8.

```
interface UsefulConstants {
    public static final int MAXWORDS = 50000;
    public static final int MAXWORDLEN = 30;
    public static final int EOF = -1;
```

Note the way a reference variable can be used to provide a shorter name for another object.

We can now say "o.println()" instead of "System.out.println()".

```
    // shorter alias for I/O streams
    public static final PrintStream o = System.out;
    public static final PrintStream e = System.err;
}


class Word {
    int mask;
    byte count []= new byte[26];
    int total;
    String aword;
```

This is an important data structure for representing one word. We keep it as a string, we note the total number of letters in the word, the count of each letter and a bitmask of the alphabet. A zero at bit N means the letter that comes Nth in the alphabet is in the word. A one means that letter is not in the word. This allows for some fast comparisons later on how much overlap there is between these two strings.

```
    Word(String s)   // construct an entry from a string
    {
        int ch;
        aword = s;
        mask = ~0;
        total = 0;
        s = s.toLowerCase();
        for (int i = 'a'; i <= 'z'; i++) count[i-'a'] = 0;

        for (int i = s.length()-1; i >= 0; i--) {
            ch = s.charAt(i) - 'a';
            if (ch >= 0 && ch < 26) {
                total++;
                count[ch]++;
                mask &= ~(1 << ch);
            }
        }
    }
}
```

The program has the following steps:

1. Read in a list of real words, and convert each word into a form that makes it easy to compare on the quantity and value of letters.

2. Get the word or phrase we are anagramming, and convert it into the same form.

3. Go through the list of words, using our helpful comparison to make a second list of those which can be part of a possible anagram. Words that can be part of a possible anagram are those which only have the same letters as appear in the anagram, and do not have more of any one letter than appears in the anagram.

4. Go through our extracted list of candidate words. Choose the most difficult letter (the one that appears least often) to start with. Take words with it in, and call the anagram finder recursively to fill out the rest of the letters from the candidate dictionary.

The class "Word" above is the class that deals with one word from the wordlist and puts it in the special "easy to compare" form.

In several places in this program, characters are used as the basis for an index into an array. The line below, from the Word() constructor, is an example of this.

```
for (int i='a'; i <= 'z'; i++) count[i-'a'] = 0;
```

In C, this is the classic example of something that would work on a system with an ASCII codeset, but fail on an EBCDIC machine since the alphabetic letters are not contiguous in EBCDIC. Java's use of Unicode ensures that this idiom works on all systems. On, say, a Sun Ultra workstation, the following code gives the expected "i = 97".

```
int i='a';
System.out.println("i = " + i);
```

This is because that is the decimal value that represents lower case A in both ASCII and Unicode. However, you would even get the same result on an IBM System/390 where an EBCDIC 'a' is decimal 121, as Java guarantees and requires the internal representation of a character to be 16-bit Unicode. The runtime system will need to do the translation from/to EBCDIC on input/output.

The class "WordList" below is the one that reads in a word list and builds up an entire dictionary of all words in the special format:

```
class WordList implements UsefulConstants {
    static Word[] Dictionary= new Word[MAXWORDS];
    static int totWords=0;

    static void ReadDict(String f)
    {
```

The half dozen lines that follow are a very common idiom for opening a file. This can throw an exception, so we either deal with it here or declare it in the method. It is usually easiest to deal with exceptions closest to the point where they are raised, if you are going to catch them at all.

Here we catch the exception, print out a diagnostic, then re-throw a RuntimeException to cause the program to stop with a backtrace. We could exit the program at this point, but re-throwing the exception ensures that it will be recognized that an error has occurred. We throw RuntimeException rather than our original exception because RuntimeException *does not have to be handled or declared.* Now that we have printed a diagnostic at the point of error, it is acceptable to take this shortcut:

```
        FileInputStream fis;
        try {fis = new FileInputStream(f)};
        catch (FileNotFoundException fnfe) {
            e.println ("Cannot open file of words '" + f + "'");
            throw new RuntimeException();
        }
        e.println("reading dictionary...");
```

It is better not to have any arbitrary fixed size arrays in your code. This one is done for convenience. Removing the limitation is one of the programming challenges at the end of this example. The buffer holds the characters of a word as we read them in from the word list and assemble them.

```
char buffer[] = new char[MAXWORDLEN];
String s;
int r =0;
while (r!=EOF) {
    int i=0;
    try {
        // read a word in from the word file
        while ( (r=fis.read()) != EOF ) {
            if ( r == '\n' ) break;
            buffer[i++] = (char) r;
        }
    } catch (IOException ioe) {
        e.println ("Cannot read the file of words ");
        throw new RuntimeException();
    }
```

This simple looking constructor to create a new Word object actually does the complicated conversion of a string into the form convenient for further processing (the dozen or so lines of code in class Word).

```
        s=new String(buffer,0,i);
        Dictionary[totWords] = new Word(s);
        totWords++;
    }

    e.println("main dictionary has " + totWords + " entries.");
    }

}
```

An example of a class that is both a subclass and an implementation follows. It extends and implements:

```
class anagram extends WordList implements UsefulConstants {

    static Word[] Candidate = new Word[MAXWORDS];
    static int totCandidates=0,
            MinimumLength = 3;
```

We just made it implement UsefulConstants to show that a class can implement and extend at the same time. In practice, since anagram's parent class implements UsefulConstants, that namespace is already present in the subclass.

This is the main routine where execution starts:

```
public static void main(String[] argv)
{
    if ( argv.length < 1 || argv.length > 3) {
        e.println("Usage: anagram  string-to-anagram "
                    + "[min-len [word file]]");
        return;
    }
    if (argv.length >= 2)
        MinimumLength = Integer.parseInt(argv[1]);
```

If the name of a words list isn't explicitly provided as an argument, the program expects to find a file called "words.txt" in the current directory. This will simply be an ASCII file with a few hundred or thousand words, one word per line, no definitions or other information.

```
    // word filename is optional 3rd argument
    ReadDict( argv.length==3? argv[2] : "words.txt" );
    DoAnagrams(argv[0]);
}

static void DoAnagrams(String anag)
{
    Word myAnagram = new Word(anag);

    myAnagram.mask = ~myAnagram.mask;
```

The next couple of lines go through the list of words that we read in, and extract the ones that could be part of the phrase to anagram. These words are extracted into a second word list or dictionary, called "Candidates." The dictionary of Candidate words is sorted.

```
    getCandidates(myAnagram);

    int RootIndexEnd = sortCandidates(myAnagram);
```

The call below says "Find an anagram of the string 'myAnagram,' using this working storage, you're at level 0 (first attempt), and considering candidate words zero through RootIndexEnd".

```
    FindAnagram(myAnagram, new String[50], 0,0, RootIndexEnd);

    o.println("----" + anag + "----");
}
```

This is how a word becomes a candidate:

1. The candidate must only have letters that appear in the anagram (this is the fast overlap test that a bit mask representation provides).

2. It must also be no shorter than the minimum length we specified.

3. It must not be too long.

4. It must not have more of any one letter than the anagram has.

If the word meets all these conditions, add it to the candidates dictionary.

```java
static void getCandidates(Word d)
{
    for (int i = totCandidates = 0; i < totWords; i++)
        if (   (  (Dictionary[i].mask | d.mask) == (int)~0)
            && (   Dictionary[i].total >= MinimumLength   )
            && ( Dictionary[i].total + MinimumLength <= d.total
                 || Dictionary[i].total == d.total)
            && ( fewerOfEachLetter(d.count,
                 Dictionary[i].count) )   )

                Candidate[totCandidates++]=Dictionary[i];

    e.println(
      "Dictionary of words-that-are-substring-anagrams has "
            + totCandidates + " entries.");
//    PrintCandidate();
}


static boolean fewerOfEachLetter(byte anagCount[], byte
entryCount[])
{
    for (int i = 25; i >= 0; i--)
        if (entryCount[i] > anagCount[i]) return false;
    return true;
}

static void PrintCandidate()
{
    for (int i = 0; i < totCandidates; i++)
        o.print( Candidate[i].aword + ", "
                + ((i%4 == 3)?"\n":" " ) );
    o.println("");
}
```

Here's where we start trying to assemble anagrams out of the words in the candidates dictionary.

```
static void FindAnagram(Word d,
                        String WordArray[],
                        int Level, int StartAt, int EndAt)
{
    int i, j;
    boolean enoughCommonLetters;
    Word WordToPass = new Word("");

    for (i = StartAt; i < EndAt; i++) {
       if ( (d.mask | Candidate[i].mask) != 0) {
          enoughCommonLetters = true;
          for (j = 25; j >=0 && enoughCommonLetters; j--)
             if (d.count[j] < Candidate[i].count[j])
                enoughCommonLetters = false;

          if (enoughCommonLetters) {
             WordArray[Level] = Candidate[i].aword;
             WordToPass.mask = 0;
             WordToPass.total = 0;
             for (j = 25; j >= 0; j--) {
```

The cast to (byte) is needed whenever a byte receives the value of an arithmetic expression. It assures the compiler that the programer realizes the expression was evaluated in at least 32 bits and the result will be truncated before storing in the byte.

```
                WordToPass.count[j] = (byte)
                 (      d.count[j] -
                     Candidate[i].count[j] );
                if ( WordToPass.count[j] != 0 ) {
                   WordToPass.total +=
                        (int)WordToPass.count[j];
                   WordToPass.mask |= 1 << j;
                }
             }
             if (WordToPass.total == 0) {
                /* Found a series of words! */
                for (j = 0; j <= Level; j++)
                   o.print(WordArray[j] + " ");
                o.println();
             } else if (WordToPass.total < MinimumLength) {
                   ; /* Don't call again */
             } else {
```

The recursive call to find anagrams for the remaining letters in the phrase.

```
                    FindAnagram(WordToPass, WordArray, Level+1,
                        i, totCandidates);
                }
            }
        }
    }
}


static int SortMask;

static int sortCandidates(Word d)
{
    int [] MasterCount=new int[26];
    int LeastCommonIndex=0, LeastCommonCount;
    int i, j;

    for (j = 25; j >= 0; j--) MasterCount[j] = 0;
    for (i = totCandidates-1; i >= 0; i--)
        for (j = 25; j >= 0; j--)
            MasterCount[j] += Candidate[i].count[j];

    LeastCommonCount = MAXWORDS * 5;
    for (j = 25; j >= 0; j--)
        if (    MasterCount[j] != 0
            && MasterCount[j] < LeastCommonCount
            && (d.mask & (1 << j) ) != 0   ) {
            LeastCommonCount = MasterCount[j];
            LeastCommonIndex = j;
        }

    SortMask = (1 << LeastCommonIndex);

    quickSort(0, totCandidates-1 );

    for (i = 0; i < totCandidates; i++)
        if ((SortMask & ~Candidate[i].mask) == 0)
            break;
```

The root breadth is the first word in the sorted candidate dictionary that doesn't contain the least common letter. Since the least common letter will be hard to match, we plan to start out by using all the words with it in as the roots of our search. The breadth part is that it represents the number of alternatives to start with.

```
        e.println("least common letter is '"
            + (char)(LeastCommonIndex+'a') + "'" );
        e.println("words with least common letter: " + i + " words");
        return i;
    }
```

Sort the dictionary of Candidate words, using the standard quicksort algorithm from any Algorithm book. This one was adapted from page 87 of K&R Edition 2. Again, it shows that recursion is fine in Java.[1]

```
static void quickSort(int left, int right)
{
    // standard quicksort from any algorithm book
    int i, last;
    if (left >= right) return;
    swap(left, (left+right)/2);
    last = left;
    for (i=left+1; i<=right; i++)   /* partition */
        if (MultiFieldCompare( Candidate[i],
                                Candidate[left] ) == -1 )
            swap( ++last, i);

    swap(last, left);
    quickSort(left, last-1);
    quickSort(last+1,right);
}

static int MultiFieldCompare(Word s, Word t)
{
    if ( (s.mask & SortMask) != (t.mask & SortMask) )
        return ( (s.mask & SortMask)>(t.mask & SortMask)? 1:-1);

    if ( t.total != s.total )
        return (t.total - s.total);

    return (s.aword).compareTo(t.aword);
}

static void swap(int d1, int d2) {
    Word tmp = Candidate[d1];
    Candidate[d1] = Candidate[d2];
    Candidate[d2] = tmp;
}
}
```

---

1. This anagram program was based on a C program that my colleague Brian Scearce wrote in his copious free time.

When I wrote the above Java code, my first version had a bug in it. In the following code, I had omitted to subtract 1 from the String length (also I did not check that the character was alphabetic before putting it in the data structure). Instead of looking like this:

GOOD CODE

```
for (int i = s.length()-1; i >= 0; i--) {
        ...s.charAt(i)...
```

I had it like this:

BAD CODE

```
for (int i = s.length(); i >= 0; i--) {
        ...s.charAt(i)...
```

In a C program, this would cause no anagrams to be found, but the program would run to completion. There would not be any indication that an error had occurred, or where. A naive tester would report that the program worked fine. Works fine? Ship it!

In my Java program, this was the output from my first test run:

```
java.lang.StringIndexOutOfBoundsException: String index out of range: 4
        at java.lang.String.charAt(String.java)
        at Word.<init>(anagram.java:35)
        at WordList.ReadDict(anagram.java:77)
        at anagram.main(anagram.java:104)
```

It told me an error had occurred, what the error was, why it was an error, where it happened, and how execution reached that point. Some other languages have this kind of comprehensive runtime checking (Ada comes to mind), but Java is the only one that is also both object-oriented and has a C flavor. At that moment, as they say, I became enlightened.

Some Light Relief

As the old saying goes, "the wonderful thing about standards is there are so many different competing ones from which to choose." Here's a story about how consensus is forged as standards are created. It turns out to be one of those things you shouldn't watch being made.

A few years back, a promising new networking technology called ATM—Asynchronous Transfer Mode—came onto the scene. ATM has not yet fulfilled its promise, but that is not to say it never will. ATM can be viewed as the "scaling up" of broadband ISDN, and ATM standardization attracted the attention of people in both the computer and the telecommunications industry. While there were many areas of cooperation, there were a few areas where the players had very different needs. One of these areas was defining the size of the basic block of bits to be transmitted. Short cells were advantageous for voice traffic; echo suppression works better on brief fragments of speech. So the telcos strongly promoted 16-byte cells.

On the other hand, the computer industry favored longer cells because of better transmission efficiencies (less overhead per byte of data), and recommended 128-byte cells. This went round and round in committee, and where it stopped nobody knows, but when the smoke cleared everyone had compromised a little bit. The telcos were now saying they could accept a 32-byte cell, and the computerheads were going along with 64-byte cells.

Well, it didn't take King Solomon to find the answer to this one. When they realized they still didn't have a standard, they agreed to split the difference, and now ATM has a 48-byte cell size. A CCITT standards committee defined the standard so it doesn't work well with any application! Nobody is happy, but at least we are all fairly treated and equally unhappy.

The compromise of 48 bytes was reached in the CCITT SGXVIII meeting of June 1989 in Geneva, and this is official CCITT recommendation I.361.

Exercises

1. (Complexity: Easy) After it's completed one anagram, make the program go back and prompt for more. Don't make it reload the wordlist!

2. (Complexity: Easy) Modify the program so it doesn't use arrays of fixed size, but uses the Vector class from package "java.util" to grow arrays as needed at runtime. Don't forget to add this line to the start of the program:

   ```
   import java.util.Vector;
   ```

3. (Complexity: Medium) Create a version of the program that has the word list compiled into it. You'll probably want to first write a java program that reads a word list and prints out the array initialization literals for you to edit into your source program. What difference does this make to program start-up time? Run time? Size? (Medium)

4. (Complexity: Medium) Create a version of the program that uses several threads to sort the candidate words. Use a heuristic like "if the partition is larger than 4 elements, spawn a thread to sort it using quicksort, otherwise sort it directly by decision tree comparison." Decision tree comparison means this:

   ```
   if ( a>b )
       if ( a>c )
           if (a>d)  // a is largest
           else      // d is largest, then a
               if (b>c) // order is d,a,b,c
               else     // order is d,a,c,b
   // and so on
   ```

CHAPTER
13

- Embedding a Java Program in a Web Page

- Starting Applet Execution

- Zip Files and Jar Files

- Some Light Relief

All About Applets

"People say you can't compare apples and oranges. But why not? They are both hand-held, round, edible, fruity things that grow on trees."

—*Anonymous*

J ava is a fine general purpose programming language. It can be used to good effect to generate stand-alone executables, just as C, C++, Visual Basic, Pascal or Fortran can. Java offers the additional capability of writing code that can live in a web page and be downloaded and executed when the web page is browsed. Here is why is it useful to put a program in a web page and publish it on the Internet:

- Anyone, on any platform, with any version of any operating system can run the program immediately, without installing anything (think of the client end of e-commerce).

- It is simple to run the program; just browse the web page it is on.

- An applet enables a web page to move beyond a static one-way presentation to live content that can interact with the user. See examples at http://home.augsburg.baynet.de/walter.fendt/physengl/ physengl.htm and http://www.gamelan.com.

Although most commercial applets are written for in-house use, and thus do not have a high public profile, applets remain a vibrant and important capability of Java. If you want to write applications, write applications. If you want to write applets and put them in web pages, write applets and put them in web pages. This chapter explains how to do that.

Reminder on Java Programs

There are three different ways to run a Java executable:

- As a stand-alone program that can be invoked from the command line. This is termed an *application.*

- As a program embedded in a web page to be run when the page is browsed. This is termed an *applet.*

- As a program that is invoked on demand on a server system and that runs in the context of a web server. This is termed a *servlet.*

Applications and applets differ in the execution privileges they have and also in the way they indicate where to start execution.

There are a number of special considerations that apply to applets. These considerations include connecting a class file to a web page, starting execution, screen appearance, parameter passing, and security. Let's take these one by one.

Embedding a Java Program in a Web Page

As mentioned in chapter 1 when we touched on this topic, an applet is a Java program that is invoked, not from the command line, but rather through a web browser reaching that page, or equivalently through the appletviewer that comes with the Java Development Kit. We will stick with using the appletviewer in this chapter because we are trying to teach the language not the use of a browser.

The first thing to understand about applets is how they are run from a web browser. The numerous Applet methods that your applet subclasses can override follow from that.

Web browsers deal with HTML (HyperText Markup Language). There are HTML tags that say, "Set this text in bold," "Break to a new paragraph," and "Include this GIF image here." There is now an HTML tag that says, "Run the Java applet that you will find in this .class file." Just as a GIF image file will be displayed at the point where its tag is in the HTML source, so the applet will be executed when its tag is encountered. The applet will start running even if it is on a part of the page that is scrolled off the screen.

The HTML to Invoke an Applet

An example of the HTML code that invokes an applet is shown below:

```
<h1>A simple applet</h1>

<applet code=myApplet.class width=300 height=50>
            ... a bunch of optional parameters can go here
</applet>
```

The width and height fields are mandatory, and they are measured in units of pixels (dots of resolution on the computer monitor). Applets run in a GUI subclass object, either a `JApplet` (newer Swing GUI) or an `Applet` (older AWT GUI). You have to tell the browser how big a panel the applet takes up on the page.

Figure 13-1 shows how the source, bytecode, and HTML files are related, and how they are used. The classfile must be found in one of these ways:

- **remotely**, in the same directory that served up this HTML page or at the CODEBASE defined in the HTML tag. CODEBASE specifies a different directory or URL that contains the applet's code.

- **locally,** somewhere along the CLASSPATH environment variable or in the standard places the browser will look for code (varies for each browser).

Applets located on remote servers can be accessed just as easily as those stored locally.

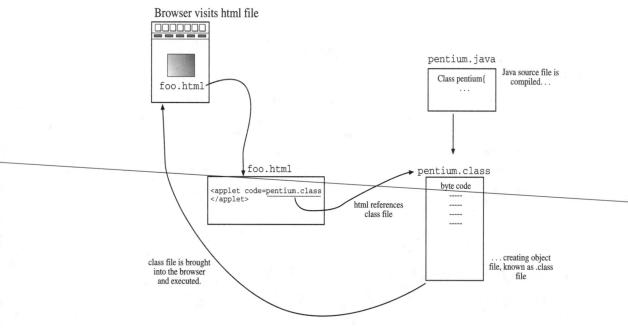

Figure 13-1: The file example.html will run like this.

The full list of tags that can be used for applets is listed at the end of the chapter.

Starting Applet Execution

Applets are started up in a different manner from applications, and the difference is more than just command-line versus HTML file. Applications start execution in a public function called main() similar to the convention used in C. Applets have a different convention, involving overriding certain pre-named functions.

The first thing to note is that an applet is a *window object* that *runs in a thread object*, so every applet will be able to do window-y kind of things and thread-y kind of things. An applet's execution starts using the thready kind of methods that we have already seen.

You always create an applet by extending the Java class javax.swing.JApplet, and providing your own versions of some of the methods. You can override the start() and stop() methods, but you do not call them yourself. This funny stuff exists because of the funny context in which applets live. The class is loaded once, instantiated by the browser (not you), and then subject to repeated execution as the web browser visits and revisits the page containing the applet. The diagram in Figure 13-2 shows how.

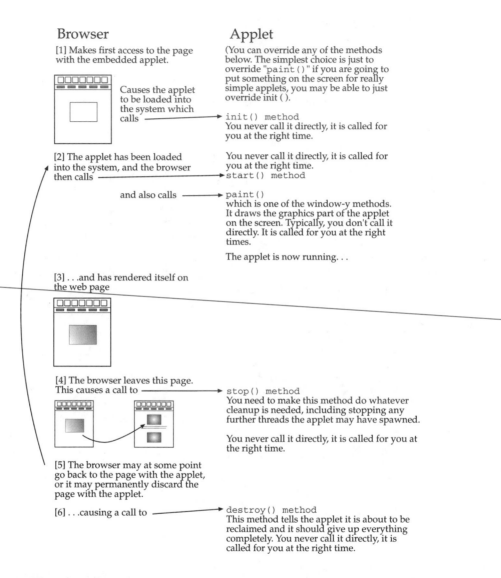

Figure 13-2:   Repeated execution caused by a hypertext web browser.

The method `init()` is a good place to create GUI objects and threads. Similarly you will only override the methods `start()` and `stop()` if you have something that actually needs to be started and stopped, namely threads. You can usually leave `destroy()` alone.

All applets have the same basic code framework that corresponds to the life cycle shown in Figure 13-2. The framework is shown in Figure 13-3 below

```
public class MyApplet extends javax.swing.JApplet {

        public void init() { ... }

        public void start() { ... }

        public void stop() { ... }

        public void paint(Graphics g) { ... }

}
```

Figure 13-3:   Basic code framework of an applet.

It is most important that you override stop() and explicitly stop any threads in the applet. Otherwise, they will continue to run and consume browser cycles even after you leave the page. Table 13-1 summarizes the applet methods, and when they are called. You do not have to have threads in your applets.

Table 13-1: Summary of Key Applet Methods

Method	Description
void init()	Called when the applet is first loaded into memory. Typically you override it with one-time initialization code.
void start()	Called each time the browser visits the page containing this applet. Typically you override it to start or resume any threads the applet contains.
void stop()	Called when the browser leaves the page containing this applet. Typically you override it to stop or suspend any threads the applet contains.
void paint(Graphics g)	Will be called by the window system when the component needs to be redisplayed. You will not call this. You will override this method with your code to dynamically change the appearance of the screen.
void run()	Nothing to do with applets. This is the routine in which thread execution starts, if the applet has one.

We won't use threads in applets here, for simplicity. They can be used if you want. We will show them in a later chapter.

In JDK 1.2, the GUI appearance was greatly improved by a new library called the Swing library, which supplements the original AWT library. The AWT Applet class is extended by the Swing JApplet class. All the basic applet functionality still comes from the java.applet.Applet class which is shown below.

```
public class java.applet.Applet extends java.awt.Panel {
// lifecycle methods:
   public java.applet.Applet();
   public void init();
   public void start();
   public void stop();
   public void destroy();

// media related methods
   public java.applet.AudioClip getAudioClip(java.net.URL);
   public java.applet.AudioClip getAudioClip(java.net.URL, String);
   public java.awt.Image getImage(java.net.URL);
   public java.awt.Image getImage(java.net.URL, java.lang.String);
   public static final java.applet.AudioClip newAudioClip(java.net.URL);
   public void play(java.net.URL);
   public void play(java.net.URL, java.lang.String);

// get information methods
   public java.lang.String getParameter(java.lang.String);
   public java.lang.String getParameterInfo()[][];
   public boolean isActive();
   public java.applet.AppletContext getAppletContext();
   public java.lang.String getAppletInfo();
   public java.net.URL getCodeBase();
   public java.net.URL getDocumentBase();
   public java.util.Locale getLocale();
   public void resize(int, int);
   public void resize(java.awt.Dimension);
   public final void setStub(java.applet.AppletStub);
   public void showStatus(java.lang.String);
}
```

The java.swing.JApplet class has this appearance:

```
public class javax.swing.JApplet extends java.applet.Applet
    // inherits all the Applet methods above, plus
    // about 2 dozen methods of its own relating to Swing (omitted)
    ...
}
```

Screen Appearance of an Applet

Here is an example of the minimal applet:

```
public class Message extends javax.swing.JApplet {
    public void paint(java.awt.Graphics g) {
        g.drawString("Yes!", 25, 35);
    }
}
```

An HTML suitable for this program might be this:

```
<applet code=Message.class width=200 height=100> </applet>
```

Now put it in a file called Message.html. Compile the Java program.

```
javac Message.java
```

Run it under the appletviewer with the following command:

```
appletviewer Message.html
```

A window like the following will appear.

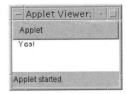

Figure 13-4: A minimal applet.

If you don't see this, step through the installation instructions again, checking that you have done everything correctly. You can also run this in your browser by directing it to browse the HTML:

```
netscape file:///home/linden/Java/Message.html
```

Because an applet is a windowing thing (we will get back to more formal terminology eventually), it does not use the standard I/O that we have been using up till now for interactive I/O. Instead it uses the facilities that are available to windows, like drawing a string at particular coordinates. The coordinate system of every window has the origin in the top left as shown in Figure 13-5.

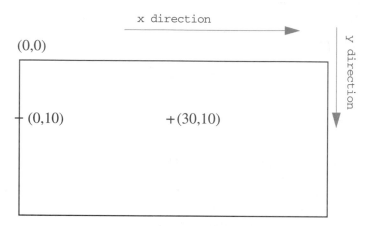

Figure 13-5: Every window's coordinates originate in the top left corner.

What are the other facilities that are available to windows? We will discuss these in greater depth in the later chapters that deal with the Abstract Window Toolkit. The AWT class called Container contains the superclass from which JApplet is (eventually) derived. Container has the method paint() which is called by the Window toolkit whenever the applet panel needs to be refreshed. By providing our own version of paint, we override Container's version.

You can look at the source for method drawString() in file java/src/awt/Graphics.java.

```
public void paint(Graphics g) {
    g.drawString("text to display", x_pos, y_pos);
}
```

The Graphics class has many methods concerned with rendering a shape, line, or text onto the screen. It will also let you select colors and fonts.

The convention throughout Java is that class names begin with a capital letter, and method names start with a lower case letter, but subsequent words in the name are capitalized. This leads to odd looking names like "drawString" that make it seem as though someone had a previous job writing ransom notes wItH rAndOmlY caPitALiZeD LeTteRs. ("wE HaVe yOuR MiSsinG piXeL. seNd $10K iN sMaLL BilLS. dO nOt TeLl tHe PolICe. ThEy'Re sTuPId.")

When the compiler complains that it can't find one of the library methods, your first thought should be "did I get the capitals right?" It is not always consistent in that we have MenuBar and yet Scrollbar in the window toolkit. Especially watch out for the "instanceof" operator that uses no capitals. In cases like this, it's better to always be consistent or always be inconsistent, but not keep changing between the two.

We mentioned that some programs need to explicitly start threads, rather than have them created and started in one operation. An applet running in a web browser is one of those programs. It allows a closer fit to the "go back to a page you already visited and which is likely to still be loaded" model. That is why init() (one-time initialization) is separated from start() (called every time the page is accessed).

Speed up Applet Development!

When you start creating applets, you usually need at least three files before anything can happen: a .java source file, a .class bytecode file, and a .html file. If you aren't careful with your naming, you'll lose track of what's where.

One suggestion (for experts only) that is useful while the code is under development is to put the HTML commands in the java source file, inside a comment, like this:

```
// <applet  code=Message.class  height=100  width=100>
// </applet>
public class Message extends javax.swing.JApplet {
    public void paint(java.awt.Graphics g) {
        g.drawString("Yes!", 10,10);
    }
}
```

It offers two advantages: First, you cut out the need for a separate HTML file (so you don't waste time flipping back and forth between HTML file and source file in the editor); and secondly, you can put the parameters for the applet right in the file with the applet code (so it's easy to check you've got them right). Then you invoke appletviewer on the source file, like so:

```
appletviewer  Message.java
```

This works because browsers just read arbitrary text files, looking for tags. They don't care if the file contains source code as well.

Browser Summary

The browser will automatically instantiate an object of your Applet subclass, and make certain calls to get it running.

You can overload some of the called methods. The methods init() and paint() are the ones you will mostly overload, unless you have threads in the applet, when you will want to overload start() and stop(), too.

Typically you never call any of these methods. They are called for you by the window system/browser at appropriate times. As the browser visits pages and moves away from them, these predefined Applet methods are invoked.

Passing Parameters to Applets

Just as we have command line arguments for applications, there is a similar feature for passing arguments from the HTML file to the applet it invokes. Parameters are indicated by an HTML tag of this form:

```
<param     name=namestring     value=valuestring>
```

The param tags come after the <applet> tag and before the </applet> tag. An example of some actual parameters in an applet version of the anagram program might be:

```
<applet  code=anagram.class  width=500, height=500>
    <param    name=datastring value="surfing the net">
    <param    name=wordfile   value="words.txt">
    <param    name=minsize    value="2">
</applet>
```

It does not matter if strings are quoted or not, unless the string contains embedded white space. Inside the program you call getParameter() with the name as an argument, and it returns the string representing the value. If there isn't a parameter of that name, it returns null. Here is an example:

```
String s = getParameter("minsize");
// parse to an int.
int minsize = Integer.parseInt(s);
```

Notice that this follows the same conventions as main(String argv[])—all arguments are passed as strings, and programmers need to do a little processing to get the values of arguments that are numbers.

To pass a double as a parameter to an applet, the HTML tag would look like this:

```
<param name=peach    value="3.1" >
```

The code to retrieve it would be:

```
String s = getParameter("peach");
double d = Double.parseDouble(s);
```

JDK 1.2 introduced a parseDouble method to create a double from a String. Before that you had to create a double object from the String, then extract the double value from that.

Build in Debugging Help

You can put a main method in any class—even a class that runs as an applet or a class that isn't the main routine of your application. Like any other method that isn't called, it doesn't do any harm.

Some programmers recommend adding a main() routine to all classes. This main should just be a test driver to check the functionality of that class. When you are debugging your system, you'll find it most convenient to test individual classes this way. Just leave it there—it won't hurt in the finished version of the system.

Alternatively, you can use a main() routine in a different class as a different entry point to your program allowing the program to do slightly different things depending on which class you tell the interpreter to start in. You can vary this from run to run.

Zip Files and Jar Files

This section explains how you can group together any number of files into one zip file. There are two reasons for doing this: a small reason and a big reason. The small reason is that, if you have a Java program that consists of five `.class` files, three `.jpg` files, four `.au` files, and a GIF file, that's a lot of files to remember to move onto your web server. It's much more convenient for passing the program around if you can roll all the pieces up into one large archive file, just as the Windows ZIP or the Unix tar utilities do.

The second, more important reason, for grouping together lots of little files into one large file is that HTTP (the protocol used between a web server and a client browser) is an inefficient protocol. It takes a large amount of effort on both server and client side to set up an HTTP connection. For files of just a few K, the time and effort to set up the connection can easily outweigh the time to transmit the file. And not just by a little, but by a lot. As with disk I/O, one large read of 100N bytes is far less time and effort than the sum of 100 small reads of N bytes each. For an individual client, the applets arrive and start running faster. At the server end, the server can handle many more client requests at a time, and throughput rises.

JDK 1.0.2 lets you wrap up several class files in a `.zip` file, using the standard PKZIP format popularized on PCs. Zip file format is a combination of compression and aggregation, though zip file compression was not supported in JDK 1.0.2. An example of the use of zip files in JDK 1.0.2 is the core Java libraries which were put into a file called `classes.zip`, to which your $CLASSPATH environment variable had to point. We won't dwell on zip files in JDK 1.0.2 because things are better and easier in JDK 1.1.

PKZIP

PKZIP stands for Phil Katz ZIP. The zip part just means "bringing things together speedily" as a clothing zip fastener does. Phil Katz was the programmer who, several years before Java, developed the zip file format, the compression format, and `.zip` file extension and put it all in the public domain for the benefit of everyone in the industry. Java now has a built-in API to read and write zip files; some examples of this are in the I/O chapter later in the book.

Keep Your Software in a Jar

In JDK 1.1, the format was extended to a JAR, or "Java ARchive." A jar file contains a group of files in zip format with compression turned on. You can create your own jar files by using standard WinZIP, other software, or the `jar` utility that comes with JDK 1.1. The `jar` program has a command line that looks like this in general form:

```
jar [ options ] [manifest] destination input-file [input-files]
```

The options that `jar` takes are similar to those of `tar`—the Unix tape archive utility—but the formats are different, and tar files are not used in Java. JDK 1.2 also introduced an option to update (replace a file in) an existing Jar file. To create a compressed archive of all the class files and `.jpg` files in a directory, you would use the command

```
jar cvf myJarFile.jar *.class *.jpg
```

An example of the applet tag used with a jar file follows:

```
<APPLET   ARCHIVE=myfile.jar
          CODE=myapplet.class
          WIDTH-600    HEIGHT=250>
</APPLET>
```

These lines will use an applet called `myapplet` that can be found in the jar file `myfile.jar`. You can supply several jar file names in a comma-separated list.

Removing the Contents from a Jar

As we mentioned earlier, a jar file can contain media files as well as code. The class files will be extracted automatically when the class loader sees a jar file in an applet tag such as:

```
<applet
     archive=Example.jar
     code=Example.class
     height=200 width=250>
</applet>
```

The noncode files, however, like `.gif`, `.au`, or `.jpg` must be extracted a slightly different way. The method `getImage (getCodeBase(), image_name)`, which works for individual image files in the HTML directory, doesn't work when the file is in a jar.

This applet example shows how to pull a media file out of a jar file. The key idea is to use the class runtime-type information to create a URL for the media file (this line is shown in bold in the example). The rest of the code is the magic associated with displaying an image and is described in the chapter on graphics programming. The approach also works for .au (sound) files and .gif files.

First, create our example source file called view.java with this HTML and code inside it.

```
 /* <applet
        archive=view.jar     code=view.class
        width=350            height=450>
   </applet>
*/
import java.net.*;
import java.awt.*;
import java.awt.image.*;
import java.applet.*;

public class view extends Applet {
    String MyFileName = "titan.jpg";
    URL MyURL;
    Image MyImg;
    ImageProducer MyImgProd;

    public void init() {
        Toolkit tool = Toolkit.getDefaultToolkit();
        MyURL = getClass().getResource(MyFileName);
        try {
            MyImgProd = (ImageProducer) MyURL.getContent();
        } catch (Exception ex) {
            System.out.println(ex.getMessage());
        }
        MyImg = tool.createImage( MyImgProd );
    }

    public void paint(Graphics g){
        g.drawImage(MyImg, 10, 10, this);
    }
}
```

The code is on the CD under book/ch13. This works because an object's class knows about its classloader, and its classloader knows how and where the class file was brought in from a file.

Compile the code, and create the jar file by entering these commands:

```
% javac view.java

% jar -cvf view.jar  view.class titan.jpg
adding: view.class (in=1418) (out=781) (deflated 44%)
adding: titan.jpg (in=59698) (out=59340) (deflated 0%)
```

Then, you can run the program by using the appletviewer:

```
% appletviewer view.java
```

The applet will successfully read and execute the code from the jar file. It will then extract the JPEG file from the jar and display it on the screen like this:

Figure 13-6: Displaying a JPEG extracted from a jar file.

Be careful: the appletviewer may just wait forever if you send it to look for a file that isn't there. You must make sure that your applet tags, jar name, and file names are all absolutely correct.

Also, if you are using the programmer's shortcut of placing the HTML into the source file, then it's better to use `/*` to open a comment at the beginning, and `*/` to close a comment at the end of all the tags. The browsers and applet viewers get confused if they find `//` on lines interspersed with applet tags.

Finally, don't forget that once you put some code in a jar, it's not enough to recompile when you change something. You must also rebuild the jar file with the new `.class`; otherwise, you'll continue to get the old version of the program.

Last, note that `getClass().getResourceAsStream()` should be used for the Netscape 4.x browsers. Netscape has disabled getResource() under some circumstances due to their own security considerations.

Applications Can Be Stored in Jars, Too

This chapter has shown several examples of applets run from a jar file. You can also store an application in a jar file, and run it without unpacking the contents. The command will execute the application contained in the jar file.

```
java -jar  MyApp.jar
```

For this to work, the manifest header in the jar file needs to which class has the main() routine where you want execution to start. You provide this information with the Main-Class header, which has the general form:

```
Main-Class: MyMainClassName
```

Put that line of text into a file called "wheretostart.txt". When you create the jar file, ensure that the information gets put into the manifest of the jar by using the command

```
jar cmf wheretostart.txt write.jar write.class
```

This is a JDK 1.2 feature.

Some Light Relief

Did Apple Copy Xerox?

The Apple Macintosh is a marvellous personal computer that featured a windowing interface right from its introduction in 1984. The Macintosh popularized the use of windows, menus, and mouse pointing devices very effectively. But where did the Macintosh team get the idea from?

There's a story in wide circulation that the Macintosh GUI was ripped off wholesale from Xerox! Before starting the Macintosh project, Steve Jobs visited the Xerox Research Center in Palo Alto California (PARC), and was shown a GUI interface running on the Xerox Star computer. Conspiracy theorists then claim that Steve Jobs realized the potential of the Xerox technology and pinched the ideas (and later some of the people) for the Macintosh.

How shocking. But what are the facts? One indication that things might not have happened quite that way, is the marked lack of innovation at Apple since Steve Jobs was pushed out in 1985. (In a surprise move, he was pushed back in again in December 1996. It's hard to keep up with the latest developments at Apple!) The stagnation at Apple without Jobs suggests that Jobs may well have been an innovator rather than a copier. On the other hand, it might just mean that it is really hard to get anything new done in a huge corporation. Since Jobs and many of his key developers left, the product improvement focus at Apple has largely centered around more memory/bigger screen/newer processor. These are just pedestrian "mid-life kickers" as we call them in Silicon Valley. The one totally new product, the Newton personal digital assistant, was an unmitigated disaster. Ironically, the failure of the Newton led to the firing of John Sculley, the Pepsi executive who had pushed out Jobs. Users don't want small products of increased complexity. They want decreased complexity in existing products.

But back to the Macintosh GUI, the man who started the Macintosh project (named for his favorite type of eating apple, modified to avoid trademark issues—those fruit farmers are apparently fanatically litigious) was Jef Raskin. The Macintosh project started early in 1979, long before Jobs ever visited Xerox. In fact, the reason Jobs finally went to PARC was that Raskin asked him to, to help convince Jobs that a WYSIWYG environment was the way to go.

Raskin had been a professor and computer center director at the University of California at San Diego and a visiting scholar at the Stanford Artificial Intelligence Laboratory (SAIL). Raskin was often a visiting academic at the Xerox Research Center in its first few years, but to avoid any possible conflict of interest Raskin stopped visiting PARC after he joined Apple in 1978.

Raskin was an early originator of the idea that user interface and graphics were of primary importance to the future of computing. His 1967 Computer Science thesis argued that computers should be all-graphic; that we should eliminate character generators and create characters graphically and in various fonts; that what you see on the screen should be what you get; and that the human interface was more important than mere considerations of algorithmic efficiency and compactness. The thesis was titled "The Quickdraw System" which is the name of the Macintosh GUI drawing toolbox.

At Apple, Raskin built on his own earlier work to create click-and-drag for moving objects and making selections. Xerox used a click-move-click paradigm that was prone to error. Raskin hired a former student of his, Bill Atkinson, who extended Raskin's work to pull-down menus.

Larry Tesler was the first PARC ex-employee to join Apple, and some people have claimed that he brought the selection-based editor with him. In reality the concept dates back to an editor Raskin had designed many years before in 1973 while at Bannister & Crun. However, Raskin had discussed his ideas with those of similar interests at Xerox, so perhaps some of the technology transfer was actually from future Apple employee to Xerox!

In summary, contrary to the widely-accepted version, Steve Jobs didn't totally rip off the Macintosh GUI from a visit to Xerox. On the contrary, key elements of the design came from Jef Raskin, a computer science professor who had evangelized WYSIWYG designs for many years, including inside Xerox. Other parts of the Macintosh interface originated with Bill Atkinson and Bud Tribble who had been students at UCSD when Raskin taught there.

The moral of this story is. . .what—you expect every story to end with a moral? Too bad. This one doesn't have one. Raskin did comment on the inaccuracies in the common story, and tried to get his perspective down on paper in "Holes in the Histories" (the fourth reference below in the following list). The only other point to mention is that Raskin gave his three children palindromic names: Aza, Aviva, and "Sums are" Erasmus (not sure about that last one. . .).

Further References

1. Raskin, Jef. "Down With GUIs!," *Wired*, December 1993, pg. 122.

2. Stross, Randall E. "Hubris of a heavyweight. A review of Steve Jobs & the NeXT Big Thing," *IEEE Spectrum*, July 1994, pp. 8-9.

3. Raskin, Jef. "Intuitive Equals Familiar," *Communications of the ACM*, Volume 37:9, September 1994, pg. 17.

4. Raskin, Jef. "Holes in the Histories," *Interactions 1.3*, July 1994, pg. 11.

HTML Applet Tags

The full list of tags that can be used for applets is:

```
<applet
    code=classfilename
    width=integer_pixels
    height=integer_pixels
    [archive=archivefile [,archivefile]]
    [codebase=applet-url]
    [vspace=integer_pixels]
    [hspace=integer_pixels]
    [align=alignment]
    [name=some_name]
    [alt="You need a browser that understands Java" ]
>
```

The applet tag can be followed by zero or more parameter tags, with the general form of attribute name/value pairs.

```
<param name=param_name  value=param_value >
```

Here is an example:

```
<param name=soundfile value=teletubbies.wav>
```

You can also put some alternate HTML here, which will only be formatted if the browser doesn't understand the applet tag. Finally, the applet ends with an "end applet" tag:

```
</applet>
```

Confusingly, letter case is not significant for any HTML tags or attribute names, but it is significant for some of the arguments they take (e.g., the name of the class file). When in doubt make uses of uppercase and lowercase consistent.

The attributes have the following meanings:

CODE=*CLASSFILENAME*
> This attribute is required, and names the class file that is to be executed. *Note:* This must be just a single file name, with no part of a longer path prefixed to it. So, "foo.class" is good, but "bin/foo.class" is bad.

WIDTH=*INTEGER_PIXELS*
HEIGHT=*INTEGER_PIXELS*
> These two attributes are required, and say how large a space in the browser the applet takes up.

All the remaining attributes are optional.

ARCHIVE=*ARCHIVEFILE* [,*ARCHIVEFILE*]

> This attribute allows an applet to bundle all its class files and media files into one ZIP or jar archive. The browser will retrieve the entire in one big transaction, rather than many slow, smaller transactions.

CODEBASE=*APPLET-URL*

> This attribute allows you more flexibility in where applet class files are located. You can provide a URL identifying a directory in which the browser looks for the class files this applet loads. Since it is a URL, the directory can be specified anywhere on the Internet, not just on the server or client system. If this attribute is omitted (a common occurrence), the class files must be in the same directory as the HTML file.

VSPACE=*INTEGER_PIXELS*
HSPACE=*INTEGER_PIXELS*

> These two attributes allow you to specify the size of the blank margin to leave around the applet in the browser. These two tags and the one below are similar to the attributes of the same names used with the <IMG> tag.

ALIGN=*ALIGNMENT*

> This attribute allows you to control where the applet appears on the page. There are several possible alignment values: "left," "right," "top," and "middle" are popular choices.

NAME=*SOME_NAME*

> The name provided here is associated with the applet. It can be used by other applets running on the same page to refer to the applet and communicate with it.

ALT=*SOME_TEXT*

> This attribute specifies the text to be displayed in the (unlikely) event that the browser does not understand Java.

The <applet> tag was invented specifically for Java, but it is possible that people will want to download other types of executable content. It would be a poor idea to have to invent a new tag for each new type of downloadable program. Accordingly, the <embed> tag has been proposed to replace the <applet> tag. The main difference is that <embed> allows you to put a full URL on the beginning of the "class=" attribute (and it calls it "src=," not "class="). As a result the codebase attribute would not be needed.

Exercises

(Medium) Make the anagram application into an applet.

1. The scheme for passing parameters to applets from HTML is very flexible and in fact allows you to pass an arbitrary number of parameters. Let's say you give your HTML parameters names that end with a number in sequence, like this:

```
<param  name=myparam1   value="some value" >
<param  name=myparam2   value="another value" >
<param  name=myparam3   value="25.2" >
```

It's then easy to concatenate a count onto the name, as an argument to getParameter like this:

```
next = getParameter( "myparam"+i );
i++;
```

That way you can keep retrieving parameters until null is returned. Write a program with the two statements above in a loop to demonstrate this. Print out the value of the parameters received.

2. Write an applet that reads a file. Run it in the appletviewer and set the properties so it runs successfully. Then sign it and configure a browser to run it.

3. Distinguish between "init()" and "start()" in an applet.

4. Does HTML have to be in a file with the extension .html or .htm? Where else might you put it and why?

CHAPTER
14

JDK 1.2 Security

T he term "security" means controlling the resources of your computer system: the files, screen, peripherals, and CPU cycles. Even on a single-user system, like Windows 3.11, this is an issue because a computer virus can destroy your valuable work. Some form of security check is especially needed with applets because they are executed automatically on your behalf. Just by browsing a web page embedded applets are sent over and executed on your system. Without a security check an applet could, either through maliciousness or poor programming, corrupt your files or transmit the contents to points unknown.

Viruses are already too prevalent in the PC world. A virus was recently detected that even infected the MS-Word word processor by taking advantage of an "execute macros on start-up" feature. MS-DOS, Windows 3.11, and Windows 95 and 98 have essentially no security. The Microsoft ActiveX framework has security in terms of identification through code signing, but no security in terms of resource access permission. A malicious or even simply buggy program can access your entire system, even if you wanted only to give it read access to one specific temp directory. This security deficiency makes ActiveX (or OLE, or DNA, etc.; whatever Microsoft's name of the month currently is) unsuitable for use across the Internet.

Right from the start, Java improves on this situation by defining and supporting several levels of resource access control. Some of Java's security is user-configurable, and some of it (to avoid a breach of security) is not. Here's how security has evolved over the different Java releases:

- All Java releases feature *language security* (strong typing, no pointer arithmetic, etc.) and *runtime type checking* of array indexes, casts, references, etc., as well as *verification* of remotely-loaded bytecode.

- JDK 1.0.2 runs applets in the *sandbox*—a restricted environment that denied applets access to client system resources like local files

- JDK 1.1 introduced the ability to *sign* applets, meaning "provide a cryptographic assurance that the applet comes from a source you trust". Signed applets can run with the same privileges as local applications. All code is still subject to the language and runtime security features, of course.

- JDK 1.2 brings in a number of improvements. All code, regardless of whether it is local or remote, an applet or an application, can now be made subject to a *security policy.* Programmers or users also have finer control over the permissions granted to code. You can give a program write access to a directory, but not read access.

  The *security policy* is a list of all the possible permissions available for code (read access, write access, which directories, etc.), matched with a list of the various URLs code can come from and the various organizations from which you will accept signed code. You apply aspects of the policy to bundles of classes, called *domains*. System administrators can put a central security policy in place, and users can customize it for their individual needs.

The philosophy has been to start off with many restrictions on access, and to selectively allow greater flexibility with control in successive Java releases. In the next sections we will look at the sandbox, code signing, and the security manager (which is how the security policy is applied).

The Sandbox

Default Capability Differences

Note that there is a difference in default capabilities between an applet loaded from over the net and an applet loaded from the local file system. Where an applet comes from determines what it is allowed to do. An applet from over the net is loaded by the applet class loader, and it is subject to the sandbox restrictions enforced by the applet security manager.

An applet stored on the client's local disk and accessible from the CLASSPATH is loaded by the file system loader. These applets are permitted to read and write files, load Java libraries and exec processes. Local applets are not passed through the bytecode verifier, which is another line of defence against code from the net.

The verifier checks that the bytecode conforms to the Java Language Specification and looks for violations of the type rules and namespace restrictions. The verifier looks at individual instructions to ensure that:

- There are no stack overflows or underflows. That is, every path through a basic block leaves the stack pushed or popped by the same amount. Thus you can keep track of stack depth and avoid illegal accesses.

- All register accesses and stores are valid.

- The parameters to all bytecode instructions are correct.

- No illegal type conversions are attempted.

Code Signing

Now that we have seen how to put Java applets into jars, the next step is to describe how jars can be used to convey the notion that an applet is trusted. Since an applet can be downloaded from anywhere on the net just by browsing a URL, the default security model needs to be very strict. JDK 1.1 introduced support for signing an applet, which gives the browser the opportunity to identify who wrote the applet and then choose to let the applet access all system resources. JDK 1.2 lets you configure more precisely the resources that can be accessed by signed code.

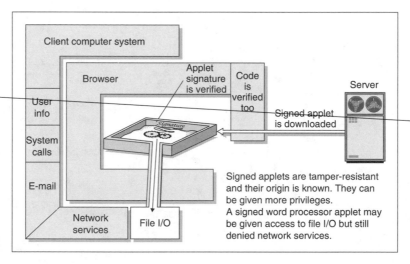

Figure 14-1: Signed applets have more privileges.

Signing an applet is like signing a bank check. It means labeling it with a tamper-proof identifying mark saying where it came from. Don't we already know this? Doesn't it come from the URL we are browsing? The answer is that we are not sure enough to give our system away to the applet.

Applets start running by virtue of visiting a page; there need not be any visible indication that the page contains an applet. Secondly, although an applet is hosted on a page, it is not necessarily located on that page. The CODEBASE applet tag can point to a URL anywhere else on the net. Finally, with enough effort, it is possible to spoof (masquerade as) web servers. If the stakes are high enough people could do this to make a malicious or fraudulent applet appear to come from http://mother.teresa.org.

A sandbox is like a room built out of firewalls. Applets are executed inside a sandbox by default, so they cannot access the private or vulnerable resources of your system. This is a representative but not exhaustive list of the restrictions on remotely accessed applets.

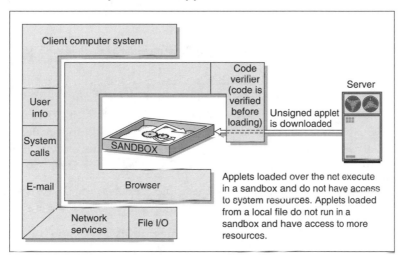

By default, an applet accessed over the net:
- cannot read or write files;
- cannot open a socket connection, except to the server that it came from;
- cannot start up a program on your system;
- cannot call native (non-Java) code.

Applets accessed from a local file system (rather than over the net) are allowed more privileges. They can only be on your local file system with your permission, so it is presumed that you trust them.

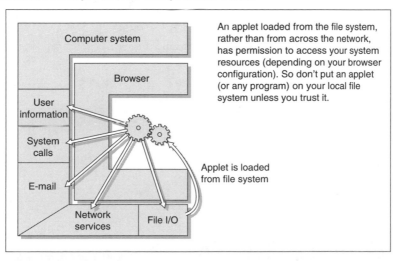

We can write our signature on a check because it is a physical piece of paper. For an applet in a jar file, we add an extra file saying what the origin is. Obviously, it wouldn't be good enough just to put an ASCII text file in there saying "Software from Honest Software Corporation," since the bomb-building, drug-peddling, code-encrypting, porno-terrorists that the FBI says are all over the Internet could easily forge that file on their own applets.

Instead, we use computer encryption to sign a file. Here is a summary of the basic steps:

1. Do all the one-time preparation necessary to set yourself up for encrypting files. The preparation consists of generating your code keys, registering them with the keystore database, getting yourself a digitally-signed certificate attesting to who you are, and a couple of other things. You will use the new JDK 1.2 `keytool` for all this.

2. Put all the files that make up the applet into a jar file. We have already seen how to do this in the previous section.

3. Sign the jar file. The `jarsigner` signing utility looks up your secret code in the `keystore` database and runs it over a hash of the jar file and the directives file. Then, it adds the coded result to the jar. Anyone can look at it, and anyone could change it, but if they do, the results won't match the hash value that was generated using your secret code, and the tampering will be obvious.

4. Export the public key certificate that you generated in step 1. People who wish to check your signature before running the code must import your certificate into their own keystore.

5. Put the signed applet jar file on your web page, and let people have at it.

This process makes the applet trusted. The longest part of the process is the one-time setup.

The Security Manager

All browsers install a security manager, and you can install one on your applications too. It's called by the runtime. Look at this code in the runtime library to create a FileInputStream:

```
public FileInputStream(String name) throws FileNotFoundException {
        SecurityManager security = System.getSecurityManager();
        if (security != null) {
            security.checkRead(name);
        }
        fd = new FileDescriptor();
        open(name);
    }
```

Before it does anything else, the code gets the SecurityManager object for the system. If there isn't one (the reference is null), it goes ahead. However, if someone has created a SecurityManager, then its checkRead() method is called. That method will judge whether this operation is permitted or not. If it is permitted, the method silently returns without a problem. If the file access is not permitted (you're an ordinary applet that was just downloaded, for example), a SecurityException is thrown, tossing you out of the FileInputStream constructor before the object creation completes.

The SecurityManager is a built-in class in package java.lang with about a dozen methods each of which checks access to a particular resource: threads, properties, socket connections, reading a file, and so on.

What Do All the Cryptographic Terms Mean?

We don't present a general tutorial on computer cryptography in this text. Bruce Schneier does that in his excellent book referenced at the end of the chapter, and it takes 750 pages. The pages are packed with information and stories that will keep you reading and learning.

You don't have to know how computer cryptography works in order to sign Java applets, but most readers will be very interested to find out more details. Cryptography is a truly fascinating topic, with an engaging blend of intrigue, high finance, and technical challenges. If you get caught up in it, it might even become your career!

The java.lang.SecurityManager class contains these public methods:

```
public class java.lang.SecurityManager extends java.lang.Object {
    public java.lang.SecurityManager();
    public void checkAccept(java.lang.String, int);
    public void checkAccess(java.lang.Thread);
    public void checkAccess(java.lang.ThreadGroup);
    public void checkAwtEventQueueAccess();
    public void checkConnect(java.lang.String, int);
    public void checkConnect(java.lang.String, int, Object);
    public void checkCreateClassLoader();
    public void checkDelete(java.lang.String);
    public void checkExec(java.lang.String);
    public void checkExit(int);
    public void checkLink(java.lang.String);
    public void checkListen(int);
    public void checkMemberAccess(java.lang.Class, int);
    public void checkMulticast(java.net.InetAddress);
    public void checkMulticast(java.net.InetAddress, byte);
    public void checkPackageAccess(java.lang.String);
    public void checkPackageDefinition(java.lang.String);
    public void checkPermission(java.security.Permission);
    public void checkPermission(java.security.Permission, Object);
    public void checkPrintJobAccess();
    public void checkPropertiesAccess();
    public void checkPropertyAccess(java.lang.String);
    public void checkRead(java.io.FileDescriptor);
    public void checkRead(java.lang.String);
    public void checkRead(java.lang.String, java.lang.Object);
    public void checkSecurityAccess(java.lang.String);
    public void checkSetFactory();
    public void checkSystemClipboardAccess();
    public boolean checkTopLevelWindow(java.lang.Object);
    public void checkWrite(java.io.FileDescriptor);
    public void checkWrite(java.lang.String);
    public boolean getInCheck();
    public java.lang.Object getSecurityContext();
    public java.lang.ThreadGroup getThreadGroup();
}
```

The methods scrutinize some specific form of resource access. So check-Read(java.io.FileDescriptor) will return normally if a read may be done using this file descriptor, and throw an exception if it should not. The three non-obvious methods carry out this processing:

checkSetFactory()   Checks whether an applet can set a networking-related
                           object factory. A *factory* is a Java term for a class that

creates objects of another class. Usually classes are responsible for their own constructors, but sometimes it is convenient to manage this from another class, especially when one of several subtype classes might be needed.

`getInCheck()` Simply says whether a check is currently taking place.

`getSecurityContext()` Returns an implementation-dependent Object which holds enough information about the current execution environment to perform some of the security checks later.

You never call these checking methods, they are called at appropriate times by the Java runtime. The calls are already in place throughout the runtime library. When a Java system first starts executing, the security manager is set to null and the only access restrictions are those imposed by the underlying operating system. In other words, anything goes.

To change the default, you can write your own class that extends SecurityManager and provide new methods to override the checking method for the resources you are interested in. The body of each new method contains your algorithm for deciding whether to grant access or not. It will either return or throw a security exception. Returning without throwing an exception means the access is allowed. If you install a new security manager of your own, then every resource *not* controlled in your new manager is disallowed. Here is an example that allows access to all system properties and nothing else.

```
class MySecurityManager extends SecurityManager {
    public void checkPropertyAccess(String key) {
        return;
    }
}


public class foo {
    public static void main(String s[]) {
        SecurityManager msm = new MySecurityManager();
        try {
            System.setSecurityManager(msm);
        } catch(Exception e){}
    }
}
```

A SecurityManager can be set at most once during the lifetime of a Java runtime. There is no way to install a new SecurityManager that includes permission to keep installing new SecurityManagers: it's a one shot deal and cannot later be replaced, changed, or overridden. In an application, you the programmer can define the level of security for your program. In an applet, the browser sets the SecurityManager, and decides what processes to follow to grant or deny access. Applets must be unable to impose a new security manager.

Different browsers have imposed slightly different SecurityManager policies, and they can take into account whether an applet was loaded from a local file or from browsing over the Internet. Local files only exist on your system because you put them there, so they are presumed to have more privileges. Table 14-2 is a matrix of browser characteristics extracted from the JavaSoft site http://www.javasoft.com/sfaq.

Table 14-1: Capabilities of an Untrusted Applet

Capabilities	Ns/net	Ns/local	Av/net	Av/local	Applic
Read or write a file in /home/me with access control list set	no	no	yes	yes	yes
Read the user.name property	no	yes	no	yes	yes
Connect to port on client	no	yes	no	yes	yes
Connect to port on 3rd host	no	yes	no	yes	yes
Load library	no	yes	no	yes	yes
Exit(-1)	no	no	no	yes	yes
Create a pop-up window without a warning	no	yes	no	yes	yes

Key:
- Ns/net: Netscape Navigator 3.x, loading applets over the net
- Ns/local: Netscape Navigator 3.x, loading applets from the Local file system
- Av/net: Appletviewer, JDK 1.x, loading applets over the net
- Av/local: Appletviewer, JDK 1.x, loading applets from the local file system
- Applic: Java stand-alone applications

The restrictions mean that an applet loaded from over the Internet:

- Can really read and write files if an access control list file permits it, and you run the applet using appletviewer.

- Cannot make network connections to hosts other than the one it came from

- Cannot start a program on your system by using the equivalent of the system() call in C. An application or local applet can do this with the method `java.lang.Runtime.exec()`.

- Cannot load a library

- Cannot execute native code

Some browsers may impose other restrictions on top of these. The SecurityManager class provides a way to recognize trusted code, so we can grant it more capabilities, without jeopardizing system security.

You can configure the Sun appletviewer to read and write files on your local disk by editing the file .hotjava/properties. This file is in your home directory on Unix (note its name starts with a dot, so it is not usually visible when you list the directory). Under Windows, the files is in the root directory of the drive on which you installed Java (the file might be C:\.hotjava\properties). Note that this works *for the appletviewer only,* not other browsers like Netscape.

Then you can set the acl.read and acl.write properties to point to the files or directories that you will allow applets to read or write. For example, if I add these two lines to my ~/.hotjava/properties file (or my C:\.hotjava\properties file on Windows) then applets are allowed to read any files in /home/linden or to write to any files in the /tmp directory.

```
acl.read=/home/linden
acl.write=/tmp
```

ACL stands for Access Control List — a mainframe feature for providing fine-grained control of resources like files.

Here's an applet that you can run under Sun's appletviewer to confirm this.

```
// <applet code=show.class  height=100 width=200> </applet>
import java.io.*;
import java.awt.*;
import java.applet.Applet;
public class show extends Applet {

    public void Read() throws IOException {

        DataInputStream dis;
        String s, myFile = "show.java";

        dis = new DataInputStream(new FileInputStream(myFile));
        s = dis.readLine();
        System.out.println("line> "+s);
    }

    public void paint(Graphics g) {
        try {
            Read();
            g.drawString("Success in read", 10, 10);
        }
        catch (SecurityException e) {
            g.drawString("Caught security exception in read", 10, 10);
        }
        catch (IOException ioe) {
            g.drawString("Caught i/o exception in read", 10, 10);
        }
    }
}
```

Don't worry about the I/O details—that will be covered in full in a later chapter.
For now the purpose is to demonstrate that browsers control the resources
accessed by applets and that file I/O is possible from an applet using the appletviewer.

Applying the Security Policy

The previous three sections explained how security restrictions are enforced. This section describes how a fine-grained security policy can be set up to specify exactly what the restrictions are and to which code and code signers they apply. The notion of security policies, and the tools to adjust them, is a new feature of Java that came in as part of JDK 1.2.

The one sentence summary of Java Security Policy is, "There are a bunch of files outside the Java system that keep a record of the way application and applet classes are grouped together into domains, and the permissions associated with those domains." The security is carefully tracked by the runtime, so a less-privileged class cannot grab more permissions because it called or was called by a more powerful domain.

The way that permission is granted is by adding an entry to a policy file. Policy files exist in a couple of standard places, and users can create additional ones and specify them as a command-line argument when they start a program. The format of an entry in a policy file is a little tricky; it resembles statements in a programming language. At least the entries are in ASCII, not binary, so you don't have to use the policytool provided, and can just edit the file if you prefer.

Each grant entry in the policy file is of the following format, where the leading grant is a reserved word that signifies the beginning of a new entry. Optional items appear in brackets. The keyword permission is another reserved word that marks the beginning of a new permission in the entry. Each entry grants a set of permissions to the specified code source.

```
grant [SignedBy "signer_names"] [, CodeBase "URL"] {

    permission permission_class_name
      ["target_name"]   [,"action"]   [,SignedBy "signer_names"];

      // there may be a series of permission statements
};
```

Here is an example of a pretty minimal policy file. We will use this in a later chapter to grant a program the ability to connect and accept connections on sockets:

```
grant  {
    permission java.net.SocketPermission "*", "connect";
    permission java.net.SocketPermission "*", "accept";
};
```

We put that text into a file called "permit," and then start the program mentioning the permission filename like this:

```
java -Djava.security.policy=permit  MySocketProgram
```

Here is another example policy file, where I say that I will grant file read and write permission in the /tmp directory or any subdirectory of it, to all applets that originate from the Sun Java site.

```
grant CodeBase  "http://java.sun.com/" {
    permission java.io.FilePermission "/tmp/*", "read,write";
}
```

So where are the standard places that a policy file can exist, and what is the list of permissions?

There is by default a single system-wide policy file, and a single user policy file. The system policy file is by default located here:

```
$JAVAHOME\lib\security\java.policy  (Windows)
$JAVAHOME/lib/security/java.policy  (Solaris)
```

The user policy file is by default located in the user's home directory, in a file called this:

```
.java.policy  (note the leading "." in the name))
```

The system makes provision for specifying a number of additional policy files, including defining the name of one as a property when you invoke the program, as shown above. This can be done for the appletviewer, too, like so:

appletviewer **-J-Djava.security.policy=file:/foo/permit** applet.html

The full list of permissions and subpermissions is shown in Table 14-2. The policy-tool software will help you navigate these, and you can see why it's useful!

Table 14-2: Permissions and Subpermissions in JDK 1.2

Permission Class Name	Target Name (a subpermission)	Actions
java.io.FilePermission	filenames	read, write, delete, execute
java.security. AllPermission	—	—
java.awt.AWTPermission	accessClipboard, accessEventQueue, showWindowWithoutWarningBanner	—
java.net.NetPermission	requestPasswordAuthentication, setDefaultAuthenticator	—
java.net. SocketPermission	—	accept, connect, listen, resolve
java.util. PropertyPermission	—	read, write
java.lang.reflect. ReflectPermission	suppressAccessChecks	—
java.lang. RuntimePermission	queuePrintJob, setFactory, setIO, modifyThread, modifyThreadGroup getProtectionDomain, setProtectionDomain readFileDescriptor, writeFileDescriptor loadLibrary.<library name> accessClassInPackage.<package name> defineClassInPackage.<package name> accessDeclaredMembers.<class name>	—
java.security. SecurityPermission	getPolicy, setPolicy getProperty.<property name> setProperty.<property name> insertProvider.<provider name> removeProvider.<provider name> setSystemScope, setIdentityInfo, setIdentityPublicKey, addIdentityCertificate, removeIdentityCertificate clearProviderProperties.<provider name> putProviderProperty.<provider name> removeProviderProperty.<provider name> getSignerPrivateKey, setSignerKeyPair	—
java.io. SerializablePermission	enableSubclassImplementation, enableSubstitution	—

Sun has also put some security documentation online at http://java.sun.com/ products/jdk/1.2/docs/guide/security/spec/security-specTOC.fm.html.

The next section is a step-by-step example of signing a piece of code, so that it can write to the local filesystem.

Signing a Java Program

Applets are not allowed to write to the local file system by default. We will walk through the example of how we can sign an applet so that it does have that ability. It's a lengthy process the first time, because you also need to create and register your cryptographic keys.

There are steps that the code signer has to do (here, linden), and steps that the code receiver has to do to run the code (here, sauceboy). You can sign any kind of Java code: applets or applications. Applets always run under the control of a security manager, but you have to provide one if you want an application to have the same level of assurance.

Step 1: Setup for Applet Signing (One-Time)

We'll start by listing the bits and pieces involved in registering yourself with the Java system as a person or organization that can sign code. Note that you can sign applications as well as applets.

- Public and private keys: Java uses public key cryptography which involves two keys, one private and one public. Anyone can use your public key, but only you know your private key. There is no practical way to discover one key from the other, but either key can turn a message into seemingly random bits, and the other key can recover it.

  Encrypting something is like translating it into Martian—the encryption key is an English-to-Martian dictionary, and the decryption key is a Martian-to-English dictionary. Only instead of Martian, we use mathematical ciphers that are a lot harder to search exhaustively.

- Certificates: Anyone can generate their own keys, and anyone can claim to be whoever they like. To provide better assurance that you are who you say you are, we use X.509 certificates (bit files) in the online world.

- The keystore database: This repository holds records of all users, their certificates, and the pairs of code keys that each has. There can be several of these files on a system. It replaces the earlier javakey database of JDK 1.1

- The keytool utility: You'll be relieved to hear that there is a utility used to do all this key generation and database registration. It has lots of different options, but there's only one command: keytool.

Now we know the players, let's go over the rules of the game shown in Table 14-3.

Table 14-3: Getting Your Keys and Register Yourself with a Keystore

Step 1a	Generate your pair of keys.
Step 1b	Generate or buy an X.509 certificate.
Step 1c	Register your keys and certificate in a keystore database.

When you have completed these three steps, you will be able to sign applets. Although the process may seem cumbersome, remember that these steps have to be done only once and then you can do any amount of code signing. The Java keytool utility does all three steps in one go, so it takes a large number of options to drive it.

Register Yourself and Your Keys in a Java Keystore

As we mentioned, there is only one utility, keytool, to do all the preparatory work, and it has many different options which you can see if you type:

```
%   keytool
keytool usage:

-certreq    [-v] [-alias <alias>] [-sigalg <sigalg>]
            [-file <csr_file>] [-keypass <keypass>]
            [-keystore <keystore>] [-storepass <storepass>]
            [-storetype <storetype>]

-delete     [-v] -alias <alias>
            [-keystore <keystore>] [-storepass <storepass>]
            [-storetype <storetype>]

-export     [-v] [-rfc] [-alias <alias>] [-file <cert_file>]
            [-keystore <keystore>] [-storepass <storepass>]
            [-storetype <storetype>]

-genkey     [-v] [-alias <alias>] [-keyalg <keyalg>]
            [-keysize <keysize>] [-sigalg <sigalg>]
            [-dname <dname>] [-validity <valDays>]
            [-keypass <keypass>] [-keystore <keystore>]
            [-storepass <storepass>] [-storetype <storetype>]
```

. . . and there are many more!

For more information, see the documentation online at http://java.sun.com/products/jdk/1.2/docs/guide/security/spec/security-specTOC.fm.html.

We use a command of the following form all on one line:

```
keytool -genkey -storepass password1 -keystore name1
        -alias name2 -keypass password2
```

The actual command is like the following, all on one line, remember:

```
keytool -genkey -storepass soupy99  -keystore lindenstore
        -alias linden  -keypass lime43
```

The options mean:

`-genkey`	Generate a public and private keypair in this operation.
`-storepass soupy99`	Supplies the password to access this keystore file. It is better not to enter this on the command-line, as it can be snooped. If you leave it off, you will be prompted for it.
`-keystore lindenstore`	This pair of options gives a name to the keystore that you are creating, or using. The name can include a pathname.
`-alias linden`	The option says how you want to refer to the particular entry containing the keys that will be generated. It gives a name to the linden keypair.
`-keypass lime43`	The option gives a password for accessing and updating the linden keypair. Again, it is better to leave it off and be prompted for it.

When you run the keytool command, you will prompted to provide more information identifying the person or organization who owns this keypair:

```
What is your first and last name?
  [Unknown]:  Peter van der Linden
What is the name of your organizational unit?
  [Unknown]:  code grinding shop
What is the name of your organization?
  [Unknown]:  AFU (Cayman Islands) Inc.
What is the name of your City or Locality?
  [Unknown]:  Silicon Valley
What is the name of your State or Province?
  [Unknown]:  California
What is the two-letter country code for this unit?
  [Unknown]:  US
Is <CN=Peter van der Linden, OU=code grinding shop, O=AFU (Cayman
Islands) Inc., L=Silicon Valley, ST=California, C=US> correct?
  [no]:  y
```

The keytool takes a few seconds to run, and then this 1.3KB keystore file is generated:

```
% ls -l
-rw-r--r--   1 linden    staff         1351 Nov 15 14:21 lindenstore
```

Now you have a keypair within a keystore and a self-signed X.509 certificate. You are ready to sign code using it.

What Is an X.509 Certificate?

To reiterate what I said before, anyone can generate their own keys, and anyone can claim to be whoever they like. To provide better assurance that you are who you say you are, we use X.509 certificates (bit files) in the online world.

X.509 is an ISO standard for computer authentication. There are companies in business simply to check your credentials and issue you an unforgeable X.509 certificate in the form of an encrypted file. Search the web looking for "X.509 certificate" for a list of vendors.

You prove who you are to a certification authority, using real-world documents, show them your public key, and they issue you a certificate. An X.509 certificate is like a passport, only better because it's harder to forge. An X.509 certificate works like a notary public. You identify yourself to the notary public and sign something, and then the notary affixes an official seal to guarantee your signature.

Buying an X.509 certificate from a certification authority is more reliable for your users and will make your code accepted in more places. Generating our own certificate is good enough for this example. The certificate does the same job as a PGP fingerprint. There's a glossary for these terms online at: http://java.sun.com/docs/books/tutorial/security1.2/summary/glossary.html.

Step 2: Put All the Files That Make up the Applet into a Jar File

We saw how to put the class files and other resources into a jar file earlier in this chapter. Here is the example code we will use. It is an applet that attempts to write to a local file on the client. Untrusted applets do not have permission to write to local files.

```
/* <applet
        archive=write.jar      code=write.class
        width=120              height=75>
    </applet>
*/
import java.io.*;
import java.awt.*;
import javax.swing.*;

public class write extends JApplet {

    public void init() {
        try {
            FileWriter fw = new FileWriter("score.txt");
            fw.write("new high score: 14 \n");
            fw.close();
        } catch (Exception e) {System.out.println(e);}
    }

    public void paint(Graphics g){
        g.drawString("Try to write a file", 15, 15);
    }
}
```

Don't worry about the I/O details—that will be covered in full in a later chapter. For now the purpose is to demonstrate that browsers control the resources accessed by applets, and that file I/O is possible from an applet when the permission is granted. Compile the applet and put the class in a jar file.

```
% javac write.java

% jar -cvf write.jar  write.class
```

The applet attempts to open a file and write to it. When you try to run the applet, it will fail with a security error. Untrusted applets are not permitted access to the client file system. After this, we will sign it and try again.

```
% appletviewer write.java
java.security.AccessControlException: access denied
(java.io.FilePermission score.txt write)
```

Step 3: Create a Signed Jar File

To sign a jar file, we use the jarsigner tool (new with JDK 1.2). A typical run might look like this:

```
jarsigner -keystore lindenstore -signedjar swrite.jar write.jar linden
```

The options are self-explanatory. The program takes an unsigned jar file and creates a signed jarfile version of it (*Tip:* Use the same name, but prefix an "s" on the beginning). It signs it with linden's key from the lindenstore keystore. The utility will prompt you for passwords for both the keystore and the linden keypair.

```
Enter Passphrase for keystore: soupy99
Enter key password for linden: lime43
```

You can see that the following jar files now exist:

```
-rw-r--r--   1 linden    staff        2249 Nov 15 14:24 swrite.jar
-rw-r--r--   1 linden    staff         977 Nov 15 14:18 write.jar
```

Jar files (even unsigned jar files in JDK 1.2) have an extra directory called META-INF that it contains "meta-information"—information about the information in the archive. The MANIFEST.MF file is a list of files to be found in the archive, in the same sense that a manifest is a list of the cargo on a ship.

Step 4: Change the Applet Tag

Now we change the applet tag in our HTML file to refer to the signed version of the jar file. We want users to reference the newly-created signed file instead of the old .jar file.

The new tag will look like this:

```
<applet
      archive=swrite.jar
      code=write.class
      width=120
      height=75>
   </applet>
```

Step 5: The Person Who Runs the Applet Must Import My Certificate

You now have a signed jar file swrite.jar. The runtime system of the code receiver will need to authenticate the signature when the write program in the signed jar file tries to write a file. The authentication is done using a policy file that grants the permission to this signed code.

The person (sauceboy, in this example) who is going to run this applet needs to set up a policy file that says in effect, "I am going to allow file access to code written by user linden." So sauceboy's system has to know about linden's X.509 certificate and public key. Here's how we tell it.

The signer of the code sends a copy of the certificate authenticating the public key to anyone who plans to run it. That certificate must be put into their own keystore. Here is how linden extracts the X.509 certificate from the keystore using the keytool utility:

```
keytool -export -keystore lindenstore  -alias linden  -file linden.cert
```

Again, the tool will challenge you for the password.

```
Enter keystore password:  soupy99
Certificate stored in file <linden.cert>
```

The file that holds the certificate is a binary file (bear that in mind if you e-mail or FTP it somewhere). Sauceboy must now import that into his keystore by running a command like this:

```
keytool -import -alias linden -file linden.cert -keystore sauceboystore

Enter keystore password:  sauce99
Owner: CN=Peter van der Linden, OU=code grinding shop, O=AFU (Cayman
Islands) Inc., L
=Silicon Valley, ST=California, C=US
Issuer: CN=Peter van der Linden, OU=code grinding shop, O=AFU (Cayman
Islands) Inc.,
L=Silicon Valley, ST=California, C=US
Serial number: 364f53f0
Valid from: Sun Nov 15 14:21:36 PST 1998 until: Sat Feb 13 14:21:36 PST
1999
Certificate fingerprints:
        MD5:   E8:83:20:2C:99:5E:AD:25:82:F7:28:B4:96:05:F5:8E
        SHA1:
CA:EE:D3:1D:D3:A2:00:0E:E7:C8:0E:CC:8D:06:FC:76:E7:2E:6A:3D
Trust this certificate? [no]:  y
```

The certificate fingerprints can be used to check there has been no monkey-business with the certificate. You can read the expected fingerprints on a company letterhead, or off its annual report, or confirm them by phone. Don't check them by going to the company web site though.

Step 6: Set up a Security Policy for the User, Allowing Signed Code

The person who wishes to run the signed code (sauceboy, in this example) must now set up a policy file allowing this runtime permission. The policy file is an ASCII file that associates URLs with code signers, with code, and with permissions. You can edit the file manually, but there is a GUI utility in JDK 1.2 to help you. The utility is called policytool, so start it up by typing that name. It has the same kind of elementary look and feel as early versions of Netscape. You can't type directly into text fields; you have to select them from the menu first.

Start policytool and a main window will come up. Using the "Edit" -> "Change KeyStore" menu, type in the new keystore URL for the sauceboy keystore that we created in step 5. Note that the keystore is accessed by a URL, so it can be located anywhere on the Internet (or more likely, your private Intranet). Also enter "File" -> "Save as" and enter the pathname for where you want the policy file to go. The screen will look like the following picture.

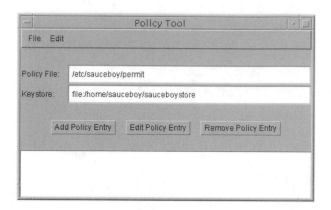

That takes care of reading the contents of sauceboy's keystore. Now we need to add a policy entry for the precise permission we want to grant. Press the button marked "Add Policy Entry" to bring up the policy entry screen.

The policy entry screen has two text fields at the top, "CodeBase" and "SignedBy". If we enter a URL in the codebase field, we are saying that the permission applies to code that arrives from that codebase. Thus you might enter "http://java.sun.com" to apply a permission to all applets that you browse on the Sun Java web site. If you leave the field blank, it means the permission you are about to specify applies to all code, regardless of where it comes from.

The second textfield "SignedBy" identifies who signed the code. We need to enter the alias that we used to identify the linden certificate when we entered it into the sauceboy keystore. If you look back a couple of pages, you'll see we just used the string "linden."

"Code signed by linden" is shorthand for saying," Code in a class file contained in a JAR file, where the JAR file was signed using the private key corresponding to the public key that appears in a keystore certificate in an entry aliased by linden." Phew!

You then click the "add permission" button and select the appropriate permission, what it applies to, and the level of access. The permissions are listed back in Table 15-2. The screen looks like the following picture.

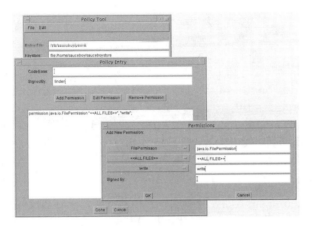

The "Target" is the file or directory to which you want to apply the permission. The "Action" is the kind of access: read, write, execute, delete. Finish up by clicking "Done" and saving the file.

Take a look at the policy file, and you will see something like this:

```
/* AUTOMATICALLY GENERATED ON Sun Nov 15 16:31:00 PST 1998*/
/* DO NOT EDIT */

keystore "file:/home/sauceboy/sauceboystore";

grant signedBy "linden" {
  permission java.io.FilePermission "<<ALL FILES>>", "write";
};
```

By the time this book gets into the hands of readers, more browsers are expected to support configurable applet security. One need is to be able to configure browsers to accept or refuse certain X.509 Certificates. You'll want to be able to tell your browser, "Accept applets that are accompanied by certificates from these five companies, and ask me explicitly about any others."

Step 7: Run the Code Using the Policy File

The final step is to execute the code, like so:

```
appletviewer -J-Djava.security.policy=file:/etc/sauceboy/permit write.html
```

The "-J" option tells the appletviewer to pass the option that follows to the JVM. The applet will run, and the file will be written successfully to the local filesystem.

Some Light Relief

Software about Nothing

Anyone who has had to do "booth duty" at a computer exhibition knows the problem: software is nebulous stuff, and very hard to demonstrate. Take a compiler for example. You don't really have anything to show that is going to make people gasp in astonishment. You type a command-line, the compiler runs and creates an object file, and that's it. The problem is even worse for utility and system administration software. There's just plain nothing to see.

A software company based in southern California, Syncronys Softcorp, took this concept to the limit (and then took one step further) with SoftRAM95, a best-selling Windows product. An advert on page 81 of the December 1995 issue of *Wired* read:

double click.

double memory.

Doubling RAM doesn't have to be hard. Install SoftRAM95 and instantly speed up Windows 95 and Windows 3.0 and higher. Run multimedia and RAM hungry applications. Open more applications simultaneously. Say good-bye to 'Out-of-Memory' messages. 4MB becomes at least 8MB. 8MB becomes at least 16MB. Get the idea? (In fact, you can get up to 5 times more memory.) SoftRAM95 works with all 386 and higher desktops and laptops. PC Novice calls SoftRAM the 'real RAM doubler for Windows.'

The trade press named SoftRAM95 as the hottest-selling utility for Windows 95. More than 600,000 people bought SoftRAM95 and Syncronys's stock price shot up from $.03 a share in March 1995 to $32 a share just five months later. SoftRAM95 works like this in action

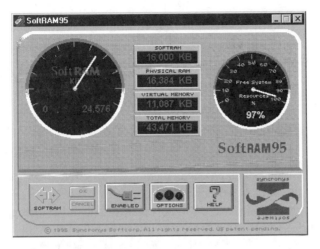

I don't mean "SoftRAM95 *looks* like this picture in a book"— I mean "SoftRAM95 *works* like this picture in a book. It looks pretty but it does nothing." The program was on the market for several months and sold hundreds of thousands of copies before word started to get out that the emperor had no clothes.

SoftRAM95 was based on an earlier Syncronys Windows 3.1 program that also did nothing. However it featured a really slick control panel that reported on the amount of memory present and the extra resources that the software said it was providing. The trade press was initially full of favorable reports, but careful consumers noticed that the dials read the same whether or not the Syncronys libraries were on the system, which tended to cast doubt on whether the control panel was reporting what the system was doing, or what it wanted users to *think* the system was doing.

The jig only started to unravel well after SoftRAM was a big hit in the market. Three independent tests reported that SoftRAM did not work as advertised, and in fact did not work at all. It did not speed up Windows. It did not double memory. The software did not do anything at all. *PC Magazine*'s technical editor Larry Seltzer reported, "I've never seen a product that was so devoid of value as Soft-RAM. After careful testing, we found no evidence that SoftRAM95 performs any of the main functions it claims to perform."

Amazingly, the product continued to sell in boatloads, and with a list price of $79.95, Syncronys was reluctant to admit that the only effect of the software was a placebo effect. Syncronys's reseller in Germany actually sued German computer magazine *c't* which was the first paper to report that SoftRAM didn't work as advertised. At first Syncronys circulated a favorable report done by XXCAL labs, claiming that the report "confirmed that SoftRAM95 effectively doubles Random Access Memory (RAM)." After criticism continued to mount, in October 1995 Syncronys issued a press release that admitted, "RAM compression is not being delivered to the operating system." Syncronys glossed over the critical fact that the software didn't even attempt any compression of memory, so of course it couldn't deliver anything at all to the operating system.

Finally the Federal Trade Commission began to lean heavily on Syncronys, who announced in December 1995 that it was recalling SoftRAM and would credit or refund purchasers. Even then Syncronys didn't give up, and wrote to its distributors saying that it would soon be re-launching SoftRAM and creating a version for the Macintosh. And in June 1996 Syncronys had its lawyers warn *Dr. Dobbs Journal* over upcoming review SoftRAM 95. *Dr. Dobbs Journal* wasn't fazed and went ahead and printed the truth in its August 1996 issue without further ado.

Eventually the FTC brought a complaint against Syncronys. It was settled by Syncronys agreeing "not to make representations about the performance, attributes, benefits, or effectiveness of SoftRAM, SoftRAM95, or any substantially similar product unless the representations were true and substantiated." In other words, they got away clean with a slap on the wrist. In a news story reporting the consent decree, Syncronys CEO Rainer Poertner was quoted as saying that SoftRAM for Windows 3.x "always worked perfectly." I suppose it depends on your definition of "perfect". While the program delivered millions of dollars into Syncronys's bank account, it certainly didn't deliver the memory benefits claimed for it.

Syncronys had perhaps the biggest of the best-selling programs that do nothing, but they are by no means alone in the field. Right now there is a vendor hawking "security" software that supposedly safeguards your system against hostile Java applets. They're using all the same tools to keep the software on the market: lawyers letters, favorable test reports, press releases, and so on. And the software has just as much use. Hostile Java applets don't exist; because of the security measures in place from the first Java release, about the worst that a cracker can do in a Java applet is a "denial of service" attack—chew up CPU cycles that don't belong to him.

Jerry Seinfeld used to take great pride in his comedy show, saying it was "a show about nothing". Sometimes life does imitate art. Synchronys had a best-selling Windows product that bore the "Designed for Windows 95" logo, and that did absolutely nothing.

Further References

Applied Cryptography, 2nd Edition

by Bruce Schneier. (John Wiley and Sons, 1996)

ISBN 0-471-11709-9 (paperback)

A wonderful book. The author has gone to considerable trouble to explain a complicated mathematical topic so that any programmer can follow it. More technical books should be written like this one.

CHAPTER
15

- The java.math API
- The java.util API
- Collections
- Calendar Utilities
- Other Utilities
- Some Light Relief

Java Data Structures Library

As chapter one explained, the Java system comes with more than a few libraries. Some of these libraries are required to be present on every Java system, so programmers can always count on them being there. Although other libraries are optional, if the implementation supports that feature at all (e.g., telephony), it must be supported in the standard way.

For the record, the core libraries that must be present in every Java 1.2 system are listed in Table 15-1. Some of these APIs started out as optional extensions and were moved into the core JDK as they were proved by practical use.

Table 15-1: Core Java APIs in JDK 1.2.

Library	Library Size	Purpose
java.lang	93 classes	The java.lang package provides basic runtime support for language, such as threads, reflection, and exceptions.
java.applet	4 classes	The java.applet classes support applet execution.
java.awt	298 classes	The java.awt classes implement the windowing operations.
javax.swing	500 classes	The javax.swing class supplements the AWT class and provides improved GUI appearance.
java.io	75 classes	The java.io package supports input/output for files.
java.util	77 classes	A very useful package of utility data structures.
java.rmi	65 classes	The java.rmi package provides remote method calls to Java programs running on other computers.
java.sql	26 classes	The java.sql library contains support for Java Database Connectivity (JDBC).
java.security	106 classes	The java.security package provides programmers with the ability to digitally sign applets and supports coding and decoding data.
java.net	38 classes	The java.net library provides programmers with a wide variety of UDP, IP, and TCP/IP networking classes.
java.beans	43 classes	The java.beans API supports "component software" allowing rapid application development through the easy connection and reuse of existing program fragments.
java.text	50 classes	The java.text package is concerned with internationalization and localization. It handles the most common kinds of text that are localized, like dates, times, and currency.
java.math	2 classes	The java.math class is provided to match the SQL database types DECIMAL and NUMERIC. Don't confuse this package with the more general java.lang.Math class.
javax.accessibility	14 classes	The javax.accessibility class supports GUI access for the visually impaired. It offers easy support for increasing the size of text and making the interface easier to understand.

These libraries are present on every Java 1.2 system. The libraries are shown here in roughly the order in which a new Java programmer will use them, with the most frequent first.

The one dozen core APIs contain a total of 1391 classes and interfaces. That's a lot of classes! We do not cover the beans and text packages in detail in this book (although we present examples of common uses of java.text). Component software, as expressed in the Beans API (and the java.lang.reflect package), is a large topic that requires book-length treatment of its own. Reflection means "what I see when I hold you up to the mirror," and the reflect API is a class that you can use to find out at runtime the methods and data fields that are in any class. Finding out dynamically the methods and data in a class is a key part of making software components work together. Component software is an area of emerging software technology, and looks likely to be very important. After you finish this book, you may feel inspired to study a JavaBeans book. The java.text library helps programmers to localize strings in the course of internationalizing software. That again is a specialized topic that takes a book of its own.

Here we'll give a summary of what each of the remaining core packages does, and a more detailed description of the packages you will use most frequently. Inside your programs, these core (required) packages all have package names starting with "java" such as "java.io" or "java.applet." That name indicates that these are all part of the Java implementation. Some of the packages are multi-level packages. We have classes in java.awt.*, and there are also classes in java.awt.event.* and java.awt.image.*. The java.lang package is the only package that is included by default in all your programs, so you can use only those classes without an explicit "import" statement.

We will now expand on some of these libraries at greater length. Most of the rest of this book is concerned with explaining the libraries and showing examples of their use. First we will cover the java.math API, introduced in JDK 1.1. The remainder of this chapter is concerned with the java.util API.

The java.math API

The java.math package is simple to understand and use. It was added to JDK 1.1 for three reasons. First, for use in the java.security Digital Signature Algorithm interfaces. Second, to complete the support for all SQL types used in database programming, and to allow arithmetic on types larger than long and double. If you do database programming, you'll be comfortable with the two classes java.math.BigDecimal and java.math.BigInteger which can represent the SQL types DECIMAL and NUMERIC. Third, even if you don't use cryptography or database programming, you can still use these classes for arithmetic on numbers of arbitrary size.

As the names suggest, BigInteger deals with integers of unbounded size, and Big-Decimal deals with unbounded numbers with fractional parts. BigDecimal is essentially BigInteger with some extra code to keep track of the scale (where the decimal point is). If you want to manipulate a number that takes a megabyte to store all its decimal places, you can. BigInteger provides versions of all of Java's primitive integer operators, and all relevant static methods from java.lang.Math. Additionally, BigInteger provides operations for modular arithmetic, greatest common divisor calculation, primality testing, prime generation, single-bit manipulation, and a few other odds and ends.

Here's an example of BigInteger used to perform a calculation that is listed in the 1989 Guinness Book of World Records under "Human Computer."

```
BigInteger bi1 = new BigInteger("7686369774870");
BigInteger bi2 = new BigInteger("2465099745779");
bi1 = bi1.multiply(bi2);
System.out.println( "The value is "+ bi1 );
```

When compiled and run, the correct answer appears:

```
The value is 18947668177995426462773730
```

BigInteger naturally does it quite a lot faster than the human record holder who took 28 seconds. *It must be stressed that record-breaking mental arithmetic is an extremely hazardous activity and should be attempted only by trained professionals, not using a Pentium computer.* (I copied that warning out of the Guinness book. They print a similar warning next to all the entries for people who set records for wrestling alligators, sword swallowing, parachute freefall, etc).

Here's an example of BigDecimal used to round a number with many decimal places of precision.

```
BigDecimal bd1 = new BigDecimal( java.lang.Math.PI );
System.out.println( "The value is "+ bd1 );

int digsrightofradix = 4;
bd1 = bd1.setScale(digsrightofradix, BigDecimal.ROUND_HALF_UP);
System.out.println( "The value is "+ bd1 );
```

When compiled and run, the output is this:

```
The value is 3.141592653589793115997963468544185161590576171875
The value is 3.1416
```

The true value is 3.1415926535 8979323846 2643383279 5028841971 693993751, so you can see that our value of pi is wrong in the 16th decimal place.

This is because we got the value from a double, and that's the limit on accuracy for doubles (refer back to chapter 4 if you don't remember this). If we calculate pi from a formula using BigDecimal, we can get arbitrary precision.

Class BigDecimal also contains many other options for rounding numbers. Don't confuse the big numbers available from package java.math with the generalized math and trig operations available in class java.lang.Math.

The java.util API

The java.util package has utility classes covering six basic areas (see Table 15-2). We'll look at support for collections first, and then some of the other utilities;

Table 15-2: Utility Classes of the java.util Package

General Area	Interface/Abstract Class	Concrete Class
Collections	`Collection`	(basic accessor and update functions)
	`Set`	`HashSet` (a set of values built on a hash table)
		`TreeSet` (a set in sorted order)
	`List`	`ArrayList` (use instead of 1.0 `Vector`)
		LinkedList
	`Map`	`HashMap` (use instead of 1.0 `Hashtable`)
		`TreeMap` (a map in sorted order)
		`WeakHashMap` (a table whose entries go away when the thing they refer to is garbage collected)
	`Other`	`Stack`, `Arrays`, `Bitset`, `Iterator` (replaces `Enumerator`)
i18n	— `ResourceBundle` `ListResourceBundle`	`Locale`, `PropertyResourceBundle`
Calendar	`Calendar`	`Date`, `GregorianCalendar`
	`TimeZone`	`SimpleTimeZone`
Jar files		`JarFile`, `JarEntry`, `JarInputStream`, `JarOutputStream`, ...
Zip files		`ZipFile`, `ZipEntry`, `ZipInputStream`, `ZipOutputStream`, ...
Other		`StringTokenizer`, `Random`, `Observer`, `Observable`, `Properties`

Collections

The most interesting data structure utility addition for JDK 1.2 is the support for Collections. Earlier releases of Java had Vector, Hashtable, and arrays as ways of storing many related objects, but there was no commonality in how you stored and retrieved from those classes. Arrays use indexing, Vector has the elementAt() method, and Hashtable uses get() and put().When you tried to write some code that operated on a data structure, it could either work on arrays, or on Vectors, or on Hashtable, but not all three. Collections fix this.

The class Collection is just an interface that defines a dozen or so methods for adding to, removing from, and querying a data structure. Now all the individual java.util data structures (and others that *you* write) can implement this interface, and everyone gets and sets data with the same method signatures. Collection also has a couple of method signatures for methods that will flatten all the elements of a data structure into an array. This array is either one it allocates, or one you give it as an argument. Collection looks like this:

```
public interface java.util.Collection {
    public abstract boolean add(java.lang.Object);
    public abstract boolean addAll(java.util.Collection);
    public abstract void    clear();
    public abstract boolean contains(java.lang.Object);
    public abstract boolean containsAll(java.util.Collection);
    public abstract boolean equals(java.lang.Object);
    public abstract int     hashCode();
    public abstract boolean isEmpty();
    public abstract java.util.Iterator iterator();
    public abstract boolean remove(java.lang.Object);
    public abstract boolean removeAll(java.util.Collection);
    public abstract boolean retainAll(java.util.Collection);
    public abstract int     size();
    public abstract java.lang.Object toArray()[];
    public abstract java.lang.Object toArray(java.lang.Object[])[];
}
```

There is a helper class, Collections, that consists exclusively of static functions to do useful things to a Collection argument (get the maximum element, reverse a collection, sort it, do a binary search, etc.). Since the package java.util has an abstract class called AbstractCollection that implements the Collection interface and provides the code for a basic Collection implementation, it's easy for you to subclass it and fill it out.

There are two new basic interfaces with JDK 1.2 that extend Collection in different directions, Set and List. We will look at these separately and at an example java.util class that implements each. There is also a new interface, Map, that represents key/value pairs and that might or might not also be stored as a set or list.

`java.util.Set`

A Set is *a collection that has no duplicate elements*. The interface adds some methods to say if a set is empty, if it contains a specified object, and to do an intersection and set difference between this set and another. An example of a set is the set of all colors that a system can display on its monitor. The methods that Set promises are:

```java
public interface java.util.Set extends java.util.Collection {
    public abstract boolean add(java.lang.Object);
    public abstract boolean addAll(java.util.Collection);
    public abstract void clear();
    public abstract boolean contains(java.lang.Object);
    public abstract boolean containsAll(java.util.Collection);
    public abstract boolean equals(java.lang.Object);
    public abstract int hashCode();
    public abstract boolean isEmpty();
    public abstract java.util.Iterator iterator();
    public abstract boolean remove(java.lang.Object);
// take the set difference between this, and the argument
    public abstract boolean removeAll(java.util.Collection);
// take the set intersection between this, and the argument
    public abstract boolean retainAll(java.util.Collection);
    public abstract int size();
    public abstract java.lang.Object toArray()[];
    public abstract java.lang.Object toArray(java.lang.Object[])[];}
```

What Is a Hash Table?

A hash table is a data structure that stores keys/values like an ordinary table, but offers fast retrieval. A symbol table in a compiler is often maintained as a hash table. When a name is first read in from the source program, it is *hashed*, or converted to a hash-key value—say, 379—by an algorithm designed to spread the values around the table. It is then entered in the table at location 379 along with its value (type, scope, etc.).

Then, when you get the same name again, it is hashed, and the same result, 379, is used as a subscript for immediate access to all its details in the hash table. It is marvellous that a hash table is a library data structure in Java!

Why is a hash table better than just maintaining a sorted list or vector? Because hashing is fast, and sorting is slow.

HashSet Implements Set

This class is a `Set` whose objects happen to be held in a hashtable. In other words the class maintains a collection of individual objects, and you can do intersection, set difference, and iteration over the collection. The hashtable makes these operations fast.

You would use HashSet when you have a collection that is not going to have duplicates (i.e., something shouldn't be in the collection in two places), and you want fast retrieval. The methods of HashSet are:

```
public class java.util.HashSet extends java.util.AbstractSet
    implements java.util.Set, java.lang.Cloneable, java.io.Serializable {
    public java.util.HashSet();
    public java.util.HashSet(int);
    public java.util.HashSet(int,float);
    public java.util.HashSet(java.util.Collection);
    public boolean add(java.lang.Object);
    public void clear();
    public java.lang.Object clone();
    public boolean contains(java.lang.Object);
    public boolean isEmpty();
    public java.util.Iterator iterator();
    public boolean remove(java.lang.Object);
    public int size();
}
```

Here's an example showing how easy it is to put something into a HashSet and later iterate through or otherwise retrieve it. I'm putting String objects in the HashSet here, but you can store any objects.

```
import java.util.*;
public class hs {
    static HashSet myHS = new HashSet();

    public static void main(String[] arg) {
        createHS();
        showHS();
        System.out.println("You have "+myHS.size() +" tools");
    }

    public static void createHS() {
        String s1="Pliers", s2="Hammer", s3="Wrench";
        myHS.add( s1 );
        myHS.add( s2 );
        myHS.add( s3 );
    }

    public static void showHS() {
        // get the iterator for the class
        Iterator i = myHS.iterator();
        while( i.hasNext() ) {
            System.out.println(" tool: "+ i.next() );
        }
    }
}
```

When you run this program, you see output like this:

```
java hs
  tool: Wrench
  tool: Pliers
  tool: Hammer
You have 3 tools
```

Notice that the order in which the elements are listed is *not* the order in which they were added. Lists have a notion of order, but sets do not.

`public interface Iterator`

As the name suggests, Iterator is a class that allows you to retrieve all the elements in a data structure without having to know all the details about how or where they're stored. There is a subclass, ListIterator, that allows you to iterate backwards over a list as well as forwards.

The class itself knows those details, and will implement the Iterator methods to supply a way to count through all the objects in its collection. For an array, iteration is simply going from a[0] to a[n-1], but for a binary tree a little more effort is needed. The Iterator interface allows that effort to be encapsulated and hidden from user classes. The methods are:

```
public interface java.util.Iterator {
    public abstract boolean hasNext();
    public abstract java.lang.Object next();
    public abstract void remove();
}
```

The method next() returns the next element of the iteration. If there is no next element, it will throw the runtime exception NoSuchElementException. When you visit an element, you can call remove() on it. This is much simpler than having every individual Java programmer trying to implement remove() for a linked list for themselves. Some data structures, such as HashSet, support *fail-fast* iterators. A fail-fast iterator notices if another thread is trying to change a collection that you are iterating through, and throws a ConcurrentModificationException rather than corrupt your data. It is fail-fast in the sense that you learn of the logic error as soon as it happens, not at some undetermined future time when the data no longer adds up. Iterator is an improved form of the Enumeration class from JDK 1.0, and should be used instead of Enumeration from now on.

TreeSet

For completeness, we'll mention the TreeSet class. This class is a set (i.e., collection of arbitrary elements), and it has the additional feature that it is stored in ascending order of elements. This is *not* the order in which you add the elements; it automatically sorts an element into its correct place in the collection whenever you add it! A TreeSet collection is implemented by ("has a") a TreeMap behind the scenes. TreeMap in turn uses a red/black tree as its data structure. If you haven't met red/black trees yet, they are a variety of binary tree that is always kept balanced.

If you look back a couple of pages to the example code for HashSet, you can turn that into an example of TreeSet by changing just one line. Use the following line instead of the HashSet declaration:

```
static TreeSet myHS = new TreeSet();
```

That's it! Because everything that's a set implements the Set interface, all the method invocations continue to work.

When you compile and run the code, you'll get this output:

```
tool: Hammer
tool: Pliers
tool: Wrench
You have 3 tools
```

Notice that the TreeSet contents are Strings, and thus have been stored in alphabetic order. There's a constructor for TreeSet that allows you to supply a different comparator if you so wish.

The ease of changing implementations here really shows the power of Collections. When you create your own data structures, you should have them implement one of the Collections interfaces, so that they will be interchangeable and present a similar API to all Java programmers.

java.util.List

A List is *a collection that has an order* associated with its elements. (Think of Letterman's Top Ten list of Java data structures, which is presented in order from 10 to 1). Lists can have duplicate elements. A List also has other methods to allow adding/removing at a particular place and for iterating through the list. The methods that List promises follow:

```
public interface java.util.List extends java.util.Collection {
    public abstract void add(int, java.lang.Object);
    public abstract boolean add(java.lang.Object);
    public abstract boolean addAll(int, java.util.Collection);
    public abstract boolean addAll(java.util.Collection);
    public abstract void clear();
    public abstract boolean contains(java.lang.Object);
    public abstract boolean containsAll(java.util.Collection);
    public abstract boolean equals(java.lang.Object);
    public abstract java.lang.Object get(int);
    public abstract int hashCode();
    public abstract int indexOf(java.lang.Object);
    public abstract boolean isEmpty();
    public abstract java.util.Iterator iterator();
    public abstract int lastIndexOf(java.lang.Object);
    public abstract java.util.ListIterator listIterator();
    public abstract java.util.ListIterator listIterator(int);
    public abstract java.lang.Object remove(int);
    public abstract boolean remove(java.lang.Object);
    public abstract boolean removeAll(java.util.Collection);
    public abstract boolean retainAll(java.util.Collection);
    public abstract java.lang.Object set(int, java.lang.Object);
    public abstract int size();
    public abstract java.util.List subList(int, int);
    public abstract java.lang.Object toArray()[];
    public abstract java.lang.Object toArray(java.lang.Object[])[];
}
```

Because List is an interface, you don't declare a List; you declare instances of one of the classes that implement list, like ArrayList or LinkedList. There is an example of ArrayList in the next section.

ArrayList implements List

ArrayList is a concrete class that implements the List interface using an array as the underlying type. The ArrayList class should be thought of as an array that grows as needed to store the number of elements you want to put there.

The ArrayList class has the following methods, in addition to those promised by the list interface:

```
public class java.util.ArrayList extends java.util.AbstractList
    implements java.util.List, java.lang.Cloneable, java.io.Serializable
{
    public java.util.ArrayList();
    public java.util.ArrayList(int);
    public java.util.ArrayList(java.util.Collection);
    public void add(int, java.lang.Object);
    public boolean add(java.lang.Object);
    public boolean addAll(int, java.util.Collection);
    public boolean addAll(java.util.Collection);
    public void clear();
    public java.lang.Object clone();
    public boolean contains(java.lang.Object);
    public void ensureCapacity(int);
    public java.lang.Object get(int);
    public int indexOf(java.lang.Object);
    public boolean isEmpty();
    public int lastIndexOf(java.lang.Object);
    public java.lang.Object remove(int);
    protected void removeRange(int, int);
    public java.lang.Object set(int, java.lang.Object);
    public int size();
    public java.lang.Object toArray()[];
    public java.lang.Object toArray(java.lang.Object[])[];
    public void trimToSize();
}
```

You don't access ArrayList elements with the array brackets "[]," instead you use the List methods to get and set the elements at particular indices. Here's an example of the use of ArrayList:

```
import java.util.*;
public class al {
    static ArrayList myAL = new ArrayList();

    public static void main(String[] arg) {
        createAL();
        showAL();
        System.out.println("You have "+myAL.size() +" primes");
        myAL.remove(1);   // remove list element 1
        showAL();
    }

    public static void createAL() {
        Integer[] primes = new Integer[] {
        new Integer(2), new Integer(3), new Integer(5), new Integer(7),
        new Integer(11),new Integer(13),new Integer(17),new Integer(19)};
        List li = java.util.Arrays.asList( primes );
        myAL.addAll( li );
    }

    public static void showAL() {
        // get the iterator for the class
        ListIterator l = myAL.listIterator();
        while( l.hasNext() ) {
            System.out.print("  "+ l.next() );
        }
        System.out.println();
    }
}
```

When you run this program, you will see this output:

```
% java al
  2  3  5  7  11  13  17  19
You have 8 primes
  2  5  7  11  13  17  19
```

The example program shows you how to create and populate an ArrayList and how you iterate through it. The ArrayList class is a replacement for the JDK 1.0 class java.util.Vector. It is not synchronized, while Vector is. If multiple threads access the ArrayList, they must synchronize on some external shared object before touching the list.

Under the covers, this class is implemented as a regular array. When you want to add an element and the array is already full, a new, larger array is allocated to make room, and the old array is copied over. To cut down on incremental reallocation, you can tell the runtime system how many elements the array should hold when it is constructed. The default allocation is ten elements.

There is also a helper class called Arrays that provides related services for arrays and can also give you back an array as a List. The class java.util.Arrays looks like this:

```
public class java.util.Arrays {
    public static java.util.List asList(java.lang.Object[]);
    public static int binarySearch(byte[], byte);
    public static boolean equals(byte[], byte[]);
    public static void fill(byte[], byte);
    public static void fill(byte[],int, int, byte);
    public static void sort(byte[]);
    public static void sort(byte[], int, int);
    public static void sort(java.lang.Object[], java.util.Comparator);
}
```

The methods are shown here for byte arguments, but Arrays has corresponding methods for other primitive types. That is, there are also these methods and more:

```
    public static int binarySearch(long[], long);
    public static int binarySearch(short[], short);
    public static int binarySearch(int[], int);
    public static int binarySearch(double[], double);
```

The arguments to sort() and fill() that are two ints are used to designate a range within the array where you wish the operation to occur from and to.

> **How Do You Choose Between Sets, Lists, Maps, Stacks, and Others?**
>
> You choose the data structure according to what you want to do with the data. If you are trying to store key/value pairs, some kind of map is indicated.
>
> If you have a collection of data and there might be some duplicate entries, (e.g., you are tracking the first names of everyone in your department), you could use some kind of list. If there are no duplicates and you want to be able to get elements out in sorted order (e.g., you are storing employees' length of service), you could use a TreeSet.
>
> If you are implementing a pocket calculator and want to be able to read and evaluate expressions, a stack is the natural data structure.
>
> Being a programmer means understanding what kind of access, storage order, restrictions, and cost different data structures have. That is independent of Java. All programmers in any language need to be familiar with common data structures.

There is another interface that you can use to get the basic behavior of pairs of values, like a table of employees and their salaries. This is the Map interface.

java.util.Map

A Map is *a way of storing key/value pairs.* They could be anything, like username/
password strings. The most obvious way of storing a Map is as a two-column
table, and you can get fancier from there. Given the key, you can ask for the value
associated with it (if there is one). The interface provides three collection views;
viewing the map as a collection of keys, as a collection of values, or as a collection
of key/value pairs. There are iterators for each of these, and the *order* of a map is
defined as the order in which the iterators on a map's collection views return their
elements. Some Map implementations, like the TreeMap class, make specific guarantees as to their order; others, like the HashMap, do not. Map is interesting
because it contains a nested (static) interface (you may have been wondering
when you'd see an example of that). The Map interface should be used instead of
the JDK 1.0 Dictionary class, and Map looks like this:

```
public interface java.util.Map {
    public abstract void clear();
    public abstract boolean containsKey(java.lang.Object);
    public abstract boolean containsValue(java.lang.Object);
    public abstract java.util.Set entrySet();
    public abstract boolean equals(java.lang.Object);
    public abstract java.lang.Object get(java.lang.Object);
    public abstract int hashCode();
    public abstract boolean isEmpty();
    public abstract java.util.Set keySet();
    public abstract java.lang.Object put(java.lang.Object,
java.lang.Object);
    public abstract void putAll(java.util.Map);
    public abstract java.lang.Object remove(java.lang.Object);
    public abstract int size();
    public abstract java.util.Collection values();

    public static interface java.util.Map.Entry {
        public abstract boolean equals(java.lang.Object);
        public abstract java.lang.Object getKey();
        public abstract java.lang.Object getValue();
        public abstract int hashCode();
        public abstract java.lang.Object setValue(java.lang.Object);
    }
}
```

A single data structure could be all of a Set, List, and a Map. Map does not implement the Collections interface, so a mapping can choose whether it is also a Set or List or not.

HashMap implements Map

The important thing about this class is that it implements the Map interface. The secondary thing is that it uses a hash table to minimize the searching on every lookup. You should now use this class instead of JDK 1.0's Hashtable.

HashMap is a supremely useful class. Hash tables allow you store together an arbitrary number of arbitrary objects. Instead of storing items with index values 0, 1, 2, 3 as you would in an array, you provide the key to be associated with the object. Then in the future, you need provide only that key again, and voila, out pops the right object.

Here are the public members in HashMap:

```
public class java.util.HashMap extends java.util.AbstractMap
    implements java.util.Map,java.lang.Cloneable,java.io.Serializable{
    public java.util.HashMap();
    public java.util.HashMap(int);
    public java.util.HashMap(int,float);
    public java.util.HashMap(java.util.Map);
    public void clear();
    public java.lang.Object clone();
    public boolean containsKey(java.lang.Object);
    public boolean containsValue(java.lang.Object);
    public java.util.Set entrySet();
    public java.lang.Object get(java.lang.Object);
    public boolean isEmpty();
    public java.util.Set keySet();
    public java.lang.Object put(java.lang.Object key, java.lang.Object
value);
    public void putAll(java.util.Map);
    public java.lang.Object remove(java.lang.Object);
    public int size();
    public java.util.Collection values();
}
```

Here is some example code that uses a hash map to hold a table of company stock symbols and stock prices.

```
import java.util.*;
public class hm {
    static HashMap myHM = new HashMap();

    public static void main(String[] arg) {
        createHM();
        showHM();
        System.out.println("You have "+myHM.size() +" stocks");
    }

    public static void createHM() {
        // stock symbols matched with prices on Nov 10, 1998
        myHM.put( "SUNW", new Double(64.5) );
        myHM.put( "IBM",  new Double(156.0) );
        myHM.put( "INTC", new Double(97.5) );
        myHM.put( "HWP",  new Double(64.5) );
    }

    public static void showHM() {
        Object o = myHM.get("SUNW");
        System.out.println(" SUNW price "+ o );
    }
}
```

Running the program, results in this:

```
% java hm
 SUNW price 64.5
You have 4 stocks
```

You can see that the collection of key/value pairs has been stored into a HashMap and can be retrieved on demand.

BitSet

This class maintains a set of bits that are identified by the value of an integer, like an array index. You can have up to about 2 billion individual bits in a set (if you have enough virtual memory), each of which can be queried, set, cleared and so on. The bit set will increase dynamically as needed to accommodate extra bits you add to it.

```
public BitSet();  // constructor
public BitSet(int N);  // constructor for set of size N bits

public void or (BitSet s); // OR's one bit set against another

public void set (int i); // sets bit number i.

public int size(); // returns the number of bits in the set.
```

Stack

The Stack class maintains a Last-In-First-Out stack of Objects. You can push (store) objects to arbitrary depth. The methods are:

```
public Object push(Object item);   // add to top of stack.

public Object pop();   // get top of stack.
```

In addition there are three other methods not usually provided for stacks.

```
public boolean empty(); // nothing on the stack?

public Object peek();   // returns top Object without popping it.

public int search (Object o); // returns how far down the stack
// this object is (1 is at the top), or -1 if not found.
```

The author of this class made an interesting mistake. He made Stack a subclass of Vector, so that he would get the vector behavior of allowing unbounded input. He failed to notice that it meant all the methods of Vector would be available in Stack— including inappropriate methods like removeElementAt() to pull something out of the middle of a vector. So Stack does not guarantee Last-In-First-Out behavior. Hans Rohnert from Germany pointed this out to me in email. As Hans put it, it is not true that Stack "is a" Vector, rather it should "have a" Vector in which to store.

The usual way to "hide" unwanted methods from a base class is to override them with private versions, or empty versions or versions that throw a runtime exception. In this case, Vector.removeElementAt(int) is final, and final methods can't be overriden. Never call `removeElementAt()` on your stack, and you'll stay out of trouble.

Some of these early 1.0 utility packages were written very quickly by skilled programmers who were more interested in getting the code working than achieving a perfect design. It's easier to find flaws in code than it is to write faultless software. Pointing out the occasional defect here is meant to instruct, not to denigrate the work of others.

Calendar Utilities

> ### Java Is Year 2000 Compliant
> Java is Y2K compliant in release JDK 1.1.6 and later, including JDK 1.2. The official statement is at URL http://www.sun.com/y2000/cpl.html. Prior to the 1.1.6 release there were some corner case bugs that had to be fixed.

The JDK 1.0 support for dates was poorly designed. With the benefit of hindsight, it might have been better to throw it out and start over again, but backwards-compatibility was seen as the more important goal. In JDK 1.1 most of the constructors and methods of java.util.Date class were deprecated and other classes were provided to offer better support for time zones and internationalization.

The classes specifically related to date/time are summarized below:

- The class `Date` represents a specific instant in time with millisecond precision.

- The class `Calendar` is an abstract class for converting between a `Date` object and a set of integer fields such as year, month, day, and hour.

- The class `GregorianCalendar` is the only concrete subclass of `Calendar` in the JDK. It does the date to fields conversions for the calendar system in common use.

- The class `DateFormat` is an abstract class that lets you convert a `Date` to a printable string with fields in the way you want (e.g., dd/mm/yy or dd.MMM.yyyy).

- The class `SimpleDateFormat` is the only concrete subclass of `DateFormat` in the JDK. It takes a format string and either parses a string to produce a date or takes a date and produces a string.

- The class `TimeZone` is an abstract class that represents a time zone offset and also figures daylight savings time adjustments.

- The class `SimpleTimeZone` is the only concrete subclass of `TimeZone` in the JDK. It is what defines an ordinary time zone with a simple daylight savings and daylight savings time period.

Not only was date/time support poorly designed, it was poorly implemented and full of bugs. The good news is that many of the bugs were corrected in 1.1.4

and 1.1.6. As of JDK 1.2, all of the common problems have been corrected. This part of the JDK is being maintained by IBM.

Deprecated Interfaces

Compatibility between releases is a major goal of JavaSoft's. In most cases this works very well, but there are a small number of cases where an API has had to be changed. When an API is replaced by a different one, JavaSoft assures software compatibility by leaving the old API in place and marking it as "deprecated."

To deprecate something means to disapprove of it. Deprecated features will eventually be removed from the API. When you compile a program that uses a deprecated API, the compiler will issue a single line error message, like this:

```
% javac foo.java
Note: foo.java uses a deprecated API.  Recompile with "-
deprecation" for details.
1 warning
```

The purpose of this warning is to tell you that you are using an old interface that has been replaced. The warning will not cause compilation to fail, but it reminds you that the class will eventually be removed from the JDK and you need to bring your code up to date. Only one deprecation warning is issued for a compilation, even if you use dozens of outmoded classes or methods. To view the full list of deprecated features that you have used, compile like this

```
% javac -deprecation foo.java
foo.java:4: Note: The constructor java.util.Date(int,int,int)
has been deprecated.
Date d1 = new Date(97,12,2);
          ^
Note: foo.java uses a deprecated API.
Please consult the documentation for a better alternative.
3 warnings
```

This tells you the deprecated feature, in this case one of the constructors in java.util.Date. You then look at the source code to see the suggested replacement. In this case, that piece of code refers you to java.util.Calendar. The Calendar class is the replacement for some methods in the Date class.

As a practical matter, some deprecated features may be unavoidable in your code—if you want your applets to run in the earliest Java-capable browsers, for example.

You can instantiate Date with no arguments, to represent the current moment.

```
Date now = new Date();
```

You used to be able to provide arguments (year, month, day, hour, etc.) to say "build me a Date that represents this date/time." That use is now deprecated and you should use the class GregorianCalendar instead.

Java uses a 64-bit long to represent an instant in time. The value is interpreted as "milliseconds since Jan 1 00:00:00, 1970." The scheme is sufficient to represent dates from 292,269,053 B.C. to A.D. 292,272,993 (64 bits covers minus 9,223,372,036,854,775,808 to plus 9,223,372,036,854,775,807 milliseconds). But note that prior to JDK 1.2, a GregorianCalendar will not accept values earlier than 4716 B.C. The class Date should really be thought of as "Instant" or "Timestamp."

Calendar and GregorianCalendar

The class Calendar translates between an instant in time, and individual fields like year, month, day, hour, etc. Date used to do this, but it did it in a way that didn't properly internationalize, so those methods have been deprecated.

Calendar also knows about time zones, and hence things like summertime. The time zone information has a class of its own: TimeZone. DateFormat class provides elementary Date formatting.

Calendar is an abstract base class, which is meant to be overridden by a subclass that implements a specific calendar system. It's a dumb approach: it makes the common case of simple date processing un-obvious. Most of the world uses the Gregorian calendar (named after the Pope who established it in 1582). Excessive generality in a design is as bad as (or worse than) excessive rigidity.

The class java.util.GregorianCalendar extends Calendar and provides more methods. Since Calendar is an abstract class, and the parent of GregorianCalendar, I recommend that you simply use GregorianCalendar all the time. Here is how you would get a date of a particular value:

```
GregorianCalendar g = new GregorianCalendar(61,7,13);
```

That represents the day the Berlin wall was constructed, August 13, 1961, in the European central time (ECT) zone. A more accurate way to construct that date is to first set the correct time zone, then set the date.

```
TimeZone z_ect = TimeZone.getTimeZone("ECT");
GregorianCalendar g = new GregorianCalendar(z_ect);
g.set(61,7,13);
```

Note that (rather stupidly) months are in the range 0 to 11, and years are represented by the four-digit year less 1900. If you don't specify a time zone, GregorianCalendar defaults to the time zone where the program is running. For example, for a program running in Japan, the default is Japanese standard time (JST). A list of all time zones can be found by looking in the source for java.util.TimeZone.java.

You can pull the individual values out of a date like this:

```
int year = g.get(Calendar.YEAR);
int month = g.get(Calendar.MONTH);
int date = g.get(Calendar.DATE);
int day = g.get(Calendar.DAY_OF_WEEK);
```

You can also check if one date is before or after another date. There is no simple way to get the amount of time between two dates. There are two "helper" classes: TimeZone and SimpleTimeZone. Again, SimpleTimeZone is a concrete subclass of TimeZone, and can be used exclusively. You can create a time zone object for any time zone you want, and then pass it to GregorianCalendar so it will work with values in that time zone.

```
TimeZone z_ect = TimeZone.getTimeZone("ECT");
GregorianCalendar g2 = new GregorianCalendar(z_ect);
g2.set(89, 10, 9, 19, 0); // Berlin Wall Down  Nov 9 1989 7pm
g2.set(89, Calendar.NOVEMBER, 9, 19, 0); // better
```

You can do simple date/time formatting with static methods from the class java.text.DateFormat, as the example below shows:

```
public static void main( String[] args ) {
    Date d = new Date();
    String s1 = DateFormat.getDateInstance().format( d );
    String s2 = DateFormat.getTimeInstance().format( d );
    String s3 = DateFormat.getDateTimeInstance().format( d );

    System.out.println("Date is " + s1 );
    System.out.println("Time is " + s2 );
    System.out.println("DateTime is " + s3 );
}
```

The program fragment runs to produce this:

```
Date is Nov 10, 1998
Time is 7:55:23 PM
DateTime is Nov 10, 1998 7:55:23 PM
```

You can also parse or convert a string into a DateFormat using that class. With methods from java.text.SimpleDateFormatMore, flexible parsing and formatting is available. You provide a format String argument to the constructor, in which different letters represent different fields of a date (day, hour, year, A.M. or P.M., etc.) and the style you want to see them in. Then you call the format() method with your date as the argument, and it passes it back as a String of the requested form.

```java
import java.text.*;
import java.util.*;
public class df {

    public static void main( String[] args ) {
        SimpleDateFormat df1 =
         new SimpleDateFormat("yyyy-MM-dd hh:mm:ss.S");
        SimpleDateFormat df2 = new SimpleDateFormat("dd MMM-yy");
        String startdatetime = "1998 11 10 19:23:27.0";
        try {
            Date d = df1.parse(startdatetime);
            String s = df2.format( d );
            System.out.println("Date is " + s );
        } catch (ParseException pe) {
            System.out.println("ParseException " + pe );
        }
    }
}
```

When you run that code, a String is parsed to get a Date, and then the Date is parsed to get a String in a different format. The resulting output is:

```
Date is 10-Nov-98
```

To parse/format other date and time fields, refer to Table 15-3. The number of times a pattern letter is repeated whether the short or long form of a text field is used. If there are at least four pattern letters, e.g., "EEEE," the long form will be used ("Tuesday"). Otherwise the short form (if there is one) will be used. For a number field, e.g., "SSSSS," the field will be zero-padded to that amount. Year is handled specially; a field of "yy" means truncate the year to two digits.

Table 15-3: SimpleDateFormat

Symbol	Meaning	Presentation	Example
G	era designator	(Text)	AD
y	year	(Number)	1996
M	month in year	(Text & Number)	July & 07
d	day in month	(Number)	10
h	hour in A.M./P.M. (1-12)	(Number)	12
H	hour in day (0-23)	(Number)	0
m	minute in hour	(Number)	30
s	second in minute	(Number)	55
S	millisecond	(Number)	978
E	day in week	(Text)	Tuesday
D	day in year	(Number)	189
F	day of week in month	(Number)	2 (2nd Wed in July)
w	week in year	(Number)	27
W	week in month	(Number)	2
a	A.M./P.M. marker	(Text)	PM
k	hour in day (1-24)	(Number)	24
K	hour in A.M./P.M. (0-11)	(Number)	0
z	time zone	(Text)	Pacific Standard Time
'	escape for text	(Delimiter)	
''	single quote	(Literal)	'

The class SimpleDateFormat is in package java.text rather than java.util because it is mostly concerned with internationalized and localized ways of formatting the date.

There is a great deal more information and code examples on dates/times/time zones in the Java FAQ that is on the CD. The database crowd fixed up date a little in java.sql.Date by overriding java.util.Date, and making it just deal with dates, not times as well. That's another possibility for you to use.

Other Utilities

Random

This is a class to provide pseudo random numbers. We call them "pseudo-random" rather than random because the source of bits is an algorithm. To the casual observer it looks like a random stream of bits and for most applications we can pretend that they are. The numbers aren't really random, though, and sequences tend to get stuck in repetitive cycles after a large number of iterations.

If you just quickly want a random number between 0.0 and (just less than) 1.0, then package Math has a method random, which is just a wrapper for instantiating Random one time, and then supplying values. You would call it like this:

```
double d = Math.random();   // 0.0 .. 1.0
```

How to Look at the API of a Class

You can run javap on a fully qualified classname to list the methods in the class. The class java.util.Random (below) was listed this way.

```
% javap java.util.Random
```

The class Random has:

```
public class java.util.Random implements java.io.Serializable {
    public java.util.Random();
    public java.util.Random(long);
    protected synchronized int next(int);
    public boolean nextBoolean();
    public void nextBytes(byte[]);
    public double nextDouble();
    public float nextFloat();
    // a Gaussian distribution has mean 0.0, standard deviation 1.0.
    public synchronized double nextGaussian();
    public int nextInt();
    public int nextInt(int);
    public long nextLong();
    public synchronized void setSeed(long);
}
```

The nextGaussian() provides numbers symmetrically distributed around zero, and successively unlikelier to be picked the further away from zero you get. If we collected a group of these numbers and plotted them, they would form the shape of a bell curve. The algorithm used here for taking random values from a Gaussian distribution is from *The Art of Computer Programming* by Donald Knuth (Addison-Wesley, 1994: Section 3.4.1, Algorithm C).

You can instantiate Random with or without a seed. Here it is with a seed:

```
java.util.Random r = new java.util.Random(344L);
```

If you don't give it a seed, it uses the current reading from the day/time clock (the millisecond part of this is going to be pretty close to random). If you choose to supply the seed, you will get the same series of random numbers every time you supply that same seed. This is useful in testing and debugging code.

To get a random int value in a certain range (say, 0 to 5) to simulate the cast of a die, you would use:

```
int myturn = r.nextInt(6);
```

The method nextDouble returns a value between 0.0 and 1.0. To get a random double value in a certain range (say, 0.0 to 100.0) to simulate a percentage, you would scale it up with multiplication:

```
double mypercent = r.nextDouble() * 100.0;
```

StringTokenizer

The fundamental idea of StringTokenizer is to instantiate it with a string, and it will then break that string up into islands of characters separated by seas of white space. If you gave it the string "Noel Bat is a fossil," successive calls to nextToken would return the individual strings "Noel" followed by "Bat" then "is" then "a" then "fossil" then a further call would throw the NoSuchElementException.

Actually you can specify the delimiters for the substring, and they don't have to be white space. One of the constructors allows for new delimiting characters to be set and also takes a boolean saying whether the delimiters themselves should be returned. The representative methods are:

```
public   StringTokenizer(String words_to_breakup); // constructor

public   StringTokenizer(String words_to_breakup,
                         String delimiting_chars,
                         boolean return_delims); // constructor

public boolean hasMoreTokens();

public String nextToken();
```

You may have noticed that tokenizing a string is a pretty similar operation to enumerating all the elements in it. The StringTokenizer class does in fact implement the Enumeration interface and provide bodies for hasMoreElements() and nextElement(). They are alternatives to the token methods and return exactly the same objects. In the case of nextElement, the return type is Object, not String, but the Object it returns is a String. The StringTokenizer is simpler than the StreamTokenizer we met earlier. StringTokenizer just breaks things up into Strings. StreamTokenizer does this and also tries to classify them as things like numbers and words.

How to Time Your Code

Here's how you can time your Java code:

```
long start = System.currentTimeMillis();
   :    // do the work here
   :
long stop = System.currentTimeMillis();
System.out.println("time: " + (stop-start) + "millisecs");
```

Observer and Observable

These two are a matched pair. Together they provide a general interface for one thread to communicate a state change to another. We'll start with Observer, because it is simpler.

Observer is an interface that looks like this:

```
public interface Observer {
    void update(Observable o, Object arg);
}
```

Any object that wants to look at (observe) something else asynchronously can declare that it is an observer and provide its own body for update. The update() method is just a callback, so let's give an example of use. When you ask an image file to load, the method returns at once and in the background (as soon as it's sure you want it) starts reading the file off disk. That incoming file is an observable event. The thread that asked to load it is an observer.

When the thing that it's looking at has something to communicate, it will call update. Since the observer might be keeping an eye on several observable objects, update needs to be told which of them is calling it. That is the purpose of the first argument. The second argument is an object to permit just about anything at all to be passed in. The body of update will do whatever needs doing when that observable object says, "Look at me."

A a JPEG file example, there will be a number of times when there is enough information to call observer.update(). It may be called when the image file header has been read, when we have decoded enough to know the height of the image, when we know the width, and when the entire transfer has been completed.

Now lets take a look at Observable. The class Observable is intended to be extended by classes you write. The key methods that Observable provides are:

```
public synchronized void addObserver(Observer o);
// this is how an Observer registers its interest
// with the Observable thing.

protected synchronized void setChanged();
// only subclasses have the privilege of saying something
// observable has changed.

public void notifyObservers();
public void notifyObservers(Object arg);
```

If the *changed* flag is true, then these two routines call the update() method of all Observers. It's done this way (with an extra flag) so the observable thing has precise control over when notification really takes place.

Observer/observable is another example of a design pattern. You could think of it as an alternative, more general, version of a wait( )/notify( ). Like wait/notify, observer/observable is always used with threads. Unlike wait/notify observer.update( ) is called rather than just allowed to contend for the lock.

There are also methods to delete one or all Observers, and set, clear, or query an internal "changed" flag that an Observer may look at.

Note: Having justified Observer and Observable in terms of loading image files, you should be aware that image loading actually uses its own special version of Observer, called ImageObserver. It works in exactly the same way as Observer and it's unclear why the general mechanism was defined, only to be passed over in favor of a special purpose implementation for image files.

One common use of Observer/Observable is in sending a message from a dialog window back to its parent Frame. The parent implements Observer, the dialog class contains an Observable object, and a method to return the text. Then, when the dialog captures some relevant information, it sets its own changed bit and calls notifyObservers().

Properties

Java has a platform-independent way to communicate extra information at runtime to a program. Known as *properties* these do a job like environment variables. Environment variables aren't used because they are too platform-specific. A programmer can read the value of a property by calling getProperty() and passing an argument string for the property in which you are interested.

```
String dir = System.getProperty("user.dir");
```

A long list of predefined properties appears in the file java/lang/System.java and is reproduced below. Some properties are not available in applets for security reasons. You can also define a property on the command line when you invoke the program like this:

```
java -Drate=10.0 myprogram
```

That value "10.0" will be returned as a string when querying the property "rate". It can then be converted to a floating-point number and used as a value in the program. In this case, it's an alternative to a command line argument, but with the advantage that its value is visible everywhere, not just in main.

Table 15-4 lists the predefined properties, guaranteed to have a value on every Java client. There are others, too.

Table 15-4: Predefined Properties

Property Name	Explanation	Visible in Applet
java.version	Version number of the Java system	yes
java.vendor	Vendor specific string	yes
java.vendor.url	Vendor URL	yes
java.home	Java installation directory	no
java.class.version	Java class version number	yes
java.class.path	Java classpath	no
os.name	Operating System Name	yes
os.arch	Operating System Architecture	yes
os.version	Operating System Version	yes
file.separator	File separator ("/" on Unix)	yes
path.separator	Path separator (":" on Unix)	yes
line.separator	Line separator ("\n" on Unix)	yes
user.name	User account name	no
user.home	User home directory	no
user.dir	User's current working directory	no

Most programs don't need to access these properties at all. But when they do, it's nice to be able to do it in a platform-independent way.

java.util.Properties

You will be happy to hear that there is a java.util class to help you read in and process properties. The java.util.Properties class is really just an instance of Hash-Table with a few extra methods wrapped around it. The concept of properties is in some other languages too, like Lisp and Forth. The Java system comes with a whole set of predefined properties holding information about the implementation.

This utility class has two purposes: First, it allows a property table to be read in and written out via streams. Second, it allows programmers to search more than one property table with a single command. If you don't need either of these benefits, then just use a HashMap instead of a Properties table. Typical methods are:

```
public String getProperty(String key);

public synchronized void load(InputStream in)
        throws IOException;
// reads key/value pairs in from a stream, stores them in this

public synchronized void save(OutputStream out, String header);
// writes the key/value pairs out as text
// the header is just a comment string you provide to label
// the property table. The current date is also appended.
```

To put entries in a Properties object, just use the put(Object key, Object element) method inherited from HashTable. So that you don't feel obliged to start adding to the predefined system property table, there's a feature that you can provide an existing properties table to a constructor. This creates an empty properties list that you can populate. Whenever you do a getProperty, it will search your table. If nothing is found, it will go on to search the table provided to the constructor. Here is an example:

```
Properties sp = System.getProperties();
Properties mytable = new Properties(sp);
mytable.list(System.out);
```

The first line gets the standard predefined properties table. The second line piggy-backs it onto a second Properties table that we create and can fill with a call like: mytable.put (propertyname, propertyvalue). When we do a lookup in mytable, it will look up first in mytable and then in the system properties table. The third line prints mytable out (intended for debugging, but it's not clear why you can't just use the save() method). The method public String getProperty(String key, String default); will return the default String if there is no entry for this key in the table.

Note on the Java Native Interface

The Java Native Interface is an API that allows you to make calls into C and C++ programs from Java. You can also make calls into any other programming language that can follow the C calling and linking conventions. Non-Java code is referred to as native code, hence it is a native interface.

If you use the JNI, you destroy portability, which is the major benefit of Java. The JNI should be used only as a last resort under special circumstances. Most programs don't need it and won't use it. Readers who want to put JNI into practice can browse to the JavaSoft web page at http://java.sun.com/products/jdk/1.1/docs/guide/jni/index.html. If this has moved, use the search facility on the home page, http://java.sun.com

Only use native methods when you really have to

Some Light Relief

There's an old story to the effect that "the people at Cray design their supercomputers with Apple systems, and the Apple designers use Crays!" Apart from this being a terrific example of recurring rotational serendipity (what goes around, comes around) is there any truth to it?

Like many urban legends, this one contains a nugget of truth. In the 1991 Annual Report of Cray Research, Inc., there is a short article describing how Apple used a Cray for designing Macintosh cases. The Cray is used to simulate the injection molding of the plastic enclosure cases. The Mac II case was the first Apple system to benefit from the modeling, and the trial was successful. The simulation identified warping problems which were solved by prototyping thus saving money in tooling and production. Apple also uses their Cray for simulating air flow inside the enclosure to check for hot spots. The Cray house magazine reported that the Apple PowerBook continues to use supercomputer simulations. (CRAY CHANNELS, Spring 1992 pp.10-12 "Apple Computer PowerBook computer molding simulation").

The inverse story holds that Seymour Cray himself used a Macintosh to design Crays. The story seems to have originated with an off-the-cuff remark from Seymour Cray himself, who had a Macintosh at home and used it to store some of his work for the Cray 3. Common sense suggests that the simulation of discrete circuitry (Verilog runs, logic analysis, etc.) which is part of all modern integrated circuit design is done far more cost-effectively on a supercomputer than on a microprocessor. Cray probably has a lot of supercomputer hardware laying around ready for testing as it comes off the production line.

It's conceivable that a Macintosh could be used to draft the layout of blinking lights for the front of a Cray, or choose some nice color combinations, or some other non-CPU intensive work. A Macintosh is a very good system for writing design notes, sending email, and drawing diagrams, all of which are an equally essential part of designing a computer system.

The good folks at Cray Research have confirmed in a Cray Users Group newsletter that they have a few Macs on the premises. So, while it's extremely unlikely that they run logic simulations on their Macs, we can indeed chalk it up as only-slightly-varnished truth that "the people at Cray design their supercomputers with Apple's systems, and the Apple designers use Crays," for some value of the word "design!"

Exercises

1. Convince yourself that the nextGaussian numbers form a bell curve by writing a program to actually do it. *Hint:* You'll find it easier plot a graph using ASCII text if you generate the values first, save them, and sort them into order before plotting the values. Do you know any data-structures that can help with storing and sorting?

CHAPTER
16

- Object Communication Middleware

- Remote Method Invocation

- Object Serialization

- Java and Databases: JDBC

- Some Light Relief

Java Enterprise Libraries

*"There's a **tomato** in every automaton."*

—**Professor Rudolph's Big Book of Finite
State Machines and Fruit Fancies**

As well as organizing the Java libraries into core library/standard extension, Sun Microsystems also groups related libraries under an umbrella name. Thus we have:

- Java Enterprise APIs

- The Java Server Product Family

- Java Electronic Commerce Framework

- Java Media APIs

There are other library families, too. In a short space of time, a rich variety of Java tools, APIs, and services has been specified and implemented in a cooperative partnership with all interested parties in the computer industry. Sun has taken the unusual (for the computer industry) step of developing industry consensus around the Java APIs. There is a complete road map showing how future libraries will be added. Java has thus evolved from a programming language to a full operating environment with the cooperation of the entire industry, except for Microsoft, which is actively working to undermine it for you. The initiative clearly positions Java as a complete software solution, scalable from the smallest applet on a palmtop to the biggest server in the corporate data center.

APIs

We're going to be using the term API a lot in this section, so let's review the meaning. An API is an *Application Programmer Interface*. It is a specification of a software library, detailing all the function calls, arguments, and results you get back from them. An API exists on paper and is just a design. To actually use an API, you need a real library that implements the API.

Chapter 7 of the ANSI C specification is an API describing many functions like printf( ) in the C runtime library. On Unix, the file libc.so is the library that implements the API. An API promises some services on paper; a library delivers them in code.

When Jorge Luis Borges commented, "I have always imagined that paradise will be a kind of library," he probably had Java 1.2 in mind.

Java Enterprise

In this chapter we'll review the libraries that offer support for enterprise computing, and we'll look at code examples of the two most important packages. By "enterprise computing," we mean large scale data processing, using multi-gigabyte databases, multiple server systems, and with high availability/reliability requirements. The Java Enterprise APIs allow Java applications to be integrated with corporate databases, including legacy applications. Within Java Enterprise, about ten individual APIs have been designated:

- **Enterprise JavaBeans** (EJB). These are server-side software components, and the concept is attracting a lot of excitement and interest. The idea is to write a set of re-usable classes that support business functions.

  Currently, developers have to know how to write both business logic and specialized system-level programs that control features such as security and the ability to handle multiple transactions—a tedious and complex task. The Enterprise JavaBeans API provides the framework for the specialized system level communications, letting corporate developers concentrate on writing the logic to solve business problems. Some people think of EJB as an open replacement for Microsoft Transaction Server.

- **Java Server Pages** (JSB). It has been described as "the front door to enterprise applications." JSP is a specification that provides an easy way to access server-side components from web pages. It separates the presentation of dynamic content from the generation of that content, and gives you the ability to use Java to generate dynamic content for the web. Java Server Pages are HTML files written in a combination of industry-standard HTML, Java Server Pages HTML tags, and Java as a "glue" language.

  A Java Server Pages file has the extension .jsp and calls reusable components that reside on the server. In this release, the components are JavaBeans or Java servlets, with support for enterprise JavaBeans planned.

- **Java Servlet API**. This API is the server-side version of applets. When you browse a particular URL, you cause a Java servlet to be run on the server on your behalf. The result of running that code will be sent to the browser as HTML. It may contain extracts from a database, calculations, or even sound or images.

- **Java Naming and Directory Interface** (JNDI). The API supports a stan dard for connection to and use of different enterprise-wide naming and directory services, such as LDAP or Banyan Vines.

- **Java IDL**. Implements the OMG Interface Definition Language specification, as a language-neutral way to specify an interface between an object and a client on a different platform. It allows Java to call out to other non-Java object frameworks.

- **JDBC**. This is a DBMS-independent database access API for Java. It uses standard SQL and provides access to many different relational databases.

- **Java RMI**. A remote method invocation between peers, or between client and server, when both ends are written in Java. RMI is an object-oriented protocol that does the same kind of thing as RPC. RMI is built on object serialization. Object serialization is a new I/O library to turn an object into a byte stream, usually written to disk, and later reconstitute it back into an object.

- **Java Message Service** (JMS). Asynchronous messaging is a proven communication model for developing large-scale, distributed enterprise applications. JMS is an interface that makes it easy for Java programs to talk to message-oriented-middleware, such as MQSeries from IBM. Oracle plans to implement JMS throughout its server products. The standard is also backed by Sybase, Software AG, BEA Systems, Vitria and other messaging software vendors.

- **Java Transaction Management**. The transaction management interfaces are defined in two complementary libraries: a transaction service specification for companies providing transaction infrastructure and a transaction API for applications that run under such a framework. The former is a Java mapping of the OMG Object Transaction Service (OTS). This latter is a Java mapping of the industry standard X/Open XA interface.

The Java Enterprise APIs make it easy to create large-scale commercial and database applications that can share multimedia and other data with applications inside an organization or across the Internet.

Java Security

Java Security APIs are a framework to let developers put security-related features in their applets and applications. The features include cryptography with digital signatures, encryption, and authentication. Respectively, these allow you to say who you are, secretly, and have other people believe it.

JDK 1.2 introduces big improvements to the security features: it has policy-based, configurable, fine-grained access control; new cryptographic services and certificate and key management classes and interfaces; and three new tools (keytool, jarsigner, and policytool). These topics are discussed in the context of applets in the Applet chapter. Access control has evolved to be far more detailed than in previous versions of the Java platform. Access control can now be applied equally to applets and applications.

As far as cryptography goes, U.S. computer companies currently have to bear the expense of preparing two versions of their products: one with cryptography for the domestic market, and one with no or weaker cryptography for export. This is because the U.S. government currently insists on putting cryptographic software in the same category as machine guns, bazookas, and nuclear submarines, forbidding export under arms trading regulations.

Now systems developers can use the Java Security APIs and provide the receptacle into which alternative encryption modules can easily be placed. The Java crypto design provides a clean separation between applications and the cryptography, so that developers (or users) can plug in one of several alternative cryptographic algorithms. This simplifies matters for U.S. vendors. If you agree with the current position of the U.S. government that software (like Netscape Navigator and the Unix operating system) is a munition, that cryptography should be restricted so the U.S. government can break it, and that the U.S. government should have a "back door" key to read anyone's encoded messages (including yours), then here are some things to consider:

- *Do not* follow Usenet newsgroups alt.security.pgp, talk.politics.crypto or sci.crypt.

- *Do not* download and use PGP (Pretty Good Privacy), a package of strong encryption available for all popular systems, written by Phil Zimmermann. Do *not* visit http://web.mit.edu/pgp and follow the directions to download. Overseas readers should instead avoid visiting the alternative site http://www.ifi.uio.no/~staalesc/PGP/language.html in Norway.

- *Do not* buy Phil Zimmermann's books available in many bookstores. Do not specify *The Official PGP User's Guide,* by Philip Zimmermann (MIT Press, 1995) with ISBN 0-262-74017-6 for $14.95. Nor should you read *PGP Source Code and Internals* by Philip Zimmerman (MIT Press, 1995) with ISBN 0-262-24039-4. This book contains the entire source code for PGP and almost put the U.S. government in the medieval position of banning the sale and distribution of a book.

- Especially *do not* type in this Perl program and execute it using the Perl interpreter on the CD.

```
#!/bin/perl -s-- -export-a-crypto-system-sig -RSA-3-lines-PERL
$m=unpack(H.$w,$m."\0"x$w),$_=`echo "16do$w 2+40i0$d*-^1[d2%Sa
2/d0<X+d*La1=z\U$n%0]SX$k"[$m*]\EszlXx++p|dc`,s/^.|\W//g,print
pack('H*',$_)while read(STDIN,$m,($w=2*$d-1+length$n&~1)/2)
```

Under current U.S. law, it is illegal to put this program on the CD, but it is not illegal to print it in a book. This Perl program has been optimized for small size, and it implements RSA coding/decoding in three lines.

Everybody in the world already has access to the Data Encryption Standard (DES), the strong encryption technique standardized by the U.S. government in

1977, and to RSA (a coding scheme that, unlike DES[1], has not yet been broken for reasonable key lengths). Prohibiting its export doesn't keep it out of any nation's hands. So why do it? Some people speculate that the real agenda driving the NSA is their fear that bundling DES in popular American software products will encourage routine use of good cryptography both inside and outside the U.S.; this makes traffic analysis much harder for them.

Therefore (the theory runs), the U.S. government wants cryptography to be awkward to deploy, not because they can't break it, but because they want to discourage people inside the U.S. from using better products by default. If you spend a long time in the counterintelligence world, I guess that's how you end up thinking.

There is a lot of shady misinformation fed to the media, who are all too ready to report it unquestioningly. *Parade Magazine* (Sept. 29, 1996) printed a reader's letter that asked, "If we know so much, how come we can't catch terrorists?" *Parade Magazine* printed an answer from "an expert" claiming that "they started using codes on the Internet." Needless to say, this is such complete nonsense, one can only presume they are trying to soften up public opinion to accept restrictions on privacy on the Internet.

JavaBeans

After the Enterprise API family, JavaBeans is probably the most significant API. It is a component object model that ties all the other APIs together. It's a little hard to describe something so abstract, but the JavaBeans family defines a portable, platform-neutral set of APIs for software components to talk to each other.

JavaBeans are little fragments of programs that can be joined together at runtime to form complete programs. Just as Legos can be plugged together to create a model building, JavaBeans can be plugged together to create a bigger program. A bean can inspect other beans and call their methods. A few typical functions that can be put into beans include sorting, searching, drawing graphs, creating spreadsheets, printing services, and so on.

1. See the book, *Cracking DES: Secrets of Encryption Research, Wiretap Politics & Chip Design* (O'Reilly & Associates, 1998), the legally-exportable parts of which are on the CD.

JavaBeans are an example of component software that has been popularized in the PC world with Borland's Delphi product. Several benefits are claimed for components, including rapid application development (RAD) and software development by users. It is an evolving area and shows great promise.

JavaBeans make it easier for developers to write applications that use a common framework to blend programs seamlessly. The usual example people give is embedding a spreadsheet in a word processor document, and a chart program in the spreadsheet. The application is much wider and more significant than that. If the promise of beans is fulfilled, it will provide a complete desktop component environment independent of the underlying operating system.

JavaBeans required some refinement of the AWT. Now that has been completed (the JDK 1.1 event model and renaming of some methods), JavaBeans and the AWT work seamlessly together. All Swing GUI components are JavaBeans.

Object Communication Middleware

This section contains a description of some Java-related products. It provides useful background information on non-Java object software.

CORBA

If you read the object-oriented trade press, one term you may have seen more and more is CORBA. CORBA is the *Common Object Request Broker Architecture*. In a single sentence, it is a framework to let objects on one computer to talk to objects on another computer, just as Unix RPC (Remote Procedure Call) lets processes talk to one another. CORBA is a true object-oriented distributed processing framework. The "common" part means that it is not tied to any one language, or any one hardware vendor, but can inter-operate among all. CORBA was designed over the course of several years in an open industry-wide process, with the main participants being the Unix hardware vendors: DEC, HP, Sun, and IBM.

Why do you want objects on different computers to talk to each other? Because it allows you to build much more complicated and capable systems that support true distributed processing. It's not intended for a single programmer working on a lone PC. It is highly useful in a large enterprise with Terabytes of data distributed in databases on dozens of mainframe class systems.

CORBA implementations have been deployed over the last couple of years. CORBA is language-neutral, and it achieves this by having an interface language (it looks close to C) that other languages must map into. Making CORBA language independent was a very far-sighted decision on the part of the original designers, and it means there is a place for CORBA in the Java world.

CORBA implementations were often deployed with C++, but with the right "glue" or interface definition language (IDL), they can talk to Java programs and supply object services across a net.

When you want objects to communicate across different systems, there are two main reasons for using CORBA instead of just using Java's RMI:

- CORBA provides an object framework that is language independent. If you're using multiple languages, or you wish to leave that option open for the future, or you want to access C++ legacy systems, CORBA makes it easy.

- The CORBA initiative started before Java, and the CORBA code is further along. CORBA ORBs are sophisticated pieces of middleware that can schedule, route, queue and despatch incoming object requests. System administrators can inspect queues and do load-balancing across servers.

JDK 1.2 adds a set of classes to provide ORB access and full support for talking to anybody's objects through CORBA. The release even includes a lightweight ORB, which can be replaced by your commercial ORB of choice. The overlap between Java RMI and CORBA is still being worked on. Sun has indicated that it will deliver a library that lets RMI run over IIOP (the Internet Inter-ORB Protocol allowing different CORBA implementations to talk to one another), though this didn't make it into 1.2. When that arrives it will make it simpler still for Java to communicate with the existing base of distributed systems. Start up Java RMI at one end, and let it talk IIOP directly to your CORBA objects, without the programmer needing to have IDL knowledge.

CORBA is a big, industrial-strength, language-independent, object communication system. Java's RMI is a smaller, simpler system that currently can be used only when both endpoints are written in Java. CORBA gives you compatibility with legacy code, Java's RMI provides simplicity of remote communication. The two are converging into a single Java solution.

IDL

IDL or *Interface Definition Language* is the way CORBA achieves language-neutrality. You describe in IDL the signature of the methods and data that CORBA will pass back and forth for you. IDL looks somewhat like C, but it is purely for describing interfaces, not writing actual programs. IDL is only for people using CORBA. Many Java systems won't see the CORBA framework directly, so many Java programmers will not need to bother with IDL.

Remote Method Invocation

Remote Method Invocation (RMI) is a java-specific version of a CORBA. RMI means that an object on one system can call a method in an object somewhere else on the network. It will send over parameters, and get a result back automatically. It all happens invisibly, and just looks like the invocation of a local method (it may take a little longer time of course). RMI directly supports client/server systems in Java. Clients can truly make procedure calls directly to their server

How does this differ from opening a socket to the server? It's a higher-level interface (RMI is actually built on top of sockets). A socket just lets you pass data to the server. RMI lets you call a method on the server, and pass objects in and out. This *is* a very big deal!

For those familiar with Remote Procedure Calls (RPC), RMI is RPC with an object-oriented flavor. It is also very simple to set up and use, compared to what it offers. Let's think about the problem for a second, show a diagram in Figure 16-1, and use that to lead into a description of how it works, with a code example. What we are trying to do is allow an object in a Java program on one system to call a method in a Java program on another system. Furthermore, we want this to look as similar as possible to a method calling a method in the same program.

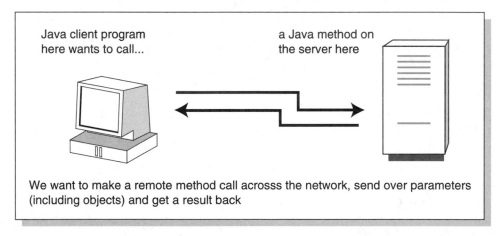

Java client program here wants to call...

a Java method on the server here

We want to make a remote method call acrosss the network, send over parameters (including objects) and get a result back

Figure 16-1: What RMI does.

Not only does RMI look like RPC, it is implemented in a similar way to this established, and ingenious software. We know that it is not possible to make the desired call directly, so we break the problem down into smaller pieces that can be done directly. We make the client call a local routine which looks just like the one it wants to call remotely. We call this local dummy routine a *stub*. The stub is responsible for getting the incoming arguments and transmitting them over to its buddy on the server machine. It does this by opening a socket, serializing the objects, and passing the data across.

The buddy routine on the server machine is called a *skeleton* because it's just the bare bones of a routine. It doesn't do anything except unmarshal the data passed to it, and call the real server routine. The algorithm is then reversed to communicate the result back to the method on the client machine. And so a remote method has been invoked on one system by another, as shown in Figure 16-2.

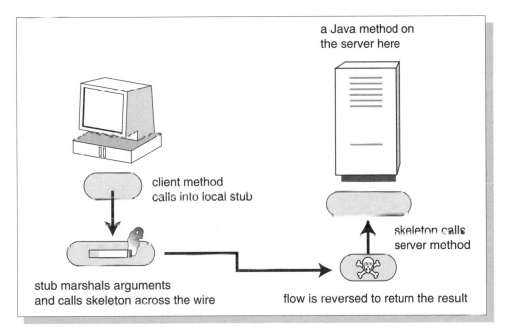

Figure 16-2: How RMI does it.

Various extra cleverness takes place to support sending Objects across the network, including sending the exact type of the object arguments with the data. If that class doesn't exist on the receiving side, the corresponding class object itself is also loaded over the network.

Outline of our RMI System

Let's look at a code example to make this abstract description a little more concrete. Suppose we have a computer system that is physically connected to all sorts of weather-monitoring equipment: rain gauges, thermometer, anemometer, barometer, and so on. This will be our server system. We will abstract an interface of this, that describes the methods that can be called remotely.

The remote method we want to invoke is getWeatherReadings(). We need to provide an implementation of this on the server, and we need to provide an interface for it on the client, so it can compile against it. The next section describes this server interface.

The Interface to the RMI Remote Server

The interface WeatherIntf is compiled on the client, and it describes the service (method calls) that we will be accessing remotely. The interface looks like this:

```
public interface WeatherIntf extends java.rmi.Remote {
    public String getWeather() throws java.rmi.RemoteException;
}
```

It is recommended that you always compile remote servers and interfaces into a named package, and not try to lazily squeak by using the anonymous package as we have to date.

The interface says that it extends (i.e. includes all the methods promised by) the java.rmi.Remote interface. WeatherIntf promises one method of its own "getWeather()" that returns a String, and may throw a RemoteException. There's nothing too special about RemoteException. It can be caught like any other exception. Rather than try to propagate arbitrary exceptions across the ether, we just have the one RemoteException type, and build into its string message some indication of what went wrong remotely.

Next we will look at the client code that uses this remote interface.

The RMI Client

The client code is straightforward. It looks like this:

```
import java.rmi.*;
public class RMIdemo {

    public static void main(String[] args) {
      try {
          Remote robj = Naming.lookup("//localhost/WeatherServer");
          WeatherIntf weatherserver = (WeatherIntf) robj;

          String forecast = weatherserver.getWeather();

          System.out.println("The weather will be " + forecast );

      } catch (Exception e) {System.out.println(e.getMessage());}
    }
}
```

The only new thing in this code is these two lines:

```
          Remote robj = Naming.lookup("//localhost/WeatherServer");
          WeatherIntf weatherserver = (WeatherIntf) robj;
```

The first line creates a Remote. This is the counterpart of an Object, but it represents a reference to something that can be anywhere outside this Java virtual machine. The naming lookup takes a string that looks something like a URL. It describes:

- The name of the server—localhost (use a different system once you have this working locally).

- The service to look for—the service called "WeatherServer."

Figure 16-3 illustrates how everything fits together.

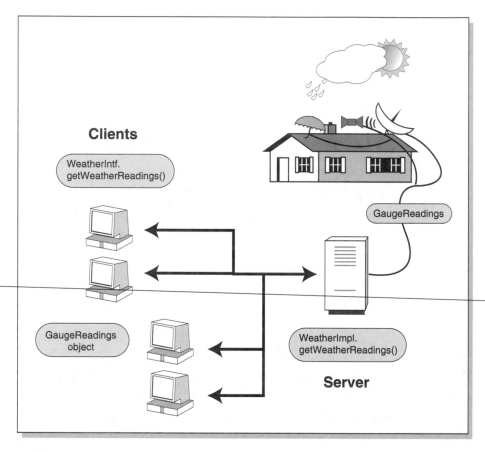

Figure 16-3: The weather station client/server.

Everyone who wishes to communicate with a server has to agree on the name of the server and the name of the service. For this example I am running server and client all on one machine, so I just use the special name localhost (a TCP/IP standard meaning "this system". I made up the name "WeatherServer" for the service.

Our Remote object implements the WeatherIntf interface. As a result, we can cast it to that interface, and use it to invoke the "getWeather()" call that the interface promises. We catch any exceptions (there shouldn't be any) and print out the String that we receive back. This example uses a String object to represent the gauge readings, but you can pass back and forth objects of arbitrary complexity, both as arguments and return values.

Apart from the references to Remote, there is nothing at all in this code that is different from a wholly local system. What a marvellous advantage to have code that works the same way in the local case and when distributed across a network.

The RMI Remote Server Code

Finally we come to the server code that has some (a very little) RMI magic dust sprinkled over it to make everything work. The code looks like:

```java
import java.rmi.*;
import java.rmi.server.UnicastRemoteObject;
public class WeatherServer extends UnicastRemoteObject
                             implements WeatherIntf {
    public WeatherServer ()  throws java.rmi.RemoteException {
        super();
    }

    public String getWeather() throws RemoteException {
        return Math.random()>0.5? "sunny" : "rainy";
    }

    public static void main(String[] args) {
        System.setSecurityManager(new RMISecurityManager());
        try {
            WeatherServer myWeatherServer = new WeatherServer();
            Naming.rebind("/WeatherServer",myWeatherServer);
        }catch (Exception e) {
            System.out.println(e.getMessage() );
        }
    }
}
```

Here we extend the `java.rmi.server.UnicastRemoteObject` class. This tips off the system that clients will expect to talk to and treat instances of this class as Remote objects. We extend the WeatherIntf. This promises that we will provide an implementation of the getWeather() method. Sure enough, we do. The getWeather() method just looks at a random number to decide whether to predict sunshine or rain, exactly the same as professional weather forecasters do. Alternatively, the software could actually be wired to all those instruments up on the roof through a serial port interface.

We set a security manager (this is required in a server). It allows us to customize the kind of accesses and services that we are going to provide. Then we create an instance of this class simply so we can pass the object as an argument to the Naming.rebind. Rebind is the way a server announces its service to the registry.

There is a central table called the Registry on each server. It contains a list of service names paired with (essentially) socket connections. It is not the Windows Registry, but it does a similar job: acts as a central place to ask for information.

Compiling and Running the Code

Here, alas, is where things get a little complicated. As part of moving to JDK 1.2, the security framework was strengthened considerably. I am going to tell you the steps to successfully execute this system, and refer you to chapter 14 for the explanation of the new security model.

On Windows 95, TCP/IP networking is somewhat fragile, and often seems not to work unless you have a dial-up connection to your ISP in place. There is some information about this in the FAQ. It is easy to screw up and find that your efforts to reproduce this example don't work. To help prevent that, I will present numbered steps to compile and run this example, and I recommend you follow them exactly. You'll need three command windows: one each for the registry, the server, and the client (on Unix you could run them all in the background out of one window if you wanted).

1. Put all three source files in a directory on your hard disk.

2. Compile the programs. Compile the interface first, then the server and the client.

    ```
    javac WeatherIntf.java
    javac WeatherServer.java
    javac RMIdemo.java
    ```

3. Generate the stub and skeleton files for the server.

    ```
    rmic WeatherServer
    ```

4. Move the class files to somewhere the JDK can find them.

    ```
    copy *.class $JAVAHOME/jre/classes
    ```

5. Start the registry by entering the following JDK command at the command line in a shell tool you are not otherwise using:

    ```
    rmiregistry
    ```

6. Create a file called "permit" that grants socket permission to the server. The file should contain these lines. The I/O permission is not needed, but is an example of another kind of permission.

```
grant  {
    permission java.net.SocketPermission "*", "connect";
    permission java.net.SocketPermission "*", "accept";
    permission java.io.FilePermission "/tmp/*", "read";
};
```

7. Start the remote server, mentioning your permission file.

    ```
    java -Djava.security.policy=permit WeatherServer
    ```

8. Then start the client.

    ```
    java RMIdemo
    ```

9. Electrons will whizz back and forth across the ether for a second or two, and then you will get the weather forecast:

    ```
    The weather will be sunny
    ```

A common mistake results in this error message:

```
Unexpected exception; nested exception is:
java.io.NotSerializableException:
```

Any classes whose objects are sent remotely must implement java.io.Serializable. This is a change between JDK 1.0 and JDK 1.1.

RMI is a very powerful technique for building large systems. The fact that the technique can be described, along with a working example, in just a few pages, speaks volumes in favor of Java. RMI is tremendously exciting and it's simple to use. You can call to any server you can bind to, and you can build networks of distributed objects. RMI opens the door to software systems that were formerly too complex to build.

Object Serialization

Serializing an object just means writing the values of all its data fields into a stream of bytes. You already know how to serialize an array or a String. Two new classes let you serialize/deserialize other objects, too.

Once you can turn an object into a stream, you can write it to a file (which gives you a persistent object that lives on after the program in which it was created), print it, pipe it to a thread, or even send it down a socket to another system on the other side of the world. All of these are useful things.

Object serialization is in the java.io class, along with all the other classes that process streams. The new classes are:

```
public class java.io.ObjectOutputStream
        extends java.io.DataOutputStream
        implements java.io.ObjectOutput {
    public java.io.ObjectOutputStream(java.io.OutputStream);

    public final void writeObject(java.lang.Object);
}
```

```
public class java.io.ObjectInputStream
        extends java.io.DataInputStream implements java.io.ObjectInput
{
    public java.io.ObjectInputStream(java.io.InputStream);
    public final java.lang.Object readObject();
    public synchronized void
registerValidation(java.io.ObjectInputValidation,int);
}
```

A whole slew of exceptions can be thrown by the readObject routine, namely ClassNotFound Exception, MethodMissingException, ClassMismatchException, StreamCorruptedException, and of course IOException. The method writeObject can throw MethodMissingException, ClassMismatchException, and IOException. Primitive data types can be written directly, and object data types can be written by applying the routine recursively. If an object points to other objects, those objects are saved, too, and so on.

> **Serializing Terminology**
>
> There are some commonly used terms for serializing an object. Writing it to disk is called *swizzling* or *pickling* or *preserving* the object. People also talk about *marshalling* and *unmarshalling* an object when it is being sent somewhere. I prefer the term *lyophilize* (pronounced "laff-alize") as it is a better description. When you pickle something, you add brine to it. Lyophilize is a term from chemistry meaning "freeze-dry." When you freeze dry something, you take the water out and just leave the dry stuff. When you lyophilize an object, you remove the code and just save the data.

The registerValidation() method lets you register an object to be validated before the entire graph is handed back to you. Validating an object means checking that it still points to all the things it pointed to before.

The new keyword *transient* marks data as not having a value that is saved when the class is serialized. One example would be anything whose value is only valid at a given moment in time, like:

```
transient int current_speed
```

The serializer knows it has to reserve space for the value, but it doesn't save the soon-to-be outdated value there. For this reason, transient fields should usually be marked private too, as you don't want other objects using the values they find there. Static (class-level) data is not serialized either. JDK 1.2 doesn't allow Threads to be serialized, useful though that would be. The difficulty with threads is that they have so much context built in to the current JVM. Since serialization is recursive, you would have to save everything the thread can access from the entire call chain, which is the entire stack, everything reachable from it, and any native methods that are active.

How do you serialize something from the class? That's what a class file is! You don't have to write out methods, because you already have those in the.class file and can get them by loading it at any time. Different data values are what distinguish two objects of the same class. To indicate a class is serializable, it should implement java.io.Serializable. Like Cloneable, this is an empty interface that just says, "I'm allowed to do this." The implementation team started out wanting to make serialization enabled for all classes by default, but had to back off that goal because of difficulties with security. When an object exists in a file on disk, anyone can update its fields, perhaps to a state that could not have been done as part of a running program. When you serialize a class, you need to consider the security implications.

Class Versioning

When you swizzle an object, you've got no guarantee that someone hasn't since modified its class and recompiled it, so the serializer calculates a hash value on the class and saves that, too. The saved hash value from the object you bring in must match the hash value for the class in memory. Otherwise you'll get an exception like this:

```
java.io.InvalidClassException:
MyClass; Local class not compatible at
java.io.ObjectStreamClass.setClass(ObjectStreamClass.java:219)
```

How do you avoid this? With the "serialver" utility that comes with the JDK. You run "serialver" on your new class file and it will provide you a version id to add to the class in a declaration like this:

```
static final long serialVersionUID = 4021215565287364875L;
```

The first version of class doesn't need this field, but any later versions do if you are going to be serializing and deserializing them. The version id lets Java identify the classes, and reject any where the serial version UID has changed. That way, if you want to let Java know that you have made an incompatible change (removed a field or added some), you just change the version UID in the class.

Note that when you read an object back in, after you have written it out, you do not get back the same object. You get back a different object with identical values in the data fields.

Serialization Code Example

This little program creates a FileOutputStream and then pushes an ObjectOutput-Stream on it to write an Integer object to the file "plum.dat." It then reads it in again.

```
import java.io.*;
public class writeobj {

    public static void main(String arg[]) {
        Integer I = new Integer(65);
        try {
          FileOutputStream fos = new FileOutputStream("plum.dat");
          ObjectOutputStream oos = new ObjectOutputStream(fos);
          oos.writeObject(I);
        } catch(Exception e) {System.out.println(e);}

        try {
          FileInputStream fis = new FileInputStream("plum.dat");
          ObjectInputStream ois = new ObjectInputStream(fis);
          Object o = ois.readObject();
          I = (Integer) o;
          int i = I.intValue();
          System.out.println("i="+i);
        } catch(Exception e) {System.out.println(e);}
    }
}
```

Notice that you just read in a raw object, and need to cast it back to its original type. You need to have some way of remembering what that type is, such as writing only one kind of object in a given file.

Java and Databases: JDBC

Right at the beginning it was realized that getting information into and out of databases would be a really useful ability to give Java. Large enterprises stand or fall by the quality of their corporate databases, and Java has a bright future in enterprise computing. So the very first library that Sun provided after the Java Development Kit was the Java DataBase Connectivity (JDBC). Sun designed the JDBC to allow access to any ANSI SQL-2 standard database.

We'll describe the JDBC in full here, and show a working example that you can copy and try. To get the most out of this section, you really need to understand database terms and techniques (like "SQL"). We'll sketch out some of these, but to get the full benefit you have to have that knowledge in your background.

You should also be alert to a newly completed project, called Java Blend, which allows database programs to be wholly written in Java (i.e., no SQL). Java Blend provides the automatic translation between Java objects and relational databases. It even allows databases to store serialized objects. Now there's a concept! Your database doesn't merely contain data, but can also hold objects that you can retrieve, unpickle, and set to work!.

Java Blend

The five word description of Java Blend is "Use databases without writing SQL!"

Java Blend was co-developed with The Baan Company, a worldwide provider of enterprise-wide business software solutions and consulting services. It's available for purchase and use now, as a separate unbundled product.

There is a Java Blend white paper at http://java.sun.com/products/java-blend/index.html.

About SQL and Relational Databases

Extracting information from a database and writing it back is usually done in Structured Query Language. SQL has been refined over more than two decades, and is the language used to access essentially all modern databases.

Years ago, there used to be several fundamentally different architectures for databases: there were hierarchical databases (like IBM's IMS), network databases (like the Codasyl model), and relational databases. It is now almost universally accepted that the relational design is superior to the other alternatives. We're also starting to see early use of object-oriented databases, some of which are accessed in a relational fashion. The collision between *object-oriented* and *relational-databases* is an area of emerging technology. Java Blend is one such example.

The database gurus have their own terminology of relations, tuples and N'th normal form, but (in plain words) the central idea to a relational database is that data appears to be kept in tables. The database can contain several tables. In a way, a table in a relational database is like an enormous spreadsheet. It might have millions of rows and hundreds of columns. Each column contains only one kind of data. A row in a table corresponds to a record. A programmer will use SQL state ments to merge tables and extract data from them. There is a whole arithmetic or algebra, based on set theory, for merging and extracting from tables.

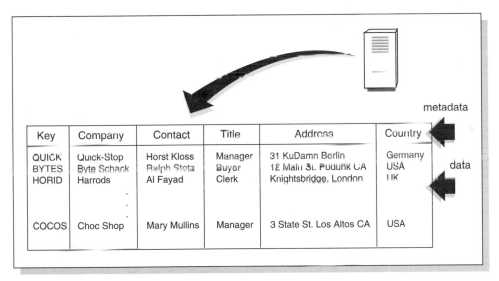

Figure 16-4: A relational database.

At first every database vendor had its own special database query language. Users eventually got fed up enough to create an industry standard around IBM's SQL. There was the SQL'89 standard, followed by the SQL'92 standard, both created under the ANSI umbrella. But SQL is still fragmented into many subtly-different slightly incompatible dialects.

The JDBC classes do their work in terms of SQL, so it takes an understanding of SQL to describe what these are. SQL is a pretty elaborate programming language in its own right, customized to handle tables, rows and columns. Suffice it to say that SQL has statements like SELECT, INSERT, DELETE, and UPDATE. SQL operates on tables; merging, matching and extracting from them and it provides its result sets in the form of further tables. We want Java to be able to bundle up SQL queries, direct them to the right database, and listen for the answers.

The JDBC API defines Java classes to represent database connections, SQL statements, result sets, database metadata (data about data), etc. It allows a Java programmer to issue SQL statements to read/write a database. The JDBC itself is written entirely in Java, will run anywhere and (from JDK 1.1 on) can be downloaded as part of an applet. JDBC access does not work in Microsoft's Internet Explorer because Microsoft declines to support the standard interface needed.

The JDBC consists of an API and a package containing about twenty Java classes to implement the application program side of the API. Some of the classes are interfaces, and the code that implements them must be provided by an additional database-specific piece of software called a driver.

Java programs call methods in the JDBC package to connect with databases through their drivers, then retrieve, process, and write information, as depicted in Figure 16-5. The package that holds the Java code for the JDBC is called java.sql.

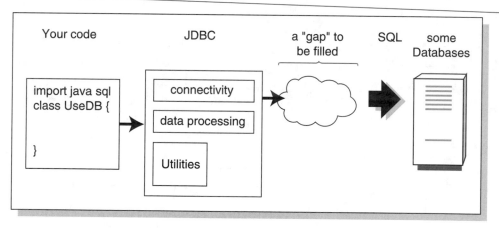

Figure 16-5: Where the JDBC fits.

Note that we are not saying what kind of database is upstream from the JDBC. Your Java code knows very little about this. What your program does know is that by talking to JDBC it can indirectly talk to a database, just as by talking to a broker you can accomplish a transaction (sell a house, shop for a new car, buy a diamond) through a third party you might never meet directly. This approach was pioneered by Borland with the Borland Database Engine and its IDAPI protocol. It was also one of the virtues claimed for ODBC.

Vendor independence is one of the reasons that the large commercial database users are excited by the Java-DBMS integration. These companies see great value in front-end software that doesn't lock them in to one particular database supplier. The network distributed feature of Java is an additional boost, making it almost trivial to build true distributed data processing systems.

The JDBC-ODBC Bridge

In the early 1990s there was a further development in the SQL world. Microsoft got involved in the process and used its monopoly leverage, the way IBM used to, to impose the *Open DataBase Connectivity* (ODBC) standard on the industry. ODBC is an Application Programmer Interface that allows C programs to make calls into an SQL server and get back results. ODBC provided a unified way for Microsoft applications such as Access, Excel, FoxPro, and Btrieve to talk to IBM, Oracle, Paradox and other back end database systems.

Every database vendor was then pretty much obliged to provide not just a driver for their own dialect of SQL, but also a driver that would allow ODBC to communicate with their protocols. If they didn't support ODBC they would be locked out of the high volume PC desktop market. Most of the ANSI SQL-2 databases out there now have ODBC drivers. In order to provide instant Java connectivity to lots of products, Sun joined with Intersolv to create the jdbc.odbc package that implements the java.sql package for ODBC databases. This was a brilliant move as it leveraged Microsoft's earlier imposition of a standard.

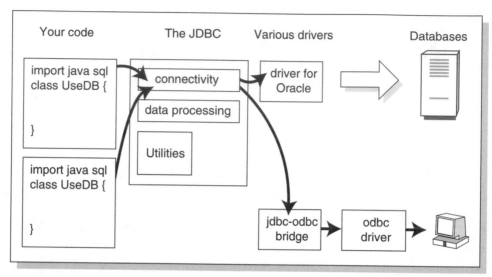

Figure 16-6: The JDBC-ODBC bridge.

By creating an open standard for its desktop applications to connect to anybody's database, Microsoft also inadvertently provided a way for Java to connect to their standard, and thence to anybody's database. The JDBC-ODBC bridge implements the JDBC by making the appropriate calls to the ODBC Standard C API.

The JDBC-ODBC bridge is a little inefficient perhaps, using a driver to talk to a driver, but it provides instant connectivity to all popular databases. ODBC is a C language interface so the bridge needs to take Java types, and unhand them into C types on the way over to ODBC, and re-hand them on the way back. The JDBC-ODBC bridge is a separate C library that needs to be accessible to your code. There's a Java part that is a driver manager for the bridge, and a native code part that's the driver. Since it's native code, there are separate versions of the bridge driver for Windows and for Solaris.

People also talk about *tiers* of database access. This has nothing to do with how many drivers and driver managers are in the chain between the application and the database. It has to do with how the application code is partitioned. Before client/server, you had to connect directly to the system with the database and run your program on it. Such a mainframe might have hundreds or even thousands of terminals like the IBM 3270 attached to it. This was a one-tier solution.

In the early days of client/server, there was a simple split between code on the client and data on the server. That was the so-called "fat client" or two-tiered approach with no middleware. Now the model has become more refined: often the client only has code for the GUI, and there is separate application logic on a server, which the client accesses (often by browsing an applet on a web page). The application logic in turn may talk to a database server on another system. The client never talks directly to the database. This is the three-tiered approach.

JDBC drivers have been classified by JavaSoft into four categories:

- **type 1**: JDBC-ODBC bridge. The cheapest alternative, as it is built on a PC standard. It requires some native code on the client side.

- **type 2**: Java-to-native API. The easiest driver for a vendor to implement. It converts JDBC calls into calls on the client API for a given database. It requires some native code on the client side.

- **type 3**: Net protocol all-Java driver. This is the most flexible type as it connects to database vendor-neutral middleware.

- **type 4**: Native-protocol all-Java driver: This gives the highest performance. Because it involves knowledge of the vendor-specific database access protocol, the database vendors will supply these kind of drivers.

The Classes in the JDBC

The JDBC Application Programmer Interface is implemented by about twenty Java classes, in the java.sql package. In Table 16-1, the twenty-odd classes are divided into three groups concerned with connectivity, data processing, and utility functions. The source for these classes and interfaces is provided, too.

Table 16-1: Three Groups of JDBCLasses

Class	Purpose
Connectivity java.sql.DriverManager java.sql.Driver java.sql.DriverPropertyInfo java.sql.Connection	Manages the drivers that are registered with it. Handles one specific type of database. Gets and sets Connection properties. Represents a session with a specific database. SQL statements are executed and results are returned for an individual connectioN.
Data Processing java.sql.DatabaseMetaData java.sql.Statement java.sql.CallableStatement java.sql.PreparedStatement java.sql.ResultSet java.sql.ResultSetMetaData	Provide information on the database as a whole. Sends over an SQL statement. A variant on Statement (used to execute an SQL stored procedure). Another variant on Statement (holds a static pre-compiled SQL statement). These are often more efficient to execute. Holds the result of executing an SQL statement. Provides information on the types and properties of a ResultSet.
Support java.sql.Types java.sql.Numeric java.sql.Date java.sql.Time java.sql.Timestamp java.sql.SQLException java.sql.SQLWarning java.sql.DataTruncation	Constants used by SQL. Supports arbitrary precision numbers. Supports dates. Supports times. Supports a combined date/time. A database access exception class with more information added about the error. A subclass of SQLException. A subclass of SQLWarning relating to a data value being unexpectedly cut short.

Using the JDBC

There are four steps that all Java programs follow to talk to a database using the JDBC.

1. Load any drivers you are going to need.

2. Tell the JDBC what database you want to use.

3. Connect to that database.

4. SQL statements across the connection, and get results back.

Step 1: Load Any Drivers You Are Going to Need

This is a system-specific step that depends on how exactly you will connect to the database. The drivers are the software component that "fills the gap," as shown in Figure 16-5. There are several possibilities for how the gap may be filled. In Java, you will simply invoke the static method Class.forName("drivername"); using the actual name of the driver. The forName() method gets the runtime class descriptor, and has the side effect of loading the associated library or class into your Java runtime.

All databases have a driver at their end to accept queries, feed them into the database's internal form and deliver results. As Figure 16-7 shows, the driver for Oracle is specific to Oracle, the driver for Sybase is specific to Sybase and so on. Although just about all databases speak SQL in theory, they all actually have slightly incompatible local dialects of SQL.

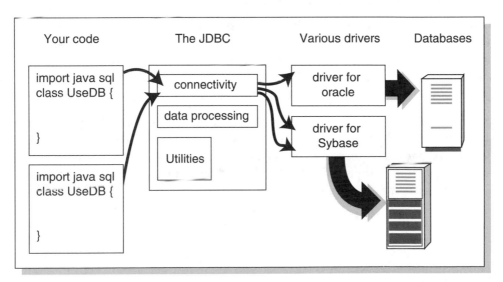

Figure 16-7: Where the drivers fit in.

What's needed is a driver or a pipeline of drivers that speak to the JDBC at one end, and can speak the database dialect at the other end. Right here is where you can start to get into trouble, because there are no drivers supplied with the JDBC. You have to obtain them from the database vendors or from the third party tools companies. These companies are flourishing filling this need and will usually let you download an evaluation copy of a driver for a limited use period.

Although these driver components are essential to use the JDBC, this is a "batteries not included" kind of deal. If you want to run a Java program that accesses a database, you need to additionally procure both the database and its drivers. The drivers could be in the form of a Java program, or (more likely at this point) a dynamically linked library of native code, which must be loaded into your running Java system.

The slickest kind of driver implements the JDBC interfaces and talks directly to the database server with no other intervening code. It's a big programming job to get the proprietary and usually unpublished database protocols working, and it must be rewritten for each kind of database. It offers the best performance, however.

Another implementation possibility is a bit simpler: provide some code that talks to the JDBC at one end, and can speak the language expected by an existing database driver at the other. This code in the middle is, of course, termed *middleware*. Such a driver would be a bridge between JDBC and the database driver at the back end. We'll say more about this later.

Step 2: Specify What Database You Want to Use

There can be several programs active on one system and talking to different databases at one time. You need to tell the JDBC which one will be used by this program. Rather than giving a file name (which doesn't scale across different machines very well), you tell the JDBC what database you want to use in the form of a URL. An example URL might be like the one shown in Figure 16-8.

As you might guess, the form and content of the URL is very specific to individual databases and the drivers you will use for access. Whether or not the port number is necessary, or even required, is a driver-dependent feature, as are the parameters in the URL after the subprotocol (ODBC, here). You just have to read the documentation that comes with the driver.

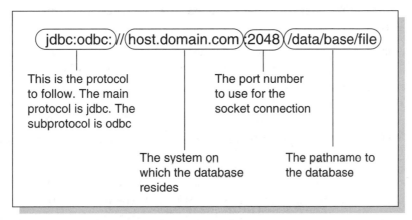

This is the protocol to follow. The main protocol is jdbc. The subprotocol is odbc

The port number to use for the socket connection

The system on which the database resides

The pathnamo to the database

Figure 16-8: A URL tells the JDBC what database to use.

Step 3: Connect to That Database

This is the point where your code registers with the JDBC. You will use the connectivity classes to connect to the database of interest. Your program can be talking to several different databases at once. For this reason, the JDBC package is sometimes called a *driver manager*, which can be anything that controls multiple drivers. However, the JDBC does a lot more than just manage a few drivers

Your application program needs to tell the driver manager to open a connection to the URL you put together in step 2. Making the connection is an iterative process: the JDBC driver manager will load all the drivers it can find and ask each in turn to try to process the URL. The driver manager looks up a property called "jdbc.drivers" in the system properties table. This should contain a list of class names for driver classes, separated by colons. You can set these in a ~/.hotjava/ properties file, which might contain a property key/value pair like:

```
jdbc.drivers=foo.bah.Driver:wombat.sql.Driver:some.other.ourDriver
```

The DriverManager class will attempt to load each of these driver classes. If you have all the right software "glue" in place, then one of them will be able to connect to that URL successfully. The rest will fail silently, without throwing an exception. Typically there will only be a handful of drivers on any given system, so the connection is established very quickly.

Step 4: Send SQL Statements Across the Connection and Receive Results Back

Once you have a connection open to your database, you will start sending SQL statements across and getting back result sets. Some database APIs have special mechanisms to support asynchronous querying, but this is not needed by Java. You simply create a new thread for any SQL statement that might take a long time. Be careful to ensure that you only use the java.sql classes in a "thread-safe" manner. That is, you are responsible for providing synchronization and avoiding data races where necessary.

Queries and updates are sent across to the database in the form of SQL statements, which are just Strings containing the SQL text. The results usually come back as something called a "Result Set." Some SQL statements just return an integer, while one SQL statement (DDL) returns nothing. If you refer back to the list of classes in the JDBC, you'll notice there is one called ResultSet that has many methods for retrieving the result of executing an SQL statement.

The result will usually be in the form of a table (several rows each of several columns of data). There are methods to access individual rows by index and to get the data back as a String or some other type. There is also a class ResultSetMetaData. *Meta* is a Greek word meaning "I will try to impress you by using Greek words." In computer science it means "information about," so the meta-data of a result set is merely the information about the data in a result set (the number of columns and rows, their names and sizes, and so on). The ResultSet lets you look at the values you got back. The ResultSetMetaData lets you look at the types.

When you have finished all the processing, close everything down in an orderly manner.

Code Example of Database Access

This section presents a step-by-step example of the actual set-up and code for an access to a database using Java. This is a one tiered access because everything is on one system: the application, the JDBC, the bridge, and the database. On the other hand we are stringing all these components together in just the way you need to for a multi-tiered approach. There is a large number of different databases, access methods, and host platforms, so the example I have chosen to present is the one that can be tried at least cost for most people. It uses a small scale database MS-Access on Windows 95, rather than an industrial-strength database like Oracle, Sybase or Informix on an enterprise server system. The principle remains the same however.

The example has a Java application that talks to the JDBC, and then a bridge from JDBC to ODBC, ending up at an ODBC database. This example shows how to configure everything if you are going in across the bridge. But, bear in mind that the JDBC-ODBC bridge is really just an interim solution while we wait for vendors to provide direct access drivers. You don't have to use the bridge and if you have a more direct driver, you wouldn't. Before a direct driver is available, developers can use the ODBC drivers to begin development, and later switch to a JDBC driver and avoid two layers of driver software.

The JDBC-ODBC bridge (which also contains a driver to interface to the ODBC driver) translates JDBC calls into ODBC calls. Thus, it allows the JDBC to talk to an ODBC driver front ending a database. It's a bridge in the sense that it allows you to pass over a rocky chasm separating two different protocols. The standard Java JDBC-ODBC bridge does not currently work if you are using a Microsoft Java compiler. This is because Microsoft has decided not to implement the standard Java Native Interface. (This may change—a federal judge ruled in November 1998 that this probably broke the agreement Microsoft had made with Sun.)

This example describes how your Java application can use the JDBC to process a Microsoft Access database running under Windows 95. Frankly, the process depends on a long chain of actions, each of which must be done exactly right to avoid mysterious failures. You should read through all these steps before trying it for yourself. And with that warning in mind, here goes.

1. Make sure you have MS-Access for Windows 95, version 7.00 or later running on your Windows 95 system.

   Typical error: Trying to use MS Access version 2.0. The 16-bit Windows 3.1 version of MS Access cannot be used as JDBC uses the 32-bit ODBC which Microsoft only supplies in Access for Windows 95/NT. The downrev version of Access will result in the following error in Step 7:

   ```
   Unable to load dll "JdbcOdbc.dll" (errcode = 45a)
   *** SQLException caught ***

   SQLState: 08001
   Message:  No suitable driver
   Vendow:   0
   ```

   The message indicates that you do not have the 32-bit ODBC driver for the database you are trying to access.

2. The "typical installation" option of MS Access for Windows 95 does not include the ODBC drivers you require. If necessary, go back and reinstall everything in MS Access to get the ODBC drivers on your system. This will make a "32-bit ODBC" icon appear on your control panel.

    The 32-bit MS-Access driver for ODBC comes with Access 95 / Office Pro. It is not a standard part of Windows 95.

    Typical error: Mistaking the "ODBC" icon on your Windows 95 control panel for the required "32bit ODBC" icon.

3. Set up a Data Source Name for the sample database. Open the "32-bit ODBC" icon on your Control Panel to bring up the "Data Sources" panel then press "add" to bring up "Add Data Source" and highlight "Microsoft Access Driver (*.mdb)" and press "OK."

    This brings up a panel labeled "ODBC Microsoft Access 7.0 Setup" in which you enter a Data Source Name. Use "myDSN." Also enter the description "bananas." Then press Database: "Select," which brings up a file chooser panel.

    Choose the pathname C:\Access\Samples\Northwind.mdb, which is one of the sample databases that comes with Access, assuming you installed in C:\Access. If you installed in a different place, use that path to the Northwind.mdb file instead.

    Press "OK" and get back to the "Data Sources" panel, where you should now see the entry "myDSN." You have successfully associated the Data Source Name and 32bit ODBC with the Access database.

4. Set up the Java side to match this DSN. Make certain that the Java program names the right database. The program is on the CD and is called simple.java. It contains the following code.

```java
import java.sql.*;
class simple {

    public static void main (String args[]) {

            String url   = "jdbc:odbc:myDSN",
            String query = "SELECT * FROM Customers "
                         + "WHERE CustomerID = 'QUICK'";
        try {
            // Load the jdbc-odbc bridge driver
            Class.forName ("sun.jdbc.odbc.JdbcOdbcDriver");

            // Attempt to connect to a driver.
            Connection con = DriverManager.getConnection (
                                        url, "", "" );

            // Create a Statement object so we can submit
            // SQL statements to the driver
            Statement stmt = con.createStatement ();

            // Submit a query, creating a ResultSet object
                ResultSet rs = stmt.executeQuery (query);

            // Display all columns and rows from the result set
                printResultSet (rs);

            rs.close();
            stmt.close();
            con.close();
        }
        catch (SQLException ex) {
             while (ex != null) {
            System.out.println ("SQL Exception:  " +
                                ex.getMessage ());
                    ex = ex.getNextException ();
                }
            }
            catch (java.lang.Exception ex) {
                ex.printStackTrace ();
            }
        }

    private static void printResultSet (ResultSet rs)
            throws SQLException
     {
        int numCols = rs.getMetaData().getColumnCount ();

        while ( rs.next() ) {
            for (int i=1; i<=numCols; i++) {
                System.out.print (rs.getString(i) + " | " );
                }
            System.out.println();
        }
    }
 }
}
```

The SQL statement in this program retrieves the record for the customer key "QUICK." There are two declarations right at the beginning of the main routine, URL and query. When you have this working, you can try changing the following to point to another database:

```
String url = "jdbc:odbc:myDSN";
```

You could also change query to:

```
String query = "SELECT * FROM Customers";
```

This would make it retrieve every customer record. Half a dozen lines down, the connection line is:

```
Connection con = DriverManager.getConnection(
                        url, "", "" );
```

The two null strings are for user-id and password. The program source is set up correctly as it is, but these are some things to try experimenting with.

5.   Compile the Java program.

```
javac Simple.java
```

Fix any compilation errors that show up (typically problems caused by not setting classpath correctly).

6.   Run the Java program.

```
java Simple
```

You should see one entry in the Customers table print out.

```
QUICK | QUICK-Stop | Horst Kloss | Accounting Manager | ....
```

You can look at this table using Access, and confirm that the record is correct.

Review of Classes

This section takes a closer look at some of the important classes used in the preceding program and in the JDBC generally. It highlights some of the important methods of each.

Connectivity Classes

`java.sql.DriverManager` manages the drivers that are registered with it.

```
public static synchronized Connection getConnection(String url)
            throws SQLException;
// try to establish a connection to the given database URL

public static Driver getDriver(String url)
            throws SQLException;

// try to find a driver that understands this URL.

public static synchronized void registerDriver(java.sql.Driver driver)
            throws SQLException;
// how a newly loaded driver tells the driver manager about itself

public static void setLoginTimeout(int seconds) {
// maximum time a database login can take before failing.

public static void setLogStream(java.io.PrintStream out) {
// Set the logging/tracing PrintStream
```

`java.sql.Driver` handles one specific type of database. This class is an interface

```
Connection connect(String url, java.util.Properties info)
            throws SQLException;
// try to connect to the database at the given URL

boolean acceptsURL(String url) throws SQLException;
// return true if the driver thinks it can process url.
```

`java.sql.Connection` represents a session with a specific database. SQL statements are executed and results are returned for an individual connection. This class is an interface.

```
Statement createStatement() throws SQLException;
// a statement is an SQL string to send to the database.

void setAutoCommit(boolean autoCommit) throws SQLException;
// By default the Connection automatically commits
// changes after executing each statement. If auto commit has been
// disabled an explicit commit must be done or database changes
// will not be saved.

DatabaseMetaData getMetaData() throws SQLException;;
// get the metadata.

void commit() throws SQLException;
// makes all changes since the previous commit/rollback

void rollback() throws SQLException;
// drops all changes made since previous commit/rollback
```

There are other, more advanced methods in this interface, too.

Data Processing Classes

`java.sql.Statement` sends over an SQL statement. This class is an interface.

```
ResultSet executeQuery(String sql) throws SQLException;
// Execute a SQL statement that returns a single ResultSet

int executeUpdate(String sql) throws SQLException;
// Execute a SQL DDL, INSERT, UPDATE or DELETE statement

void close() throws SQLException;
// close the database

void cancel() throws SQLException;
// can be used by one thread to cancel a statement being
// executed by another thread.

SQLWarning getWarnings() throws SQLException;
// executing a statement clears the old value of Warnings
// and possibly creates a list of new warnings.
```

java.sql.ResultSet holds the result of executing an SQL statement. This class is an interface. A ResultSet provides access to a table of data generated by executing a Statement. The table rows are retrieved in sequence. Within a row its column values can be accessed in any order.

```
String getString(int columnIndex) throws SQLException;
// Get the value of a column in the current row as a String

boolean getBoolean(int columnIndex) throws SQLException;
// ... as a boolean
// there are also corresponding methods to get value of the
// entry in that column as any kind of Java primitive type,
// and as an SQL.Numeric, a byte array, a Time, Date, or Timestamp,
// ASCII stream, Unicode Stream, a binaryStream, or an Object!
// if you can put it into a database, Java can pull it out.

SQLWarning getWarnings() throws SQLException;
// get warning messages

void clearWarnings() throws SQLException;
// clear warning messages

ResultSetMetaData getMetaData() throws SQLException;
// get metadata describing the number, types and properties of
// a ResultSet's columns. The first column number is 1, not 0.

boolean next() throws SQLException;
// true if the current row is valid. False when no more rows.
```

java.sql.ResultSetMetaData provides information on the types and properties of a ResultSet.

```
int getColumnCount() throws SQLException;
// the number of columns in this result set

boolean isCaseSensitive(int column) throws SQLException;
// does upper/lower case matter in this column?

boolean isSearchable(int column) throws SQLException;
// can this column be used in a 'WHERE' clause?

boolean isCurrency(int column) throws SQLException;
// is this column a cash value?

int isNullable(int column) throws SQLException;
// can you store null in this column

String getColumnLabel(int column) throws SQLException;
// what is the full name of the column?

String getColumnName(int column) throws SQLException;
// what is the column known as internally?

String getSchemaName(int column) throws SQLException;
// get the schema (loosely "plan") name for the table that
// this column came from.

boolean isReadOnly(int column) throws SQLException;
// is this column definitely not writeable?
```

Useful URLs

You will find more information about Java database connectivity at the following URLs:

- http://www.xdb.com/home.htm

- http://www.weblogic.com

- http://dataramp.com/

- http://splash.javasoft.com/jdbc/

- http://www.vincent.se/

These URLs are for companies that are producing commercial JDBC (or jdbc-odbc) drivers and tools. If you're on a tight budget, use the Postgres database software, which is available with source from http://www.postgresql.org.

Some Light Relief

Those Messy Messages

How many times have you encountered some kind of software failure, and ended up with an error message that told you precisely nothing? If you've been programming for any length of time at all, you'll recognize this as an all-too-familiar source of frustration.

The all time classic used to be the Unix "bus error-core dumped" but that has been replaced in recent years by the infamous Microsoft Windows "GPF." What are systems programmers thinking of when they design error messages like that? Are they deliberately trying to confuse and annoy applications programmers?

Well, no. We hardly ever try to do that deliberately. The problem arises because at the point where the problem is detected in the operating system kernel, there is no application-specific knowledge to report the problem in terms meaningful to the user. Let me give you an example of what I mean.

Inside Sun's operating system development group, there is a special interest committee known as the Ease-of-Use group. I was a co-founder and strong supporter of this free-ranging think tank some years ago, and was for a long period the representative from kernel software development.

One day the Ease-of-Use committee decided to study kernel messages and see if there were any candidates for improvement. The person who did the study was an experienced technical writer, skilled in the art of communication, and she found many kernel error messages to complain of, including these ones:

- Bad terminal owner
- bread error, fatstart
- Error walking tree %s.
- FAT size error
- Flushing job
- Hit BOTTOM
- lpExec confused.
- object exists in wastebasket

- Out of register space (ugh) allocator

- POSSIBLE ATTACK from %s: newline in string "%s"

- That must be tomorrow

- real error

- repeated leap second moment

- runt packet

- Bogus wildcard from %s

I read through this list, and the first thing that jumped out at me was that these were all reasonable error messages, so what was the problem? Then I read the list again, and thought about it a bit longer and the reason became clear: Every one of these messages was ambiguous. If you didn't have programming experience, you would only see the English meaning. If you did have programming experience, in this context you would only see the programming meaning. Table 16-2 explains this more clearly.

Table 16-2: Interpreting Error Messages

Error	English Meaning	Programming Meaning
Bad terminal owner device.	The person who bought the system has been naughty.	The system has lost track of the process that controls this device.
bread error, fatstart.	Something to do with putting on weight if you eat too much bread.	There was an error when we tried to read one of the blocks near the beginning of the File Allocation Table.
Error walking tree.	Something went wrong when we were trying to take a tree for a walk.	An invalid pointer was found as we were traversing the data structure known as a "tree."
Hit BOTTOM	User needs spanking.	Unexpectedly encountered the end of a table
Flushing job.	More toilet humor.	This process is being completely removed from the queue of the shell.
real error	As opposed to a fake one?	An error in a real (floating-point) number calculation.
repeated leap second moment	What? We have leap years and leap days, but surely we don't have leap seconds?	Actually we do, perhaps James Gosling was right after all to comment on it at length in the Date.java class.
object exists in wastebasket	How can the computer possibly know how untidy my office is?	The wastebasket icon on the window desktop has a discarded object in it.
Out of register space (ugh) allocator.	What is "ugh" supposed to add to this?	I'm tempted to pretend that "ugh" is the Universal Graphic Hash code, but actually it conveys that a distasteful and irrecoverable error situation has occurred in the code generator. It has encountered an expression so complex that it has bedeviled the compiler.
That must be tomorrow	Too whimsical?	This message is the response from shutdown when you give an invalid time.

. . . and so on. The point is that both parties have merit here. The programmer has chosen brief messages that describe the situation well—to other programmers. The Ease-of-Use fan has demonstrated that the messages are surprisingly easy to misinterpret. Neither party has understood the perspective of the other. It's clearly a mistake to demand that users have a programming background. On the other hand we can't expect every diagnostic message from the kernel to be meaningful to the lay person, but neither should it be ambiguous.

The moral is clear: As systems programmers we must avoid ambiguous messages. We must spell out the full name of data structures where possible. We don't necessarily have to make a message meaningful to the end user, but at least it must be incapable of misinterpretation. Don't tell users "hit bottom" when "item not found in table" will do just as well. Whenever you write an error message that will be seen by the user, take an extra minute to phrase it with care.

I'll finish by presenting one final example. I like this because it reveals a programmer who's trying hard, but can't quite let go of the techno-babble:

```
Printer out of media (paper).
```

That error used to be in PrintTool, but we have since sent the programmer to a re-education camp, and it has now been changed to

```
Printer out of paper (media).
```

Hey, even small improvements count.

CHAPTER 17

GUI Basics and Event-Handling

A ll GUI libraries have four basic areas of functionality:

- Creation of user interface "controls" or components such as scrollbars, buttons, and labels.

- Support for giving behavior to the controls by tying GUI events (like clicking on a button) to code that you write.

- Support for grouping and arranging the controls on the screen.

- Support for accessing window manager facilities like specifying which window has the input focus, reading JPEG and other image files, and printing.

Related graphics libraries also provide support for graphics operations like draw an arc, fill a polygon, clip a rectangle, and so on. There may even be a complete 2D drawing library, such as Java has.

For the first couple of major releases, Java supported GUI operations solely with a package called `java.awt`. The "AWT" stands for "Abstract Window Toolkit." The AWT supported the portability goals of Java. It gave user programs a common binary Windowing interface on systems with wildly different native window systems. That's an unusual feature, like having your favorite Macintosh program run on a Windows PC and still do GUI operations. You might be wondering how it is done.

Inside the AWT runtime, there are methods that you can call to pop-up a menu, resize a window, get the location of a mouse click, and so on. Since these methods are implemented with a little bit of Java wrapping, you can call them from Java user programs. Java can thus keep track of what is happening, and then the methods call through to a native code library. The *Java bytecode* is the same on each platform, and the *native library* behind the Java runtime library is specific to each platform. The AWT code uses the underlying native (or "peer") window system to manipulate GUI objects. The AWT is a series of abstract interfaces along with Java code to map them into the actual native code on each system. This is why it is an *abstract* window toolkit: it is not tailored for a specific computer but offers the same API on all.

At the start of the chapter, we mentioned the list of services that any GUI library must support. In this chapter we will focus on one of these services: An event-handling system that notices when the user adjusts one of the components and conveys that information to the program

You have to know how to handle the events that controls can generate before you can make sense out of the controls themselves. Event-handling is a dull but necessary prerequisite, like eating your vegetables before you can have dessert.We will deal with controls in the next chapter. The basic idea with Java GUI programs is that you do the following:

1. Declare controls. These are such things as your buttons, menus, and choices. You can subclass them to add to the behavior, but this is often unnecessary.

2. Implement an interface to provide the event handler that responds to control activity. The implementing class will often be an anonymous class. This is because this simplifies coding and puts the class declaration close to where it is used.

3. Add the controls to a container. Subclassing the container is possible but frequently unnecessary. Containers are what you display on the screen. They can hold several related controls that you want to appear next to each other on screen.

It's a challenge to explain all this. The first three topics—declaring controls, handling their events, and putting them in containers—fit together so closely that you have to understand a bit of each before you can fully understand any. They are such big topics that I've given them a chapter each and will take them serially.

All About Event-Handling

First, a few necessary words of explanation about the programming model for window systems. Unlike procedural programs in which things happen sequentially, windowing programs are *asynchronous*, meaning that things happen at unpredictable times. You never know which of the on-screen buttons, menus, frames, or other elements the user will touch next. Accordingly, a model known as *event-driven programming* is used.

In event-driven programming, the logic of your code is inverted. Instead of one flow of control from beginning to end, the runtime system sits in a "window main loop" simply waiting for user input. When the user clicks the mouse, the operating system passes it to the window manager which turns it into an *event* and passes it on to a handler you supplied earlier. This is known as a *callback*. Your handler is a *callback routine*, because the window system calls back to it when the event happens. Your event handler will deal with the graphics event and any work that is associated with it. If a button says "press here to read the file," your code must read in the file when called. Handling a button event just means noticing that it occurred and doing the associated action, but other events may involve some drawing on the screen. For example, dragging something with the mouse is just repeatedly drawing it under the mouse coordinates as it moves.

JDK 1.1 Event Model

The *event model* is the name we give to the framework that turns a GUI interaction (mouse click, menu selection, button press, etc.) into a call for your code to process it. The event model can also be used for something unrelated to the GUI, like a timer going off. In other words, the event model is the design for connecting your code to any kind of asynchronous actions, termed *events*, for handling.

Obviously, the window manager can't directly call your event-handling routines because the runtime library doesn't even see your code until it is asked to run it. So, at runtime the event model has to be told which of your routines are there to handle events.

Java originally used inheritance to tie together your code and the event model. JDK 1.1 introduced a better approach called the *delegation-based* model. To get any events, your code has to tell the window system, "Send those events of yours to these methods of mine." You connect the controls that generate events by registering a callback with your event-handling classes, as shown in Figure 17-1.

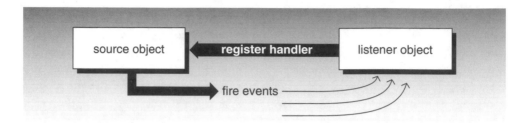

Figure 17-1: How events are passed in JDK 1.1.

 If you are not 100% clear on callbacks, go back and read the section in chapter 8 on "Using Interfaces Dynamically." It is *essential* that you fully understand callbacks since they form the basis of the new event-handling model.

The events that are fired (sent) from the source to the listener are simply objects. An event object has several data fields holding such information as where on the screen the event took place, what the event is, how many mouse clicks there were, the state of a checkbox, and so on. There is a general `java.util.EventObject` type, and all AWT events are children of that as shown in Figure 17-2.

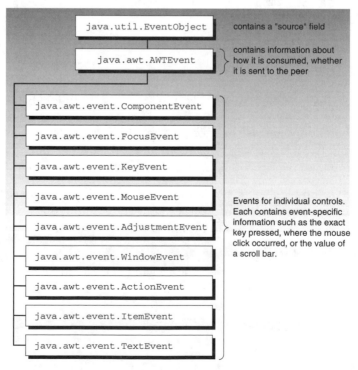

Figure 17-2: The hierarchy of event objects in JDK 1.1.

The JFrame Example

A JFrame, a subclass of the AWT class Frame, has a title string and a menu bar on which you can add several menus. Here is the code to put a JFrame on the screen from an application:

```java
import javax.swing.*;
public class FrameDemo {
    public static void main(String[] args) {
        JFrame jframe = new JFrame("Example");
        jframe.setSize(400,100);
        jframe.setVisible(true);
    }
}
```

Compiling and executing this program will cause a Frame like that in Figure 17-3 to appear on the screen. Here, we just gave it the name on the title bar of "Example." Pretty simple, yes?

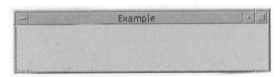

Figure 17-3: The JFrame is a subclass of Frame which is a subclass of Window.

Since it is a Window, JFrame is capable of receiving events generated by Windows. When you click on a Window to close it, that generates an event. If you try this with the program above, you'll notice that the JFrame goes away, but your program stays active. You have to press control-C to get out of the program. That's because you need to write code to handle the "window closing" event. The code should quit the program when it is invoked.

Let's add an event handler to our JFrame that notices when the WindowClosing event takes place. That event will be delivered when you click to close a Window.

First, I'll tell our JFrame that Window events are handled by an object that I call "mwh" here—a nice short name which is an abbreviation of "my window handler." The code appears exactly as before, and we add this one line to the main() routine:

```java
jframe.addWindowListener(mwh);
```

The callback for a Window event is registered by calling the AWT method addWindowListener. This is a method in the Window superclass of JFrame that takes as a parameter an interface called WindowListener. Your applet must declare an instance of a class that implements the WindowListener interface and that will be the event handler for this button. You still have to write that class, but assuming it has the name shown below, you can instantiate an object like this:

```
myCodeToHandleWinClose mwh = new myCodeToHandleWinClose();
```

The last step is to write the myCodeToHandleWinClose class that implements the java.awt.event.WindowListener interface and provides the promised methods. The class can be in a separate file or the same one.

```
class myCodeToHandleWinClose implements WindowListener {
    public void windowClosing(WindowEvent e) {System.exit(0);}
    public void windowClosed(WindowEvent e) { }
    public void windowOpened(WindowEvent e) { }
    public void windowIconified(WindowEvent e) { }
    public void windowDeiconified(WindowEvent e) { }
    public void windowActivated(WindowEvent e) { }
    public void windowDeactivated(WindowEvent e) { }
}
```

The windowClosing() method of the myCodeToHandleWinClose class is called whenever the Window "close" choice is made. Notice that it was necessary to provide declarations for all the routines in the interface. Since we are interested only in WindowClosing, there are empty bodies for the other methods. We'll show a way of simplifying this later in the chapter.

The WindowListener interface (like many of the *Something*Listener interfaces) is declared in the java.awt.event package. There are other event and Listeners declared in the javax.swing.event package. The WindowListener interface promises that there will be half a dozen methods with specific names. The methods will be called for different Window events, now that we have delegated the task to the object mwh that contains the methods.

One advantage of the Java event framework is that the GUI-related code is easily separated from the application logic code. This flows from good use of OOP. Put everything in a class of its own, and declare instances of the class as needed. In that way, encapsulation works for you. If you want to change what happens on window close, you just update the class that deals specifically with it. In a non-OOP implementation, it's too easy to mix everything together, making program maintenance and testing ten times harder than it needs to be. The same event framework is used for JavaBeans (component software), as well as the AWT.

Putting the whole thing together, and into our JFrame example, the code to handle the window closing event is as follows:

```java
import javax.swing.*;
import java.awt.event.*;
public class CloseDemo {
    public static void main(String[] args) {
        JFrame jframe = new JFrame("Example");
        jframe.setSize(400,100);
        jframe.setVisible(true);
        myCodeToHandleWinClose m = new myCodeToHandleWinClose();
        jframe.addWindowListener(m);
    }
}


class myCodeToHandleWinClose implements WindowListener {

    public void windowClosing(WindowEvent e) {System.exit(0);}
    public void windowClosed(WindowEvent e) { }
    public void windowOpened(WindowEvent e) { }
    public void windowIconified(WindowEvent e) { }
    public void windowDeiconified(WindowEvent e) { }
    public void windowActivated(WindowEvent e) { }
    public void windowDeactivated(WindowEvent e) { }
}
```

Notice that the code inside the WindowClosing method calls System.exit() to quit the program. When you run this, you'll see the same frame as before, but when you click on the window to close it, the program will now exit gracefully. Well done! You have finished your first example of an event handler.

You may wonder, "How do I know what events there are, what interfaces deal with them, and what methods the Listener interfaces use?" Table 17-1 summarizes the answers to all three questions. The source code for the interfaces and their methods can also be reviewed in the directory $JAVAHOME/src/java/awt/event.

The same basic framework is used by all the event handlers:

1. Write a class that implements a *Something*Listener interface.

2. Declare an object—called, say, myHandler—of your class.

3. On your component, call the add*Something*Listener(myHandler) method.

You can shortcut the amount of code with inner classes. The next section explains how.

Table 17-1: Categories, Events, and Interfaces

General Category	Events That It Generates	Interface That the Event-Handler Implements
Mouse	Dragging, moving mouse causes a `MouseEvent`	MouseMotionListener
	Clicking, selecting, releasing causes a `MouseEvent`	MouseListener
Keyboard	Key press or key release causes a `KeyEvent`	`KeyListener`
Selecting (an item from a list, check-box, etc.)	When item is selected causes an `ItemEvent`	`ItemListener`
Text Input Controls	When newline is entered causes a `TextEvent`	`TextListener`
Scrolling Controls	When a scrollbar slider is moved causes an `AdjustmentEvent`	`AdjustmentListener`
Other Controls (button, menu, etc.)	When pressed causes an `ActionEvent`	`ActionListener`
Window Changes	Open, close, iconify, etc., causes a `WindowEvent`	`WindowListener`
Keyboard Focus Changes	Tabbing to next field or requesting focus causes a `FocusEvent`. A component must have the focus to generate key events.	`FocusListener`
Component Change	Resizing, hiding, revealing, or moving a component causes a `ComponentEvent`	`ComponentListener`
Container Change	Adding or removing a component to a container causes a `ContainerEvent`	`ContainerListener`

Tips for Slimming down Handler Code

Inner classes are intended for event handlers. They allow you to put the event-handling class and method right next to the place where you declare the control or register the callback listener. Anonymous classes are a refinement of inner classes allowing you to combine the definition of the class with the instance allocation. Here is the code rewritten using an anonymous class.

```
import javax.swing.*;
import java.awt.event.*;
public class CloseDemo2 {

    public static void main(String[] args) {
        JFrame jframe = new JFrame("Example");
        jframe.setSize(400,100);
        jframe.setVisible(true);

        myCodeToHandleWinClose m = new myCodeToHandleWinClose();

        jframe.addWindowListener( new WindowListener() { // anon. class
            public void windowClosing(WindowEvent e) {System.exit(0);}
            public void windowClosed(WindowEvent e) { }
            public void windowOpened(WindowEvent e) { }
            public void windowIconified(WindowEvent e) { }
            public void windowDeiconified(WindowEvent e) { }
            public void windowActivated(WindowEvent e) { }
            public void windowDeactivated(WindowEvent e) { }
        } ); // end of anonymous class.
    }
}
```

Try compiling and running the example above. Your `CloseDemo2.java` file generates class files called `CloseDemo2.class` and `CloseDemo2$1.class`. The second of these represents the anonymous `WindowListener` inner class.

You should only use inner classes and anonymous classes where the event handler is just a few lines long. If the event handler is more than a screenful of text, it should be in a named top-level class. We have to admit, however, that the notational convenience for smaller cases is considerable—just don't get carried away with it.

There are two further refinements: making your top level class implement the appropriate listener interface and using an adapter class. These techniques further reduce the amount of "housekeeping code" you need to write. You'll see them in other programmers' code. I'll present them here so you can recognize the pattern.

Making a Top-Level Class into a Listener

You don't *have* to declare a separate class to implement the Listener interface. You can make any of your existing classes do the work. The code below shows an example:

```java
import javax.swing.*;
import java.awt.event.*;
public class CloseDemo3 implements WindowListener {

    public static void main(String[] args) {
        JFrame jframe = new JFrame("Example");
        jframe.setSize(400,100);
        jframe.setVisible(true);

        myCodeToHandleWinClose m = new myCodeToHandleWinClose();

        jframe.addWindowListener( new CloseDemo3() );
    }

    public void windowClosing(WindowEvent e) {System.exit(0);}

    public void windowClosed(WindowEvent e) { }
    public void windowOpened(WindowEvent e) { }
    public void windowIconified(WindowEvent e) { }
    public void windowDeiconified(WindowEvent e) { }
    public void windowActivated(WindowEvent e) { }
    public void windowDeactivated(WindowEvent e) { }
}
```

Here you make the demo class implement WindowListener. The body of the class provides all the methods that WindowListener demands. When you want to add the WindowListener, you just instantiate an object of the demo class and away you go. The work is done in the main method which is static. If you were making that call in an instance method, the line would be even simpler:

```java
jframe.addWindowListener( this );
```

It's a handy technique, but you're not done yet. You can make the code shorter still, as the next section explains.

Using a Listener Adapter Class

Even though you were interested only in the `windowClosing` event, you had to supply null bodies for all the methods in the `WindowListener` interface. To make things a little more convenient, a concept called *adapter classes* can be used. An adapter is one specific example of a design pattern. An adapter is the design pattern that converts the API of some class into a different, more convenient API.

In Java AWT event-handling, for some of the Listener interfaces (such as `WindowListener`), you might want to implement only one or two functions to handle the one or two events of interest, but the `SomethingListener` interface may specify half a dozen methods. The language rules are such that you must implement all the functions in an interface even if you just give them empty bodies, as in the `WindowListener` above. The package java.awt.event provides adapters that help with the situation by allowing you to override as few methods as you like. They are:

- `ComponentAdapter`
- `MouseMotionAdapter`
- `WindowAdapter`
- `ContainerAdapter`
- `MouseAdapter`
- `FocusAdapter`
- `KeyAdapter`

These adapters are classes that provide empty bodies for all the methods in the corresponding `SomethingListener` interface. Here is WindowAdapter.java:

```
public abstract class WindowAdapter implements WindowListener {
    public void windowOpened(WindowEvent e) { }
    public void windowClosing(WindowEvent e) { }
    public void windowClosed(WindowEvent e) { }
    public void windowIconified(WindowEvent e) { }
    public void windowDeiconified(WindowEvent e) { }
    public void windowActivated(WindowEvent e) { }
    public void windowDeactivated(WindowEvent e) {}
}
```

If you can declare your event handler as a subclass of one of these adapters, you can provide only the one or two methods you want, instead of implementing all the methods in the interface. Let inheritance do the work. Another way of doing this would be to have one `Adapter` class that implements *all* the `Listener` classes with null methods for all of them. In that way, you don't have to remember all the individual adapter names. That's the way I would have done it, which is probably why I'm not on the Swing design team.

Since Java classes have only one parent, you can't use this technique if you already inherit from some other class (although you can always create a new class just to make it a subclass of some adapter). Here is an example showing how the `WindowAdapter` class is used when all you are interested in is the `windowClosing` event:

```
import javax.swing.*;
import java.awt.event.*;
public class CloseDemo4 extends WindowAdapter {

    public static void main(String[] args) {
        JFrame jframe = new JFrame("Example");
        jframe.setSize(400,100);
        jframe.setVisible(true);

        myCodeToHandleWinClose m = new myCodeToHandleWinClose();

        jframe.addWindowListener( new CloseDemo4() );
    }

    public void windowClosing(WindowEvent e) {System.exit(0);}
}
```

The code is much shorter and easier to understand. What could be simpler than an adapter? Well, it turns out that there is a major pitfall with adapter classes, and it's one of those awful problems that leaves you swearing at the keyboard the first time you encounter it. You'll know to check for it thereafter, but the first time is a little frustrating. I'll use KeyAdapter as an example, because you've seen enough of WindowListener. The KeyListener is an interface used to send keyboard events. A keyboard event is generated when a key is pressed, released, and typed (pressed and released). There are KeyListener methods for all three of these. For this example, say you are going to use an adapter because you're interested only in the keyPressed event. Let's create an anonymous class for the KeyAdapter.

When you create an inner class for an adapter class, you simply supply the one or two methods that you wish to override, like this:

```
new KeyAdapter() {
    public void keyPressed(java.awt.event.KeyEvent e)
    { System.out.println("got "+e.getKeyChar()); }
} // end anon class
```

You may, however, make a small spelling or letter case error in supplying your method, like this:

```
new KeyAdapter() {
    public void KeyPressed(java.awt.event.KeyEvent e)
    // Notice capital "K" in "KeyPressed" WRONG!
    { System.out.println("got "+e.getKeyChar()); }
} // end anon class
```

Such a spelling mistake means that your method will not override the intended method in the adapter class. Instead, you have added a new method that never gets invoked. The empty body of the correctly spelled method in the adapter class will be invoked instead, and it will do nothing.[1] If your event handler seems to do nothing and you used an adapter, your first check should be that the method name and signature exactly matches something in the adapter class.

As mentioned at the start of the chapter, learning how to handle events is like clearing your plate of vegetables before being allowed to sit down to dessert. You've now eaten enough vegetables, so I'll wrap up this chapter with a summary.

---

1. The Swing team could have made the adapter methods throw an exception, so you wouldn't spend hours debugging this error.

Summary of Event-Handling

We have seen a specific example of handling the event generated by closing a Window. It can be written more compactly if you write it as an inner class or even as an anonymous class. You can junk even more unneeded code if you use an adapter class.

There are several kinds of events for the different controls: a button generates one kind of event, a text field another, and so on. To impose a little order and to split them up according to what they do, there are a dozen or so individual Listener interfaces shown in Table 17-1. They all work the same way: You write a handler class that implements the interface, and register it with the control. When the control fires an event, the method in the handler object that you registered is called.

The key points to note on GUI handling are:

- Each interface `SomethingListener` has one or more methods showing the signature of a method that is called when the corresponding `SomethingEvent` occurs.

- Your handler code implements the `SomethingListener` interface and therefore has methods with signatures that duplicate those in the interface.

- Each control has a method called `addSomethingListener()`. The `addSomethinglistener()` method takes a single argument; an object that fulfills the `SomethingListener` interface.

- As mentioned in chapter 11, Swing requires that all code that might affect GUI components be executed from the event-dispatching thread. Refer back to the section, "Swing Threads—A Caution!," if you need more information on this.

- You call `addSomethingListener()`, using an instance of your handler class as the parameter. This registers your object as the handler for that kind of event for that control.

The `SomethingEvent` class is a subclass of class `AWTEvent` and stores all the information about what just happened, where, and when. An object of the `SomethingEvent` class is passed to the method in the `SomethingListener` interface. It sounds more complicated than it is. The design pattern is shown in Figure 17-4.

You can register several handlers to receive the same singles event if you wish. You can dynamically (at runtime) remove or add an event handler from a control.

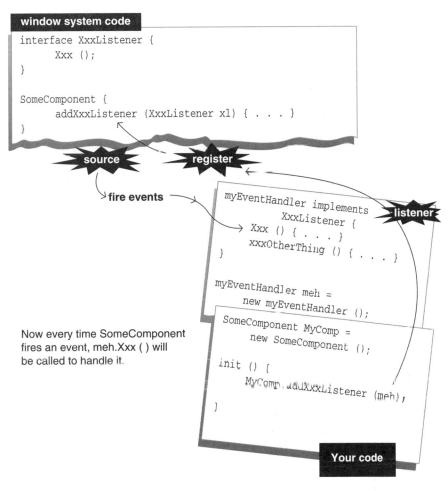

Figure 17-4: Design pattern of JDK 1.1 event-handling.

You add an event handler with a call like this:

```
myComponent.addWindowListener( myEventHandler );
```

You won't be too surprised to learn that the method to remove one is this:

```
myComponent.removeWindowListener( myEventHandler );
```

We won't show all the dozen or so *Something*Event classes and *Something*Listener interfaces here. You can and should look at them by typing the following:

```
javap java.awt.event.MouseEvent
```

Compiled from `MouseEvent.java`:

```
public synchronized class java.awt.event.MouseEvent
        extends java.awt.event.InputEvent
{
    public static final int MOUSE_FIRST;
    public static final int MOUSE_LAST;
    public static final int MOUSE_CLICKED;
    public static final int MOUSE_PRESSED;
    public static final int MOUSE_RELEASED;
    public static final int MOUSE_MOVED;
    public static final int MOUSE_ENTERED;
    public static final int MOUSE_EXITED;
    public static final int MOUSE_DRAGGED;
    int x;
    int y;
    int clickCount;
    boolean popupTrigger;
    public int getX();
    public int getY();
    public java.awt.Point getPoint();
    public synchronized void translatePoint(int, int);
    public int getClickCount();
    public boolean isPopupTrigger();
    public java.lang.String paramString();
    // constructor
    public java.awt.event.MouseEvent(java.awt.Component,
        int,long,int,int,int,int,boolean);
}
```

Similarly, you can check on the interface that is implemented by your handler by typing the following:

```
javap java.awt.event.MouseListener
```

Compiled from `MouseListener.java`:

```
public interface java.awt.event.MouseListener extends
        java.lang.Object implements java.util.EventListener {
    public void mouseClicked(java.awt.event.MouseEvent);
    public void mousePressed(java.awt.event.MouseEvent);
    public void mouseReleased(java.awt.event.MouseEvent);
    public void mouseEntered(java.awt.event.MouseEvent);
    public void mouseExited(java.awt.event.MouseEvent);
}
```

We don't need to show the `java.awt.event.MouseAdapter` class because it has all the same methods, only with empty bodies (of course). You should use `javap` to look at the public fields and methods of all the other Events and Listeners. A full list of the events and listeners is given in the next chapter.

There are a lot of new ideas presented by event-handling, so don't worry if it doesn't all make sense now. Sleep on it, re-read it, try the sample programs, and it will all come together. Get the event-handling down before moving on.

Some Light Relief

The Origami Kamikaze Water Bomber

Origami is an ancient and honorable technique of delicate paper folding. It takes finesse, skill, and subtlety—so, we certainly won't be discussing *that* any further. Instead, this section explains how to make a paper airplane that takes a payload. Not only can you impress your coworkers with paper airplanes, but you can bombard them with an air delivery of confetti, glue, or shaving cream from the far side of the room. People will be talking about you for days to come, and your manager will certainly remember your achievements when the review period comes around.

One warning here: At the age of 14, I dropped a paper water bomb on the head of schoolfriend "Piffer" Tully from an upstairs classroom. He didn't see who did it, and I felt it better not to burden him by claiming responsibility. Now, 25 years later, it is probably safe to own up (ha, ha, ha, Piffer!), and also alert you to the fact that not everyone appreciates the drollness of saturation bombing by paper airplane. So, pick your targets carefully, or stick to launching blanks.

As always, observe the three cardinal safety rules when working around electronic equipment:

1. Make sure you know where the main circuit breaker is located.

2. Keep a grounding strap around your wrist.

3. Most of all, wait till your boss goes on a lunch break before starting this project.

Figure 17-5 shows how you make the Kamikaze water bomber. There is an applet that animates these steps on the CD that comes with this book.

First, take an ordinary sheet of 8.5" by 11" paper, and make it narrower by cutting off 1.5" or so, to make 7" by 11". Then follow these instructions:

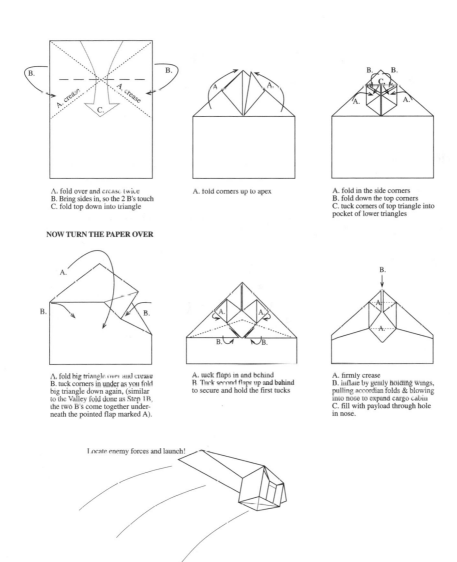

A. fold over and crease twice
B. Bring sides in, so the 2 B's touch
C. fold top down into triangle

A. fold corners up to apex

A. fold in the side corners
B. fold down the top corners
C. tuck corners of top triangle into pocket of lower triangles

NOW TURN THE PAPER OVER

A. fold big triangle over and crease
B. tuck corners in under as you fold big triangle down again, (similar to the Valley fold done as Step 1B, the two B's come together underneath the pointed flap marked A).

A. tuck flaps in and behind
B. Tuck second flaps up and behind to secure and hold the first tucks

A. firmly crease
D. inflate by gently holding wings, pulling accordian folds & blowing into nose to expand cargo cabin
C. fill with payload through hole in nose.

Locate enemy forces and launch!

Figure 17-5: The Kamikaze water bomber.

Fold up the edges of the wings for better flight, and fill with payload through hole in nose. Umm, the hole in the *plane's* nose, that is. Launch and enjoy.

Origami is relaxing and fun—just the thing for unwinding after a busy day chasing electrons. If you really have a lot of spare time, check the origami models at http://www.origami.vancouver.bc.ca/. There's a praying mantis there that takes 100 steps to complete!

CHAPTER
18

JFC and the Swing Package

In the previous chapter, we saw that the basic idea behind Java GUI programs is that you:

- Declare controls. You can subclass them to add to the behavior, but this is often unnecessary.

- Implement an interface to get the event-handler that responds to control activity.

- Add the controls to a container. Again, subclassing is possible but frequently unnecessary.

The previous chapter explained how to handle the events that controls generate. This chapter dives into the details of the controls themselves: what they look like, how you use them, and what they do. The next chapter wraps up by describing containers and how you use them to lay out controls neatly on the screen.

Java Foundation Classes

Supporting a Java interface to the underlying native window libraries achieves the goal of making Java GUI programs highly portable, but it comes at the cost of inefficiency. Peer events must be translated into Java events before they can be handled by Java code. Worse, native libraries aren't identical on each platform, and sometimes the differences leak into the Java layer.

> **Example of How Native Library Behavior Leaked into the AWT**
>
> Sun never did get filename filtering working for the AWT "file selection dialog" on Windows systems. This is bug 4031440 on the Java Developer Connection at http://java.sun.com/jdc.
>
> To support FilenameFilter, the AWT FileDialog needs to issue a callback for each file it wants to display, and you supply a FilenameFilter that can accept or reject the file. But on Win32, the FileDialog control works in a completely different way. It doesn't issue callbacks. Instead, it accepts simple wildcard patterns to match against filenames. That's a reasonable alternative to FilenameFilters, but that model isn't supported by the current Java API. As a result AWT filename filtering never worked on Win32.
>
> This all works in Swing, since there is no reliance on native library support.

The Java Foundation Classes (JFC) are a new set of GUI-related classes created to solve the AWT problem of platform idiosyncrasies. JFC also supports:

- A pluggable look and feel, meaning that when you run the program, you can choose whether you want it to look like a Windows GUI, a Macintosh GUI, or some other style.

- An accessibility API for things like larger text for the visually impaired.

- The Java 2D drawing API.

- A drag-and-drop library and an "undo last command" library.

- The Swing component set.

The Swing components (scrollbar, button, textfield, label, etc.) replace the AWT versions of these components. The AWT is still used for the other areas of GUI functionality, like layout control and printing. There's an appendix in this book that contains descriptions of the AWT components. They are simpler than the Swing components, but more basic and more bug-prone.

JFC is bundled with JDK 1.2 as a standard part of Java and was also available unbundled for JDK 1.1. Although it's a core library now, the "x" in the package name in JDK 1.2, `javax.swing`, reflects the fact that the package first became available as an optional extension library. There was quite a bit of churn over the correct package name for Swing, and the unbundled version for JDK 1.1 was released as package `com.sun.java.swing`. You should use Swing, rather than AWT components, in new programs you write, but you need to be aware of whether or not your browser supports it in applets.

How Do AWT, JFC, and Swing Fit Together?

AWT (Abstract Window Toolkit) provides the totality of GUI support in JDK 1.0. It offers a basic set of GUI objects, and also supports all the other features of a Window toolkit: the ability to layout objects, group them together, print them, and so on.

JFC (Java Foundation Classes) is a big set of libraries that adds to one part of AWT and replaces another part. JFC provides support for things that are missing in AWT, like accessibility features for the visually impaired, a 2D drawing library, and the "pluggable look and feel."

One of the key pieces of JFC is the *Swing component set.* The Swing GUI components (button, textfield, scrollpane, etc.) are intended to completely replace the corresponding AWT GUI components. The Swing components are better and often simpler. AWT is still needed for all the non-component services that it provides. Swing only replaces one piece of AWT.

The choices you have for GUI objects are:

JDK 1.0—AWT

JDK 1.1—AWT or the unbundled version of Swing

JDK 1.2—The core Swing package or AWT

For the sake of simplicity, I use AWT exclusively in JDK 1.0 and 1.1, and Swing in JDK 1.2 for GUI components.

The Java Foundation Classes are aimed squarely at programmers who want to build enterprise-ready software, at least as good as (often better than) software built with native GUI libraries. The JFC has the additional advantage of being a lot simpler than competing window systems, and producing code that runs on all systems. JFC is the most important thing to happen in user interfaces since the Macintosh operating system.

Some Terminology

In Win32, the term *control* means the group of all the GUI things that users can press, scroll, choose between, type into, draw on, and so forth. In the Unix XWindows world, a control is called a *widget*.

Neither control nor widget is a Java term. Instead we use the term *Component*, or, when talking specifically about Swing, *JComponent*. Each control is a subclass of `javax.swing.JComponent`, so each control also inherits all the methods and data fields of `JComponent`. JComponents are serializable, meaning the object can be written out to disk, can be later read in again, and can become an object again. They follow the rules for JavaBeans, so they can be coupled together in visual builder tools.

> **Heavyweight Versus Lightweight Components**
>
> In AWT, all components are based on peer components. A Java AWT button really is a Win32 button on Windows. This is termed a *heavyweight component.*
>
> A *lightweight component,* like all the Swing JComponents, is one which doesn't use a peer or native component. Instead, it is drawn by Java code on a piece of the screen that already belongs to Java. It is drawn onto its container in fact. The most important differences are:
>
> - Lightweight components can have transparent areas in them, so they don't have to look rectangular in shape.
>
> - Mouse events on a lightweight component are delivered to its container.
>
> - When they overlap, lightweight components are never drawn on top of heavyweight components. This is because you can't draw half of a lightweight component on one component and the other half on another. Lightweights exist wholly within their parent heavyweight component.
>
> Poor behavior when overlapping is the main reason JavaSoft gives for recommending that you not mix Swing JComponents with AWT components.

This whole chapter is about explaining the Swing components and how you use them. You will build up your GUI programs using these components. The first thing to note is that the Swing components are no longer peer-based, but are written in Java and are thus consistent on all platforms. Under the AWT, a button ended up being a Win32 button on Windows, a Macintosh button on the Macintosh, and a Motif button on Unix. With Swing, the button is rendered on a little bit of screen area that belongs to some ancestor Java component, and Swing puts all the button semantics on top of that. Swing draws the button so it looks pushed, armed (ready to push), or disabled. Because the code is written in Java, the button has identical behavior no matter where it runs.

Frankly, JFC is a very big topic. There are more than three hundred classes in the Swing library alone. We'll present nine or ten individual Swing JComponents here, and provide pointers on the rest. This amounts to quite a few pages, so I recommend you read one or two in depth, then just look at the screen pictures to see what each does. Return to the appropriate section in the chapter as you need actual code examples.

Overview of `JComponent`

Object-Oriented Programming fits well with window systems. The concept of making new controls by subclassing existing ones and overriding part of their behavior saves time and effort. Another similarity is the way that controls have to handle events just as objects handle messages. Method calls are equivalent to sending a message to an object, and some OOP languages even refer to a method call as "sending a message."

There is an abstract class called `JComponent` which is the parent class for most things that can appear on screen. The basic ingredients of a GUI are all subclasses of the class called `JComponent`. `JComponent` is the superclass that holds the common information about an on-screen control and provides higher level features common to each control, such as:

- Size (preferred, minimum, and maximum).

- Double buffering (a technique to make frequently changing components look smoother with less flickering).

- Support for accessibility and internationalization.

- Tooltips (pop-up help when you linger on a JComponent).

- Support for operating the control with the keyboard instead of the mouse.

- Some help for debugging by slowing component rendering so you can see what's happening.

- The thickness of any lines or insets around the edge of the Control.

Components correspond to "things that interact with the user" and Containers are "backdrops to put them on." The superclass of `javax.swing.JComponent` is `java.awt.Container`. A lot of people find that highly confusing! Why isn't its parent class java.awt.Component? It's a container to give "look and feel" implementors the option of using child components. For example, a ScrollBarUI subclass can choose to use button children to create the knob or arrow buttons. The component/container distinction turned out to be not very useful in practice.

The behavior and appearance of each specific control is one level down in the subclasses of JComponent.

The Swing lightweight controls can be divided up as shown in Table 18-1.

We will look at just one or two components from each of these categories.

Each control has methods appropriate to what it does. The `JFileChooser` control has methods to get and set the current directory, get the selected filename(s), apply a filename filter, and so on. We'll examine these individual JComponents later in the chapter.

Table 18-1: Swing Lightweight Controls

GUI Category	Control	Swing Class Name

Basic Controls	Button
	Combo box
	List
	Menu
	Slider
	Toolbar
	Text field
		`JButton, JCheckBox, JRadioButton`
		`JComboBox`
		`JList`
		`JMenu, JMenuBar, JMenuItem`
		`JSlider`
		`JToolbar`
		`JTextField, JPasswordField,`
		`JTextArea`

Uneditable Displays	Label
	Tooltip
	Progress bar
		`JLabel`
		`JToolTip`
		`JProgressBar`

Editable Displays	Table
	Text
	Tree
	Color chooser
	File chooser
		`JTable`
		`JTextPane, JTextArea,JEditorPane`
		`JTree`
		`JColorChooser`
		`JFileChooser`

Space-Saving Containers	Scroll pane
	Split pane
	Tabbed pane
		`JScrollPane, JScrollBar`
		`JSplitPane`
		`JTabbedPane`

Top-Level Containers	Frame
	Applet
	Dialog
		`JFrame`
		`JApplet`
		`JDialog, JOptionPane`

Other Containers	Panel
	Internal frame
	Layered pane
	Root pane
		`JPanel`
		`JInternalFrame`
		`JLayeredPane`
		`JRootPane`

All About Controls (JComponents)

We now have enough knowledge to start looking at individual controls in detail and to describe the kinds of events they can generate. Almost the whole of window programming is learning about the different controls that you can put on the screen and how to drive them. This section (at last) describes some individual controls. The controls shown in Figure 18-1 are all subclasses of the general class JComponent that we have already seen.

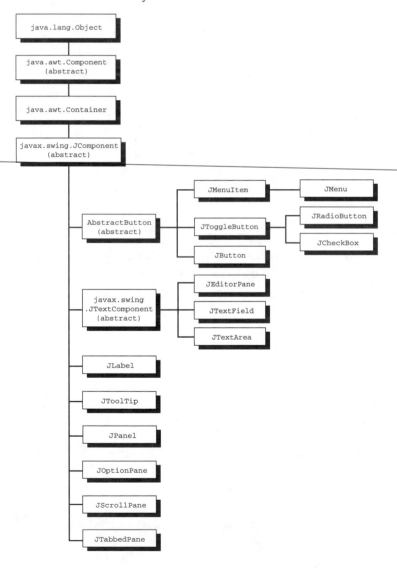

Figure 18-1: Some JComponent controls (visible GUI objects) of Java.

These classes are the controls or building blocks from which you create your GUI. What you do with all these components is the following:

1. Add them to the content pane of a container (often JFrame or JApplet) with a call like:

    ```
    MyJContainer.getContentPane().add( myJComponent );
    ```

2. Register your event-handler using the addSomeListener() method of the control. This tells the window system which routine of yours should be called when the user presses buttons or otherwise makes selections to process the event.

Fortunately, both of these activities are quite straightforward, and we'll cover them here in source code, words, and pictures. The add method can be applied to a Frame in an application like this:

```
JFrame jf = new JFrame();
        . . .
jf.getContentPane().add( something );
```

Or, it can be applied to the JApplet's panel like so:

```
public static void init () {
     this.getContentPane().add( something );
```

Recall the Applet/JApplet life cycle described in an earlier chapter. That discussion made clear that there is an init() method which each Applet should override. It will be called when the Applet is loaded, and it is a good place to place the code that creates these GUI objects. We will use init() for that purpose. If you are writing an applet with Swing components you must use JApplet (not Applet) as your parent class to ensure that all drawing and updates take place correctly.

Whenever a user operates a JComponent (presses a button, clicks on a choice), an event is generated. The SomeEvent argument is a class that can be seen in the $JAVAHOME/src/java/awt/event directory. It contains much information about the coordinates of the event, the time it occurred, and the kind of event that it was. If the event was a key press, it has the value of the key. If the event was a selection from a list, it has the string chosen.

How to Display Components

Containers are the objects that are displayed directly on the screen. Controls must be added to a Container if you want to see them. The container in this example driver program is called *JFrame*. JFrame will be the main window of most of your Swing applications.

Let's create a JFrame, set its size, set it visible, tell it how to arrange JComponents that are added, and add some event-handler code to exit the program when it detects that you have clicked on the JFrame to close it. Phew! That's quite a list of tasks, so we'll split them off into a separate method. Make everything static. In this way, we can use it from the main() method, and we get the following:

```
import java.awt.*;
import java.awt.event.*;
import javax.swing.*;
public class Demo {
    static JFrame jframe = new JFrame("Example");

    public static void setupJFrame() {
        jframe.setSize(400,100);
        jframe.setVisible(true);
        jframe.getContentPane().setLayout( new FlowLayout() );

        WindowListener l = new WindowAdapter() {
            public void windowClosing(WindowEvent e) {
                System.exit(0);}
        };
        jframe.addWindowListener(l);
    }

    public static void main(String[] args) {
        setupJFrame();
        JButton jb = new JButton("pressure");
        jframe.getContentPane().add( jb );
    }
}
```

The JButton Component that we are trying to demonstrate is printed in bold type. The line that follows adds the JComponent to the JFrame's content pane. To cut down on the extraneous code in the pages ahead, I'll show only the statements that directly deal with the JComponent. That means I'll show only the two bold statements in the example above. You should supply all the missing code when you compile and run the examples. On to the first example!

JLabel

What it is:

JLabel is the simplest JComponent. It is just a string, image, or both that appears on screen. The contents can be left-, right-, or center-aligned according to an argument to the constructor. The default is left-aligned. JLabel is a cheap, fast way to get a picture or text on the screen

What it looks like on screen:

The code to create it:

```
//   remember, we are only showing relevant statements from main()
    ImageIcon icon = new ImageIcon("star.gif");
    JLabel jl = new JLabel("You are a star", icon, JLabel.CENTER);

    frame.getContentPane().add( jl );
    frame.pack(); // size the JFrame to fit its contents
```

Note the way we can bring in an image from a GIF or JPEG file by constructing an ImageIcon with a pathname to a file. Labels do not generate any events in and of themselves. It is possible, however, to get and set the text of a label. You might do that in response to an event from a different component. The constructors for JLabel are:

```
public javax.swing.JLabel(java.lang.String);
public javax.swing.JLabel(java.lang.String,int);
public javax.swing.JLabel(java.lang.String,javax.swing.Icon,int);
public javax.swing.JLabel(javax.swing.Icon);
public javax.swing.JLabel(javax.swing.Icon,int);
```

The int parameter is a constant from the JLabel class specifying left-, right- or center-alignment in the area where the label is displayed.

JLabels are typically used to augment other controls with descriptions or instructions. People often want to know how to get a multi-line label (or a multi-line button). There is no direct way. Either use multiple labels, or program the functionality in for yourself by extending the class JComponent to do what you want.

JButton

What it is:

This is a GUI button. You supply code for the action that is to take place when the button is pressed.

What it looks like on screen:

The code to create it:

```
JButton jb = new JButton("pressure");
jframe.getContentPane().add( jb );
```

The code to handle events from it:

```
jb.addActionListener( new ActionListener() {
     int i = 1;
     public void actionPerformed(ActionEvent e)
          { System.out.println("pressed "+ i++); }
} );
```

When you press this button, the event-handler will print out the number of times it has been pressed. You can easily create buttons with images as well, like this:

```
Icon spIcon = new ImageIcon("spam.jpg");
JButton jb = new JButton("press here for Spam", spIcon);
```

 You can add a keyboard accelerator to a button, and you can give it a symbolic name for the text string that it displays. This helps with internationalizing code.

Program an "Alice in Wonderland" JFrame with two buttons, one of which makes the frame grow larger, the other smaller. The Component method setSize(int, int) will resize a component. (Easy—about twenty lines of code).

JToolTip

What it is:

This is a text string that acts as a hint or further explanation. You can set it for any JComponent. It appears automatically when the mouse lingers on that component and it disappears when you roll the mouse away.

Tooltips don't generate any events, so there is nothing to handle.

What it looks like on screen:

We'll add a tooltip to the JLabel that we showed on the previous page.

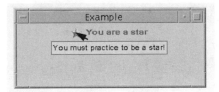

The code to create it:

```
JLabel jl = ...
jl.setToolTipText("You must practice to be a star!");
```

Notice that you don't directly create a JToolTip object. That is done for you behind the scenes. You invoke the setToolTipText() method of JComponent. It's so quick and easy to create tooltips, there's no reason not to

JTextField

What it is:

This is an area of the screen where you can enter a line of text. There are a couple of subclasses; JTextArea (several lines in size) and JPasswordField (which doesn't echo what you type in). You can display some initial text. The text is selectable (you can highlight it with the cursor) and can be set to be editable or not editable.

What it looks like on screen:

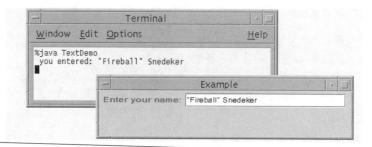

The code to create it:

```
JLabel jl = new JLabel("Enter your name:");
JTextField jtf = new JTextField(25); // field is 25 chars wide
```

The code to retrieve user input from it:

Text fields generate key events on each keystroke and an ActionEvent when the user presses a carriage return. This makes it convenient to validate individual keystrokes as they are typed (as in, ensuring that a field is wholly numeric) and to retrieve all the text when the user has finished typing. The code to get the text looks like this:

```
jtf.addActionListener( new ActionListener() {
    public void actionPerformed(ActionEvent e)
    {   System.out.println(
        " you entered: " + e.getActionCommand() ); }
    } );

Container c = jframe.getContentPane();
c.add( jl );
c.add( jtf );
```

In this example, running the program, typing in a name, and hitting carriage return will cause the name to be echoed on system.out. You should write some code to try implementing a listener for each keystroke.

JCheckBox

What it is:

A checkbox screen object that represents a boolean choice: pressed, not pressed, on, or off. Usually some text explains the choice. For example, a "Press for fries" JLabel would have a JCheckBox "button" allowing yes or no. You can also add an icon to the JCheckBox, just the way you can with JButton.

What it looks like on screen:

The code to create it:

```
JCheckBox jck1 = new JCheckBox("Pepperoni");
JCheckBox jck2 = new JCheckBox("Mushroom");
JCheckBox jck3 = new JCheckBox("Black olives");
JCheckBox jck4 = new JCheckBox("Tomato");
Container c = jframe.getContentPane();
c.add( jck1 ); c.add( jck2 ); // etc...
```

The code to retrieve user input from it:

Checkbox generates both ActionEvent and ItemEvent every time you change it. This seems to be for backward compatibility with AWT. We already saw the code to handle ActionEvents with Button. The code to register an ItemListener looks like this:

```
jck2.addItemListener( new ItemListener()
{ // anonymous class
    public void itemStateChanged(ItemEvent e) {
        if (e.getStateChange()==e.SELECTED)
            System.out.print("selected ");
        else System.out.print("de-selected ");
        System.out.print("Mushroom\n");
    }
} );
```

In this example, running the program and clicking the "Mushroom" checkbox will cause the output of selected Mushroom in the system console.

Handlers in real programs will do more useful actions as necessary like assigning values and creating objects. The ItemEvent contains fields and methods that specify which object generated the event and whether it was selected or deselected.

JPanel

What it is:

There was (and is) an AWT component known as `Canvas`. It is a screen area that you can use for drawing graphics or receiving user input. A `Canvas` usually is subclassed to add the behavior you need, especially when you use it to display a GIF or JPEG image. A `Canvas` contains almost no methods. All its functionality is either inherited from `Component` (setting font, color, size) or from functionality you add when you extend the class.

Everyone expects there to be a JCanvas replacing Canvas, just as JButton replaces Button, JFrame replaces Frame, and so on. There is no JCanvas. The AWT component Canvas was just like the AWT component Panel, except Panel was also a container. The Swing version of Panel, JPanel, does double duty. It replaces both Canvas and Panel.

To draw on a JPanel, you may want to supply your own version of the method `paintComponent(Graphics g)`. To do that, you need to extend the class and override the `paintComponent()` method[1] for this Container. That gives you a Graphics context—the argument to `paintComponent()`—which is used in all drawing operations. The many methods of Graphics let you render (the fancy graphics word for "draw") lines, shapes, text, etc., on the screen.

A simpler alternative, for simpler drawings, is to use JLabel to create the picture, and add it to JPanel as shown in the code opposite.

I like this picture because it looks the same in black and white as it does in color.

---

1. A more descriptive name for the `paintComponent()` method would be `how_to_draw_me()`.

The code to create it:

```
class MyJPanel extends JPanel {
    JLabel jl = new JLabel(new ImageIcon( "bmw.jpg"));
    { add(jl); // instance initializer just for fun

        addKeyListener( new KeyAdapter() {
            public void keyPressed(KeyEvent e) {
                char c = e.getKeyChar();
                System.out.println("got char "+c);
            }
        } );
    }
}


...

    public static void main(String[] args) {
        setupFrame();
        MyJPanel mjp = new MyJPanel();
        jframe.getContentPane().add(mjp);
        jframe.setVisible(true);
        mjp.requestFocus();
    }
```

I have also added a KeyListener for the JPanel here. That allows you to make keystrokes on top of the JPanel and have the callback take place for each one individually. All you do is echo the characters to prove you got them. With the picture backdrop and the capture of individual keystrokes, you have the basics of a computer game right there. There are a couple of real computer games on the CD.

You have to request the focus for a component before key events will be sent to it, and the component has to be visible at the time you do that.

JRadioButton and ButtonGroup

What it is:
JRadioButtons are used when you have a group of checkboxes, and you want a maximum of one of them to be selected. This was done with a CheckboxGroup in the AWT, but the design has been cleaned and simplified in Swing. JRadioButton, JCheckBox, and JButton are now subclasses of AbstractButton and have common consistent behavior, can be given images, can be embedded in menus, and so on.

The term "radio buttons" arises from the old manual station selection buttons in car radios. When you pressed in one of the buttons, all the others would pop out and be deselected. ButtonGroups work the same way.

What it looks like on screen:

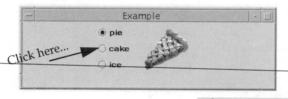

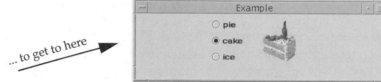

On Windows 95, mutually exclusive checkboxes are round, while multiple selection checkboxes are square. This is one of those "look and feel" differences between window systems.

The code to create it:
This example shows some more sophisticated things you can do in your event-handler. In this example, we have a JLabel with a picture of the choice. In the event-handler, we set the label to correspond to the RadioButton choice.

The ButtonGroup class automatically takes care of arming the previous radio button when you press another.

```
// JRadioButton code
    final JLabel piclabel
        = new JLabel(new ImageIcon( pieString + ".gif"));

    /** Listens to the radio buttons. */
    class RadioListener implements ActionListener {
        public void actionPerformed(ActionEvent e) {
        // getting the event causes update on Jlabel icon
        piclabel.setIcon(
            new ImageIcon( e.getActionCommand()+".gif"));
        }
    }

    JRadioButton pieButton = new JRadioButton(pieString);
    pieButton.setMnemonic('b');
    pieButton.setActionCommand(pieString);
    pieButton.setSelected(true);

    JRadioButton cakeButton = new JRadioButton(cakeString);
    JRadioButton iceButton = new JRadioButton(iceString);

    // Group the radio buttons.
    ButtonGroup group = new ButtonGroup();
    group.add(pieButton);
    group.add(cakeButton);
    group.add(iceButton);

    // Register a listener for the radio buttons.
    RadioListener myListener = new RadioListener();
    pieButton.addActionListener(myListener);
    cakeButton.addActionListener(myListener);
    iceButton.addActionListener(myListener);

    // Put the radio buttons in a column in a panel to line up
    JPanel radioPanel = new JPanel();
    radioPanel.setLayout(new GridLayout(0, 1));
    radioPanel.add(pieButton);
    radioPanel.add(cakeButton);
    radioPanel.add(iceButton);

    jframe.getContentPane().add(radioPanel);
    jframe.getContentPane().add(piclabel);
    jframe.setVisible(true);
```

JOptionPane

What it is:

This is utility pane that can pop up some common warning and error messages. It's as easy to use as JToolTip, and it works the same way. You don't instantiate it directly, but you call a method to make it happen.

What it looks like on screen:

The code to create it:

The method to show a JOptionPane takes four arguments:

- A parent frame (null means use a default). The Pane appears below its parent.

- The thing to display. It can be a String or an icon or a JLabel or other possibilities that are converted to String and then wrapped in a JLabel.

- The title String to put on the Pane title bar.

- The type of message, like ERROR_MESSAGE, WARNING_MESSAGE, or INFORMATION_MESSAGE.

```
Icon s = new ImageIcon("spam.jpg");
JLabel jl = new JLabel("Are you getting enough?", s,JLabel.CENTER);

JOptionPane.showMessageDialog( null, // parent frame
                jl,    // Object to display
                "Plenty of spam", // title bar message
                JOptionPane.QUESTION_MESSAGE );
```

The code to retrieve user input from it:

No input comes back from this component. When the user clicks on the button, the Pane is dismissed automatically. There are a great many choices and methods that fine-tune this JComponent to let you convey exactly the nuance of information you want.

JScrollPane

What it is:

Of all the JComponents, this one is probably my favorite. It works so hard for you with so little effort on your part.

A JScrollPane provides a scrollable view of any lightweight component. You just instantiate a JScrollPane with the thing you want to scroll as an argument to the constructor. Then set the ScrollPane's preferred size with a method call, add it to your container, and you're done! This is so much easier than the messing around with individual and highly buggy scrollbars that we had to do in JDK 1.0

By default, a scroll pane attempts to size itself so that its client displays at its preferred size. Many components have a simple preferred size that's big enough to display the entire component. You can customize a scroll pane with many refinements on how much to scroll, which of the scroll bars to show, custom decorations around the sides, and so on. The visible area in the Pane is called the "viewport."

What it looks like on screen:

The code to create it:

In this code, we put the JPanel subclass that we created earlier into a JScrollPane.

```
MyJPanel mjp = new MyJPanel();
JScrollPane jsp = new JScrollPane( mjp );
jsp.setPreferredSize( new Dimension(150, 150));
jframe.getContentPane().add(jsp);
```

The code to retrieve user input from it:

You frequently won't need to interact with your scroll pane at all, as it does so much of the right thing by default. However, you can implement the Scrollable interface if your enthusiasm extends to wanting to get callbacks for individual clicks on the scroll bars.

JTabbedPane

What it is:

A Tabbed Pane is a component that lets you economize on screen real estate. It simulates a folder with tabbed page dividers. You have a series of "tabs" (labels) along the top, associated with Components on a larger rectangular area beneath. By clicking on a tab label, you bring its associated component to the front. We'll show an example using the JEditorPane and the JPanel we already saw.

What it looks like on screen:

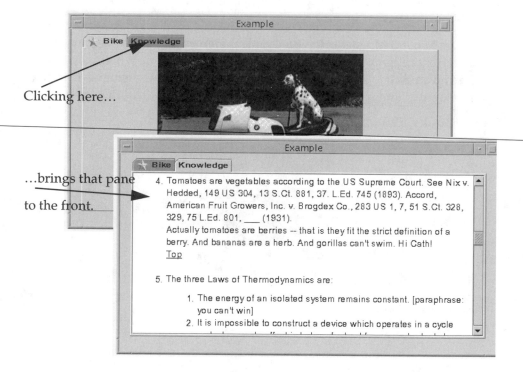

Clicking here...

...brings that pane to the front.

You can make the tabs appear on any of the four sides of the TabbedPane. You can have even more than one row of tabs, but the human factors of that are appalling. When you have multiple rows, any tab that's clicked moves to the bottom row of tabs. As a result, clicking on some tabs causes all of them to change places. Ugh.

The code to create it:

```
// set up the editor pane, as before
    JEditorPane jep =null;
    try {
        jep = new JEditorPane( "file:///tmp/know.html" );
    } catch (Exception e) {System.out.println("error: "+e); }

    jep.setEditable(false); // turns off the ability to edit
    JScrollPane jsp = new JScrollPane( jep );
    jsp.setPreferredSize( new Dimension(550, 250));

// set up the JPanel, as before
    MyJPanel mjp = new MyJPanel();
    jframe.getContentPane().add(mjp);

// create a tabbed pane and add them to it.
    JTabbedPane jtp = new JTabbedPane();
    ImageIcon ic = new ImageIcon("star.gif");
    jtp.addTab("Bike", ic, mjp,
                "1989 BWM RS100/1996 Dalmatian Annie");
    jtp.addTab("Knowledge", null, jsp, "who knew?");

    jframe.getContentPane().add(jtp);
    jframe.setVisible(true);
}
```

The method to add a tab and the Component together takes four arguments:

```
public void addTab(String title,
                    Icon icon,
                    Component component,
                    String tip)
```

The title is the phrase to put on the tab. The icon is a little picture with which you can decorate the phrase. For example, on the "Bike" pane I use a star, and on the "Knowledge" pane I use null to signify no picture. The third parameter is the component that you want associated with that tab. The final parameter is a String representing tooltip text that you get for free with this component.

JEditorPane

What it is:

This is a very powerful JComponent! JEditorPane allows you to display and edit documents that contain HTML, Rich Text Format, or straight Unicode characters. It formats the text and displays it.

What it looks like on screen:

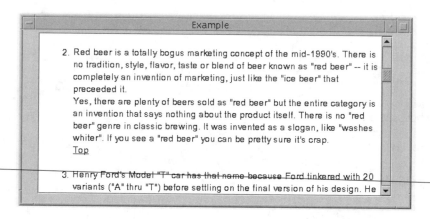

You can load the component from a URL or from a String containing a URL as shown below, or from the contents of a String itself. In the example below, the JEditor pane is placed in a ScrollPane so it displays and scrolls well

The code to create it:

```
JEditorPane jep =null;
try {
    jep = new JEditorPane( "file:///tmp/know.html" );
} catch (Exception e) {System.out.println("error: "+e); }

jep.setEditable(false); // turns off the ability to edit
JScrollPane jsp = new JScrollPane( jep );
jsp.setPreferredSize( new Dimension(550, 250));
jframe.getContentPane().add(jsp);
```

Notice how trivial it is to display an HTML file and to wrap a JScrollPane around it. JEditorPane is a subclass of the less specialized JTextComponent.

Let's quickly review the match between components and events.

More about Swing Components

Cast your mind back to Table 18-1 at the beginning of this chapter. It named all the significant JComponents, and there were about forty in all (including all the subclasses of subclasses). We've presented, briefly, some of the more important ones here. That's certainly enough to get you started writing GUI programs. To keep the book to a manageable size, however, and still fit in all the other information, we don't show all of them.

Here are some pointers on how to find out more about the other components when you're ready to. The first resource is the good (if somewhat fluid) online tutorial on Java generally, and Swing in particular, that Sun Microsystems maintains at http://java.sun.com/docs/books/tutorial/ui/swing/.

The second resource is the Swing section of the Java Programmers FAQ that is on this CD and is also online in a more up-to-date form at http://www.afu.com. The FAQ has lots of nuggets of information about Java problems that everyone initially encounters. It gives advice on solutions and workarounds.

The third resource is to buy or borrow a book that examines JFC, including the Swing components in depth. These books are frequently intimidating in size. One such book that I like is Kim Topley's *Core Java Foundation Classes* (Prentice Hall, 1998) with ISBN 0-13-080301-4. It weighs in at over 1,100 pages, so be prepared to put in a few evenings and weekends.

Debugging Lightweight Components

JComponent supports a method to help the implementation team debug the Swing library, but you can use it, too. You can call the following:

```
RepaintManager.currentManager(yourContainer.getRootPane()).
            setDoubleBufferingEnabled(false);

anyJComponent.setDebugGraphicsOptions( options );
```

The first statement turns off double buffering for the container your component is in. The "options" parameter on the second statement is an int which is 0 to switch debugging off, or contains any of these flags OR'd together:

DebugGraphics.FLASH_OPTION // flash the component as it is accessed

DebugGraphics.BUFFER_OPTION // show the offscreen graphics work

DebugGraphics.LOG_OPTION // print a text summary of graphics work

The flash option is pretty spectacular and allows you to see lightweights being drawn.

Table 18-2 Components and Events

Component Generating This Event	Interface the Event-Handling Code Implements	Method(s) the Interface Promises
JButton JMenu JMenuItem JRadioButton JCheckBox	`ActionListener`	`public void actionPerformed(ActionEvent e);`

Component	`ComponentListener`	`public void componentResized(ComponentEvent);`
		`public void componentMoved(ComponentEvent);`
		`public void componentShown(ComponentEvent);`
		`public void componentHidden(ComponentEvent);`

Container	`ContainerListener`	`public void componentAdded(ContainerEvent);` `public void componentRemoved(ContainerEvent);`
Component	`FocusListener`	`public void focusGained(FocusEvent e);` `public void focusLost(FocusEvent e);`
JButton JMenu JMenuItem JRadioButton JCheckBox	`ItemListener`	`public void itemStateChanged(ItemEvent e);`

Component	`KeyListener`	`public void keyTyped(KeyEvent e);`
		`public void keyPressed(KeyEvent e);`
		`public void keyReleased(KeyEvent e);`

Component	`MouseListener`	`public void mouseClicked(MouseEvent e);`
		`public void mousePressed(MouseEvent e);`
		`public void mouseReleased(MouseEvent e);`
		`public void mouseEntered(MouseEvent e);`
		`public void mouseExited(MouseEvent e);`

Component	`MouseMotionListener`	`public void mouseDragged(MouseEvent e);` `public void mouseMoved(MouseEvent e);`
JTextField	`ActionListener`	`public void actionPerformed(ActionEvent e);`

Dialog
JDialog
Frame
JFrame
Window
JWindow
	`WindowListener`	`public void windowOpened(WindowEvent e);`
		`public void windowClosing(WindowEvent e);`
		`public void windowClosed(WindowEvent e);`
		`public void windowIconified(WindowEvent e);`
		`public void windowDeiconified(WindowEvent e):`
		`public void windowActivated(WindowEvent e);`
		`public void WindowDeactivated (WindowEvent e);`

Finally, I have the same advice that Obi-Wan gave Luke Skywalker on his quest to defeat the forces of evil: *Use the source.* The Java platform is almost unique among commercial products in that the complete source code for the runtime library is distributed with the system. If you installed the compiler in C:\jdk1.2fcs then the source is in C:\jdk1.2fcs\src.jar. Jar (Java archive) files have the same format as zip files, so you can unpack it by using `unzip src.jar`. That will put the Swing source files into the C:\jdk1.2fcs\src\javax\swing directory.

Having the source is a triple blessing. You can read the code to find out how something works and what features it offers (the code is heavily commented). You can recompile the code with more of your own debugging information, and use that instead of the standard runtime library (not everyone will want to tackle this). You will also be exposed to the ideas, style, and designs that are used by the best Java programmers in the world. The best programmers in the world learn from each other by reading each other's code. Now you have this opportunity, too. Seize it.

I really like Swing. It passes the golden rule of software: It's simple to do simple things. Just be aware that all the components have many more features than are presented here and you can get some very sophisticated effects when you start combining them and using them to full advantage.

Some Light Relief

The Bible Code

The previous chapter ended with a praying mantis, so I'll continue the religious theme with a description of the Bible code. The concept of "Bible codes" was something that became popular in 1997, helped by a mass marketed book on the subject. It's a completely bogus idea that there are hidden strings in the first five books of the Bible, and these hidden strings foretell the future.

The hidden strings, or *Bible codes*, are supposedly found by looking at individual characters of the Bible, starting at some offset, and taking every Nth letter thereafter to form a phrase. It works much better with a Bible in Hebrew because the classic written form of that language does not have any vowels. Hence you can construct many possible phrases depending on which vowels you choose to put in and where you choose to end a word. "BLLGTS" can be interpreted as "Boil leg & toes" or "Be a li'l gutsy" or even "Bill Gates".

When you find a Bible "code" you frequently find other related phrases around it. Of course, you can often find clouds in the sky that have shapes that look like animals, and the reason is exactly the same: people tend to see what they want to see, there's a huge amount of sky and clouds to look at, and you can always find something if you look at enough random stuff.

I thought it would be fun to write some Bible code software in Java, and I put it on the CD. There's a program in \goodies\bible that you can run to search for arbitrary patterns in the Bible (a copy of the King James Version is also on the CD). Here are the results when I set it to search for the string "Java"—a place and language unknown in biblical times.

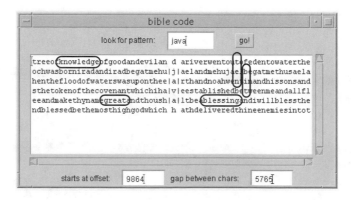

As you can see, it has found the word along with other astonishing and highly meaningful phrases ("knowledge of Java, a great blessing, bit, net"). You can run the program for yourself and find other phrases of your choice.

One of the promoters of the Bible code concept challenged his critics to find hidden messages in non-Bible texts like *Moby Dick*. He thought there weren't any. He was dead wrong!

You will find that *Moby Dick* contains predictions for the deaths of Indira Gandhi, President Rene Moawad of Lebanon, Martin Luther King, Chancellor Engelbert Dollfuss of Austria, Leon Trotsky, Sirhan Sirhan, John F. Kennedy, Robert Kennedy, and Princess Diana, among others! Here is the Diana prediction from *Moby Dick*:

"Lady Diana, Dodi, foolishly wasted, mortal in these jaws of death!" The two likeliest conclusions follow. Either Herman Melville was the Supreme Creator of the Universe and he encoded Bible code style predictions in *Moby Dick* as well as in the Bible. Another option is that the notion of hidden messages encoded in revered works is a bunch of nonsense put about by some people who should know better. I don't know about you, but I'm going with the simpler of the two explanations. Let me add that the meaninglessness of the codes doesn't impugn the origin of the Bible. It just says that people can be wrong when they try to project their own interpretations onto any text.

Take a look at the CD directory goodies\bible\MobyDick for details. There's a copy of Moby Dick there, along with the Bible code software to search it. I'd like to find out what hidden messages there are in the Sherlock Holmes books. This is what programmers do when they have too much time on their hands.

CHAPTER 19

- Pluggable Look and Feel
- All About Containers
- Layout in a Container
- Tying up the Loose Ends
- Some Light Relief

Containers,
Layouts, and AWT
Loose Ends

We're now two thirds of the way through our tour of JFC and Swing. This chapter completes the topic by presenting some containers and an explanation of how you use them to lay out your components neatly on the screen. We also give some information on a couple of topics that are related to the window system generally.

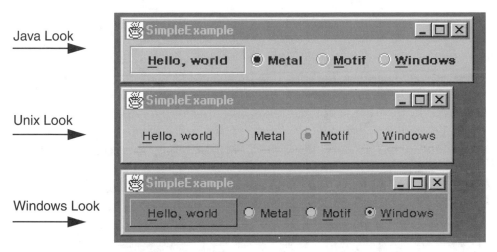

Java Look →

Unix Look →

Windows Look →

Figure 19-1: A Pluggable Look and Feel (PLAF).

Here's the really cool thing: there is only one program here! When you select one of those JRadioButtons, it transforms the program to display in that style. I started up three copies of the program, chose a different look and feel in each, put them next to each other, and took a screen snapshot. This is less than 150 lines long, and the key area is a couple of lines. It declares the JComponents and a listener for the radio buttons. The listener has the code (shown below) that does the magic. That's all there is to it!

```
String metalPLAFName = "javax.swing.plaf.metal.MetalLookAndFeel";
String motifPLAFName = "com.sun.java.swing.plaf.motif.MotifLookAndFeel";
String winPLAFName =
"com.sun.java.swing.plaf.windows.WindowsLookAndFeel";
String lnfName = e.getActionCommand();
try {
    UIManager.setLookAndFeel(lnfName);
    SwingUtilities.updateComponentTreeUI(frame);
    frame.pack();
} catch (Exception exc) { ...
```

This program is distributed as part of the JDK, and you can find it in $JAVAHOME/demo/jfc/Simple/src.java.

Model/View/Controller Architecture

You may hear people talk about the *Model/View/Controller,* or *MVC,* architecture of Swing. MVC is a design pattern or framework originally developed by Professor Trygve Reenskaug at Xerox PARC in 1978. The purpose of MVC was to provide convenient GUI support in Smalltalk.

Model/View/Controller is used extensively in Swing. For the basic components, you don't notice it. For more complicated components like JTree and JTable, you need to know a little about it. A one line summary of MVC is "Rather than having one big class for each JComponent, different GUI responsibilities have been split out into different classes." MVC makes the Platform Look and Feel possible, or at least a lot simpler.

Basically, the *model* contains your data, the *view* is the graphical representation, and the *controller* is responsible for the interaction between the other two. As an example, think of visually editing a Tree control that represents a directory. The display is the view. Selecting a file, and dragging it to the trash can will delete the file. In order for the delete to happen, the controller must tell the model what just happened in the view.

In practice, the view and the controller are put in the same class in Swing. They initially tried having them separate, but realized it caused more trouble than it was worth. The model (data) is separate, though.

There are a couple of methods in the library to let you force the look and feel to match the system on which you are running. Here's the code to do that:

```
UIManager.setLookAndFeel(UIManager.getSystemLookAndFeelClassName());
```

Here's the code to force a program to use the common, Metal look:

```
UIManager.setLookAndFeel(UIManager.getCrossPlatformLookAndFeelClassName());
```

Since the look and feel is rendered by Java code, not by use of native libraries, it is feasible to have any look and feel on any platform. Microsoft and Apple, however, have chosen not to grant permission for their look and feel to be used on other platforms. The Java FAQ has some information about how the runtime system checks this, and how you can influence it.

All About Containers

We come now to the third of the three ideas common to all Java GUI programs: grouping together controls and arranging them neatly by adding them to a container.

Controls, Containers, Component...Where Will It All End?

Here's the way to tell these three similar sounding names apart!

Control	This is not a Java term. This is the PC term for what is called a widget in the Unix world. It's a software element on the screen, like a button or a scroll bar.
Container	These are screen windows that physically contain groups of controls or other containers. You can move, hide, or show a Container and all its contents in one operation. Top-level containers can be displayed on the screen. Non top-level containers have to be in a top-level container to be displayed.
Component	This is a collective name for Controls and Containers. Since they have some common operations, Component is their common parent class. Swing's JComponents are a subclass of Component.

We've seen this when we added the JComponents to the contentpane of a JFrame, and the JFrame showed up on the screen. The piece that is new that a container can have different *layout policies* for where components go on the screen when you add them. A layout policy might be, "Add components from left to right across the container. When you reach the right-hand margin, start a new line of them". Another layout policy might be "Components can go to the north, south, east, west, or in the center of the component. You have to tell me where when you add one." There are a number of classes, called *Layout Managers*, that implement layout polices like these. We are going to describe them at length in this chapter. Before we do, we'll look at Containers a bit more closely.

The Container Class Hierarchy

The previous chapter described many controls of JDK 1.2. Now let's take a look at the Containers that hold them. The class hierarchy for containers is shown in the following Figure 19-2. Notice that most of the Swing containers are not JCompo-nents, but are specializations of existing AWT containers.

On the following pages, we will outline these containers, suggest typical uses, and show code examples. Container is the class that groups together a number of controls and provides a framework for how they are positioned on the screen.

Container has fields and methods to deal with the following:

- The layout manager used to automatically position controls.

- Forcing the layout to be done.

- The thickness of any lines or insets (*Borders*) around its edges.

- Adding a ContainerListener for ContainerEvents.

- Adding, removing, and retrieving a list of any of the controls.

- Size (current, preferred, minimum, and maximum).

- Requesting the keyboard focus.

- A paint() routine that renders it on the screen.

The AWT class called Container is the superclass for components whose purpose is to hold several controls. A Container is essentially a rectangular portion of the screen that allows you to treat several individual controls as a group. You don't display a control directly; you add it to a Container, and it is the container that is displayed.

Container also has methods to get and set many attributes and to add and remove Components from itself. Containers must have either their pack() method called, or have their initial size set before they will show up on the screen. Set their size by using the following:

```
public void setSize(int width, int height)
```

The units are pixels (dots on the screen). Since a Container is a subclass of Compo-nent, it also has all the Component fields. You can and should review the Container methods by running javap java.awt.Container.

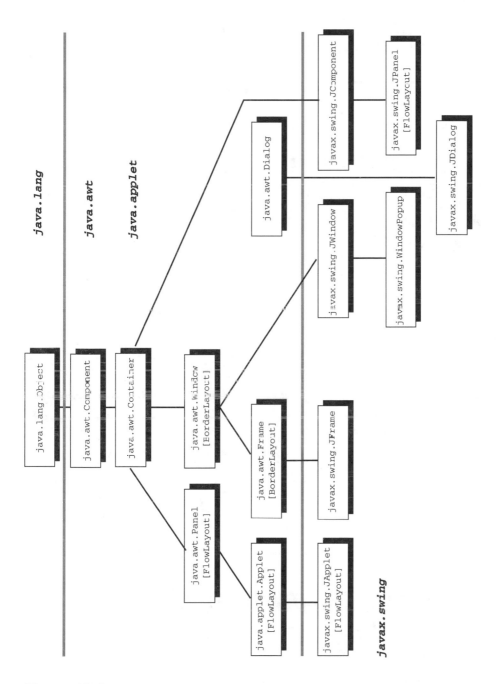

Figure 19-2: Class hierarchy of containers.

When you have finished adding or changing the components in a Container, you typically call the first three of these three methods on the Container.

```
myContainer.invalidate();   // tell AWT it needs laying out
myContainer.validate();     // ask AWT to lay it out
myContainer.show();         // make it visible

myContainer.pack();         // squeeze it down smaller
```

These methods aren't needed if you are just adding to an applet, but you will need to use them in your more complicated programs.

What's in a Swing Container?

In this section, we look at what a Swing container has that an AWT container doesn't, and why you must use a Swing container to contain Swing components. Most of it comes down to the difference between lightweight and heavyweight components and making lightweight components work properly.

You add an component to an AWT container with a statement like:

```
myAWTContainer.add(myAWTComponent)
```

Swing containers are different. They have several layers, shown in Figure 19-3. The different layers are used for different effects.

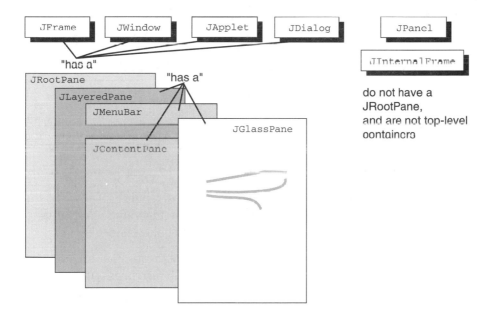

Figure 19-3: Layers of Swing containers.

The JRootPane is the fundamental Swing container. The JGlassPane lays over everything and allows you to intercept mouse events or draw over the whole container without getting distracted by the components within it.

The JContentPane is the object within a Swing container to which you add your Jcomponents and set layout policies. The default layout policy is border layout. Border layout components are added around the four edges and in the center of the container. The JMenuBar is an object that keeps track of any menus associated with the container.

The JLayeredPane manages the menubar and the content pane. It also maintains a notion of z-order (which components are on top of other components within the container). It has several default depth ranges, including one for floating toolbars, one for modal dialogs, one for things being dragged, and so on. The JLayeredPane does the right thing by default, but also allows you to "get under the hood" and set things explicitly where you want them.

A JPanel is a lightweight container whose purpose is to be drawn on, and to group controls together. There is no JContentPane class. If you peek at the JRoot-Pane source, you'll see the work is actually done by a JPanel. The Swing containers have methods to get and adjust these individual pane layers. We saw many times in the previous chapter how you add components to a Swing container. This is how you add them to the content pane:

```
mySwingContainer.getContentPane().add(child);
```

Now we'll look at some individual Swing containers.

JFrame

A JFrame is a window that also has a title bar, a menubar, a border (known as the inset), and that can be closed to an icon. JFrame is the Swing version of Frame. You should avoid mixing Swing and AWT controls and containers.

We've seen the code to create, resize, and show a JFrame throughout the previous chapter. That was done as an application, but frames can also be displayed from an applet. When you create a JFrame, it is not displayed physically inside the applet or other Container but is a separate free-floating window on the monitor.

A JFrame is a specialization of Frame in the Swing package. It has more refined default behavior on closing the Frame, and it adds a number of methods for getting the different "layers" of a Swing container. Here is how you associate a file containing an icon with a Frame so that when you close the Frame, it collapses to the icon.

```
// load the image from a file Toolkit
t = MyFrame.getToolkit();
Image FrameIcon = t.getImage(filename);
MyFrame.setIconImage(FrameIcon);
```

The file name should point to a GIF or JPEG file that is the icon you want to use. Typically, this image will be thumbnail-sized, 32 × 32 pixels or so.

Other Ways to Bring in an Image

We saw in the previous chapter that it is convenient to use ImageIcon to import an image file into a Java program. Here are the constructors for ImageIcon:

```
// constructors of ImageIcon
public javax.swing.ImageIcon();
public javax.swing.ImageIcon(java.awt.Image);
public javax.swing.ImageIcon(java.awt.Image,java.lang.String);
public javax.swing.ImageIcon(java.lang.String); // a filename
public javax.swing.ImageIcon(java.lang.String,java.lang.String);
public javax.swing.ImageIcon(java.net.URL);
public javax.swing.ImageIcon(java.net.URL,java.lang.String);
public javax.swing.ImageIcon(byte[]);
public javax.swing.ImageIcon(byte[],java.lang.String);
```

Once you have an ImageIcon, you can retrieve the image from it with the following:

```
Image myImage = myImageIcon.getImage();
```

JPanel

A JPanel is a generic container that is always in some other container. It does not float loose on the desktop, as JWindow and JFrame do. A JPanel is used when you want to group several controls inside your GUI. For example, you might have several buttons that go together. Adding them to a Panel can treat them as one unit, display them together, and lay them out on the screen under the same set of rules (more about this later).

Note that the Swing JPanel isn't descended from the AWT Panel. They still fulfill the same kind of role: to be a generic non-top-level container. By being a JComponent, JPanel can also provide other support not present in AWT. It can provide automatic double buffering and the accessibility help. Double buffering is a technique that uses more memory to obtain flicker-free updates to components that are being updated frequently on the screen.

Applet and JApplet

Applet is a subclass of Panel. This means that applets come ready-made with some GUI features. JApplet is the Swing subclass of Applet. We've seen applets many times now. Figure 19-4 is another sample screen capture of one.

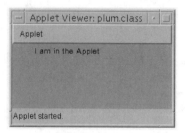

Figure 19-4: Another applet.

Here is the code that created that applet:

```
// <applet code=plum.class height=100 width=200> </applet>

import java.awt.*;
import javax.swing.*;

public class plum extends JApplet {

    public void init() {
       setBackground(Color.green);
       resize(250,100);
    }

    public void paint(Graphics g) {
       g.drawString("I am in the Applet", 35,15);
    }
}
```

As with Panel and JPanel, JApplet adds some Swing conveniences and is required when your applet consists of Swing components. Since Japplet is a subclass of Applet, it has all the Applet methods described on the next page.

One advantage of an applet over an application for a GUI program is that you can start adding and displaying components without creating an underlying back-drop. With an applet, one already exists.

Here are some popular methods of Applet:

```
public URL getDocumentBase() //the URL of the page
                              containing the applet
public URL getCodeBase() //the URL of the applet code

public String getParameter(String name)
public void resize(int width, int height)

public void showStatus(String msg)
public Image getImage(URL url) //bring in an image
public Image getImage(URL url, String name)

public static AudioClip newAudioClip(URL url) // NEW in 1.2
public AudioClip getAudioClip(URL url) //bring in a sound file
public void play(URL url)
```

These four methods are for the stages in the applet life cycle:

```
public void init()
public void start()
public void stop()
public void destroy()
```

As you can see, Applet has several methods that deal with sounds and pictures. For both of these, it uses a URL to pinpoint the file containing the goodies. You can now obtain an audio clip from a URL with a static method. That means you can do it in an application, not just in an applet. You do not have to do anything special to make an Applet retrieve media from its server over the Internet—it is a built-in method. A URL can locate something that is local to your system or anywhere on Internet.

The DocumentBase referred to in the first method is simply the directory containing the HTML page that you are currently visiting. Similarly, the CodeBase is the directory that contains the applet you are currently executing. For security purposes, the machine with the codebase is regarded as the server. Often these two directories will be the same, but since the codebase is a URL, it can be anywhere on the Internet. The source for Applet can be seen in $JAVAHOME/src/java/applet/Applet.java and for Japplet in $JAVAHOME/src/javax/swing/JApplet.java.

Window and JWindow

This container is a totally blank window. It doesn't even have a border. You can display messages by putting Labels on it. Typically you don't use `Window` directly but instead use its more useful subclasses, `Frame` and `Dialog`. The Swing class JWindow is really only there to help with pop-up menus.

Windows can be modal, meaning they prevent all other windows from responding until they are dealt with (e.g., dismissed with a checkbox). `Window` has a few methods for bringing it to the front or back, packing (resizing to preferred size), or showing (making it visible).

For security purposes, the browser typically makes sure any `Window` or subclass of `Window` originating from an untrusted applet contains a line of text warning that it is an "untrusted window" or an "applet window." This message ensures the applet user is never in any doubt about the origin of the window. Without this clear label, it would be too easy to pop up a window that looked like it came from the operating system and ask for confidential information to send back to the applet server.

Now that we've met containers, we are ready to move on to the next section and tackle layouts!

Another Debugging Tip

If you ever want to see what components are in a Java GUI, you can press control + shift + F1.

These three keys will dump out on system.error the text representation of the components that are on the screen. You will see results like this:

```
java.awt.Frame[frame0,0,0,500x275,layout=java.awt.FlowLayout,
resizable,title=bible code]
  java.awt.Label[label0,130,32,98x24,align=left,text=look for pattern:]
  java.awt.TextField[textfield0,233,29,76x31,text=,editable,selection=0-0]
  java.awt.Label[label1,314,32,20x24,align=left,text=  ]
  java.awt.Button[button0,339,32,31x24,label=go!]
  java.awt.TextArea[text0,20,65,459x175,text=,editable,selection=0-
0,rows=10,columns=62, scrollbarVisibility=both]
  java.awt.Label[label2,67,248,91x24,align=left,text=starts at offset:]
  java.awt.TextField[textfield1,163,245,69x31,text=,editable,selection=0-0]
  java.awt.Label[label3,237,248,121x24,align=left,text=gap between chars:]
  java.awt.TextField[textfield2,363,245,69x31,text=,editable,selection=0-0]
```

It's a bit of a "brute force" technique, but it's nice to know about.

Layout in a Container

Here in Figure 19-5 is an frame to which we have added several controls. They are positioned automatically as we add them.

Figure 19-5:   Arranging controls on the screen.

The code for this is on the CD in the directory containing all the other AWT programming material. Problem: The end result doesn't look very professional because nothing is neatly aligned. Solution: Layout managers!

Layout Managers are classes that specify how components should be placed in a Container. You choose a layout manager for a Container with a call like this, invoked on the content pane:

```
setLayout( new FlowLayout() );
```

We'll look at six layout managers: the five that are part of AWT and a sixth one that comes with Swing. The first and most basic layout manager is FlowLayout.

Flow Layout

Figure 19-6 is the same code as above using FlowLayout and with the JFrame pulled out wide to the right.

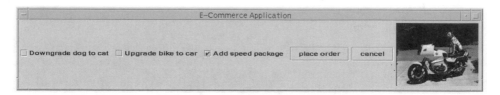

Figure 19-6:   In this applet, buttons are positioned left to right and centered.

A flow layout means that Components are added left to right, keeping them centered in the Container and starting a new line whenever necessary. When you resize the applet, components might move to a new line. There are possible "left" and "right" arguments to the constructor to make the components be left- or right-justified instead of centered, as shown here:

```
setLayout (new FlowLayout (FlowLayout.RIGHT));
```

Most of the layouts allow you to specify the gap in pixels between adjacent components by specifying the values to the constructor. One FlowLayout constructor looks like this:

```
public FlowLayout(int align, int hgap, int vgap);
```

Our first example on the previous page was actually a FlowLayout, too. As we made the JFrame less wide, it folded the flowing line of Components with the result seen there.

This is the code that sets a flow layout on a JFrame:

```
myJframe.getContentPane().setLayout( new FlowLayout() );
```

Some layout managers adjust their components to fit the container, and some layout managers just lay out components unchanged. `FlowLayout` doesn't change the sizes of contained components at all. The `BorderLayout` tells its enclosing container the size to allow for each control by invoking the `preferredSize()` methods of each control. Other layout managers (`GridBagLayout` and `GridLayout`) force the components to adjust their size according to the actual dimensions of the container.

Here is the code used to generate the previous screen capture and the following two examples (commenting and uncommenting code as needed):

```
import java.awt.*;
import java.awt.event.*;
import javax.swing.*;
public class BorderDemo {
    static JFrame jframe = new JFrame("E-Commerce Application");

    public static void setupjframe() {
        jframe.setSize(400,400);
        jframe.setVisible(true);
// jframe.getContentPane().setLayout( new FlowLayout() );
    jframe.getContentPane().setLayout( new BorderLayout(10,7) );
// jframe.getContentPane().setLayout( new GridLayout(3,2, 10, 7));
        WindowListener l = new WindowAdapter() {
        public void windowClosing(WindowEvent e){System.exit(0);}
        };
        jframe.addWindowListener(l);
    }

    public static void main(String[] args) {
        setupjframe();
// JCheckBox jck1 = new JCheckBox("Downgrade dog to cat");
        JCheckBox jck2 = new JCheckBox("Upgrade bike to car");
        JCheckBox jck3 = new JCheckBox("Add speed package");
        // p.add( jck1, "North" ); //max. 5 components
        Container p = jframe.getContentPane();
        p.add( jck2, "East" );
        p.add( jck3, "South" );

        JButton jb1 = new JButton("place order");
        p.add( jb1, "North" );
        JButton jb2 = new JButton("cancel");
        p.add( jb2, "West" );

        JLabel jl = new JLabel(new ImageIcon( "bmw.jpg"));
        p.add(jl, "Center");
        jframe.pack();
    }
}
```

Grid Layout

Figure 19-7 is the same code with a one-line change to give it a grid (m-by-n) layout.

Figure 19-7: A grid layout puts things in equally-sized boxes starting from the top-left.

In the constructor you specify the number of rows and columns, like this:

```
setLayout( new GridLayout(2,3) );
```

That creates a two row grid with three boxes in each row.

Grid layouts are simple and somewhat rigid. One thing that always surprises and annoys programmers is the way the components change in size to match the grid size. Compare the size and shape of the buttons here with those in the previous layout. To avoid this, add a component to a panel, and add the panel to the container with the grid layout.

This is the code that sets a grid layout on a JFrame:

```
jframe.getContentPane().setLayout( new GridLayout(3,2, 10, 7) );
```

The "3, 2" are the rows and columns. The "10, 7" are the horizontal gap and the vertical gap in pixels to leave between components.

Border Layout

The third popular type of layout is BorderLayout. As the name suggests you can put four components around the four edges of the Frame, with a fifth component taking any remaining space in the middle. The default layout for a Window and its subclasses Frame and JFrame is BorderLayout. You can set a border layout in a ContentPane with a line like this:

```
setLayout( new BorderLayout() );
```

You then add up to five widgets, specifying whether they go at the north (top), east (right), and so on. The same application with a one line change to use Border-Layout looks like that shown in Figure 19-8. Note the size of the buttons.

Figure 19-8:   Frame using BorderLayout.

Obviously it's inconvenient to have a maximum of five widgets and that brings us to the real way layouts are used. There probably isn't a single layout manager that will do exactly what you want. Instead, group related components onto panels, and then add the panels to a Frame, using another layout manager. We'll explain how this works using BoxLayout, introduced with Swing. This is the code that sets a border layout on a JFrame:

```
jframe.getContentPane().setLayout( new BorderLayout(10, 7) );
```

Again, the "10, 7" are the horizontal and vertical gaps. This is the code for a component to Container with a Border Layout:

```
myFrame.getContentPane().add( myComponent, "East" );
```

The directions can be "North," "South," "East," "West," and "Center."

There are two important points to watch with BorderLayout. First, you have to set BorderLayout before adding components. Otherwise you mysteriously see nothing (this isn't true, however, for the other two layout managers). Second, letter case is significant when setting the position. For example, you can't use "north" instead of "North."

Box Layout

A fourth kind of layout manager is BoxLayout, named because of its ability to align a group of components horizontally or vertically, shown in Figure 19-9.

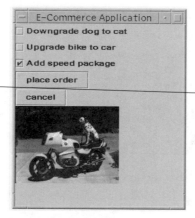

Figure 19-9:   A screen shot using BoxLayout.

The code to apply a BoxLayout to a Container looks like this:

```
Container c = jframe.getContentPane();
c.setLayout( new BoxLayout(c, BoxLayout.Y_AXIS));
```

Note that, unlike the other layout managers, this one takes the content pane as an argument, as well as being invoked on the content pane. The second argument says whether to stack vertically (as here) or horizontally, BoxLayout.X_AXIS.

You add components exactly the same way as in the previous layout managers:

```
JButton jb1 = new JButton("place order");
p.add( jb1 );
```

Box layout gives us the ability to, say, stack all the radio buttons on one panel, the Jbuttons on another panel, and add them to a Frame in three columns with grid layout or border layout. Let's try that.

Combining Layouts

The screen capture in Figure 19-10 below shows the results of putting the three radio buttons on their own panel, putting the two buttons on their own panel, then adding the two panels and the Jlabel to the Frame with a border layout. Already this is starting to look more normal. The size, shape, and positioning of the components won't fly all over the place when you resize the frame.

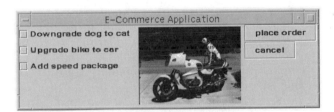

Figure 19-10: A screen capture using several layouts.

Here's the important part of the code to produce the above results.

```
JPanel p1 = new JPanel();
p1.setLayout( new BoxLayout(p1, BoxLayout.Y_AXIS));
JCheckBox jck1 = new JCheckBox("Downgrade dog to cat");
JCheckBox jck2 = new JCheckBox("Upgrade bike to car");
JCheckBox jck3 = new JCheckBox("Add speed package");
p1.add( jck1 );
p1.add( jck2 );
p1.add( jck3 );

JPanel p2 = new JPanel();
p2.setLayout( new BoxLayout(p2, BoxLayout.Y_AXIS));
JButton jb1 = new JButton("place order");    p2.add( jb1 );
JButton jb2 = new JButton("cancel");      p2.add( jb2 );

JLabel j1 = new JLabel(new ImageIcon( "bmw.jpg"));

Container c2 = jframe.getContentPane();
c2.add(j1, "Center");
c2.add(p1, "West");
c2.add(p2, "East");
jframe.pack();
```

That layout can still be improved in a couple of ways. You can:

- Move the radio buttons in from the edge of the panel. This can be done by adding a *border* to the panel. The following code adds a ten-pixel border all around the component:

```
JPanel p1 = new JPanel();
p1.setBorder(BorderFactory.createEmptyBorder(10, 10, 10, 10));
```

- Make the two buttons the same length by setting the maximum size of the shorter button to the preferred (or regular) size of the longer button, like this:

```
JButton jb2 = new JButton("cancel");
jb2.setMaximumSize( jb1.getPreferredSize() µ);
```

- Add a bit of spacing between the buttons, by adding a blank area, as follows:

```
p2.add(Box.createRigidArea(new Dimension(0, 15)));
```

Box is a helper class for BoxLayout.

- Finally, we can add a border around the panel on which the buttons are located, as follows:

```
JPanel p2 = new JPanel();
p2.setBorder(BorderFactory.createEmptyBorder(14, 14, 14, 14));
```

Putting it all together, and you have quite a pleasing and professional looking GUI, as shown in Figure 19-11.

Figure 19-11:   Adding multiple elements to a layout.

The only thing that is at all new is the `BorderFactory.createEmptyBorder(14, 14, 14, 14)` call. A *factory* is a class that can create other classes and return them to you. Here, it will send you some instance of a border class, possibly shared if you're using the same kind of border in two places. I've only scratched the surface of the many ways you can improve alignment and appearance in Swing. Although there are many more features available to the expert, the features we have reviewed will serve your basic needs.

Other Layout Managers

AWT has a CardLayout manager. It does exactly the same thing as a tabbed pane, but without the finesse. There's no reason to use CardLayout now that we have tabbed panes.

The final kind of AWT layout manager is GridBagLayout, which is a variation of GridLayout. Rather than force you to fit components one per grid position, it allows you to let a component take up the space of several adjacent grid positions. It uses a series of constraints and weights to work out what goes where.

GridBagLayout is excessively complicated for what it does, and I recommend helping it fall into disuse by not bothering with it. If you really want to spend time on GridBagLayout, there is a tutorial about it online at http://www.java soft.com/nav/read/Tutorial/ui/layout/gridbag.html

Most of the use of GridBagLayout comes from programmers who use IDEs like Visual Cafe or SuperCede. The GBL monster is generated automatically, and the coders don't have to wrangle it by hand (unless they later try to fix it up without the visual tool). It's just drag-and-drop-and-hope.

Layouts are funky. You probably won't find any one layout that does exactly what you want. The solution is to divide your Panels and Frames into subpanels, use an appropriate layout manager for each panel, and then display the different panels together in a single frame. You may then use borders and boxes to hone the results. Skilled programmers can write their own layout managers. AWT contains enough power for you to do that. You might consider it if you're trying to match the look and feel of some existing custom application. In Java, you can write your own look and feel, not just layout, if you care to go down that path.

Finally, you always have the option of setting a null layout manager and positioning controls at absolute coordinates, using `public void setLocation(int x, int y)`. It is almost always better to use a layout manager than to use absolute positions. It's less work for you, and the GUI will look better when run on different platforms. An absolute layout that looks good on one platform frequently looks terrible on another platform.

Tying up the Loose Ends

At this point, we have dealt with events, components, and containers both in summary and in depth. There are just four minor topics to cover to conclude the chapter. The topics are applet and application differences, the toolkit, cursors, and multibutton mice.

Differences Between Applets and Applications and How to Convert Between Them

Many programmers are unduly worried about the differences between applets and applications. People often post questions on the Java newsgroups complaining that the book they are reading focuses on one of these when they are interested in the other. The truth is that 95% of the information carries over between applets and applications. All the GUI information is common.

In fact, apart from the security restrictions on applets, each kind of execution framework can be transformed easily into the other. All the examples here can be rewritten as an applet or an application.

To Turn an Applet into an Application

This is the simpler rewrite because the security restrictions are relaxed. The basic process is to provide the same kind of execution context that an applet provides. Then, call explicitly the methods that are called automatically in an applet. Follow these steps.

1. Make your top-level class extend JFrame, not JApplet. Since the default layout in a Panel (and hence its subclasses, like Applet) is FlowLayout, explicitly set that layout manager on the JFrame.

2. Add a main routine in the class.

3. The main routine should read its arguments, and you should arrange to pass it the same arguments that were passed to the applet as params in HTML.

4. The main routine should instantiate an object of the class. The constructor should call start() and then init().

5. Add a menu with an Exit item or an exit button; otherwise, there may be no internal way to exit.

The JDK demo directory has a class in file $JAVAHOME/demo/applets/ GraphicsTest /AppletFrame.java that provides the surrounding framework to run an applet as an application. `AppletFrame` actually lets your program run as either an applet or an application. In application mode, it creates a frame and puts the applet inside. You could use this class as the basis for your code. This doesn't quite take you all the way, as you still need to take care of applications that need applet services like `appletContext()`, but it does 99% of what you need.

To Turn an Application into an Applet

It's more common to want to turn an application into an applet because this allows you to invoke the program just by browsing the web page that contains it. This direction is a little tougher because of the security restrictions on applets. You need to remove file and network I/O except that permitted by the applet framework. The simplest approach is to sign your applet to make it trusted. Then, follow these steps:

1. Create the HTML that will invoke the applet. To be quick and dirty, we put it in the source file. That's not the right place for it in a production program.

2. The top-level class should extend `JApplet`, rather than `JFrame`, which is the starting point for most application GUIs. Give the `JApplet` the `BorderLayout` that the `JFrame` has by default.

3. Replace the class constructor with a method called `init()` to do the one time setup.

4. Move any initialization statements from `main()` into `init()`. Other statements that do "revisit page" setup must be placed in a method called `start()`.

5. Fix any code that may not be used in an `Applet`, such as setting the title bar, adding menus to the Frame bar, calling native routines, I/O, or operating system commands.

6. Don't forget to put the "leaving a page" cleanup in `stop()`.

It is also possible to have a program containing all the elements of both an application and an applet that can be run as either, according to convenience.

The Toolkit

A Component method called get Toolkit() returns a reference to the toolkit. The name *toolkit* just means "a bunch of generally useful window-related things" and is the "T" in AWT. Once you have a Toolkit, you can call any of its methods, which can do things like:

- Set things up for printing the screen.

- Get information about the screen size and resolution.

- Beep the keyboard.

- Get information about the color model in use.

- Get information about font size.

- Transfer data to and from the system clipboard.

- Set the icon image of the Frame.

For example, java.awt.Toolkit.getDefaultToolkit().getScreenSize() returns a java.awt.Dimension object, which has ints representing height and width. As usual, you can view all the methods by typing javap java.awt.Toolkit.

JFC introduced the ability to transfer data to and from the system clipboard and to drag-and-drop components. The topics are a bit outside the scope of this book, but you can find the source files in $JAVAHOME/src/java/awt/datatransfer and dnd, respectively.

Printing the Screen

Printing is one of the services provided by the window toolkit. JDK 1.1 introduced the ability to directly print the screen from an applet. JDK 1.1.1 took it away again, at least for untrusted applets. To prevent a rogue applet from spawning large or offensive print jobs behind your back, an untrusted applet cannot directly start a print job. The printing support just pops up the native "print this" dialog box, allowing the user to review the job and initiate it.

Setting up a print job is a little elaborate. This is how it is done:

- First, you get the Toolkit.

- From the Toolkit, you get a PrintJob.

- From the `PrintJob`, you get a `Graphics` object, called, say, go. Since this a regular graphics object, you can do all the things with it that you can do with any graphics object, including drawing in it directly with the kinds of statements that you typically use inside `paint()`, like `draw-String()`.

- Then, you call `printAll(go)`. This method will pop up the native printing dialog. Every component has a `print()` method that just calls its `paint()` routine by default. You can override these as needed for special effects.

- Finally, invoke dispose on the go, and invoke `end()` on the PrintJob.

Yes, I know. This all seems to have been designed with the "principle of most astonishment" in mind. Worse, printing seems to have more than its share of bugs in it (but that could improve with the next maintenance release). The code looks like this:

```java
import java.awt.*;
import java.awt.event.*;
import javax.swing.*;

public class exprint extends JFrame {

    Image si;
    public exprint(Image i) { this.setSize(200,200), si=i;}
    public void paint(Graphics g) { g.drawImage(si,0,0,this);}

    public static void main(String args[]) {

        Image i =Toolkit.getDefaultToolkit().getImage("RSM.jpg");
        exprint f = new exprint(i);
        f.show();
        f.printMe();
    }

    public void printMe() {
        Toolkit t = getToolkit();
        PrintJob pj = t.getPrintJob(this, "my printing", null);
        Graphics pg = pj.getGraphics();
        printAll(pg);
        pg.dispose();
        pj.end();
    }
}
```

The third argument to `getPrintJob` is a property table you supply that can be used for such things as specifying the printer to use. A null reference works here.

This kind of printing allows you to put anything that you can see on your screen onto your printer. If all you want to do is print text, you don't need to get so elaborate. Just write it to a file, and print the file.

The standard print properties are shown in Table 19-1.

Table 19-1: Print Properties

Print Property	Description or Effect
awt.print.destination	Can be "printer" or "file"
awt.print.printer	Name of printer to use
awt.print.fileName	Name of the file to print
awt.print.numCopies	Number of copies to print
awt.print.options	Options to pass to the print command
awt.print.orientation	Can be "portrait" or "landscape"
awt.print.paperSize	Can be "letter," "legal," "executive," or "a4"

The defaults are destination=printer, orientation=portrait, paperSize=letter, and numCopies=1.

Running the code will pop up a print dialog box like this:

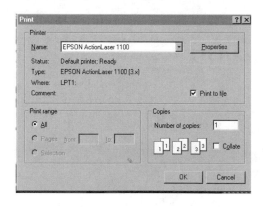

541

Changing Cursor Appearance

In JDK 1.0.2, the cursor could be set only for a `Frame`. In JDK 1.1, this restriction was lifted, and the cursor can now be set for each individual `Component`. The cursor is the little icon that moves about the screen tracking the mouse movements. There are fourteen different cursor icons shown in Table 19-2.

Table 19-2: Fourteen Cursor Icons

Appearance	Name
Eight different directions for resizing	Cursor.SW_RESIZE_CURSOR, etc.
One default cursor	Cursor.DEFAULT_CURSOR
One crosshair cursor	Cursor.CROSSHAIR_CURSOR
One text cursor	Cursor.TEXT_CURSOR
One busy waiting cursor	Cursor.WAIT_CURSOR
One hand cursor	Cursor.HAND_CURSOR
One move cursor	Cursor.MOVE_CURSOR

Some of these icons are shown in the Figure 19-12 below.

Arrow	Busy	Resize	SizeEast	Text	CrossHair
⇖	⌛	✛	↔	I	+

Figure 19-12: Some of the many cursor icons.

The cursor appearance can be set for any component with the following method:

```
public synchronized void setCursor(Cursor cursor)
```

For example, to set the hand cursor, use the following:

```
this.setCursor(new Cursor(Cursor.HAND_CURSOR) );
```

There is a `getCursor()` method, too. There is no way in JDK 1.1 to supply your own bitmap for a custom cursor, though obviously this is a reasonable thing to want to do. Custom cursors arrived in JDK 1.2 with the following toolkit method:

```
Cursor createCustomCursor(Image cursor, Point hotSpot, String id)
        throws IndexOutOfBoundsException
```

You must override that method, and then call `setCursor()`.

How to Simulate Multibutton Mice

Here, as a further example, is the code to show which mouse button has been pressed. This applet will run on Macintoshes, MS Windows, and Unix (one-,two-, and three-button mice systems, respectively). It will allow you to generate events from button two and button three, even on single-button mice.

How the AWT Smooths over Hardware Differences

Where there are big differences in window toolkits, Java adopts conventions to smooth over those differences. For example:

- Macs have one button on the mouse.
- PCs have two buttons on the mouse.
- Unix systems have three buttons on the mouse (left, right, and center).

Java deals with this hardware difference by adopting the convention that mice have three buttons. If the GUI invites a user to "click on the right button," a one-button mouse user can simulate it by holding down the META key while clicking. The following code is an example.

```
//<applet code=exmouse.class height=100 width=200> </applet> import
java.applet.*;
import java.awt.*;
import java.awt.event.*;

public class exmouse extends Applet {

    public void init() {
        addMouseListener( new MouseAdapter() {
        public void mouseClicked(MouseEvent e) {
            if ((e.getModifiers() & InputEvent.BUTTON1_MASK) != 0)
                System.out.println( "button1 pressed" );
            if ((e.getModifiers() & InputEvent.BUTTON2_MASK) != 0)
                System.out.println( "button2 pressed" );
            if ((e.getModifiers() & InputEvent.BUTTON3_MASK) != 0)
                System.out.println( "button3 pressed" );

            if ((e.getModifiers() & InputEvent.ALT_MASK) != 0)
                System.out.println( "alt held down" );
            if ((e.getModifiers() & InputEvent.META_MASK) != 0)
                System.out.println( "meta held down" );
            }
        } // end anon class
        ); // end method call
    }
}
```

Under JDK 1.1.1, if you hold down the ALT key while you click button one, you will get a mouse button two event. If you hold down the META key while you click button one, you will get a mouse button three event.

On a two-button mouse system, clicking the left button will result in the following output:

```
button1 pressed
```

Holding down the ALT key while clicking the same left mouse button will result in this output:

```
button2 pressed
alt held down
```

How do you know which is the ALT key and which is the META key? Often one or both of these is marked on the keyboard. The META key is just as often not marked or is marked as something else. Use a bit of experimentation.

Some Light Relief

The Chang Modification: A Design Breakthrough?

Once every five or ten years someone in the computer industry comes out with a new development that has a dramatic impact on performance and is eventually adopted by everybody. In the past we've seen large scale integration circuits, many-layer printed circuit boards, CPU modules, multilevel (cache) memory, and high-performance special-purpose interconnects between CPU and memory, to name a few. There are a lot of evolutionary performance improvements, too. Every year processors get faster, disks get bigger, and memory gets cheaper. There's a guy in my office who buys a new PC every two years. He always spends about the same amount of money, around $2K, but he gets more for his money every time.

There is pressure in the computer industry to be the fastest at something, and huge sums are therefore spent to improve hardware and software designs. Every now and again, either by accident or by design, someone comes up with something that doesn't quite deliver, but the trade press runs with the idea anyway.

Cast your mind all the way back to September 1988. What were you doing then? Perhaps you were still in school? Or maybe you were putting the finishing touches to the port of a mainframe system to the very latest, state of the art, 12MHz IBM 286PC? In September 1988, *PC Magazine* columnist John C. Dvorak was writing these fateful words about the latest performance bombshell: "It's the fastest board I've ever seen, and nobody knows (yet!) how it works... it uses the Chang modified 286 circuit." The Chang modification surfaced in late summer 1988 at a Taiwan computer show. Tucked away in a corner was a booth offering $500 to anyone who had a PC that could outperform Taiwanese engineer Mei-Chung Chang's modified 286 system. Now even back in 1988, PCs were commodity items. Everyone had access to the same CPU, the same memory, the same disks, the same ASICs, and the same system bus. If everyone is buying the same speed parts, everyone ends up with a system that performs the same, within 1%. Yet here was Chang with his challenge. People were taking him up on it, and his hardware was reporting faster results than their hardware. Here's the thing that really got people's attention: They could bring along their own benchmark program, run it on a system with the Chang modification, and it would get better results than when they ran the same program on their hardware. Dvorak himself (no relation to the keyboard, by the way) commented, "I ran one benchmark test after another on this and it outperformed anything I've ever seen."

There was an explanation of how the Chang Modification worked: it was said to be a chip level modification that force-fed more instructions into the chip than it could immediately execute. When the chip had spare cycles, it didn't have to go to (slow) memory for more instructions—they were already on chip. That's a garbled version of how processor pipelines work in RISC architectures, so it's not completely off the wall.

Still, you have to remember that the computer industry contains a lot of ingenious minds, who can invent explanations for anything, including things that are completely false. I do it myself when we're working on something secret that has a long lead-time to market. First, you provide a bit of harmless misdirection. In Chang's case he glued a heat sink on top of the CPU and told everyone that the supercharged instruction stream made it necessary. Next, you re-use a code name from a project that's been cancelled. If anyone hears it, they'll associate it with something else. Finally, you concoct a cover story that isn't completely impossible and also isn't completely unlike what you're doing. If anyone asks what you are doing, let them have the cover story.

For the Chang Modification, virtually every computer journalist with an expense account got on the next plane to Taiwan and interviewed Chang. It didn't do them much good, because he didn't speak much English. In any case, the only thing they could get out of him was that the modification was cheap, very secret, and would affect all future chip designs. The people in the best position to know, Intel, pooh-poohed the story even as they were trying to get a board to test.

The cheap and very secret modification came apart almost as quickly as the story came together. In fairness, John Dvorak was the first to break this news, too. Mei-Chung was simply slowing down the chip that kept the real-time clock on the motherboard. It was supposed to interrupt, say, every millisecond, and the operating system would count a thousand such interrupts as the passage of a second. If you actually made it interrupt every two milliseconds, then the CPU would be working for two seconds but the operating system would report that only one second had passed! Benchmarks are "twice as fast" when timed by a clock that runs slow. Anyone looking at the second hand on their watch or trying a side-by-side comparison wouldn't be fooled.

The best light to cast on the whole thing is that perhaps Chang himself didn't really understand how his modification worked, and then got caught up in a whirlwind of media attention. *PC Magazine's* retrospective on the affair also included a shame-faced announcement of certain changes to their benchmarking policy. The highly-rated modification captured the attention of the entire computer industry for six or eight weeks. In the end though, it was not a design breakthrough, but a broken design.

CHAPTER
20

Graphics Programming

"A disciple of the temple once asked a Zen master "What is Risk?" The master patiently explained, "It is that which has caused men to venture everything in its pursuit. It is associated with intense speed, and it is prominent in the overlapping flow of events. It embraces the simplest and most consistent of designs in life."

"I see," said the disciple, "so that is peril, hazard, chance, or risk." "Risk?" said the master, "I thought you said RISC."

-Anonymous

his chapter covers the more advanced features of window programming, namely those associated with graphics rather than window widgets. In this chapter we will cover color, fonts, and how to draw shapes on a Canvas or Panel. We will then look at Images and some Image Processing. We'll finish up with an explanation and some sample programs showing Java's support for audio output. Table 20-1 lists the methods that cause the screen to be displayed.

Table 20-1: Common Graphics Methods

Method	Description
void repaint()	You may call this to request that the window be refreshed. Typically, you would call it if you have changed the appearance of something, and you want to see it on the screen. It calls update()
void update(Graphics g)	This routine exists to let you participate in painting the window. It defaults to clearing the area then painting it, but you can conceivably override it to do something additional. Most of your programs, however, will not override this, and will not call this.
void paint(Graphics g)	Will be called by the window system when the component needs to be redisplayed. You will not call this. You will override this if you dynamically change the appearance of the screen, and want to see it appear.

Colors

Naturally, Java allows you to put colors on the screen and there is a class called Color in the java.awt package. The basic color model used by Java is a common one in the computer industry. Colors are made up of a red, a green, and a blue component, each of which is described by a byte value saying how vivid that color is, ranging from 0 (darkest shade) to 255 (lightest shade). This is known as the RGB model. The actual color used in rendering will be the best match in the color space available for a given output device. Images (like JPEG files) also have an "alpha" component that describes how transparent a pixel[1] is.

Again this is stored in a byte, so it takes 32 bits just to store a single pixel on the screen. This is why some graphics programs can swamp your system. For large images, megabytes of data need to be moved around. The "alpha" comes in later with images, it isn't part of the Color class.

You need to experiment with this a little to get a feel for it. Figure 20-1 shows an applet that allows you to set the R, G, and B values and see the resulting color mix.

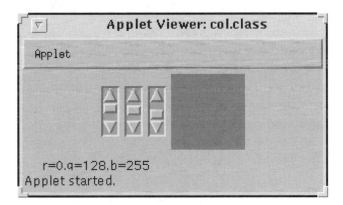

Figure 20-1:   The RGB can be set like this.

To get these results, type in the following 30-line program (or copy it off the CD).

---

1.   A Pixel is a "Picture Element." It is a dot on a computer screen. When people say screens are 1024 by 768 (or whatever) they are referring to the number of pixels it can display. A pixel is like a grain of sand. By itself it is almost unnoticeable, nothing happens until you have thousands of them.

```
// <applet code=col.class    height=100 width=300>  </applet>
//
//   An applet to show how colors are made up of three values,
//   0-255 representing each of red, green, and blue.
//   Uses the JDK 1.1 event model

import java.awt.*;
import java.awt.event.*;
import java.applet.*;
public class col extends Applet {

    Scrollbar s1 = new Scrollbar(Scrollbar.VERTICAL,0,50,0,255);
    Scrollbar s2 = new Scrollbar(Scrollbar.VERTICAL,0,50,0,255);
    Scrollbar s3 = new Scrollbar(Scrollbar.VERTICAL,0,50,0,255);
    Canvas c = new Canvas();

    int r,g,b;
    public void init () {
        s1.setUnitIncrement(10); s1.setBlockIncrement(25);
        s2.setUnitIncrement(10); s2.setBlockIncrement(25);
        s3.setUnitIncrement(10); s3.setBlockIncrement(25);
        add(s1); add(s2); add(s3); add(c);
        ScrAdj sa = new ScrAdj();
        s1.addAdjustmentListener(sa);
        s2.addAdjustmentListener(sa);
        s3.addAdjustmentListener(sa);
        c.setSize(75,75);
    }

    public void paint(Graphics gr) {
        c.setBackground(new Color(r,g,b) );
        gr.drawString("r="+r+ ",g="+g+ ",b="+b, 20,100);
    }


    class ScrAdj implements AdjustmentListener {
      public void adjustmentValueChanged(AdjustmentEvent ae) {
        System.out.println("ae="+ae);
        Scrollbar s = (Scrollbar) ae.getAdjustable();
             if (s==s1) r=ae.getValue();
        else if (s==s2) g=ae.getValue();
        else            b=ae.getValue();
        repaint();
      }
    }

}
```

We've already seen how you can use a Color object to set the color of a component. Here's an example of how that might be done in practice.

```
Frame f = new Frame("my frame");
f.setForeground( Color.white );

f.setBackground( new Color(255,175,175) ); //pink
```

The class Color has the following methods and constants, among others:

```
public final class Color {

    public final static Color white = new Color(255, 255, 255);
    public final static Color gray = new Color(128, 128, 128);
    public final static Color black = new Color(0, 0, 0);
    public final static Color red = new Color(255, 0, 0);
    public final static Color pink = new Color(255, 175, 175);
    public final static Color orange = new Color(255, 200, 0);
    public final static Color yellow = new Color(255, 255, 0);
    public final static Color green = new Color(0, 255, 0);
    public final static Color magenta= new Color(255, 0, 255);
    public final static Color cyan = new Color(0, 255, 255);
    public final static Color blue = new Color(0, 0, 255);

    public Color(int r, int g, int b);
    public Color(int rgb);
    public Color(float r, float g, float b);

    public int getRed();
    public int getGreen();
    public int getBlue();
    public int getRGB();

    public Color brighter();
    public Color darker();

    public static int HSBtoRGB(float hue, float saturation, float
brightness);
    public static float[] RGBtoHSB(int r, int g, int b, float[]
hsbvals);
    public static Color getHSBColor(float h, float s, float b);
}
```

There's an alternative color model, known as HSB, meaning *Hue Saturation and Brightness*. Java doesn't use this, but it allows easy translations using the methods just described.

So When Will I Use the `paint()`, `repaint()`, or `update()` Methods?

If you just use the static display typical of a GUI, you might never need to override any of the three above methods. You can often just hide() and show() Components as needed. Let's explain when you use paint().

Normally the window system keeps track of what you have put on the screen. If you obscure it with other windows and then bring it to the front, the window system is responsible for restoring the state.

If, however, you wish to *change* what you have put on the screen (say you have displayed a GIF that you now want to replace with something else), this would be accomplished by overriding paint(). Code in init() can get something on the screen to begin with. Code in paint() can change the screen and get something different up there. You call repaint() to signal to the window system that it needs to update the screen. The window system will then call your paint() method to put the new image on the screen. It's done this way because paint takes an argument (a Graphics context) that you don't normally have (or need to have) access to. Repaint() doesn't need any arguments.

Repaint() calls update() which calls clear() and then paint(). You might override update() if you are doing some advanced graphics work, and you know that you only need a small portion of the screen to be changed (e.g., in an animation). Update gives you the opportunity to achieve this, by providing a point where you can insert your own code between repaint() and paint(). In addition, the following will repaint just the stated size rectangle at the given coordinates:

```
repaint(x,y,w,h);
```

Paint may be called by the runtime independent of update.

In summary, you never call paint() yourself. You may override it, but the understanding is always that it will be called for you at the times the window system thinks it needs to update the screen. If you want to force the window system to think that, then call "repaint()."

Repaint() simply lodges a request to update the screen, and returns immediately. Its effect is asynchronous, and if there are several paint requests outstanding it is possible that only the last `paint()` will be done.

Fonts and Font Metrics

Fonts and information about font size are encapsulated into two classes: Font and FontMetrics. Just as with Colors, whatever font is current will be used in all text drawing operations in the AWT. However, it will not be used in operations like System.out.println. Think about it: those are Stream operations that merely push data in and out of files, and not to the screen. Only the window system cares about the physical appearance of that data.

Notice in the following example that the "foo" text will appear in the current font.

```
paint(Graphics g) {
  g.drawString("foo",10,10);
}
```

You're given a default font to start you off, then you can change any of the characteristics, or construct a new font and set it as the font to use.

> Try modifying the "mobile button" program q.java, so that the button has a background color of red, a foreground color of white, and is labeled in italic courier size 18 point. The source is on the CD. Setting colors on buttons was buggy in JDK 1.0.2.

You can construct a new font with this:

```
Font loud – new Font  ("TimesRoman", Font.BOLD, 18);
```

You can make that the current font for any Component (any Button, Label, Menu-Item, Canvas) or Graphics object, with this:

```
this.setFont(loud);
```

The constructor for a Font is simply this:

```
public Font( String name, int style, int size);
```

You can set the font (Courier, Helvetica, etc.), the style (plain, bold, italic, or combinations of the three), and the size (8 point, 10 point, 12 point, etc.) any way you like.

Different computer systems will have fonts that are similar but have different names. The reason font names vary is that owners of the font can charge for using its name. For example, the closest thing available to the Windows Windings font on Unix is called Zapf Dingbats (really). It's a screwy font, so everyone gives it a screwy name. Java copes with this by mapping your font request to the closest font, size and style that is on the underlying system. These five font names can be taken for granted:

- TimesRoman
- Courier
- Helvetica
- Symbol (The font will be different on different systems.)
- Dialog

Fonts are very straightforward. The FontMetric class allows you to compute the exact position of Strings, namely how wide and high they are in terms of pixels. This will allow you to lay out strings exactly centered or to mix Strings of different styles and get the spacing right. You might do this if you were writing a word processor in Java, but it's a bit fussy for everyday use. Figure 20-2 shows how the terms relate to typeface measurements.

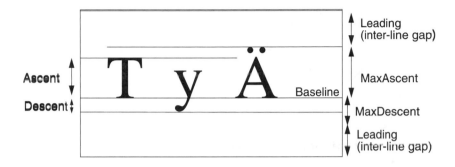

FontMetrics

getLeading()   is the standard line spacing for the font. This is the
amount of space between the max descent of one line
and the maximum ascent of the next line.

getAscent()   is the distance from the baseline to the top of most
characters in the font.

getMaxAscent() is the distance from the baseline to the highest
pixel painted of any character in the font. This may be
the same as the ascent.

Figure 20-2:   FontMetrics terms as they relate to typeface measurements.

FontMetrics has these methods, which return values in units of a pixel (a dot on
the screen).

```
public abstract class FontMetrics {
    public Font getFont() {

    public int getLeading();  // print term for line spacing
    public int getAscent();
    public int getDescent();
    public int getHeight()    // leading + ascent + descent

    public int getMaxAscent() {
    public int getMaxDescent() {

    // For backward compatibility only.
    public int getMaxDecent()  // some programmers can't spell...

    public int charWidth(char ch);
    public int stringWidth(String str);
}
```

The font metrics give you the real measurements of the font that is actually in use on your system, not the theoretical measurements of the font you asked for. The two may well be different.

The Graphics Context

A Graphics object is what you ultimately draw lines, shapes, and text on. It is also called a "graphics context" in some window systems because it bundles together information about a drawable area, plus font, color, clipping region, and other situational factors. If you look at the code in $JAVAHOME/src/java/awt/ Graphics.java, you will see that it is an abstract class:

```
public abstract class Graphics { ...
```

It cannot therefore be instantiated directly, and you will never see code like the following:

```
Graphics gr = new Graphics(); // NO!
```

The most common way to obtain a Graphics object is as the argument to a paint() routine in a Canvas or Panel. (You'll actually get some concrete subclass of graphics, the details of which you never need worry about). Less commonly, you can explicitly ask for the Graphics object belonging to any Component or any Image with the call:

```
myComponent mc ...

Graphics mg = mc.getGraphics();
```

When you call getGraphics() it is usually for an Image, Panel or Canvas. It's unlikely you'll want to get the Graphics object for anything else, such as a button. There is too much peer behavior associated with it for you to be able to add to it sensibly. When you have a Graphics object, you can draw on it, and later paint it to the screen. You can clip it (shrink the drawing area). You can modify the colors and fonts. A common reason for explicitly getting the Graphics context of an Image is to do double-buffering, or to draw over an Image you have read in. All these techniques are explained in this chapter. If you do explicitly call this:

```
Graphics g = myPanel.getGraphics();
```

Make sure you also call this when you are done with it:

```
g.dispose();
```

Graphics objects take up operating system resources (more than just memory), and a window system may have a limited number of them. When you clean them up explicitly without waiting for garbage collection to kick in, your system will usually tick along more smoothly.

Drawing Text, Lines, and Shapes

These are the methods of Graphics that draw text, lines, and shapes. Most of these come in two varieties: a drawXXX and a fillXXX. The first puts an empty outline on the screen, the second puts the outline and fills the interior with a solid color. In both cases the foreground color is used. A graphics object has the method `setColor(Color c)` to change the foreground color, but it doesn't have any direct way to change the background color. The underlying panel (or whatever) must do that, as shown in the following cases.

```
public void drawString(String str, int x, int y);
```

Here, the string is placed at location x,y on this component. For example:

```
public void paint(Graphics g) {
    g.drawString("The dentist whined incessantly", 10, 15);
}
```

A common pitfall with this method and the next two is drawing with y coordinate zero. That makes the characters disappear as they will be almost completely off the top of the canvas.

```
public void drawChars(char data[], int offset, int length, int x, int y)
public void drawBytes(byte data[], int offset, int length, int x, int y)
```

These two methods place characters or bytes from the array data[offset] to data[offset+length-1] on the component starting at location (x,y).

```
public void drawLine(int x1, int y1, int x2, int y2);
```

A line one pixel wide is drawn from (x1,y1) to (x2,y2). There is no support for drawing lines thicker than one pixel. The workaround is to use the fillPolygon described later. Like all of these methods, the rendering is done in whatever you have set the color to. The default foreground color is black.

```
public void drawRect(int x, int y, int width, int height);
public void fillRect(int x, int y, int width, int height);
```

A rectangle of the stated width and height is drawn with its top left corner at (x,y). There is also a `void clearRect(x,y,w,h)` that gets rid of a rectangle.

```
public void draw3DRect(int x, int y, int width, int height, boolean
raised);
public void fill3DRect(int x, int y, int width, int height, boolean
raised);
```

A rectangle of the stated width and height is drawn with its top left corner at (x,y). The rectangle is artfully shaded on two sides to make it appear to be standing out (raised=true) or to be impressed (raised=false). A raised rectangle is shaded with brighter color, and a non-raised one with a darker color. Figure 20-3 shows some 3D rectangles.

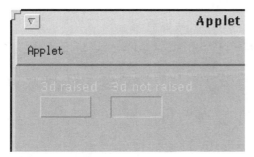

Figure 20-3: 3D raised and unraised.

Here is the code that generated the screen capture:

```
// <applet code=graf.class height=300 width=500> </applet>
import java.awt.*;
import java.applet.*;
public class graf  extends Applet {

    public void paint(Graphics g) {
        g.setColor(Color.cyan);
        g.drawString("3d raised", 25,25);
        g.draw3DRect(25,30,50,20,true);
        g.drawString("3d not raised", 95,25);
        g.draw3DRect(95,30,50,20,false);
    }
}
```

Here are two more ways to draw a rectangle

```
public void drawRoundRect(int x, int y, int width, int height, int
  arcWidth, int arcHeight);
public void fillRoundRect(int x, int y, int width, int height, int
  arcWidth, int arcHeight);
```

There are Like drawRect and fillRect, only these rectangles have rounded corners.

You control the diameter of the rounded corners by setting the width and height of the curved portion in pixels. If you use values that are comparable to the width and height of the rectangle, you end up with an oval not a rectangle, as shown in Figure 20-4. Rule of thumb: Use arc width and height that are 15-25% of the rectangle width and height.

Figure 20-4: A rounded rectangle.

Here is the code that generated the diagram:

```
// <applet code=graf.class   height=300 width=500> </applet>
import java.awt.*;
import java.applet.*;
public class graf  extends Applet {

    public void paint(Graphics g) {
        g.setColor(Color.cyan);
        g.drawString("round", 25,25);
        g.fillRoundRect(25,30, 50,100,15,25);
    }
}
```

```
public void drawOval(int x, int y, int width, int height);
public void fillOval(int x, int y, int width, int height);
```

These two methods draw ovals. The arguments are easy to understand if you compare the methods to drawRect(). The oval that is drawn is one that fits exactly in the rectangle of that width and height. The imaginary rectangle's top left corner is at the (x,y) location (see Figure 20-5).

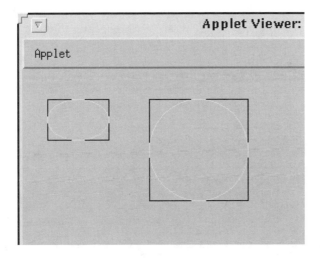

Figure 20-5:   Two ovals and their bounding rectangles.

Here is the code that generated the diagram:

```
// <applet code=graf.class height=300 width=500> </applet>
import java.awt.*;
import java.applet.*;
public class graf  extends Applet {

    public void paint(Graphics g) {
        g.drawRect(25,30,  60,40);
        g.drawRect(125,30,  100,100);

        g.setColor(Color.cyan);
        g.drawOval(25,30,  60,40);
        g.drawOval(125,30,  100,100);
    }
}
```

As can be seen, an oval with the width=height is a circle.

```
public void drawArc(int x, int y, int width, int height,
            int startAngle, int arcAngle);
public void fillArc(int x, int y, int width, int height,
            int startAngle, int arcAngle);
```

Again, the starting point for understanding these two methods is the rectangle located at (x,y). Then imagine dividing the rectangle into four quadrants. This x axis from the origin of the quadrants represents 0 degrees. The starting point for the arc is the offset from this line: 90 is straight up (along the y axis), 270 is straight down.

Finally, the arcAngle is how many degrees to sweep from that starting point. See Figure 20-6. Note that it is *not* the end angle as many people assume. A negative arcAngle sweeps clockwise, and a positive one counter clockwise. You never need use a negative angle because an arc sweeping 40 degrees forward from 90 degrees is the same as an arc sweeping 40 degrees back from 50 degrees.

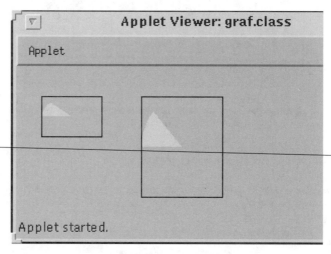

Figure 20-6:   An arc has the same concept of bounding box as an oval.

Here is the code that generated the diagram:

```
import java.awt.*;
import java.applet.*;
public class graf  extends Applet {

    public void paint(Graphics g) {
        g.drawRect(25,30,  60,40);
        g.drawRect(125,30,  80,100);
        g.setColor(Color.cyan);
        g.fillArc(25,30,  60,40,  135,45);
        g.fillArc(125,30,  80,100,  135,45);
    }
}
```

```
public void drawPolygon(int xPoints[], int yPoints[], int nPoints);
public void fillPolygon(int xPoints[], int yPoints[], int nPoints);
```

Polygons are shapes with an arbitrary number of straight sides. To draw or fill one using these methods, you provide an array of x coordinates, and an array of corresponding y coordinates, along with the total number of points.

If you want the polygon to be drawn closed you have to duplicate the starting point at the end of the arrays. Figure 20-7 is an example of polygons:

Figure 20-7: A filled polygon connects its end points automatically as it fills.

Here is the code that generated the diagram:

```
// <applet    code=graf.class height=300 width=500> </applet>
import java.awt.*;
import java.applet.*;
public class graf  extends Applet {

    public void paint(Graphics g) {
        g.setColor(Color.cyan);
        int x_vals[] = {75,45,15,45,45 };
        int y_vals[] = {40,70,40,10,40 };

        g.drawPolygon(x_vals, y_vals, x_vals.length);

        for (int i=0;i<5;i++) x_vals[i]+=80;
        g.fillPolygon(x_vals, y_vals, x_vals.length);
    }
}
```

```
public void drawPolygon(Polygon p);
public void fillPolygon(Polygon p);
```

These two overloaded methods draw or fill a Polygon object. A Polygon object is constructed from the same arrays of (x,y) pairs as used previously:

```
Polygon(int xPoints[], int yPoints[], int nPoints);
```

You pass in the number of points if you only want the first N elements of the array to form the polygon. However, you can also add new points to a polygon, simply by calling this method with an (x,y) pair:

```
pol.addPoint(10,20);
```

A Polygon also knows what its bounding box is.

That concludes most of the important routines for drawing text, lines and shapes. The next section covers the topic of loading images into memory and rendering (drawing) them onto a graphics context.

Loading and Drawing Images

An Image, as the name suggests holds a picture in memory. Originally, a picture will have been scanned in and stored in a file in GIF, JPEG, raster, PostScript, or other format. Java can currently only process the GIF and JPEG format.

Image File Formats

A GIF is a file format for storing pictures. GIF stands for Graphic Interchange Format and it was originally developed by CompuServe to be a system-independent way to store images. GIFs only store 8 bits of color information per pixel. Just adequate for run-of-the-mill PCs that only allow 256 different colors on screen at once, it is rapidly heading for technical obsolescence. Only use GIFs for cartoons and line drawings. GIF includes compression based on the Lempel-Ziv-Welch (LZW) algorithm, so the files are smaller than they would otherwise be. LZW compression is protected by a software patent filed by Unisys a few years ago. A copy of the public record for this patent is on the CD in book/ch1. If you've never seen a software patent before, take a look at this example, for some incredible claims about what has been "invented."

A JPEG is a newer and superior file format for compressing images. It's an acronym for Joint Photographic Experts Group (the committee that wrote the standard). An image in JPEG format can take much less storage space than the same picture in GIF format. However, the JPEG format also allows you to trade off image quality against storage needs—more requires more. When you save an image in JPEG format, you can specify a percentage for the image quality. JPEG stores full color information: 24 bits per pixel.

Before you can draw an Image onto a Graphics object, you must have an Image to draw. The most common way of getting one is to load it from a file. Another way of getting an Image is to call createImage() for a particular Component. We'll start by dealing with an image in GIF or JPEG format in a file. An image can be displayed in either an applet or an application. The two alternatives vary slightly.

Loading an Image File in an Application

Here is some code to display a file in an application. We create a Frame, read in the image file from our URL, instantiate a canvas, and off we go.

The only novelty about this is the way we get the image. We use the toolkit which is available in the AWT. It provides a getImage() method for applications. Note that you can get an Image from a URL (i.e. anywhere) as well as from a local file specified by a pathname as shown here.

```java
import java.awt.*;
import java.net.*;
public class display {

    static public void main(String a[]) {
        Image i = Toolkit.getDefaultToolkit().getImage("dickens.jpg");
        Frame f = new Frame("my frame");

        myCanvas mc = new myCanvas(i);
        f.resize(350,200);
        f.add(mc);
        f.show();
    }
}

class myCanvas extends Canvas {
    Image saved_i;
    public myCanvas(Image i) {
        this.resize(300,200);
        saved_i = i;
    }

    public void paint(Graphics g){
        g.drawImage(saved_i, 10, 10, this);
    }
}
```

There are plenty of pitfalls to avoid when you type in this code. If you get one of these wrong, your image will not appear and you will not get any kind of helpful error message either. Here are some potential problems:

- You must give the frame a size in order to see it!

- If you provide a file name which doesn't exist or can't be accessed, it will fail silently. The same if you use the URL alternative for getImage.

- If you don't give the canvas a size, it won't show up.

If you get all this correct, Figure 20-8 will appear.

Figure 20-8:   See Dickens lay down—on the Internet sometimes they *do* know
you're a dog.

Loading an Image File in an Applet

To load an image file in an Applet, we simply reference its URL. File access is usually restricted in an Applet, so there is no getImage that takes a pathname as an
argument. Recall, however, that a URL can point to a resource anywhere on the
Internet, so if the file is local to your system it can find it (if your security manager
allows your applet to read local files). The Applet method is:

```
public Image getImage(URL url);
```

It allows you to specify a complete absolute URL to the image file. Some examples
would be these:

```
URL u1 = new URL("http://sparcs/images/ball.jpg");    //remote
URL u2 = new URL("file:///home/linden/puppy.jpg"); // local
```

The other alternative lets you specify a URL and an image filename that is relative
to where the URL points.

```
public Image getImage(URL url, String name);
```

This is more common in an applet because the images files are usually stored in
the same directory as the HTML document or the class files. For these cases you
can use the following code.

```
getDocumentBase() // the URL of the document containing the applet
getCodeBase() // the URL of the applet class file
```

So an example would be this:

```
Image i;
    ...
i=getImage( getDocumentBase(), "puppy.jpg");
```

Note there is a pitfall here! A very common mistake is to try to call getImage() to initialize the image as you declare it, like this:

```
Image i1 = getImage(getDocumentBase(), "spot.jpg");
```

That compiles without a problem, but (if the Image is declared outside any method, as normal) it fails at runtime like this:

```
java.lang.NullPointerException
    at java.applet.Applet.getDocumentBase(Applet.java:59)
    at jpg.<init>(jpg.java:7)
    at sun.applet.AppletPanel.runLoader(AppletPanel.java:386)
```

The reason is that before the init() method of an Applet is called there isn't enough structure in place for calls to other methods of Applet to succeed. You can't do much with an Applet until its init() method has been called, which is the right place to put this getImage() call.

If you can't remember which methods belong to Applet, just use the following rule of thumb: In an applet don't call any methods to initialize data fields in their declaration. Instead declare them, then initialize them separately in the init() method.

A related pitfall concerns the createImage() method. Many people want to create an Image in the constructor of, for example, a Canvas.

```
public class MyCanvas extends Canvas{
    Image myImage;
    Graphics myGraphics;

    public MyCanvas(){
        myImage=this.createImage(100,50); //  this returns Null.
        myGraphics=myImage.getGraphics(); // so this throws NullPtrExcptn.
    }
```

The createImage() method does not work until *after* the Canvas has been added to a Container. So in general you can't create the Image in the constructor. One workaround is to also add the Canvas to its Container in the constructor. This is because a peer for the Canvas component must have been created before we can get its image. But we are still in the class constructor, so unless we force peer creation by doing an add(), createImage here will always fail and return a null pointer. These limitations are defects in the design of this Java library.

The code using getImage () brings the image into memory, and holds it in the Image object. The next step is to render it on the screen.

How Do You Get a Java Applet to Load an HTML Page Into the Browser?

The method `this.getAppletContext().showDocument(URL)` will make the browser load the page from the specified URL. There is also a version that takes a String argument:

```
public abstract void showDocument(URL url, String target)
```

The string says where to show it:

- `_self`   Bring the URL up in the current frame.
- `_parent`   Bring it up in the parent frame.
- `_top`   Show it in the top-most frame.
- `_blank`   Show it in a new unnamed frame.

Similarly, the following will put the message on the browser status line:

```
this.getAppletContext().showStatus("Get out in the fresh air more.");
```

Drawing an Image Onto a Graphics Object

The Graphics object has four variations of the drawImage() method:

- ```
  public boolean drawImage(Image img, int x, int y,
  ImageObserver observer);
  ```

  This draws the specified image at the specified coordinates (x, y). The image is cut off as necessary if it is larger than the area it is being drawn onto.
  ```

- ```
  public boolean drawImage(Image img, int x, int y,
  int width, int height,
  ImageObserver observer);
  ```

  This scales the image as needed to fit within the width and height specified as it draws it. Depending on the values you supply, that might change the proportions of the picture, stretching or shrinking it in one direction.

- ```
  public boolean drawImage(Image img, int x, int y,
  Color bgcolor,
  ImageObserver observer);
  ```

- ```
  public boolean drawImage(Image img, int x, int y,
  int width, int height,
  Color bgcolor,
  ImageObserver observer); .
  ```

These last two methods are just variations on the first, with the addition of providing a solid background color behind the image being drawn.

An Applet is an example of an ImageObserver, so wherever one is required, we can just provide the "this" of an Applet. The entire code to load and display a file in an Applet is thus just this:

```
// <applet code=jpg.class height=250  width=300> </applet>
import java.awt.*;
import java.applet.*;

public class jpg extends Applet {

    Image i;

    public void init() {
        i=getImage( getDocumentBase(), "puppy.jpg");
    }

    public void paint(Graphics g) {
        boolean b = g.drawImage(i,25,25, this);
    }
}
```

Running this code results in Figure 20-9 appearing on the screen.
```

Figure 20-9: See Young Dickens do the "Type-5 Keyboard Macarena."

The ImageObserver Argument

Let's get back to the ImageObserver argument used in drawImage. When you call getImage() to bring an image file into memory, the method returns at once, and in the background at some point a separate thread starts reading the file off disk somewhere on the Internet. That incoming image data is said to be an observable event. And you can specify who or what is going to observe it.

As a matter of fact, Component implements the ImageObserver interface. Every button, frame, canvas, panel, label, etc., is an ImageObserver and able to register its interest in observing incoming images. An applet being a subclass of Panel is also therefore an ImageObserver. We normally just put "this" down as the argument and the right thing happens by default. As the image comes in gradually, more and more of it is painted onto the screen.

Why have an ImageObserver? Why not just use Observer/Observable? Through an oversight or by design, Observable is a class, not an interface. Any class wishing to be observable must use up its one chance to inherit. In the case of Image it was felt better to provide the specialized interface ImageObserver.

Why bother with an Observer at all, though? The reason it's done this way, instead of the obvious implementation of making getImage() stall until the bytes are loaded, is twofold:

1.   The human factors of waiting for an image file to load are truly horrible. In other words, few things make users angrier than being forced to sit idle while some hideous GIF loads scanline by scanline.

2.   Everyone would end up writing every getImage() as a separate thread. This way, your applet is decoupled from the slow net for free.

Better yet, as pieces of the image are gradually loaded into memory, there will be a number of times when there is enough information to call ImageObserver.imageupdate(). It may be called when the image file header has been read, when we have decoded enough to know the height of the image, when we know the width, and when the entire transfer has been completed.

The Component class contains an imageUpdate() method. When it is called, it schedules a repaint, allowing a little more of the image to be drawn without interfering at all with your thread of control. There are a couple of properties shown in Table 20-2 that affect this.

Table 20-2: **System Properties**

Property	Effect
awt.image.incrementaldraw	True: (default) Draw parts of an image as it arrives. False: Don't draw until all the image is loaded.
awt.image.redrawrate	The default value is 100. It is the minimum period in milliseconds between calls to repaint for images. This property only applies if the first one is true.

JDK 1.0 doesn't support setting an individual property. You change a property by instantiating a new property table based on the system one, then appending your modifications.

The code below updates the entire system properties table. If you just want to add one or two properties, you can't do it directly, but you can do it indirectly. You create a new properties table, supplying the system properties table to the constructor. You add properties one by one to your new table. When you search, if a property isn't found in your new table, the program will proceed to look in the system properties table. Clumsy, but it works.

```
import java.io.*;
import java.util.*;

public class read {

  public static void main(String args[]) {
    try {

      // get the standard system properties into a property table
      Properties MyProps = new Properties(System.getProperties());

      // add my new properties to that table
      MyProps.put( "awt.image.incrementaldraw", "true" );
      MyProps.put( "awt.image.redrawrate", "50" );

      // set that table as the system property table.
      System.setProperties(MyProps);

      // list all properties
      System.getProperties().list(System.out);

    } catch (Exception e) {e.printStackTrace();}

  }
}
```

When you change a property, the change only lasts for as long as your program runs. If you want to permanently change a property you need to write the property file out to disk (with your change) and read it back in at the start of each program.

You can save a property table to a file with this:

```
// save a property table to a file
FileOutputStream fos = new FileOutputStream("banana.txt");
MyProps.save(fos, "my own properties");
fos.close();
```

You can read a property table back from a file with this:

```
// read in a property table from a file
FileInputStream fis = new FileInputStream("banana.txt");
MyProps.load(fis);
fis.close();
```

Image Update

If you want to retain really tight control over an incoming image you can overload imageUpdate() in your applet that will override the regular version in the Component parent class. Whenever there is more information available, your imageUpdate() will be called repeatedly until you return a value of false to indicate that you've got enough information. The following code example will clarify how this works:

```java
import java.applet.*;
import java.awt.*;

public class iu extends Applet {
    Image   i;
        int times=0, flags=0,x=0,y=0,w=0,h=0;

    public void init() {
        i = getImage(getDocumentBase(), "spots.jpeg" );
        w = i.getWidth(this);  System.err.println("INIT:w="+w);
        h = i.getHeight(this);  System.err.println("INIT:h="+h);
    }

    public boolean imageUpdate(Image i, int flags,
                        int x, int y, int w, int h) {
            if (times++<5)
                System.err.println("my IMAGEUPDATE: flags="
                                +flags+ " w="+w+ " h="+h);
            return true;
    }

    public void paint (Graphics g) {
        g.drawImage(i,50,50, this);

    }

}
```

This clearly shows how imageUpdate is a callback routine. Experiment with this example (invoke with the usual HTML file), including removing the limitation of five prints in the middle of imageUpdate (done so that the information doesn't scroll off the screen the first time you try it).

The Media Tracker

The ImageObserver interface is good for really low-level control of loading media files. But for some purposes it's a bit too low-level. If you just want to wait till a file is loaded completely, and you don't care to hear about the 57 intermediate stages of loading it, then the MediaTracker class is for you.

MediaTracker is actually built using ImageObserver, and it allows you to track the status of a number of media objects. Media objects could include audio clips, though currently only images are supported.

To use MediaTracker, simply create an instance and then call addImage() for each image to be tracked. Each image can be assigned a unique ID for indentification purposes. The IDs control the priority order in which the images are fetched as well as identifying unique subsets of the images that can be waited on independently. You then waitForID(n), which will suspend the thread until the image is completely loaded. The methods isErrorAny() and isErrorID(i) let you know if everything went OK for all the images or for a particular ID group.

Here is an example of the MediaTracker in use:

```
public void init() {
    MediaTracker t = new MediaTracker (this);
    Image i = getImage (getDocumentBase "spots.gif");
    t.addImage (i,1);
    try     {t.waitForID(1);}
    catch   (InterruptedException ie) {return;}
    //Image is now in memory, ready to draw
}
```

Image Processing

By putting together the basic classes that have already been described, and sprinkling a couple of new ones in, some pretty sophisticated image processing can be achieved. This section will describe the standard techniques for getting smoother animation by overriding update and double buffering. Start with this brief applet. The code and JPEG image files are on the CD in directory book/ch10.

```
//<applet  code=pin.class    width=600 height=350>  </applet>
import java.awt.*;
import java.awt.event.*;
import java.awt.image.*;

public class pin extends java.applet.Applet {
    Image spirit, rolls;
    int new_x=550;
    int new_y=100;

    public void init () {
        spirit = getImage(getDocumentBase(), "spirit.jpg");
        rolls = getImage(getDocumentBase(), "rolls.jpg");
        addMouseMotionListener( new MouseMotionListener () {
         public void mouseDragged(MouseEvent e){
            System.out.println("what a drag");
            new_x=e.getX();
            new_y=e.getY();
            repaint();
        }
        public void mouseMoved(MouseEvent e){}
    } );
    }


    public void paint (Graphics g) {
        g.setColor(Color.gray);
        g.fillRect(0,0,getSize().width, getSize().height );
        g.drawImage (rolls,5, 5, this);
        g.drawImage (spirit, new_x-25, new_y-25, this);
    }


}
```

The code implements a simple "pin-the-tail-on-the-donkey" game. In other
words, you can use the mouse to drag the image of the Spirit of Ecstasy over to its
place on the Rolls-Royce radiator. Incidentally, the Spirit of Ecstasy was modeled
on a real person: Eleanor Thornton. She was the paramour of early motoring pio-
neer, the second Lord Montagu. He artfully suggested to his pals on the Rolls-
Royce board in 1911 that their cars would be enhanced by a graceful radiator mas-
cot, and he "just happened to know a good one." Sadly, Eleanor Thornton per-

ished in a tragic torpedo mishap in 1915 (Lord Montagu on the same boat was wearing an inflatable cork waistcoat and he made it back to England in time to read his obituary in *The Times*). Thornton's spirit lives on, immortalized on the bonnet of every Rolls-Royce motor car for the last eighty-five years. But I digress. The applet screen looks like that in Figure 20-10.

Figure 20-10:   A moment of silence for Eleanor Thornton.

When you run the code you will notice that the applet flickers annoyingly as you drag the mouse. The flickering problem is a well known artifact of imaging programs in all languages. To fix this, there are some Java-specific things to try and some algorithmic things to try. The first and easiest improvement is to look at the default implementation of one of the utility routines, update().

As we drag the mouse, each event causes the new_x and new_y coordinates to be noted, then a request to repaint() is made. Repaint will call Component.update, which looks like the following code.

```
public void update(Graphics g) {
    g.setColor(getBackground());
    g.fillRect(0, 0, width, height);
    g.setColor(getForeground());
    paint(g);
}
```

It sets the color to the background color, then fills the whole Graphics context with it (in other words erases whatever image is currently there). It then sets the foreground color, and calls paint.

However, we are already painting the whole background in our paint routine. So, repaint calls update which paints the whole panel, then calls paint, which again paints the whole panel. Voila: a flicker or flash is seen as an unnecessary paint is done. We could remove the fillRect() in paint, for it was put there precisely to demonstrate this flicker as a teaching example (and it represents some more general background painting that you may do). A better solution is to override update(), and provide your own version that doesn't clear the applet panel.

```
public void update(Graphics g) {
    paint(g);
}
```

You can (and should) do this whenever your paint routine updates the entire component. If your paint didn't update the entire component, then you couldn't override update in this manner. You'd get pieces of the old image left in place as you dragged it to a new location. Overriding update with a more sensible version reduces flashing considerably, but doesn't eliminate it. For that we'll use a technique called double buffering or offscreen imaging (they mean the same thing).

Double Buffering

Double buffering, or *offscreen imaging* (a more accurate description), is the process of doing all your (slow) drawing to a graphics area in memory. When the entire image is complete, it zaps it up onto the screen in one (fast) operation. The overall time is slightly longer because of the overhead, but the overall effect is stunning because the new graphics context appears instantly.

The following code makes the image rendering double buffered.

```
//<applet  code=pin2.class   width=600 height=350>  </applet>
// same as pin, but uses double buffered output.
// PvdL.
import java.awt.*;
import java.awt.event.*;
import java.awt.image.*;

public class pin2 extends java.applet.Applet {
    Image spirit, rolls;
    Image myOffScreenImage;
    Graphics myOffScreenGraphics;
    int new_x=550;
    int new_y=100;

    public void init () {
        spirit = getImage(getDocumentBase(), "spirit.jpg");
        rolls = getImage(getDocumentBase(), "rolls.jpg");
        myOffScreenImage= createImage(
                    getSize().width, getSize().height );
        myOffScreenGraphics = myOffScreenImage.getGraphics();
        addMouseMotionListener( new MouseMotionListener () {
            public void mouseDragged(MouseEvent e){
                System.out.println("what a drag");
                new_x=e.getX();
                new_y=e.getY();
                repaint();
            }
            public void mouseMoved(MouseEvent e){}
        } );
    }

    public void paint (Graphics g) {
        g.setColor(Color.gray);
        g.fillRect(0,0,getSize().width, getSize().height );
        g.drawImage (rolls,5, 5, this);
        g.drawImage (spirit, new_x-25, new_y-25, this);
    }

    public void update(Graphics g) {
        paint(myOffScreenGraphics);    // draws on the db
        // draws the double buffer onto applet
        g.drawImage(myOffScreenImage,0,0, this);
    }

}
```

We don't change paint() at all. Paint will still do its rendering thing onto whatever Graphics context you give it. Here's where the magic comes in. We have added two off-screen objects:

```
Image myOffScreenImage;
Graphics myOffScreenGraphics;
```

In init() these two are initialized. We create an Image the same size of the applet. Then we get a graphics context for it. Now the clever part. We modify update so *first* it paints the offscreen image myOffScreenGraphics. It simply uses the regular call to paint, with myOffScreenGraphics as the argument. That painting won't appear on the screen, as it would if the AWT had called paint with the Graphics object for the applet. Instead it goes to myOffScreenGraphics object. (Sorry to belabor the point, but it is important to understand this thoroughly.)

Finally, instead of update() calling only paint() as it did in the previous version, we now do a very quick g.drawImage() to get the just-painted myOffScreenImage onto the Applet's graphics context! Drawing a single pre-constructed image onto the screen is a lot faster than building up a screenful of images one at a time. And that is double buffering.

Clipping Rectangles

The final possible optimization is to use a clipping rectangle to only draw where the image has changed. Clipping is a standard graphics technique to optimize the amount of (slow) drawing that takes place. When you clip, you are telling the paint routine "I know that the only changes in this image are inside this rectangle, so you need only paint inside the rectangle. Everything else remains unchanged."

The clipRect method of Graphics follows:

```
public void clipRect(int x, int y, int width, int height);
```

This cuts down the size of the area that is painted to just the *intersection* of what it was and the new rectangle specified by the arguments. This is an optimization used in animations and other graphics programming to speed up output and make it smoother. Many people have complained about the way the clipping rectangle can only be reduced in size. So JDK 1.1 added this method to set the current clip to the specified rectangle:

```
setClip(int x, int y, int width, int height)
```

Rendering doesn't take place outside this area.

Depending on how much can be clipped and how long it takes to calculate the overall image, clipping can save a lot of time and effort. Clipping works best on big images where only a little changes at a time. It's tailor-made for animations.

Taking Images Apart: java.awt.image

Java features some pretty substantial support for pulling Images apart to get at individual pixels. It also has a class that takes bytes from memory and assembles them into an Image. One problem with mastering this area of Java is that there is a lot of classes, generality, and infrastructure. As with the stream I/O classes, the profusion of abstractions creates a learning barrier for programmers.

We'll look at two concrete classes in java.awt.image that allow you to have absolute control over your screen images, namely:

- PixelGrabber: implements the abstract class ImageConsumer.

- MemoryImageSource: implements the abstract class ImageProducer.

As the names suggest, ImageConsumer takes an Image away from you (giving you something else you'd rather have, like an array of pixels), while ImageProducer takes something and gives you back the Image that it created from it.

Here's how PixelGrabber works:

1. You construct a new instance of the class supplying the image (or ImageProducer) and lots of sizes and an int array as arguments:

    ```
    PixelGrabber pg = new PixelGrabber ( .... );
    ```

2. You call grabPixels() which fills the int array with the pixels from the image:

    ```
    pg.grabPixels();
    ```

3. You check the status to see if all bits were grabbed without problems:

    ```
    if (pg.status() & ImageObserver.ALLBITS) != 0)
            // we grabbed all the bits OK
    ```

The two constructors of PixelGrabber are:

```
public PixelGrabber(Image img, int x, int y, int w, int h,  int[] pix,
int off, int scansize);

public PixelGrabber(ImageProducer ip, int x, int y, int w, int h, int[]
pix, int off, int scansize);
```

As you can see, the second constructor has an ImageProducer as its first parameter, but the other arguments (defined here) are the same.

- img is the image to retrieve pixels from

- x is the x coordinate of the upper-left corner of the rectangle of pixels to retrieve from the image, relative to the default (unscaled) size of the image

- y is the y coordinate of the upper-left corner of the rectangle of pixels to retrieve from the image

- w is the width of the rectangle of pixels to retrieve

- h is the height of the rectangle of pixels to retrieve

- pix is the array of integers which are to be used to hold the RGB pixels retrieved from the image

- off is the offset into the array of where to store the first pixel

- scansize is the distance from one row of pixels to the next in the array

Here's how MemoryImageSource works. It is essentially the complement of PixelGrabber. It reads an int array of pixels and gives you back the corresponding image. First, you construct a new instance of the class MemoryImageSource supplying arguments of the int array, and lots of sizes (height, width, scanline size, etc.). That will get you a MemoryImageSource object, which implements ImageProducer, and hence can be fed into the Component.createImage() method to obtain a real renderable Image.

There are six constructors for MemoryImageSource. The simplest one is:

```
public MemoryImageSource(int w, int h, int pix[],
                         int off, int scan)
```

This instantiates a w-by-h MemoryImageSource starting from the pix[off] element in the array of pixels, and with scan pixels in each line. The other five constructors allow various combinations of with and without HashTables and ColorModels.

Transparent Backgrounds

We are going to use these two classes on our image of the Spirit of Ecstasy. We are going to grab the pixels, and turn all the pink ones transparent, by setting the alpha byte to zero. If the alpha value of a pixel is 0 it is totally invisible. If the alpha value is 255, it is totally solid color. Values in between allow for varying degrees of translucence or opacity. Since the background is mostly pink, this will turn it transparent and allow Eleanor Thornton to be seamlessly reunited with her pedestal.

How Do I Turn the Background of My Image Transparent?

In general, there is no way to say, "Filter this image and give it a transparent background." You need a way to identify what is a background pixel and what is a foreground pixel. Here we are using color to identify the background. If the foreground is a regular shape you could use (x,y) position. For more on this, read on.

I touched up these images in Adobe Photoshop beforehand to give them a uniform pink background and sharper edges. If your company won't spring for Adobe Photoshop so you can play around with stuff like this, use the shareware "xv" software that can do many of the same things.

To minimize the learning curve here, let's highlight the new code by making this class extend the class pin2 above. Notice what we are doing here. We already have a class pin2 that does most of what we want. Instead of copying all that code into a new file, and starting hacking from scratch, we just create a new class that *extends* pin2. Then in our new class we place new versions of the methods that we want to replace in pin2. Our new methods will override the corresponding methods in pin2. We have reused pin2 by extending it and adding the changed functionality. The compiler has done most of the work for us. We only have to test the features that have changed. (Isn't Object-Oriented Programming wonderful?)

```
//<applet  code=transp.class   width=600 height=350>  </applet>
// double buffered
// transparent image
// Peter van der Linden, Sept 1996, Silicon Valley, Calif.
import java.awt.*;
import java.awt.image.*;

public class transp extends pin2 {

    public void init () {
        spirit = getImage(getDocumentBase(), "spirit.jpg");
        rolls = getImage(getDocumentBase(), "rolls.jpg");
        myOffScreenImage= createImage(size().width, size().height );
        myOffScreenGraphics = myOffScreenImage.getGraphics();

        spirit = getRidOfPink(spirit);    // filter the image

    }


    int  width=475, height=265;

    public Image getRidOfPink(Image im) {
        try {
// grab the pixels from the image
            int[] pgPixels = new int [width*height];
            PixelGrabber pg = new PixelGrabber (im, 0, 0,
                width, height, pgPixels, 0, width);

    if (pg.grabPixels() && ((pg.status() & ImageObserver.ALLBITS) != 0))
{
        // Now change some of the bits
            for (int y=0;y<height;y++) {
                for (int x=0;x<width;x++) {
                    int i = y*width+x;
                    int a = (pgPixels[i] & 0xff000000)>>24;
                    int r = (pgPixels[i] & 0x00ff0000)>>16;
                    int g = (pgPixels[i] & 0x0000ff00)>>8;
                    int b = pgPixels[i] & 0x000000ff;
                    // turn the pink-ish pixels transparent.
                    if (r>200 && g>100&&g<200&&b>100&&b<200) {
                        a=0;
                        pgPixels[i] = a  | (r<<16) | (g<<8) | b;
                    }
                }
            }
            im = createImage (new MemoryImageSource (width, height,
pgPixels, 0, width));
            }
        } catch (InterruptedException e) { e.printStackTrace (); }
        return im;
    }
}
```

We have overridden init() to add the filtering statement:

```
spirit = getRidOfPink(spirit);   // filter the image
```

And we have added the routine getRidOfPink(). That routine looks fearsome at first, but it quickly breaks down into four simple stages:

1. Grab the pixels

2. Look at each individual pixel. You may be wondering why the pixel array isn't two dimensional, just as an image is. The reason is to keep it closer to the model the hardware uses. Frame buffer (graphics adapter) and CPU memory is one dimensional.

3. If the RGB values are within the range of "generally pink" then make the pixel transparent by setting its alpha value to 0.

4. Reassemble the pixel array into an image with MemoryImageSource.

It's as simple as that. When you run this, you see a picture like Figure 20-11.

Figure 20-11:   Eleanor transparently on her pedestal.

Comparing this image with Figure 20-10, you'll see that the ugly pink background has disappeared.

Note that it is a very expensive operation to grab pixels and look at them. To help your program performance you should do this as sparingly as possible, and look at as few pixels as you can. Don't grab pixels from the whole image if you don't need to. On a SPARCstation 5 desktop computer, this applet took about five seconds to initialize. On an Intel Pentium 66Mhz system, it took about twice as long.

How Do I Save to a File an Image I Have Created on the Screen?

The beauty of pixel grabbing is that it turns a picture into an array of ints. You can do anything you like with that array of ints including process it, send it down a socket, or write it out to a file. If you write it out to a file, you have saved your image to disk. It will not be in a recognized standard format like GIF or JPEG, and you will not get the benefit of compression. But it does let you save an image to a file.

The final point is that the java.awt.image package has a couple of other specialized classes for filtering RGB values and for chaining ImageProducers together so you can do multiple filtering.

> *Exercise:* Try filtering an image by adapting the code above. Turn the black Rolls-Royce into a pink one.

Animation

Animation is the last major Image Processing topic we are going to cover, and it is thankfully simple. In fact if you already know how to get an image on the screen, you already know how to animate. Just as in cartoon movies, Java animation consists of showing several images (known as "frames") in quick succession. The human eye has a quality called *persistence* that means a series of slightly different frames fools us into thinking we see movement. When we change the entire image it is called "frame animation." When we just change a small area of the image, that area is called a "sprite" and we do "sprite animation."

So all we do for animation is bring all our frames in memory and display them one after the other. If we need to we will also use double buffering and clipping to make things appear smoother. There is a cheesy example of Animation that comes with the JDK in directory $JAVAHOME/demo/Animator. If you go to that directory, you can run the following to see some jumping beans.

```
appletviewer   example4.html
```

The CD that comes with this book has a Java program to save images to disk in JPEG format in the goodies directory.

You can also review the Animator.java source code. As an example here, let's make Dickens the Dalmatian wag his tail in Figure 20-12.

Figure 20-12:   See Dickens wag his tail.

Before we show the code, let's look at the Java idiom for starting a thread in an Applet. You don't need a user thread in an applet if all you do is respond to GUI events. You *do* need one if you are animating, though.

A regular applet has the framework shown in Figure 20-13.

```
public class foo extends java.applet.Applet
{

    public void init() { ... }

    public void start() { ... }

    public void stop() { ... }

    public void paint (Graphics g) { ... }

}
```

Figure 20-13:   Framework of a normal applet.

To give yourself a thread, the idiom is that you do these five things:

- Make your applet class implement Runnable.

- Add the run() method of the thread. Inside here will be the statements to do all the work that your thread must do.

- Declare a Thread object: `Thread t;`.

- Inside start(), instantiate the thread with this Applet:

  ```
  t = new Thread(this);
  ```

  The thread running:

  ```
       t.start();
  ```

- Inside stop(), stop the thread running by this:

  ```
       t.stop();
       t=null;  // so it can be garbage collected.
  ```

So the applet framework with a thread looks like Figure 20-14.

```
public class foo extends java.applet.Applet
implements Runnable{

    Thread t;

    public void run()  { ...}

    public void init() { ... }

    public void start() {
        t = new Thread(this);
        t.start();    }

    public void stop() {
        t.stop();
        t=null;         }

    public void paint (Graphics g) { ... }

}
```

Figure 20-14: Threaded applet.

Here is the code to animate the tail. It closely follows the preceding framework. Again, by making this extend the "transp" class of the previous example, we can present the minimum new code. It's not too surprising that we can use the framework of the "pin-the-silver-lady-on-the-Rolls" code as the basis of the "animate the dog's tail" program. They both involve putting images on the screen and moving them about. All animation programs will have the same general form.

```
//<applet   code=wag.class    width=280 height=200>   </applet>
// double buffered, transparent image, animation
import java.awt.*;
import java.awt.image.*;
import java.awt.event.*;

public class wag extends transp implements Runnable {
    Image dal, appendage, tail1, tail2;
    Font f;

    public void init () {
        tail1 = getImage(getDocumentBase(), "tail.jpg");
        tail2 = getImage(getDocumentBase(), "tail2.jpg");
        dal = getImage(getDocumentBase(), "dickens.jpg");
        dal = getRidOfPink(dal);
        tail1 = getRidOfPink(tail1);
        tail2 = getRidOfPink(tail2);
        appendage=tail2;

        addMouseMotionListener( new MouseMotionListener () {
            public void mouseDragged(MouseEvent e){
                System.out.println("what a drag");
                new_x=e.getX();
                new_y=e.getY();
                repaint();
            }
            public void mouseMoved(MouseEvent e){}
        } );

        f = new Font("Helvetica", Font.BOLD, 18);

        myOffScreenImage = createImage(getSize().width, getSize().height );
        myOffScreenGraphics = myOffScreenImage.getGraphics();

    }

    public void paint (Graphics g) {
        g.setColor(Color.lightGray);
        g.fillRect(0,0,getSize().width, getSize().height );
        g.setColor(Color.yellow);
        g.setFont(f);
        g.drawString("Dickens is a happy dog",10,20);
        g.drawImage (appendage, 10, 50, this);
        appendage= (appendage==tail2?tail1:tail2); // swap frames
        g.drawImage (dal, 35, 65, this);
    }

        public void run() {
        while (true) {
            try{Thread.sleep( 100 ); }
            catch(InterruptedException ie){}
            repaint();
            }
        }

        Thread t;

        public void start() {
            t = new Thread(this);
            t.start();
        }
        public void stop() {
            t.stop();
            t = null;
        }
}
```

The init() method brings in an extra image, tail2.jpg, which looks similar to tail, but is slightly displaced. All the images are filtered to give them a transparent background.

The two tails look like those shown in Figures 20-15 and 20-16.

Figure 20-15:   Dickens tail can look like this. . .

Figure 20-16:   . . . or this.

I created Figure 20-15 from Figure 20-14 by rotating it ten degrees in Adobe Photoshop (image rotation is one of the features that xv doesn't offer). If you don't have Photoshop, it doesn't matter—you now know enough Java to whip up a special purpose program to do any image processing you want!

In the paint method, I added some text at the top just for fun. The only other change is we now draw an "appendage" instead of a tail. The appendage just holds a reference to either tail1 or tail2. Immediately after we have drawn the appendage, this line:

```
appendage= (appendage==tail2?tail1:tail2); // swap frames
```

swaps it over to point to the other one. In this way, when paint is called, it alternates between Figure 20-15 and Figure 20-16. Another way to accomplish this is to change what appendage refers to in the run() routine. It doesn't have to alternate between two images; you may have dozens in your animation.

The run routine just spins in an infinite loop, sleeping for a tenth of a second, then issuing a repaint request. About twenty-four frames per second is all you need to fool the eye into seeing continuous motion. Here we're running at ten frames per second.

The start() instantiates and kicks the thread off. The stop() is equally important. It's very poor programming to leave a thread running after the user leaves a page, so you kill the thread in the stop routine. And that is image animation. Finally, putting the whole thing together, so you can see all the code in one place, here is the program written without inheritance:

```
//<applet  code=fullwag.class   width=280 height=200>  </applet>
// double buffered
// transparent image
// animated tail
// Peter van der Linden

import java.awt.*;
import java.awt.image.*;
import java.awt.event.*;
import java.applet.*;

public class fullwag extends Applet implements Runnable {
    Image dal, appendage, tail1, tail2;
    Image myOffScreenImage;
    Font f;
    Graphics myOffScreenGraphics;

    public void update(Graphics g) {
        paint(myOffScreenGraphics);      // draws on double buffer
            // draws the db onto applet
                g.drawImage(myOffScreenImage,0,0, this);
}
    int  width=475, height=265;

    public Image getRidOfPink(Image im) {
        try {
     // grab the pixels from the image
            int[] pgPixels = new int [width*height];
            PixelGrabber pg = new PixelGrabber (im, 0, 0,
                    width, height, pgPixels, 0, width);

    if (pg.grabPixels() &&
              ((pg.status() & ImageObserver.ALLBITS) != 0)) {
     // Now change some of the bits
        for (int y=0;y<height;y++) {
            for (int x=0;x<width;x++) {
                    int i = y*width+x;
                    int a = (pgPixels[i] & 0xff000000)>>24;
                    int r = (pgPixels[i] & 0x00ff0000)>>16;
                    int g = (pgPixels[i] & 0x0000ff00)>>8;
                    int b = pgPixels[i] & 0x000000ff;
                    // turn the pink-ish pixels transparent.
                    if (r>200 && g>100&&g<200&&b>100&&b<200) {
                        a=0;
                        pgPixels[i] =  a  | (r<<16) | (g<<8) | b;
```

```
                }
            }
        }
        im = createImage (new MemoryImageSource (width, height,
pgPixels, 0, width));
        }
    } catch (InterruptedException e) { e.printStackTrace (); }
    return im;
}

public void init () {
    tail1 = getImage(getDocumentBase(), "tail.jpg");
    tail2 = getImage(getDocumentBase(), "tail2.jpg");
    dal = getImage(getDocumentBase(), "dickens.jpg");
    dal = getRidOfPink(dal);
    tail1 = getRidOfPink(tail1);
    tail2 = getRidOfPink(tail2);
    appendage=tail2;
    f = new Font("Helvetica", Font.BOLD, 18);
            myOffScreenImage = createImage(getSize().width,
getSize().height );
        myOffScreenGraphics = myOffScreenImage.getGraphics();
}

public void paint (Graphics g) {
    g.setColor(Color.lightGray);
    g.fillRect(0,0,getSize().width, getSize().height );
    g.setColor(Color.yellow);
    g.setFont(f);
    g.drawString("Dickens is a happy dog",10,20);
    g.drawImage (appendage, 10, 50, this);
    appendage= (appendage==tail2?tail1:tail2); // swap frames
    g.drawImage (dal, 35, 65, this);
}

    public void run() {
    while (true) {
        try{Thread.sleep( 100 ); }
        catch(InterruptedException ie){}
        repaint();
        }
    }
    Thread t;
    public void start() {
        t = new Thread(this);
        t.start();
    }
            public void stop() {
        t.stop();
        t = null;
    }
```

Table 20-3: Some Image Processing Utilities

Windows	The windows equivalent to xv is LView Pro, downloadable from http://www.lview.com
	Other people like Paint Shop Pro from Jasc, downloadable from http://www.zdnet.com
Solaris	xv is an interactive image manipulation program for XWindows (i.e., Unix).
	It understands all popular formats and can be downloaded for free from ftp.cis.upenn.edu in directory pub/xv.
Macintosh	Macintosh image processing software can be downloaded from: ftp://rever.nmsu.edu/pub/macfaq/JPEGView or ftp://rever.nmsu.edu/pub/macfaq/GIF_Converter.sit.bin.

Now Try These Exercises

1. Add to the filtering to turn Dickens into a black lab by turning all his white fur black.

2. Change the animation so the "tail wags the dog."

Sounds

Applets have some simple methods to play sound files. The 1.1 release can only deal with sounds in the .au format. The Java library that supports sound files has been greatly improved for JDK 1.2. It now enables playback of sound files in WAV, AIFF, AU, MIDI, and RMF format with much higher sound quality. The API has not changed, the methods are the same, but there is a big increase in the types of different sound files they can handle. Also in JDK 1.2, applications can now access sound files by calling the new static method "newAudioClip()" from class java.applet.Applet.

You can browse the site http://cuiwww.unige.ch/OSG/AudioFormats which describes the implementation of all the popular sound file formats including .wav (Windows), .au (Sun and NeXT), and .aif (Macintosh and SGI).

There are four kinds of information making up a Digital Audio stream. The man (manual) page explains that digital audio data represents a quantized approximation of an analog audio signal waveform. In the simplest case, these quantized numbers represent the amplitude of the input waveform at particular sampling intervals. I hate it when man pages (the UNIX online documentation) read like dictionary entries instead of making a reasonable attempt at explaining something.

Sample Rate

This says how many times per second we sample (take a reading from) our noise source. Java 1.1 supports only 8000Hz, while Java 1.2 supports many more.

Encoding

The encoding says how the audio data is represented. Java uses µ-law encoding (pronounced mew-law) which is the standard CCITT G.711 for voice data used by telephone companies in the United States, Canada, and Japan.

There is an alternative A-law encoding (also part of G.711) which is the standard encoding for telephony elsewhere in the world. A-law and µ-law audio data are sampled at a rate of 8000 samples per second with 12-bit precision, with the data compressed to 8-bit samples. The resulting audio data quality is equivalent to that of standard analog telephone service, meaning, in technical terms, pretty crappy.

Precision

Precision indicates the number of bits used to store each audio sample. For instance, µ-law and A-law data are stored with 8-bit precision. 16-bit precision is common elsewhere and now available in Java.

Here is a minimal applet to play a sound effect:

```
import java.applet.*;
public class noise extends Applet {
    public void init() {
        play( getCodeBase(), "danger.au");
    }
}
```

The file "danger.au" is on the CD. It makes a noise like a drumstick rattling on the side of a tin cup. The program would be invoked from the usual HTML file:

```
<applet code=noise.class  width = 150 height =100> </applet>
```

The applet directory $JAVAHOME/src/java/applet contains several other useful methods:

```
public AudioClip getAudioClip(URL url)
```

Once you have retrieved an AudioClip from a URL, you can play it once, play it in a loop continuously, or cease playing it with these methods `play()`, `loop()`, or `stop()`.

If you play it continuously, make sure that you stop playing it in the stop() method, called when the applet's Panel is no longer on the screen. Otherwise the noise will continue longer than you probably want.

Write an applet that plays a sound file, and evaluates it for hidden Satanic messages. There is an easy way to do this and a hard way. The easy way is to play the sound file, and then conclude:

```
    println("That contained 0 Satanic messages \n");
```

The hard way would actually involve some analysis of the sound waveforms, but it would probably produce exactly the same result.

In the first edition of this book I threw down the challenge to readers inviting them to submit code to play a sound file backwards. It would be a non-trivial task to figure out the .au format and do that, but alert programmer Manfred Thole from Germany realized that the task would be considerably simplified by using one of the vendor-specific classes that turns a FileInputStream into an AudioStream. This was a clever piece of programming to get the job done more simply.

```
import java.io.*;
import sun.audio.*;


/**
*
 * This application plays audio files backwards!
 * Only applicable for "8-bit u-law 8kHz mono" encoded audio files.
 * Usage: BackwardAudio audio-file-to-play-backwards
 */


public class BackwardAudio {

  static void swap(byte [] b) {
    int l = b.length;
    int i;
    byte tmp;

    for (i = 0; i < l/2; i++) {
      tmp = b[i];
      b[i] = b[l-i-1];
      b[l-i-1] = tmp;
    }
  }


  public static void main(String[] args) {

    AudioPlayer ap = AudioPlayer.player;
    AudioStream as = null;
    byte [] ad = null;

    if ( args.length != 1 ) {
      System.err.println("Usage: BackwardAudio audio-file-to-play-backwards");
      return;
    }
    try {
      as = new AudioStream(new FileInputStream(args[0]));
      // Some files give strange results...
      // Maybe they have an incorrect file header.
      if ( as.getLength() < 1 ) {
        System.err.println("Length: "+as.getLength()+"!");
        return;
      }
      ad = new byte[as.getLength()];
      as.read(ad, 0, as.getLength()-1);
      swap(ad);
      //ap.start(new ByteArrayInputStream(ad));
      ap.start(new AudioDataStream(new AudioData(ad)));
      // We have to wait for the ap daemon thread to play the sound!
      Thread.sleep(as.getLength()/8+100);
    }
    catch (FileNotFoundException fne) {
      System.err.println(fne);

    }
    catch (IOException ioe) {
      System.err.println(ioe);
    }
    catch (InterruptedException ie) {
      System.err.println(ie);
    }
  }
}
```

As well as the java.*.* hierarchy of packages, Java vendors can supply vendor-specific packages under <vendor>.* Sun has a large number of sun.* packages that it does not tell you about explicitly. Good programmers will find them because good programmers tend to investigate on their own.

The classes are in the $JAVAHOME/jre/lib/rt.jar. Copy this file somewhere safe, and unzip it. By the way, this is the file that the JDK README warns you not to unzip. I think they are trying to use reverse psychology on you.

You'll see all the standard java.*.* classes in there, and several dozen interesting looking Sun ones, too, including these:

```
Extracting: sun/misc/Ref.class
Extracting: sun/misc/MessageUtils.class
Extracting: sun/misc/CEStreamExhausted.class
Extracting: sun/misc/UUEncoder.class
Extracting: sun/misc/CharacterEncoder.class
Extracting: sun/misc/HexDumpEncoder.class
Extracting: sun/misc/UUDecoder.class
Extracting: sun/misc/BASE64Encoder.class
Extracting: sun/misc/UCDecoder.class
Extracting: sun/misc/CacheEnumerator.class
Extracting: sun/misc/Timeable.class
Extracting: sun/misc/TimerThread.class
Extracting: sun/misc/UCEncoder.class
Extracting: sun/misc/CRC16.class
Extracting: sun/misc/ConditionLock.class
Extracting: sun/misc/BASE64Decoder.class
Extracting: sun/misc/CacheEntry.class
Extracting: sun/misc/CEFormatException.class
Extracting: sun/misc/Timer.class
Extracting: sun/misc/TimerTickThread.class
Extracting: sun/misc/Lock.class
Extracting: sun/misc/CharacterDecoder.class
Extracting: sun/misc/Cache.class
  Creating: sun/audio/
Extracting: sun/audio/AudioStream.class
Extracting: sun/audio/InvalidAudioFormatException.class
Extracting: sun/audio/AudioStreamSequence.class
Extracting: sun/audio/ContinuousAudioDataStream.class
Extracting: sun/audio/AudioDevice.class
Extracting: sun/audio/AudioPlayer.class
Extracting: sun/audio/AudioData.class
Extracting: sun/audio/AudioTranslatorStream.class
Extracting: sun/audio/NativeAudioStream.class
Extracting: sun/audio/AudioDataStream.class
```

That gives you the package name. Of course, you remember that you can use javap to look at any of the methods of these!

```
    % javap sun.audio.AudioStream
Compiled from AudioStream.java
public class sun.audio.AudioStream extends java.io.FilterInputStream {
    sun.audio.NativeAudioStream audioIn;
    public sun.audio.AudioStream(java.io.InputStream);
    public int read(byte [],int,int);
    public sun.audio.AudioData getData();
    public int getLength();
}
```

Fuller documentation on these Sun classes has been put together by some Swedish programmers and is available at: http://www.cdt.luth.se/java/doc/sun.

Note that Sun's position is that the classes in the vendor-specific hierarchy are intended solely for Sun's use to implement the public APIs in the JDK. So Sun might change these classes around without notice. Use these at your own risk, they may change, and they make programs nonportable. Other Java vendors have other policies—Microsoft really wants you to use its vendor classes to lock you into its platforms.

Some Light Relief

Satan: Oscillate My Metallic Sonatas

Some people claim that "backwards masking" conceals satanic messages in popular music. They believe that if you play the music backwards (like reading the phrase above backwards) a hidden message will be revealed.

You can easily play a piece of music backwards by recording it onto a cassette tape. Then take the cassette apart by unscrewing the little screws, and swap the reels left to right (don't flip them upside down). You will have to thread the tape a little differently onto one spool.

You've done it correctly if the feed and take-up spools revolve in opposite directions to each other when you hit "play." Rewind once to remove this anomaly, and away you go with your backwards masking. This experiment is so much fun, you should drop whatever you're doing (you're probably reading a book) and go and try this *right now*.

For advanced students: overdub a tape to produce a gimmicked version on which you have added some suitable wording ("Sacrifice homework. Cthulu is our thesis advisor. Wear leather and stay out late on Fridays. Stack dirty dishes in the sink, and cut in line at supermarkets"). Leave the tape out for a suitable colleague to "discover" your backwards masked work.

Finally, I urge you to try running the Backward audio class on the file yenrab.au on the CD:

```
java BackwardAudio yenrab.au
```

If that sound file isn't evidence of demonic possession, I don't know what is.

CHAPTER
21

File I/O

I t is not completely fair to remark, as some have, that support for I/O in Java is "bone headed." Support for I/O in Java does make loose sense eventually, if you pound on it hard enough, and once you understand the whole panorama.

I/O in Java is modular: there are lots of classes that each do one specialized kind of I/O, and your job is to know what they do and how to connect objects of these classes. It works like a pipe of several connected OS commands, so that as the data flows through, it is modified or filtered in the way you need. The key to understanding I/O in Java is getting comfortable with connecting different file processing objects. But I/O is not one of the better-designed APIs. There are three major criticisms of the Java I/O design.

The first issue is that in computing it should be simple to do simple things. Reading a number from the keyboard is a simple thing, and there should be a core library function that does this simply and elegantly. But there is not.

The second issue is that the JDK 1.1 release did not cleanly fix up the JDK 1.0 release that got I/O wrong. JDK 1.0 built everything off 8-bit streams, which did not properly support the 16-bit character streams needed for internationalization. Accordingly, the I/O package virtually doubled in size in JDK 1.1, with a whole set of new 16-bit Reader/Writer classes added to the old 8-bit Stream classes. But the changeover was not completed: the old classes were left around, and keyboard I/O was still based on 8-bit streams. Programmers are supposed to use the Reader and Writer classes when coding character I/O, but the Stream classes are still used for binary I/O—except that interactive character I/O is still based on the Stream classes.

The third issue is that, in striving for generality, the I/O classes have become too numerous and too general. The excessive generality is a problem that is becoming worse, not better. In JDK 1.0, there was a class called `PushbackInputStream` that provided the ability to "unread" or push back a single byte. Pushing back the last character read is a rare operation. It's only in the JDK because its needed by someone writing an `LALR(1)` parser for a compiler. It should never have been set up as a class of its own; the function should have been made part of an existing class, probably `DataInput`. In JDK 1.1, `PushbackInputStream` was augmented by `PushbackReader`, which can push back an arbitrary number of Unicode characters into the input stream, not just a single 8-bit byte onto a Stream. Hardly anyone needs that.

The reason for the unhappy I/O situation is that designers of programming languages and runtime libraries form a very different community from application programmers. They get close to their work and lose the perspective of someone seeing it for the first time. What appears clear and obvious to the designer can be obscure to someone else. And that's why all software should be approved by a human interface engineer before release. Well, enough of the gripes. Let's take a look at what services the `java.io` API offers.

Files and Streams

The way that an operating system stores data is by putting it in a file. The way that Java puts data in a file is by connecting a stream to the file. We'll look at how you name a file, before we consider how to fill it with data.

Files have path names that identify where they are stored and also what they are called. Files have many other attributes such as whether they are readable, what directory they live in, and when they were last modified. The Java class called File allows you to look at these attributes of a file.

The File *Class*

The class called File does not let you do any I/O. File just has methods to look at and modify filename and pathname-related information (the so-called meta-data), not file contents. The class should really be called Filename. Methods of File allow you to:

- Return a File object, given a String containing a path name.

- Test whether a File object exists, can be read/written.

- Test whether a File object is a file or a directory.

- Say how many bytes are in the file or when it was last modified.

- Delete the file.

- Get various forms of the file path name.

- Create a directory.

As always, running the following will reveal the method signatures:

```
javap java.io.File
```

A number of methods are available in the class File to provide information about a file or a directory. The class was considerably enriched over Java 1.1 and the following shows the methods.

```
public class java.io.File implements java.io.Serializable, java.lang.Comparable {
    public static final char separatorChar; // '\' win32, '/' Unix
    public static final java.lang.String separator;
    public static final char pathSeparatorChar; // ';' win32, ':' Unix
    public static final java.lang.String pathSeparator;
```

// constructors:

```
    public java.io.File(java.io.File,java.lang.String);
    public java.io.File(java.lang.String);
    public java.io.File(java.lang.String,java.lang.String);

    public int compareTo(java.io.File);
    public int compareTo(java.lang.Object);
    public boolean equals(java.lang.Object);
    public int hashCode();

    public boolean createNewFile() throws java.io.IOException;
    public static File createTempFile(String, String) throws IOException;
    public static File createTempFile(String, String, File) throws IOException;
    public boolean delete();
    public void deleteOnExit();
```

// getting the attributes of a file:

```
    public boolean exists();
    public boolean canRead();
    public boolean canWrite();
    public java.io.File getAbsoluteFile();
    public java.lang.String getAbsolutePath();
    public java.io.File getCanonicalFile() throws java.io.IOException;
    public java.lang.String getCanonicalPath() throws java.io.IOException;
    public java.lang.String getName();
    public java.lang.String getParent();
    public java.io.File getParentFile();
    public java.lang.String getPath();
    int getPrefixLength();
    public boolean isAbsolute();
    public boolean isDirectory();
    public boolean isFile();
    public boolean isHidden();
    public long lastModified();
    public long length();
```

// to do with the directory:

```
    public java.lang.String list()[];
    public java.lang.String list(java.io.FilenameFilter)[];
    public java.io.File listFiles()[];
    public java.io.File listFiles(java.io.FileFilter)[];
    public java.io.File listFiles(java.io.FilenameFilter)[];
    public static java.io.File listRoots()[];
    public boolean mkdir();
    public boolean mkdirs();
```

// miscellaneous:

```
    public boolean renameTo(java.io.File);
    public boolean setLastModified(long);
    public boolean setReadOnly();
    public java.lang.String toString();
    public java.net.URL toURL() throws java.net.MalformedURLException;
}
```

You will only bother instantiating a `File` object if one of the foregoing operations is of interest to you. If you simply want to do I/O, you will use a different class.

Although you can use the `File` class to create and delete files and directories, there is currently no method that allows you to change the current working direc tory of the program. You always stay in whatever directory you were in when you started the program.

Most of the time the method names indicate what they do and what the arguments are. Here are the details on some of the less obvious ones.

```
public int compareTo(java.io.File);
```

This method compares two pathnames for lexicographically less, equal, or greater than. Filename comparisons are going to be platform-dependent, as Win95 ignores letter case in filenames.

```
public static File createTempFile(String, String, File) throws IOException;
```

This creates a temporary file in the directory specified by the File argument. The first two arguments are Strings used as used as a prefix and a suffix to the temp file name, and they must each be at least three characters long. The purpose of the arguments is to ensure that all the temp files created by something like your mail program have a name that starts with something like "mail".

```
public void deleteOnExit();
```

Calling this method marks the file to be deleted when the program ends. You can't rescind this request after you've made it.

```
public boolean mkdir();
public boolean mkdirs();
```

The first method creates one directory. The second method creates the directory plus any non-existent parent directories as needed.

```
public java.lang.String[] list();
public java.io.File[] listFiles();
```

The first method returns an array of Strings representing the files and directories in the directory that the method is invoked on. The second method returns the same information, but as File objects, not Strings.

```
public static java.io.File listRoots()[];
```

Finally! A method to list the available filesystems on this system! On Windows systems, the array will hold File objects for "A:\", "C:\", "D:\" and so on, allowing the programmer to learn what active drives there are. On Unix, the root drive is just "/", the root filesystem. File objects denoting the root directories of the mapped network drives of a Windows platform will be returned by this method, while File objects containing Win32 UNC[1] pathnames will not be returned by this method.

```
public java.net.URL toURL() throws java.net.MalformedURLException;
```

This converts a File object into a URL of the form file:///*something*. If the File is a directory, the URL will end in a slash, "/".

```
public boolean createNewFile() throws java.io.IOException;
```

This method creates a new file, if it doesn't already exist and returns true or false according to whether or not it created the file. The check for file existence and its possible subsequent creation is an atomic (indivisible) operation within the filesystem. That means that you can use this to implement a simple cooperative file-locking protocol.

File Locking in Java

Here's how your program might work with other programs to cooperate on synchronizing file access. The other programs can be running as separate processes in another JVM (and even on another system entirely), so the thread synchronization primitives, which only work within one JVM, can't help us.

---

1.   UNC is NT's "Universal Naming Convention," a pathname that starts with "\\".

```
import java.io.*;
public class exclude {
    public static void main(String a[]) throws Exception {
    // this is the file we are locking on
    File locker = new File("/tmp/mailfile.lock");
    boolean IgotIt = false;

    AcquireLockLoop: for ( ; ; ) { // repeat forever
        IgotIt = locker.createNewFile();
        if (IgotIt) { // we created the file (got the lock)
            break AcquireLockLoop;
        } else { // otherwise, sleep for a bit and try again
                System.out.println(a[0] + " didn't get file, trying again"
                Thread.sleep(3000);
        }
    }
    if (IgotIt) { // do regular work here,
    // assured that we have sole access to the resource.
        System.out.println(a[0]+ " got the file!");
        locker.deleteOnExit();
        Thread.sleep(2000);
    }
    }
}
```

There are several things to note about this program. First, instantiating a File object doesn't create a File. It merely gives us a handle to make enquiries about a file or directory of that name, if it exists.

Next note that instead of acquiring a lock, we try to create the file. This kind of file creation attempt is thread-safe and process-safe. If there are several Java programs running at the same time, only one of them will succeed in creating the file. The others will print the "didn't get message," sleep, and go round the loop again.

When a program succeeds in creating the file, it breaks from the loop and enters the "if I got the file" statement. It prints a message, marks the file to be deleted on exit, sleeps for a bit, and exits.

When you run several copies of this program, you will see these messages:

```
% java exclude A &; java exclude B &; java exclude C
    B got the file!
    A didn't get file, trying again
    C didn't get file, trying again
    A got the file!
    C didn't get file, trying again
    C got the file!
```

When running a file-locking scheme this way to gain exclusive access to some resource, the main thing is to create the file. You don't actually write to the file to fill it with data. It's only purpose is to be created or not to be created because it already exists.

Up to now Java has not had any support for file-locking. The approach shown here gives you file-locking. The comments in the runtime source code make it clear that this is a recommended use.

Getting the Drive Letters in Windows

A lot of people have been finding ingenious workarounds to get the drive letters of filesystems on Windows machines, so it's very helpful to find that the following method is added as part of JDK 1.2:

```
public static java.io.File listRoots()[];
```

Formats, Encodings, and I/O

Before looking at I/O, we need to review the formats for data. Table 21-1 describes the bit-level appearance of data in the different formats. Do not confuse a "format" with a "type." I may want to output a character, an integer, a boolean, or any of the primitive types. The type defines the range of admissible values, e.g., "A to Z" or "false, true." The format (also known as an *encoding*) defines how those values will be represented in terms of bits.

Table 21-1: Different Formats for Data

• Format: **ASCII** Size: 1 byte   Example Description: letter "A" Binary value: 0x41   Printable Representation: A The American Standard Code for Information Interchange is an 8-bit code in which most of the characters are human readable. There are also a few dozen control characters. ASCII is essentially a 7-bit subset of the 8-bit ISO 8859_1 encoding, shown in the appendix at the end of this book.
• Format: **Unicode** Size: 2 bytes   Example Description: capital letter "E acute" Binary value: 0x00C9   Printable Representation: É The problem with 8859_1 is that it can represent only 256 distinct characters. That's barely enough for all the accented and diacritical characters used in western Europe, let alone the many alphabets used around the rest of the world. Unicode is a 16-bit character set developed to solve this problem by allowing for 65,536 different characters. A String in Java holds adjacent Unicode characters.
• Format: **UCS** Size: 2 or 4 bytes   Example Description: capital letter "E acute" Binary value: 0x00C9   Printable Representation: É UCS is the Universal Character Set. There are two forms: UCS-2 and UCS-4. UCS-2 is a 2-byte encoding, and UCS-4 is a 4-byte encoding. The ISO/IEC standard 10646 provides for a full 4-bytes-per-character encoding, called UCS-4. Fortunately, this enormous encoding space is divided into 64K "planes" of 64K characters each. The ISO people want everyone to think of Unicode as just a shorthand way of referring to Plane Zero of the complete 4-byte ISO/IEC 10646 encoding space. UCS-2, in other words, is a subset of the full UCS-4. They call this the "Basic Multilingual Plane" or BMP. Personally, I think they all need a good talking to for taking a very simple concept and dressing it up with a lot of confusing terminology. I have never seen UCS or Unicode simply explained in plain language anywhere. Since Unicode is essentially just UCS-2, you may also hear people say (correctly) Java uses UCS-2 as its internal encoding.

Table 21-1: Different Formats for Data

• Format: **UTF**	
Size: 1-3 bytes	Example Description: letter "A"
Binary value: 0x41	Printable Representation: A

UCS Transformation Format is an interim code that allows systems to operate with both ASCII and Unicode. In UTF, a character is either 1, 2, or 3 bytes long. ASCII values less than 0x7F are written as one byte. Unicode values less than 0x7FF are written as two bytes. Other Unicode values are written as three bytes.

The initial bits of a UTF character identify how long it is. If the first bit of a value is 0, it is a 1-byte ASCII value. If the first bits are 110, it is the first byte of a 2-byte sequence. If the first bits are 1110, it is the first byte of a 3-byte sequence. The second and third bytes of a multibyte sequence start with the bits set to 10.

UTF is a hack best avoided if possible. It complicates code quite a bit when you can no longer rely on all characters being the same size. However, UTF offers the benefit of backward compatibility with existing ASCII-based data, and forward compatibility with Unicode data.

• Format: **binary**	
Size: 1-8 bytes	Example Description: value 65 (decimal byte)
Binary value: 0x41	Printable Representation: has to be converted to char

Java has the ability to do I/O on binary values. Binary output makes a big difference when you are using numbers. Just as an int representation of a number is very different from the String representation, binary I/O is very different from Unicode I/O. In fact, binary I/O is simply transferring the data as an int (or long, float, etc.) to or from disk. The binary value of a character is the same as the Unicode or ASCII value of the character, which occasionally leaves room for confusion. The binary value of an int is different from the Unicode or ASCII value of the int. A binary byte holding a single ASCII digit is (of course) 1 byte long, whereas a binary double-precision floating-point number is 8 bytes long.

A very common mistake in Java is to use binary I/O where Unicode or ASCII I/O was intended. The numeric values transferred will not necessarily be human readable, and you'll usually get a different length of data and different value of data than you were expecting. The character values transferred will be fine because an ASCII character has the same bit representation whether it was written using an ASCII method or a binary method.

• Format: **objects**	
Size: varies	

Java allows objects to be written out, and read back in, in a process known as serialization/deserialization. It's quite powerful to be able to do I/O on an entire object in one go.

Table 21-2 shows the code sets or "encodings" that various popular operating systems support:

Table 21-2: Encodings Supported by Some Operating Systems

Operating System	Encoding
Solaris (Sun Unix)	ASCII, ISO 8859_1, and UTF
Macintosh	A nonstandard character set in which the first 128 characters are ASCII and the rest are Apple's own invention.
Windows 95	MS-Windows (using code page 1252) normally uses the first 256 characters of Unicode, which is (for all practical purposes) equivalent to ISO 8859-1. Can also convert to UCS2 as needed.
Windows NT	Uses Unicode internally. Can also cope with ASCII, UCS, and other encodings.

Characters are always 16-bit Unicode internally in Java. Characters may be represented as Unicode, ASCII, UTF or something else entirely on a particular operating system. Therefore, I/O routines must translate the native character set into Unicode. The actual scheme that is used is called the *encoding*. An encoding is a protocol for translating characters to bit patterns.

The Reader/Writer Unicode stream classes should be used instead of the old JDK 1.0 InputStream/OutputStream classes because the Reader/Writer classes make it easy to write code that can be internationalized. Specifically, the Reader/Writer classes process Unicode internally. At the lowest level, they also provide the "hooks" for getting between Unicode and characters in a different protocol, such as ASCII or UTF. Many of today's popular operating systems use ASCII or UTF as their native codeset. Operating systems of the future will likely use Unicode as their native codeset.

Streams of Data

A file is but one possible source for data. We may equally acquire data from sources that are not files, such as the keyboard, a socket on the network, consecutive elements of an array, and so on. Accordingly, Java has another, higher abstraction called a *Stream*.

A stream in real life could be supplied by a lake, by another stream, by a spring, by a pumping station, and so on. Similarly a Stream in Java could be getting its bytes from (or sending them to) a file, a String, a socket on the net, an array, the keyboard, and so on. A Stream is a flow of data, never mind where it comes from or goes to. A Stream lets you put or take data as it goes by.

In JDK 1.0, Streams were a flow of 8-bit bytes, but this was not adequate for the conversion between different external codesets and Unicode. Proper internation-alization relies on this conversion, so JDK 1.1 introduced Readers (input streams of Unicode characters) and Writers (output streams of Unicode characters). Read-ers and Writers should now be used everywhere you want to do character I/O. Readers and Writers are 16-bit character streams that also know how to properly convert those characters into the native codeset.

`PrintWriter.println()` now emits an end-of-line marker that matches the con-ventions of the platform it is on. On Windows 95, it outputs \r\n, on Unix, it out-puts \n, and on Macintoshes, it outputs \r. The old `PrintStream` class just used \n on all systems.

The Essentials of Java I/O

If you do not memorize anything else about Java I/O, memorize this:

- All I/O in Java is done using a stream.
- There are two kinds of stream: 8-bit streams and 16-bit streams.
- The 8-bit streams are known as InputStreams or OutputStreams. The 16-bit streams are known as Readers (input) or Writers (output).
- Because the class name has Reader, Writer, InputStream, or Output-Stream in it, it's easy to know which set of services you are using.
- Each stream offers just one kind of service (e.g., character I/O, binary I/O, I/O to a byte array, to a file). You are supposed to connect several streams to get the exact processing you want.
- I/O streams are connected by passing one stream as an argument to the constructor of another.

I/O in Java is a little harder to grasp than in other languages because it has forsaken simplicity in the basic case, for generality of all cases. It remains to be seen if that was a wise course, but it is the way things are, so we must all deal with it.

The old JDK 1.0 Stream classes are 8-bit byte streams and are still used for binary I/O (and interactive I/O). When you hear the term "stream," make sure you are clear about whether you're dealing with a byte stream or a Unicode stream.

Predefined Streams

Three predefined Streams are already open and ready to use in every program. These Streams are declared in the java.lang.System class, and they are all byte streams.

- System.in   InputStream used to read bytes from the keyboard.

- System.out   PrintStream used to write bytes to the screen.

- System.err   PrintStream used to report errors. System.out can also be used to report errors, but having a separate channel for errors makes it easier to notice errors when program output has been redirected to a file.

> **Why Standard I/O Still Uses 8-bit Streams**
>
> The predefined objects System.in, System.out, and System.err are built on the now-deprecated 8-bit byte streams left over from JDK 1.0. Beta versions of JDK 1.1 replaced these three streams by Unicode streams, but many people complained that the change was incompatible with their existing code. So, to minimize transition costs Sun left in, out, and err as 8-bit streams, placed a "deprecated" tag on the constructors, and provided an adapter class to accept an 8-bit stream and give back a 16-bit Reader stream. This adapter class is called InputStreamReader.
>
> In JDK 1.2 the deprecated tag is removed so programmers can reassign the stdin, stdout and stderr without getting a compiler warning. Here's an example of those reassignments
>
> ```
> // reassign stdout to a file
> FileOutputStream fs1 = new FileOutputStream("stdlog.txt");
> System.setOut( new PrintStream( fs1 ) );
>
>
> // reassign stdin from a file
> FileInputStream fi = new FileInputStream("input.txt");
> System.setIn(  fi  );
> ```

Although these streams are intended for interactive I/O, you can redirect them to a file. This can be done on the command line, using the OS feature for I/O redirection, or in the program. The method `System.setOut(PrintStream)` will redirect `System.out` after checking with the SecurityManager. There are also methods `System.setErr()` and `System.setIn()`.

Converting from an 8-Bit Stream to a 16-Bit Reader/Writer

Reading a Line or Converting to 16 Bits? BufferedReader!

Two new adapters can be connected to an 8-bit stream to give you a 16-bit stream.

The `InputStreamReader` class can be layered onto an input stream to give you a Reader.

```
InputStreamReader isr = new InputStreamReader( System.in );
```

The `java.io.OutputStreamWriter` class connects a Writer to an Output-Stream.

```
PrintWriter pw = new PrintWriter(
    new OutputStreamWriter(conn.getOutputStream()));
```

Often, you then layer a BufferedReader or BufferedWriter on top of that to get the best performance, or to be able to read or write a line at a time. Connecting a PrintWriter will let you output printable characters to the stream.

JDK 1.1 Input

Let's focus on input only to begin with. Output works in a similar way, and we'll look at it later. In this section on input, we will cover the following topics

- Character input
- Reading characters from the keyboard
- Reading characters from a file
- Reading binary data from a file
- Reading numbers and other types from the keyboard

We use different classes to read the different I/O formats, as shown in Table 21-3.

Table 21-3: Classes for Different I/O Formats

If You Have a Value in This Format...	...Use This Class or One of Its Subclasses to Read It
ASCII or Unicode character	`FileReader` (if it's in a file) `InputStreamReader` (if it's in a byte stream)
binary data	`DataInputStream`
persistent object	`ObjectInputStream`

Character Input

Character input is done by using one (or more) of the `Reader` classes. There is a different Reader subclass for each different source of characters (file, String, array, etc.). You are expected to call the constructor with the character source as an argument. It will hand you back a Reader, which means from that point on you never have to worry about lower-level details like how an array differs from the keyboard. The `Reader` class hides or encapsulates all the implementation details from you. A Reader is a class that works on a Unicode character stream.

Reader is abstract, so you will always be dealing with one of its concrete subclasses. Making the class abstract forces the subclasses to have a method of the given name and to implement it in its own way. Reader has the following public methods, along with others:

```
int read() throws IOException
      // returns Unicode value, or -1 if end of stream

int read(char cbuf[]) throws IOException
      // fills the array with chars, and returns the
      // number of chars read, or -1 if end of stream

int read(char cbuf[], int off, int len) throws IOException
      // puts up to len chars in the array starting at element off,
      // and returns the number of chars read,
      // or -1 if end of stream

long skip(long n) throws IOException
      // tries to advance over n chars and
      // return the number actually skipped

boolean markSupported()
      // tells whether this stream supports the mark() operation

void mark(int);
      // marks the present position in the stream.
      // if you read more than int more characters, you are
      // allowed to forget the marked place.

void reset();
      // goes back to the point previously marked.

void close();
      // closes the stream. Throws IOException if further reads
      // are attempted.
```

These are the same method names that InputStream has, but the Reader methods convert to native codesets properly. The read routine returns an int rather than a char because it has to allow for every possible legal 16-bit value, plus an additional value to say that end of stream was hit. If a character was successfully read, the return value is the Unicode value of that character in the range 0 to 0xFFFF. If a character was not successfully read, read() returns the value 0xFFFFFFFF (minus one). Note that this class does not throw the EOFException (end of file exception), but returns an out-of-range value to indicate EOF.

The read() method will read one "chunk" from the stream and convert it into a Unicode character by following the default encoding conversion that is in effect. On an ASCII system, it will read one byte and promote it to a Unicode character. On a system with Unicode in effect, it will read two bytes and no conversion is needed. Where the encoding has been set to UTF, the method will read one to three bytes and assemble them into a Unicode character. You cannot currently change the encoding that is in effect for a file, as the InputStreamReader constructor that does this is marked private.

Interactive I/O—Reading from the Keyboard

System.in is an InputStream (actually a BufferedInputStream) that offers just
three methods for getting data: read a byte, read enough to fill my array of bytes,
and read enough to fill a specified range within my array of bytes.

```java
import java.io.*;

public class exreadin {

    public static void main(String f[]) {
        int i=0;
        char c;

        try {
            while ( i != -1 ) {
                i = System.in.read();
                c = (char) i;
                System.out.println( "read: " + c
                        + " hex value: "+Integer.toString(i,16));
            }
        } catch (IOException ioe) {
                System.out.println( "IO error:" + ioe );
        }

    }

}
```

Running the program and typing some input will look like this:

```
java exreadin
def 123
read: d hex value: 64
read: e hex value: 65
read: f hex value: 66
read: hex value: 20
read: 1 hex value: 31
read: 2 hex value: 32
read: 3 hex value: 33
read:
hex value: a
read:? hex value: -1
```

When we type the end of file indicator (Ctrl-Z on PCs, Ctrl-D on Unix) the program stops reading from System.in and returns –1.

Good Java programmers will want to make sure that incoming characters are correctly converted to Unicode by reading through a Reader rather than a Stream. The way to get Unicode characters from an InputStream (like `System.in`) is to layer an InputStreamReader on top of it.

`InputStreamReader` is an adapter from a byte stream to a character Reader. You pass the constructor one of the old-style JDK 1.0 8-bit byte input streams, and it gives you back a Reader. The input bytes are translated into characters according to a default character encoding (e.g., ISO 8859_1, ASCII, Unicode). It assumes sensible defaults.

The other methods of `InputStreamReader` are just the methods of `Reader` that we saw above. So, this is how to read characters (not bytes) from the keyboard.

- Wrap an InputStreamReader around `System.in`.

  ```
  InputStreamReader isr = new InputStreamReader( System.in );
  ```

- Read a character or (a portion of) a character array at a time from the InputStreamReader object.

Why does this seem so hard? Because it caters for the general case of fully internationalized software, not the simple case of I/O in the U.S. You want to sell your software in Japan, don't you?

Notice that so far we just have character-by-character input. Ideally, we would like to read numeric values, such as 123, and have them handed back to us as an int without us having to program it in detail. We'll get to that.

Reading Characters from a File

`Reader` is an abstract class, so it is subclassed by other classes in the `java.io` package before it is used in practice. Here are four popular subclasses of `Reader`, corresponding to four possible sources for the data.

- `FileReader`   Translates bytes from file into character stream.
- `InputStreamReader`   Fetch characters from byte stream.
- `StringReader`   Gets characters from String.
- `CharArrayReader`   Gets characters from char array.

All of these subclasses offer the Reader methods just outlined above. Here is an example program that uses `FileReader` to access and count the number of bytes in a file. It compares the total to the `File.length()` value. They should be equal.

```java
import java.io.*;

public class exfileread {

    public static void main(String args[]){
        int i=0;
        int bytesRead=0;

        try {
            FileReader fr = new FileReader( "animals.txt" );
            while ( i != -1 ) {
                i = fr.read();
                if (i!=-1) bytesRead++;
            }
        } catch (IOException ioe) {
                System.out.println( "IO error:" + ioe );
        }
        System.out.println("bytes read from file: "+bytesRead);

        File f = new File("animals.txt");
        System.out.println("bytes in File.length(): "+f.length() );
    }
}
```

If you create a text file called `animals.txt` with the names of a few animals in it, and run the program, you will see:

```
java exfileread
bytes read from file: 27
bytes in File.length(): 27
```

`FileReader` offers several constructors: it can take a path name as an argument, as in the example above. Another constructor takes a `File` object as an argument. A third constructor takes a `FileDescriptor` as an argument. Application programmers don't use file descriptors, but one may be constructed on your behalf to represent an open file or open socket.

Notice that there is no concept of a separate `open()` step as occurs in C. You just instantiate the stream object and if it didn't throw an exception, you are ready to do I/O immediately. And there is no concept of "I am opening this file for ASCII/binary data" as occurs on the PC. You read the data in different formats by using different methods. However, don't be fooled—although there is no `open()`, there is a `close()`! You should always explicitly use `close()` to close your output streams to ensure that the last few bytes are flushed into the system.

Reading or writing is synchronous. You don't return from the call until you have passed the bytes to the operating system. Depending on the implementation, I/O may block all threads in a program until it has completed. Watch out for this. The best implementations will block only the thread making the I/O call.

Simple Rules for Character I/O

The two rules of character I/O from files are:

- If you want to do character input, all the classes you use should have names that end in `Reader` (not in `InputStream`).

- If you want to do character output, all the classes you use should have names that end in `Writer` (not in `OutputStream`).

These rules don't apply to the predefined `stdin`, `stdout`, `stderr` objects.

Reading Binary Data From a File

So far, so good, but what if you don't want to read characters? What if you want to read binary numbers? Table 21-3 showed that binary data is read with `DataInputStream`. `DataInputStream` has these public methods, along with others:

```
boolean readBoolean()
byte readByte()
int readUnsignedByte()
short readShort()
int readUnsignedShort()
int readInt()
long readLong()
float readFloat()
double readDouble()
```

Each method either reads in a binary representation of the value of the stated type or throws an `EOFException` or other `IOException`. The EOF exception would be thrown when you order (say) a four-byte value to be read, but fewer bytes are available before the end of the input stream.

When you have binary data in a stream, `DataInputStream` can be used to read it into your program. DataInputStream would really have been better named Bina- ryInputStream, as that might have prevented the confusion that arises when people wrongly use it on a character stream. The question of conversion between character sets does not arise for binary data, although the question of conversion between endians may. A number like 0xFF00 takes two bytes to store, and those two bytes might be stored in the order FF then 00 (known as big endian, because the big end comes first), or the other way around, with 00 then FF (known as little endian). Java stores everything as big endian. If a computer system is little endian (as PCs are), some care must be taken to convert values to big endian on input, if the file was not written by Java.

Layering Streams on Top of Each Other

If you run `javap` on `java.io.DataInputStream`, you'll see that it has only one constructor, which looks like this:

```
public java.io.DataInputStream(java.io.InputStream);
```

How, then, can I get a `DataInputStream` that operates on a file? The answer is to layer one stream on top of another. Many of the Java I/O classes have constructors that take one kind of stream as an argument and return a different kind of stream. You are supposed to connect several streams to get the exact processing you need (see Figure 21-1), just the way you might connect a garden spigot to a hose, and the hose to a lawn sprinkler.

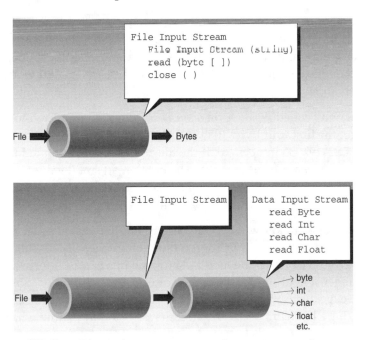

Figure 21-1: Connecting streams to get the exact processing you want.

In this case, just construct a `FileInputStream` with the path name of your file (passed in as an argument to the program in the example below). Then, construct a `DataInputStream` from the `FileInputStream`. The code looks like this:

```
import java.io.*;

public class exreaddata {
    public static void main(String f[]) {
        FileInputStream fis;
        DataInputStream dis;
        try {
            fis = new FileInputStream(f[0]);
            dis = new DataInputStream( fis );
            System.out.println( "file: " + f[0] );
            int i;
            while ( true ) {
            i = dis.readInt();
            System.out.println( "read: " + i );
        }
    } catch (EOFException eof)
            {System.out.println( "EOF reached " ); }
        catch (IOException ioe)
            {System.out.println( "IO error: " + ioe ); }
    }
}
```

If you run this program on a data file with characters in it, the characters will be interpreted as binary data. It's all bits inside a processor, and it just does what you tell it. If the data file contained the ASCII characters "1 CAT," that would be 0x31 0x20 0x43 0x41 0x54.

If you (mistakenly) called `readInt` on a `DataInputStream` connected to this file, you would get the first four bytes (0x31204341) and interpret them as one int, giving a result of 824197953 in decimal. If the file actually does contain binary data, you'll get those values instead. If you are trying to read small values and you find you are getting huge ones, the first thing to check is "Am I reading binary values instead of character values?" It is a very common error.

In all cases, you need to know what the data was written as, in order to read it in successfully. This is true for most programming languages because data is just a collection of arbitrary bits on the media. The same bits can be interpreted equally well as an integer, a floating-point number, or four bytes from the 8859-1 encoding. If you're expecting an int at that point in the input stream, use `readInt()`. If you're expecting a boolean, use `readBoolean()`. If you don't know what to expect, whatever wrote the file needs to be redesigned.

Reading Numbers and Other Types from the Keyboard

Now that we are comfortable with the concept of pushing streams on top of streams to get the methods we need, let's go back to system.in and see how we can assemble numbers out of the characters we know how to read in. This book comes with an easy keyboard input class called EasyIn. Before describing that, we'll describe how you must read values from the keyboard if you don't want to use EasyIn.

In all cases, we have to know in advance what type we are reading in. We need to know what to expect because the methods for reading a boolean, an int, a floating-point number, and so on, are all different. Follow this process:

1. Layer an InputStreamReader on System.in. This gives us a Reader class, on which we can layer other Readers.

2. Layer a BufferedReader on the InputStreamReader. This gives us a method that reads an entire line, allowing us to get all the text as a String when the user presses Return.

3. Layer a java.util.StringTokenizer on the String just read in. Call the nextToken() method to extract just the nonspace characters. This makes the input format a little more forgiving by removing trailing and leading whitespace.

4. Use the parseXxx method of the primitive types wrapper classes to extract the expected value.

The exact combination of features to read from the keyboard is painful, to say the least. It is a major wart on Java's mostly reasonable claim to simplicity. Table 21-4 shows how to read values from the keyboard and get them into a primitive type in your program.

Table 21-4: Reading from the Keyboard

Preliminary Declarations

```import java.io.*;```
 ```import java.util.*;```
 `. . .`
 	
 ```InputStreamReader is = new InputStreamReader(System.in);```
 ```BufferedReader br = new BufferedReader(is);```
 `. . .`
 ```String s = br.readLine();```
 ```StringTokenizer st = new StringTokenizer(s);```

Note: An exception handler is also needed. Wrap a `try...catch` around the input statements.

Primitive Type	Code to Read It from System.in
char	```int i = is.read(); // -1 denotes EOF``` ```char c = (char) i;```
~~String~~	```String s = br.readLine();```
boolean	```boolean bo = new``` ```Boolean(st.nextToken()).booleanValue();```
int	```int i = Integer.parseInt(st.nextToken());```
byte	```byte by = Byte.parseByte(st.nextToken());```
short	```short sh =``` ```Short.parseShort(st.nextToken());```
long	```long lo = Long.parseLong(st.nextToken());```
float	```float fl = new``` ```Float.parseFloat(st.nextToken());```
double	```double db = new``` ```Double.parseDouble(st.nextToken());```

Note: Each statement or group of statements must have an exception handler wrapped around it, as shown in the column opposite. Or the method must declare that it throws an IOException.	```try {```
	 ``` // put I/O statement here```
	 ```} catch(Exception e)```
	 ``` { e.printStackTrace(); }```

For the sake of completeness, here is the full code to prompt for and read an int value.

```
import java.io.*;
import java.util.*;

public class exreadin2 {

    public static void main(String f[]) {
        int i=0;
        char c;
        InputStreamReader is = new InputStreamReader( System.in );
        BufferedReader br = new BufferedReader( is );
        StringTokenizer st;

        try {
                System.out.print( "int: ");    System.out.flush();
                String myline = br.readLine();
                st = new StringTokenizer(myline);
                i = Integer.parseInt(st.nextToken());
                System.out.println( "got: " + i );
        } catch (IOException ioe) {
                System.out.println( "IO error:" + ioe );
        }


    }

}
```

Most programmers would agree that this is excessively complicated for a simple thing like interactive I/O. When Java 1.0 came out, I filed a bug against the I/O library on this topic and included in the bug report my suggested fix: the code for a new class that supported simple keyboard I/O.

Easy Keyboard Input

Alas, my efforts were in vain, for matters did not improve with JDK 1.1; indeed, they became worse.

The I/O classes changed between JDK 1.0 and JDK 1.1, such that many existing programs with I/O became deprecated. However, the new features introduced did not address the basic problem that the common, simple cases of I/O were complicated and involved to program. Drat!

The code that I included in the bug report collected the keyboard input methods in a class called `EasyIn`, which is on the CD. The class `EasyIn` has these methods:

```java
public class EasyIn {
    boolean readBoolean();
       byte readByte();
      short readShort();
        int readInt();
       long readLong();
      float readFloat();
     double readDouble();
       char readChar();
     String readString();
}
```

You are welcome to copy this source file from the CD and use it without restriction in your programs. It supports easy keyboard input for the basic types. You would compile it with your code and use it like this:

```java
EasyIn easy = new EasyIn();

int i = easy.readInt(); // gets an int from System.in
boolean b = easy.readBoolean(); // gets a boolean from System.in
```

`EasyIn` is not part of the JDK but is a utility I put together to provide the missing functionality. I didn't make it work with any arbitrary stream because I wanted it to be customized for simplicity in the most frequent case: use with `System.in`.

JDK 1.1 Output

At this point we have seen how to read both character and binary data from the keyboard and from files. Now it is time to look at the corresponding output classes. In this section on output, we will cover the following topics:

- Character output

- Writing characters to the console

- Writing characters to a file

- Formatted character output

- Writing binary data to a file

Again, there are different classes according to the format that you wish to output. Table 21-5 lists them.

Table 21-5: Classes for Different Output Formats

If You Have a Value in This Format...	...Use This Class or One of Its Subclasses to Write It
ASCII or Unicode character	`FileWriter` (if it's to a file) `OutputStreamWriter` (if it's to a byte stream)
binary data	`DataOutputStream`
persistent object	`ObjectOutputStream`

Character Output

Character output is done using one or more of the `Writer` classes. There is a different Writer subclass for each different destination of characters (file, String, array, etc.). You are expected to call the constructor with the character destination as an argument. It will hand you back a Writer, which means from that point on you never have to worry about lower-level details like how an array differs from the keyboard or how the Unicode is converted into the native codeset. The `Writer` class hides or encapsulates all the implementation details from you.

Writer has these public methods, along with others:

```
void write(java.lang.String);
  // Write out a String

void write(java.lang.String, int, int);
  // Write out a portion of a String

void write(int);
  // The single char to be written out. The low 16 bits of
  // the int are output, and the high 16 bits are ignored.

void write(char[]);
  // The array of chars to be written out.

abstract void write(char[], int, int);
  // Write a portion of an array of characters

abstract void flush();
  // Flush internal buffers for this stream

abstract void close();
  // Close this stream (no further processing)
```

As with the Reader classes, `Writer` is abstract, so you will always be dealing with one of its concrete subclasses.

Accessing the Serial/Parallel Port

Programmers writing applications frequently ask how they can access the RS232 serial port (or modem, etc.) on a system.

There is a Java library for this known as the Java Communications package. It provides read/write access to RS232 serial ports and IEEE1284 parallel ports. The package isn't part of the JDK (maybe it will be one day), but you can download it through the Sun Java site at http://java.sun.com, and use it today.

Writing Characters to the Console

We have seen code like the following frequently enough to be confident about writing to the console:

```
System.out.println("send more beer");
```

The line of code breaks down like this. `System` is a class in the `java.lang` package. The class System roughly corresponds to the AppletContext or Toolkit classes. It contains a number of useful objects and methods for the program, *not* for the system as the name suggests.

`out` is an object declaration within `System`. The declaration is this:

```
public final static PrintStream out = nullPrintStream();
```

`PrintStream` is marked as `final`, but that just means Java can't change it. `PrintStream` is actually given an initial value in a native code method in `System` in the Sun JDK. This code is called from an initializer that can be seen in file $JAVAHOME/src/java/lang/System.java.

```
FileOutputStream fdOut = new FileOutputStream(FileDescriptor.out);
setOut0(new PrintStream(new BufferedOutputStream(fdOut, 128), true));
```

The `PrintStream` class has Stream in the name, so we know it deals with 8-bit byte streams. It has methods like the following to print a value of every primitive type, and for Strings and Objects, too.

```
public void print(int);
public void print(byte);
public void print(float);
public void print(double);
public void print(String);
```

It also has a `println()` method for each of these that will print the value and then print a new line. When you invoke `print()` on an object it calls the `toString()` method of that object, and prints the resulting string.

Writing Characters to a File

Let's take a look at how to write characters to a file. This is a place where you may need to know about the underlying encoding or codeset of the operating system. There will be a default encoding in place, and if you want something different, you must change it (not supported in JDK 1.1.1).

`Writer` is an abstract class, so it is subclassed by other classes in the `java.io` package before it is used in practice. Here are four popular subclasses of `Writer`, corresponding to four possible destinations for the data.

- FileWriter   Writes a character stream into a file.
- InputStreamWriter   Writes characters into a byte stream.
- StringWriter   Writes characters into a String.
- CharArrayWriter   Writes characters into a char array.

All of these subclasses offer the `Writer` methods outlined above. Here is an example program that uses `FileWriter` to write whatever you type into a file. Provide the file name as a command-line argument.

```
import java.io.*;

public class exfilewrite {
    public static void main(String f[]) {
        FileWriter fw;
        int i;
        try {
          fw = new FileWriter( f[0] );

            while ( (i=System.in.read()) != -1 ) {
                fw.write( (char) i );
            }
            fw.close();
        } catch (IOException ioe) {
                System.out.println( "IO error:" + ioe );
        }
    }

}
```

The file can be compiled and run on Windows 95 like this:

```
c:\> javac exfilewrite.java

c:\> java exfilewrite cars.txt
jaguar
ford chevy rolls
^Z

c:\> type cars.txt
jaguar
ford chevy rolls
```

So far, so good. But that just shows you how to write characters as characters. How can we write binary values as character data so it will be human readable?

Say we have an int that we want to write into a file as a series of characters. We have already seen that the System.out object can do exactly that, so perhaps there is some way to construct an object of class PrintStream from a FileOutputStream.

Indeed there is, but it is now deprecated. The code looks like this:

```
import java.io.*;
// write binary data as characters (deprecated)
public class exfilewrite2 {
    public static void main(String f[]) {
        try {
            FileOutputStream fos = new FileOutputStream("foo.txt");
            PrintStream ps = new PrintStream(fos);

            boolean b=true;
            int i=27;
            double d=432.5;

            ps.print( b );
            ps.print( i );
            ps.print( d );

            ps.close();
        } catch (IOException ioc) {
            System.out.println( "IO error:" + ioe );
        }
    }

}
```

Compiling it gives you this warning message:

% javac exfilewrite2.java

```
Note: exfilewrite2.java uses a deprecated API.
     Recompile with "-deprecation" for details.
1 warning
```

% javac -deprecation exfilewrite2.java
```
exfilewrite2.java:7:
Note: The constructor java.io.PrintStream(java.io.OutputStream)
      has been deprecated.
          PrintStream ps = new PrintStream(fos);
                           ^
Note: exfilewrite2.java uses a deprecated API.
      Please consult the documentation for a better alternative.
2 warnings
```

That was the way we would have written binary data to a file as characters with JDK 1.0. If you run this program and look inside `foo.txt`, you'll see it contains human-readable characters. Notice this breaks the character I/O rules at the beginning of the chapter. We are trying to do character output, but the name of the class does not end in `Writer`.

The new approved way is to use a `PrintWriter`, as shown in the example below.

```
import java.io.*;
// write binary data as characters (new way)
public class exfilewrite3 {
    public static void main(String f[]) {
        try {
            FileWriter fw = new FileWriter("foo.txt");
            PrintWriter pw = new PrintWriter(fw);

            boolean b=true;
            int i=27;
            double d=432.5;

            pw.print( b );
            pw.print( i );
            pw.print( d );

            pw.close();
        } catch (IOException ioe) {
            System.out.println( "IO error:" + ioe );
        }
    }
}
```

Quick and Dirty Ways to Fake out Untrusted Applet Client-Side I/O

For security reasons, untrusted applets are not allowed to write to the client's local disk. One quick and dirty approach to saving information permanently is for the applet to open a socket connection back to the server's SMTP port and e-mail the data to the client. The user at the client can then decide if he or she wishes to save the e-mail into a file. The chapter on networking explains how to connect to a mail server port and gives an example program.

If you want to do client-side I/O, you should simply use a signed (trusted) applet. That's not possible if you only have JDK 1.0-level browsers. So here's an ingenious approach that works.

The steps are:

1. Install a CGI script on the server, which simply stashes all its input into a temporary file.

2. Have your applet write the data to the URL of this CGI script, as shown in the networking chapter. Use Java strings to GET or POST the data to the CGI program.

3. The CGI program should give the file a MIME type which ensures the browser won't try to display it as HTML when you try to browse the file. Giving the temporary file an extension of ".zip" accomplishes this.

4. Finally, in your applet, open a URL to this temporary .zip file on the server, and do a showDocument () command on it, like this:

    ```
    URL data = new URL(getDocumentBase(), "write/tmp.zip");

    getAppletContext().showDocument(data);
    ```

The MIME type will cause Netscape to put up a dialog box, asking if the user wants to save the document (your file) to local disk. Just say yes. (This workaround was put together by my colleague Robert Lynch. All the scripts and classes that Robert generated are on the CD at goodies/saveit.)

If you have permission to install perl scripts on your applet server, these scripts give your applet users the ability to save files locally on their system. Note that this does not subvert system security—users must still explicitly choose whether or not to allow the file to be written to their system.

Formatted Character Output

Being able to write binary data as characters leads directly to the next requirement? How do we control the format of the character output? How do I specify that I want exactly two decimal places for my floating-point number? "Format" in this section means "appearance on the printed page," not character encoding.

The support for formatted output was introduced with JDK 1.1, and it uses the classes in the new package `java.text`. The package contains classes to help with collation (sorting order), formatting numbers and dates, and messaging.

Formatting a number allows localization to Western, Arabic, or Indic numbers, as well as specifying such things as the number of decimal places. A class called `java.text.DecimalFormat` has a constructor that takes a string which is a template for the format you want. Then you call its `format()` method, passing in your number. (The method is overloaded for doubles and longs, so you can call it with any kind of primitive type number.) Here's an example:

```
DecimalFormat df = new DecimalFormat( "#0.00;#0.00CR" );
System.out.println( df.format( -1.267) );

1.26CR // the output
```

The format string you pass to the constructor will be made up of the symbols shown in Table 21-6 to indicate the significant digits, where to put the sign, and how positive numbers differ from negative numbers.

Table 21-6: Some Characters Used in a Format String

Symbol	Meaning
;	Separates positive and negative formats in the format string
0	A digit
#	A digit; zero shows as absent (not space)
.	Placeholder for decimal separator
,	Placeholder for grouping separator
–	Default negative prefix
%	Multiply by 100 and show as percentage

You can put two of these formats together, separated by a semicolon. The first format will then be used for positive and zero numbers, and the second format will be applied to negative numbers. Some useful complete format strings are shown in Table 21-7.

Table 21-7: Some Typical Format Strings

Format String	Meaning	Value	Output String
##0.00	At least one digit before the decimal point, and two after.	1234.567 .256	1234.56 0.25
#.000	Possibly no digits before the point, three after.	1234.567 .256	1234.567 .256
,###	Use thousands separator and no decimal places	1234.567 .256	1,234 0
0.00;0.00–	Show negative numbers with sign on the right	–27.5	27.5–

The class java.text.DecimalFormat is designed for common uses; for very large or small numbers, instead use a format that can express exponential values. Here is an example of using the number format class to get numbers printed with two decimal places. Notice that if rounding is needed, we have to do it ourselves. The format just truncates, though it would be a good idea to add a format character that says "round this digit in that direction."

```
import java.io.*;
import java.text.*;
// write binary data as formatted characters

public class exformat {
    public static void main(String f[]) {

        double db[] = { -1.1, 2.2, -3.33, 4.444, -5.5555, 6.66666};

        DecimalFormat df = new DecimalFormat( "#0.00;#0.00CR" );

        for (int i=0; i<db.length; i++) {
            System.out.println( df.format( db[i]) );
        }

    }

}
```

Running this code gives the output shown below. The symbol CR (credit) used for negative numbers is a common business usage.

```
% java exformat
1.10CR
2.20
3.33CR
4.44
5.55CR
6.66
```

A comment in the DecimalFormat class warns that the normal use is to get a proper format string for a specific locale, using one of the factory methods such as getInstance(). You may then modify it from there (after testing to make sure it is a DecimalFormat). They are suggesting that the proper usage is something like this:

```
NumberFormat nf = NumberFormat.getInstance();
System.out.println( nf.format( mydouble ));
```

Finally, note that the format in which a number is printed can depend on the locale (geographical region). In some parts of Europe, a decimal point is a "." and in other parts it is a "," so formatting a number is bound up with internationalization and localization (a topic that deserves a book in its own right). Here is how you can get a list of locales known to your system:

```
import java.io.*;
import java.util.Locale;
import java.text.*;

public class exlocales {
    public static void main(String f[]) {

        java.util.Locale[] locales =
                java.text.NumberFormat.getAvailableLocales();

        System.out.println("The locales on this system are:");

        for (int i = 0; i < locales.length; ++i) {
            if (locales[i].getCountry().length() == 0) {
                // skip locales with no country
                continue;
            }
            System.out.println(locales[i].getDisplayName());
        }
    }
}
```

Running this program on a Unix system and on a PC produced exactly the same result:

```
C:\> java exlocales
The locales on this system are:
German (Austria)
German (Switzerland)
English (Canada)
English (United Kingdom)
English (Ireland)
English (United States)
French (Belgium)
French (Canada)
French (Switzerland)
Italian (Switzerland)
Dutch (Belgium)
Norwegian (Nynorsk) (Norway,NY)
Chinese (ROC)
```

How Many Digits Are Output?

The Java Language Specification (section 20.10.15) says that when you output a double or float as a character string, by default it should print as many decimal places as are necessary to ensure that the number can be read back in without loss of precision:

> How many digits must be printed for the fractional part of m or a? There must be at least one digit to represent the fractional part, and beyond that as many, but only as many, more digits as are needed to uniquely distinguish the argument value from adjacent values of type double.

Go to http://www.javasoft.com/doc/language_specification/index.html to read this online.

Before JDK 1.1, the floating-point output routines output at most six decimal places. From JDK 1.1 on, you get floating-point output that ensures exactly that value can be read back in again, which sometimes leads to what looks like an excessive number of decimal places being printed. When you use a NumberFormat class, you get neater output, but you lose the ability to read the number back in with the same exact value it had when output.

Writing Binary Data to a File

Finally, what if you want to write binary data to a file? Binary data cannot be read directly by people, but it is faster for computers to read in, and the values are of a fixed length. Table 21-5 showed that binary data written with `DataOutputStream`. `DataOutputStream` has these public methods, along with others:

```
public java.io.DataOutputStream(java.io.OutputStream);
public synchronized void write(int);
public synchronized void write(byte[], int, int);
public void flush();
public final void writeBoolean(boolean);
public final void writeByte(int);
public final void writeShort(int);
public final void writeChar(int);
public final void writeInt(int);
public final void writeLong(long);
public final void writeFloat(float);
public final void writeDouble(double);
public final void writeBytes(java.lang.String);
public final void writeChars(java.lang.String);
public final void writeUTF(java.lang.String);
public final int size();
```

Each method writes a binary representation of the value of the stated type or throws an `IOException`. `DataOutputStream` is guaranteed to be able to read anything that `DataInputStream` wrote because they both use network byte order (big endian format). `DataOutputStream` might not be able to read data that you have written using a program in a different language or on a system with a different byte order. The Intel x86 architecture uses the reverse order to standard network byte order. So, to read binary integers written by a C program on an Intel machine, read byte by byte and manually assemble into integers, using bit shifting.

`DataOutputStream` would really have been better named BinaryOutputStream as that more accurately says what it does. Here is an example of writing ints to a file, using a `DataOutputStream`. As before, we just construct a `FileOutputStream` with the path name of your file (passed in as an argument to the program in the example that follows). Then, construct a `DataOutputStream` from the `FileOutputStream`.

The code looks like this:

```
import java.io.*;

public class exwritedata {
    public static void main(String f[]) {
        FileOutputStream fos;
        DataOutputStream ds;
        try {
            fos = new FileOutputStream(f[0]);
            ds = new DataOutputStream( fos );

            int a[] = {0,1,2,3,4,5,6,7,8,9};

            for (int i=0; i<a.length; i++) {
                ds.writeInt(a[i]);
            }

        } catch (IOException ioe) {
                System.out.println( "IO error: " + ioe );
        }

    }

}
```

If you run this program, you will find that the data file it creates can be read perfectly by the exreaddata program given earlier in the chapter. Running this program, followed by the read program looks like this:

```
% java exwritedata myfile.dat

% java exreaddata myfile.dat
file: myfile.dat
read: 0
read: 1
read: 2
read: 3
read: 4
read: 5
read: 6
read: 7
read: 8
read: 9
EOF reached
```

Random Access File and Appending

The class RandomAccessFile allows the file pointer to be moved to arbitrary positions in the file prior to reading or writing. This allows you to "jump around" in the file, reading and writing data with random (nonsequential) access. You provide a mode string when you open the file, specifying whether you are opening it for read access only r, or read and update access rw.

Here is an example of how you would append to a file, using the class RandomAccessFile. Create a file called animals.txt with the names of a few animals in it. We will write a few more animals on the end of the animals.txt file, using RandomAccessFile.

```java
import java.io.RandomAccessFile;
class exraf {

    static public void main(String a[]) {
        RandomAccessFile rf;
        try  {
                rf = new RandomAccessFile("animals.txt", "rw");

                rf.seek( rf.length() );

                rf.writeBytes("ant bee\ncat dog\n");

                rf.close();

        } catch (Exception e) {
            System.out.println("file snafu");
            System.exit(0);
        }
    }
}
```

This example will extend the animals.txt file by appending the string on the end.

Note that you cannot jump to a specific line number in the file. RandomAccessFile only keeps track of the number of bytes in the file, not the interpretation of those bytes as line endings. Also note that the class Reader has mark() and reset() methods, allowing you to jump back to a file position you have already visited once. RandomAccessFile allows you to jump to an offset in the file without having previously passed it.

JDK 1.1 introduced a new constructor for `FileOutputStream` that lets you open a file in append mode, like this:

```
FileOutputStream fos = new FileOutputStream ("animals.txt, true);
```

There is a similar constructor in `FileWriter`:

```
public FileWriter(String fileName, boolean append)
        throws IOException;
```

Platform-Specific I/O

Since file I/O results in something that has an existence outside a program, we should (alas) expect some visible differences between the different platforms. There are several such differences, as listed in Table 21-8.

Table 21-8: Platform Differences Relating to I/O

Property	Usual Value		
	Unix	Windows	Macintosh
`file.separator`	/	\	:
`line.separator`	\n	\r\n	\r
`path.separator`	:	;	:

The file separator is the character used to separate components in a path name (e.g., in `c:\windows\bin\foo.exe` the character "\" is the file separator). Remember "\" is also the escape character, so you must double it up when you use it in strings, e.g., "c:\\windows\\bin\\foo.exe". The path separator is an OS concept, used when you want to specify several path names as starting points for searching for a command or library. Path separators are used when you set, for example, CLASSPATH. The file and path separators are also available as static literals in the File class.

On Unix, a newline is just a linefeed character. On Windows, a newline is usually represented by two characters, carriage return followed by linefeed. On the Mac, a newline is represented by a carriage return. The standard I/O streams are capable of coping with any of these manifestations.

On the other hand, you can use "/" to separate the components in a file name in Windows, just as in Unix. The Windows file system calls all use it internally anyway, and only COMMAND.COM (the shell) can't handle it. This is an interesting artifact of history, dating from the origins of DOS as a ripped-off port (known as QDOS) of CP/M with a few trivial changes.

Reading/Writing Objects

It is perfectly possible to input and output entire objects. If an object can be written to a stream, it can also be sent through a socket, backed up onto a file, and later read back in again and reconstituted.

To make an object serializable, all you need do is make its class implement the Serializable or Externalizable interface. If you are happy with the default methods for writing its fields out, implement `java.io.Serializable`. If you want your own `writeExternal()` method to participate in writing the object out, then implement `java.io.Externalizable`. There is a corresponding `readExternal`, too.

Making an object serializable only requires implementing an interface. It is not turned on by default because there are certain classes that should not be serialized for security reasons. It is more secure to allow serialization by explicitly saying so than to allow it by default. Reading and writing objects is thankfully very simple. It is extensively used in Remote Method Invocation, and the chapter describing RMI walks through a practical example.

Distributing Software: Software Travels Best in Jars

When you write Java software, it runs on all systems. But if you are giving away interesting source code (as many of us do who want to encourage the growth of Java), you need to find a format for distributing your application that can be understood and unpacked on all systems.

In the past people giving away source code have usually had to package it in two formats: a tar file or gzipped tar file for Unix, and a zip file or self-extracting exe file for Windows.

Now, with Java, you can just package everything up in a jar file, like this:

```
jar -cvf myJarFile.jar  myDirectory
```

The standard Java jar utility can extract it, whatever system you are running on, like this:

```
jar -xvf myJarFile.jar
```

Saving objects (including GUIs and data structures) to files is so easy, you just do it:

```
Vector myVector = new Vector ();
  // ...
ObjectOutputStream out =
    new ObjectOutputStream (new FileOutputStream("myVector.dat"));
out.writeObject (myVector);
out.close ();
```

More Examples of Layering Streams

A significant Java idiom is the use of streams to connect one stream to another. The result is also a stream that can be further connected. Each Stream in a chain has the chance to modify the data as it goes by, and it can also offer a selection of more sophisticated methods to operate on the stream.

Really Important: Streams can be "pushed" or layered on top of each other to provide filtered processing.

Let's show how this works in practice. Suppose that I have two or three data files, each containing the names of some animals. I want to read each of the files one after the other and do the same processing on each, let us say, print out the contents. And I also want to read the files buffered, meaning that I want the run-time system to read great chunks of the file at a time and dole out individual characters to me as I ask for them. Buffered I/O often provides a big performance speed-up because one large read from a (slow) disk is faster than many small reads.

The best way to write the specified program is as follows:

- Create a `FileInputStream` for each input file.

- Group all the `FileInputStreams` together as a single `SequenceInputStream`. This class makes two streams look like one long concatenated stream.

- Convert the stream to a reader by using InputStreamReader.

- Layer a BufferedReader on the InputStreamReader.

- Read from the BufferedReader.

The code is remarkably compact and looks like this:

```
import java.io.*;
public class exlayer {

    public static void main(String args[]) {
        try {
            FileInputStream fr1 = new FileInputStream( "mammals.txt"
);

            FileInputStream fr2 = new FileInputStream( "reptiles.txt"
);

            SequenceInputStream sis = new SequenceInputStream( fr1,
fr2 );
            InputStreamReader isr = new InputStreamReader(sis);
            BufferedReader br = new BufferedReader( isr );

            int i=0;
            while( (i=br.read() )!= -1 ) {
                System.out.print( (char) i);
            }
        } catch(FileNotFoundException fnf){System.out.println(fnf); }
            catch(IOException ioe) {ioe.printStackTrace(); }
    }
}
```

This little program does a lot of layered processing, using the built-in classes. If you had to program all this functionality from scratch (stream aggregation and so on), it would take hundreds of lines. I wrote and tested this program in about fifteen minutes, and so can you after you become familiar with the classes in `java.io`.

There is another class that is sometimes layered on top of others. The class LineNumberReader counts the lines as you read from the stream and, at any time, can tell you how many lines it has seen. Programmers can also implement their own classes that extend `Reader` or `Writer` to filter the characters as they flow through the stream.

Piped I/O for Threads

A pipe forms a shared buffer between two threads. One thread writes into the pipe, and the other reads from it. This forms a producer/consumer buffer, ready-programmed for you. There are two stream classes that we always use together in a matched consumer/producer pair:

- PipedInputStream   Gets bytes from a pipe (think "hosepipe"; it's just a data structure that squirts bytes at you).

- PipedOutputStream   Puts bytes into a pipe (think "drainpipe"; it's just a data structure that drinks down bytes that you pour into it).

An object of one of these classes is connected to an object of the other class, providing a safe way (without data race conditions) for one thread to send a stream of data to another thread.

As an example of the use of piped streams, the program below reimplements the Producer/Consumer problem, but uses piped streams instead of wait/notify. If you compare, you'll see that this is considerably simpler. There is no explicit shared buffer—the pipe stream between the two threads carries out that job.

The next example shows one thread sending longs to another. You can also send Strings, using the classes PipedWriter and PipedReader.

```
import java.io.*;
public class expipes {

  public static void main(String args[]) {
      Producer p = new Producer();
      p.start();

      Consumer c = new Consumer(p);
      c.start();
  }
}




///// This class writes into the pipe until it is full, at which
///// point it is blocked until the consumer takes something out.

class Producer extends Thread {
      protected PipedOutputStream po = new PipedOutputStream();
      private DataOutputStream dos = new DataOutputStream(po);

      public void run() {
          // just keep producing numbers that represent the
          // amount of millisecs program has been running.
          for(;;) produce();
      }

      private final long start = System.currentTimeMillis();
      private final long banana() {
          return (System.currentTimeMillis() - start);
      }

      void produce() {
          long t = banana();
          System.out.println("produced " + t);
          try {dos.writeLong( t );}
          catch (IOException ie) { System.out.println(ie); }
      }

}
```

```
///// This class consumes everything sent over the pipe.
///// The pipe does the synchronization.  When the pipe is full,
///// this thread's read from the pipe is blocked.

class Consumer extends Thread {
   private PipedInputStream pip;
   private DataInputStream d;

   // java constructor idiom, save argument.
   Consumer(Producer who) {
      try {
           pip = new PipedInputStream(who.po);
           d = new DataInputStream( pip );
      } catch (IOException ie) {
          System.out.println(ie);
      }
   }

    long get(){
       long i=0;
       try {   i= d.readLong();   // read from pipe.
       } catch (IOException ie) {System.out.println(ie);}
       return i;
    }

   public void run() {
      java.util.Random r = new java.util.Random();
      for(;;) {
          long result = get();
          System.out.println("consumed: "+result);
          // next lines are just to make things asynchronous
          int randomtime = r.nextInt() % 1250;
          try{sleep(randomtime);} catch(Exception e){}
      }
   }
}
```

The output of this program is a list of numbers that represent the number of milliseconds the program has been running. The numbers are passed in a buffer in a thread-safe way from the producer thread to the consumer thread. The piped streams allow for real simplification in interthread communication.

A Word About IOExceptions

Let's say a few words on the subject of IOExceptions. If you look at the runtime source, you'll see that there are sixteen I/O-related exceptions. The basic I/O related exceptions are:

- CharConversionException

- StreamCorruptedException

- WriteAbortedException

- FileNotFoundException

- InterruptedIOException

- UTFDataFormatError

- EOFException

These names are self-explanatory, except for the last one. The name EOFException suggests that it is thrown whenever EOF (end of file) is encountered, and that therefore this exception might be used as the condition to break out of a loop.

That's *not* what happens, and no, it can't always be used that way. The EOFException would be better named UnexpectedEOFException, as it is only raised when the programmer has asked for a fixed definite amount of input, and the end of file is reached before all the requested amount of data has been obtained. EOFException is raised in only three classes: DataInputStream, ObjectInputStream, and RandomAccessFile, (and their subclasses, of course). It is never raised when the normal end of file is reached.

Other than in the classes mentioned, the usual way to detect EOF is to check for the –1 return value from a byte read, not try to catch EOFexception.

How to Execute a Program from Java

This section explains how to execute a program from Java and read the output of that program back into your application. Just as a reminder, untrusted applets cannot do this.

Executing a program from your Java program has four general steps.

1. Get the object representing the current runtime environment. A call in class java.lang.Runtime does this.

2. Call the exec method in the runtime object with your command as an argument. This call creates a Process object. Give the full path name to the executable, and make sure the executable really exists on the system.

3. Connect the output of the Process (which will be coming to you as an input stream) to an input stream reader in your program.

4. You can either read individual characters from the input stream or layer a BufferedReader on it and read a line at a time, as in the code below.

```java
import java.io.*;
    public class exwho {

        public static void main(String argo[]) {
          try {
              Runtime rt = Runtime.getRuntime();         // step 1

              Process prcs = rt.exec("/bin/who");        // step 2

              InputStreamReader isr =                    // step 3
                 new InputStreamReader( prcs.getInputStream() );

              BufferedReader br = new BufferedReader(  // step 4.
                                        isr );
              String line;
              while  ((line = br.readLine()) != null)
                  System.out.println(line);
          } catch(IOException ioe) { System.out.println(ioe); }
        }

    }
```

This code program uses a class inside System called Runtime which does a couple of runtime-related things. The main use is to provide a way to execute other programs, but it can also force garbage collection or finalization and tell you how much total memory and free memory is available. It also uses the class Process that allows you to get in, out, err streams, and to destroy, or to wait for a process.

Several books use the example of listing files in a directory, but there is already a Java method to do that in class File. The following code will return an array of Strings, one string for each file name in the directory.

```
File f = new File(".");
String lst[] = f.list();
```

The file with the magic name of "." is used on many operating systems to refer to the current working directory.

The program /bin/who is a Unix program that lists the users on a system. Compiling and running the program above gives this output:

```
% javac exwho.java
% java exwho
pvdl       console      Aug 17 12:29
pvdl       pts/1        Aug 17 12:30
pvdl       pts/2        Aug 17 12:30
pvdl       pts/3        Aug 17 12:30
```

Here, it shows that I logged on to my workstation in four different windows at the stated times.

Watch out for these common errors when executing a program from your Java code:

- Remember that an untrusted applet does not have permission to run executables.

- You must provide the complete path name for the command. The exec method does not use a shell, so does not have the ability to look for executables in the search path that your shell (or command interpreter) knows about.

- Note that this also means you cannot use commands that are built into a shell unless you explicitly call a shell as the program you wish to run (see upcoming tip).

- Remember to instantiate an input stream to read the output from running the command. You will only be able to communicate with programs that use standard in, out, and err. Some programs like xterm open a new tty, so can't be used as you would wish.

How to Execute an MS-DOS Batch File from a Java Application

As previously mentioned, the Java exec method does not use a shell, so you can't directly use it to execute shell-supported features. In MS-DOS, the DIR and DEL commands are not programs, but are internal commands which are processed by the command interpreter (COMMAND.COM).

To execute one of these internal commands or to run a batch file (another feature of the shell), you make the shell itself be the command you execute, and you give the appropriate parameters to it. To run the batch file c:\foo\mybatch.bat, you would change step 2 in the code above to say:

```
Process prcs = rt.exec("command.com /c c:\\foo\\mybatch.bat");
```

The name command.com is the shell under Windows 95.

ZIP Files and Streams

ZIP is a multifile archive format popularized by the PC but available on almost all systems now. The ZIP format offers two principal benefits: it can bundle several files into one file, and it can compress the data as it writes it to the ZIP archive. It's more convenient to pass around one file than twenty separate files. Compressed files are faster and cheaper to download or e-mail than their uncompressed versions. Java Archives (.jar) files are in ZIP format.

JDK 1.1 introduced several new utilities in the package java.util. It collected some classes that can read and write ZIP and gzip archives. gzip, an alternative to ZIP, uses a different format for the data, and can only hold one file (not a series of them). To conserve programmer sanity, most people writing compression and archiving utilities make sure that their software can deal with both .zip files and .gz files. ZIP traditionally uses the file extension .zip, and gzip uses .gz for its files. The gzip program was written by the GNU folks, and it compresses its input by using the patent-free Lempel-Ziv coding.

JDK 1.1 included both utilities because ZIP is something of a standard on PCs, while gzip (and the OS commands gzip, gunzip) is found most often on Unix systems. Go to http://www.sdsu.edu/doc/texi/gzip_toc.html for more information about gzip.

You should be comfortable with the idea of connecting streams to each other now, and it's no surprise that the ZIP utilities just work this way. Here is a program that creates a .zip file of its own source (you could easily change it to pass the file name in as an argument).

```java
import java.io.*;
import java.util.zip.*;
public class exzip {

    public static void main(String args[]) {
      try {
          FileInputStream fis = new FileInputStream("exzip.java");

          FileOutputStream fos = new
              FileOutputStream("output.zip");
          ZipOutputStream z = new ZipOutputStream(fos);

          z.putNextEntry( new ZipEntry("myfile.java") );
          int i;
          while  ((i = fis.read()) != -1)
              z.write((byte)i);

          z.close();

      } catch(IOException ioe) { System.out.println(ioe); }
    }

}
```

The following line tells the ZIP archive what name to give this file when it is extracted.

```java
    z.putNextEntry( new ZipEntry("myfile.java") );
```

We are putting only one file in the archive in this example.   We use a different name (myfile.zip) than the name of the original source file because we want to have both of them together for this example, so we can compare them.

Compiling and running this program gives:

```
% javac exzip.java

% java exzip

% ls -l *.zip
-rw-rw-r--   1 linden    staff          415 May  6 12:09 output.zip

% ls -l exzip.java
-rw-rw-r--   1 linden    staff          557 May  6 12:06 exzip.java

% unzip output.zip
  Inflating: myfile.java

% diff myfile.java exzip.java
  (no differences found)
```

The `ls` command lists the files in a directory in Unix. The `diff` command compares two files for any differences. You don't need to write ZIP streams to a file. You can equally send them through a socket, put them in a String or byte array for later retrieval, or send them through a pipe to another thread.

The class `ZipOutputStream` has these methods:

```
    public java.util.zip.ZipOutputStream(java.io.OutputStream);

    public void setComment(java.lang.String);
    public void setMethod(int);
    public void setLevel(int);

    public void putNextEntry(java.util.zip.ZipEntry);
    public void closeEntry();
    public synchronized void write(byte[], int, int);
    public void finish();
    public void close();
```

The method `setLevel()` sets the compression level, 0–9. A higher level of compression takes longer to zip and unzip but potentially yields more space saving. Some kinds of data, such as human-readable characters, compress better than others. The default compression level is set to eight.

Some Light Relief

Crossing the Chasm

If you've read my book, *Expert C Programming*, you'll have seen the appendix that describes how to conduct yourself in a Silicon Valley programmer job interview (don't critique the interviewer with your imaginary friend while you are actually interviewing, etc.). I also described some of the puzzles that are used in job interviews. Some companies interview programmers by posing a few logic puzzles to them and seeing how they handle it. Microsoft is famous for interviewing programmers this way. It's great if you can solve the puzzle, but even if you can't, you're supposed to make intelligent remarks and look as though you care.

Here is a puzzle that Microsoft has been using in recent job interviews. There are four men who want to cross a bridge at night, by the light of a flashlight that one of them has. They all begin on the same side, and the bridge can only hold two of them at once. They all walk at different speeds and take different amounts of time to cross the bridge, namely, 1, 2, 5, and 10 minutes. Whenever two are on the bridge together they walk at the pace of the slower person. Any party who crosses the bridge must carry the flashlight, and the flashlight must be walked back to the other side to bring over any remaining people. The flashlight cannot be thrown, sent by Federal Express, etc.

For example, if the 1 minute man and the 10 minute man walk across first, 10 minutes have elapsed when they get to the far side of the bridge. If the 1 minute man then crosses back with the flashlight, a total of 11 minutes has passed and there are still three people on the wrong side of the bridge. Describe how everyone can get across in 17 minutes.

Before reading on, take a little while to try this problem. Stop reading now. Don't read any further. Hey! I said stop. What, can't you read? OK, you asked for it. The "obvious" solution is to have the fastest people travel with the slowest, so men 10 and 1 go over (10 minutes), 1 returns (total 11 minutes), 2 and 5 go over (16 minutes), 2 returns (18 minutes, and you've blown the mission), 2 and 1 go over for a total of 20 minutes.

How can it be done in less time? The answer is that this is one of those puzzles where your intuition is just plain wrong! You need to drop the preconceived idea about what works best and explore other alternatives. The insight to move you to the correct answer is to view the problem from the point of view of your slowest walkers instead of your fastest. If you make your two slowest walkers go over together, they will only take 10 minutes, instead of the 15 minutes taken if they go separately. But if they go over together, you need to have someone quick on the other side ready to bring the light back. Hence, 1 and 2 should go first. So, one answer is men 1 and 2 go over (2 minutes), 1 returns (3 minutes), men 10 and 5 go over (13 minutes), men 2 returns (15 minutes), men 1 and 2 go over (17 minutes).

Well, it's just a puzzle, but as I mentioned, Microsoft has been using it lately in their interviews. I was reminded of this when I called the Microsoft telephone support line. The support line was my last resort. My problem was that when I upgraded from Windows 3.1 to Windows 95, some pieces of networking stopped working. The problem had nothing to do with Java, except that it meant many Java applets would not run.

At first I could see only the symptoms, and I did not know what the problem was. I worked hard to gather more information about the problem and was soon able to conclude that my Netscape browser could not resolve domain names. Domain Name Service (DNS) is the Internet protocol for mapping between computer names (like ds.internic.net) and computer IP addresses (like 198.49.45.10). When a domain name needs to be resolved (translated into the other form), a DNS server (anyone's DNS server) first goes to the central Network Information Center (NIC) to ask where to go to resolve the domain name. The NIC itself cannot resolve domains, but it tells DNS server where to go to get that service for that name. The DNS server then goes to the specified remote site to resolve the domain name, which typically belongs to the site that owns the domain name in question. The remote site replies with the answer, which the local DNS server caches for future reference, and returns to the original requester.

But DNS names weren't being resolved for me. To cut a long story short, I invested many hours over a period of months to solve this problem. It seemed that DNS worked for everyone else at my Internet Service Provider. I followed cookbooks, I reconfigured the software, I reinstalled Windows 95 several times. Nothing solved the problem, but it worked for everyone else at the ISP. Eventually, I made an appointment with the top troubleshooter at the ISP and physically took my system into their premises, where we hooked it up to a phone line, dialed in, and brought up Netscape. The problem was right there still. I could access a site via its IP address but not by name.

The top troubleshooter quickly went to work and was quickly able to demonstrate that the problem was nothing to do with Netscape or my configuration. The Windows 95 FTP command failed the same way. Under his eye, I reinstalled Windows 95 from scratch, and DNS resolution still failed. Aha! This was a Windows 95 bug!

Later that day, at home, I browsed the Microsoft web site looking for a patch to fix the problem. There were many patches, but none seemed to address the problem I was seeing. After months of troubleshooting, it looked like I had to call the Microsoft support line. I carefully set up everything I would need: two phone lines (one for the support line, one for the PC to my ISP), manuals, invoices, notes of things I had tried, notes of configurations and versions, and so on.

As everyone in the computer industry knows, 90 percent of all calls to support lines are made by novices and can be solved by checking the basics like "Is your computer plugged in?" and "Did you remove the old floppy disk from the drive before inserting the new one?" Front-line support staff usually deal with trivial problems, so I made sure I was ready with a clear, full description of the bug. The conversation went like this:

me: Hi, I'm having a network software problem with Windows 95.

Microsoft support guy (brightly): OK! Did you know that your system has to be powered on before it will work?

me: Yes, the system is on and running.
The problem relates to Windows 95 networking, and...

Microsoft support guy: (cutting in) We recommend you contact your ISP to fix any networking problems at their end.

me: Yes. I have already taken the system in to the ISP's office, and we have eliminated any problems in their configuration or mine. I have reinstalled Windows 95 multiple times, including immediately before this call.

The problem has been traced to the Windows 95 networking library not successfully using DNS to resolve symbolic domain names into their equivalent numeric IP addresses. We know this because even the basic Window TCP commands like ping and FTP fail.

I want to know if failure to do DNS resolution to resolve fully-qualified domain names into network IP addresses is a known bug, and if there's a Windows 95 patch for it.

Microsoft support guy (goes very quiet for several seconds, then asks in a small voice): ...could you hold the line for few minutes? I'm going to get some help.

A few minutes pass while I hold the line. Then the Microsoft support guy comes back.

Microsoft support guy   (still in a small voice): Um. I'm still waiting to hear from the network group. In the meantime, have you heard this one? There are four fellows with a flashlight who want to cross a bridge,...

me: Send the two fastest guys over together, bring back the light, and send the two slowest over together. Call me when you get an answer.

I never did hear back from them. I found a workaround and have been living with it ever since. Giving and getting telephone support for computer software is tough!

List of I/O Classes

There are now 75 classes in the `java.io` package. Here is a list of some of the classes, grouped into categories by function.

Input Streams (for 8-Bit Input)
BufferedInputStream
ByteArrayInputStream
DataInputStream
FileInputStream
FilterInputStream
InputStream
InputStreamReader
LineNumberInputStream
ObjectInputStream
PipedInputStream
PushbackInputStream
SequenceInputStream
StringBufferInputStream

Readers (for 16-Bit Character Input)
BufferedReader
CharArrayReader
FileReader
FilterReader
InputStreamReader
LineNumberReader
PipedReader
PushbackReader
Reader
StringReader

Output Streams (8-Bit Output)

OutputStream
DataOutputStream
FileOutputStream
PipedOutputStream
ObjectOutputStream
FilterOutputStream
BufferedOutputStream
ByteArrayOutputStresm
OutputStreamWriter

Writers (for 16-Bit Character Output)

BufferedWriter
CharArrayWriter
FileWriter
FilterWriter
OutputStreamWriter
PipedWriter
PrinterWriter
StringWriter
Writer

Table 21-9: Reading from Various Sources

READ from	As a Stream (8-Bit)	As a Reader (16-Bit)

a socket	`s = new Socket("somehost", port);`
	`InputStream is = s.getInputStream();`
	May need to specify a proxy server on command-line
		Same as column to left, plus
		`new InputStreamReader(is);`

a URL	`URL url = new URL`
	`("http://www.x.com:/y.html");`
	`URLConnection urlc = url.openConnection();`
	`urlc.setDoInput(true);`
	`is = urlc.getInputStream();`
	May need to specify a proxy server on command-line
		same as column to left, plus
		`new InputStreamReader(is);`

a Char file	`FileInputStream fis = new`
	`FileInputStream("f.txt");`
	`DataInputStream dis = new`
	`DataInputStream(fis);`
	(deprecated)
		`FileReader fr = new`
		`FileReader("f.txt");`
		`BufferedReader br =new`
		`BufferedReader(fr);`

a binary file	`FileInputStream fis = new`
	`FileInputStream("f.txt");`
	~~`DataInputStream dis = new`~~
	`DataInputStream(fis);`
		Same as column to left
		8-bit/16-bit distinction not applicable to ~~binary files~~

keyboard	*Device does not need to be opened*	`new` `InputStreamReader(System.in)`

an Object	`FileInputStream fis = new`
	`FileInputStream("f.txt");`
	`ObjectInputStream ois = new`
	`ObjectInputStream(fis);`
		Same as column to left
		8-bit/16-bit distinction not applicable to object files

a String	*Not applicable*	`String s = "data to read ";`
		`StringReader sr = new`
		`StringReader(s);`

a Char array	*Not applicable*	`char[] ca = new char[100];`
		`// ... code to fill ca with data`
		`CharArrayReader car = new`
		`CharArrayReader(ca);`

Note: Wrapping a BufferedReader around a Reader makes reading more efficient, and also provides you with the readLine() method.

Table 21-10: Writing to Various Sources

WRITE to	As a Stream (8-Bit)	As a Writer (16-Bit)

a socket	`s = new Socket("somehost", port);`
	`OutputStream os = s.getOutputStream();`
	May need to specify a proxy server on commandline
		Same as column to left, plus
		`new OutputStreamWriter(os);`

a URL	*A server accessed by URL usually won't have write access permission. Use sockets, RMI or servlets*	*Same as column to left*

a Char file	`FileOutputStream fos = new`
	`FileOutputStream("f.txt");`
	`DataOutputStream dos = new`
	`DataOutputStream(fos);`
	(deprecated)
		`FileWriter fw = new`
		`FileWriter("f.txt");`

a binary file	`FileOutputStream fos = new`
	`FileOutputStream("f.txt");`
	`DataOutputStream dos = new`
	`DataOutputStream(fos);`
		Same as column to left
		8-bit/16-bit distinction not applicable to binary files

keyboard	*Device does not need to be opened*	`OutputStreamWriter osw = new`
		`OutputStreamWriter(System.out);`
		`PrintWriter ps = new`
		`PrintWriter(osw);`

an Object	`FileOutputStream fos = new`
	`FileOutputStream("f.txt");`
	`ObjectOutputStream oos = new`
	`ObjectOutputStream(fos);`
		8-bit/16-bit distinction not applicable to object files

a String	*Not applicable*	`StringWriter sw = new` `StringWriter();`
a Char array	*Not applicable*	`CharArrayWriter caw = new` `CharArrayWriter();`

Answer To Programming Challenge

Here is a Java program that creates a subdirectory, and a file in it.

```java
// create a subdirectory Fruit
// then create a file called yam in that directory
import java.io.*;
class files {
    public static final PrintStream o = System.out;

    public static void main(String a[]) throws IOException {
        File d = new File("Fruit");
        checkDirectory(d);
        checkFile("Fruit/yam");
    }

    static void checkFile(String s) {
        File f = new File(s);
        if (!f.exists() ) {
            o.println("File " + f.getName() + " doesn't exist");
            FileOutputStream fos;
            try { fos = new FileOutputStream(f);
                    fos.write(' ');
            } catch (IOException ioe) {
                    o.println("IO Exception!");
            }
        } else {
            o.println("File " + f.getName() + " already exists");
        }
    }

    static void checkDirectory(File d) throws IOException {
        boolean success;
        if (!d.exists() ) {
            o.println("Directory "
          + d.getName() + " doesn't exist");
            if (success=d.mkdir())
                o.println("Have created directory " + d.getName());
            else
                o.println("Failed to create directory "
          + d.getName());
        } else {
            o.println( d.getName() + " exists already");
            if (d.isDirectory()) {
                o.println( "and is a directory.");
            } else {
                o.println( "and is a file.");
                throw new IOException();
            }
        }
    }
}
```

Answer To Programming Challenge

This program uses a SequenceInputStream to jam two different sources of data seamlessly together. It pushes a LineNumberInputStream on top of that, to keep track of line numbers.

```java
// shows the use of various input streams
import java.io.*;
public class test7c {
    static String s=new String("aardvark butterfly\n" +
      "carp dalmatian\n" +
              "eagle fish\ngopher hippo\ninyala jackal\nkyloe " +
              "lamb\nmoose nanny-goat\nopossum pandora\n" );

    static StringBufferInputStream sbis=
     new StringBufferInputStream(s);

    public static void main (String a[])
     throws FileNotFoundException {
        int c;
        FileInputStream fis = new FileInputStream("animals.txt");

        SequenceInputStream sis =
            new SequenceInputStream( sbis, fis );

        LineNumberInputStream lsis =
     new LineNumberInputStream( sis );

        try {
            while ((c=lsis.read())!= -1) {

                System.out.print((char)c);
                if (c=='\n') {
                    System.out.print("that finishes input line "
                            + lsis.getLineNumber() + "\n\n");
                }

            }
        } catch (IOException ioe) {
            System.out.println("Exception reading stream");
            ioe.printStackTrace();
            System.exit(0);
        }
    }
}
```

CHAPTER
22

- All About TCP/IP

- Ping in Java

- Sending E-Mail by Java

- How to Make an Applet Write a File on the Server

- HTTP and Web Browsing: Retrieving HTTP Pages

- A Client/Server Socket Program

- A Multi-Threaded Client/Server System

- Page Counters in Web Pages

- Some Light Relief

Networking
in Java

"If a packet hits a pocket on a socket on a port,
and the bus is interrupted and the interrupt's not caught,
then the socket packet pocket has an error to report.

–Programmer's traditional nursery rhyme

T he biggest difficulty most people face in understanding the Java networking features lies more in understanding the network part than the
Java part. If you learn French, it doesn't mean that you can understand an article
from a French medical journal. Similarly if you learn Java, you need to have an
understanding of the network services and terminology before you can blithely
write Internet code. This chapter provides a solid review, followed by a description of the Java support.

Everything You Need To Know about TCP/IP But Failed to Learn in Kindergarten

Networking at heart is all about shifting bits from point A to point B. Usually we bundle the data bits into a packet with some more bits that say where they are to go. That, in a nutshell, is the Internet Protocol or IP. If we want to send more bits than will fit into a single packet, we can divide the bits into groups and send them in several successive packets. These are called "User Datagrams."

User Datagrams can be sent across the Internet using the User Datagram Protocol (UDP), which relies on the Internet Protocol for addressing and routing. UDP is like going to the post office, sticking on a stamp, and dropping off the packet. IP is what the mail carrier does to route and deliver the packet. Two common applications that use the UDP are: SNMP, the Simple Network Management Protocol, and TFTP, the Trivial File Transfer Protocol. See Figure 22-1.

Just as when we send several pieces of postal mail to the same address, the packages might arrive in any order. Some of them might even be delayed, or even on occasion lost altogether. This is true for UDP too; you wave good-bye to the bits as they leave your workstation, and you have no idea when they will arrive where you sent them, or even if they did.

Uncertain delivery is equally undesirable for postal mail and for network bit streams. We deal with the problem in the postal mail world (when the importance warrants the cost) by paying an extra fee to register the mail and have the mail carrier collect and bring back a signature acknowledging delivery. A similar protocol is used in the network work to guarantee reliable delivery in the order in which the packets were sent. This protocol is known as Transmission Control Protocol or "TCP." Two applications that run on top of, or use, TCP are: FTP, the File Transfer Protocol, and Telnet.

TCP uses IP as its underlying protocol (just as UDP does) for routing and delivering the bits to the correct address. However, TCP is more like a phone call than a registered mail delivery, in that a real end-to-end connection is held open for the duration of the transmission session. It takes a while to set up this stream connection, and it costs more to assure reliable sequenced delivery, but often the cost is justified. See Figure 22-2.

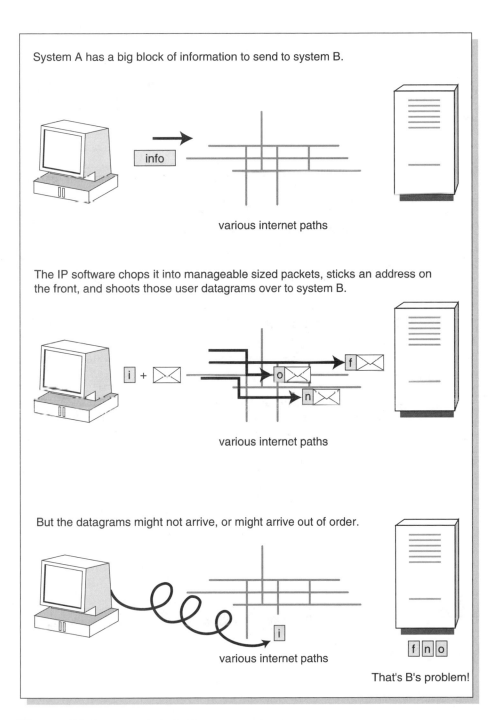

Figure 22-1: IP and UDP (datagram sockets).

The access device at each end-point of a phone conversation is a telephone. The access object at each end-point of a TCP/IP session is a socket. Sockets started life as a way for two processes on the same Unix system to talk to each other, but some smart programmers realized that they could be generalized into connection end-points between processes on different machines connected by a TCP/IP network.

IP can deliver the following via socket connections:

- Fast bits wrapped up in packets using UDP (this is a *datagram socket*)

- Slower, fussier, and reliably using TCP (this is termed a *stream socket*)

- Fast raw bits using ICMP (Internet Control Message Protocol) datagrams.

ICMP is a more of an administrative protocol than UDP or TCP. Java doesn't need or support it and we won't say anything more about it.

Socket connections have a client end and a server end. Generally the server end just keeps listening for incoming requests (an "operators are standing by" kind of thing). The client end initiates a connection, and then passes or requests information from the server.

Note that the number of socket writes is not at all synchronized with the number or timing of socket reads. A packet may be broken into smaller packets as it is sent across the network, so your code should never assume that a read will get the same number of bytes that were just written into the socket.

There! Now you know everything you need to use the Java networking features.

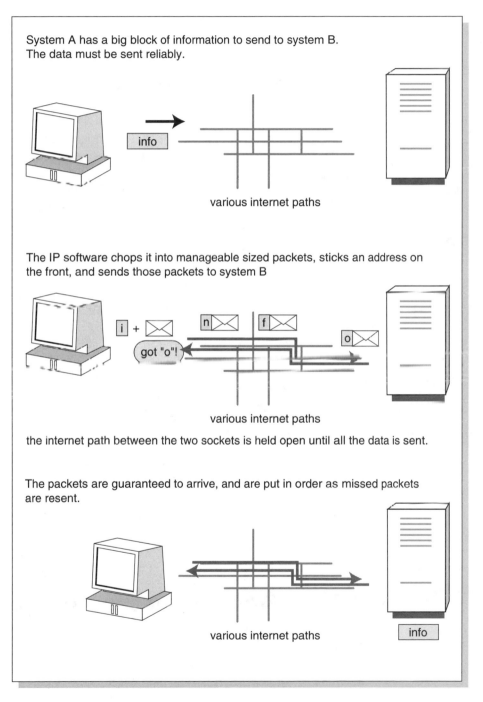

System A has a big block of information to send to system B.
The data must be sent reliably.

info

various internet paths

The IP software chops it into manageable sized packets, sticks an address on
the front, and sends those packets to system B

i + ⊠   n⊠   f⊠   o⊠

got "o"!

various internet paths

the internet path between the two sockets is held open until all the data is sent.

The packets are guaranteed to arrive, and are put in order as missed packets
are resent.

various internet paths

info

Figure 22-2:   TCP/IP (stream sockets).

What's in the Networking Library?

If you browse the network library source in $JAVAHOME/src/java/net, you'll find the following classes (there are a few other classes, but these are the key ones):

- InetAddress   The class that represents IP addresses and the operations on them. The class should have been called IP or IPAddress, but was not (presumably because such a name does not match the coding conventions for classnames).

- URL   The class represents a Uniform Resource Locator—a reference to an object on the web. You can create a URL reference with this class

- URLConnection   You can open a URL and retrieve the contents, or write to it, using this class

- HttpURLConnection   The class extends URLConnection and supports functions specific to HTTP, like get, post, put, head, trace, and options.

- URLEncoder/URLDecoder   These two classes have static methods to allow you to convert a String to and from MIME x-www-form-urlencoded form. This is convenient for posting data to CGI scripts.

- Socket   This is the client Socket class, and it uses a SocketImpl class to implement the actual socket operations. This permits you to change socket implementations depending on the kind of firewall that is used.

- ServerSocket   This is the server Socket class. It uses a SocketImpl to implement the actual socket operations. It is done this way so that you can change socket implementations depending on the kind of firewall that is used.

TCP/IP Client/Server Model

Before we look at actual Java code, a diagram is in order showing how a client and server typically communicate over a TCP/IP network connection. Figure 22-3 shows the way the processes contact each other is by knowing the IP address (which identifies a unique computer on the Internet) and a port number (which is a simple software convention the OS maintains, allowing an incoming network connection to be routed to a specific process).

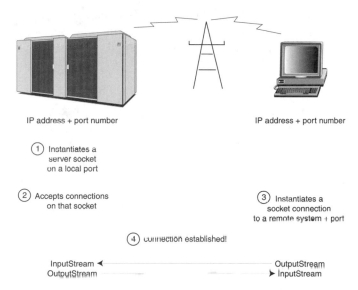

Figure 22-3: Client and server communication using a TCP/IP connection.

An IP address is like a telephone number, and a port number is like an extension at that number. Together they specify a unique destination. As a matter of fact, a socket is *defined* as an IP address and a port number.

The client and server must agree on the same port number. The port numbers under 1024 are reserved for system software use, and on Unix can only be accessed by the superuser. For simplicity, network socket connections are made to look like I/O streams. You simply read and write data using the usual stream methods, and it automagically appears at the other end. Unlike a stream, a socket supports two-way communication. There is a method to get the input stream of a socket, and another method to get the output stream. This allows the client and server to talk back and forth. Be warned: If you close either direction of a socket connection, both directions will be taken down.

Many Internet programs work as client/server pairs. The server is on a host system somewhere in cyberspace, and the client is a program running on your local system. When the client wants an Internet service (such as retrieving a web page from an HTTP server), it issues a request, usually to a symbolic address such as www.sun.com rather than to an IP address (though that works, too).

There will be a Domain Name Server locally (usually one per subnet, per campus, or per company) that resolves the symbolic name into an Internet address.

The bits forming the request are assembled into a *datagram*, and routed to the server. The server reads the incoming packets, notes what the request is, where it came from, and then tries to respond to it by providing either the service (web page, shell account, file contents, etc.) or a sensible error message. The response is sent back across the Internet to the client.

Almost all the standard Internet utilities (telnet, rdist, FTP, ping, rcp, and so on) operate in client/server mode connected by a TCP socket or by UDP. Programs that send mail don't really know how to send mail—they just know how to take it to the Post Office. In this case, mail has a socket connection, and talks to a daemon at the other end with a fairly simple protocol. The standard mail *daemon* knows how to accept text and addresses from clients and transmit it for delivery. If you can talk to the mail daemon, you can send mail. There is little else to it.

Many of the Internet services are actually quite simple. But often considerable frustration comes in doing the socket programming in C and in learning the correct protocol. The socket programming API presented to C is quite low-level, and all too easy to screw up. Needless to say, errors are poorly handled and diagnosed. As a result many programmers naturally conclude that sockets are brittle and error-prone.

The C code to establish a socket connection is:

```
int set_up_socket(u_short port) {
    char    myname[MAXHOSTNAME+1];
    int     s;
    struct  sockaddr_in sa;
    struct hostent *he;

    bzero(&sa,sizeof(struct sockaddr_in));    /* clear the address */
    gethostname(myname,MAXHOSTNAME);          /* establish identity */
    he= gethostbyname(myname);                /* get our address   */
    if (he == NULL)                           /* if addr not found... */
        return(-1);
    sa.sin_family= he->h_addrtype;            /* host address */
    sa.sin_port= htons(port);                 /* port number */

if ((s= socket(AF_INET,SOCK_STREAM,0)) <0)    /* finally, create socket */
        return(-1);
    if (bind(s, &sa, sizeof(sa), 0) < 0) {
        close(s);
        return(-1);                           /* bind address to socket */
    }

    listen(s, 3);                             /* max queued connections */
    return(s);
}
```

Horrid C Sockets

By way of contrast, the Java code is:

```
ServerSocket servSock = new ServerSocket(port, 3);
```

That's it! Just one line of code to do all the things the C code does.

Java handles all that socket complexity "under the covers" for you. It doesn't expose the full range of socket possibilities, so Java avoids the novice socketeer choosing contradictory options. On the other hand, a few recondite sockety things cannot be done in Java. You cannot create a raw socket in Java, and hence cannot write a ping program that relies on raw sockets (you can do something just as good though). The benefit is overwhelming: you can open sockets and start writing to another system just as easily as you open a file and start writing to hard disk.

Loopback Address

Every computer system on the Internet has a unique IP address consisting of four groups of digits separated by periods, like this: 204.156.141.229

They are currently revising and increasing the IP address specification so that there will be enough new IP addresses to give one to every conceivable embedded processor on earth, and a few nearby friendly planets.

One special IP address is: 127.0.0.1

This is the "loopback" address used in testing and debugging. If a computer sends a packet to this address, it is routed out and back in again, without actually leaving the system. Thus this special address can be used to run Internet software even if you are not connected to the Internet. Set your system up so that the Internet services it will be requesting are all at the loopback address. Make sure your system is actually running the daemons corresponding to the services you want to use.

The special hostname associated with the loopback address is "localhost," if you are requesting services by name rather than IP address. On any system, you should be able to enter the command "ping localhost" and have it echo a reply from the loopback IP address. If you can't do this, it indicates that your TCP/IP stack is not set up properly.

Ping in Java

As our very first example, let's write a Java program to ping a system. Ping is a standard TCP/IP command to send an echo request to a network host or gateway. In other words ping says, "Tell me you got this message and are alive." In retrospect, the command has been deemed an acronym for "Packet InterNet Groper." (Don't ask why everything has to be an acronym in computing, it's just one of our fine traditions.)

The standard ping uses the ICMP (Internet Control Message Protocol) which is a low-level network administration protocol not supported in Java nor in Microsoft's Winsock. ICMP on Win32 is provided by an unsupported and undocumented library icmp.dll.

However, all is not lost! Look at the functionality of ping. All it does is send a message to a network host, and tell you if it got an answer. Sending a message to a host is trivial: just open a socket on the host, and write to it. Java does all the work of assembling the bytes into packets and sending them. The only question is what port should be used. There are several standard TCP/IP services. Port 7 is the echo service and port 23 is the telnet port. I like port 13, which is the daytime port and can accept either TCP or UDP enquiries. When you connect to port 13 on a computer, it responds with a single message telling you what it thinks the date and time is. Here is my version of ping in Java:

```java
import java.io.*;
import java.net.*;
public class ping {

  public static void main(String a[]) throws Exception {
  if (a.length!=1) {
  System.out.println("usage:  java ping <systemname> ");
  System.exit(0);
  }

  String machine = a[0];
  final int daytimeport = 13;
  Socket so = new Socket(machine, daytimeport);
  BufferedReader br =
    new BufferedReader( new InputStreamReader( so.getInputStream() ) );
  String timestamp = br.readLine();
  System.out.println( machine + " is alive at " + timestamp );
  }
}
```

When you run the program, giving a hostname as argument you see this:

```
% java ping positive
positive is alive at Wed Nov 11 19:31:38 1998
```

This program demonstrates how easy it is to open a socket connection to a port on another computer using the Java networking library. We'll look at a series of slightly more involved examples, and I think you'll be pleasantly surprised at how simple it is to write Java network programs.

Sending E-Mail by Java

As our next example, let's write a Java program to send some e-mail. E-mail is sent by socketed communication with port 25 on a computer system. All we are going to do is open a socket connected to port 25 on some system, and speak "mail protocol" to the daemon at the other end. In an applet, open a socket back to the server. In an application, you can open a socket on the same system on which you're running the program. If we speak the mail protocol correctly, it will listen to what we say, and send the e-mail for us.

Note that this program requires an Internet standard mail (SMTP) program running on the server. If your server has some non-standard proprietary mail program on it, you're out of luck. You can check which program you have by telnetting to port 25 on the server, and seeing if you get a mail server to talk to you. The code to send e-mail is:

```java
import java.io.*;
import java.net.*;
public class email {

    public static void main(String args[]) throws IOException {
        Socket sock;
        DataInputStream dis;
        PrintStream ps;

        sock = new Socket("localhost", 25);
        dis = new DataInputStream( sock.getInputStream());
        ps = new PrintStream( sock.getOutputStream());

        ps.println("mail from: trelford");
        System.out.println( dis.readLine() );

        String Addressee= "linden";
        ps.println("rcpt to: " + Addressee );
        System.out.println( dis.readLine() );

        ps.println("data");
        System.out.println( dis.readLine() );

        ps.println("This is the message\n that Java sent");
        ps.println(".");
        System.out.println( dis.readLine() );

        ps.flush();
        sock.close();
    }
}
```

Many of the Internet services are like this one. You set up a socket connection, and talk a simple protocol to tell the server at the other end what you want.

Note that the main() routine has been declared as throwing an Exception. This is a shortcut, permissible in development, to save the necessity of handling any exceptions that might be raised. It only works because exceptions are not considered part of the signature of a method. In production code, it is *crucial* to catch and handle any exceptions.

You can find all the Internet Protocols described in documents *Request For Comments* (RFCs), the format in which they were originally issued, available online at: http://www.internic.net/std. The mail RFC is RFC821.txt.

You can find all the WWW protocols described in documents linked to from the URL http://www.w3.org/pub/WWW/Protocols/. A careful study of some of these documents will often answer any protocol questions you have.

If you write a simple Swing GUI around this mail-sending code, you've written a mailer program! It's not that hard to get the RFCs for the POP3 and IMAP[1] protocols, and write the code to read and display incoming mail, too.

---

1. POP3 is "Post Office Protocol 3," and IMAP is "Internet Mail Access Protocol."

How to Make an Applet Write a File on the Server

Everyone who writes an applet sooner or later wants to have it write a file back on the server. This is perhaps the most frequently asked question in Java. You might wish want the high score in a high score file, or have a guestbook that visitors to the page can sign, or count the number of HTTP requests for this page.

If you think about it, giving write access to your server system to anyone any-where on the Internet is a very bad idea. It would be the equivalent of leaving the keys in your car with the engine running and a sign on the windshield saying, "Help yourself." One of Java's goals is to improve, not undermine, system secu-rity and so there is *no* built-in support allowing an applet to directly write to a file on a server. None! You can read a file on the server inside an applet, but you abso-lutely cannot directly create or write a file on the server unless the server does it for you. But all is not lost. We could write the ping program even though Java doesn't support ICMP.

How can you persuade the server to write a file for you? One possibility is to write a system demon that runs on the server 24 hours a day and listens to a spec-ified port. When one of your applets wants to write a file, it opens a socket on that port on the server, sends commands saying what it wants to do, gives the file-name, and then sends the data. This is open to abuse, though. Anyone who knows about this service could similarly connect to that port, and fill up your filesystem with their files. You could lessen the probability of that happening if you pro-tected the service by a password challenge.

The Linlyn Class for File Transfer

Well, what do you know? The previous paragraph is a pretty good description of the standard FTP (file transfer protocol) service. This service will frequently be running on any system that has full TCP/IP support. The standard FTP port is port 21 for commands and port 20 for data. Simply open a socket connection from your applet to port 21 on the server, and you can have FTP write the files for you. Of course you have to know the FTP commands to send, and you have to be able to deal with the password challenge.

Luckily, that work has already been done for you. The request for code to write to the server from an applet is made so frequently that I got together with my col-league Bob Lynch, and we created the Linlyn class. (Hey, at least the name's not an acronym.) The Linlyn class does easy FTP file transfer from an applet to a server. The Linlyn class was designed with absolute ease-of-use as its foremost consideration, and a copy of it (along with a sample applet) is on the CD in the goodies directory.

The Linlyn class is published under the GNU public license for anyone to use or improve. Be advised that in its standard form, you compile the userid and password as a String into the class file. That is appropriate only for use on a secure intranet, and must not be used for an applet that you publish on the Internet. It would be a simple matter, however, for you to prompt the user for the password, instead of hard-coding it in the program. Then you or anyone that you trust with your FTP password (and your credit card, car keys, wallet, etc.) can write files on your server from your applet.

How to Find the IP Address Given to a Machine Name

This code will be able to find the IP address of all computers it knows about. That may mean all systems that have an entry in the local hosts table, or (if it is served by a name server) the domain of the name server, which could be as extensive as a large subnet or the entire organization.

```
import java.io.*;
import java.net.*;

class who {

    public static void main(String a[]) throws IOException {

        InetAddress InetAddr =
            InetAddress.getByName (a[0]);
        System.out.println(
            "inet address is " + InetAddr.toString() );

    }
}
```

Some Notes on Protocol and Content Handlers

Some of the Java documentation makes a big production about support for extending the MIME types known to browsers. If it is asked to browse some data whose type it doesn't recognize, it can simply download the code for the appropriate handler based on the name of the datetype, and use that to grok the data.

This is exactly what happens with plug-ins. If you stumble across a RealAudio file, the browser prompts you to download the plug-in that can play it. Java can make this completely automatic. Or so the theory runs. It hasn't yet been proved in practice.

The theory of the handlers is this. There are two kinds of handler that you can write: protocol handlers and content handlers.

A *protocol handler* talks to other programs. Both ends follow the same protocol in order to communicate structured data between themselves ("After you," "No, I insist—after you.") If you wrote an Oracle database protocol handler, it would deal with SQL queries to pull data out of an Oracle database.

A *content handler* knows how to decode the contents of a file. It handles data (think of it as the contents of something pointed to by a URL). It gets the bytes and assembles them into an object. If you wrote an MPEG content handler, then it would be able to play MPEG movies in your browser, once you had brought the data over there. Bringing MPEG data to your browser could be done using the FTP protocol, or you might wish to write your own high performance protocol handler.

By the way, the reason that MPEG and video shows so poorly on even top-end PC's is the heavy bandwidth it consumes. The back-of-the-envelope calculations are:

```
Frame size          = NTSC screensize   * reasonable color size
                    = (768 * 486)        * 8 bits for each of R,G,Blue
                    = 8.9 Megabits
Data transfer rate  = Frame size         * rate
                    = 8.9 Megabits       * 24 frames per second
                    = 214 Megabits/sec
```

So a proper quality moving digital image on your monitor requires 214 Mbits (26MB/sec.) minimum sustained bandwidth from the source to your display card (graphics adapter, framebuffer, whatever you want to call it). This is not possible in the current generation of PCs, and to even think of putting this kind of load on the network is absurd.

Content handlers and protocol handlers may be particularly convenient for web browsers, and they may also be useful in stand-alone applications. There is not a lot of practical experience with these handlers yet, so it is hard to offer definitive advice about their use. Some people predict they are going to be very important for decoding file formats of arbitrary wackiness, while other people are ready to be convinced by an existence proof.

HTTP and Web Browsing: Retrieving HTTP Pages

Here is an example of using the HTTP daemon to retrieve a web page from a system on the network. The HTTP daemon sits on port 80 by convention. It understands a dozen or so requests, including "GET" followed by a path name. The argument "sparcs" is the name of a web server system on my subnet inside Sun Microsystems in Menlo Park, California, so change that to the name of your local web server.

```
import java.io.*;
import java.net.*;
public class http {

  public static void main(String args[]) throws IOException {
     String webserver = "sparcs";
     int http_port = 80;
     Socket sock;
     DataInputStream dis;
     PrintStream ps;

     sock = new Socket(webserver, http_port);
     dis = new DataInputStream( sock.getInputStream() );
     ps = new PrintStream( sock.getOutputStream() );

     ps.println("GET /index.html");
     String s=null;
     while ( (s=dis.readLine())!=null)
               System.out.println( s );

     sock.close();
  }
}
```

Note: If you are not on a network, before you run this code, start the HTTP server daemon on your local system and use the local host address. If you are on a local network, your firewall will probably limit the visibility of outside systems, so pick a local server system that is running HTTPD as your test case.

The program prints out everything the HTTP daemon sends back to it. In this case, running the program yields:

```
<Html>
<Head>
<Title>SPARCS</Title>
<!-- Author: Susan P. Motorcycles -->
</Head>
<Body>

<h2>Resources</h2>
<p>
<hr>Go to
<a HREF="estar/public_html/index.html"><u>Estar Homepage</u>
 </a></p>
```

This is indeed the page at http://sparcs.eng/index.html inside Sun. As may be expected, Java has some awareness of various net protocols. In particular it can deal with a URL directly, and not require the programmer to descend into the underlying netherworld of sockets. So in practice, if we wanted to look at the contents of a URL, we would use the URL class, like this:

```
import java.net.*;
import java.io.*;
public class page {

    public static void main(String a[]) {
        DataInputStream dis;
        try {
            URL u  = new URL( "http://sparcs.eng/index.html" );
            dis = new DataInputStream(
                        u.openConnection().getInputStream() );

            String s ;
            while ( (s=dis.readLine())!=null ) {
                System.out.println( s );
            }
        } catch (Exception e) { System.out.println( e ); }
    }
}
```

Coding the program this way is not only shorter, but allows us to interrogate certain other URL properties, such as the protocol that is being used and the host system (these methods are of use when you don't use literal values as in this example).

```
System.out.println("    file: "+ u.getFile() );
System.out.println("    host: "+ u.getHost() );
  System.out.println("     ref: "+ u.getRef() );
  System.out.println("protocol:" + u.getProtocol() );
```

This gives this result:

```
    file: /index.html
    host: sparcs.eng
     ref: null
protocol:http
```

The "ref" is the reference or label that you can put in the middle of an html file to take you there instead of starting at the beginning.

What if there is a GIF at that URL? Won't we print out image information as though it were text? Yes, the program would. You need to build just a little more intelligence into it so it recognizes file types, and handles them appropriately. If we wanted to retrieve a GIF from a URL, we just use Applet's `getImage(url)` method.

A URL can pose a security risk, since you can pass along information even by reading a URL. Requesting http://www.cia.gov/cgi-bin/cgi.exe/secretinfo passes "secretinfo" along to the CGI script, for example. Since requesting a URL can send out information just as a Socket can, requesting a URL has the same security model as access to Sockets. Namely, in an applet you can only open a socket connection back to the server from which the applet came.

If you are behind a firewall (and who isn't these days?) you will need to tell Java the details of your proxy server and port in order to access hosts outside the firewall. You do this by defining properties, perhaps when starting the code:

```
java -DproxySet=true -DproxyHost=SOMEHOST -DproxyPort=SOMENUM code.java
```

Without this, you'll get an UnknownHostException. The proxy settings are needed for both java.net.URLConnection and for java.net.Sockets.

If you modify the basic program above so that it transmits the other ten or eleven HTTP commands and give it a GUI front end to display the formatted HTTP text, you will have written a web browser! A web browser is at heart a fairly simple program. The prototype HotJava web browser, at that time called "Webrunner," was written in just one week according to Patrick Naughton (who was there and worked on it).

Both this example and the mailer program are client applications. The server end of the HTTP protocol is not much more complicated. A basic HTTP daemon can be implemented in a few hundred lines of code. The Apache web server (the most popular web server in the known universe) is only ten or twenty thousand lines of code. There is a copy of the Apache web server and the source code on the CD, too.

A Client/Server Socket Program

Now it's time for an industrial-strength socket example! Recall the phenomenon in which the Internet entered the public consciousness in a big way. One of the early indicators of this was a 1993 cartoon in *New Yorker Magazine*, with the punchline, "On the Internet nobody knows you're a dog!" This cartoon was cut out and displayed in every network programmer's office from Albuquerque to Zimbabwe.

Our program here is a Canine Turing Test—a Java program to distinguish whether the networked host is a dog or not. People greet each other by shaking hands, while dogs sniff each other. Dogs are loyal companions, and part of their loyalty is absolute truthfulness. To tell if a dog is at the other end of a socket, just ask the question, "If you met me, would you shake my hand or sniff it?" Depending on the answer that the client sends back over the socket to the server, the server will know if the client is a dog or a human.

TCP/IP on Windows

Your Java network programs are going to work only if you are using a computer that has an IP address and a connection to a TCP/IP network, or if you run it all on one system, and you have socket support working.

On a Unix workstation, TCP/IP support is a standard part of the operating system. On a PC, you'll need to have the TCP/IP protocol stack installed. Calling this software a "protocol stack" is a bit of a misnomer as it has nothing to do with LIFO stacks. "TCP/IP library" would be a more accurate name.

Under Windows 95, the TCP/IP protocol stack (wsock32.dll) is present on the system, but needs to be configured to work. You configure it by clicking on My Computer -> Control Panel -> Network -> Network. Where the window shows a list reading "The following network components are installed," make sure you have at least "Dial-Up adapter" and "TCP/IP" in the list. Click on "TCP/IP" to highlight it and activate the "Properties" button underneath the network component list.

Press the button to bring up TCP/IP properties. There are six tabbed entries here, and they all need to be set up for your networking code to work correctly. Your Internet Service Provider should supply full instructions.

Frankly, networking in Windows is fragile and unsatisfactory. You may find that you have to have an active dial-up connection to get it to work. There are supposed to be workarounds that make this unnecessary (see the network section of the Java Programmers FAQ on the CD), but none of them have ever worked for me.

The code comes in two parts: a server that listens for clients and asks them the question, and clients that connect to the server. The server is going to detect whether clients are dogs or not. The heart of this server code just creates a server socket and then, in a loop, accepts connections to it and handles them. When a connection is accepted, it returns a new socket over which the client and server can talk without affecting new incoming connection requests.

The Socket Server Code

```java
/**
 *   a network server that detects presence of dogs on the Internet
 *
 *   @author     Peter van der Linden
 *   @author     From the book "Just Java"
 */
import java.io.*;
import java.net.*;

class server {
    public static void main(String a[]) throws IOException {
        int q_len = 6;
        int port = 4444;
        Socket sock;
        String query = "If you met me would you shake my hand, "
                    + "or sniff it?";

        ServerSocket servsock =
            new ServerSocket(port, q_len);

    while (true) {
        // wait for the next client connection
            sock=servsock.accept();

        // Get I/O streams from the socket
        PrintStream out =
         new PrintStream( sock.getOutputStream() );
        DataInputStream in  =
        new DataInputStream( sock.getInputStream() );

        // Send our query
        out.println(query);
        out.flush();

        // get the reply
        String reply = in.readLine();
        if (reply.indexOf("sniff") > -1)
            System.out.println(
          "On the Internet I know this is a DOG!");
            else System.out.println(
          "Probably a person or an AI experiment");

    // Close this connection, (not overall server socket)
      sock.close();
    }
  }
}
```

The Socket Client Code

Now the client end of the socket, which looks like this:

```
// On the Internet no one knows you're a dog...
// unless you tell them.

import java.io.*;
import java.net.*;

class dog {

    public static void main(String a[]) throws IOException {
        Socket sock;
        DataInputStream dis;
        PrintStream dat;

        // Open our connection to positive, at port 4444
        sock = new Socket("positive",4444);

        // Get I/O streams from the socket
        dis = new DataInputStream( sock.getInputStream() );
        dat = new PrintStream( sock.getOutputStream() );

        String fromServer = dis.readLine();

        System.out.println("Got this from server:" + fromServer);

        dat.println("I would sniff you");
        dat.flush();

        sock.close();
    }
}
```

When you try running this program, make sure that you change the client socket connect to refer not to "positive" (my workstation) but to a system where you intend to run the server code. You can identify this system by using either the name (as long as the name will uniquely locate it on your net) or the IP address. (If in doubt, just use the IP address.)

Here's how to run the example:

1. Put the server program on the system that you want to be the server. Compile the server program and start it.

   ```
   javac server.java
   java server
   ```

2. Put the client program on the system that you want to be the client. Change the client program so it references your server machine, not machine "positive." Then compile it.

   ```
   javac dog.java
   ```

3. When you execute the client program, you will see the output on the client system:

   ```
   java dog
   ```

4. Got this from server: If you met me would you shake my hand, or sniff it?

5. On the server machine, you will see the output.

   ```
   On the Internet I know this is a DOG!
   ```

Make sure the server is running before you execute the client, otherwise it will have no one to talk to.

 Write a second client program that would reply with the "shake hands" typical of a person. Run this from the same or another client system. (Easy.)

A Multi-Threaded Client/Server System

There's one improvement that is customary in servers, and we will make it here. For all but the smallest of servers, it is usual to spawn a new thread to handle each request. This has three big advantages:

1. The program source is less cluttered, as the server processing is written in a different class

2. By handling each request in a new thread, clients do not have to wait for every request ahead of them to be served

3. Finally, it makes the server scalable: It can accept new requests independent of its speed in handling them. (Of course, you better buy a server that has the mippage to keep up with requests.)

The following code demonstrates how we would rewrite the Internet dog detector using a new thread for each client request.

```
/**
 *   a network server that detects presence of dogs on the Internet
 *   and which spawns a new thread for each client request.
 *   @author    Peter van der Linden
 *
 */
import java.io.*;
import java.net.*;

class Worker extends Thread {
Socket sock;
Worker(Socket s) { sock =s; }
public void run(){
System.out.println("Thread running:"+currentThread() );
// Get I/O streams from the socket
  PrintStream out = null;
  DataInputStream in  = null;
try {
  out = new PrintStream( sock.getOutputStream() );
  in  = new DataInputStream( sock.getInputStream() );
// Send our query
String query = "If you met me would you shake my hand, or sniff it?";
  out.println(query);
  out.flush();

  // get the reply
  String reply = in.readLine();
  if (reply.indexOf("sniff") > -1)
    System.out.println("On the Internet I know this is a DOG!");
  else System.out.println("Probably a person or an AI experiment");

    // Close this connection, (not the overall server socket)

    sock.close();
  } catch(IOException ioe){System.out.println(ioe); }
}
}

public class server2 {
public static void main(String a[]) throws IOException {
  int q_len = 6;
  int port = 4444;
  Socket sock;

  ServerSocket servsock = new ServerSocket(port, q_len);

while (true) {
  // wait for the next client connection
    sock=servsock.accept();
  new Worker( sock ).start();
 }
}
}
```

Page Counters in Web Pages

Finally, lets wind up by answering a question that many people have, namely: "How do I use Java to implement a counter on my web page?" It seems like this should be trivial to do—there's probably even a class to increment a count every time a web page is accessed and display the new value on the page. Alas, no, for the same reason that there is no file write access.

Here are the obvious steps to set up a page counter in Java:

1. Keep the "page access count" in a file on the server, which is referred to by an HTML document.

2. When the page is accessed, an applet in the page executes on the client.

3. Send a message to a daemon running on the server to say "add one to the number in the page access count file."

4. The daemon on the server reads and updates the file.

People always want to be able to do this totally from the applet, but that is not possible. The cooperation of the server is required. This kind of communication was traditionally done with CGI scripts. You can interface Java to your existing CGI scripts with the following steps replacing steps 3 and 4, respectively.

*   A CGI GET request can be made, and the output can be read by code like this:

```
try { URL u=new URL ("http:// ... some URL" + "... some query
    string");
 // read results back
 DataInputStream dis = new DataInputStream (u.openStream());
 string firstline = dis.readLine ();
```

Open a socket and write an HTTP GET or POST request to the server. GET requests encode their arguments to the CGI script as the last part of the URL. POST requests send the arguments along so the CGI script can read them from standard input. In either case, the argument must be encoded according to the standard CGI rules: parameter name/value fields are separated by "=," pairs of these are separated by ampersands "&," and non-alphanumerics are converted to percent escape form "%nnn." The URLEncoder class will do the encoding for you.

- The HTTP request will start up the CGI script. The output of the script (with a MIME header stripped off) will be sent back down the socket to the applet.

Java, however, now offers the Java Web Server framework for servers. The JWS API for "servlets" is fast replacing the work done formerly by CGI scripts.

More information on JWS, including a white paper is available at the JavaSoft web site http://java.sun.com/. JWS allows you to program everything in Java, and leave the CGI muddle alone. You get the benefit of doing everything in one language, plus Java's security.

Some Light Relief

The Nerd Detection System

Most people are familiar with the little security decals that electronic and other high-value stores use to deter shoplifters. The sticker contains a metallic strip. Unless deactivated by a store cashier, the sticker sets off an alarm when carried past a detector at the store doors.

These security stickers are actually a form of antenna. The sticker detector sends out a weak RF signal between two posts through which shoppers will pass. It looks for a return signal at a specific frequency, which indicates that one of the stickers has entered the field between the posts.

All this theory was obvious to a couple of California Institute of Technology students Dwight Berg and Tom Capellari, who decided to test the system in practice. Naturally, they selected a freshman to (unknowingly) participate in the trials. At preregistration, after the unlucky frosh's picture was taken, but before it was laminated into his I.D. card, Dwight and Tom fixed a couple of active security decals from local stores onto the back of the photo.

The gimmicked card was then laminated together hiding the McGuffin, and the two conspirators awaited further developments. A couple of months later they caught up with their victim as he was entering one of the stores. He was carrying his wallet above his head. In response to a comment that this was an unusual posture, the frosh replied that something in his wallet, probably his bank card, seemed to set off store alarms. He had been conditioned to carry his wallet above his head after several weeks of setting off the alarms while entering and leaving many of the local stores.

The frosh seemed unimpressed with Dwight and Tom's suggestion that perhaps the local merchants had installed some new type of nerd detection system. Apparently the comment got the frosh thinking, because on the next occasion he met Dwight, he put Dwight in a headlock until he confessed to his misdeed. **Moral**: Never annoy a nerd.

And that seems like the ideal note on which to end this book. Thank you. You've been a great audience, and may we all have many happy years of writing Java programs ahead of us.

Exercises

1. Extend the example mail program above so that it prompts for user input and generally provides a friendly front end to sending mail.

2. Write a socket server program that simply returns the time on the current system. Write a client that calls the server, and sends you mail reporting on how far apart the time on the local system is versus the time on the current system.

3. In the previous exercise, the server can only state what time it is at the instant the request reaches it, but that answer will take a certain amount of time to travel back to the client. Devise a strategy to minimize or correct for errors due to transmission time. (Hard—use a heuristic to make a good guess.)

Further Reading

TCP/IP Network Administration

by Craig Hunt (O'Reilly & Associates, Sebastopol CA, 1994)

ISBN 0-937175-82-X

The modest title hides the fact that this book will be useful to a wider audience than just network administrators. It is a very good practical guide to TCP/IP written as a tutorial introduction.

Teach Yourself TCP/IP in 14 Days

by Timothy Parker (Sams Publishing, Indianapolis, 1994)

ISBN 0-672-30549-6

When a book starts off with an apology for the dullness of the subject material, you just know that the author has some unusual ways about him.

Unix Network Programming

by W. Richard Stevens (Prentice Hall, NJ 1990)

The canonical guide to network programming.

Acknowledgments

I would like to express my thanks to Bob Lynch who read the new chapters for the 4th edition, and made many suggestions for improvements. I take responsibility for all remaining errors (except the ones to do with double and single quotes in source listings—blame FrameMaker for those). If you notice an error that isn't in the errata sheet (obtainable from the web site), please let me know by email to pvdl@best.com.

The layout and design of this book was greatly improved by the hard work of Cass Kovel, Joanne Anzalone, and previous editors who have earned my warmest appreciation.

Thanks to the people who encouraged me to write this book: Jane Erskine, Rachel Borden, Greg Doench.

I would also like to thank the following people who provided significant help, code for the CD, moral support, beer recipes, programming assistance, etc.:

Roger Abbott,
Franck Allimant,
Ragavendra Angadi,
Antranig Basman,
Keith Bierman,
Josh Bloch,
Roland Bock,
Matthew Burtch,

Mark Chamness,
Elwood C. Downey,
John F. Dumas,
Matisse Enzer,
Gordon Fccyk,
Walter Fendt,
Roedy Green,
Karl Hörnell,
Dean Jones,
Tom Karpowitz,
Rajeev Karunakaran,
Kevin Kelley,
Kevin Kelm,
John S.Kern,
Robert Kiesling,
Henry Lai,
Roger Lindsjö,
David Mikkelson,
Nicholas J. Morrell (what a taste he has in expensive Scotch),
J.C.Morris,
Alex Muttet,
Matthias Neeracher,
Tor Norbye,
Peter Norvig,
The Old Hats of AFU (Cayman Islands) Inc.,
Jef Poskanzer,
Burkhard Ratheiser,
G. Sarathy,
Andrew Schulman,
Daniel P. B. Smith,
Jean-Guy Speton,
Jeremy H. Sproat,
Kathy Stark,
Al Sutton,
Greg Turner,
Tom van der Linden (who instilled in me his love for reading, writing, and
    consolidated statements of stockholder equity),
Wendy van der Linden (who pointed out that Citrus was a subclass of Fruit),

William C. Wake,

Brent Welch,

Sean Willard

I am fortunate to work in the department at Sun Microsystems directed by Deepak Bhagat. My team of colleagues at Sun Microsystems also deserves my gratitude for helping me in numerous ways while I worked on this text: Sudershan Goyal, Jim Marks, Saeed Nowshadi, Sarito, Set Priority Level, David Smith, Sumit Gupta, Barada Mishra, Shiv Rajpal, Ian Skreen, Tanjore Suresh, and Srinivasa Vetsa. If you've seen any of my earlier books, you'll note that I have worked with some of these people for several years now. We're doing something right.

APPENDIX A

The Obsolete JDK 1.0 Event Model

We describe the old JDK 1.0 event model here because you might see it in old code, or have to maintain programs that use it. The 1.0 event model was based on inheritance. The class Component is the percent of most screen controls (scrollbar, button, etc.). Component has a method handleEvent() that the runtime system calls whenever the user does something with a control. handleEvent() looks at the incoming event and splits it off into a call to various mouse methods like mouse-Drag(), or action().

Your code can override handleEvent() and get a first look at all incoming events, or it can override the specific lower-level event handler (such as action() or mouseDrag()) that is called by handleEvent(). The most common case for handling control input is just to override action(). Inside action, you examine the event parameter to decode exactly what kind of event has occurred.

The event handling routines return a boolean value: true if it consumed the event, and, not false but an explicit call to the parent handler if the event was not handled. This complication arises because there are two kinds of hierarchy: physical nesting (Canvas is in a Panel that is in a Frame) and inheritance (myOtherCanvas is a subclass of MyCanvas which is a subclass of Canvas). An event needs to be propagated up both the hierarchies to find the right handler. People found this confusing (it *is* confusing) and few Java books explained it well.

Just Java 1.2

Here is the simplest example: the event handling code for a button press. In the old JDK 1.0 inheritance-based model, in an applet this was:

```
public class myClass extends Applet {

    Button apple = new Button("press me");

    public boolean action(Event e, Object o) {
        if (e.target instanceof Button)
            if ("press me".equals((String) o)) {
                // do button handling stuff...
                return true;
            }
```

Adding `action()` to an applet was just like adding `init()` or `start()`: it overrode the preexisting method of that name in the `Component` parent class several parent classes up from `Applet`.

A Few Words on Getting a GUI Event

Just as adding widgets to a panel or frame is easy, so getting back user input is also straightforward. Everything hinges on the method with this signature:

```
public boolean action( Event e, Object o)
```

The method is part of every Component, so all of the buttons, choices lists, etc., inherit it and can override it.

Whenever a user operates a Component (presses a button, clicks on a choice), the action method is called. The "Event e" argument contains much information about the coordinates of the event, the time it occurred, and the kind of event that it was. If the event was a keypress, it has the value of the key. The other argument is a generalized object that contains extra information in some cases.

The event contains a field called "id" that indicates the type of event it is (e.g. KEY_PRESS, MOUSE_DOWN, LIST_SELECT, etc), and hence which other Event variables are relevant for the event. For keyboard events, the field called "key" will contain a value indicating the key that was pressed/released and the modifiers field will contain the modifiers (whether the shift key was down, etc).

For KEY_PRESS and KEY_RELEASE event ids, the value of key will be the unicode character code for the key; for KEY_ACTION and KEY_ACTION_RELEASE, the value of key will be one of the defined action-key identifiers in the Event class (PGUP, PGDN, F1, F2, etc).

The class Event can be seen in full in directory $JAVAHOME/src/java/awt/Event.java.

A summary of the event class is:

```
public class Event {
    public static final int SHIFT_MASK;
    public static final int CTRL_MASK;
    public static final int META_MASK;
    public static final int ALT_MASK;

    public static final int F1; // the F1 function key
    public static final int F2;
     // ...
    public static final int F12; // the F12 function key

    public static final int KEY_PRESS;
    public static final int KEY_RELEASE;
    public static final int KEY_ACTION;
    public static final int KEY_ACTION_RELEASE;

    public static final int MOUSE_DOWN;
    public static final int MOUSE_UP;
    public static final int MOUSE_MOVE;
    public static final int MOUSE_ENTER;
    public static final int MOUSE_EXIT;
    public static final int MOUSE_DRAG;

    public static final int ACTION_EVENT;
    public static final int GOT_FOCUS;
    public static final int LOST_FOCUS;

    public int id; // what the event was (uses the constants above)

    public Object target;  // the component generating the event.
    public long when;     // the timestamp

    public int x;
    public int y;     // x and y are where the event happened.

    public int key;  // the key that was pressed

    public int modifiers;   // the state of the modifiers

    public int clickCount; // number of clicks from the mouse

    public Object arg;    // an arbitrary argument, not always used

    public boolean shiftDown();    // true if shift key down
    public boolean controlDown(); // true if ctrl key down
    public boolean metaDown();     // true if meta key down

}
```

You get an object of this class sent to the action routine for each GUI event.

So for example, if the "Q" key is pressed, these fields (others will be set too) will have the values shown in the event object sent to the container of the key:

```
id=KEY_PRESS, key=81, modifiers=SHIFT_MASK
```

For some events (like key presses, and mouse movements), the target is the container. For others (like buttons, scrollbars, and text fields), the target is the widget itself. Don't be fooled by the implication that the "target" is where the Event is going to. Sometimes it is where it has come from.

If the mouse is dragged, this event object will be sent to the container of the key:

```
id=MOUSE_DRAG, x=x_coord, y=y_coord,  modifiers=0
```

When you drag a mouse or a scrollbar, many, many events are sent. It doesn't wait until you have stopped moving the object, it generates an event for each slight movement (not necessarily each pixel of movement).

If the center button of a 3-button mouse is pressed, these are some of the fields of the Event object:

```
id=MOUSE_DOWN, modifiers=ALT_MASK
```

If the right button of a 3-button mouse is pressed, these are some of the fields of the Event object:

```
id=MOUSE_DOWN, modifiers=META_MASK
```

The modifiers field in the event is how Java portably handles the different number of mouse buttons Mac: one, Windows: two, and Unix: three. You should be able to hold down the ALT or META (shift or control) key and click the left mouse button to make it appear as a center or right mouse button event. This is totally broken in JDK 1.0.2.

The object o in the action routine is not always used. When the event is a button, it holds a string that is the label of the button. When the event is a menu item being selected, it holds a string that is the menu item's name.

For each container that a widget is added to, the programmer has the opportunity to provide an overriding version of:

```
public boolean action(Event e, Object o)
```

and to use that to determine exactly what the event was, and from that take action to deal with it. The action method must return true to indicate it has consumed (dealt with) the event.

Obtaining Mouse and Keyboard Input

The previous section described how various widgets interact with the user. This section describes how mouse and keyboard events are passed to your program. It is done in a very similar way to what we have already seen for widgets.

Events go to the Component that is the immediate Container of the place where the event happened. The class Component has a method `handleEvent()` with this signature:

```
public boolean handleEvent(Event evt)
```

If you look at handleEvent in file $JAVAHOME/src/java/awt/Component.java, you'll see that it contains a switch statement based on what the event was, and it really factors out all the keyboard and mouse events calling individual methods to handle all the possibilities for those.

A list of some of the specific Event handlers that `handleEvent()` factors out is:

```
public boolean mouseDown(Event evt, int x, int y)
public boolean mouseDrag(Event evt, int x, int y)
public boolean mouseUp(Event evt, int x, int y)
public boolean mouseMove(Event evt, int x, int y)
public boolean mouseEnter(Event evt, int x, int y)
public boolean mouseExit(Event evt, int x, int y)

public boolean keyDown(Event evt, int key)
public boolean keyUp(Event evt, int key)

public boolean action(Event evt, Object what) //when a widget is touched
```

The programmer can override these to provide the callback routines that window systems use for event handling.

To see what's really going on with events, insert this line at the start of your version of handleEvent.

```
System.err.println("Event: " + e.toString() );
```

You'll be amazed at the number of events that are generated by the simplest mouse motions. This method converts each to a string and prints it.

Use inheritance to create your own version of the Button and Choice classes in an example Applet. Override "action()" within each of these two classes. Now it is much easier to decode which event has come in. If the "myButton.action()" has been invoked, it must have been an instance of myButton that was operated. (Easy).

Capturing Individual KeyPresses

Write an action() method that will handle all of the widgets in the previous section, and for each print out what the event is. (Medium).

Here is an example of how a game program might capture individual key presses as they are made. Note that only certain events are available from certain widgets. This can be even more annoying than those smirking kids in the Mentos commercials.

```
import java.awt.*;
import java.applet.*;
public class game  extends Applet {

    public void init() {
        resize(450,200);
    }

    public boolean keyDown(Event evt, int key) {
        System.out.println("Got: " + (char)key );
        return true;
    }

}
```

What could be simpler?

Handling the Quit Event

You will usually want to put the three or four lines of code that deal with a window being quit or destroyed (when the user has finished with it—this is usually a standard choice on the frame menu bar). The code looks like:

```
public boolean handleEvent(Event e) {
    if (e.id == Event.WINDOW_DESTROY) {
        System.exit(0);
    }
    return false;
}
```

You don't have to exit the program. That would be appropriate when the user quits from the top-level window. For a lower-level window, the right thing to do may be to hide the window, and release the resource for garbage collection by removing any pointers to it.

All the Event handling methods have a boolean return type. This is used to answer the question "Did this method fully handle the event?" If it did, return true. If it did not, (Whoa! Trick answer coming!) return the result of calling the superclass's event handler to propagate the event up the containment hierarchy. To understand why, let's look at a partial solution to the previous Programming Challenge.

```
import java.awt.*;
import java.applet.Applet;

public class mb extends Applet {
    myButton mb;

    public void init() {
        add(new myButton("press me") );
    }
}

class myButton extends Button {

    public myButton(String s) {
        super(s);
    }

    public boolean action(Event e, Object arg) {
        System.out.println("myButton pressed!");
        return true;
    }
}
```

Here we see a very common form of inheritance: subclassing an AWT widget to provide some slight refinement of behavior. Normally, our "action()" method is a common method that might handle a dozen kinds of event. In this case, when the button is pressed, control is transferred to the myButton.action() method and no decoding of "what Event was this?" is needed. We know it must have been a myButton that was pressed.

Now, we may have created several levels of subclass of Button, myOtherButton extends... extends myButton extends Button. Each adds some slight twist, and each has its own overriding action() routine. Our intent will be to first try handling the special button event in the lowest subclass. If that doesn't want it, then we almost certainly want to pass the event up the inheritance hierarchy. (If that isn't what we want then why did we bother creating the inheritance hierarchy?) However, what will actually happen is that the runtime system will propagate the unconsumed event up the containment hierarchy.

For Advanced Students Only

The fact that you return "true" from the Event handler leads the normal programmer to assume that one should return "false" if more processing is required by the containing class.

Bzzzt! The idiom is that you "return super.handleEvent(e)" to pass the event up the inheritance chain if your method doesn't consume the event.

This is because there are two possible chains to follow to look for the event handler:

1. Up the chain of containers: (Event is in a Panel which is in a Frame which is in a Window...)

2. Up the chain of subclasses: (Event is from myOtherButton which is a subclass of myButton, which is...)

What you usually want to happen is for the runtime to try both hierarchies. The runtime system should make the event go up the chain of superclasses for a given widget, and then go to the enclosing container, exhaust all its superclasses, and so on.

This will occur if your Event handler, instead of returning false, does:

```
return super.handleEvent(e);
```

None of this is necessary if you do not have a chain of subclassed widgets. On the other hand, it doesn't hurt to write the statement this way regardless. If you don't have a big inheritance hierarchy myButton.action() will call Button.action() which simply returns false anyway.

APPENDIX

B

Obsolete Components of the Abstract Window Toolkit

This appendix describes the components of the Abstract Window Toolkit (AWT) that have been replaced by the Swing components. The AWT components are described here because there are two circumstances when you may run into them: when you maintain old code, and when you are asked to write code that must run in the obsolete JDK 1.0 environment.

The Java AWT interface offers the functions that are common to all window systems. The AWT code then uses the underlying native (or "peer") window system to actually render the screen images and manipulate GUI objects. The AWT thus consists of a series of abstract interfaces along with Java code to map them into the actual native code on each system. This is why it is an *abstract* window toolkit; it is not tailored for a specific computer but offers the same API on all.

How the Java Abstract Window Toolkit Works

The AWT currently requires the native window system to be running on the platform because it uses the native window system to support windows within Java. Figure B-1 shows how the AWT interacts with the native window system.

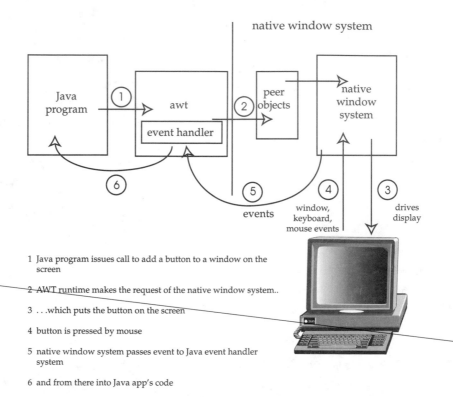

1 Java program issues call to add a button to a window on the screen

2 AWT runtime makes the request of the native window system..

3 . . .which puts the button on the screen

4 button is pressed by mouse

5 native window system passes event to Java event handler system

6 and from there into Java app's code

Figure B-1:   How the Java abstract window toolkit works.

Mnemonic: Peer objects let your Java runtime "peer" at the underlying window implementation. They are only of interest to people porting the Java Development Kit. To a Java applications programmer, all window system code is written in Java.

Controls, Containers, Events

In this appendix, I use the PC term *control* to mean the group of all the GUI things that users can press, scroll, choose between, type into, draw on, etc. In the Unix world, a control is called a *widget*. Neither control nor widget is a Java term, and in reality there is no control class. It's so useful, however, to be able to say "control" instead of "GUI thing that the user interacts with" or "Components plus menus" that we use the term here wherever convenient. Because each control is a subclass of Component, each control (button, etc.) also inherits all the methods and data fields of Component.

The important top-level classes that make up the AWT are shown in Figure B-2.

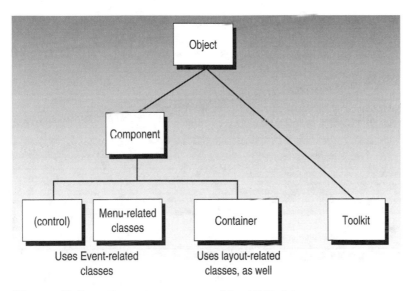

Figure B-2:   The most important of the AWT classes

The basic idea is that you:

- Declare controls. You can subclass them to add to the behavior, but this is often not necessary.

- Add the controls to a container. Again, subclassing is possible but frequently not necessary.

- Implement an interface to get the event handler that responds to control activity.

We will look at all the dozen or so individual controls in depth.

Overview of Controls

The controls are: Button, Canvas, Checkbox, Choice, Label, List, Scrollbar, Text-Field, TextArea, and the variations on Menu. Each control has methods appropriate to what it does. The Scrollbar control has methods to set the width, orientation, and height of scrollbars, for instance. We'll examine each individual control in depth later in the appendix. One obvious control that is missing is a control into which you can write HTML and have it automatically formatted. More controls were added with the Java Foundation Classes, adopted from Netscape's Internet Foundation Classes. These were announced for the JDK 1.2 release.

At this point we now have enough background knowledge of the various GUI elements to present an in-depth treatment of how they talk to your code. Read on for the fascinating details!

Summary of AWT Event Handling: JDK1.0 vs JDK 1.1

Event-handling changed completely in JDK 1.1 mostly in order to better accommodate JavaBeans. In the JDK 1.0.2, the event-handling callbacks were based on inheritance. Your event-handling code had to be subclassed from `Component` so it would override the `Component's handleEvent()` or `action()` method. You may see this code when you maintain older Java programs, so a description of it appears in Appendix A of this book.

In the JDK 1.1, the callbacks are based on delegation: there is an interface for listening to each kind of event (mouse event, button event, scrollbar event, etc.). When an event occurs, the window system calls a method of a class that implements the specific listener interface. You create a class of your own that implements the appropriate interface, and register it with the window system. When that event occurs, the method that you have delegated (appointed) will be called back by the window system.

JDK 1.1 event-handling is a big improvement on the former model. The problem is that there are a lot of browsers still in use that support only JDK 1.0. Until the whole world has upgraded at least to JDK 1.1, there will be an issue with older browsers not being able to run applets with the event-handling. So, you need to carefully consider who will try to run your applets and what browsers they might use. My advice and practice is to give people an incentive to upgrade by using the new event model exclusively, but that might not be the right answer for all organizations and programmers.

Never use a mixture of the two event models in the same program. That is not supported and will lead to bugs that can only be solved by a rewrite.

All About AWT Controls (Components)

We now start looking at individual controls in detail and to describe the kinds of event they can generate. Almost the whole of window programming is learning about the different objects that you can put on the screen (windows, scrollbars, buttons, etc.) and how to drive them. This section explains how to register for and process the events (input) that you get back from controls. A control isn't a freestanding thing; it is always added to a Container such as an Applet, Frame, Panel, or Window, with a method call like MyContainer.add(myComponent). The controls that we will cover here are buttons, text fields, scrollbars, mouse events, and so on. The class hierarchy is quite flat. The controls shown in Figure B-4 are all subclasses of the general class Component that we have already seen.

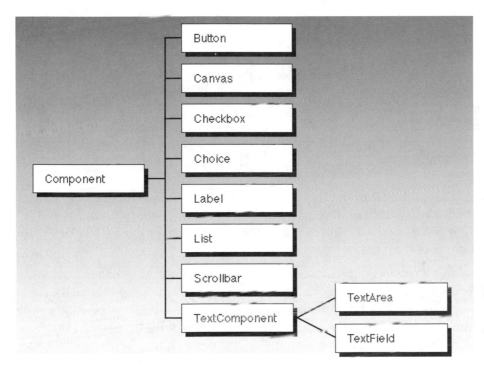

Figure B-3:   The controls (visible AWT objects) of Java.

These classes are the controls or building blocks from which you will create your GUI. What you do with all these components is:

1.   Add them to a container (usually Frame or Applet), then display the container with the show() method.

2.   Register your event handler, using the addXxxListener() method of the control. This will tell the window system which routine of yours should be called when the user presses buttons, makes selections, etc., to process the event.

Fortunately, both of these activities are quite straightforward, and we'll cover them here in source code, words, and pictures. The add method can be applied to a Frame in an application, like this:

```
Frame f = new Frame();
        ...
f.add( something );
```

Or, it can be applied to the Applet's panel in an applet, like so:

```
public static void init () {
    this.add( something );
```

Or, more simply:

```
public static void init () {
    add( something );
```

Recall the Applet life cycle. That discussion made clear that there is an init() method which each Applet should override. It will be called when the Applet is loaded, and it is a good place to place the code that creates these GUI objects. We will use init() for that purpose.

Whenever a user operates a Component (presses a button, clicks on a choice), an event is generated. The XxxEvent argument is a class that can be seen in the awt/ event directory. It contains much information about the coordinates of the event, the time it occurred, and the kind of event that it was. If the event was a keypress, it has the value of the key. If the event was a selection from a list, it has the string chosen.

Having explained the general theory of controls and control events, let's take a look at how they appear on the screen and the typical code to handle them.

Button

What it is:

This is a GUI button. You can program the action that takes place when the button is pressed

What it looks like on screen:

The code to create it:

```
Button b = new Button("peach");
```

```
add(b);
```

The code to retrieve user input from it:

```
MyBHClass myButtonHandler = new MyBHClass();

public void init() {
    add(apple);
    apple.addActionListener(myButtonHandler);
}
}

class MyBHClass implements java.awt.event.ActionListener {
    int i=1;

    public void actionPerformed(ActionEvent e) {
        // this gets called when button pressed...
            String s = e.paramString(); // gets the button label
    }
}
```

An event-handler this small would typically be written using an inner class, and we will use inner classes for the rest of the examples.

In an applet, you will typically override the init() method and, inside it, call the add() method to add these objects to your Applet's panel. In an application, there is no predetermined convention, and you can set the objects where you like. (*Note:* in future examples in this section, we won't bother repeating the context that this is part of the init() method in an applet).

Program an "Alice in Wonderland" applet: a panel with two buttons, one of which makes the panel grow larger, the other smaller. The Component method

```
setSize(int, int)
```

will resize a Panel or other Container. (Easy—about 20 lines of code).

Canvas

What it is:

A Canvas is a screen area that you can use for drawing graphics or receiving user input. A Canvas usually is subclassed to add the behavior you need, especially when you use it to display a GIF or JPEG image. A Canvas contains almost no methods. All its functionality is either inherited from Component (setting font, color, size) or from functionality you add when you extend the class.

To draw on a canvas, you supply your own version of the paint(Graphics g) method. To do that, you need to extend the class and override the paint() method for this Canvas. A more descriptive name for the paint() method would be do_this_to_draw_me(). That gives you a Graphics context (the argument to paint()), which is used in all drawing operations. The many methods of Graphics let you render (the fancy graphics word for "draw") lines, shapes, text, etc., on the screen.

What it looks like on screen:

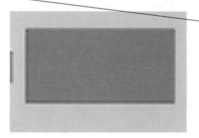

The screen capture is not very exciting, merely showing a rectangular area that has been highlighted with a different color to make it visible (see code below). Canvases are relatively inert until you extend them and use them to display images or do other graphics programming.

The code to create it:

This code gives the Canvas a red color, so you can distinguish it from the Panel (as long as your *Applet* panel isn't red to begin with, of course). The code then gives the Canvas a size of 80 pixels wide by 40 pixels high and adds it to the Applet.

```
Canvas n = new Canvas();

n.setBackground(Color.red);
n.setSize(80,40);
add(n);
```

Note that you cannot draw on objects of class Canvas. You must extend Canvas and override the paint() method and do your drawing in that routine. The paint() method needs to contain all the statements to draw everything that you want to see in the canvas at that time. Here is how you would extend Canvas to provide a surface that you can draw on:

```
// <applet code=can.class width=250 height=100> </applet>
import java.awt.*;
import java.applet.*;
public class can extends Applet {
    myCanvas c = new myCanvas();

    public void init() {
        c.setSize(200,50);
        add(c);
    }
}

class myCanvas extends Canvas{
    public void paint(Graphics g) {
        g.drawString("don't go in the basement", 10,25);
        g.drawLine(10,35, 165,35);
    }
}
```

You can compile and execute this by typing

```
javac can.java appletviewer can.java
```

A window like this is displayed on the screen:

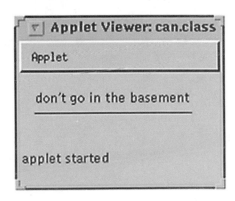

A Canvas is similar to a Panel, in that you can draw on it, render images, and accept events. A Canvas is not a container, however, so you cannot add other components to it. Here is how you would accept mouse events on a Canvas.

```
//   <applet code=can.class width=250 height=100> </applet>
import java.awt.*;
import java.awt.event.*;
import java.applet.*;
public class can extends Applet {
    Canvas c = new Canvas();

    public void init() {
        c.setSize(200,50);
        c.setEnabled(true);
        c.setBackground(Color.blue);
        c.addMouseListener ( new MouseListener() {
            public void mouseEntered(java.awt.event.MouseEvent e)
                {System.out.println(e.toString() );}
            public void mouseClicked(java.awt.event.MouseEvent e) {}
            public void mousePressed(java.awt.event.MouseEvent e) {}
            public void mouseReleased(java.awt.event.MouseEvent e) {}
            public void mouseExited(java.awt.event.MouseEvent e) {}
            });
        add(c);
    }
}
```

The preceding code handles the event fired when the mouse enters the blue canvas. If you run it, you'll see something like this.

```
% appletviewer can.java
java.awt.event.MouseEvent[MOUSE_ENTERED,(131,49),mods=0,clickCount
    =0]  on canvas0
```

Adapter Classes

Here is an example showing how the MouseAdapter class is used when all we are interested in is the mouse entering the Canvas.

```
//  <applet code=can.class width=250 height=100>  </applet> import java awt.*;
import java.awt.event.*;
import java.applet.*;
public class can extends Applet {
     Canvas c = new Canvas();

     public void init() {
          c.setSize(200,50);
          c.setEnabled(true);
          c.setBackground(Color.blue);
          c.addMouseListener ( new MouseAdapter() {
               public void mouseEntered(java.awt.event.MouseEvent e)
                    {System.out.println(e.toString() );}
               });
          add(c);
     }
}
```

Here is an example of how a game program might capture individual key presses in an applet as they are made. Note that the output is to System.out, which isn't displayed in a browser unless you bring up the right window. This example is best run in the applet viewer.

```
// <applet code=game.class height=200 width=300> </applet>
import java.awt.*;
import java.awt.event.*;
import java.applet.*;
public class game  extends Applet {

     public void init() {
          requestFocus(); // a component must have the focus to get
                              //key events
          addKeyListener(
              new KeyAdapter() {
              public void keyPressed(java.awt.event.KeyEvent e)
                   { System.out.println("got "+e.getKeyChar()); }
              } // end anon class
          ); // end method call
     }
}
```

The requestFocus() call is a Component method to ask that keyboard input be directed to this control. Having to explicitly ask for the focus is a change from JDK 1.0.2. The Component must be visible on the screen for the requestFocus() to succeed. A FocusGained event will then be delivered if there's a listener for it.

Let's continue with our description of the individual controls.

Checkbox

What it is:

A checkbox screen object that represents a boolean choice: "pressed" or "not pressed" or "on" or "off." Usually some text explains the choice. For example, "Press for fries" would have a Checkbox "button" allowing yes or no.

What it looks like on screen:

The code to create it:
```
Checkbox cb  = new Checkbox("small");
add(cb);
```

The code to retrieve user input from it:

Checkbox generates ItemEvent. The code to register an ItemListener looks like this:

```
//  <applet code=excheck.class width=250 height=100>  </applet> import
java.awt.*;
import java.awt.event.*;
import java.applet.*;
public class excheck extends Applet {
    Checkbox c1 = new Checkbox("small");

    public void init() {
        c1.addItemListener ( new ItemListener() {
            public void itemStateChanged(java.awt.event.ItemEvent ie)
            { System.out.println(ie.paramString() );}
    });
        add(c1);
    }
}
```

In this example, as in most of them, we simply print out a String representation of the event that has occurred. Running the applet and clicking the checkbox will cause this output in the system console:

```
appletviewer excheck.java
ITEM_STATE_CHANGED, item=small, stateChange=SELECTED
ITEM_STATE_CHANGED, item=small, stateChange=DESELECTED
```

Handlers in real programs will do more useful actions: assign values, create objects, etc., as necessary. The ItemEvent contains fields and methods that specify which object generated the event and whether it was selected or deselected.

CheckboxGroup

What it is:

There is a way to group a series of checkboxes to create a CheckboxGroup of *radio buttons*. The term "radio buttons" arises from the old manual station selection buttons in car radios. When you pressed in one of the buttons, all the others would pop out and be deselected. CheckboxGroups work the same way.

What it looks like on screen:

On Windows 95, mutually-exclusive checkboxes are round, while multiple-selection checkboxes are square. This is one of those "look and feel" differences that vary between window systems.

The code to create it:

You first instantiate a CheckboxGroup object, then use that in each Checkbox constructor, along with a parameter saying whether it is selected or not. This ensures that only one of those Checkbox buttons will be allowed to be on at a time.

```java
//   <applet code=excheck2.class width=250 height=100>   </applet>
import java.awt.*;
import java.awt.event.*;
import java.applet.*;
public class excheck2 extends Applet {
    CheckboxGroup cbg = new CheckboxGroup();

    Checkbox c1 = new Checkbox("small", false,  cbg);
    Checkbox c2 = new Checkbox("medium", false, cbg);
    Checkbox c3 = new Checkbox("large",  true,  cbg);

    ItemListener ie = new ItemListener () {
        public void itemStateChanged(java.awt.event.ItemEvent ie)
            { System.out.println(ie.toString());}
        };
    public void init() {
        c1.addItemListener ( ie );
        c2.addItemListener ( ie );
        c3.addItemListener ( ie );
        add(c1);
        add(c2);
        add(c3);
    }
}
```

Note here that we are using the same, one instance of an inner class as the handler for events from all three of these Checkboxes. It is common to have one handler for several related objects, and let the handler decode which of them actually caused the event. We couldn't do this if we had created an anonymous class, because we would not have kept a reference to use in the later addItemListener() calls.

Choice

What it is:

This is a pop-up list, akin to a pull-down menu, which allows a selection from several text strings. When you hold down the mouse button on the choice, a list of all the other choices appears and you can move the mouse over the one you want.

What it looks like on screen:

Choices are very similar to the List control. Lists look a little more like text; Choices look a little more like buttons and menus. When you click the mouse on a Choice, it pops up the full range of choices, looking like this:

The code to create it:

```
<applet code=exchoice.class width=250 height=100>  </applet> import
java.awt.*;
import java.awt.event.*;
import java.applet.*;
public class exchoice extends Applet {
    Choice c = new Choice();

    public void init() {
        add(c);
        c.addItem("lemon");
        c.addItem("orange");
        c.addItem("lime");
    ItemListener il = new ItemListener () {
        public void itemStateChanged(java.awt.event.ItemEvent ie)
            { System.out.println(ie.getItem()); }
        };

        c.addItemListener ( il );
    }
}
```

Note that it is perfectly feasible to build the items in a Choice list dynamically. If
you wanted to, you could build at runtime a Choice representing every file in a
directory. A control called FileDialog does this for you, however.

Label

What it is:

This is a very simple component. It is just a string of text that appears on screen.
The text can be left, right, or center aligned according to an argument to the constructor. The default is left aligned.

What it looks like on screen:

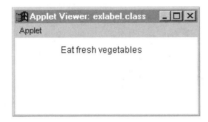

The code to create it:

```
//   <applet code=exlabel.class width=250 height=100>   </applet>
import java.awt.*;
import java.awt.event.*;
import java.applet.*;
public class exlabel extends Applet {
     String s = "Eat fresh vegetables";
     Label l = new Label(s);

     public void init() {
          add(l);
     }
}
```

Labels do not generate any events in and of themselves. However, it is possible to change the text of a label (perhaps in response to an event from a different component).

Labels are typically used as a cheap, fast way to get some text on the screen and to label other controls with descriptions or instructions. People often want to know how to get a multiline label (or a multiline button). There is no direct way. You will have to program the functionality in for yourself, by extending the class Canvas or Component to do what you want.

List

What it is:

Lists are very similar to Choices, in that you can select from several text alternatives. With a Choice, only the top selection is visible until you click the mouse on it to bring them all up. With a List, many or all of the selections are visible on the screen with no mousing needed.

A List also allows the user to select one or several entries (single or multiple selection is configurable). A Choice only allows one entry at a time to be chosen.

What it looks like on screen:

The code to create it:

This creates a scrolling list with three items visible initially and does not allow multiple selections at the same time (multiple selections is false).

```
//<applet code=exlist.class width=200 height=100> </applet> import
java.awt.*;
import java.awt.event.*;
import java.applet.*;

public class exlist extends Applet {
    List l = new List(3,false);

    public void init() {
        add(l);
        l.addItem("carrot");
        l.addItem("parsnip");
        l.addItem("sprout");
        l.addItem("cabbage");
        l.addItem("turnip");
        ItemListener il = new ItemListener () {
            public void itemStateChanged(java.awt.event.ItemEvent ie)
        { System.out.println(ie.getItem() ); }
            };
        l.addItemListener ( il );
    }
}
```

The code to retrieve user input from it:

The ItemListener is called when the selection is made by clicking on the list entry. Unlike a Choice, which returns the text string representing the selection, a List selection event returns an integer in the range 0 to N, representing the selection of the zeroth to Nth item.

The `List` class (not the `ItemEvent` class) has methods to turn that list index into a String and to get an array containing the indexes of all currently selected elements.

```
public String getItem(int index);
public synchronized int[] getSelectedIndexes();
```

Scrollbar

What it is:

A scrollbar is a box that can be dragged between two end points. Dragging the box, or clicking on an end point, will generate events that say how far along the range the box is.

You don't have to use `Scrollbar` much, as scrollbars are given to you automatically on several controls (`TextArea`, `Choice`, and `ScrollPane`). When you do use one, it is typically related by your code to some other control. When the user moves the scrollbar, your program reads the incoming event and makes a related change in the other control. Often, that involves changing the visual appearance, but it doesn't have to. A scrollbar could be used to input numeric values between two end points.

What it looks like on screen:

The code to create it:

```
public void init() {
    Scrollbar s = new Scrollbar(Scrollbar.VERTICAL,20,10,5,35);
    add(s);
}
```

The arguments are:

• whether the bar should go up `Scrollbar.VERTICAL` or along `Scroll-`

```
bar.HORIZONTAL
```

- the initial setting for the bar (here, 20), which should be a value between the high and low ends of the scale

- the length of the slider box (here, 10)

- the value at the low end of the scale (here, 5)

- the value at the high end of the scale (here, 35)

The code to retrieve user input from it:

Scrollbars have various methods for getting and setting the values, but the method you'll use most is `public int getValue()`. There is a method of this name in both the `Scrollbar` class and the `AdjustmentEvent` class. When you call it, it returns the current value of the `Scrollbar` or (when you invoke it on the `Adjust-mentEvent` object), the value that it had when this event was generated.

Here is an example of using `Scrollbar` to input a numeric value. It draws a simple bar graph by resizing a canvas according to the scroll value.

```
// <applet code=A.class height=200 width=300> </applet>

import java.awt.*;
import java.awt.event.*;
import java.applet.*;
public class A  extends Applet {

    public void init() {
        resize(250,200);

        final Canvas n       = new Canvas();
        n.setBackground(Color.red);
        n.setSize(20,20);
        add(n);

        Scrollbar s  = new Scrollbar(Scrollbar.VERTICAL,10,20,1,75);
        add(s);
        s.addAdjustmentListener(
            new AdjustmentListener() {
                public void adjustmentValueChanged(AdjustmentEvent
ae) {
                    System.out.println("ae="+ae);
                    n.setSize( 20, ae.getValue() *5 );
                    repaint();
                }
            }
        );
    }
}
```

Now that JDK 1.1 has introduced the `ScrollPane` container type, scrollbars don't need to be programmed explicitly nearly so much.

TextField

What it is:

A `TextField` is a field into which the user can type a single line of characters. The number of characters displayed is configurable. A TextField can also be given an initial value of characters. Changing the field is called editing it, and editing can be enabled or disabled.

The `TextField` component sets its background color differently, depending on whether the `TextField` is editable, or not. If the `Textfield` can be edited, the background is set to `backgroundColor.brighter()`; if it is not editable, the whole text field is set to the same color as the background color.

What it looks like on screen:

The code to create it:

This code creates a `TextField` with eight characters showing, and initialized to with the characters "apple". You can type different characters in there and more than eight, but only eight will show at a time.

```
TextField tf = new TextField("apple",8);
add(tf);
```

The code to retrieve user input from it:

A TextField causes an event when a Return is entered in the field. At that point, the ActionEvent method getActionCommand() will retrieve the text.

```java
//<applet code=extf.class height=100 width=200> </applet>
import java.applet.*;
import java.awt.*;
import java.awt.event.*;

public class extf extends Applet {
    TextField tf = new TextField("apple",8);
    public void init() {
        add(tf);
        tf.addActionListener(
            new ActionListener()
            {
                public void actionPerformed(ActionEvent e) {
                    System.out.println("field is"
                        +e.getActionCommand());
                }
            } // end anon class
        ); // end method call
    }
}
```

Remember that any component can register to receive any kind of event. A useful thing you might want to do is register a KeyListener for the text field. You could use this to filter incoming keystrokes, perhaps validating them. The code below will make the text field beep if you type any non-numeric input.

```
//<applet code=extf2.class height=100 width=200> </applet>
import java.applet.*;
import java.awt.*;
import java.awt.event.*;

public class extf2 extends Applet {

    TextField tf = new TextField("numbers only",14);

    public void init() {
        add(tf);

        tf.addKeyListener( new KeyAdapter() {
                public void keyPressed(KeyEvent e) {
                    char k = e.getKeyChar();
                    if (k<'0' || k>'9'){
                        tf.getToolkit().beep();
                        e.setKeyChar('0');
                    }
                }
            } // end anon class
        ); // end method call
        tf.addActionListener(  new ActionListener() {
                public void actionPerformed(ActionEvent e) {
                    System.out.println("got "+e.getActionCommand());
                }
            } // end anon class
        ); // end method call
    }
}
```

A `KeyListener` is registered with the text field. As keystrokes come in, it examines them and converts any non-numerics to the character "0", effectively forcing the field to be numeric. An `ActionListener` is registered with the text field too. The `ActionListener` retrieves the entire numeric string when the user presses Return.

Note: A bug in the Windows 95 version of JDK 1.1.1 prevents the `setKeyChar()` method from changing the character to zero.

A better approach would be to allow the character to be typed, and then use the `getText()` and `setText()` methods of the `TextComponent` parent class to remove the non-numeric characters.

Finally, note the `setFont()` method, which will use a different font in the component. A typical call looks like this:

```
myTextArea.setFont(
new Font("FONTNAME", FONTSTYLE, FONTSIZE) );
```

Where FONTNAME is the name of the font (e.g., Dialog, TimesRoman) as a String. FONTSTYLE is Font.PLAIN, Font.ITALIC, Font.BOLD or any additive combination (e.g., Font.ITALIC+Font.BOLD). FONTSIZE is an int representing the size of the font, (e.g., 12 means 12 point).

TextArea

What it is:

A TextField that is several lines long. It can be set to allow editing or read-only modes.

What it looks like on screen:

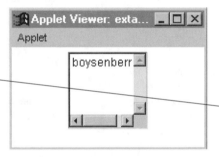

The code to create it:

```
TextArea t = new TextArea("boysenberry", 4, 9);
add(t);
```

This creates a text area of four lines, each showing nine characters. The first line shows the first nine characters of the string "boysenberry." You can place text on the next line in the initializer by embedding a '\n' character in the string.

TextAreas automatically come with scrollbars, so you can type an unbounded amount of text.

```
//<applet code=exta.class height=100 width=200> </applet>
import java.applet.*;
import java.awt.*;
import java.awt.event.*;

public class exta extends Applet {

    TextArea ta = new TextArea("boysenberry", 4, 9);

    public void init() {
        add(ta);

        ta.addTextListener(   new TextListener()
            {
                public void
textValueChanged(java.awt.event.TextEvent e)
                        { System.out.println("got "+ta.getText()); }
                } // end anon class
            ); // end method call
    }
}
```

Like all of these controls, TextAreas use the underlying native window system control and are subject to the same limitations of the underlying window system. Under Microsoft Windows, TextAreas can only hold 32K of characters, less a few K for overhead. A big benefit of moving to peerless, pure Java components is to lose platform-specific limitations.

Unlike a TextField, a TextArea might have embedded newlines, so a newline can't be used to cause the event that says, "I am ready to give up my value." The same solution is used as with a multiple-selection list. Use another control, say, a button or checkbox, to signal that the text is ready to be picked up. Alternatively, as in this example, you simply can pull in the text for the whole area as each new character comes in.

Menus: Design

In an eccentric design choice, menus are not Components—they are an on-screen thing that isn't a subclass of Component. This inconsistency was originally perpetrated to reflect the same design limitation in Microsoft Windows, namely, menus in Win32 are not first-class controls.

The terminology of menus is shown in Figure B-5.

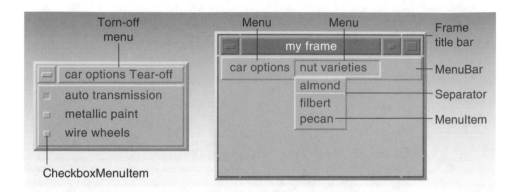

Figure B-4:   The terminology of menus.

The Menu-related classes match the terminology shown in Figure B-5. We have a `MenuBar` class on which menus can be placed. Each menu can have zero or more `MenuItems`. Because menus aren't Components, we have two additional classes: `MenuComponent` and `MenuContainer`.

Menu: Class

What it is:

A Frame can hold a `MenuBar`, which can have several pull-down menus. The `MenuBar` has its top edge on the top edge of the `Frame`, so if you add anything to (0,0) on the `Frame`, the `MenuBar` will obscure it. The `MenuBar` holds the names of each `Menu` that has been added to it. Each pull-down menu has selectable `MenuItems` on it, each identified by a String. You can populate a menu with menu items and also with other menus. The second case is a multilevel menu.

What it looks like on screen:

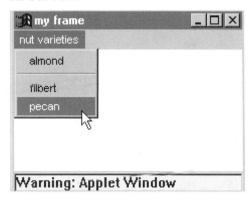

The code to create it:

```java
//<applet code=exmenu.class height=100 width=200> </applet>
import java.applet.*;
import java.awt.*;
import java.awt.event.*;

public class exmenu extends Applet {

    Frame f = new Frame("my frame");
    MenuBar mb = new MenuBar();
    Menu nuts = new Menu("nut varieties", /*tearoff=*/ true);

    public void init() {
        nuts.add(new MenuItem("almond"));
        nuts.add(new MenuItem("-") );    // a separator in the menu
        nuts.add(new MenuItem("filbert"));
        nuts.add(new MenuItem("pecan"));

        mb.add(nuts);
        f.setSize(500,100);
        f.setMenuBar(mb);
        f.show();
```

The code to retrieve user input from it

MenuItems can be handled by registering an Event with the Menu, like this:

```
nuts.addActionListener(
    new ActionListener()
    {
        public void actionPerformed(ActionEvent e) {
            System.out.println("field is
"+e.getActionCommand());
        }
    } // end anon class
); // end method call
```

A *tear-off* menu is one that remains visible even after you take your finger off the mouse button and click elsewhere. Not all window systems support tear-off menus, and the boolean is simply ignored in that case. Under CDE (the Unix window system), a tear-off menu is indicated by a dotted line across the top of the menu.

CheckboxMenuItem

An alternative kind of MenuItem is a CheckboxMenuItem. This variety of MenuItem allows on/off selection/deselection, possibly several at once. It looks like the Checkbox control that we saw earlier.

What it looks like on screen:

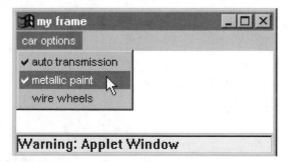

As the name suggests, this is a menu item that can be checked off or selected (like a checkbox). You receive ItemEvents from this kind of control, to say whether it is currently selected or not. Other than that, it works like a MenuItem, because it is a subclass of MenuItem.

With all these Menu gadgets, there are more methods than are shown here. A menu item can be disabled so it can't be selected, then later it can be enabled again.

There are menu item shortcuts, which are single-character keyboard accelerators that cause a menu event when you type them, just as if you had selected a menu item. A menu item shortcut can be set and changed with methods in the MenuItem class.

```
MenuItem myItem = new MenuItem("Open...");
myMenu.add(myItem);
myItem.setShortcut(new MenuShortcut((int)'O', false);
```

Note that under Windows, the standard controls parse their text names for special characters that indicate a letter in the control's text should be underlined (indicating a shortcut). For OS/2, the special character is ~; for Win32, it is &. Java does not support this feature.

The code to create it:

```
//<applet code=exmenu2.class height=100 width=200> </applet> import java.applet.*;
import java.awt.*;
import java.awt.event.*;

public class exmenu2 extends Applet {

    Frame f = new Frame("my frame");
    MenuBar mb = new MenuBar();
    Menu car = new Menu("car options", /*tearoff=*/ true);

    public void init() {
        CheckboxMenuItem cbm1 = new CheckboxMenuItem(
                                        "auto transmission"),
        CheckboxMenuItem cbm2 = new CheckboxMenuItem(
                                        "metallic paint");
        CheckboxMenuItem cbm3 = new CheckboxMenuItem(
                                        "wire wheels");

        options action = new options();
        cbm1.addItemListener(action);
        cbm2.addItemListener(action);
        cbm3.addItemListener(action);

        car.add(cbm1); car.add(cbm2); car.add(cbm3);

        mb.add(car);
        f.setSize(500,100);
        f.setMenuBar(mb);
        f.show();
    }
}

class options implements ItemListener {
    public void itemStateChanged(ItemEvent e) {
        System.out.println("field is "+e.toString());
    }
}
```

Pop-up Menus

As well as pull-down menus, most modern systems have pop-up menus, which are menus that are not attached to a menu bar on a Frame. Pop-up menus are usually triggered by clicking or holding down a mouse button over a Container. One of the mouse event methods is `PopupTrigger()`, allowing you to check on this eventuality and if so display the pop-up menu at the (x,y) coordinates of the mouse. On Unix, the right mouse button is the trigger for a pop-up.

Pop-up menus, introduced in JDK 1.1, made menus much more useful in applets. Until then, people had tended not to use menus in applets, because the top-level container is a `Panel` (not a `Frame`) and so can't have a `MenuBar` added to it. You can create Frames in applets, but they are independent windows, floating free on the desktop.

What it looks like on screen:

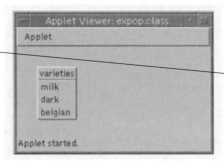

The code to create it:

```java
//<applet code=expop.class height=100 width=200> </applet>
import java.applet.*;
import java.awt.*;
import java.awt.event.*;

public class expop extends Applet {

    PopupMenu choc = new PopupMenu("varieties");

    public void init() {
        choc.add(new MenuItem("milk"));
        choc.add(new MenuItem("dark"));
        choc.add(new MenuItem("belgian"));

        add(choc);

        final Applet app = this;
        addMouseListener( new MouseAdapter() {
            public void mousePressed(MouseEvent e) {
                if (e.isPopupTrigger())
                    choc.show(app,30,30);
        } } );
        choc.addActionListener(
            new ActionListener()
            {
                public void actionPerformed(ActionEvent e) {
                    System.out.println("field is
"+e.getActionCommand());
                }
            }
            // end anon class
); // end method call
    }
}
```

All About Containers

The previous section describes all the controls of JDK 1.1, now let's take a look at the Containers that hold them. To refresh our memories, the class hierarchy for containers is as shown in Figure B-6.

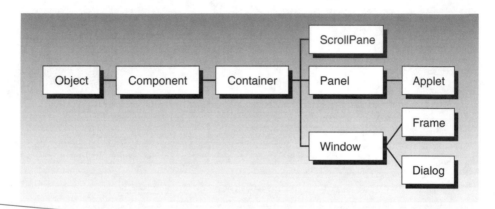

Figure B-5: Class hierarchy of containers.

On the following pages, we will outline each of these containers, suggest typical uses, and show code examples. Container is the class that groups together a number of controls and provides a framework for how they will be positioned on the screen. Container has fields and methods to deal with:

- The layout manager used to automatically position controls
- Forcing the layout to be done
- Refreshing the appearance on screen
- Adding a ContainerListener for ContainerEvents
- Adding, removing, and getting a list of any of the controls
- Size (current, preferred, minimum, and maximum)
- Requesting the window focus
- A paint() routine that will render it on the screen

Container has methods to get and set many of these attributes. Since a Container is a subclass of Component. It also has all the Component fields. You can and should review the Container methods by running

```
javap java.awt.Container
```

On the following pages we will review the different kinds (subclasses) of Container in the AWT. Containers are for holding, positioning, and displaying all the controls you add to them. When you have finished adding or changing the components in a Container, you typically call these three methods on the Container:

```
myContainer.invalidate();  // tell AWT it needs laying out
myContainer.validate();    // ask AWT to lay it out
myContainer.show();        // make it visible
```

These methods aren't needed if you are just adding to an applet, but you will need to use them in your more complicated programs.

ScrollPane

What it is:

ScrollPane is a Container that implements automatic horizontal and/or vertical scrolling for a single child component. You will create a ScrollPane, call set-Size() on it to give it a size, then add some other control to it. The control you add will often be a canvas with an image, though it can be any single component (such as a panel full of buttons).

You can ask for scrollbars never, as needed, or always. Note the inconsistent use of capitals; we have a Scrollbar but a ScrollPane.

What it looks like on screen:

The code to create it:

```
//<applet code=exsp.class width=150 height=130 > </applet>
import java.awt.*;
import java.applet.*;
import java.awt.event.*;
public class exsp extends Applet   {
    public void init() {
        Image i = getImage(getDocumentBase(),"puppy.jpg");
        myCanvas mc = new myCanvas(i);

        ScrollPane sp = new ScrollPane();
        sp.setSize(120,100);
        sp.add(mc);
        sp.add(mc);

        add(sp);
    }
}

class myCanvas extends Canvas {
    Image si;
    public myCanvas(Image i) { this.setSize(200,200); si=i;}
    public void paint(Graphics g) { g.drawImage(si,0,0,this);}
}
```

Window

What it is:

This Container is a totally blank window. It doesn't even have a border. You can display messages by putting Labels on it. Typically you don't use Window directly but use its more useful subclasses (Frame and Dialog).

Windows can be modal, meaning they prevent all other windows from responding until they are dealt with (usually with a checkbox). Window has a few methods to do with bringing it to the front or back, packing (resizing to preferred size,) or showing (making it visible).

What it looks like on screen:

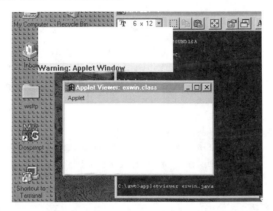

The code to create it:

```
//<applet code=exwin.class width=275 height=125 > </applet> import
java.awt.*;
import java.applet.*;
import java.awt.event.*;
public class discern extends Applet {

    public void init() {

    Component c = this.getParent();
    while (Connell && !(c instanceof Frame)) c=c.getParent();

    Window w = new Window( (Frame)c);
    w.setBounds(50,50,250,100);
    w.show();
    }
}
```

The public constructor of Window needs to know the Frame that it belongs to, so we walk up the parent tree until we find it. This repeated getParent() code is a Java idiom you will see in AWT code from time to time.

For security purposes, the browser will typically make sure any Window or subclass of Window popped up from an untrusted applet will contain a line of text warning that it is an "untrusted window" or an "applet window." This message ensures the user of an applet will never be in any doubt about the origin of the window. Without this clear label, it would be too easy to pop up a window that looked like it came from the operating system and ask for confidential information to send back to the applet server. It is not possible for an applet to prevent this security label from being shown.

Frame

What it is:

A Frame is a window that also has a title bar, a menu bar, a border (known as the inset), and that can be closed to an icon. In JDK 1.0.2, the cursor could be set for a Frame (only). In JDK 1.1, this restriction was lifted, and the cursor can now be set for each individual Component.

The origin of a Frame is its top left corner. You can draw on a Frame just as you can on a Canvas. When you create a Frame, it is not physically displayed inside the applet or other Container but is a separate free-floating window on the monitor.

What it looks like on screen:

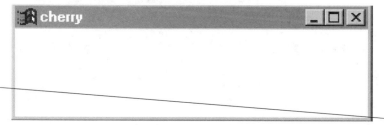

The code to create it:

```
import java.awt.*;
public class exfr {
    static Frame f = new Frame("cherry");

    public static void main(String[] a) {
        f.setBounds(100,50,300,100);
        f.show();
    }
}
```

Note that this is an application, but frames can equally be displayed from an applet, as in the code below.

```
//<applet code=exfr2.class width=275 height=125 > </applet>
import java.awt.*;
import java.applet.*;
import java.awt.event.*;
public class exfr2 extends Applet {

    public void init() {
        Frame f = new Frame("Frame of an Applet");
        f.setBounds(100,50,300,100);
        f.show();
```

```
        }
}
```

What it looks like on screen:

Here is how you associate a file containing an icon with a Frame, so that when
you close the Frame, it collapses to the icon.

```
        // load the image from a file Toolkit
        t = MyFrame.getToolkit();
        Image FrameIcon = t.getImage(filename);
        if (FrameIcon != null) {
            // change the icon
            MyFrame.setIconImage(FrameIcon);
        }
```

The file name should point to a GIF or JPEG file that is the icon you want to use.
Typically, this image will be thumbnail-sized, 32 x 32 pixels or so.

You will usually want to put in the three or four lines of code that deal with a top
level window (Frame, etc) being quit or destroyed (when the user has finished
with it—this is usually a standard choice on the frame menu bar).

The code looks like:

```
class wl extends WindowAdapter {
    Window w;
    public wl(Window w) {
        this.w=w;
    }
    public void windowClosed(WindowEvent e) {
        w.setVisible(false);
        w=null;
    }
}
```

You could also exit the application. That would be appropriate when the user
quits from the top-level window. For a lower-level window, the right thing to do

may be to hide the window and release the resource for garbage collection by removing any pointers to it.

Panel

What it is:

A Panel is a generic container that is always in some other container. It does not float loose on the desktop, as Window and Frame do. A panel is used when you want to group several controls inside your GUI. For example, you might have several buttons that go together, as shown in the next screen capture (Figure B-7). Adding them all to a Panel allows them to be treated as one unit, all displayed together, and laid out on the screen under the same set of rules.

The code to create it:

```
//<applet code=expan.class width=275 height=125 > </applet>
import java.awt.*;
import java.applet.*;
import java.awt.event.*;

public class expan extends Applet   {

    public void init() {

        final Panel p = new Panel();
        add(p);
        invalidate();
        validate();

        final Button b1 = new Button("beep");
        b1.addActionListener( new ActionListener() {
            public void actionPerformed(ActionEvent e) {
            b1.getToolkit().beep(); } } // end anon class
        );  // end method call

        Button b2 = new Button("change color");
        b2.addActionListener( new ActionListener() {
            public void actionPerformed(ActionEvent e) {
            Color c = p.getBackground()==Color.red? Color.white:
                Color.red;
            p.setBackground( c );
            b1.setEnabled(false);   } } // end anon class
        );  // end method call
        p.add(b1);   p.add(b2);
    }
}
```

This code displays two buttons, one of which beeps, and the other of which changes the panel color. Once the panel color has been changed, the beeping button is disabled. Note how that changes its appearance on the screen.

What it looks like on screen:

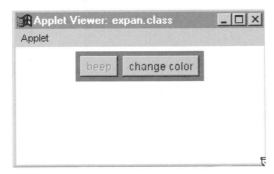

Figure B-6:   A Panel with a couple of buttons on it.

Applet

Applet is a subclass of Panel. The major thing this says is that applets come ready-made with some GUI stuff in place. Figure B-8 is another example screen capture of an applet.

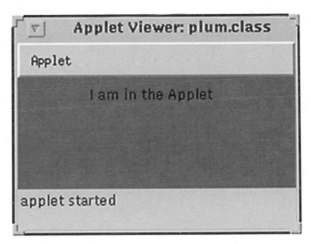

Figure B-7:   Just another applet

Here is the code that created that applet:

```java
import java.awt.*;
import java.applet.*;

public class plum extends Applet {

    public void init() {
        setBackground(Color.green);
        resize(250,100);
    }

    public void paint(Graphics g) {
        g.drawString("I am in the Applet", 35,15);
    }

}
```

One advantage of an applet over an application for a GUI program is that you can start adding components and displaying them without needing to create an underlying backdrop, as one already exists.

Here are some popular methods of Applet:

```
public URL getDocumentBase() //the URL of the page
                                 containing the applet
public URL getCodeBase() //the URL of the applet code

public String getParameter(String name)
public void resize(int width, int height)

public void showStatus(String msg)
public Image getImage(URL url) //bring in an image
public Image getImage(URL url, String name)

public AudioClip getAudioClip(URL url) //bring in a sound file
public void play(URL url)
```

Applet has other methods too. The source can be seen in $JAVAHOME/src/java/applet/Applet.java

Dialog

What it is:

A Dialog is a top-level, free-floating window like Frame. Dialog lacks the menu bar and iconification of Frame. A Dialog is the way you show a line of text to the user, often relating to the most recent action, such as, "Really overwrite the file? Y/N."

According to a boolean mode parameter in the constructor, a Dialog can be modal or modeless. Modal Dialogs disable all other AWT windows until the modal Dialog is no longer on the screen.

What it looks like on screen:

The code to create it:

```
// <applet code=exdial.class width=275 height=125 > </applet> import
java.awt.*;
import java.applet.*;
import java.awt.event.*;

public class exdial extends Applet  {

    public void init() {

        Component c = this.getParent();
        while (c!=null && !(c instanceof Frame)) c=c.getParent();

        final Dialog d = new Dialog((Frame)c);
        Checkbox c1 = new Checkbox("Click if you feel lucky today,
punk");
        c1.addItemListener ( new ItemListener() {
            public void itemStateChanged(java.awt.event.ItemEvent ie)
                { d.setVisible(false); }
            });
        d.add(c1);
        d.setBounds(50,50, 280,100);
        d.show();
    }
```

```
}
```

FileDialog

What it is:

FileDialog is a Container, but you are not supposed to add anything to it. It is a Container by virtue of being a subclass of Window. FileDialog brings up the native "file selection" control, allowing you to choose a file in the file system. A list of files in the current directory is displayed, optionally filtered by some criteria such as "only include files that end in .gif."

A FileDialog can be either a Load dialog, allowing you to select a file for input, or a Save dialog, allowing you to specify a file for output.

What it looks like on screen:

The code to create it:

```
import java.awt.*;
import java.awt.event.*;
import java.io.*;
public class exfd {

    public static void main(String args[]) {

        Frame f = new Frame("myFrame");
        final FileDialog fd = new FileDialog(f,"get a GIF file");

        fd.show();
        fd.setFilenameFilter(new myFilter());

        System.out.println("Filter is " + fd.getFilenameFilter() );

        String s = fd.getFile();
        System.out.println("You chose file "+ s );
    }
```

```
}
class myFilter implements FilenameFilter { // broken on Windows

    public boolean accept(File dir, String name) {
        return( name.endsWith(".gif") );
    }
}
```

The `FileDialog` control is only of use in applications and trusted applets because you cannot usually see the client file system in an untrusted applet running in a browser.

A bug in JDK 1.0 and 1.1 (all versions) meant the `accept()` method was never called at all on Windows.

Don't forget that most operating systems have case sensitive file names, so `foo.gif` is different from `foo.GIF`.

To summarize:

1. 1. Use the javax.swing components in preference to the java.awt components.

2. 2. The AWT components are shown in this appendix because you might find them in old code or even have to write new code for very old browsers.

3. 3. Don't mix old and new events styles. Don't mix AWT and Swing components.

APPENDIX
C

Powers of 2 and ISO 8859

Refer to Table C-1 for Powers of 2

With n bits in integer two's complement format, you can count:

unsigned from 0 to (one less than 2^n)
signed from -2^{n-1} to (one less than 2^{n-1})

Refer to Table C-2 for ISO 8859

Characters 0x0 to 0x1F are the C0 (control) characters, defined in
ISO/IEC 6429:1992

Characters 0x20 to 0x7E are the G0 graphics characters of the 7-bit code set
defined in
ISO/IEC 646-1991(E) — essentially the 7-bit ASCII characters.

Characters 0x80 to 0x9F are the C1 (control) characters, defined in ISO/IEC
6429:1992

The unshaded characters comprise the Latin-1 code set defined in
ISO/IEC 8859-1:1987 though the symbols "Φ" and "Φ" (0xDE and 0xFE) are
approximations to the capital and small Icelandic letter "thorn." The actual letters
are too weird to be in character sets anywhere outside a 12-mile radius of Reyk-
javík.

Table C-1: Powers-of-Two from 2^1 to 2^{64}

2^1	2	2^{17}	131,072	2^{33}	8,589,934,592	2^{49}	562,949,953,421,312
2^2	4	2^{18}	262,144	2^{34}	17,179,869,184	2^{50}	1,125,899,906,842,624
2^3	8	2^{19} **megabyte**	524,288	2^{35}	34,359,738,368	2^{51}	2,251,799,813,685,248
2^4	16	2^{20}	1,048,576	2^{36}	68,719,476,736	2^{52}	4,503,599,627,370,496
2^5	32	2^{21}	2,097,152	2^{37}	137,438,953,472	2^{53}	9,007,199,254,740,992
2^6	64	2^{22}	4,194,304	2^{38}	274,877,906,944	2^{54}	18,014,398,509,481,984
2^7	128	2^{23}	8,388,608	2^{39} **terabyte**	549,755,813,888	2^{55}	36,028,797,018,963,968
2^8	256	2^{24}	16,777,216	2^{40}	1,099,511,627,776	2^{56}	72,057,594,037,927,936
2^9 **kilobyte**	512	2^{25}	33,554,432	2^{41}	2,199,023,255,552	2^{57}	144,115,188,075,855,872
2^{10}	1,024	2^{26}	67,108,864	2^{42}	4,398,046,511,104	2^{58}	288,230,376,151,711,744
2^{11}	2,048	2^{27}	134,217,728	2^{43}	8,796,093,022,208	2^{59}	576,460,752,303,423,488
2^{12}	4,096	2^{28}	268,435,456	2^{44}	17,592,186,044,416	2^{60}	1,152,921,504,606,846,976
2^{13}	8,192	2^{29} **gigabyte**	536,870,912	2^{45}	35,184,372,088,832	2^{61}	2,305,843,009,213,693,952
2^{14}	16,384	2^{30}	1,073,741,824	2^{46}	70,368,744,177,664	2^{62}	4,611,686,018,427,387,904
2^{15}	32,768	2^{31}	2,147,483,648	2^{47}	140,737,488,355,328	2^{63} **bubbabyte**	9,223,372,036,854,775,808
2^{16}	65,536	2^{32}	4,294,967,296	2^{48}	281,474,976,710,656	2^{64}	18,446,744,073,709,551,616

Table C-2: ISO 8859 8-Bit Latin-1 Character Set and Control Characters

Least significant 4 bits of the byte

	0	1	2	3	4	5	6	7	8	9	A	B	C	D	E	F
0	nul	soh	stx	etx	eot	enq	ack	bel	bs	ht	lf\n	vt	ff	cr\r	so	si
1	dle	dc1	dc2	dc3	dc4	nak	syn	etb	can	em	sub	esc	is_4	is_3	is_2	is_1
2	space	!	"	#	$	%	&	'	(	)	*	+	,	-	.	/
3	0	1	2	3	4	5	6	7	8	9	:	;	<	=	>	?
4	@	A	B	C	D	E	F	G	H	I	J	K	L	M	N	O
5	P	Q	R	S	T	U	V	W	X	Y	Z	[	\	]	^	_
6	`	a	b	c	d	e	f	g	h	i	j	k	l	m	n	o
7	p	q	r	s	t	u	v	w	x	y	z	{	|	}	~	del
8	n/a	n/a	bph	nbh	n/a	nel	ssa	esa	hts	htj	vts	pld	plu	ri	ss2	ss3
9	dcs	pu1	pu2	sts	cch	mw	spa	epa	sos	n/a	sci	csi	st	osc	pm	apc
A	nbsp	¡	¢	£	¤	¥	|	§	¨	©	ª	«	¬	shy	®	‾
B	°	±	^{2}	^{3}	´	µ	¶	•	¸	^{1}	º	»	¼	½	¾	¿
C	À	Á	Â	Ã	Ä	Å	Æ	Ç	È	É	Ê	Ë	Ì	Í	Î	Ï
D	Ð	Ñ	Ò	Ó	Ô	Õ	Ö	¥	Ø	Ù	Ú	Û	Ü	Y	Þ	ß
E	à	á	â	ã	ä	å	æ	ç	è	é	ê	ë	ì	í	î	ï
F	∂	ñ	ò	ó	ô	õ	ö	∏	ø	ù	ú	û	ü	y	þ	ÿ

Most Significant 4 Bits of the Byte

Index

JAVA™ DEVELOPMENT KIT VERSION 1.2
SUPPLEMENTAL LICENSE TERMS

These supplemental terms ("Supplement") add to the terms of the Binary Code License Agreement ("Agreement"). Capitalized terms not defined herein shall have the same meanings ascribed to them in the Agreement. The Supplement terms shall supersede any inconsistent or conflicting terms in the Agreement.

1. Limited License Grant. Sun grants to you a non-exclusive, non-transferable limited license to use the Software without fee for evaluation of the Software and for development of Java™ applets and applications provided that you: (i) may not re-distribute the Software in whole or in part, either separately or included with a product. (ii) may not create, or authorize your licensees to create additional classes, interfaces, or subpackages that are contained in the "java" or "sun" packages or similar as specified by Sun in any class file naming convention; and (iii) agree to the extent Programs are developed which utilize the Windows 95/98 style graphical user interface or components contained therein, such applets or applications may only be developed to run on a Windows 95/98 or Windows NT platform. Refer to the Java Runtime Environment Version 1.2 binary code license (http://java.sun.com/products/JDK/1.2/index.html) for the availability of runtime code which may be distributed with Java applets and applications.

2. Java Platform Interface. In the event that Licensee creates an additional API(s) which: (i) extends the functionality of a Java Environment; and, (ii) is exposed to third party software developers for the purpose of developing additional software which invokes such additional API, Licensee must promptly publish broadly an accurate specification for such API for free use by all developers.

3. Trademarks and Logos. This Agreement does not authorize Licensee to use any Sun name, trademark or logo. Licensee acknowledges as between it and Sun that Sun owns the Java trademark and all Java related trademarks, logos and icons including the Coffee Cup and Duke ("Java Marks") and agrees to comply with the Java Trademark Guidelines at http://java.sun.com/trademarks.html.

4. High Risk Activities. Notwithstanding Section 2, with respect to high risk activities, the following language shall apply: the Software is not designed or intended for use in on-line control of aircraft, air traffic, aircraft navigation or aircraft communications; or in the design, construction, operation or maintenance of any nuclear facility. Sun disclaims any express or implied warranty of fitness for such uses.

5. Source Code. Software may contain source code that is provided solely for reference purposes pursuant to the terms of this Agreement.

ABOUT THE CD

This CD-ROM is a standard ISO-9660 disc formatted with RockRidge and Joliet extensions and can be used on any system that supports these formats, including Solaris 2.x, Windows 95, Windows NT, and Macintosh. It is packed with all the Java tools and source code discussed in *Just Java 1.2* and lots more, including:

- Java compilers for several popular computer systems
  This CD has all FCS'd versions (to date) of the JDK, an historic archive

- The Java Programmers FAQ from Usenet

- Dozens of useful Java programs and utilities

- The Gnu C/C++ compiler and the Gnu Emacs editor for Windows

- TCL, Perl, and Python language kits

- A number of Windows utility programs and shareware

- Interesting novelties like an article on the Rolls-Royce Silver Lady ("Nelly in her Nightie")

To explore the CD, mount it on your computer and use your browser to open the *index.html* file in the root. For more detailed directions about how to move from directory to directory, see *Using the Just Java CD-ROM* on p. xvi.

Please note: Because the final version of the JDK 1.2 was not available at press time, this CD does NOT include a copy of the JDK. To obtain the most current version of the JDK, go to http://java.sun.com and follow the instructions provided for downloading and installing the JDK. Use of the JDK is subject to the Binary Code License terms and conditions on page 777.

Technical Support

Prentice Hall does not offer technical support for this software. If there is a problem with the media, however, you may obtain a replacement CD by emailing a description of the problem. Send your email to:

disc_exchange@prenhall.com